The Higley
Lesson Commentary
2008–2009

Based on the

**International Sunday
School Lessons**

**King James Version
76th Annual Volume**

Editor

Wesley C. Reagan

Contributing Writers

Ron Durham, Ph.D.
John Comer
Tommy King, D.Min.
Gene Shelburne

The Higley Lesson Commentary, in this 76th year of its life, renews its commitment to careful and reverent scholarship, clear and understandable language, practical and insightful application, and interesting and readable writing. We send it to you with a prayer that it will be a powerful resource for you.

© 2008 by Higley Publishing Corp.
Jacksonville, FL 32204
Tel. 1-800-842-1093

Printed in U.S.A.

i

Foreword

What if you aspired to be an excellent teacher of the Scriptures and you enjoyed access to the following resources?

1) A balanced guide emphasizing key elements in each part of the Bible, with stress on the special holy days of the Christian faith such as Christmas, Easter, and Pentecost.

2) Tutors with years of training, experience, and a personal faith.

3) Libraries that the writers have access to with material gleaned to give you the best access that your schedule will allow.

4) Useful teaching helps such as exegesis, discussion questions, real life application, and evangelistic encouragement.

5) Words of uplift and inspiration that improve morale and provide motivation.

And, suppose that those resources were coordinated with the texts in your regular Sunday School Quarterly. And, suppose further, that you can enjoy that treasury of information for only pennies a week.

We are grateful to *The Higley Lesson Commentary* writers for their careful and poignant sharing of their hearts and faith in the pages that you now hold in your hand.

Wesley C. Reagan, Editor
The Higley Lesson Commentary

Soft Cover ISBN: 978-1-886763-34-0
Hard Cover ISBN: 978-1-886763-35-7

Lessons and/or Readings based on International Sunday School Lessons. The International Bible Lessons for Christian Teaching, © 2005 by the Committee on the Uniform Series. Unless otherwise indicated, all Scripture references are taken from the King James Version of the Bible..

Preface

Assignments sometimes come as privileges. This assignment certainly did.

I have known the editor of this commentary in enough different contexts to know that he has a profound desire to give Sunday School teachers and students the most helpful resources possible for teaching the Bible. For me to be asked to write a preface for a quality Bible resource like *The Higley Commentary* is pure privilege.

As a former New Testament professor for 12 years in a well-known seminary, I think I have some qualifications for critiquing Sunday School material. The goal of a teacher is to "rightly divide the word of truth" (2 Tim. 2:15). All of us need help to do this because none of us has the whole truth within ourselves. The insight of another might be just what we need in order to handle the Scriptures correctly.

After all my years of studying, teaching, and writing about Scripture, I am still learning. I presume you are also. I desire to make the Word as clear as possible and I am sure you do as well.

With that goal in mind, I have found *The Higley Lesson Commentary* to be a resource I can rely on year after year. The writers have understanding and insight that is based on solid scholarship, a committed faith in God, and a love of the Scriptures. Therefore you can turn to these pages with confidence that every effort has been made to expound God's will faithfully and clearly.

Read, study, and enjoy this work with the confidence that God's Word will not return to Him void. May God bless you with a deeper understanding and a higher motivation as a result of your study.

Douglas Ezell, Ph.D.

*Doug Ezell has had a multifaceted career as a professor, a pastor, a writer, and a personal counselor. Some years ago he served with distinction as a contributing writer of **The Higley Lesson Commentary**.*

FALL QUARTER
The New Testament Community
Unit I: The Birth of a New Community (Lessons 1–4)
Unit II: The Development and Work of the New Community (Lessons 5–8)
Unit III. Growing Pains in the New Community (Lessons 9–13)

WINTER QUARTER
Human Commitment
Unit I. Commitment to the Messiah (Lessons 1–4)
Unit II. Old Testament People of Commitment (Lessons 5–13)

SPRING QUARTER
New Creation in Christ
Unit 1. The Promise of New Life Lessons (1–5)
Unit II. The Path to New Life (Lessons 6–9)
Unit III. The Way of New Life (Lessons 10–14)

SUMMER QUARTER
Call Sealed With Promise

Unit I. Called Out of Egypt (Lessons 1-4)
Unit II. Called to be God's People (Lessons 5-8)
Unit III. Called to Choose Life (Lessons 9-13)

LESSON CYCLE, 2007–2010

Arrangement of Quarters according to the
Church School Year, September 2008 through August 2010

	Fall	Winter	Spring	Summer
Year One 2007–2008	*Creation* God Created a People Genesis	*Call* God's Call to the Christian Community (Luke)	*Covenant* God, the People, and the Covenant (1 and 2 Chronicles, Daniel, Haggai, Nehemiah)	*Christ* Images of Christ (Hebrews, Gospels)
Year Two 2008–2009	*Community* New Testament Survey	*Commitment* Human Commitment (Luke, Old Testament)	*Creation* Christ and Creation (Ezekiel, Luke, Acts, Ephesians)	*Call* Call of God's Covenant Community (Exodus, Leviticus, Numbers, Deuteronomy)
Year Three 2009–2010	*Covenant* Covenant Communities (Joshua, Judges, Ezra, Nehemia, Mark, 1 and 2 Peter)	*Christ* Christ the Fulfillment (Matthew)	*Community* Teachings on Community (John, Ruth, New Testament)	*Commitment* Christian Commitment in Today's World (1 and 2 Thessalonians, Philippians)

Lesson 1

A New Community

Mark 1:1-8; Matt. 3:1-3

The beginning of the gospel of Jesus Christ, the Son of God;

2 As it is written in the prophets, Behold, I send my messenger before thy face, which shall prepare thy way before thee.

3 The voice of one crying in the wilderness, Prepare ye the way of the Lord, make his paths straight.

4 John did baptize in the wilderness, and preach the baptism of repentance for the remission of sins.

5 And there went out unto him all the land of Judaea, and they of Jerusalem, and were all baptized of him in the river of Jordan, confessing their sins.

6 And John was clothed with camel's hair, and with a girdle of a skin about his loins; and he did eat locusts and wild honey;

7 And preached, saying, There cometh one mightier than I after me, the latchet of whose shoes I am not worthy to stoop down and unloose.

8 I indeed have baptized you with water: but he shall baptize you with the Holy Ghost.

Matt. 3:1-12

1 In those days came John the Baptist, preaching in the wilderness of Judea.

2 And saying, Repent ye: for the kingdom of heaven is at hand,

3 The voice of one crying in the wilderness, Prepare ye the way of the Lord, make his paths straight.

Memory Selection
Matt. 3:2

Background Scripture
Mark 1:1-8; Matt. 3:1-12

Devotional Reading
1 Pet. 2:1-10

Jesus and John the Baptist, who were probably cousins, lived during a time of intense religious fervor and excitement among their fellow countrymen, the Jews. John's main message, "The kingdom of heaven is at hand," was connected to the coming of the Messiah and the beginning of a New Age of freedom and, for some, righteousness.

Later Old Testament prophets identified the ninth-century prophet Elijah with a prophet who would come to prepare the way for the Messiah. Jesus identified this prophet with John the Baptist (Matt. 11:14-15). John was also compared with Isaiah, who cried for the people to make straight the ways of the Lord. John was therefore highly important as an instrument of preparation for the Messiah.

ഇരുരു

For a Lively Start

You can start this lesson by discussing John the Baptist's colorful ministry and life-style. What connection was there between John's untamed life-style and his call for the people to repent? (Perhaps he wanted his severe way of living and dressing to point the way to greater self-control in life. Perhaps he was showing that right living is more important than fine clothes.)

What brought so many people out to the wilderness to hear John preach? Would this kind of messenger be as effective today? How would John's message "prepare the way" for Jesus and His message? Why did John seem to doubt whether Jesus was the Messiah, later in life (Matt. 11:1-3)? Perhaps John had expected the Messiah to live a stricter life, as he did (see Matt. 9:14).

Teaching Outline	Daily Bible Readings	

I. The Beginning—Mark 1:1-8
  A. Cry in the wilderness, 1-3
  B. Baptism of repentance, 4-5
  C. Humble place, 6-8
II. The Message—Matt. 3:1-3
  A. "Repent," 1-2a
  B. "Kingdom at hand," 2b
  C. "Prepare," 3
	Mon.	God's Coming Messenger
		Mal. 3:1-5

	Tue.	Preparing the Way *Isa. 40:1-5*
	Wed.	Voice Crying Out *Isa. 40:6-11*
	Thu.	Proclaiming Good News *Matt. 3:4-10*
	Fri.	Pointing to Christ *Matt. 3:11-19*
	Sat.	'You Are God's People' *1 Pet. 2:1-10*
	Sun.	John Prepares the Way *Mark 1:1-8; Matt. 3:1-3*

Verse by Verse

I. The Beginning—Mark 1:1-8

A. Cry in the wilderness, 1-3

1 The beginning of the gospel of Jesus Christ, the Son of God;

2 As it is written in the prophets, Behold, I send my messenger before thy face, which shall prepare thy way before thee.

3 The voice of one crying in the wilderness, Prepare ye the way of the Lord, make his paths straight.

Ironically, the "beginning of the gospel" is not with Jesus, but with His cousin John, son of Elizabeth. This was a highly important feature of the gospel because the prophet Malachi— widely considered to be the last inspired Old Covenant writer—had predicted that a "messenger of the covenant" like John would appear to prepare the way for the coming of the Messiah (Mal. 3:1). Without John and his preparatory work, Jesus would have been dismissed as a false Messiah, one of many at this time in the life of Judaism. Many made a living by stirring up the people with false prophecies and other pretenses, often speaking oracles they knew the current king would like. Jeremiah was their special enemy, warning that "they commit adultery, and walk in lies: they strengthen also the hands of evildoers" (Jer. 23:14; see also 2 Pet. 2:1; Rev. 2:20). John's ragged and rugged appearance (vs. 6) was testimony that he was not prophesying to please anyone or make money from his work, so his testimony that Jesus was real was more likely to be accepted.

"As is is written in the prophets" is an ample signal that Mark (as well as Matthew) will show that this Gospel will dovetail with Old Covenant prophecies. In terms of modern literature, it is not so much "creative writing" or a short story as it is a metaphor, for it seeks to elucidate previous truth.

"Straight paths" is probably a reference to the way crooked roads would be straightened and leveled for a king or other royal personage so their passage would be less strenuous. John's work was a spiritualized version of this kind of preparation. His testimony to the truthfulness of Jesus' teaching is therefore quite properly called "the beginning of the gospel."

B. Baptism of repentance, 4-5

4 John did baptize in the wilderness, and preach the baptism of re-

3

pentance for the remission of sins.

5 And there went out unto him all the land of Judaea, and they of Jerusalem, and were all baptized of him in the river of Jordan, confessing their sins.

John also showed his lack of concern for what a paid prophetic ministry could purchase by living and working in the wilderness, instead of choosing the soft life of a court prophet. There, in a setting that perhaps reminded the people of stories of their ancestors' wandering in the wilderness of Sinai, far from other people but close to God, they could be called to repentance. The washing of baptism in the Jordan River symbolized this cleansing of the spirit, and won for John the nickname of "the Baptizer."

C. Humble place, 6-8

6 And John was clothed with camel's hair, and with a girdle of a skin about his loins; and he did eat locusts and wild honey;

7 And preached, saying, There cometh one mightier than I after me, the latchet of whose shoes I am not worthy to stoop down and unloose.

Although John's clothing, appearance, and diet marked him as a "wilderness man," he attracted large crowds from the cities. In fact, he made such a mark on many Jews that he found it necessary to deny that he himself was not the Messiah (see Acts 13:25). Here, in verse 7, he uses other language to make the same point, affirming that he was not even worth serving as the personal valet of the true Messiah who would follow him.

8 I indeed have baptized you with water: but he shall baptize you with the Holy Ghost.

Another way John chose to show that he and his role were not equal to that of the Christ was to compare their baptisms. Although the forgiveness of sins was associated with John's baptism (vs. 4), such wondrous displays as the Spirit-inspired tongue-speaking in Acts 2 sometimes accompanied baptism in the name of Jesus.

II. The Message—Matt. 3:1-3

A. "Repent," 1-2a

1 In those days came John the Baptist, preaching in the wilderness of Judæa,

2a And saying, Repent ye:

Matthew's account of John's work is highly similar to Mark's. John's work of baptism is called "the baptism of repentance for the remission of sins" (Mark 1:4), while here John is quoted as giving the simple call, "Repent ye." Repentance is also frequently included in the examples of conversion given in the book of Acts. The term in the original means literally to have a change of mind or heart. It shows that conversion for John required a personal transformation, not just a change of political or social allegiance.

2b for the kingdom of heaven is at hand.

Closely connected with the call to repent is the explanation that "the kingdom of heaven is at hand (or "near"). The phrase "kingdom of God" refers to the same realm. Unfortunately, in our day the term is often thought of as still in the future; but in New Testament times people who were converted are said to become members of the Kingdom then

4

and there (see Col. 1:13; 1Thess. 2:12). In the present passage, John could say that the kingdom is "at hand" because *the King* was at hand. The Kingdom is simply the realm over which Jesus reigns; and those who follow Him are made members of it at the time of conversion.

B. "Prepare," 3

3 For this is he that was spoken of by the prophet Esaias, saying, The voice of one crying in the wilderness, Prepare ye the way of the Lord, make his paths straight.

Again, as in Mark 1, the prophecy of Isaiah (40:3) is referred to as the charter for John the Baptist's ministry. Although the wilderness was a rough and sometimes punishing habitat, John seems to have accepted it as an honor to be chosen to "straighten" and smooth the path for Him who was cousin by birth, but Lord by spiritual appointment.

The saga of John the Baptist is not complete without reference to Matthew 11:1ff., when John seems to have doubted whether Jesus was the Messiah. It is likely that Jesus did not measure up to John's expectations—and that of many others—that when the Messiah came He would lead a rebellion against the Roman occupiers of the land God had given to the Jews. Instead of being such a firebrand and military leader, Jesus speaks of performing miracles designed to produce personal faith, of works of healing, and of preaching to the poor. In the end it will be the event of the crucifixion/resurrection, not human testimony, that proves Jesus' Messiahship.

☙❧

Evangelistic Emphasis

Have you noticed that most denominations were born because somebody felt a deep need to emphasize some practice or doctrine their previous fellowship seemed to ignore?

Perhaps this explains why many of the preachers I listened to as a boy seemed to be obsessed with the subject of baptism.

Don't misunderstand what I'm saying here. Any of us who pay attention to the New Testament know how central baptism is in the teaching and practice of Jesus and His earliest followers.

Notice, though, that John the Baptist did not preach about baptism. He called his hearers to repentance. Men and women who came to hear John at the Jordan River chose to be immersed by him because that powerful preacher convicted them of their sins.

John talked to the crowds about how much they needed a life change. Liars needed to start telling the truth. Lawmen needed to stop taking bribes. Clergymen needed to live honest, upright lives in their villages. Why did people need to change their ways? Because the Messiah was coming.

This was John's main message. He preached to the multitudes about their sins because he wanted them to get ready for the coming of God's Son. Can you think of a better way for us to help our friends prepare their hearts and lives for Jesus? Choosing to abandon their bad habits and wrong attitudes may be an important part of their choice to live holy lives with the help of the Lord.

ജരു

Memory Selection

In those days came John the Baptist, preaching in the wilderness of Judaea, And saying Repent ye: for the kingdom of heaven is at hand. For this is he that was spoken of by the prophet Esaias, saying, The voice of one crying in the wilderness, Prepare ye the way of the Lord, make his paths straight.—*Matthew 3:1-3*

If my grandchildren had bumped into John the Baptist, I think they would have called him "weird." We might have, too. What other word can you think of to describe a fellow who never cuts his hair or shaves his beard, who wears homemade skins instead of store-bought clothing, and who dines on bugs and wild honey?

Is it possible that his oddity helped draw the crowds who came to hear him preach? No doubt, people whose hearts were touched by the power of his proclamation helped spread John's fame. They probably hurried back home to the surrounding cities and encouraged their neighbors to come hear the mighty prophet in the wilderness. God often used the weirdness of His spokesmen to get the attention of His people. John the Baptist was no exception. People streamed into the desert to check out this nut-case, and then God's spokesman was able to reach them with His message.

Weekday Problems

Today I received a phone call from a lady who was hoping I might be able to connect her with other pastors in our community so she could share her message and ministry with them and their churches. I don't know what she calls her organization, but her burning passion is to warn people about meth-amphetamines. She wants people to know how permanently destructive these common street drugs can be to anybody who dares to dabble with them.

Have you ever tried to work with a meth addict? Have you tried to help some relative or neighbor break the hold of this pernicious drug on his mind and behavior? If you have, you know how totally such chemicals can enslave their victims, taking over their mind and actions. Just preaching John the Baptist's message, "Repent," seldom works in such cases. Meth addicts, in their few lucid moments, are desperate to repent. They would give anything to be free from the devilish drive that is destroying their lives. But a moment later they seem to be willing to do almost anything to get another fix.

Most of our sinful habits are addictive. They start off disguised as fun, but sins hook us and hold us prisoner. Repentance is therefore painful and, at times, it seems almost impossible. Yet, though tough and hard, it is also essential.

SAP—from sapience, *wisdom; Therefore Wise or Stupid—Take Your Choice*

You're getting fat. You're in terrible shape.
  Well, fat is a shape.

Time may be a great healer, but it's a lousy beautician.

Conscience is what hurts when everything else feels good.

Talk is cheap because supply exceeds demand.

Even if you're on the right track,
  You'll get run over if you just sit there.

An optimist thinks this is the best possible world.
  A pessimist fears this is true.

Yes, there will always be death and taxes.
  But death doesn't get worse every year.

Hang in there. In just two days, tomorrow will be yesterday.

This Lesson in Your Life

I live in West Texas, but I was preaching a revival in southern Arkansas. On the opening Sunday morning I labored in my message to explain John the Baptist's picture of Jesus in Matthew 1:12. John says of Jesus that His "fan is in his hand, and he will throughly purge his floor, and gather his wheat into the garner; but he will burn up the chaff with unquenchable fire." Newer versions of the Bible use different words to describe what Jesus is holding. Some say He has a "winnowing shovel" or a "winnowing fork" in His hand. All of the translations have Jesus involved in threshing a grain crop, but the precise tool He is using to do it seems to be unclear.

In my youthful naivete, I set about that morning to clarify this Gospel picture of our Lord. Wanting to be crystal clear, I explained to my hearers that the fan in Jesus' hand is not one you could plug in. Instead it was a much larger version of the cardboard fans funeral homes used to provide un-air-conditioned churches when I was a boy. I labored to explain the ancient threshing process. In Jesus' day farmers didn't have combines, I pointed out. I described how they separated the good seeds of grain from the leaves and stalk.

First they mulched the dried plants by having oxen tread on them. Then they tossed up the combined mess with a winnowing fork or shovel so that the wind—created on a still day by a winnowing fan—could blow the chaff (the waste portions) to one side. This let the good grain fall into a pile at the farmer's feet. The farmer then stored the good seed and burned up the useless chaff. John's point in using this image is to describe Jesus as One who came to separate the good from the bad. He came to save the good, just as the farmer exerts all his efforts to save the good grain from his field.

That morning in that small Arkansas church I did my best to help the assembled worshipers see John's picture of Christ. While I was preaching my heart out, however, I detected ill-concealed snickers and smiles erupting in my audience. I could see that even some of the deacons were getting entirely too much pleasure out of my carefully crafted sermon. It was enough to make me get paranoid. After worship that morning some of them apologized, but the ones who had known me for years began ribbing me because of my agricultural ignorance. What I didn't know—West Texas parson that I am—was that all of them raised huge crops of peas, and every year after harvest, all of them winnowed their peas. They separated the hulls from the seeds by "fanning their peas." I was probably the only person in the house that day who had never held and used a fan like the one John the Baptist described in Jesus' hand. I needed my audience to teach me this lesson.

All of us, of course, need to learn how seriously Jesus wants us to winnow our attitudes and habits and desires. If we don't, one day He will have to do it for us.

GETTING THE FACTS STRAIGHT

1. How does Mark identify Jesus in his very first verse?
He calls Him "the Son of God."

2. How does Mark describe John the Baptist's baptism in 1:4?
Mark calls John's baptism "the baptism of repentance for the remission of sins."

3. How does Mark describe John's clothes and his diet?
John's clothes were made of camel's hair, cinched up with a leather belt. His diet was grasshoppers (locusts) and wild honey. He lived off the land.

4. What contrast did John the Baptist make between his baptism and the baptism Jesus would offer?
John said his baptism was done in water, but in Mark's account he said Jesus would offer baptism in the Holy Spirit.

5. According to Matthew, how did the prophet Isaiah describe John the Baptist?
Isaiah described John as "the voice of one crying in the wilderness, Prepare ye the way of the Lord."

6. What did John call the Pharisees and Sadducees who came to hear him preach beside the River Jordan?
He called them snakes or vipers, comparing them to reptiles that run from forest and grass fires to the nearest water.

7. According to John, what kind of tree gets chopped down? How did this metaphor apply to John's listeners?
John said a useless tree that doesn't bear good fruit gets cut down and burned. He was predicting God's judgment on the godless religious leaders of that time.

8. Compare the verses in Mark and Matthew that refer to what John cannot do to Jesus' shoes (or sandals). What point was John making in these remarks?
Mark has John saying he is not worthy to untie (or loose the latchet—KJV) of Jesus' shoes. In Matthew's account, John says he is not worthy to carry Jesus' shoes. Either job would be the work of a slave, so John is illustrating how unworthy he is compared to God's Son, the Messiah.

9. According to Matthew 1:11, how will Jesus baptize His followers?
John says Jesus will baptize people with both the Holy Spirit and with fire.

10. What does John the Baptist mean in Matthew 1:8 when he commands his listeners to "bring forth therefore fruits meet for repentance"?
That those who *say* they have repented must demonstrate it by their good works.

9

During a recent summer, wildfires swept through the ranch land in my part of the world, scorching hundreds of square miles of pasture, consuming fences, and broiling whole herds of cattle in the field. Many horses and cattle died in those wind-swept flames, but the smaller critters in the range land—rabbits, prairie dogs, foxes, and especially the snakes—seemed to have a greater instinct for survival. Either they huddled deep in their burrows until the inferno blew past, or they scurried ahead of the flames to the nearest creek or "playa" (shallow lake). A day when a wildfire was roaring across the terrain was not a good day to visit the downwind creeks or lakes. Quicker than you can imagine you would find yourself sharing that water with a frantic horde of rattle snakes fleeing the flames.

This is the metaphor John the Baptist chose to describe the hypocritical religious leaders who came to hear him preach. The wilderness preacher compared them to snakes running from a range fire. "You snakes," he called them. "You brood of vipers! Who warned you to run from the fire of God?"

Any of us who have strayed from the righteous life and chosen to enjoy "the pleasures of sin" (Heb. 11:25) need to hear John's warning about the wrath of God that awaits those who opt for a life of sin. But surely those corrupt religious leaders were by far the minority in the crowds that flocked to the river to hear John's message. From all of Judea came people with tender spirits and hungry hearts—people who craved a right relationship with God. People like that did not need to be threatened with fire from on high. John surely would not call them vipers. These penitent souls came to the river to confess their sins. They left the water with the glorious peace that comes from knowing they had been washed clean.

Through the centuries since John's day, the Body of Christ has been made up of generation after generation of believers who have come to the waters of baptism to find the holy cleansing. Since the earliest days of the Church, converts to Jesus have been told, "Arise and be baptized, and wash away your sins, calling on the name of the Lord" (Acts 22:16, NKJV).

What a blessed cleanness is ours when we know that our sins have been removed by the cleansing blood of Jesus! What a blessing to know that we who have been baptized in Jesus' baptism have been empowered by the Holy Spirit to resist the lure of sin!

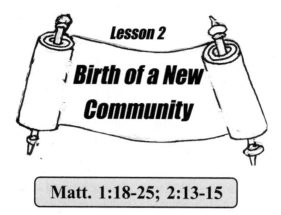

Lesson 2

Birth of a New Community

Matt. 1:18-25; 2:13-15

Now the birth of Jesus Christ was on this wise: When as his mother Mary was espoused to Joseph, before they came together, she was found with child of the Holy Ghost.

19 Then Joseph her husband, being a just man, and not willing to make her a publick example, was minded to put her away privily.

20 But while he thought on these things, behold, the angel of the Lord appeared unto him in a dream, saying, Joseph, thou son of David, fear not to take unto thee Mary thy wife: for that which is conceived in her is of the Holy Ghost.

21 And she shall bring forth a son, and thou shalt call his name JESUS: for he shall save his people from their sins.

22 Now all this was done, that it might be fulfilled which was spoken of the Lord by the prophet, saying,

23 Behold, a virgin shall be with child, and shall bring forth a son, and they shall call his name Emmanuel, which being interpreted is, God with us.

24 Then Joseph being raised from sleep did as the angel of the Lord had bidden him, and took unto him his wife:

25 And knew her not till she had brought forth her firstborn son: and he called his name JESUS.

2:13 And when they were departed, behold, the angel of the Lord appeareth to Joseph in a dream, saying, Arise, and take the young child and his mother, and flee into Egypt, and be thou there until I bring thee word: for Herod will seek the young child to destroy him.

14 When he arose, he took the young child and his mother by night, and departed into Egypt:

15 And was there until the death of Herod: that it might be fulfilled which was spoken of the Lord by the prophet, saying, Out of Egypt have I called my son.

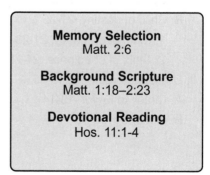

Memory Selection
Matt. 2:6

Background Scripture
Matt. 1:18–2:23

Devotional Reading
Hos. 11:1-4

FOCUS

Too often Christians think of Jesus as their own "personal Savior," to the exclusion of realizing that He is the Savior and head of a *community* of believers. In this lesson, the angel who appeared to Joseph said that the child to be born of Mary would "save *his people* [note the plural] from their sins."

Therefore, to read of the birth of Jesus is to read also of the birth of the New Community, the Church. King Herod had good reason to be fearful of this infant. He was destined to head a corps of millions of spiritual soldiers. For the Babe of Bethlehem was more than Mary's son; He was the star-crossed prince who would lead not just one individual here and another there, but *"my people [the new] Israel"* (Matt. 2:6).

ഇൽ

For a Lively Start

The teacher can focus on the impact the birth of Jesus had by a discussion of how infants born into the families of group members impacted the lives of others. Sometimes having a child will awaken a father, for example, to a new sense of responsibility for the family. The lives of siblings are invariable changed by the arrival of a new baby. Sometimes, in the case of absentee parents, the grandparents are suddenly called on to function as caregivers of the new arrival.

Turning to the manger scene in this story, in what ways would the newborn change the lives both of those who were present, and of millions who would come after Him?

Teaching Outline	Daily Bible Readings	
I. Unusual Conception—Matt. 1:18-25	Mon.	God's Care for His People *Hos. 11:1-7*
A. Conceived by the Spirit, 18-20	Tue.	To All Who Receive Him *John 1:10-14*
B. Child of destiny, 21-25	Wed.	Consider Your Call *1 Cor. 1:26-31*
1. Child of prophecy, 21-23		
2. Child of obedience, 24-25	Thur.	Gifted by God's Spirit *1 Cor. 12:4-13*
II. Unmapped route—2:13-15	Fri.	Members of the Body *1 Cor. 12:14-27*
A. Circuit to Egypt, 13-14	Sat.	Kingdom of God's Son *Col. 1:9-14*
B. Out of Egypt, 15	Sun.	God Is with Us *Matt. 1:18-25, 2:13-15*

Verse by Verse

I. Unusual Conception—Matt. 1:18-25

A. Conceived by the Spirit, 18-20

18 Now the birth of Jesus Christ was on this wise: When as his mother Mary was espoused to Joseph, before they came together, she was found with child of the Holy Ghost.

19 Then Joseph her husband, being a just man, and not willing to make her a publick example, was minded to put her away privily.

20 But while he thought on these things, behold, the angel of the Lord appeared unto him in a dream, saying, Joseph, thou son of David, fear not to take unto thee Mary thy wife: for that which is conceived in her is of the Holy Ghost.

Matthew and Luke (1:34-35) both record the account of the virgin birth. In an age that finds it difficult to accept the miraculous, it is not surprising that the difficulty is often extended to this teaching as well. It is often dismissed as a "magical" element inserted to increase the distance between Jesus and His "merely human" followers. Actually, it fulfills the prophecy of Isaiah 7:14, as shown by Matthew 1:22-23, and serves as one of the many "signs" or miracles that provide evidence that Jesus was the true Messiah.

Some critics also note the supposed similarity between this story and various myths that describe pagan gods consorting with human women. This could hardly have been the case since most of the early Christians were Jews, who would have dismissed such stories out of hand. It is more logical to accept the accounts as they appear, affirming, as one early church father noted, that in the virgin birth God became man in order that man could become like God.

The word for "espoused" comes from a term referring to a memento or souvenir to mark a special occasion, and took the place of an engagement ring in our own culture. It marked, however, a somewhat more serious period in a couple's relationship. From betrothal on, for example, having sexual relations with someone else was grounds for divorce. Joseph would have had ample ground to sue for divorce as he seems to be considering here. However, even before he could do so quietly, instead of engaging in the lawful repetition "I divorce thee!"

three times, his plan is interrupted by an angel's message.

B. Child of destiny, 21-25

1. Child of prophecy, 21-23

21 And she shall bring forth a son, and thou shalt call his name JESUS: for he shall save his people from their sins.

22 Now all this was done, that it might be fulfilled which was spoken of the Lord by the prophet, saying,

23 Behold, a virgin shall be with child, and shall bring forth a son, and they shall call his name Emmanuel, which being interpreted is, God with us.

The Greek name "Jesus" (*Iesous*) was transliterated from the Hebrew "Joshua." Although it was a common name among the Jews, the role of savior was anything but common. From earliest times among Christians, parallels were drawn between Jesus and the deliverance wrought by Joshua after he took over the leadership of Israel from Moses. Of course the comparisons were limited by the teaching that in Jesus was somehow to be found God Himself, "Emmanuel," one basis for Trinitarian teaching.

2. Child of obedience, 24-25

24 Then Joseph being raised from sleep did as the angel of the Lord had bidden him, and took unto him his wife:

25 And knew her not till she had brought forth her firstborn son: and he called his name JESUS.

Stirred from his dream, or sleep, Joseph does not seem to have spent much time speculating what all this might mean. He is a practical man, more given to obeying what the angel commanded than to dwelling on the metaphysics involved by a divine being having a conversation—not to mention sexual relations—with a human. This simplicity of spirit was characteristic of Joseph; had it been otherwise the story might well still be snagged on unanswerable questions and futile attempts at answers. As it was, to say that he "knew (Mary) not" until after Jesus was born means that they abstained from such relationships until after the marriage ceremony.

II. Unmapped route—2:13-15

A. Circuit to Egypt, 13-14

2:13 And when they were departed, behold, the angel of the Lord appeareth to Joseph in a dream, saying, Arise, and take the young child and his mother, and flee into Egypt, and be thou there until I bring thee word: for Herod will seek the young child to destroy him.

14 When he arose, he took the young child and his mother by night, and departed into Egypt:

"They" refers to the three "wise men" (Grk. *magoi*) whose visit to Jesus Matthew alone records (2:1ff.). No doubt the account is provided to lay the groundwork for Jesus' tense relationship with the Roman civil powers in Jerusalem and Judea, and perhaps also to show the universal appeal—to Jews and non-Jews—this universal Messiah would have.

Note Herod's deceitful pretense at wanting to worship the child (vs. 8), when in fact rumors that he was born to be king threatened Roman rule from the ground up. The wise men are therefore warned in another dream to take an alternate route home (vs. 12), While this ruse spares Jesus' life, it unfortunately leads to a tragic massacre that became known in literature and art as the "slaughter of the innocents" (vs. 16). Note also that twice in verse 13 Jesus is referred to not as an infant or a babe but as "the young child," showing the passage of at least several months.

B. Out of Egypt, 15

15 And was there until the death of Herod: that it might be fulfilled which was spoken of the Lord by the prophet, saying, Out of Egypt have I called my son.

As in verse 6, we are shown that all these events are taking place under a careful providence, one which does not remove the free will of the players in the drama but which nonetheless shows the stamp of God's directorship of the play. The careful Jewish rabbi/reader would no doubt already have seen some parallels between the infants Moses and Jesus. Now, with Jesus being brought "out of Egypt" the similarities are too sharply drawn to be missed.

෧෨

Evangelistic Emphasis

Do you have friends or relatives like a brother-in-law I had? He was a decent fellow, straight as an arrow. He was truthful, patriotic, cheerful, and kind. I often said to myself that he was a better man than many of us who were active in church.

During his first decade in our family, however, this good man avoided church. Only when I got to know him as my fishing buddy did I find out why. My brother-in-law didn't think he was good enough to go to church. All of us saw him as a great guy. He saw himself as a human being with weaknesses and failings. And he was too honest to show up at church pretending to be righteous.

When I read the story of that good man Joseph and I see him struggling with his fiance's surprise pregnancy, I think of people like my brother-in-law. Would it help people like him to know that the Christian faith was born under a cloud of ugly rumors and allegations of immorality?

I'm afraid that the secular stereotype of the Church is that we're a bunch of folks who think we're better than everybody else. Those of us on the inside know just how wrong this is. We Christians have come to Jesus because we realize how much we need Him to save us from our sins.

Matthew's account of Jesus' birth reminds us that Christianity was born under a moral cloud. Dear Mary and her Son had to endure the stigma that went with a premarital pregnancy. Those of us who follow Him call our friends and neighbors into a fellowship that understands the plight of sinners.

℘

Memory Selection

All this was done, that it might be fulfilled which was spoken of the Lord by the prophet, saying, Behold, a virgin shall be with child, and shall bring forth a son, and they shall call his name Emmanuel, which being interpreted is, God with us.—*Matthew 1:22-23*

That grand defender of the Christian faith, C. S. Lewis, makes a good point early in his classic book, *Miracles*. All of the Gospel accounts of Jesus' spectacular miracles become believable, Lewis says, if we accept what Matthew and Luke tell us about Jesus' birth. Even the most unschooled among us know that in the normal scheme of things, women who have not mated with a man don't have babies. If we believe that Mary got pregnant before she lay with Joseph, we obviously are people who accept the possibility of miracles. Beyond that, if we accept the angel's explanation that the baby who "is conceived in her is of the Holy Ghost" (Matt. 1:10), we know from the start who Jesus really is. The Messiah we worship is "God with us." This is what His name Emmanuel means.

The miracle is still present among us. He still is "God with us."

Weekday Problems

The congregations I grew up in were mostly white and mostly poor folks below the median income level of th 1940s. Nobody planned it that way. I don't recall anyone in those churches being stand-offish or unkind to the occasional rich family or African American family who came to worship with us. But in those pre-Rosa Parks days, it was a segregated world.

Today I look back on those 1940 times and realize how proud I should have been of the people in those small churches. They exhibited almost none of the ugly prejudice that had produced the harsh ethnic divisions of that era. Anybody of any race was welcome in our fellowship. At the time I was too young and naive to know that I was seeing the love of Jesus at work in those dear people.

Matthew's account of the wise men (called magi in more recent Bible versions) contains the Holy Spirit's subtle but undeniable reminder that God works His wonders through people in all nations. Do you realize that those visitors who came bearing gifts for the Christ child were not Jewish? They came "from the east"—possibly from Persia (modern Iraq or Iran). God guided these foreigners to His Son so they could pay homage to Him.

Later, the apostle Peter confessed, "I now realize that it is true that God treats everyone on the same basis. Whoever fears him and does what is right is acceptable to him, no matter what race he belongs to" (Acts 10:34-35, TEV). The Holy Spirit reveals this same truth to us in the story of the wise men.

From Wedding to Marriage

Bill: My wife has gained 20 pounds since our wedding last month.

Gill: She should try that new reducing roller.

Bill: Oh, did that work with your wife?

Gill: Well, not with her body, but the roller is much thinner.

* * *

My new bride is amazing at figuring out new ways to do house work.

Howzzat?

Well, like in the kitchen. She doesn't turn on the stove, she just lights the grease.

* * *

I had to give my new husband plastic surgery.

You mean you did it yourself?

Sure. I just cut up all his credit cards.

This Lesson in Your Life

Can you imagine a ruler cruel enough or crazy enough to slaughter all the toddlers in a town just because he's afraid they might grow up to want his crown someday? We call this wicked man Herod the Great to distinguish him from all the other Herods who roam the pages of Bible history. But *"Great"?* The blood in the streets of Bethlehem and the wailing of the mothers weeping for their little ones are evidence of how tragically this king abused his power. Can you imagine how the helpless residents of Bethlehem felt when Herod's soldiers finished their carnage?

In December 2004 devastating tsunamis wiped out entire villages and killed thousands of people in Indonesia. Immediately we heard some of the traumatized victims wondering out loud, "Where was God when all of this happened?"

On September 11, 2001, terrorist hijackers took down the World Trade Center, leaving a death toll of almost 3,000 innocent men and women. During the awful aftermath at Ground Zero, firemen and chaplains searched vainly for survivors. Repeatedly we heard grieving family members asking how God could let something like this occur.

Matthew 2 may be God's answer to those who decide to dismiss Him because they have suffered some horrid disaster. God's own Son topped Herod's hit list when the wise men visited Bethlehem. Joseph and Mary barely escaped the blood-lust of Herod's henchmen.

Look at the faces of people in New York City videos in the days right after 9/11 and you have seen the faces of the brutalized populace of Bethlehem after Herod's thugs came to town. "Post-traumatic syndrome" the experts call it psychologically. I wonder what we should call it theologically.

Giving up on God because of tragedy is not a response confined to disasters of epic proportions like the tsunamis. I remember a mother who quit church and renounced her faith when her 3-year-old daughter died an agonizing death from a brain tumor. "How can there possibly be a God of love if things like this happen?" she reasoned.

Unfortunately, this woman's name is Legion. When life falls apart for many people and agony engulfs their souls, their faith falters. God makes sense to them only when the seas of life are smooth and the sun of their days shines brightly. But all was not sweet and rosy when Christ was born, either. Life was not safe and secure. Instead, deceit and intrigue were the political norm. Brutal death lurked close at hand. Yet into this kind of world—a world subject to spasms of deadly, unexpected violence—God sent His Son.

Where is God when evil has a heyday? Right where He was when He was busy sending Jesus into Herod's realm to deliver humanity from the curse of pain and fear and death.

GETTING THE FACTS STRAIGHT

1. What kind of man was Joseph? Can you tell anything from how he dealt with Mary when he discovered that she was pregnant before they got married?
Joseph was a good, just man. His care not to subject Mary to public scorn shows his loving nature.

2. In a Bible dictionary or a good study Bible, find out what the names "Jesus" (or "Joshua") mean.
The root of these names means to save or to rescue. Hence "he will save his people."

3. Does Matthew 2:25 say anything to us about the possibility of sexual abstinence?
Joseph and Mary were able to control their desires for one another during the entire time of her pregnancy.

4. How did the wise men know that Jesus had been born in Judea?
They had seen a star that signaled Christ's birth.

5. What was Herod's reaction to the news that a new king had been born?
Herod was frightened that the new king would take away his throne.

6. How did Herod find out which town to search for the Christ child?
Herod consulted the top priests and scholars in the Temple to find out what the prophets had foretold about the king's birth.

7. What reason did Herod give to the wise men when he told them to let him know where they found the new king, and what was his real reason?
Wicked Herod said he wanted to come "worship" the baby, but he really wanted to kill the child.

8. What gifts did the wise men give to Jesus? If you have found them listed in the Bible text, do you know what they actually are?
All of us have seen and handled *gold*. *Frankincense* was incense that was burned to produce fragrance, and *myrrh* was a sweet-smelling perfume or ointment applied to the bodies or to the clothing of noble, wealthy people.

9. How did the wise men know not to return to let Herod know Jesus' whereabouts? How did Joseph know to flee to Egypt to escape Herod's slaughter?
Both the magi and Joseph were warned in dreams. In Joseph's dream, an angel spoke to him.

10. Why did Joseph and Mary move north to Nazareth instead of returning to Bethlehem?
Herod's son, Archelaus, who succeeded his wicked father, turned out to be as dangerous as his daddy. Again Joseph had a dream with a warning of the potential danger in Jerusalem.

The New Testament offers us a host of names and descriptions of the Church. Would it be accurate to refer to Christ's Church as the fellowship of those who are saved? Such a description would actually be a veiled reference to the name God chose for His Son. The angel told Joseph to name Mary's baby "Jesus."

We may not understand the angel's reason for selecting this name unless we know that Jesus (Greek for the Hebrew name "Joshua") comes from the verb *to save.*

In the Old Testament, Joshua was Israel's deliverer, their rescuer, the one who saved them in difficult times. In the New Testament, Jesus is the one who rescues or delivers or saves us. So to say that we belong to the Church of Jesus (the One who saves) is another way of saying that we are the saved ones.

Let's explore this line of thought a bit further, though, by asking, "Saved from what?" Repeatedly in Old Testament times, God came to the rescue of His people. When slavery in Egypt became unbearable for the Jews, God heard the cries of His people and delivered them from bondage. In the book of Judges, when the abuse of their enemies became too bitter to bear, over and over God raised up champions to lead His people to victory.

Stories of God the Rescuer fill the pages of Scripture. He saved Hagar from Sarah's abuse. He rescued Jacob's family from starvation. He saved Samson from a lion and David from a bear.

Divine rescue may be either physical or spiritual in nature. When the jailer in Philippi's collapsed prison pled, "Sirs, what must I do to be saved?" he was facing almost certain death because his prisoners were loose. "Believe in Jesus," Paul and Silas instructed him (Acts 16:30-31). In other words, "Believe in the One who saves." By keeping his prisoners from escaping, Jesus saved the man physically.

Later that night the preachers told the jailer and his family what to do to save their souls, and the entire household accepted Jesus—the One who saves. This time they claimed His spiritual saving.

"He will save his people from their sins," the angel promised Joseph (Matt. 1:21). All of us who belong to Jesus' Church have received that blessing. We are the saved.

Lesson 3

Core Values of the New Community

Matthew 5:1-16

And seeing the multitudes, he went up into a mountain: and when he was set, his disciples came unto him:

2 And he opened his mouth, and taught them, saying,

3 Blessed are the poor in spirit: for theirs is the kingdom of heaven.

4 Blessed are they that mourn: for they shall be comforted.

5 Blessed are the meek: for they shall inherit the earth.

6 Blessed are they which do hunger and thirst after righteousness: for they shall be filled.

7 Blessed are the merciful: for they shall obtain mercy.

8 Blessed are the pure in heart: for they shall see God.

9 Blessed are the peacemakers: for they shall be called the children of God.

10 Blessed are they which are persecuted for righteousness' sake: for theirs is the kingdom of heaven.

11 Blessed are ye, when men shall revile you, and persecute you, and shall say all manner of evil against you falsely, for my sake.

12 Rejoice, and be exceeding glad: for great is your reward in heaven: for so persecuted they the prophets which were before you.

13 Ye are the salt of the earth: but if the salt have lost his savour, wherewith shall it be salted? it is thenceforth good for nothing, but to be cast out, and to be trodden under foot of men.

14 Ye are the light of the world. A city that is set on an hill cannot be hid.

15 Neither do men light a candle, and put it under a bushel, but on a candlestick; and it giveth light unto all that are in the house.

16 Let your light so shine before men, that they may see your good works, and glorify your Father which is in heaven.

Memory Selection
Matt. 6:33
Background Scripture
Matt. 5:1–7:28

Devotional Reading
Num. 6:22-27

FOCUS

The "Beatitudes," the topic of this lesson, is one of those texts whose grandly simple wording masks some of the most profound and difficult teaching in all of Scripture. They have been called "Kingdom ethics" because they are so basic to being a follower of Jesus and dwelling faithfully under His rule. No one can rightly claim to be a follower of the King while ignoring these principles. Yet no one, however devoted to the Kingdom, can claim to follow these teachings as a list of perfectly kept rules. Perhaps the best we can do is hold them up as a light which we do our best to use as "a lamp unto our feet and a light unto our pathway."

ജരുൽ

For a Lively Start

One good way to start this lesson is simply to read the printed text as a responsive or unified reading, in order to get these highly familiar verses before the group once again. If read responsively, choose a leader who reads every other verse, (verses 1, 3, 5, 7, etc.) and have the group join in alternate verses (2, 4, 6, 8, etc.).

After reading the text, explain that the goal of the lesson is review these teachings as a "possible impossibility"—treating them as a realistic goal while not allowing their difficulty to create guilt by their very reading.

Teaching Outline	Daily Bible Readings	
I. Teaching with Authority—1-2	Mon.	Asking for God's Blessing *Num. 6:22-27*
II. True Blessedness—3-12	Tue.	Blessed by the Father *Matt. 25:31-40*
A. Poor in spirit, 3		
B. Mournful and meek, 4-5	Wed.	Acting on Jesus' Words *Matt. 7:24-29*
C. The highest hunger, 6-7		
D. Pure and peaceful, 8-9	Thu.	Returning Evil with Good *Rom. 12:9-13*
E. The persecuted, 10-12	Fri.	Living in Harmony *Rom. 12:14-21*
II.The 'You Are's'—13-16		
A. Salt, 13	Sat.	Inheriting a Blessing *1 Pet. 3:8-15*
B. Light, 14-16		
	Sun.	Blessing for God's People *Matt. 5:1-16*

Verse by Verse

I. Teaching with Authority—1-2

1 And seeing the multitudes, he went up into a mountain: and when he was set, his disciples came unto him:

2 And he opened his mouth, and taught them, saying,

As justly famous as is the Sermon on the Mount, it has always been accompanied by nagging questions regarding its setting and exact wording. Is it the same sermon as the "Sermon on the Plain" of Luke 6:17ff., or are the two passages parts of separate sermons preached at differing times? Many a preacher has integrated parts of separate sermons, resulting in talks that are both similar and different. Space forbids a thorough examination of the arguments for and against each view; and at any rate the important point is the content rather than the setting.

The two passages share an authoritative note, reminding us of the closing verse in Matthew's version: "He taught them as one having authority, and not as the scribes." In fact, here Jesus is portrayed as settling himself in a sitting position, which was a common position for an authoritative rabbi to assume. Some have even found the book of Matthew to be divided into five parts, and compared them with the five "books of Moses" or the Torah, traditionally thought to have been written by Moses. Perhaps Matthew is painting a picture of a "new Moses," complete with Mosaic authority.

II. True Blessedness—3-12
A. Poor in spirit, 3

3 Blessed are the poor in spirit: for theirs is the kingdom of heaven.

Although the word for "blessed" literally means "happy," Jesus seems to use it with a sense of gravity that is hardly communicated by a word that we associate more with the term "cheerful." It sounds more like the Hebrew *shalom,* which can mean whole-hearted well-being. Through all these "Beatitudes" Jesus chooses a term that bears a surprising and almost opposing definition, to get our attention. The "poor in spirit" are those who are humble enough to call on God instead of the forces of the world, and in that way showing their choice for God's Kingdom, not man's. (Note that in Luke's version the term is not an attitude but simply the non-materialistic term "poor.")

B. Mournful and meek, 4-5

4 Blessed are they that mourn: for they shall be comforted.

5 Blessed are the meek: for they shall inherit the earth.

In Jesus' day many Jews wanted to take up arms to forcibly drive out the Romans, while others, like old Simeon, were meekly "waiting for the consolation of Israel" (Luke 2:25). Here Jesus commends the latter attitude, not the former. The earth they shall "inherit" will be a realm that is like the attitude—a spiritual, not a material or political realm.

C. The highest hunger, 6-7

6 Blessed are they which do hunger and thirst after righteousness: for they shall be filled.

7 Blessed are the merciful: for they shall obtain mercy.

Akin to the meekness with which Simeon and his kind awaited the Kingdom are those for whom Messiah's Kingdom was more important than feasting and banqueting in celebration of the expected New Age. The attitude of mercy is also kin to that of meekness and humility—with the whole tone of Jesus' teaching exalting a non-violent, peaceful, and merciful demeanor. These are "the politics of the Kingdom." We could hardly describe a more contradictory attitude when we look about us today at violent attempts to bring one or another political force to power.

D. Pure and peaceful, 8-9

8 Blessed are the pure in heart: for they shall see God.

9 Blessed are the peacemakers: for they shall be called the children of God.

Continuing to commend peacefulness as the true path for His followers, Jesus also describes the "weapons" of the Kingdom of heaven as purity of heart, not sharpness of sword. Note the similar metaphors used to describe their reward: "kingdom of heaven" . . . "kingdom of God" . . . "children of God" . . . "filled" and "mercy."

E. The persecuted, 10-12

10 Blessed are they which are persecuted for righteousness' sake: for theirs is the kingdom of heaven.

11 Blessed are ye, when men shall revile you, and persecute you, and shall say all manner of evil against you falsely, for my sake.

12 Rejoice, and be exceeding glad: for great is your reward in heaven: for so persecuted they the prophets which were before you.

Those who dare follow Jesus' peaceful way need not expect success. They will be persecuted both by their fellow Jews who want to violently expel the Romans from their borders, and by the Romans themselves. For Jesus, their method is more important than success. He is the Prince of Peace, and He calls His followers to take up the methods of peace that will lead Him to the Cross. Yet those who take up their own crosses are members of an elite corps that have their own definition of "success"—they are fellow-peace-warriors with the prophets who, through the years, have also been put to death "for righteousness' sake."

II. The 'You Are's'—13-16

A. Salt, 13

13 Ye are the salt of the earth: but if the salt have lost his savour, wherewith shall it be salted? it is thenceforth good for nothing, but to be cast out, and to be trodden under foot of men.

Jesus uses two metaphors to further encourage His followers to take up His way of "activism" instead of the way of the world. First, in that way they maintain the preservative quality of salt. They are little good if they merely *appear* to be His followers, but have lost their "savor" or preservative power. That kind of salt is like sand, and is fit only for packing down into trails.

B. Light, 14-16

14 Ye are the light of the world. A city that is set on an hill cannot be hid.

15 Neither do men light a candle, and put it under a bushel, but on a candlestick; and it giveth light unto all that are in the house.

16 Let your light so shine before men, that they may see your good works, and glorify your Father which is in heaven.

Second, Christ's followers must remember to be *light*. If they forget and act like their enemies, they are like a candle covered by a basket. Note that maintaining Christ-like works is for the purpose of glorifying their Leader, not themselves.

ഇൗരു

Evangelistic Emphasis

Are any words in the New Testament more familiar to more people than Matthew 5–7, commonly known as Jesus' famous "Sermon on the Mount"? Long before I understood their full meaning, my parents had taught me parts of this section of Scripture such as Jesus' well-known and life-changing words calling His followers to be "the salt of the earth" and "the light of the world."

We can use the truths in this sermon to touch the hearts of loved ones and neighbors who don't yet know Jesus. His words here are simple. They address humanity's most basic concerns and needs, so they will "hook" the felt-needs of just about anyone.

Often our friends who never go to church seem to be more concerned about insincere worship than are some of us to never miss a church service. Their frequent criticism of church folks tends to be that we who worship are too often hypocrites. So our unchurched friends should appreciate the fact that Jesus is equally concerned about this. He warns us to "beware of practicing your piety before men in order to be seen by them" (Matt. 6:1, RSV).

Let me encourage you to check out the rest of Jesus' sermon to identify truths that will connect with people you want to win for Jesus.

ଗୈଓଃ

Memory Selection

Lay not up for yourselves treasures upon earth, where moth and rust doth corrupt, and where thieves break through and steal: But lay up for yourselves treasures in heaven, where neither moth nor rust doth corrupt, and where thieves do not break through nor steal: For where your treasure is, there will your heart be also.—*Matthew 6:19–21*

A friend of mine recently turned 90. He is still physically and mentally fit, but his wife's failing health caused them to put a For Sale sign in front of the home they have enjoyed so much. To prepare for their move to a nearby assisted living village, they began the difficult task of culling their possessions. Into the stack of garage sale stuff they consigned treasures it took them decades to accumulate.

On the appointed day strangers came and hauled away truckloads of furniture and china and books and baubles my friends had loved and protected. Now that they were downsizing from a spacious home to a one-bedroom apartment, some of their most precious items had become burdens they needed to unload.

Reflecting on this soul-stretching process, my friend wrote touching words about how little the things they parted with actually mattered. He says, "It is sobering to see how much we can do without that we supposed we needed." Thankfully my friend and his dear wife have spent most of their lives laying up their real treasures in heaven. This gives them clear perspective now and a lot to look forward to.

Weekday Problems

Shortly after their mother's funeral, the two middle-aged sons began growling at each other like pit bulls on a chain. Mama didn't leave much behind—not like wealthy people do—but she left enough to fuel the anger of her boys as they fussed about how to divide it.

I don't know what might have happened if a friendly neighbor and a long-time pastor friend had not stepped in to make peace between these warring brothers. One man was threatening serious damage to the other.

How fortunate is the family, or the church, or the business that has a peacemaker among them. Some people by nature stir up trouble. They ignite anger and plant seeds of distrust. They can keep a home or a congregation in a ferment most of the time. "Blessed are the peacemakers," Jesus said. Their kind spirits and calm words smooth ruffled feathers and dampen angry arguments.

Most of our fusses are so pointless. Joseph Addison contemplated this as he walked among the tombs of great men. "When I see kings lying beside those who deposed them, when I see rival wits placed side by side," he wrote, "I reflect with sorrow and astonishment on the frivolous competitions, factions, and debates of mankind."

Each of us would do well to look honestly at ourselves.

• Do we make peace or war among our associates? Do we usually calm tempers or light fuses by the words we speak?

Heavenly Harmony

God help the man who won't marry until he finds the perfect woman, and God help him still more if he finds her.—*Benjamin Tillett*

* * *

Marriages are made in heaven, but they are lived on earth.—*George P. Weiss*

* * *

Even if marriages are made in heaven, man has to be responsible for the maintenance.—*Kroehler News*

* * *

A good marriage is not a contract between two persons but a sacred covenant beween three. Too often Christ is never invited to the wedding and finds no room in the home. Why? Is it because we have misrepresented Him and forgotten His joyful outlook on life?—*Donald T. Kauffman: Gist of the Lesson*

This Lesson in Your Life

Of the many books written on our Lord's Sermon on the Mount, none outshines the two-volume classic by the late British pastor, Dr. D. Martyn Lloyd-Jones. The books contain 30 sermons this great preacher shared with his church in Westminster Chapel.

Can we learn anything from the fact that it took this expositor half of his first volume just to capture the truths in the "Beatitudes"—the "blessed" statements that begin Jesus' sermon?

Where could we find a better description of the Christian way than in these opening lines of the sermon? In them Jesus defines the true contentment and genuine satisfaction that should fill the hearts of those who are committed to living life His way. Do you remember all the advertisements that began with the catchy words, "Happiness is . . ."? In every case the message was that a person could find happiness in something they purchased. To hear Wall Street tell it, happiness is owning a new Lexus, the latest iPod, a showy Rolex, or maybe a plasma TV screen. Happiness by this carnal definition is cruising the Caribbean, touring Scandinavia, or lounging on South Sea islands. How different from the world's view are the definitions Jesus gives us for that which truly satisfies the soul.

Some of the newer versions of the New Testament begin each of the Beatitudes with the expression, "Happy is the person who . . . ." While this seems to dilute Jesus' meaning, still it may help us to home in on His central message.

What does Jesus tell us in the Beatitudes? That a true sense of spiritual well-being belongs to those who swim upstream in this world. The world applauds the proud; Jesus lauds the "poor in spirit." The world bows to the powerful; Jesus commends those who do acts of mercy. The world defines "the good life" as debauchery; Jesus finds it in a hunger for righteousness.

Most of what the world touts as ways to be happy amounts to temporary fun, at best. Dr. Lloyd-Jones wisely observes, "Anything which, by evading the difficulties, merely makes people happy for the time being, is ultimately going to add to their misery and problems."

Jesus came to give us eternal life. That is the kind of life He is describing in the Beatitudes. Quick fixes and one-night stands are a recipe for lasting misery and disappointment.

Look at the marvelous promises attached to each of the Beatitudes. Do you want to be part of the Lord's Kingdom? Do you want Heaven's comfort for your soul? Would you like for the emptiness in your heart to be filled? Do you want Heaven's mercy to meet your needs? Would you like to see God? These blessings and more Jesus promises to us if we will become the kind of people He describes in the Beatitudes.

GETTING THE FACTS STRAIGHT

1. **The word "ye" in "Ye are the salt . . ." and "Ye are the light . . ." (5:13-14) is plural. How does this affect the meaning of what Jesus says about us here?**

That Jesus intends for the Church as a whole to be examples of goodness in the world.

2. **Jesus tells us He came not to destroy but to fulfil the Law. In what ways does He fulfil it?**

In 5:17-48, each paragraph tells us how to behave in a way that fulfills the real intent of God's Law—such as controlling not only adultery but also lust.

3. **According to Jesus, what was God's real intent behind the basic law, "Thou shalt not kill"?**

Instead of just prohibiting murder, God wanted His people not to be abusive or hateful to each other.

4. **According to Jesus, what was God's real intent behind the basic law, "Thou shalt not commit adultery"?**

The Seventh Commandment was intended to control our sexual desires and free us from enslaving lusts.

5. **In the same way, according to Jesus, how was God trying to shape our behavior when He gave the law, "Swear not at all"?**

He wanted us to learn to tell the truth, simply and directly, without embellishing our speech with elaborate oaths.

6. **According to Jesus, what did God really intend when He told us to love our neighbors?**

He wants us to love even those people who are unlovable to us.

7. **What main mistake did Jesus identify in many who come to worship God?**

People often do acts of worship in order to be praised rather than to give praise.

8. **What does it mean to "lay up treasures in heaven"?**

This expression might apply to *tithing*, but it may reach beyond this to describe personal financial priorities that value eternal things more than temporary worldly possessions.

9. **Explain Jesus' command, "Take no thought for your life . . ." (6:25). Will it help to compare some of the newer versions?**

The simplest translations say, "Don't worry." Jesus was not prohibiting medical care or life insurance.

10. **What does Jesus teach us in this sermon about prayer?**

He tells us our prayers will be answered. He tells us to pray for God to hear us and not man. He tells us to keep our prayers short and simple, and He gives us His famous sample prayer, "The Lord's Prayer."

Uplift

A national hero like Benjamin Franklin achieves almost mythical stature, so it is hard to know if the tales told about him are true or not.

The story about Franklin's role in introducing street lighting in Philadelphia has the ring of truth about it. If it turns out that it didn't really take place, still it serves as a good parable for us today.

It troubled Ben Franklin that the streets of his growing city were dark and hard to navigate at night. He considered approaching the city fathers about the need he perceived, but he knew their penny-pinching ways well enough to know that he would be wasting his time.

So finally, when his own prosperity permitted it, Ben did the one thing he could do without waiting for their permission or their financing. He hung his own fancy street light on an extended bracket attached to the front of his own house.

According to the tale, Franklin's neighbors quickly saw the advantage of the nocturnal lighting. After dodging potholes and stumbling on curbs along the dark street, they would come to the well-lit area by Franklin's home.

That's all it took. Franklin's neighbors knew a good idea when they saw it. Before long—without any kind of civic improvement campaign being waged by the old printer—people in his neighborhood began mounting light-holders on their houses too. Philadelphia became a lighted city because their illustrious citizen "lit the way."

Albert Schweitzer somewhere wrote, "Example is not the main thing in influencing others. It is the only thing." In His most famous sermon, Jesus seems to recognize this truth. Nowhere in the sermon does He tell his followers to go talk about their faith. Instead, He tell us to go demonstrate it—to be the salt of the earth and the light of the world.

A lot of the people in your town will never hear the sermons preached in your pulpit or the Bible studies taught in your church. But they will see how the people in your church live.

If the girls in your church avoid pregnancies before marriage, this will be a shining example to a world full of unwed mothers.

If the young people on your pews refuse to be drawn into the drug and gang cultures that entice so many, other families in your community will want this for their kids.

We need to be sure, of course, that the light we shine into the world around us draws praise not to us but to our Lord—that they may glorify our Father in heaven.

Lesson 4

Creating a Community Of Servants

Matt. 20:17-28

And Jesus going up to Jerusalem took the twelve disciples apart in the way, and said unto them,

18 Behold, we go up to Jerusalem; and the Son of man shall be betrayed unto the chief priests and unto the scribes, and they shall condemn him to death,

19 And shall deliver him to the Gentiles to mock, and to scourge, and to crucify him: and the third day he shall rise again.

20 Then came to him the mother of Zebedee's children with her sons, worshipping him, and desiring a certain thing of him.

21 And he said unto her, What wilt thou? She saith unto him, Grant that these my two sons may sit, the one on thy right hand, and the other on the left, in thy kingdom.

22 But Jesus answered and said, Ye know not what ye ask. Are ye able to drink of the cup that I shall drink of, and to be baptized with the baptism that I am baptized with? They say unto him, We are able.

23 And he saith unto them, Ye shall drink indeed of my cup, and be baptized with the baptism that I am bap-

tized with: but to sit on my right hand, and on my left, is not mine to give, but it shall be given to them for whom it is prepared of my Father.

24 And when the ten heard it, they were moved with indignation against the two brethren.

25 But Jesus called them unto him, and said, Ye know that the princes of the Gentiles exercise dominion over them, and they that are great exercise authority upon them.

26 But it shall not be so among you: but whosoever will be great among you, let him be your minister;

27 And whosoever will be chief among you, let him be your servant:

28 Even as the Son of man came not to be ministered unto, but to minister, and to give his life a ransom for many.

Memory Selection
Matt. 20:28

Background Scripture
Matt. 20:1-28; Mark 10:35-45

Devotional Reading
Philippians 2:1-11

31

Christianity comes with a built-in predicament. It comes in a group called the *church,* which, like any group, functions best only when it has effective leaders. Yet even the most dynamic leaders in the church are called to be *servants,* like Jesus. We seem forced to combine two words to define their role: they are to be *"servant-leaders."* It can be difficult to be both a servant and a leader; but that is what church leaders are called to be.

This concept, though difficult, has found its way from the church into many businesses. "Servant-leaders" —people who can combine leadership with humble service—have proved useful in many circles. In this lesson, Jesus describes it.

හ)ශ

For a Lively Start

Ask group members to give brief descriptions of two kinds of people: *servants* and *leaders.* For example, they may describe a servant as someone who does what he is told . . . who has an attitude of helpfulness . . . who seeks the good of others. On the other hand, they may describe a *leader* as someone who knows how to get things done, and how to get others to get things done. They have a vision for what the organization should be and do. They know how to motivate and inspire others.

Now ask whether it's reasonable to seek both sets of descriptions in the same person. Have they known someone who can blend the qualities of both a servant and a leader? Christ seeks that kind of person for work in the Kingdom.

Teaching Outline	Daily Bible Readings	
I. Ultimate Servant—17-19	Mon.	Christ's Humility *Philip. 2:1-11*
II. Misunderstood Service—20-23	Tue.	Greatest in the Kingdom *Matt. 18:1-5*
A. Positions sought, 20-21	Wed.	Serving and Following *John 12:20-26*
B. Over-confidence stated, 22-23	Thu.	Serving Fearlessly *Matt. 10:24-33*
III. Models of Leaders, 24-28	Fri.	Serving in God's Strength *1 Pet. 4:7-11*
A. Lordly leaders, 24-25	Sat.	The Last Will Be First *Matt. 20:1-16*
B. Christian leaders, 26-28	Sun.	The Serving Son of Man *Matt. 20:17-28*

Verse by Verse

I. Ultimate Servant—17-19

17 And Jesus going up to Jerusalem took the twelve disciples apart in the way, and said unto them,

18 Behold, we go up to Jerusalem; and the Son of man shall be betrayed unto the chief priests and unto the scribes, and they shall condemn him to death,

19 And shall deliver him to the Gentiles to mock, and to scourge, and to crucify him: and the third day he shall rise again.

This is the second time that Matthew records Jesus predicting His suffering and death in Jerusalem (see also 16:21). It is so far from the expectations of the Messiah, however, that the disciples ignore it. Here, the prediction follows a long parable that portrays the owner of a vineyard hiring workers. It would have been easy for the disciples to picture themselves in such a role, too. Such a position is a far cry from being persecuted, and their desire for a position of authority overcomes what Jesus has just said.

II. Misunderstood Service—20-23

A. Positions sought, 20-21

20 Then came to him the mother of Zebedee's children with her sons, worshipping him, and desiring a certain thing of him.

21 And he said unto her, What wilt thou? She saith unto him, Grant that these my two sons may sit, the one on thy right hand, and the other on the left, in thy kingdom.

"Zebedee's children" were James and John (Matt. 4:21). The ambition of their mother seems to be stronger than the two brothers' personality, despite their nickname, "sons of thunder" (Mark 3:17). At any rate, their mother seems not to have drawn anything from Jesus' prediction of His suffering and death; she knows only that He is destined for holy leadership (not that they came worshiping him, vs. 20), and that she yearns for the prestige her sons would have if they sit on Jesus' right and left hand in the Kingdom whose nature she completely misunderstands.

B. Over-confidence stated, 22-23

22 But Jesus answered and said, Ye know not what ye ask. Are ye able to drink of the cup that I shall drink of, and to be baptized with the baptism that I am baptized with? They

say unto him, We are able.

23 And he saith unto them, Ye shall drink indeed of my cup, and be baptized with the baptism that I am baptized with: but to sit on my right hand, and on my left, is not mine to give, but it shall be given to them for whom it is prepared of my Father.

Jesus tries in vain to correct the Zebedee family's concept of His Kingdom. To ask for positions of leadership in the true Kingdom is to ask both for humble service and persecution. Both "the cup" and "baptism" were common ways of referring to one's lot or fate (see Ps. 11:6, 23:5, 16:5). While James and John envision a "cup" of glory as their fate in the Kingdom, Jesus warns subtly that it would actually be a "cup" or baptism of fire or persecution.

James and John are too quick to answer "we are able," having no clue of what this means. In fact, history and tradition will show that violent deaths await them as their "cup" in the kingdom. Herod had James killed with a sword (Acts 12:2), while one ancient tradition has it that John was martyred by being plunged into boiling oil.

At any rate, Jesus says that it will not be His responsibility, but the Father's, to appoint leaders in His Kingdom. Furthermore, when He does, they will not be tyrants but servants—men and women who lead by serving others (see 2534).

III. Models of Leaders, 24-28
A. Lordly leaders, 24-25

24 And when the ten heard it, they were moved with indignation against the two brethren.

25 But Jesus called them unto him, and said, Ye know that the princes of the Gentiles exercise dominion over them, and they that are great exercise authority upon them.

Although the other 10 apostles are indignant that James and John (apparently encouraged by their mother) would ask for special favor, the fact that Jesus addresses all of them indicates that they also have little concept of the nature of leadership in the Kingdom. To correct it, Jesus has only to refer to the character of pagan leaders. In his day, to be named king, or to seize a kingdom, was virtually a death sentence, since one who dared to elevate himself to king by murdering his predecessor could expect the same fate. The reason is clear: as a rule they led by arrogance, fear, and intimidation. As a matter of fact, the same could be said of many Jewish leaders in the time of Christ. He probably refrains from using them as an example only to give Himself a little longer to complete His ministry.

The main point, however, is that rule by arrogance and fear is contrary to the spirit of the Kingdom of God. Note that authority and "greatness" are linked in verse 25, while Jesus seeks leaders whose authority is won by *service*. Such "dominion" among the Gentiles is quite the opposite of the dominion Jesus won by quiet and humble service. The dominant symbols of His style of leadership are the basin and the towel (John 13:5), not the crown and the sword. Despite Jesus' negative reference to the opposite nature of Gentile leadership, history too often records similar styles of leadership among power-hungry Christian leaders, too.

B. Christian leaders, 26-28

26 But it shall not be so among you: but whosoever will be great among you, let him be your minister;

27 And whosoever will be chief among you, let him be your servant:

28 Even as the Son of man came not to be ministered unto, but to minister, and to give his life a ransom for many.

In direct contrast to the typical tyrant among Gentiles or pagan peoples, "it shall not be so" among the followers of Jesus. Verses 26 and 27 are cast as proverbs, with words that have "rhyming meanings." Those who will be "great" are those who would be a "minister" (lit. *diakanos),*" and the way to greatness is servanthood, (lit. a slave).

Although not all such servant-leaders will be expected to become martyrs as Jesus did, His *spirit* of ministry, which led Him to the Cross, is to serve as the model and spirit of Christian leadership.

The term "ransom" has generated much discussion. It and related terms have given rise to the "ransom" (Grk. *lutron*) theory of the atonement, with the accompanying question of whether Jesus paid the ransom to God or to Satan. The New Testament stops short of drawing such a fine line to the question, leaving it at the point of the *necessity* rather than the *explanation* of the death of Christ in the act of redemption. At any rate, the question hardly arises here, where the "ransom" serves as the model of servanthood, with no thought of the price that mere human leaders pay amounting to the price of redemption.

℘ℭ

Evangelistic Emphasis

"Ask not what your country can do for you; ask what you can do for your country," was the memorable challenge of President John F. Kennedy. We who heard this challenge were surprised and impressed by the young President's daring appeal to the servant spirit of our nation. Tens of thousands of bright American youths responded by signing up for grueling, dangerous jobs in Peace Corps assignments around the globe.

President Kennedy's uninviting invitation touched hearts and galvanized volunteers. Who would have dreamed that offering people low pay, dangerous job sites, and a dearth of modern comforts would trigger a flood of eager workers?

In many of our churches we are observing the same phenomenon. Our best and brightest young people seem most likely to get on board if we offer them dirty, dangerous, demanding labor on foreign mission fields.

Like Jesus, Christians with a right spirit step forward to serve and not to be served.

ঙ৩৫৩

Memory Selection

Ye know that the princes of the Gentiles exercise dominion over them, and they that are great exercise authority upon them. But it shall not be so among you: but whosoever will be great among you, let him be your minister; And whosoever will be chief among you, let him be your servant.—Matthew 20:25-27

One fellow I heard discussing these verses had a catchy way of summarizing them. He said, "Jesus is telling us here that the way up is down." Does that sound at first like a contradiction? Of course it does, because most of us are accustomed to seeing success and failure, greatness and worthlessness, measured by the standards of the world.

Only when we adopt Kingdom lenses do we begin to rank Mother Teresa or Billy Graham ahead of Paris Hilton or Bill Gates.

Slavery is a distasteful concept to all free people. Although it has been outlawed for a century and none of us and our kin have to had to worry about being bought or sold, still something inside us squirms a bit when we hear Jesus calling us to fill the role of a slave.

That is the basic meaning of our Lord's words in this passage. We normally use the word minister to designate a clergyman, but that is not at all what Jesus meant to imply. Both minister and servant in the KJV text are translated "slave" in many of the newer translations.

After we get past the shock of that ugly word, it can convey to us just how radical the teaching of Jesus is on this subject.

Weeekday Problems

Some communities today are facing a crisis. They lack volunteers to staff many of the social service programs vital to the well-being of their people. Programs that flourished in the middle of the past century struggle to survive today, at least in part because the capable women who kept them going have become part of our nation's work force.

Non-profit agency and church volunteers also are in short supply because we are burying a generation imbued with a sense of volunteerism. Community service ranked high on their priorities. They willingly filled unsalaried slots in everything from city government to Meals on Wheels. Today we are missing their unselfish service.

Perhaps the best way to train a new generation of volunteers is to train them first to serve our Savior and to imitate His Servant nature. He tells us that He came "to give himself." United Way, Red Cross, scouting programs, and hospital auxiliaries will have all the workers they need if we teach the coming generation the idea of service before self.

"'Nobody gave me anything to do,' is the complaint of the immature Christian," Pastor Wes Reagan insists. As he points out, "The world is full of people to love and serve."

Servants and Other Leaders

If you want to work for the kingdom of God, and to bring it, and enter into it, there is just one condition to be first accepted. You must enter into it as children, or not at all.—*John Ruskin*

* * *

It is not the possession of extraordinary gifts that makes extraordinary usefulness, but the dedication of what we have to the service of God.—*Frederick William Robertson*

* * *

There is no structural organization of society which can bring about the coming of the Kingdom of God on earth, since all systems can be perverted by the selfishness of man.—*William Temple*

* * *

Go, labor on; spend and be spent—
Thy joy to do the Father's will;
It is the way the Master went;
Should not the servant tread it still?
—*Horatius Bonar*

This Lesson in Your Life

Years ago in *Our Daily Bread*, Paul van Gorder recounted a Civil War story that well illustrates the main point Jesus tried to teach His followers after James and John made their upstart request for positions of power and honor. The Civil War had ended, so the story goes, and as General Sherman's army made its way home, they planned to march through one large city in a victorious parade.

The night before the parade, Sherman summoned Oliver Howard, one of the generals under his command. "You faithfully led your division beside me during our hardest days in Georgia, so you rightfully deserve to ride at the head of that division in tomorrow's parade."

General Howard nodded agreement, and Sherman continued, "I have been asked to allow the man who preceded you in that command to represent that division tomorrow. I don't know what to do."

"I led my division to victory," General Howard objected. "Surely I am entitled to lead them when we are honored tomorrow."

"Indeed, you are," Sherman agreed, "but I know you are a Christian, and I was wondering if Christian considerations might lead you to yield your rights for the sake of peace."

"Oh," Howard consented, "in that case, of course I'll yield."

"All right," General Sherman smiled, "I will so arrange, and will you please report to me in the morning at 9? You will ride with me at the head of the army."

Repeatedly Jesus tried to get this truth across to His men. "Every one that exalteth himself shall be abased; and he that humbleth himself shall be exalted," was His most consistent message (Luke 18:14). It may be the hardest one for us to accept today.

Something inside us yearns for honor. Like James and John, we crave the recognition and the power we think we deserve for our good works. Jesus warns us that seeking glory will bring us the opposite.

Watch Jesus closely, theologian Robert Capon Farrar bids us, and all through the Master's ministry we will see Him paying special tribute to "the last, the least, the lost, the little, and the dead." Just the opposite of how the world honors its heroes.

"The last will be first," Jesus told His apostles (Matt. 20:16). That seems to be a mixed up way to run things, doesn't it? But if this is the rule of the Kingdom, then the corollary must also be true: "The first will be last."

We are never more confused than when we scheme and clamor for an honored position in Christ's Kingdom. He tells us Himself that this is the surest way for us to come out in last place, to find ourselves humiliated before the very people we want to impress.

GETTING THE FACTS STRAIGHT

1. In a Bible dictionary, a study Bible, or footnotes in a modern translation, see if you can define the time and money equivalents in Matthew 20:1-10.

Today's English Version defines a "denarius" as "the regular wage, a silver coin a day" (20:2).

2. What does the Parable of the Laborers say about the length of our own service in the Lord's vineyard?

Some of us start serving Jesus as children; others find Jesus only in their last years. He does not love one less than the other.

3. How might this parable apply to the resentment of first-century Jews toward Gentile latecomers?

Jews had been serving God for centuries. Gentiles were coming into the Church as first-generation believers. Was it fair for both Jew and Gentile to receive the same reward?

4. Does Matthew (in 20:17-19) blame the Jews or the Gentiles for Jesus' suffering and death?

Both Jews and Gentiles get equal blame in these verses.

5. What does the example of James and John's mother teach us about the efforts of modern mothers to secure what is best for their children?

Sometimes mothers are not wise to seek advantages or special treatment for their children. Their efforts to "help" their kids may actually do their offspring harm.

6. What does it mean "to sit at the right hand or the left hand of Jesus"?

The positions next to the King were positions of high rank and power.

7. Why do you suppose this argument about position and authority occurs at the specific time it does in Jesus' minisistry?

In the last weeks of Jesus' ministry, the apostles are often seen fussing about which one should be running things.

8. What are "the cup" and "the baptism" Jesus refers to in His reply to the request of Zebedee's sons?

These terms are figures of speech that refer to the suffering Jesus and His followers would have to endure.

9. How are the suffering of Jesus and the suffering of His followers linked in this passage?

Jesus predicts that His servants will have to share the kind of suffering He endured to save us.

10. How does this scene show that Jesus' followers did not understand His repeated references to His suffering and death?

They were begging for honor; He was promising suffering. Are we any clearer on this than they were?

Some humorist with a kink in his funny bone dared to warn us that "those who get too big for their britches will be exposed in the end."

All of us have seen some pompous soul trying to strut his stuff and in the process making an absolute fool of himself. Sadly, those who embarrass themselves with such performances are usually the last people in the house to know how ridiculous they look.

Does it surprise you that Jesus' wisdom is so down-to-earth and practical? His advice about how to attain honor works not just in church circles but in every social arena. Instinctively we recognize that true greatness belongs to those who do not profess it or seek it.

At least, we recognize that this principle is at work when somebody else is doing the glory-seeking. It's the guy or the gal on an ego trip who often seems least able to perceive how much damage they may be doing to their image.

But the flip side of Jesus' wisdom turns out to be just as pragmatic and effective. People who are genuinely humble tend to rise in our esteem. The less they try to enhance their image, the better they look to the rest of us. In the community Jesus established, greatness is measured in terms of service.

We honor the missionary who gives up the comforts of middle-class America to bring truth and education and medical care to people in primitive cultures.

We salute the foster parents who pass up the luxuries and the pleasure-seeking of our age to provide hope and stability and love to children who would otherwise live without it.

We admire those believers who devote many dollars and days in the name of Jesus to the brighten the days of those whose advanced years and failing health have left them little reason for cheer.

We lift up the servants among us—those who selflessly bear the burdens of those who have no right to ask for assistance and who could never repay those who aid them.

"Whoever desires to become great among you shall be your servant" (Mark 10:43, NKJV).

Lesson 5

Empowered to Be a Community

Acts 2:1-17a

And when the day of Pentecost was fully come, they were all with one accord in one place.

2 And suddenly there came a sound from heaven as of a rushing mighty wind, and it filled all the house where they were sitting.

3 And there appeared unto them cloven tongues like as of fire, and it sat upon each of them.

4 And they were all filled with the Holy Ghost, and began to speak with other tongues, as the Spirit gave them utterance.

5 And there were dwelling at Jerusalem Jews, devout men, out of every nation under heaven.

6 Now when this was noised abroad, the multitude came together, and were confounded, because that every man heard them speak in his own language.

7 And they were all amazed and marvelled, saying one to another, Behold, are not all these which speak Galilaeans?

8 And how hear we every man in our own tongue, wherein we were born?

9 Parthians, and Medes, and Elamites, and the dwellers in Mesopotamia, and in Judaea, and Cappadocia, in Pontus, and Asia,

10 Phrygia, and Pamphylia, in Egypt, and in the parts of Libya about Cyrene, and strangers of Rome, Jews and proselytes,

11 Cretes and Arabians, we do hear them speak in our tongues the wonderful works of God.

12 And they were all amazed, and were in doubt, saying one to another, What meaneth this?

13 Others mocking said, These men are full of new wine.

14 But Peter, standing up with the eleven, lifted up his voice, and said unto them, Ye men of Judaea, and all ye that dwell at Jerusalem, be this known unto you, and hearken to my words:

15 For these are not drunken, as ye suppose, seeing it is but the third hour of the day.

16 But this is that which was spoken by the prophet Joel;

17 And it shall come to pass in the last days, saith God, I will pour out of my Spirit upon all flesh:

Memory Selection
Acts 2:4

Background Scripture
Acts 2:1-47

Devotional Reading
Eph. 2:11-22

FOCUS

The lessons in this unit all focus on the early Church as a *community*. In God's wisdom, He chose a Jewish "international holiday"—the annual Day of Pentecost—as the time to announce to the world what Jesus had accomplished on the Cross, and how all who believe can now be members of His international community, the Church.

That stroke of genius was also accompanied by a problem: the diverse nationalities represented at Pentecost posed a language problem. How could such a diverse group understand the announcement of the New Community? This lesson shows how this issue was solved by the Holy Spirit.

୨୦୯ଽ

For a Lively Start

How can a modern group grasp something of the excitement and chaos of the event in Acts 2, when people from many different lands heard the Good News in their own language? One way is to collect four or five versions of the Bible—including a foreign language or two such as Spanish and French if possible—and to *read the core of Peter's message in Acts 2: 31-36 from each version at the same time.*

Then ask how any sense could be made from such a confusion of languages? The answer is by the power of the Holy Spirit, which enabled people from each country to understand what was said. A diverse community is now well on its way to becoming one!

Teaching Outline	Daily Bible Readings
I. Tongues of Fire—1-4	Mon. Fellowship with God and Jesus *1 John 1:1-4*
A. Pentecostal event, 1	Tue. Living in Hope *Acts 2:22-35*
B. Spirit-language, 2-4	Wed. Living in Fellowship *Acts 2:37-47*
II. A Puzzle to Solve—5-8	Thu. 'Receive the Holy Spirit' *John 20:19-23*
III. Salad-bowl of Nations—9-11	Fri. One Body in Christ *Rom. 12:3-8*
IV. Question and Answer—12-17a	Sat. The Coming of the Spirit *Acts 2:1-13*
A. Wrong answer, 12-13	Sun. Living in the Last Days *Acts 2:1-21*
B. Fulfilled prophecy, 14-17a	

Verse by Verse

I. Tongues of Fire—1-4
A. Pentecostal event, 1

1 And when the day of Pentecost was fully come, they were all with one accord in one place.

Pentecost was a major Jewish feast that was observed 50 days after the feast of the Passover. No doubt it was chosen as the day for the explosion of "tongues" or languages inaugurating the New Age of the Spirit, or of the Messiah, because it was so well attended by Jews from throughout the known world. Jerusalem itself would have been taxed to hold all the visitors, who spilled beyond the city's boundaries and into surrounding villages. The phrase *"fully* come" probably refers to the morning after the day would have *officially* begun at 6 p.m. the night before, as the Jews reckoned a day's hours, but people would have not have been out and stirring until the next morning.

"They were all in one place" probably refers not to the 120 disciples of verse 16, which would have required a large hall, but to the 11 apostles, plus Matthias who was chosen to take the place of Judas, since this is the group most recently referred to (1:26). The number is an important symbol: just as the patriarchs of the 12 tribes of Israel were responsible for leadership under the Jewish system, so the 12 apostles are about to be charged and equipped with the responsibility of continuing the work the Messiah began, and which would become the Christian system.

B. Spirit-language, 2-4

2 And suddenly there came a sound from heaven as of a rushing mighty wind, and it filled all the house where they were sitting.

3 And there appeared unto them cloven tongues like as of fire, and it sat upon each of them.

4 And they were all filled with the Holy Ghost, and began to speak with other tongues, as the Spirit gave them utterance.

Three main symbols—sound, wind, and fire—characterize the amazing event which will officially launch the New Community. The *sound* is like the mighty *wind* of a tornado, and the *fire* is like Jahweh's descent in Exodus 19:18, when "mount Sinai was altogether on a smoke, because the LORD descended upon it in fire." Apparently

43

fire is also chosen because it can easily spread from one center into the 12 "tongues" that hover above the apostles' heads.

It is only by context that *pneuma* in verse 2 is translated "wind," since the word also means "spirit." However, it is a good choice since it contrasts nicely with the same words as they are used in verse 4. The word for "tongues" is *glossai,* which can also mean "languages," which unfolding events will justify. If the primary symbol of the Old Age is the Law, the primary symbol of the New Age is the Spirit, which generates these languages as He sees fit.

II. A Puzzle to Solve—5-8

5 And there were dwelling at Jerusalem Jews, devout men, out of every nation under heaven.

6 Now when this was noised abroad, the multitude came together, and were confounded, because that every man heard them speak in his own language.

7 And they were all amazed and marvelled, saying one to another, Behold, are not all these which speak Galilaeans?

8 And how hear we every man in our own tongue, wherein we were born?

Now the focus broadens from the 12, past the 120, into a "multitude," who are understandably "confounded" by the unprecedented event of hearing in one's own language the speech of one of the 12 relatively unschooled disciples from Galilee. As word spread of the unprecedented events, Jews must have streamed from all parts of the city to the point

from which the miraculous tongues were emanating.

III. Salad-bowl of Nations—9-11

9 Parthians, and Medes, and Elamites, and the dwellers in Mesopotamia, and in Judaea, and Cappadocia, in Pontus, and Asia,

10 Phrygia, and Pamphylia, in Egypt, and in the parts of Libya about Cyrene, and strangers of Rome, Jews and proselytes,

11 Cretes and Arabians, we do hear them speak in our tongues the wonderful works of God.

Luke, undoubtedly the author of Acts, begins to catalog the range of nations represented at what is surely one of the most astounding religious events in history. They are from the "diaspora" or dispersion—the scattering of Jews into virtually all nations. The Spirit is bringing them together by allowing them to hear the apostles describe "the wonderful works of God"—no doubt the death, burial and resurrection of Christ.

Luke apparently chooses the particular nations he does because they compose a rough pattern: a list that makes a circle beginning with Iran to the northeast and circling to the west, then to the south, with Jerusalem at the center. The author's reference to "proselytes"— Gentiles who have converted to Judaism—shows that many Jews have been busy preaching the message of Moses, the Law, and the One God in these otherwise pagan lands.

IV. Question and Answer—12-17a
A. Wrong answer, 12-13

12 And they were all amazed, and were in doubt, saying one to another, What meaneth this?

13 Others mocking said, These men

are full of new wine.

Terms such as "amazed," "confounded," and "marveled" continue to show the stunning impact of the outpouring of Spirit-generated languages. The only explanation some have is that many of these Jews have partied all night. We can imagine that a person from Libya hearing his native tongue might sound drunk to another from Medea.

B. Fulfilled prophecy, 14-17a

14 But Peter, standing up with the eleven, lifted up his voice, and said unto them, Ye men of Judaea, and all ye that dwell at Jerusalem, be this known unto you, and hearken to my words:

15 For these are not drunken, as ye suppose, seeing it is but the third hour of the day.

16 But this is that which was spoken by the prophet Joel;

17a And it shall come to pass in the last days, saith God, I will pour out of my Spirit upon all flesh:

Countering the charge of drunkenness, Peter reminds the diverse crowd that they have in common the religion of Judaism. Far from having partied too much, the people caught up in this amazing event are in fact fulfilling prophecy—specifically that in Joel 2 which predicts the very events that are confounding the hundreds of Jews from the Dispersion.

(In passing we might note that Peter uses the only sure and certain way of learning that a prophecy is being fulfilled: An inspired man of God says "This is that which was spoken by the prophet . . . ." A great deal of confusion in modern prophetic interpretation would be clarified by a strict observance of the "this is that" rule.)

It is also important to notice that Peter describes the timing of this great event as occurring "in the last days." Although not all of the events predicted by Joel, such as the "wonders in heaven" and the "blood, and fire, and vapor of smoke" occur here; those that do occur are a part of an era properly termed "the last days." We learn from this that the world has been in "the last days" for more than 2,000 years. Those events that mark the end of the world will are reserved for *"the last days of the last days,"* with the precise dating left to God and not to man.

৯৩৫৪

Evangelistic Emphasis

The events in Acts 2 may describe the grandest revival ever experienced by the Church. The huge crowd was drawn by the visible display of the Holy Spirit, and over 3,000 people were baptized before that landmark day was done.

History recalls many churches with roots in similar moments of charismatic revival in their formative years. The powerful preaching of George Whitefield is associated with what church historians call The Great Awakening—a revival that began in 1737 and continued for at least a de-cade. Many churches began to take their American shape during these lively years.

The Disciples of Christ, Christian Churches, and Churches of Christ can trace their common American roots to the famous Cane Ridge Revival, which has also been called a part of a Second Great Awakening. From 1800 to 1830 in Cumberland County, Kentucky, massive outdoor gatherings were the scene of fervent prayers, fiery preaching, and all manner of charismatic activities.

Methodist Churches traditionally point to the movings of the Holy Spirit in the life and ministry of the Wesley brothers, John and Charles, as the genesis of their fellowship.

Space here does not permit a complete review of all the Christian groups who were born and shaped by events similar to that described in Acts 2 .

ഇൻയ

Memory Selection

They were all filled with the Holy Ghost, and began to speak with other tongues, as the Spirit gave them utterance. And there were dwelling at Jerusalem Jews, devout men, out of every nation under heaven. Now when this was noised abroad, the multitude came together, and were confounded, because that every man heard them speak in his own language.—*Acts 2:4-6*

Bible readers find it hard not to think of the events of the Tower of Babel (Gen. 11) as they read the Acts 2 account. In the early event God split the single language of the world into many. Some say that Babel was reversed in Jerusalem on that Pentecost Day, when God was heard as though in one tongue by people of many languages. But only in a sense. For on that Pentecost, 12 apostles—who before that moment spoke the same language—suddenly began to speak multiple languages. Evidently it was something like an instant Berlitz school. Men who had never studied the dialects of the Roman territories were empowered by the Holy Spirit to discourse in several of those tongues.

The Bible never refers to this experience as the gift of *ears*. Always it is the gift of *tongues*. What an astounding display of divine power that miraculous day must have been. The day you or I start speaking languages we haven't ever studied we will know God is mightily at work among us.

Weekday Problems

When that crowd in Acts 2 clustered in Jerusalem to celebrate the Feast of Pentecost, they did not come there to do anything remotely Christian. They were Jews by faith—all of them—and Pentecost was for them something like Thanksgiving for us. Pentecost came in May or June, about the time when the first grain crops would be ripening. So the Old Testament sometimes refers to this festival as The Feast of Ingathering (Exod. 23:16).

In a world with no supermarkets and without international shipments of food every day, the new harvest was indeed something to celebrate. Without it, hunger could not be far away.

Pentecost was also called The Feast of Weeks (Exod. 34:22). In a strange display of holy numerology, the Jews marked their holy 7th day (the Sabbath) for seven weeks. When they squared the holy number, the next day—the 50th day after Passover—they celebrated. So Pentecost was for the Jewish people a jubilant, happy day, not like the more somber Yom Kippur, the Day of Atonement.

But for Christian people through the centuries the meaning of Pentecost was forever changed when God poured out His Holy Spirit that day. First to His chosen spokesmen and then, after baptism, God gave the gift of His Spirit to those who accepted His Son.

• Can you recall a time when your own religious journey included an exciting event similar to that in Acts 2?

Fiery Tongues (and Not)

Warning: The shortest inaugural address was George Washington's, which was only 135 words. The longest was William Henry Harrison's, who delivered a two-hour, 9,000-word speech into the teeth of a freezing northeast wind. He came down with a cold the following day, and died of pneumonia within a month.

* * *

Said one orator, "I have discontinued long speeches on account of my throat. Several people have threatened to cut it."

* * *

Will Rogers concluded a meeting at which the speaker went tediously on and on by explaining to the audience, "You have been listening to the famous Chinese orator, "On Too Long."

This Lesson in Your Life

Have you taken time to locate the nations listed in 2:9-11? Pinpoint these 15 or 16 nations (depending on how the translations split some of them) on a map of the first-century Mediterranean world and you will find them all over it—north and south, east and west, with some of them way off the eastern edge.

The list mentions "proselytes," which means people of other races who had converted to Judaism. So we have in the Acts 2 crowd some people without Jewish DNA. The majority of the multitude, however, would have been people who boasted Jewish blood but who were residents of the provinces named by Luke.

When Peter and James address their New Testament books to "the Diaspora"—the Jews scattered or dispersed abroad—they have in mind Jews like these who came to Jerusalem for Pentecost. During the eight or nine centuries just past, invaders on several occasions had taken their ancestors captive and relocated them all over the world.

The ancient Torah required every Jewish male 12 years old or older to appear three times a year at the Temple—for Passover, Pentecost, and the Feast of Tabernacles (Yom Kippur). These tri-annual migrations were out of the question for Hebrews living in the far-flung provinces. Still, every Jewish man lived with the dream of making the pilgrimage to the Holy City at least once in his lifetime.

This brought a huge influx of visitors to Jerusalem for Passover each year. Since Pentecost came only 50 days later, and since most Jews had relatives in the homeland, many extended their visit to include the second holiday. Hence the diverse crowd in Acts 2.

What this tells us is that from its very first day, the new Church was made up of people from all over the map—people from cultures as diverse as metropolitan Rome and rural Iraq. By the time we get to Acts 6 we will find these cultures clashing and causing a rumpus in the new fellowship.

Life in Christ's Church has never been simple, because His Church has always included people who are very different from one another. Dealing with social and cultural diversity can be a real challenge to our grasp of love and grace in Christ.

Not everybody in your church likes the music you do. Have you noticed that? Not everybody in your church likes the worship style that pleases you. Some families in your church have customs and requirements quite different from those in your family. Some congregations span huge political gulfs, or educational levels, or economic conditions.

Can those of us today who follow Christ include "unity in diversity" as those early disciples did in Acts 2?

GETTING THE FACTS STRAIGHT

1. Do you realize that the words for the Holy Spirit in both the Old and New Testament mean *wind*? Compare this to 2:2.

In Old Testament Hebrew, *ruach* means a rushing, mighty wind. In the New Testament, the Greek word for Spirit, *pneuma*, also means breath or wind.

2. What happened in the Old Testament "Tabernacle" that can be compared to Acts 2:3? (Exod. 40:34-38)

When Moses dedicated the tabernacle, God signaled His Presence by fire that burned above the place of worship.

3. What drew the huge crowd in Acts 2?

The roar that sounded like a mighty wind.

4. How did the crowd explain the phenomenon of 12 men speaking in languages most of them could not understand?

When the people heard all the different languages, it sounded to them like the apostles might be drunk.

5. What Old Testament passage did Peter quote to explain the coming of the Holy Spirit?

Joel 2:28-32.

6. According to Joel and to Peter, who was eligible to be saved?

Salvation was offered to anyone "who called on the name of the Lord." Peter emphasized that this included people in every place or nation.

7. In his sermon, what reasons did Peter give for believing that the crucified Jesus was really alive again?

Peter told the crowd (1) the apostles had seen the risen Lord, (2) the Holy Spirit had come, just as Jesus promised, (3) David had foretold the Messiah's resurrection.

8. When many in the crowd were convicted by Peter's sermon, what did he tell them to do?

He told them, "Repent, and be baptized every one of you in the name of Jesus Christ for the remission of sins" (2:38).

9. How many new converts came to Jesus on that first day?

3,000.

10. Describe the new Christian community in its very first days.

They spent a lot of time together. They were happy. They shared their possessions to be sure that all had what they needed.

Several years ago I was invited to present a marriage seminar to a robust but small congregation in upstate New York.

Before I arrived there that September day, I had not met a single person in that church. A mutual friend had recommended me to them, but when they got me, they got what farmers in my area used to call "a pig in a poke." They had little idea what to expect. Nor did I.

It turned out that I was pleasantly surprised. I hope they were too. At least from my side of the equation, it was love at first sight. These were gracious, faith-filled people who treated me so kindly. Theirs was a fun fellowship to fit into. The friendship we built that week has lasted for decades.

On the final Sunday afternoon of my first visit to their church, we gathered in their sanctuary to sing hymns for awhile before my last presentation in that seminar. I'll never forget what happened during that hour.

While we were singing, a young man in his early 20s slipped in and whispered a message to one of the church leaders. Immediately he stood and motioned for attention.

He relayed the message he had just received—that a young couple who had come to the seminar from a distant state had left to drive home right after lunch. Their old car had developed major woes before they had driven many miles, and they were stranded.

Instantly one of the men in the crowd stood up and pulled his car keys out of his pocket. "Here," he beckoned. I could hardly believe what I was witnessing. "Take my car to them. We have another one at home." Just like that—he gave his car to that young couple. For a very simple reason—they needed it.

Chills went down my spine as I watched that scene unfold. No longer was I among strangers. Without doubt I knew at that moment that I was assembled with a band of real Christians.

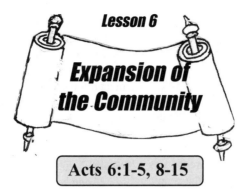

Lesson 6

Expansion of the Community

Acts 6:1-5, 8-15

And in those days, when the number of the disciples was multiplied, there arose a murmuring of the Grecians against the Hebrews, because their widows were neglected in the daily ministration.

2 Then the twelve called the multitude of the disciples unto them, and said, It is not reason that we should leave the word of God, and serve tables.

3 Wherefore, brethren, look ye out among you seven men of honest report, full of the Holy Ghost and wisdom, whom we may appoint over this business.

4 But we will give ourselves continually to prayer, and to the ministry of the word.

5 And the saying pleased the whole multitude: and they chose Stephen, a man full of faith and of the Holy Ghost, and Philip, and Prochorus, and Nicanor, and Timon, and Parmenas, and Nicolas a proselyte of Antioch:

8 And Stephen, full of faith and power, did great wonders and miracles among the people.

9 Then there arose certain of the synagogue, which is called the synagogue of the Libertines, and Cyrenians, and Alexandrians, and of them of Cilicia and of Asia, disputing with Stephen.

10 And they were not able to resist the wisdom and the spirit by which he spake.

11 Then they suborned men, which said, We have heard him speak blasphemous words against Moses, and against God.

12 And they stirred up the people, and the elders, and the scribes, and came upon him, and caught him, and brought him to the council,

13 And set up false witnesses, which said, This man ceaseth not to speak blasphemous words against this holy place, and the law:

14 For we have heard him say, that this Jesus of Nazareth shall destroy this place, and shall change the customs which Moses delivered us.

15 And all that sat in the council, looking stedfastly on him, saw his face as it had been the face of an angel.

Memory Selection
Acts 6:7a

Background Scripture
Acts 6:1–15:8:1-8

Devotional Reading
Acts 13-11

FOCUS

The explosive growth of the early Church in Jerusalem was not an unmixed blessing. With rapid growth comes organizational problems and other people-issues that are no less upsetting simply because the people involved are spiritual. The massive influx of people had especially brought with it practical problems on how to feed and house them efficiently. An issue that would gnaw at the Church for centuries arose: dealing with opposition from Roman and Jewish governmental forces.

Now another issue aggravated the problem: Jewish and Gentile factions *within* the new Christian movement arose. After all, people who had dwelt separately for centuries, were now called to be "one body." For the sake of order it was essential that leaders be appointed immediately, and that all concerned be treated fairly.

For a Lively Start

What kind of leaders would be required to "put out the fires" in a situation like that in Acts 6? Lead your group in a discussion that identifies leadership skills you would like to see in such a situation. For example, *motivational skills* would help—the ability to see that the end result of people cooperating with each other is more important than "winning points." *Being personally acquainted with owners of granaries* or other kinds of food stores would help. The ability to *trade, compromise and bargain*—not just win—could be important. If ethnic groups are involved, *having contacts within those groups* could help.

We may well wonder how many such skills could be found among the seven leaders chosen in Acts 6:5.

Teaching Outline	Daily Bible Readings
I. Food Crisis—Acts 6:1-5	Mon. No Other Name *Acts 4:1-12*
A. Greeks neglected, 1	Tue. What We Saw and Heard *Acts 4:13-22*
B. Balance needed, 2	Wed. Speaking the Word Boldly *Acts 4:23-31*
C. The seven chosen, 3-5	Thu. Breaking Community Trust *Acts 5:1-11*
II. Stephen's Power, 8-10	Fri. Obeying God *Acts 5:27-39*
A. Dispute arises, 8-9	Sat. Scattered but Proclaiming *Acts 8:1-8*
B. Wisdom exerted, 10	Sun. Full of the Spirit and Wisdom *Acts 6:1-15*
C. Underhanded means, 11-15	
1. False charges, 11-14	
2. Heavenly aid, 15	

Verse by Verse

I. Food Crisis—Acts 6:1-5
A. Greeks neglected

1 And in those days, when the number of the disciples was multiplied, there arose a murmuring of the Grecians against the Hebrews, because their widows were neglected in the daily ministration.

The term "mega-church" has been coined in modern times to describe certain evangelical churches that have had such explosive growth that they have had to rent coliseums or build their own giant "campuses" to accommodate their expansion. It is not uncommon for such churches to report membership of 8,000 to 15,000 members. Some of them begin their weekend services on Saturday nights, and have three to five services on Sunday.

Such huge enterprises are often thought to be new. Actually, they are at least as old as Acts 2, where "about three thousand souls" were baptized and added to the kingdom (2:41). The logistics for the original mega-church were much more difficult, since they had to provide not for a single weekend meeting but for living accommodations. Thousands of Jews stayed in Jerusalem indefinitely to learn how God was doing a new thing through the Pentecostal crowds. This required a "daily ministration" consisting of the distribution of food, especially to widows and others who had no trade or other way to make a temporary living. Since most of the new converts were Jews, it was understandable, if unfortunate that first precedence be given to Jewish widows. This is what created the "murmuring" or protest on the part of Greek widows.

"The twelve" refers of course to the apostles, upon whom Jesus conferred the mantle of leadership of this suddenly formed body of disciples or believers. The awkward construction "It is not reason" is better rendered in the NIV, "It would not be right." The point is that the apostles realize from the very beginning that without the proper leadership it would be all too easy for this new movement to attract people for physical instead of spiritual reasons.

C. The seven chosen, 3-5

3 Wherefore, brethren, look ye out among you seven men of honest report, full of the Holy Ghost and wis-

dom, whom we may appoint over this business.

4 But we will give ourselves continually to prayer, and to the ministry of the word.

5 And the saying pleased the whole multitude: and they chose Stephen, a man full of faith and of the Holy Ghost, and Philip, and Prochorus, and Nicanor, and Timon, and Parmenas, and Nicolas a proselyte of Antioch:

So it happens that the first steps toward "polity" or adminisrative organization in the early Church are taken because of the need for structure in the area of benevolence. Yet there is a remarkable balance in "authority," as the seven who are put in charge of the ministry are in fact chosen by "the whole multitude." Because the term "ministry" or *diakonos* is used in verse 7, many scholars believe the seven who are appointed were the first "deacons." The question naturally arises as to whether this structure was meant to be a permanent arrangement, but the question is not answered.

Also, "deacons" are sometimes assumed to have a more mundane and less spiritual role than that of "bishops" or "pastors." However, it should be noted that there is heavy emphasis here on the need for deacons to have the Holy Spirit and faith—not just the key to the front door. As we shall see, Stephen is a special example of the spiritual nature of at least some of those appointed here.

II. Stephen's Power, 8-10

A. Dispute arises, 8-9

8 And Stephen, full of faith and power, did great wonders and miracles among the people.

9 Then there arose certain of the synagogue, which is called the synagogue of the Libertines, and Cyrenians, and Alexandrians, and of them of Cilicia and of Asia, disputing with Stephen.

"Stephen" (*Grk. stephanos*) means "crown"; and it is a fitting name for this dedicated servant who was among the seven who were perhaps the first deacons (chap. 7 will fill out his story). Because he was "crowned" to receive several spiritual gifts, he attracts the attention not only among those who need miracles but those who, perhaps jealous of Stephen's gifts, want to stir up trouble in the infant Church. These trouble-makers are from four Jewish synagogues, and were no doubt in Jerusalem for the Passover. They are likely jealous not only of Stephen's spiritual gifts, but of the drain of Jews into the Christian movement; so they attack one of its most successful spokesmen.

B. Wisdom exerted, 10

10 And they were not able to resist the wisdom and the spirit by which he spake.

Recalling that Luke is likely the author of Acts, it is no surprise that he supplies proof here of the truth of Christ's promise that "the Holy Ghost shall teach you in the same hour what ye ought to say" when His followers are verbally attacked by Jewish opponents (Luke 12:12).

C. Underhanded means, 11-15

1. False charges, 11-14

11 Then they suborned men, which said, We have heard him speak blasphemous words against Moses, and

against God.

12 And they stirred up the people, and the elders, and the scribes, and came upon him, and caught him, and brought him to the council,

13 And set up false witnesses, which said, This man ceaseth not to speak blasphemous words against this holy place, and the law:

14 For we have heard him say, that this Jesus of Nazareth shall destroy this place, and shall change the customs which Moses delivered us.

Whatever their motives for attacking these early Christians, they are strong enough for them to bring Stephen before the Sanhedrin and even to lie about what he has been preaching. The charges seem to be drawn from Christ's prediction that "this place," or the Temple in Jerusalem, will be "trodden down of the Gentiles" (Luke 21:24). Stephen's repetition of Jesus' mere prophecy seems to have been transformed into an event for which He is responsible. These are "blasphemous words" because the Temple is considered holy.

The gospels do not explicitly quote Jesus as saying that the customs Moses taught would be changed, but Moses and the Law were so closely connected that Stephen's attackers connect Jesus' prediction that the Temple would be destroyed with the "customs" of Moses. By Jesus' day, the rabbis' *interpretation* of the Law of Moses carried as much weight as the Law itself. This is why it could produce such resentment for Jesus to say, in the Sermon on the Mount, "Ye have heard it said . . . [but] I say unto you." Understood as a rejection of Moses, such preaching could still cause resentment.

2. Heavenly aid, 15

15 And all that sat in the council, looking stedfastly on him, saw his face as it had been the face of an angel.

Once again we see a fulfillment of Jesus' promise to be with His followers when they are called on to answer for faithful preaching. We can imagine how the face of a Council member might in turn be changed when Stephen's face reflects God's divine support in the sermon he is about to preach.

80G3

Evangelistic Emphasis

At the end of Luke's account of the first recorded church fuss, Acts 6:7 tells us that "The word of God increased; and the number of the disciples multiplied in Jerusalem greatly." Obviously, the apostles' handling of the first rift in the early Jerusalem church was wise and fruitful.

Instead of letting this conflict tarnish the early Church's public image, they crafted a solution that brought greater credit to the new fellowship, and enabled the apostles to maintain their own focus on prayer and ministry of the word.

Church troubles don't always turn out this well. One good church scandal—especially in a smaller community—can put a lid on a church's growth for years to come. I once served as interim minister in a church where a previous preacher had behaved badly. His name appeared in front-page headlines when his illicit lover shot and killed her husband. I came to that pulpit several years later, but local folks still avoided that church. Meaningful growth was impossible.

Credit the Jerusalem apostles with an inspired solution to what could have been a disastrous dispute. Instead of curtailing that church's meteoric growth, their well-honed program for feeding hungry widows caused others in the community to want to be part of such a fellowship.

ഇൗന്ദ്ര

Memory Selection

Wherefore, brethren, look ye out among you seven men of honest report, full of the Holy Ghost and wisdom, whom we may appoint over this business. But we will give ourselves continually to prayer, and to the ministry of the word.—*Acts 6:3-4*

Part of the genius in the apostles' proposed solution was their quick instruction for the complainers to be the ones who fixed what they perceived to be a problem. In effect, the apostles told them, "If you don't like the way the widows are being fed, then you manage the food service yourselves."

Church administration sometimes calls for a Solomon. The issues often are not what they first appear to be. Only a person who knows where the rocks are under the water can keep from sinking the ship. Only a leader who knows where the bodies from previous wars are buried can stop the present blood-letting instead of causing more. The apostles wisely perceived that far more was at stake in this conflict than who got the most hamburgers. Language barriers and deep-seated cultural preferences had fostered distrust between brothers and sisters in Christ.

The complaints were silenced and the church again was at peace when Greek-speaking deacons began distributing meals for the Greek-speaking widows. The apostles' plan worked. Effective conflict management, either in the church or elsewhere, requires us to pay close attention to who feels abused.

Weekday Problems

Bible teachers commonly refer to the seven men listed in 6:5 as the first deacons in the Church. Although the word deacon does not appear in most English translations of Acts 6, the Greek word for deacon, *diakonos*, appears in some form three times in the first four verses of the chapter.

"The daily ministration" in 6:1 could literally be rendered "the daily deaconing." Likewise, in the next verse, the phrase "to serve tables" could read "to deacon." If we recognize these seven godly men as deacons, however, we still have not found our way out of the woods of confusion. Unfortunately, the word deacon doesn't mean the same thing to Bible readers from different denominations.

One of my most trusted friends, Pete Smith, is chairman of the deacons for a nearby growing Baptist church. I'm sure he does a good job of deaconing for them, but Pete's duties and authority in that role bear little resemblance to those of Deacon Floyd Ashley. Floyd serves as personal assistant to our local Catholic bishop and helps in roles that used to be reserved for the priests. The confusion doesn't end there. Neither Pete or Floyd fill the same role as the deacons in Churches of Christ.

The original word we translate "deacon" actually means a servant. Regardless of how our various churches may define the official deacon role, all of us are called in Christ to be humble servants to all who need our loving care.

When the Wind Blows

Once during a debate Abraham Lincoln was accused by his opponent as being two-faced. Without hesitation, Lincoln said, "I leave it to my audience . . . if I had two faces, would I be wearing this one?"

* * *

A very poor speaker was losing his audience. One by one they got up and filed out, until only one man was left. In desperation the speaker said, "Sir, why are you still here, when everyone else has left?:

"I have to stay," said the man, "I'm the next speaker."

* * *

The speaker was warning against over-population. "Do you realize," he said, "that somewhere in the world a woman is having a baby every four seconds?"

"Great guns!" cried a member of the audience, jumping to his feet. "We have to find that woman and stop her!"

This Lesson in Your Life

Not long ago, several of my clergy colleagues and I agreed to help a charitable foundation identify recipients of their scholarship awards.

Years ago a generous Christian couple set aside millions of dollars for Christian ministries. Among other things, they desired to educate and equip young people for what they described as "pulpit ministry."

In the earliest days of this foundation, the definition of pulpit ministry was construed quite simply as that of their own denomination. Most of the scholarships helped students attend schools linked to that fellowship. As the decades slipped past, however, the descendants of the foundation's founders became leaders in several types of churches, thus blurring the terms limiting the scholarships.

I relate this background so you can understand the questions our new scholarship committee faced. Some of the distinctions were easy. If a student told us he planned to become a marine biologist or a medical doctor, he obviously was not a candidate for our scholarship—not because we had anything against those professions, but because we simply were looking for potential pulpit ministers.

What if a student told us she planned to become an education minister or a youth minister? Would we automatically blackball such an applicant? It didn't take us long to find out that half the pulpit ministers around our table began ministry in one of those roles. Only the Lord could know what roles might open later for these young people.

Two members of our clergy committee revealed that they had spent two or three years pursuing engineering degrees before they accepted a call to ministry. This made us cautious about excluding promising young people who sought our scholarship aid.

Why do I tell you this tale? Because it mirrors the experience of two of the Acts 6 deacons, Stephen and Philip. They surface in Scripture serving beans to needy women. Five verses later Stephen is empowered by God to perform mighty miracles. Soon he became such a gifted preacher that his opponents "could not stand up against his wisdom or the Spirit by whom he spoke" (6:10, NIV).

Philip's shift from deacon to evangelist parallels that of Stephen. In the first Christian preaching beyond the city limits of Jerusalem, Philip ministered with power in the capital of Samaria. Healing the sick and casting out demons, he captured the attention of the entire town. Everybody wanted to hear this deacon-turned-evangelist preach Christ.

Did either Philip or Stephen have even a hint that feeding widows might morph into a preaching assignment from the Lord? What role could God have in mind for you or me around the bend?

GETTING THE FACTS STRAIGHT

1. Since most of the people involved in the Acts 6 fuss were Jews, what was the trouble?

They were Jews who spoke different languages. "Grecians" spoke Greek and "Hebrews" spoke Hebrew.

2. What complaint did the Greek-speaking Jews bring against the local majority that spoke Hebrew?

The Greek-speakers felt that their widows were not getting their fair share of a food distribution.

3. What kind of men did the apostles designate to be put in charge of the food distribution?

They needed to be wise, honest fellows who were full of the Spirit, and they needed to be part of the complaining group.

4. Can you tell from the description in 6:9 what group of Jews got upset with Stephen?

They were from a Greek-speaking synagogue and probably shared his own non-Judean identity.

5. Why did these non-Judean Jews get angry at Stephen?

They could not answer Stephen's powerful testimony about Jesus.

6. What charge did they lodge against Stephen?

They accused him of blaspheming against Moses and God.

7. How did they go about "proving" their charge in the Jewish court known as the Sanhedrin?

They bribed false witness who lied about Stephen.

8. When Stephen was defending himself in the Jewish court, what did they think he looked like?

His face looked to his accusers like the face of an angel. Some of the modern Bible versions explain that his face was radiant.

9. What famous church persecutor shows up in the first verses of Acts 8?

Saul of Tarsus.

10. How does Luke describe the impact of Philip's ministry in the city of Samaria?

Everybody in town paid attention to his miracles and his preaching and rejoiced at the fine results of his ministry there.

If we had interviewed an average member of the Jerusalem church during the week when the Greek-speakers were upsetting things with their protests, how do you think they would they have described the status of their once-peaceful church?

What if we had conducted similar interviews a day or two after their beloved deacon Stephen died under that hail of stones? How upbeat do you think folks would have been about the church's future?

Things are not always as they appear to be.

Consider some astounding calculations by premier Christian statistician George Otis, Jr. His figures show that of all the numerical growth of the Kingdom from Pentecost through 1995, 70 percent occurred in the 20th century alone.

Of 20th century church growth, Otis calculates that 70 percent of that took place since the end of World War II. Don't stop there. Since WW II, 70 percent of Christianity's expansion happened in the five years between 1990 and 1995.

This means, according to Otis, that some 34 percent of all the people who ever said Yes to the gospel made their profession of faith in the five years before he compiled these figures.

If the numerical trend continued, Otis predicted in 1995 that the number who came to Christ in the last 10 years of the 20th century alone would outstrip the total of converts in the previous 1,900 years.

If someone had interviewed you or me about the state of the Church today, would we have told them that we live today in the era of the most explosive growth Christianity has ever known?

Bad times fell on the Church in Acts 6, 7, and 8. For the first time a key leader paid for his faith with his life. Enemies of the new faith were rising up to imprison disciples and threaten converts. The bottom surely fell out of worship attendance stats in Jerusalem as converts from distant provinces hurried home to escape the danger. Members of that first church had no way to know that the outbreak of persecutions and problems would soon propel the growth rate of the Christian faith to levels they had never dreamed of. Right when the clouds seemed darkest, their best days were just beginning.

None of us knows what God has in store for His people in the decades just ahead of us. These chapters in Acts teach us to expect Him to accomplish far more than any of us can imagine.

Lesson 7
Transformed To Witness

And Saul, yet breathing out threatenings and slaughter against the disciples of the Lord, went unto the high priest,

2 And desired of him letters to Damascus to the synagogues, that if he found any of this way, whether they were men or women, he might bring them bound unto Jerusalem.

3 And as he journeyed, he came near Damascus: and suddenly there shined round about him a light from heaven:

4 And he fell to the earth, and heard a voice saying unto him, Saul, Saul, why persecutest thou me?

5 And he said, Who art thou, Lord? And the Lord said, I am Jesus whom thou persecutest: it is hard for thee to kick against the pricks.

6 And he trembling and astonished said, Lord, what wilt thou have me to do? And the Lord said unto him, Arise, and go into the city, and it shall be told thee what thou must do.

7 And the men which journeyed with him stood speechless, hearing a voice, but seeing no man.

8 And Saul arose from the earth; and when his eyes were opened, he saw no man: but they led him by the hand, and brought him into Damascus.

9 And he was three days without sight, and neither did eat nor drink.

10 And there was a certain disciple at Damascus, named Ananias; and to him said the Lord in a vision, Ananias. And he said, Behold, I am here, Lord.

11 And the Lord said unto him, Arise, and go into the street which is called Straight, and inquire in the house of Judas for one called Saul, of Tarsus: for, behold, he prayeth,

16 For I will shew him how great things he must suffer for my name's sake.

17 And Ananias went his way, and entered into the house; and putting his hands on him said, Brother Saul, the Lord, even Jesus, that appeared unto thee in the way as thou camest, hath sent me, that thou mightest receive thy sight, and be filled with the Holy Ghost.

18 And immediately there fell from his eyes as it had been scales: and he received sight forthwith, and arose, and was baptized.

19 And when he had received meat, he was strengthened.

Oct. 19

Memory Selection
Acts 19:17b

Background Scripture
Acts 9:1-31

Devotional Reading
Gal. 1:11-24

This lesson focuses on one of the three New Testament accounts of the conversion of the apostle Paul from a Jew to a Christian. (The other accounts are in Acts 22 and 26.)

Paul became arguably the most influential Christian in the world, next to Jesus Himself. By what measure might such a claim be made? In Paul's case, we could point to the personal impact he had on others, whether individually or through public speaking; to the writing and preaching which such converts like Apollos did, and to the fact that he himself wrote a major part of the New Testament. Of course the latter impact is still being made through the fact that the Bible is still the world's best-selling book.

Paul himself would protest such a claim. In his own view, any positive influence he made was off-set by his self-concept as being "the chief of sinners" (1 Tim. 1:15).

ഇറ

For a Lively Start

In this lesson we have already made the claim that, next to Jesus, the apostle Paul was the most influential Christian in the world. Yet we have also noted that Paul claimed to be "chief of sinners." This lesson can be introduced by a brief debate over two such opposing passages—just as the Pharisees used to do.

The passage arguing for Paul as "chief of sinners" might be **1 Timothy 1:12-16,** while the text portraying him as "Influential sinner" could be **Philipians 3:3-4.** *Which text more accurately reveals the "real Paul"?*

Teaching Outline	Daily Bible Readings
I. Zealous Persecutor—1-2	Mon. Revelation of Jesus Christ *Gal. 1:11-17*
A. Purpose, 1	Tues. Persecutor Now Proclaimer *Gal. 1:18-24*
B. Destination, 2	Wed. Surpassing Value of Christ *Philip. 3:2-11*
II. Voice from Heaven—3-4	Thurs. Befriended by Barnabas *Act 9:22-31*
III. Response from Earth—5-9	Fri. Content in All *Philip. 4:10-20*
IV. Disciple's Commission—10-11	Sat. A Light from Heaven *Acts 9:1-9*
V. A Greater Destiny—16	Sun. God's Chosen Instrument *Acts 9:10-21*
VI. Sight and Spirit—17-19a	

Verse by Verse

I. Zealous Persecutor—9:1-2
A. Purpose, 1

1 And Saul, yet breathing out threatenings and slaughter against the disciples of the Lord, went unto the high priest,

The author Luke assumes that the reader will remember that the last recorded incident involving Saul of Tarsus finds him persecuting Christians (Acts 7:59–8:3)—hence "yet" engaging in the same terrorism. The colorful language calls forth a fire-breathing dragon. A highly trained rabbi of the sect of the Pharisees, Saul considered himself "a Hebrew of the Hebrews" (Philip. 3:5). His zeal in defending what he considered to be the truth is what drove him to the high priest to obtain official authorization enabling him to persecute even to the death those who dared to follow Jesus as the Messiah. The importance of this authority, showing that it was not just a one-man juggernaut, is seen in the fact that Paul's conversion story is told three times in Acts, this being the first.

2 And desired of him letters to Damascus to the synagogues, that if he found any of this way, whether they were men or women, he might bring them bound unto Jerusalem.

Always sensitive to the danger of stirring up a Judean-wide distress that would bring down widespread persecution by the Romans, the authority Saul seeks is limited to Damascus, one of 10 cities that had a long tradition of maintaining a somewhat independent jurisdiction. It is interesting that the author takes the trouble to specify that the persecution is against both men and women, although the difference in the application of the law is not spelled out.

Referring to the Christians as those of "the way" reminds us that this was a common term for any group who maintained a certain exclusivist quest on their search for salvation. The book of Acts is the only New Testament book that uses the term in reference to Christians, but some scholars think they were almost exclusively called "the Way" during this early period.

II. Voice from Heaven—3-4

3 And as he journeyed, he came near Damascus: and suddenly there

63

shined round about him a light from heaven:

4 And he fell to the earth, and heard a voice saying unto him, Saul, Saul, why persecutest thou me?

What follows seems to be a true "theophany," or vision of God, and all attempts to explain it in human terms are bound to miss the forest for the trees. In one of history's most important changes in direction, God confronts Saul directly. He is a highly trained rabbi but going in precisely the opposite direction from that which God had planned. A divine intervention is called for, and in changing Saul's direction, history is changed as well. Apparently the light Saul sees counts for an appearance or apparition of Jesus Himself, since seeing Christ was one of the qualification for being an apostle, and Paul later seems to call on this as evidence that this fulfilled that qualification (1 Cor. 9:1).

III. Response from Earth—5-9

5 And he said, Who art thou, Lord? And the Lord said, I am Jesus whom thou persecutest: it is hard for thee to kick against the pricks.

6 And he trembling and astonished said, Lord, what wilt thou have me to do? And the Lord said unto him, Arise, and go into the city, and it shall be told thee what thou must do.

7 And the men which journeyed with him stood speechless, hearing a voice, but seeing no man.

8 And Saul arose from the earth; and when his eyes were opened, he saw no man: but they led him by the hand, and brought him into Damascus.

9 And he was three days without sight, and neither did eat nor drink.

The passage offers an interesting progression in the meaning of the term "lord." In its first usage in verse 5 Paul has no idea that he is addressing Jesus. He uses "lord" (Grk. *kyrios*, "sir") as simply a term that shows deference to a mere man. By verse 6, however, the same word, *kyrios*—sir or lord—has obviously taken on more honor and even awe. Verse 7 says that the men accompanying Saul heard the voice, but saw no one—adding to the awesome setting.

Adding to the mysterious setting, verse 7 says that those with Paul heard a voice but saw no man, while Paul's recounting of the event in 22:9 says that Paul's companions "heard not the voice." Various suggestions for harmonizing the discrepancy have been suggested, but it seems possible that the power of the supernatural clashing with the natural has removed the event from ordinary ways of smoothing out such divergences.

A final mystery is why Paul, apparently having been temporarily blinded by the light from heaven, had to be led into the city and could not see men even after his eyes were opened. Little wonder that it took him three days to recuperate from the event that kept creating new questions with each new retelling.

IV. Disciple's Commission—10-11

10 And there was a certain disciple at Damascus, named Ananias; and to him said the Lord in a vision, Ananias. And he said, Behold, I am here, Lord.

11 And the Lord said unto him, Arise, and go into the street which is

64

called Straight, and inquire in the house of Judas for one called Saul, of Tarsus: for, behold, he prayeth,

An admirable new character enters the story when Ananias, a Damascene disciple, joins the list of those who are entrusted with direct messages from heaven. Apparently this unusual number of believers who speak to and are spoken to by the Lord appears because of the unusual nature of the conversion of an important Jewish figure who will become such an influential Christian leader. When applied to the firebrand Jewish persecutor Saul, the simple phrase, "he prayeth," must have been stunning to the Christians he was persecuting.

V. A Greater Destiny—16

16 For I will shew him how great things he must suffer for my name's sake.

Making it attractive to have a mission to "suffer" for Christ reminds us that the term *martys,* which originally meant "witness," came to mean a witness called on to give his life for the cause of Christ. However, after fasting in blindness for three days, nearly any mission must have seemed attractive.

VI. Sight and Spirit—17-19a

17 And Ananias went his way, and entered into the house; and putting his hands on him said, Brother Saul, the Lord, even Jesus, that appeared unto thee in the way as thou camest, hath sent me, that thou mightest receive thy sight, and be filled with the Holy Ghost.

18 And immediately there fell from his eyes as it had been scales: and he received sight forthwith, and arose, and was baptized.

19 And when he had received meat, he was strengthened.

Calling Saul "brother" must have been heartening for Saul after such a heart-shaking experience. Ananias wastes no time before identifying Jesus with the "lord," or "sir, associated with Saul's blindness and fall to the earth. The promise of being filled with the Holy Spirit, however, may not have been so attractive since the experience had become somewhat suspect among the Jews after the exciting incident in Acts 2 which was associated with the formal organizing of the Christians as a "way" that was separate from the Jews.

Accepting Ananias' promise by faith, Paul not only is filled with the Spirit; his blindness disappears as scales falling from his eyes. Although baptism had been practiced long before the Christians popularized it, by now it was associated with being part of the initiating rite of becoming a Christian. It would thus have been something of a heretical move by Saul the Jew. It was therefore, for him, not a passive ritual but a bold statement of faith.

છ૭૦૪

Evangelistic Emphasis

Scripture describes no conversion in more detail than that of Saul of Tarsus. After showing us Saul as a zealot breathing threats and bent on violence toward all who confessed Jesus, Acts 9 treats us to a second portrait of the man. Now we see a changed, humbled man—still zealous, but now filled with zeal to tell others about the risen Messiah.

Listen to Saul himself as he explains this in 1 Timothy 1:15-16: "Here is a trustworthy saying that deserves full acceptance: Christ Jesus came into the world to save sinners—of whom I am the worst," Saul confesses.

Then he explains, "But for that very reason I was shown mercy so that in me, the worst of sinners, Christ Jesus might display His unlimited patience as an example for those who would believe on him and receive eternal life" (NIV).

The Scriptures tell us that Jesus saved the sinner Saul in order to save other sinners through him.

Is it possible that the Lord might use your conversion or mine for the same reason?

In his gripping book, *Born Again,* former White House counsel and Watergate criminal Chuck Colson tells how God used his public humiliation and his later conversion to Christ in just this way. My sins or yours may not be so well known. At least, we hope not. But the Lord still can use the changes in us to beckon others to His grace.

ഇരുന്നു

Memory Selection

Ananias went his way, and entered into the house; and putting his hands on him said, Brother Saul, the Lord, even Jesus, that appeared unto thee in the way as thou camest, hath sent me, that thou mightest receive thy sight, and be filled with the Holy Ghost. And immediately there fell from his eyes as it had been scales: and he received sight forthwith, and arose, and was baptized.—*Acts 9:17-18*

One morning more than a decade ago I awoke, opened my eyes, and discovered to my horror that the sight in my right eye—my good eye—was gone. The night before it was 20/20. By morning all I could see was a haze, as though I were peering through crinkled, smoked cellophane. As it turned out, I had suffered a retinal hemorrhage, and I had the assurance of a trusted ophthalmologist that several months of laser treatment would probably restore my sight.

Do I need to tell you that until I got that good news, my sudden loss of sight arrested my total attention? If it happened to one eye so quickly, and without warning, what if it happened to the other? The prospect of such immediate blindness chilled my soul. So I know something of what was going on in Saul's mind when he was struck blind. On that day the Lord had Saul's complete attention.

Weekday Problems

Has God ever given you an assignment you didn't want?

He commissioned Jonah to go preach in Nineveh, but the prophet wasn't about to offer God's salvation to people who hated and threatened his own nation. He caught a boat going the opposite way.

God told His servant Ananias to go to Judas' house and heal Saul's blind eyes. "No way," Ananias objected. To him, Saul was a menace—an enemy. Ananias was, at first, not about to aid a man who meant him nothing but harm.

God's projects often stretch our comfort zones, don't they? He called a pastor friend of mine to a leadership role in a Franklin Graham Festival—a role that would require him to cross fellowship lines he had seldom dared to cross before.

At first my friend was hesitant—not quite sure what he was getting into. Working alongside Methodists and Baptists and Catholics and Presbyterians was a new ballgame for him. I watched with delight as his new circle of friends embraced him and he relaxed.

The Bible doesn't tell us if Ananias lived to see the heyday of Saul's later ministry. Don't you know his heart swelled with joy and pride if he saw his own convert carrying the gospel to the world?

The next time God calls you to do a job that intimidates or repulses you, remember Ananias.

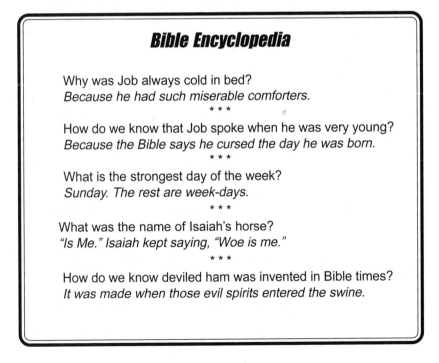

Bible Encyclopedia

Why was Job always cold in bed?
Because he had such miserable comforters.

* * *

How do we know that Job spoke when he was very young?
Because the Bible says he cursed the day he was born.

* * *

What is the strongest day of the week?
Sunday. The rest are week-days.

* * *

What was the name of Isaiah's horse?
"Is Me." Isaiah kept saying, "Woe is me."

* * *

How do we know deviled ham was invented in Bible times?
It was made when those evil spirits entered the swine.

This Lesson in Your Life

At least twice every year I have the pleasure of teaching an academic Bible course to a class of serious students. Every year when we come to Acts 9, I ask my students to dig deeper than we often do—to make sure they know what the rest of the New Testament reveals to us about this remarkable conversion story.

Luke tells us the basic story of Saul's conversion here in Acts 9, and, as we have noted, he repeats the story two more times before he concludes Acts. In Acts 22, more than 20 years later, Luke tells us of the time when Saul—now the veteran apostle Paul—was rescued from a mob of Jewish zealots who were trying to kill him. With his rescuer's permission, he addressed the mob. He told them the story of his conversion—basically the same story we have read in Acts 9.

Again in Acts 26 the apostle tells the same story of how he came to faith in Jesus. This time he is a prisoner at a legal hearing before the Roman governor, Festus, and a visiting king, Agrippa II. To explain how he came to be in chains before them, he told how Jesus called him on the Damascus Road to a lifetime of ministry worldwide.

In addition to these three tellings in Acts 9, 22, and 26, Saul gives us a few more details about the story in Galatians 1:11-17. A Bible student cannot know the complete story of Saul's conversion without merging all four of these Bible passages.

So, when I teach Acts 9, I assign my students to pull together all of the facts in all four of these chapters. I ask them to make a list of everything that happens—who does what and who says what—from the time Saul leaves Jerusalem until the time when he returns three years later.

My students groan when I give them this assignment, but that's normal for any of us in any class, isn't it? Most of them tell me later how much they learned doing this project.

In our usual Bible studies many weeks or months separate our studies of the early and late chapters of Acts, so many confess to me they had never before seen how all this material links together—even though some of the details aren't easy to fit in. For example, in Galatians 1, Paul tells us he went to Arabia to receive his gospel from the Lord. Where does this fit into the timeline of his conversion? Also, can you tell if the dramatic basket-escape through a window in Damascus' wall took place the first time he left Damascus, or the second?

Lining up in correct order all the statements Jesus made to Saul and all of Saul's replies will also be a challenge. When you get through, you'll probably know more about Saul's conversion than you ever expected to.

GETTING THE FACTS STRAIGHT

1. What was the purpose of Saul's journey to Damascus?

Saul was commissioned by the chief priests in Jerusalem to arrest any Damascus Jews who had accepted Jesus.

2. What blinded Saul, and how long was he blind?

When the risen Christ appeared to Saul, the brightness of the light impaired his eyesight. He was blind for three days.

3. Why did Saul call Jesus "Lord" if he didn't know who he was talking to?

The word "Lord" was used in Saul's day when people spoke to anyone in authority. It was not reserved for God or Jesus. In this case it did not indicate deity.

4. Whom did the Lord send to heal Saul?

The Damascus preacher, Ananias.

5. What was this man's reaction when God asked him to go help the blind man?

Ananias protested to God that he didn't want anything to do with Saul, for he had heard what a dangerous enemy Saul was to all Christians.

6. After Saul was healed and baptized, what did he begin to do in Damascus?

He began immediately to preach that Jesus is indeed the Christ.

7. When his former friends decided to kill him, how did Saul escape from Damascus?

The Christians in the city lowered him in a basket through a window in the city wall.

8. Were the Christians in Jerusalem glad to see Saul when he returned home?

Not at first, for they remembered him as the fierce anti-Christian persecutor who had helped to kill Stephen.

9. Who persuaded the Jerusalem church to accept Saul?

Barnabas.

10. Why did Saul leave Jerusalem and sail to Tarsus?

His former friends—the ones he helped to kill Stephen—now wanted to kill him because of his new faith in Jesus.

69

When the Lord was trying to convince Ananias to go to Saul's aid, He told the frightened preacher, "This man is my chosen instrument to carry my name before the Gentiles and their kings and before the people of Israel. I will show him how much he must suffer for my name" (Acts 9:15-16, NIV).

Saul tells us later in Acts 22 that when Ananias came and healed him, the hesitant preacher shared this information with the apostle-to-be. He told him, "The God of our fathers hath chosen thee, that thou shouldest know his will, and see that Just One, and shouldest hear the voice of his mouth. For thou shalt be his witness unto all men of what thou hast seen and heard."

In the Acts 9 account Luke also omits what Jesus said to Saul about his future assignment when He talked to him on the road. Later in Acts 26 Saul himself divulges that Jesus said to him, "Rise, and stand upon thy feet: for I have appeared unto thee for this purpose, to make thee a minister and a witness both of these things which thou hast seen, and of those things in the which I will appear unto thee; Delivering thee from the people, and from the Gentiles, unto whom now I send thee" (26:16-17).

When Saul is recalling his conversion in Galatians 1, he tells us in verse 15 that God had all these things in mind for him even before he was born.

This is the kind of God you and I serve. He has plans for His servants, marvelous plans that dwarf our faith and shame our lack of imagination on His behalf.

"I know the plans I have for you," declares the LORD, "plans to prosper you and not to harm you, plans to give you hope and a future" (Jer. 29:11, NIV).

Saul spent approximately half of his life unaware of the exciting plans God had for him. He devoted himself diligently to prepare himself to serve God, studying at the feet of the finest rabbi of that day. Then God surprised him by using that education to accomplish things Saul never dreamed of.

What do you suppose the Lord has in mind for you a decade or so from now? Saul could tell you that He is a God of surprises. He is a big God who plans big for His servants. Our assignment is to be ready for whatever He is has in mind for us to do.

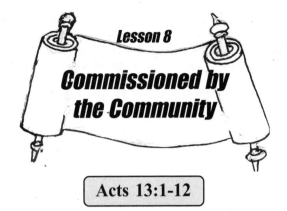

Lesson 8

Commissioned by the Community

Acts 13:1-12

Now there were in the church that was at Antioch certain prophets and teachers; as Barnabas, and Simeon that was called Niger, and Lucius of Cyrene, and Manaen, which had been brought up with Herod the tetrarch, and Saul.

2 As they ministered to the Lord, and fasted, the Holy Ghost said, Separate me Barnabas and Saul for the work whereunto I have called them.

3 And when they had fasted and prayed, and laid their hands on them, they sent them away.

4 So they, being sent forth by the Holy Ghost, departed unto Seleucia; and from thence they sailed to Cyprus.

5 And when they were at Salamis, they preached the word of God in the synagogues of the Jews: and they had also John to their minister.

6 And when they had gone through the isle unto Paphos, they found a certain sorcerer, a false prophet, a Jew, whose name was Bar-jesus:

7 Which was with the deputy of the country, Sergius Paulus, a prudent man; who called for Barnabas and Saul, and desired to hear the word of God.

8 But Elymas the sorcerer (for so is his name by interpretation) withstood them, seeking to turn away the deputy from the faith.

9 Then Saul, (who also is called Paul,) filled with the Holy Ghost, set his eyes on him,

10 And said, O full of all subtilty and all mischief, thou child of the devil, thou enemy of all righteousness, wilt thou not cease to pervert the right ways of the Lord?

11 And now, behold, the hand of the Lord is upon thee, and thou shalt be blind, not seeing the sun for a season. And immediately there fell on him a mist and a darkness; and he went about seeking some to lead him by the hand.

12 Then the deputy, when he saw what was done, believed, being astonished at the doctrine of the Lord.

Oct. 26

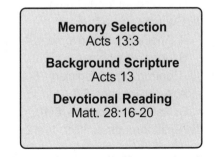

Memory Selection
Acts 13:3

Background Scripture
Acts 13

Devotional Reading
Matt. 28:16-20

The role of the Holy Spirit is especially important in this lesson. If it were not for the Spirit, these new members of "the Lord's army" would have no direction. Yet, as we become aware of the Spirit we also become aware of His subjective nature. Virtually in the same breath, the author,

Luke, must relate the Spirit's work of sending workers out in the Lord's vineyard, then of dealing with false prophets whose claim to have God's Spirit is false.

The lesson highlights several turning points. The city of Antioch (of Syria) becomes a center of Christian activity. The focus on Christian ministers shifts from Peter to Paul, for reasons unstated. In the absence of Jesus, the importance of such spiritual disciplines as fasting and prayer becomes more evident. The Church is on the march!

ജരു

For a Lively Start

If your class is "freed up" enough, this lesson offers good opportunities for role playing or skits in getting things started. The overall story of one scene depicting the way the early Church got started can be drawn from verses 1-3. A more dramatic vignette is portrayed

in the conflict between Saul and Elymas the Sorcerer, in verses 6-10.

Alternately, you can start the lesson by providing a wall-size map and tracing major places on this, the "first missionary journey." Point out such places as Antioch of Seleucia, Cyprus, Salamis and Paphos.

Note from the map how Christ's followers are becoming a missionary church.

Teaching Outline	Daily Bible Readings	
I. Getting Organized—1-3	Mon.	Filling a Vacancy *Acts 1:15-26*
A. A prophetic church, 1	Tue.	Go and Proclaim the News *Matt. 10:1-15*
B. A Spirit-guided church, 2-3	Wed.	Persevere in Persecution *Matt. 10:16-25*
II. Going Afar—4-5		
A. Another Spirit movement, 4	Thu.	Finding Life *Matt. 10:32-39*
B. John as a helper, 5	Fri.	The Gift In You *1 Tim. 4:6-16*
III. Confronting a Magician—6-10		
A. A call for light, 6-7	Sat.	Salvation to the Gentiles *Acts 28:25-31*
B. Satanic opposition, 8-10	Sun.	Set Apart for God's Work *Acts 13:1-12, 42-43*
IV. Faith through conflict, 11-12		

Verse by Verse

I. Getting Organized—1-3
A. A prophetic church, 1

1 Now there were in the church that was at Antioch certain prophets and teachers; as Barnabas, and Simeon that was called Niger, and Lucius of Cyrene, and Manaen, which had been brought up with Herod the tetrarch, and Saul.

A little less than halfway through the book of Acts an important new chapter begins in the story of the new believers. With the stoning of Stephen, many followers of "the Way" fled from Jerusalem north to Antioch, the third largest city in the Empire (11:19; this is "Antioch of Syria," in northern Palestine, not "Antioch of Phrygia," in central Asia Minor.) Much of the activity at Antioch was led by Barnabas, who had paved the way for Saul to be accepted by the very disciples he had persecuted (9:27-28). At Antioch a vibrant and influential center developed, resulting in an important study center where thoughtful students of the Old Covenant Scriptures pored over the text to see how the new events they were caught up in fit Old Testament prophecies. Since it was more and more obvious that the new "Way" was different from the old, a new name was called for; and "the disciples were called Christians first at Antioch" (11:26).

Following the Old Testament pattern, the center at Antioch was led by "prophets and teachers"—apparently men like Barnabas, whose leadership qualifications were too obvious to require, at first, any appointment process. One result of their leadership was a missionary thrust led by the men listed here. Already the early church is distinguishing itself from Judaism by becoming a missionary enterprise: the people of God are those who respond to the preaching of the gospel, not those born as Jews. This difference can hardly be over-stated. It will result in a multi-cultural, worldwide movement instead of remaining an ethnic-based enterprise. It will also mean that certain differences will develop between the Christians at Antioch, who were open to Gentile influence, and those at Jerusalem, who continued to favor their Jewish roots.

2. A Spirit-guided Church, 2-3

2 As they ministered to the Lord, and fasted, the Holy Ghost said, Separate me Barnabas and Saul for the work whereunto I have called them.

3 And when they had fasted and prayed, and laid their hands on them, they sent them away.

A second important shift with which

"Acts II" begins is the emergence of Saul of Tarsus as a new and dynamic leader. At first he is one of the "prophets and teacher" listed in verse 1; then he, along with Barnabas, are "separated" for special ministry by the Holy Spirit; and finally his increasing association with Gentiles will result in changing his name from the Jewish name "Saul" to the Greek "Paul" (13:9). This increasingly Greek cast to the early Christian movement will also contribute to Paul's becoming more influential than Peter, especially in Gentile areas.

Here, however, the emphasis is on the co-ministry inaugurated by Barnabas and Saul, who become leaders in the missionary activity already mentioned. Notice that they go simply by the authority of the Holy Spirit, who at this early stage takes the place of formally appointed bishops or people with other titles. In fact, this element is so prominent that Acts as had been called "the book of the Holy Spirit." As important as it is to have the Spirit's guidance, however, someone must interpret His message; and the subjectivity and bias that can creep into this process will lead to some unfortunate differences as well.

II. Going Afar—4-5
A. Another Spirit movement

4 So they, being sent forth by the Holy Ghost, departed unto Seleucia; and from thence they sailed to Cyprus.

5 And when they were at Salamis, they preached the word of God in the synagogues of the Jews: and they had also John to their minister.

The repeated mention of the Holy Spirit raises the question of whether there was some opposition to the enterprise, and a dispute that could be settled only by showing that Saul and Barnabas' trip was authorized by the Spirit.

The Christian movement is still "Jewish" enough to enjoy invitations to preach in the synagogues they find on the islands in the northeastern Mediterranean. This will continue to be an important doorway through which to carry the message of Jesus until 13:46, when Jewish rejection of the message virtually assures that the two movements will become two different faith traditions.

The John mentioned here is John Mark (see 12:12). Since the kind of ministry he performed for Saul and Barnabas is not described, he is probably mentioned here to lay the groundwork for the conflict between Saul and Barnabas when John Mark decided not to complete the mission (Acts 15:37;40).

III. Confronting a magician, 6-10
A. A call for light,

6 And when they had gone through the isle unto Paphos, they found a certain sorcerer, a false prophet, a Jew, whose name was Bar-jesus:

7 Which was with the deputy of the country, Sergius Paulus, a prudent man; who called for Barnabas and Saul, and desired to hear the word of God.

In remarkably few words, we learn that the man who plays such an important part in the story to follow is named Bar ("Son of") Jesus, that he is a Jew who therefore was forbidden from practicing the black arts of sorcery, and that he was furthermore (Grk. *pseudo-*, "false") even in his practice of the black arts.

Since the sorcerer was *"with"* Sergius Paulus, the deputy or proconsul, the chief political figure of the island, he was probably employed as an adviser or even a seer. As misguided as the deputy could become with a sorcerer as an adviser, it shows a certain humility, and may be why he could be called "prudent."

B. Satanic opposition, 8-11
1. Contest with a magician, 8-10

8 But Elymas the sorcerer (for so is his name by interpretation) withstood them, seeking to turn away the deputy from the faith.

9 Then Saul, (who also is called Paul,) filled with the Holy Ghost, set his eyes on him,

10 And said, O full of all subtilty and all mischief, thou child of the devil, thou enemy of all righteousness, wilt thou not cease to pervert the right ways of the Lord?

The deputy's desire "to hear the word of the Lord" was reason enough for Elymas (or bar-Jesus) to oppose the truth of what Saul and Barnabas had to say. This pre-decided opposition causes Saul to pile on phrase after phrase that dismisses Elymas as a child of the devil from the start.

As mentioned earlier, the change in Saul's name to "Paul" was no doubt associated with the fact that "Paul" (*paulus*), being Greek, suits the social context in which he will be working better than the Hebrew *Saulus*. At any rate, here is another major shift that makes this part of "Acts Book II." From now on he is the one whose sermons are almost exclusively quoted, and who otherwise takes the lead in the missions. When the dispute with Barnabas leads to their division, Luke chooses to follow Paul's work, not Barnabas'.

2. Faith through conflict, 11-12

11 And now, behold, the hand of the Lord is upon thee, and thou shalt be blind, not seeing the sun for a season. And immediately there fell on him a mist and a darkness; and he went about seeking some to lead him by the hand.

12 Then the deputy, when he saw what was done, believed, being astonished at the doctrine of the Lord.

Paul is not satisfied with calling Elymas a child of the devil; to show that his power extends beyond mere name-calling, he takes the bold step of calling down from heaven a spell of temporary blindness on the sorcerer. This is the man who only weeks earlier (depending on the dating of his sojourn in Arabia, Gal. 1:17) had been a persecutor of Christians; yet now he has the power to call down a blight from heaven on a man who dares oppose Christian teaching!

This display of righteous indignation and miraculously expressed anger so impresses the proconsul that he "believes," associating Paul's *act* with Christian "doctrine." It is possible that this "belief" stops short of permanent conversion, since Luke is careful to note that the *reason* for the proconsul's belief is "astonishment," as though he is simply more impressed with what he interprets as Paul's "magic" than with Elymas' power, who after all is left wandering in a blinding mist seeking someone to lead him about.

Evangelistic Emphasis

In his book, *The Closing of the American Mind,* Dr. Alan Bloom explores one of the biggest hurdles to evangelism today. In both educational and religious arenas, the top forbidden sin in this generation is to suggest that someone else might be wrong—that they need to change their ideas or their faith.

Obviously this is a huge barrier to the church's traditional strategies for sharing our faith. Yesterday's methods of winning others to Jesus seem gauche and rude to many today. So how should we go about the task of evangelizing our part of the world?

While the prophets in the church at Syrian Antioch fasted and prayed, the Holy Spirit revealed to them and to their church that at that moment evangelism needed to be their primary focus. God was ready for His people to spread the Good News about His Son to the entire Mediterranean world, and that task would begin with them.

Evangelism is still a high priority for the Lord and His people, but we too will need the guidance of the Spirit as we seek new and effective ways to tell this generation about Jesus.

How can we win our neighbors to Christ in a time when any attempt to share faith or to contend for the correctness of a religious idea may be seen as the ultimate social offense?

Perhaps the Holy Spirit will direct us to new and fruitful ways to share the message of Jesus if we imitate those Antioch prophets and get on our knees.

✖

Memory Selection

We declare unto you glad tidings, how that the promise which was made unto the fathers, God hath fulfilled the same unto us their children, in that he hath raised up Jesus again.—*Acts 13:32-33*

That superb Bible expositor, the late Dr. Merrill Tenney, wrote a compelling book called *The Reality of the Resurrection.* In it he traces the preaching of the apostles to show us that our Lord's first messengers had only one subject. Wherever the apostles went and whenever they preached, they told their hearers that Jesus had been raised from the dead, and called men and women to serve a living Lord.

When they spoke to the mixed crowd of Jews and Gentiles in the synagogue in Pisidian Antioch, the message of Paul and Barnabas was simple. They told how Jesus had been slain and how God raised Him to life again. In the Hebrew Scriptures they pointed to the predictions of David that God would free the Messiah from His tomb.

What about those of us who speak for Jesus today? Is there any message more urgent for us to share than the Resurrection? The Savior we serve is the Living One. "I died," He tells us, "and behold I am alive for evermore" (Rev. 1:18, RSV).

Weekday Problems

Years ago a delightful Christian couple confided to me that they decided to get married after visiting a local fortune teller. Evidently they had not read the Bible's clear warnings about dabbling in sorcery and black magic. They told me their tale without the slightest embarrassment or shame.

In the Scriptures, from Moses' time onward, witchery and occult practitioners are seen as enemies of the work of God and of His people. Under the Leviticus laws, such practices were capital crimes. So these are not minor matters in God's sight.

Despite the clear prohibitions in Scripture, sorcery was big business in the Jewish communities in New Testament times. The ancient lore of magic spells called the Caballa was preserved in ancient times with largely Jewish sorcerers.

In the Book of Acts we see the apostle colliding with Jewish witch doctors on several occasion. In the Cypriot capital of Paphos, Paul and Barnabas found themselves opposed by a Jewish sorcerer named Elymas, or Bar-jesus. He came out second best to the powers of the Holy Spirit.

Earlier in Acts 8 the apostle Peter confronted Samaria's famous Jewish sorcerer, Simon. Then in Acts 19 in Ephesus we will see still another Jewish sorcerer, Sceva, along with his witch-doctor sons, opposing the ministry of Paul and Silas.

In every instance, the power of the Holy Spirit triumphed over that of Satan. Christ's followers need to make sure that they stay on the right side—the winning side.

The Magic of Electricity

I know an electrician who became a famous baseball player.

That's a switch!

Yeah, he really gave 'em a charge.

Once he got his wires crossed and made the audience disappear.

Did he ever play against that famous pitcher O'Watts?

Oh, yeah, but he was really jealous of him. He wanted to kill O'Watts.

What happened?

Well, he pulled it off and they sent him to that chair with a large charge.

Shocking!

This Lesson in Your Life

What would you do if the Holy Spirit suddenly designated you as the next missionary your congregation should send to preach in Costa Rica or Belarus? Would you be pleased or perplexed?

Several years ago unexpected health concerns caused a devout missionary couple to end many years of fruitful service in Africa. Their sponsoring church began a serious search for someone to replace them.

A number of obvious prospects were contacted. Because of previous commitments, none of them could accept the assignment at hand. As the time drew near for the veteran missionaries to fly home, the church began to be anxious because they still had not identified someone who could take their place.

After an intense week of fasting and prayer by the leaders of that church, one man in their prayer circle felt the calling of the Spirit.

This man was a devout believer, but he had not prepared himself as a minister of the word. Instead, his training and skills lay in computer technology and programming. So he wondered at first if he might have been mistaken about the Spirit's call.

In Africa at the mission station, however, it soon became clear that the Spirit chose correctly. It turned out that the most urgent need of the long-time, proven mission program was a Bible concordance in the limited language of that area.

Producing such a volume would require a lifetime of labor, or it might be done in a year or so by a person with the right computer skills. Sure enough, the right man was there, ready to use his unique gifts to advance the already excellent Bible instruction at the mission.

The same Holy Spirit who selected Barnabas and Saul picked that computer-savvy Christian to help the world learn about Jesus.

The Spirit, who knows our hearts and minds, could see that Barnabas' early life on Cyprus would make him especially useful in reaching the inhabitants of that island for the Lord.

He knew that Paul's rabbinical training in Jerusalem coupled with his childhood in the Gentile city of Tarsus had prepared him to witness powerfully both in the synagogues and the Gentile cities along the route of that first historical mission journey.

The same Spirit can also see how that the combination of your personal talents and life experiences makes you a one-of-a-kind candidate for Kingdom tasks—tasks nobody else could accomplish quite as well as you.

When the Syrian Antioch church laid hands on Barnabas and Saul and set them apart to go preach about Jesus, they willingly went. Are you and I equally ready to go and to do when the Spirit calls?

GETTING THE FACTS STRAIGHT

1. What was the Antioch church doing when the Holy Spirit told them to set apart Barnabas and Saul to go preach?

Their prophets and teachers were fasting and praying.

2. What sort of position did Sergius Paulus occupy?

To keep from confusing the KJV's "deputy" with a sheriff's sidekick, note that other versions call him the "proconsul" (NIV, RSV) or the "governor" (TEV) of the island.

3. How did Elymas interfere with the work of the missionaries?

He tried to keep Sergius Paulus from accepting their message about Jesus.

4. According to Saul, why was Elymas temporarily blinded?

Saul said Elymas had "tried to pervert the right ways of the Lord." The sorcerer had opposed the work of God in Sergius Paulus' heart.

5. Does the text tell us why Saul's name was changed?

No. There is not even a hint why this change took place.

6. According to verses 5 and 13, what roles did John play in this first mission journey?

John came along with Saul and Barnabas as their "minister" or their helper. Part way on the journey he quit and went home.

7. In his sermon in the synagogue at Antioch of Pisidia, how did Paul identify Jesus?

As King David's descendant, the one John the Baptist predicted, and the One God raised from the dead after the Jewish authorities killed Him.

8. In verse 26, what two groups did Paul address as he preached in that synagogue?

He spoke both to Jews and to those who had converted to Judaism—known then as "god-fearers."

9. According to Paul in his sermon, who in the Old Testament predicted the Resurrection of Jesus?

David predicted it in Psalm 16:10.

10. Can you explain the difference in the response of the Jews and the Gentiles to Paul's sermon in Antioch of Pisidia?

The Jewish leaders were jealous of Paul and his huge popularity, but the non-Jews were eager to hear his message.

Acts 13 tells us the story of the highly successful work of the first mission team in Christian history. Do you realize that it also tells the story of the first major failure by a mission team member?

In 13:5, Luke tells us that a young man named John "was with them as their helper" (NIV). This is not the first time Bible readers have met John. In Acts 12:12 we learn that John lived in Jerusalem and his mother Mary welcomed groups of Christians into her home.

Because of their involvement with the Jerusalem church, Paul and Barnabas may have known John before the Acts 12 events, but the last verse in that chapter tells us that they took John back to Syrian Antioch with them. We also learn in this verse (12:25) that John's other name—his surname, according to the NIV—was Mark.

If all we knew about it was the information in 13:13, we might not suspect anything negative about John's departure from the mission team. In the final four or five verses of Acts 15, however, we learn that Paul took a very dim view of John's decision to return home.

Paul was so unhappy with John's performance, in fact, that he refused to travel with him on the next journey. Barnabas, who was kin to John, took the lad back to Cyprus with him, and Paul chose a new missionary partner for his next trip. From their earliest days, mission teams have at times been beset by friction between the team members.

This would be a rather dismal tale if it ended here. Thankfully, it doesn't. In fact, the young man who disappointed Paul on this journey later matured into one of the finest spokesmen for the Christian faith.

Years later the apostle Peter would refer to him as his son in the faith (1 Pet. 5:13). Although Paul would not take him along on his second missionary journey, later this man traveled with Paul during some of his most difficult days (Philem. 24; Col. 4:10).

This man who failed in Acts 13 eventually became such a valuable worker that Paul, near the end of his life, actually asked Timothy to bring him when he came Rome. Paul said of this former failure, "He is helpful to me in my ministry" (2 Tim. 4:11).

Today we usually refer to this "failure" by his surname, Mark—the man who wrote the second Gospel by that same name.

Lesson 9

Fitting into the Community

Eph 4:1-16

I therefore, the prisoner of the Lord, beseech you that ye walk worthy of the vocation wherewith ye are called,

2 With all lowliness and meekness, with longsuffering, forbearing one another in love;

3 Endeavouring to keep the unity of the Spirit in the bond of peace.

4 There is one body, and one Spirit, even as ye are called in one hope of your calling;

5 One Lord, one faith, one baptism,

6 One God and Father of all, who is above all, and through all, and in you all.

7 But unto every one of us is given grace according to the measure of the gift of Christ.

8 Wherefore he saith, When he ascended up on high, he led captivity captive, and gave gifts unto men.

9(Now that he ascended, what is it but that he also descended first into the lower parts of the earth?

10 He that descended is the same also that ascended up far above all heavens, that he might fill all things.)

11 And he gave some, apostles; and some, prophets; and some, evangelists; and some, pastors and teachers;

12 For the perfecting of the saints, for the work of the ministry, for the edifying of the body of Christ:

13 Till we all come in the unity of the faith, and of the knowledge of the Son of God, unto a perfect man, unto the measure of the stature of the fulness of Christ:

14 That we henceforth be no more children, tossed to and fro, and carried about with every wind of doctrine, by the sleight of men, and cunning craftiness, whereby they lie in wait to deceive;

15 But speaking the truth in love, may grow up into him in all things, which is the head, even Christ:

16 From whom the whole body fitly joined together and compacted by that which every joint supplieth, according to the effectual working in the measure of every part, maketh increase of the body unto the edifying of itself in love.

Memory Selection
Eph. 4:7
Background Scripture
1 Cor. 12:3-21; Eph. 4:1-16
Devotional Reading
1 Cor. 12:4-20

Nov. 2

FOCUS

One of the first hard realities the early Church faced was the fact of diversity. Suddenly Jew and Gentile found themselves asked to work and worship together as one. Furthermore, diverse races and cultures among both Gentiles and Jews had to be welded into one. Of course diversity need not be "hard"; but just as in the modern Church—it isn't always easy to accept diversity as a gift instead of an obstacle.

Paul's letter to the Ephesians is one of the richest resources in the New Testament for encouragement and teaching on the value of diversity. How many true Gods are there? How many Messiahs? Just so, "There is one body" (4:4).

ഇരു

For a Lively Start

Ask your group, *Wouldn't it be wonderful if all of us in the church here were just alike? Same gifts and talents? Same interests? Same abilities?*

Of course if no one in the group objects to this line of reasoning, the teacher must answer *No!* Note what price would be paid if everyone in the church had the same interests and gifts. The many different kinds of ministries that need doing wouldn't get done. The enrichment of variety couldn't be enjoyed. And things would be just plain dull!

Yet the gift of diversity also comes with a price: unity must walk hand in hand with diversity if Christ's work is to be done. As a Jew called to work among Gentiles, the apostle Paul was uniquely qualified to keep both elements in balance: unity in diversity. More than any other New Testament writer, Paul perceived that if believers are to reflect Christ to the world, we must balance the two.

Teaching Outline	**Daily Bible Readings**	
I. Walk in Unity—1-6	Mon.	Drawn by God's Power *Acts 8:12-25*
A. Unity from the Spirit, 1-3	Tue.	Drawn from a Distant Land *Acts 8:26-38*
B. The 'Seven Ones,' 4-6	Wed.	Drawn from Other Nations *Acts 22:3-16*
II. Enjoy Diversity—7-13		
A. Various gifts . . . 7-10	Thurs.	Drawn to be Christians *Acts 11:19-26*
B. . . . Toward perfection, 11-13	Fri.	Seekers Among All People *Acts 17:22-28*
III. Grow the Body—14-16	Sat.	A Worthy Calling *Eph. 4:1-6*
A. Childish turbulence, 14	Sun.	Joined and Knit Together *Eph. 4:7-16*
B. Mature Christlikeness, 15-16		

Verse by Verse

I. Walk in Unity—1-6

A. Unity from the Spirit, 1-3

1 I therefore, the prisoner of the Lord, beseech you that ye walk worthy of the vocation wherewith ye are called,

2 With all lowliness and meekness, with longsuffering, forbearing one another in love;

3 Endeavouring to keep the unity of the Spirit in the bond of peace.

Why does Paul call himself God's "prisoner" here? We are more accustomed to hearing him speak of himself as a servant or slave of Christ. Perhaps he changes to this metaphor because the topic, unity, lends itself easily to a group of people who have put themselves in the service of a master and in doing so have bound themselves to work together in a common cause. Prisoners wear the same kind of clothes. Some march in step with each other. Although their peace with each other is forced, Paul makes his point. Being a Christian is a vocation or calling that requires humility, lowliness of mind, and living in peace voluntarily with each other. It is to this kind of life that Paul calls the Ephesians.

B. The 'Seven Ones,' 4-6

4 There is one body, and one Spirit, even as ye are called in one hope of your calling;

5 One Lord, one faith, one baptism,

6 One God and Father of all, who is above all, and through all, and in you all.

This famous list emphasizes the divine and doctrinal oneness out of which unity among Christians grows. It is impossible to have harmony among believers without reflecting on, and giving allegiance to, the unity among God, Christ, and the Holy Spirit, and the solid relationship among Christian doctrines such as faith and baptism.

The way in which the unity Paul urges here has been violated in Christian history is tragic. Speculation on the nature of God, and of Christ—depths of doctrine that are often impossible to agree on—split many early churches. Leaders often split churches for the mere purpose of satisfying their egos. Still, this list of "ones" often called quarreling Christians back into fellowship with each other. There is one body, or Church, and divisiveness cannot bear witness to this fundamental fact.

II. Enjoy Diversity—7-13
A. Various gifts . . . 7-10

7 But unto every one of us is given grace according to the measure of the gift of Christ.

8 Wherefore he saith, When he ascended up on high, he led captivity captive, and gave gifts unto men.

9 (Now that he ascended, what is it but that he also descended first into the lower parts of the earth?

10 He that descended is the same also that ascended up far above all heavens, that he might fill all things.)

It is ironic that one source of disunity is the very gifting which we see Christ bestowing upon members of His Body. Paul uses a passage from Psalm 68:18 to illustrate this irony. He pictures the Messiah as a king returning from battle with the spoils of war. There would have been bowls of gold, pitchers of silver, and many other treasures that the king could distribute in his grace as gifts to the leaders that had made victory possible. Likewise, Christ has won a much greater war by descending into Hades where He captured Satan. Then, returning with spiritual gifts—love, grace, peace, kindness, various talents, etc.—He distributes them to members of his "army," the Church. How tragic to allow such "spoils of war" to cause division, instead of using them to build a stronger army!

B. . . . Toward perfection, 11-13

11 And he gave some, apostles; and some, prophets; and some, evangelists; and some, pastors and teachers;

12 For the perfecting of the saints, for the work of the ministry, for the edifying of the body of Christ:

13 Till we all come in the unity of the faith, and of the knowledge of the Son of God, unto a perfect man, unto the measure of the stature of the fulness of Christ:

Among the graces distributed among His people by the Prince of Peace are various levels of leadership skills. Despite the fact that the gift of the apostleship is listed first, it is doubtful that Paul meant for us to think of these as "ranks," with the grace of teaching coming last. One indication of this is the value Paul places on the gift of teaching in Romans 12, in a well-known list of gifts. Prophets, evangelists, and pastors (elders or bishops) round out the list of gifts.

It is interesting to note the reason Paul gives for Christ having given such gifts to those in His Body, the Church. They are for the edifying or building up of that Body in order to help it grow toward perfection. The term "perfect" can mean "full-grown" or "mature," not just without sin, and it is in the former sense that Paul seems to use it here. The gifts of leadership and teaching that God gives to the Church are to help it mature into the "perfect man"—a term that probably refers to Christ. It would be hard to place a higher value on leadership than Paul does in this language, despite its difficulty in places.

III. Grow the Body—14-16
A. Childish turbulence, 14

14 That we henceforth be no more children, tossed to and fro, and carried about with every wind of doctrine, by the sleight of men, and cunning craftiness, whereby they lie in wait to deceive;

84

The early Church faced several sources of "childlikeness" or doctrinal instability. First, we recall that on that day of Pentecost when Peter preached the first gospel sermon after Christ's resurrection, throwing open the doors of the Christian Church, most of those who responded to his appeal were Jews. Among other things, this means that from the beginning the ideas in the early Church were heavily tilted toward Jewish thought.

After the martyrdom of Stephen, much of the Church's leadership was scattered throughout Gentile areas. Almost from the beginning, therefore, people trained to, for example, make a small sacrifice to the gods at the meat market were asked to worship alongside Jews for whom such a gesture was anathema. Some of these Gentiles who became Christians gave in to the natural human tendency to compete for leadership honors, and to do so with "cunning craftiness."

Later, Gentile ideas about the nature of persons clashed with Jewish teaching, as both sides tried to reconcile the full humanity of Jesus with the claim that He was also divine. Add the variety of ethnic and nationalistic pieces to this picture, and it is little wonder that, to Paul, they were often stalled in "childish" debates.

B. Mature Christlikeness

15 But speaking the truth in love, may grow up into him in all things, which is the head, even Christ:

16 From whom the whole body fitly joined together and compacted by that which every joint supplieth, according to the effectual working in the measure of every part, maketh increase of the body unto the edifying of itself in love.

The key to church unity is to speak the truth—not in arrogance but in love. In that way, every "joint" or body-part can contribute whatever gifts God has given it, and to whatever extent. When one loving, informed believer teaches another person also to teach in love, the Church becomes a self-edifying organism.

శారు

Evangelistic Emphasis

Jesus cited effective evangelism as a key reason for unity in His Body. In His famous John 17 prayer He prayed to the Father "that they also may be one in us: that the world may believe that thou hast sent me" (vs. 21).

What happens, though, when God's children don't get along with one another? Christians have been fussing and feuding for so long in some communities that the favorite coffee shop sport of non-church-goers is laughing at the antics of believers.

A preacher friend of mine was still a novice at his job when, just outside his tiny town he discovered a "tent city"—a tenement where paupers lived in shipping crates and dilapidated shacks. Kids there were unwashed and hungry. Christmas was not far away, and my friend hurried to town and told a banker and several other Main Street business-men what he had found. Together they provided food and clothing for all of the domestic refugees in that camp.

My preacher friend made one mistake. To assist the homeless, he joined hands with Catholics and Baptists and Methodists—with citizens from half a dozen denominations. Back then, when Christians were expected to stay on their side of the existing lines, this drew a storm of criticism, and jeopardized my friend's job.

Can you imagine what unbelievers talked about in the coffee shops of that one-horse town during the weeks that followed?

ഇൗരു

Memory Selection

As the body is one, and hath many members, and all the members of that one body, being many, are one body: so also is Christ. For by one Spirit are we all baptized into one body, whether we be Jews or Gentiles, whether we be bond or free; and have been all made to drink into one Spirit. For the body is not one member, but many.—*1 Corinthians 12:12-14*

My congregation is a singing church. Our people love to sing praise to the Lord, and they do it with skill and gusto. One of our key church leaders, however, is tone deaf, and he knows it. We kid him a lot about not allowing him to lead our music or participate in our praise team. All of the banter is good-spirited, much of it instigated by this man himself.

Although the Spirit did not see fit to give this good man the gift of music, this does not mean, that He overlooked this music-less soul when He was passing out gifts. Nobody among us has a clearer mind or a kinder heart. This Christian leader's gift is the one Paul calls "governments" (KJV) or "administration" (NIV, RSV) just a few verses later in 1 Corinthians 12.

This man's wisdom and balance have guided our church for several decades. His spiritual gift has blessed all of us. We won't let him lead our singing, but because of his spiritual gift, we gladly let him lead us.

Weekday Problems

Like many who will read these words, I was born into a world with high walls between various groups of Christians—walls designed to keep us from really knowing one another or learning to trust each other. All of my life those walls have troubled me, and I've done everything I could to tear them down. As the years have passed, however, I have begun to think that the greatest barriers to unity in Christ's Church are not the theological rifts and the doctrinal disputes that fuel our fusses. The splintering in Christian is more often the result of our failure to control our tongues and egos. Unity is impossible among Christians whose hearts and wills are not shaped by the gentle, loving fruit of God's Spirit.

Some of the theological issues that divide the Church will not likely be sorted out this side of Heaven. Godly men and women with keen minds and clean hearts have tried for centuries to unravel the questions that separate us in Christ. The result has usually been more questions on which to disagree. Just like the brothers and sisters in our physical families, though, God's children can cherish one another and enjoy blessed activities together despite unsettled disagreements.

"Love one another, as I have loved you," Jesus instructs us. He died for us and welcomed us to Himself although He knew we were wrong about many matters. That's how He expects to us to treat one another.

Unity and Diversity

Union does everything when it is perfect. It satisfies desires, simplifies needs, foresees the wishes, and becomes a constant fortune.—*Etienne Senancour*

* * *

The multitude which does not reduce itself to unity is confusion; the unity which does not depend upon the multude is tyranny.—*Anonymous*

* * *

The union of Christians to Chist, their common head . . . may be illustrated by the lodestone. It not only attracts the particles of iron to itself by the magnetic virtue, but by this virture it unites them one to another.—*Richard Cecil*

* * *

Had we not faults of our own, we should take less pleasure in complaining of others.—*Francis deS. Fenelon*

Ths Lesson in Your Life

It's easy to harbor hateful, negative thoughts about Catholics or Pente-costals or Baptists—if we don't know one.

As a young preacher I was amazed to see church leaders who had been scathingly merciless toward divorced people turn into lovable souls who, after the marriage of their own son or daughter failed, could find all man-ner of scriptural basis to love and accept divorcees.

Have you noticed how much kinder your assessment of Methodists or Presbyterians or Catholics becomes when your own daughter or grand-daughter becomes one? I'm convinced that most of us are far nicer than our theology. We always have been. And this pleases me no end. Even when our preaching was full of vitriolic abuse for people in other denomi-nations on Sunday, folks in my fellowship tended to be gentle and amiable to those same people in the coffee shop on Monday.

It's easy to hate in the abstract. But the love of Christ constrains us when we are face to face with a real human being, regardless of how much our views may clash.

Prejudice—whether racial or cultural or spiritual—seldom can survive personal friendship. That is one huge reason why you and I need to have frequent and purposeful contacts with all of our neighbors who believe in Jesus. The better we get to know each other, the more likely are many of our differences to dissolve.

In her fine little book *Walking on Water,* Madeleine L'Engle shares a great quotation from the pen of Samuel Coleridge. It echoes the apostle Paul's concern that because of minor doctrinal differences, one Christian might "set at nought" (KJV) or "look down on" (NIV) a brother for whom Christ died (Rom. 14:10).

In the syntax of his day, Coleridge advised his fellow-believers, "Trample not on any; there may be some work of grace there, that thou knowest not of. The name of God may be written upon that soul thou treadest on; it may be a soul that Christ thought so much of as to give His precious blood for it; therefore, despise it not."

Unfortunately, our estrangement from God's children in other fellow-ships has far too often caused us to discount them as "real" Christians. To use Coleridge's term, we have been tempted to "trample" on other believ-ers because they were not one of us.

Do you agree with me that we are far less likely to mistreat a believer in Jesus who differs with us if we have wept with them, laughed with them, broken bread with them? As much as anything else, it is our continuing isolation from other believers that perpetuates the fracturing of the family of God.

STRAIGHT

1. How is our confession of Jesus linked to the Presence of the Spirit in our hearts?
None of us can make this confession unless the Spirit of God is in our heart.

2. From Paul's illustration of the body, does he expect all Christians to possess all of the Spirit's gifts? Is there any one gift that every Christian must possess?
No. The point of his illustration is that it takes different members with different gifts to make up a functioning body.

3. According to Paul in 1 Corinthians, who decides who will get which ones of the spiritual gifts?
The Holy Spirit gives to each believer as He sees fit.

4. How does Paul use the concept of the human body to show what would happen if every member of the Church had the same gift?
He asks us to envision a human being that is one big eyeball or just one ear. The Church would be just as grotesque if every member had the same gift.

5. What does Paul's body illustration teach us about failing to value some of the Spirit's gifts?
Some parts of our bodies that we seldom think about or honor turn out to be just as essential as the ones we esteem. Even so, some of the less spectacular spiritual gifts matter immensely.

6. From Ephesians 4:2-3, what attitudes are essential to unity in Christ's Church?
Humility, meekness, patience, and love.

7. List the seven "ones" in Ephesians 4:4-6? How do they unite us in Jesus?
One body, one Spirit, one hope, one Lord, one faith, one baptism, and one God. All Christians share these.

8. In Ephesians 4:11-14, what picture Paul is painting?
The apostle compares the ascending Christ to a conquering king who comes home from victory distributing generous gifts to his people.

9. According to Paul in these verses, what gifts does Jesus give to the Church and what are the purposes of these gifts?
Paul lists apostles, prophets, evangelists, pastors, and teachers.

10. In order for Christians to "speak the truth" effectively and beneficially, how must we speak it?
In love.

When I began to write sermons as a young minister, Ephesians 4 quickly became one of my favorite places to find a Sunday morning text. Paul's emphasis on the unity of Christ's followers resonated in my soul.

I suspect, however, that I may have been attracted to this chapter for a less noble reason. After several centuries of being esteemed as often the best educated and best equipped leader in their communities, clergy by the time I came along had plunged low on the list of respected local professionals.

Here was a Bible text that counter-balanced the rising tendency to see ministers as nuisances or nincompoops or non-productive citizens, at best. Ephesians 4:11 tell us that evangelists, pastors, and teachers are Christ's gift to His Church. They are not a scourge. They are not dead weight. Christ gives them to us for the good of His Body.

Preaching that text in that light may have been a bit self-serving, I now must admit. In my youthful years, I'm not sure I convinced anybody that Paul really intended for the text to convey this message.

While studying this intriguing text to prepare those self-assuring sermons, however, I did discover with some amazement how much difference a single comma can make in a Bible verse. Ephesians 4:12, with all the commas supplied in the KJV, seems to be telling us that Christ gave leaders and teachers to the Church for three purposes: "For the perfecting of the saints, for the work of the ministry, for the edifying of the body of Christ."

What if the comma after "saints" vanishes, as it does in many of the newer translations? Then we hear Paul telling us that evangelists and pastors were given to the church "to prepare God's people for works of service" (NIV). Then we see that Christ sends these equippers "so that the body of Christ may be built up."

If we keep reading beyond that vanishing comma, we can see that Christ's ultimate goal in sending leaders to His Church is to help all of us to mature spiritually and be united in Him.

What a blessed day it will be for all of us if the evangelists and pastors in every community become the main reason for all Christians to love one another and to be united in Jesus. Then Paul's vision in this Scripture will have come true.

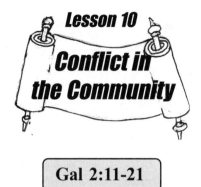

Lesson 10

Conflict in the Community

Gal 2:11-21

But when Peter was come to Antioch, I withstood him to the face, because he was to be blamed.

12 For before that certain came from James, he did eat with the Gentiles: but when they were come, he withdrew and separated himself, fearing them which were of the circumcision.

13 And the other Jews dissembled likewise with him; insomuch that Barnabas also was carried away with their dissimulation.

14 But when I saw that they walked not uprightly according to the truth of the gospel, I said unto Peter before them all, If thou, being a Jew, livest after the manner of Gentiles, and not as do the Jews, why compellest thou the Gentiles to live as do the Jews?

15 We who are Jews by nature, and not sinners of the Gentiles,

16 Knowing that a man is not justified by the works of the law, but by the faith of Jesus Christ, even we have believed in Jesus Christ, that we might be justified by the faith of Christ, and not by the works of the law: for by the works of the law shall no flesh be justified.

17 But if, while we seek to be justified by Christ, we ourselves also are found sinners, is therefore Christ the minister of sin? God forbid.

18 For if I build again the things which I destroyed, I make myself a transgressor.

19 For I through the law am dead to the law, that I might live unto God.

20 I am crucified with Christ: nevertheless I live; yet not I, but Christ liveth in me: and the life which I now live in the flesh I live by the faith of the Son of God, who loved me, and gave himself for me.

21 I do not frustrate the grace of God: for if righteousness come by the law, then Christ is dead in vain.

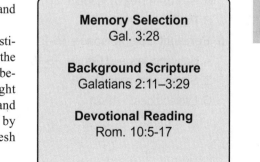

Memory Selection
Gal. 3:28

Background Scripture
Galatians 2:11–3:29

Devotional Reading
Rom. 10:5-17

FOCUS

It was both Paul's glad assignment and burden to insist that Jesus united both Jew and Gentile in one Body. While the other apostles also knew this, they were not always as consistent in putting it into practice.

The main obstacle that persisted in dividing these two groups was the Law of Moses. For Paul, this was highly ironic since the Law had been fulfilled in Christ, and was no longer binding on either Jew or Gentile. For the sake of getting along with strict Jews, the apostle Peter had failed to put this principle into practice. In this lesson Paul rebukes Peter for his inconsistency, and insists again that neither Jew nor Gentile is justified by Law, but by grace.

80CR

For a Lively Start

For almost a century, since the turbulent days of the civil rights movement in the 1950s, a majority of people of all races in the U. S. have agreed in principle on the principle of racial equality. You can start this class by an illustration that puts this verbal principle to a practical test.

Picture for your group a church that is predominantly, say, Vietnamese. One Sunday morning a family of five, led by an Anglo man in his 60s walks into the service. There is no group of five seats available, so they file through the audience trying to find a place where at least a couple of them can sit together. The man is a veteran of the Vietnam War. Describe how you think the average Anglo family and Vietnamese church would handle this situation, and justify their reasons for what they do.

Teaching Outline	**Daily Bible Readings**	
	Mon.	Dissension and Debate Acts 15:1-5
I. Prejudice Among Christians—2:11-14	Tue.	Evidence of God's Work Acts 15:6-11
A. Bad examples by leaders, 11-13	Wed.	Basis for Unity Acts 15:12-21
B. Paul's bold rebuke, 14	Thu.	Confession that Saves Rom. 10:5-9
II. Pertinent Comparisons—15-21	Fri.	Everyone May Be Saved Rom. 10:10-17
A. Between Jew and Gentile, 15-16	Sat.	Not Running in Vain Gal. 2:1-10
B. Sin after salvation, 17-18	Sun.	Living by Law or Faith Gal. 2:11-21
C. Life and death, 19-21		

Verse by Verse

I. Prejudice Among Christians—2:11-14

A. Bad examples by leaders, 11-13

11 But when Peter was come to Antioch, I withstood him to the face, because he was to be blamed.

12 For before that certain came from James, he did eat with the Gentiles: but when they were come, he withdrew and separated himself, fearing them which were of the circumcision.

13 And the other Jews dissembled likewise with him; insomuch that Barnabas also was carried away with their dissimulation.

Paul wrote to the Christians in "New Gaul" or Galatia, a province in Asia Minor (now Turkey) to correct certain errors. Unfortunately he learned that some Galatians rejected his teachings because he was not among the original 12 apostles; so Paul recounts an arrangement by which the other apostles agreed that he would go to such non-Jews as the Galatians (2:9).

Even so, all was not well. We have noted earlier how the city of Antioch, north of Jerusalem, became an important center for both Jewish and Gentile believers. It had come about that the apostle Peter, whom the agreement designated a missionary among Jews, came to Antioch after having had "table fellowship" with Gentile Christians, apparently in Jerusalem. This would have been strictly forbidden until the new Christian openness lowered the walls that had separated Jew and Gentile. Despite this new freedom and "democratic" sociability, when Peter came to Antioch he would not eat with Gentiles, lest he be criticized by fellow Jews. His act of prejudice became so contagious that others, such as Barnabas, followed suit, threatening both to establish the old prejudices in the Church, and to give the Law more force and authority than Jesus (and hence Paul) ever intended.

B. Paul's bold rebuke, 14

14 But when I saw that they walked not uprightly according to

93

the truth of the gospel, I said unto Peter before them all, **If thou, being a Jew, livest after the manner of Gentiles, and not as do the Jews, why compellest thou the Gentiles to live as do the Jews?**

Peter had even received a special revelation showing the equality of Jew and Gentile, in the vision of the sheet in which were erased the old distinctions between "clean" and "unclean" animals (and people; Acts 10:11ff.) His act of discrimination in Antioch was therefore clearly not "according to the truth of the gospel." It had the effect of "compelling" Gentiles to further the old prejudicial laws that had made Gentiles feel like second-class citizens under the Old Law.

II. Pertinent Comparisons—15-21
A. Between Jew and Gentile, 15-16

15 We who are Jews by nature, and not sinners of the Gentiles,

16 Knowing that a man is not justified by the works of the law, but by the faith of Jesus Christ, even we have believed in Jesus Christ, that we might be justified by the faith of Christ, and not by the works of the law: for by the works of the law shall no flesh be justified.

We must not be misled by Paul's referring to Gentiles (such as the Galatians) as "sinners" (and, in vs. 9, "heathen"). He is merely using terminology familiar to both Jew and Gentile, not singling out Gentiles as especially sinful. His argument is that the Jewish leaders who had become Christians—men such as Peter and Paul—have known for years that their Law does not save. Anyone who is

justified now is "made right" with God by faith in Christ, "and not by the works of the law: for by the works of the law shall no flesh be justified."

Why does Paul speak so clearly against salvation by law? Because it is that way of thinking that made Jews think it made them unclean to eat with Gentiles. It was that system of salvation by the Law of Moses that made even righteous Gentiles follow in the steps of people like Peter who refused to have fellowship with them. If "by the works of the law shall no flesh be justified," then by the works of the law shall no one look down on other races or anyone else and feel prejudiced toward them.

B. Sin after salvation, 17-18

17 But if, while we seek to be justified by Christ, we ourselves also are found sinners, is therefore Christ the minister of sin? God forbid.

18 For if I build again the things which I destroyed, I make myself a transgressor.

Now Paul asks how Peter or anyone else who had been set free from sin by Jesus could dare return to the old ways of bondage and be found deliberately living in the sin from which Christ had set them free. Paul is not speaking of the natural imperfections common to human nature, but the deliberate decision to live by the sinful system from which Christ had liberated them. By refusing to associate with Gentiles, Peter and other Jews could be charged with rebuilding the very system Christ had destroyed on the cross. If they claim that Christ endorsed their prejudicial behavior, they not only return to sin themselves, they portray Christ as a minister of sin—an unthinkable act.

C. Life and death, 19-21

19 For I through the law am dead to the law, that I might live unto God.

20 I am crucified with Christ: nevertheless I live; yet not I, but Christ liveth in me: and the life which I now live in the flesh I live by the faith of the Son of God, who loved me, and gave himself for me.

21 I do not frustrate the grace of God: for if righteousness come by the law, then Christ is dead in vain.

Paul faces the delicate task of showing that the Law itself, valuable though it was, pointed to its own inadequacy. One way he does this is to compare it with a husband whose wife is bound to him as long as he lives, but who is set free from their marriage bond if and when her husband dies (Rom. 7:1ff.). The only thing that would make such a husband-and-wife union wrong would be to think that it still exists after the death of one of the partners. The Law itself says that the former bond is now as dead as the spouse who died. The dispensation of the Law of Moses was a case of planned obsolescence, and we do it no honor by extending it into the dispensation of grace.

Furthermore, in following this planned death, believers themselves such as Paul have died, too; they have been crucified with Christ. The life that now empowers believers is the life of Christ in them. To insist on following the Old Law is to express the will to die, since God planned for it to die! By insisting on continuing such demands of the Law as not associating with Gentiles is to "frustrate the grace of God." The supreme gift of grace, the death of Christ "while we were yet sinners" (Rom. 5:8) was a complete waste of His precious blood if we could have been saved by Law anyway. In effect, Paul asks a probing question: Why would anyone cling to works such as circumcision (or keeping oneself separate from that which was considered "unclean"), when it is Christ's work, not ours, that brings righteousness to the world?

ഇൻ

Evangelistic Emphasis

How many of us are willing and eager to cross ethnic, language, or color lines to spread the gospel of Jesus?

Almost half a century ago my brother and his bride flew halfway around the world to begin 20 years of evangelism among the gentle but impoverished people in southern Malawi.

Dozens of small, mostly white congregations in several states combined their meager post-World War II resources to support this ambitious mission project. All of this was happening in a decade when people like Rosa Parks and Martin Luther King were rising up to challenge centuries of racial discrimination in America.

I was proud of the leaders in these supporting churches. In those days prejudice ran deep and the racial divide in most our communities was seldom breached. But these godly people refused to let color dampen their zeal to send the gospel to a black nation.

The people in Malawi's villages were poor—literally the poorest per capita in the entire world. The Christians who sent my brother to preach Jesus to them also paid generously to provide medical care, drought relief and education.

They proved that ethnic and cultural barriers are not strong enough to keep the gospel from being preached and acts of mercy from being done in the name of Jesus.

℘℞

Memory Selection

As many of you as have been baptized into Christ have put on Christ. There is neither Jew nor Greek, there is neither bond nor free, there is neither male nor female: for ye are all one in Christ Jesus.—*Galatians 3:27-28*

On a brisk Palm Sunday morning I slipped quietly into the early service at our downtown Presbyterian Church. I knew my colleague, Dr. Jim Bankhead, would have an uplifting message for us from God's word. I looked forward to it. Since I was almost late, I got one of the last empty seats in the house, right on the back pew (in my church you have to come early to find a back pew).

I had come there primarily to worship the Lord. As a minister, however, and as a guest in a church not my own, I could not keep from looking around and taking stock of those who had gathered there in God's house. Little things tipped me off that the petite, 40-ish black lady who had taken the very last seat right beside me was also a guest. In the sea of worshipers, though, I recognized many of their regulars. I spotted a host of friends—a banker, a successful restauranteur, a ranch family, a retired piano teacher now in her 90s, and many others. That morning I could see that the assembly represented the ethnic make-up of our community—Hispanics, Asian immigrants, African Americans, and Middle East folks—all of us gathered there to praise the One who died for us all. Paul is right. We are "one in Christ."

Weekday Problems

We hear a lot today about conflict resolution. Did you notice how Paul handled his differences with Peter? "I withstood him *to his face*," Paul tells us (2:11). It takes a real man to handle disagreements that way—the way Jesus tells us to. "If your brother sins against you, go to him and show him his  fault," Jesus commands (Matt. 18:15, TEV). One version says that we should "confront" the one who offends us (TLB).

This doesn't mean for us to be ugly and accusing to the person who has wronged us. Jesus means for us to get face to face with that person, airing our complaints only to that person. "Do it privately, just between yourselves," Jesus warns.

How different this is from the way hurt feelings often are handled both in the Church and out. When someone upsets us, most of us feel the carnal impulse to run and tell other friends how badly this person has treated us. This, of course, intensifies the problem and makes it harder than ever to resolve. It's like letting fleas out of a box. Paul, however, had the courage and honesty to confront his fellow-apostle personally. It seems clear from their later writings that they remained trusted friends in the years that followed.

Don't Knock It!

Knock knock.
Who's there?
Mayonnaise.
Mayonnaise who?
Mayonnaise have seen the glory of . . . .

* * *

Knock knock,
Who's there?
Amos.
Amos who?
A mosquito bit me.

* * *

Knock knock.
Who's there?
Andy.
Andy who?
And he bit me again.

Knock knock
Who's there
Gorilla.
Gorilla my dreams, I love you.

* * *

Knock knock.
Who's there?
Duane.
Duane who?
Duane the tub! I'm dwowning!

* * *

Knock knock.
Who's there?
Banana.
Banana who?
Banana Havana.
Havana who?
Havanapple. It's on me.

This Lesson in Your Life

Last summer two of my granddaughters were among the group from our congregation who went to a Christian youth leadership training week called Summer Excitement.

As always, they came home excited, and wearing weird T-shirts emblazoned with an upside-down slogan that screamed, "It's Not About Me!"—upside down so they could read it themselves. Unlike most shirt messages, this one was addressed to the shirt's wearer. We found out that it had been the theme of their week's activities.

On reflection, I wonder if the T-shirt message should not have been worn right side up. I certainly need to hear that message. Don't you?

I am embarrassed to admit how often I find myself more concerned about my own comfort than that of others. I want the thermostat set to suit me. I want the volume of the café music adjusted to my taste. I want other drivers to proceed at my selected speed. So much of the time, it really is about me.

How can this be, when I have been a Christian all of my life? Was I not paying attention when Jesus told me, "If any man will come after me, let him deny himself, and take up his cross, and follow me" (Matt. 16:24)? Let him do what? "Deny himself."

If I want to be a follower of Jesus, His first requirement is that I quit putting myself and my preferences first. Is this as tough for you as it is for me? Paul's metaphor at the end of Galatians 2 probably owes something to Jesus' words in Matthew 16. Jesus says we must take up our cross. Paul talks about being "crucified with Christ" (2:20). In other words, those of us who follow Jesus must die with Him so that we may live with Him.

These are not just pretty words that fit in church hymns and Sunday School prayers. Crucifixion was a form of torture—painful and often humiliating. Dying to bad habits and wrong attitudes can be too.

My alcoholic friend Ken cried to me when he fell repeatedly. In his earliest days of sobriety he told me, "I die a dozen times a day."

A colleague who lost his family, his self-respect, and his job because of his addiction to pornography found it almost impossible to put to death this devilish craving in his soul. It look him several agonizing years to learn how to stay clean.

What a marvelous victory it is for people like this to be able to proclaim with Paul, "It is no longer I who live, but Christ who lives in me." If these winners are wise, of course, they give Christ the credit for their victory, confessing, "The life I now live in the flesh I live by faith in the Son of God, who loved me and gave himself for me" (Gal. 2:20-21, RSV).

GETTING THE FACTS STRAIGHT

1. For what mistake did Paul rebuke Peter at Antioch?
Peter associated with Gentiles and shared their customs until influential Jews from Jerusalem came to Antioch. Then he started acting like all Christians needed to follow Jewish rules.

2. What basic Christian truth did both Paul and Peter know about how a person can be justified or set right with God?
Both apostles knew and believed that a person can be set right with God only by faith in Jesus and not by works of the Law.

3. According to Paul, what could we do that would "frustrate the grace of God" and cause Jesus to have died for nothing?
If we act like we can save ourselves by our own perfect obedience and good works, we reject the Cross and grace.

4. Had the Galatian Christians received salvation and the Spirit—by works of the law or by faith in Jesus?
Paul asked this question to remind his converts that they were saved and received the Spirit by believing in Jesus.

5. According to the Scriptures, why did God consider Abraham to be a righteous man?
God counted Abraham a righteous man because Abraham believed God.

6. What promise contained the gospel that Abraham heard many years before Christ's birth?
God told Abraham, "In thee shall all nations be blessed." Paul says this promise included the gospel of Christ.

7. According to 3:13, what curse did Christ redeem us from?
The curse of the Law—the idea that only a perfect person who never broke a single rule of God could be saved.

8. Why is it important, according to Paul, that the Law came 430 years after God's promise to Abraham?
God's plan for saving us by faith in Christ was clearly in place and promised long before the Law was given, so the Law could not take its place.

9. What can we learn from Paul's comparison of the Law to a schoolmaster?
All of us hope to grow up and graduate from school, but we need the discipline and insights of school to get ready for life. So the Law serves its purpose, but we do outgrow it.

10. According to Paul in the last four verses of Galatians 3, how does a person get to be a child of God?
"Ye are all the children of God by faith in Christ Jesus. For as many of you as have been baptized into Christ have put on Christ" (3:26-27).

My personal testimony is that no truth in God's word has blessed me more than Paul's assurance that we are made right with God through faith and not by works of the law. I grew up trying to do it exactly backwards. No one ever preached or taught me a backwards gospel—one that based my salvation on my goodness instead of the Lord's, but that is how I was trying to get right with God in my early days.

Do I need to tell you that this approach to religion is a recipe for misery and failure?

I can tell you from sad experience that anybody who intends to please God by keeping all the rules perfectly, by figuring out all the doctrines correctly, by always being right—anybody who thinks he can get to Heaven by being right about everything—will find himself instead in a self-created hell on earth.

Because I loved the Lord, I had a passion to be right. That's good. Unless you get things twisted like I did and decide that God will love you only if you always do the right things the right way in the right church—only if you are always right.

I tried hard to be right, but I was smart enough to know that I kept making mistakes, morally, doctrinally, ritually. I was just too human always to be right. As Paul discerned from Scripture, "The whole world is a prisoner of sin" (Gal. 3:22). That included me.

Finally, through the pages of Romans and Galatians, God spoke to me. He confirmed what I had learned by hard experience—that I could never be good enough, right enough, to save myself. If I was going to be saved, I was going to have to let Jesus do it for me.

When I discovered God's blessed promise that we are saved not by our own perfection but by our faith in the One who alone is perfect, a tremendous load was lifted from my soul and I found true joy in the Savior. Not my righteousness but His satisfied God.

Trying to save myself had cursed me with perpetual anxiety. When I learned that we are justified by faith in Jesus and His cross, I found peace with God, just as the Scriptures promised (Rom. 5:1).

Instead of worrying all the time because I knew I was not good enough to please the Lord, now I had the assurance that "there is now no condemnation for those who are in Christ Jesus" (Rom. 8:1, NIV).

"Christ hath redeemed us from the curse of the law," Paul exults (Gal. 3:13). Having lived under that curse, I now rejoice that I found the grace that can be ours only through faith.

Lesson 11

Communion with God in the Midst of Struggle

Philip. 3:17–4:9

Brethren, be followers together of me, and mark them which walk so as ye have us for an ensample.

18 (For many walk, of whom I have told you often, and now tell you even weeping, that they are the enemies of the cross of Christ:

19 Whose end is destruction, whose God is their belly, and whose glory is in their shame, who mind earthly things.)

20 For our conversation is in heaven; from whence also we look for the Saviour, the Lord Jesus Christ:

21 Who shall change our vile body, that it may be fashioned like unto his glorious body, according to the working whereby he is able even to subdue all things unto himself.

4:1 Therefore, my brethren dearly beloved and longed for, my joy and crown, so stand fast in the Lord, my dearly beloved.

2 I beseech Euodias, and beseech Syntyche, that they be of the same mind in the Lord.

3 And I intreat thee also, true yokefellow, help those women which laboured with me in the gospel, with Clement also, and with other my fellowlabourers, whose names are in the book of life.

4 Rejoice in the Lord alway: and again I say, Rejoice.

5 Let your moderation be known unto all men. The Lord is at hand.

6 Be careful for nothing; but in every thing by prayer and supplication with thanksgiving let your requests be made known unto God.

7 And the peace of God, which passeth all understanding, shall keep your hearts and minds through Christ Jesus.

8 Finally, brethren, whatsoever things are true, whatsoever things are honest, whatsoever things are just, whatsoever things are pure, whatsoever things are lovely, whatsoever things are of good report; if there be any virtue, and if there be any praise, think on these things.

9 Those things, which ye have both learned, and received, and heard, and seen in me, do: and the God of peace shall be with you.

Memory Selection
Philip. 4:7

Background Scripture
Philip. 3:3–49

Devotional Reading
Ps. 46

Nov. 16

FOCUS

Although Paul's brief letter to the Philippians has some passages that are unmatched in tenderness, there were also, as in every church, some difficulties there. Paul has to deal in particular with issues such as divisiveness and fleshliness that inhibited the closeness of community and fellowship in the ideal church.

Part of the difficulty here may have stemmed from the thoroughgoing Roman character of the church there. Unlike most other towns where Paul had established churches on his second missionary journey, there was no Jewish synagogue at Philippi. Some have speculated that the lack of any Jewish spirituality left the way open for a pagan atmosphere in the Church. Paul writes to establish more spiritual values among the Christians there.

For a Lively Start

Illustrate the problem between "Eudodias and Syntyche" (4:2) by asking two women in the group to do an off-the-cuff role play that illustrates trifling disputes that often break out among Christians. Have them argue about the way someone is dressed or has her hair done . . . whether a particular man and woman in the church should be dating . . . which musicians perform best . . . and whether the minister should support from the pulpit someone who is running for a political office.

The point, of course, is to show the folly of a church getting bogged down in trivia that can damage internal fellowship and hurt the church's influence in the community.

Teaching Outline	**Daily Bible Readings**	
I. The Spiritual Walk—3:17-21	Mon.	God Is Our Refuge *Ps. 46*
A. Enemies of Christ, 17-18	Tue.	Sharing God's Grace *Philip. 1:3-11*
B. Enemies of the Spirit, 19-21	Wed.	Rejoice! Christ Is Proclaimed *Philip. 1:12-18*
II. Stand Fast—4:1-3	Thu.	The Help of the Spirit *Philip. 1:19-26*
A. Paul's 'joy and crown,' 1	Fri.	Striving Side by Side *Philip. 1:27-30*
B. Two quarrelling women, 2		
C. Help the helpers, 3	Sat.	Stand Firm in the Lord *Philip. 3:17—4:1*
III. Christian Values—4-7		
IV. The 'Whatevers'—8-9	Sun.	The Peace that Guards *Philip. 4:2-9*

Verse by Verse

I. The Spiritual Walk—3:17-21

A. Enemies of Christ, 17-18

17 Brethren, be followers together of me, and mark them which walk so as ye have us for an ensample.

18 (For many walk, of whom I have told you often, and now tell you even weeping, that they are the enemies of the cross of Christ:

Despite the diversity in modern Christianity, a general form of worship and statements of belief have developed that enable a visitor from Ireland to Spain, for example, to "visit church" and find forms that are enough alike to distinguish the religion of Jesus from paganism. Centuries of using the same Scriptures, creeds, and traditions have made this possible. However, if we were traveling with Paul on, say, his third missionary tour, the variety of practices might surprise us because of the absence of these unifying factors. Thus, Paul relies here on the pattern of his own life and beliefs in urging his loved ones in the church at Philippi to be faithful. During these days when the New Covenant Scriptures were still in a formative stage, Paul could only plead with these Christians to "be fol-lowers of me," and of those Christian leaders who "have us for an ensample."

The example Paul had set began several years earlier with his vision of the man in Macedonia saying "Come over . . . and help us" (Act 16:9). Immediately he and his companions left Asia Minor and, for the first time, took the Good News into Europe, starting at Philippi, "the chief city of that part of Macedonia, and a [Roman] colony," (Acts 16:12). Now Paul has been imprisoned, probably in Rome, and writes to those in the church he founded at Philippi, to ensure their doctrinal soundness and everyday faithfulness to the message he had preached. Unfortunately, enemies of Paul and his message followed him like a plague everywhere he went; now he writes to oppose these who in being his enemies were also "enemies of the cross of Christ."

B. Enemies of the Spirit, 19-21

19 Whose end is destruction, whose God is their belly, and whose glory is in their shame, who mind earthly things.)

20 For our conversation is in heaven; from whence also we look for the Saviour, the Lord Jesus Christ:

21 Who shall change our vile body, that it may be fashioned like unto his glorious body, according to the working whereby he is able even to subdue all things unto himself.

These enemies of the Cross were distorting the true view of the body, and the material world. Some held that all flesh was evil, ignoring the fact that God had pronounced His material creation "very good" (Gen. 1:31). Others took the opposite course, reveling in orgies and drunkenness: if our bodies are "vile," then why not burn out their wickedness with further baseness, and with making their belly their "god"?

Paul calls for a balance that enables us to remember that our true destiny, our "conversation" or citizenship, is in heaven, and that we are to prepare for that eternal dwelling place by respecting our bodies and the entire material creation. Life on earth is like a Greek gymnasium, an arena where we practice living godliness so it will not be such a shock when the "eternal life" granted us at salvation is fully developed at death.

II. Stand Fast—4:1-3
A. Paul's 'joy and crown,' 1

4:1 Therefore, my brethren dearly beloved and longed for, my joy and crown, so stand fast in the Lord, my dearly beloved.

Paul uses a variety of terms to show his love for those he had converted. Sometimes they are his "letters" (2 Cor. 3:2). Here, perhaps remembering converts such as the businesswoman Lydia, his first convert at Philippi, he calls them his "joy and crown." Nothing is more important for Paul than that these early and beloved Christians remain fast in the faith. For now, they are the only "Bibles" available to the pagans around them.

B. Two quarrelling women, 2

2 I beseech Euodias, and beseech Syntyche, that they be of the same mind in the Lord.

As important as standing fast in the faith is the internal harmony among the Philippian Christians. Somehow word has come to Paul that two women are stirring up trouble in the young church. That women and their disagreement would be considered important enough to address is a remarkable indication of their rise in importance in the early Christian communities. Yet they are not to allow this new "equal opportunity" to be the cause of division in the church; and Paul reins them in with the counsel that they be "of the same mind."

C. Help the helpers, 3

3 And I intreat thee also, true yokefellow, help those women which laboured with me in the gospel, with Clement also, and with other my fellowlabourers, whose names are in the book of life.

Someone at Philippi is already at work trying to enact in the church the very reforms Paul is calling for. We may have his name: he is called either a "true yokefellow," as most translations have it, or the phrase is actually his name and Paul makes a pun of it (such as "good worker"). The "Clement" is thought by some to be an early church father whose letter to the church at Rome has been preserved, and in fact was considered in many areas of the early church to be "canonical," or a part of the Scriptures. And again we see the importance of women as co-workers with Paul. These stalwarts' names are in "the book of life," which is another way of saying that their ministries will be remembered forever.

III. Christian Values—4-7

4 Rejoice in the Lord alway: and again I say, Rejoice.

5 Let your moderation be known unto all men. The Lord is at hand.

6 Be careful for nothing; but in every thing by prayer and supplication with thanksgiving let your requests be made known unto God.

7 And the peace of God, which passeth all understanding, shall keep your hearts and minds through Christ Jesus.

Approaching the end of his letter, Paul begins a sort of list of pieces of advice which, if followed, will help accomplish his goal of a faithful church at Philippi. The call to joy is remarkable in light of the frequent persecutions these early Christians endured. That pleasure is not to be allowed to erupt into hedonism, but instead is to be a part of a life of moderation.

A life of confidence and peace of mind will be the natural result of the faithfulness to which Paul calls these Phillippians. The word "keep" makes a pun. It means to "guard," or even to be jailed—an experience known by some of these Christians. Paul reduces such persecution to a joke compared with the true protection and safe-keeping God gives the faithful.

IV. The 'Whatevers'—8-9

8 Finally, brethren, whatsoever things are true, whatsoever things are honest, whatsoever things are just, whatsoever things are pure, whatsoever things are lovely, whatsoever things are of good report; if there be any virtue, and if there be any praise, think on these things.

9 Those things, which ye have both learned, and received, and heard, and seen in me, do: and the God of peace shall be with you.

Again, Paul shows his intent on closing his letter by a list—he just, like many preachers today, has some difficulty getting there. And how valuable is the list of basic stepping stones for threading our way across the river of life. Honesty, justice, purity, loveliness, virtuousness and praise—these were traits Paul had exhibited as part of the Christian life when he first went to Philippi; and again he calls for those he left behind in the church there to imitate them, with the expectation that this will help administer to them the God of peace—a persistent theme in this lovely letter.

೮ාඥ

Evangelistic Emphasis

Recently I heard a television evangelist making a winsome appeal to what must have been a vast audience. I can't quote the man precisely, but the gist of his message was that those who give their hearts and lives to the Lord will be blessed with economic prosperity.

As I listened to his eloquent message, I wondered how it would have been heard by my dear friends who have been out of work for over a year—ever since the company the husband served for decades decided to close its plant. They love Jesus with all their hearts, but these good people are struggling to pay their utilities.

I had the same reaction when I heard another evangelist guaranteeing good health to all who say Yes to Jesus. That afternoon I had visited in the hospital room of one of the dearest Christians I know. He had just learned that he has liver cancer and, at best, only a few more months to live.

How different these evangelistic messages were from that of the apostle Paul. "I want to know Christ and the power of his resurrection and the fellowship of sharing in his sufferings, becoming like him in his death" (Phil. 3:10, NIV).

Will people accept an invitation to a life of persecution and pain? Millions have. Around the globe today thousands of Christians are paying a dreadful price for their faith, and they stand strong, knowing that sharing Jesus' Cross means also sharing His Resurrection.

ᏕᎧᏟᎡ

Memory Selection

Be careful for nothing; but in every thing by prayer and supplication with thanksgiving let your requests be made known unto God. And the peace of God, which passeth all understanding, shall keep your hearts and minds through Christ Jesus.—*Philippians 4:6-7*

"Be careful," my mother used to warn my siblings and me whenever we left the house. This was always her parting admonition. I don't know if her concern was a comment on the way we tore around the neighborhood— first on our bicycles and later in our jalopies. It was her way of saying she wanted us to come home in one piece.

My mother's words of caution did not contradict the apostle Paul's instruction, "Be careful for nothing." In Elizabethan/King James English this was their way of saying, "Don't be full of care." In other words, Don't let your heart be filled with needless anxiety. Don't worry.

Not long ago a good friend of mine heard me cite this passage. I knew that he and his family were going through an especially difficult time. He knew that I knew, so he volunteered, "I do that. I do exactly what that verse says to do. I get on my knees and give all my troubles to the Lord. And then," he smiled, "I keep taking them back."

Weekday Problems

The Book of Philippians is basically a thank-you note. That good church had sent aid to Paul in Rome while he was in Roman chains, unable to work and pay his own expenses.

This was not the first time this band of disciples had helped to finance Paul's ministry. Again and again, he said, they had supported him when nobody else did. Paul was grateful. So he wrote to say so.

It is obvious from the tone of this short letter that Paul loves these people. Bible scholars often have commented on the fact that this letter contains no rebukes, no criticism—not even a hint of disapproval.

The only comment even slightly negative is the remark about Euodias and Syntyche, two ladies who seem to have had a misunderstanding of some sort. Even in this instance, Paul does not tell the church to scold them or to punish them. "Help them," he says, as he compliments their past service in the Kingdom.

When you go to church, do you expect to be reproved and criticized? Or do you go there anticipating thankfulness and approval?

If you and I want to bless the churches where we work and worship, we should imitate Paul and never miss a chance to say thank you. Our positive outlook and our grateful hearts can go a long way toward spreading good will and warmth in our congregations.

Having Pun
Giggles and Groans from the
Lowest Form of Humor

I wondered why the baseball was getting bigger. Then it hit me.

* * *

Police were called to a day-care where a three-year-old was resisting a rest.

* * *

The roundest knight at King Arthur's round table was Sir Cumference.

* * *

To write with a broken pencil is pointless.

* * *

When fish are in schools they sometimes take debate.

* * *

A thief who stole a calendar got 12 months.

* * *

The short fortune teller who escaped from prison became a small medium at large.

This Lesson in Your Life

If you wanted to brag to someone, what details in your accomplishments and your pedigree would you cite? Would you begin by boasting of athletic honors you won during your school days? Could you point to ancestors who were quite wealthy or who were numbered among the socially elite in your area? Would you cite the place of your birth or perhaps your present citizenship as proof of that you are a special person?

What about your religious background and accomplishments? Have several generations before you been influential leaders of your church? Do you presently hold an office that deserves high respect? Are you better versed in Scripture than most of your friends? Do they consider you a reliable source of Bible knowledge?

Have you outdone your associates in charitable gifts or in missionary endeavors? Are you known to be a person with impeccable integrity and unquestionable moral probity? What plaques and honors hang on your walls—proof of your exceptional accomplishments and vocational achievements?

All of these meritorious deeds and awards are laudable, to be sure, but the apostle Paul is telling us in Philippians 3:4-8 that they all belong in the garbage dumpster if they stand between you and Christ.

Far better than all of our heady honors, Paul says, is for us to know Christ, to "be found in him, not having [our] own righteousness, which is of the law, but that which is through the faith of Christ, the righteousness which is of God by faith" (Phil. 3:9).

After citing his own lengthy and impressive list of social and spiritual credentials, Paul tells us he turned his back on all of it and considered it junk when he discovered how valuable Jesus is.

My dear friend, the late Dr. Leo Miller, had moved among the mighty and walked with the great during his years of leadership at the University of Indianapolis. When he and his wife moved to an upscale assisted living condo, he told her, "Alberta, let's tuck these plaques and photos into this closet instead of displaying them." In his modesty, he was afraid someone might think they were boasting. Because they were so near and dear to me, I was one of the few people who knew what was in that closet: a photo of President Reagan, signed personally to Leo; autographed photos of Leo with senators and governors, who were his personal friends; certificates for stellar service in high circles; and notes from several famous people.

My friend had much to brag about, but in his mind, knowing Christ, and the power of His resurrection, and the fellowship of His sufferings outweighed any worldly honor he had attained.

Of all the things you are and all the deeds you have done, what would you most like to be known for?

GETTING THE FACTS STRAIGHT

1. According to Paul, who were "the circumcision"—the real Jews?

True Jews were not those with Jewish ancestry but those who "worship God in the spirit, and rejoice in Christ Jesus, and have no confidence in the flesh" (3:3).

2. If Paul had wanted to boast about the merits of his ancestry and his religious rank, what could he have pointed to?

His tribe, his family, his rabbinical training, his strict religious party, his zeal, his obedience to the Law, his opposition to the Christian faith.

3. What did Paul consider to be worth far more than all of his personal accomplishments?

Getting to know Jesus and the power of His resurrection.

4. Although he was an apostle chosen by Jesus, did Paul think he had reached his spiritual goals?

No. He said he kept pressing on to reach his goals in Jesus.

5. What sort of example had Paul set for his converts in Philippi—what example did he urge them to follow (3:14-17)?

To urgently press forward to reach the best things in Christ.

6. How did Paul describe the false teachers who were trying to mislead the Philippian church?

He called them enemies of the Cross. He said they would be destroyed because their desires ruled them and they were proud of their shameful lifestyle.

7. The only local Christians mentioned by name in Philippians were Euodias, Syntyche, and Clement. What was Paul's opinion of these believers?

He spoke highly of them, even the ladies who had been fussing a bit. He honored them as his fellow-workers in Christ.

8. When are Christians supposed to rejoice?

All of the time.

9. What does Paul recommend as our best alternative to worrying?

Praying about whatever troubles us.

10. According to Paul, what sort of things should fill our hearts and minds?

Things that are true, honest, just, pure, lovely, of good report—things that are virtuous and praiseworthy.

Uplift

Do you remember that remarkable minister, Dr. Norman Vincent Peale? Dr. Peale has been gone for several years now, but he was best known probably for his classic book, *The Power of Positive Thinking*. During his long ministry, his message stayed focused on that theme. In Jesus he found hope and love and light to lift people out of darkness and despair.

Dr. Peale's popular message is capsulized in Paul's famous words in Philippians 4:8: "Whatsoever things are true, whatsoever things are honest, whatsoever things are just, whatsoever things are pure, whatsoever things are lovely, whatsoever things are of good report; if there be any virtue, and if there be any praise, think on these things."

My special friend Ellen Thomas is now in her 90s, but she has always been the sort of person who sees something hopeful in the most dismal situation. She never fails to see something admirable in a person the rest of us can't stand.

Every time I visit with dear Ellen, I leave her house wishing I were more like her. I wish my mind fastened instinctively and immediately on the positive, uplifting, commendatory aspects of the family members and parishioners I deal with daily.

Positive thinking is a habit, just as surely as negative thinking is a learned response. No doubt our DNA and our parental molding dispose us to one or the other, but we can choose what to dwell on.

I can choose to be a critical person, one who habitually homes in on the flaws in the people around me, or like dear Ellen, I can develop the habit of choosing to see what is true, honest, lovely, praiseworthy in them. Who would you rather work beside day after day, a negative person or a positive one? Will folks in your carpool, or your golf foursome, or your Moms-in-Touch clatch enjoy your company more if you tend to see the bright side of things or if you always focus on the underbelly of humanity?

Of course, it's not just our friends and associates who have to endure our negative mully-grubbing. You and I have to live with ourselves. I don't especially like me when I'm down and dour.

Paul is on to something important here. Filling our hearts and minds with the noble, the excellent, the praiseworthy seems to be a simple but effective strategy for lifting our Christian lives to a new plane of happiness and joy.

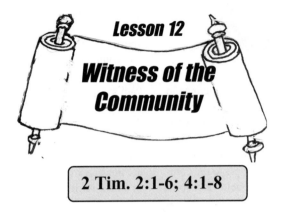

Lesson 12

Witness of the Community

2 Tim. 2:1-6; 4:1-8

Thou therefore, my son, be strong in the grace that is in Christ Jesus.

2 And the things that thou hast heard of me among many witnesses, the same commit thou to faithful men, who shall be able to teach others also.

3 Thou therefore endure hardness, as a good soldier of Jesus Christ.

4 No man that warreth entangleth himself with the affairs of this life; that he may please him who hath chosen him to be a soldier.

5 And if a man also strive for masteries, yet is he not crowned, except he strive lawfully.

6 The husbandman that laboureth must be first partaker of the fruits.

2 Tim 4:1-8

1 I charge thee therefore before God, and the Lord Jesus Christ, who shall judge the quick and the dead at his appearing and his kingdom;

2 Preach the word; be instant in season, out of season; reprove, rebuke, exhort with all longsuffering and doctrine.

3 For the time will come when they will not endure sound doctrine; but af-

ter their own lusts shall they heap to themselves teachers, having itching ears;

4 And they shall turn away their ears from the truth, and shall be turned unto fables.

5 But watch thou in all things, endure afflictions, do the work of an evangelist, make full proof of thy ministry.

6 For I am now ready to be offered, and the time of my departure is at hand.

7 I have fought a good fight, I have finished my course, I have kept the faith:

8 Henceforth there is laid up for me a crown of righteousness, which the Lord, the righteous judge, shall give me at that day: and not to me only, but unto all them also that love his appearing.

Memory Selection
2 Tim. 2:2

Background Scripture
2 Tim. 2:1-3; 4:1-8

Devotional Reading
Acts 4:13-20

FOCUS

One of the greatest challenges in the early Church was developing faithful leaders. Just as in any organization, maintaining strong leaders was important both within the Church, and as a witness to the community in which the believing community lived and worked.

This lesson focuses on some of the apostle Paul's most eloquent appeals to the younger minister Timothy, whom Paul mentored, urging him to follow Paul's steps in ministry and service. Paul develops several models of leadership that apply not only to the Church but to any organization that wants to make an impact on the community. The pictures are not of a wealthy CEO, but, as noted in an earlier lesson, a "servant-leader."

☙❧

For a Lively Start

In this lesson, the apostle Paul has his say about the traits of an effective church leader. You can begin the lesson by allowing members of your group to have their say, too—then toward the end of the class you can compare the two lists of traits.

Some members of your group may have had leadership training on the job, or in civic organizations. Whatever their experience, encourage them to search their background for attributes of leadership that may apply to the church. For example, the idea of "servant leadership," although originating in the church, has spread to many businesses as well. Point out that as Paul aged, it became more urgent for Timothy, whom Paul mentored, to develop and apply his own leadership skills.

Teaching Outline	Daily Bible Readings
I. Metaphors of Strength—2 Tim. 2:1-6	Mon. Power, Love, Self-Discipline *2 Tim. 1:3-7*
A. A good soldier, 1-4	Tue. I Am Not Ashamed *2 Tim. 1:8-14*
B. A winning contestant, 5	Wed. The Power of the Gospel *Rom. 1:8-17*
C. A successful farmer, 6	Thu. The Unchained Word *2 Tim. 2:8-13*
II. General Charge—4:1-8	Fri. An Approved Worker *2 Tim. 2:14-19*
A. Preach the word!, 1-2	Sat. Continue in the Faith *2 Tim. 3:14-17*
B. Approaching apostasy, 3-4	Sun. Proclaim the Message! *2 Tim. 2:1-5; 4:1-8*
C. Specific charge, 5	
D. Paul's future, 6-8	

Verse by Verse

I. Metaphors of Strength—2 Tim. 2:1-6

A. A good soldier, 1-4

1 Thou therefore, my son, be strong in the grace that is in Christ Jesus.

2 And the things that thou hast heard of me among many witnesses, the same commit thou to faithful men, who shall be able to teach others also.

3 Thou therefore endure hardness, as a good soldier of Jesus Christ.

4 No man that warreth entangleth himself with the affairs of this life; that he may please him who hath chosen him to be a soldier.

Many scholars believe that 2 Timothy is the apostle Paul's last letter, written not long before his death in perhaps A.D. 67 or 68. Certainly the tone of the letter is one of both resignation and hope. He is ready and willing to "go home," saying "I am now ready to be offered, and the time of my departure is at hand" (4:6).

Yet Paul's work must go on, and the letter shows that he is counting on the younger minister Timothy, whom Paul has mentored, to teach fellow ministers, who would teach other ministers, and so on into an indefinite future. In the verses at hand Paul develops four metaphors of the kind of strength that will be required for this task. The first word picture is of a soldier, a metaphor that was always at hand in the world over which the armies of Rome ruled. These troops were for the most part tough and hardened soldiers. They subsisted on minimal rations, usually slept on the ground, out of doors, and stayed physically ready for the hardest duty.

Paul calls on Timothy to have something of this character as a minister, although the emphasis is on spiritual toughness more than physical. With opposition from both Jew and Gentile, a Christian leader could not be a person who gave up at the first sign of conflict. Verse 4 may imply, but not necessarily so, that Timothy is to be paid for his ministry so he is not "entangled" with secular work.

B. A winning contestant, 5

5 And if a man also strive for masteries, yet is he not crowned, ex-

cept he strive lawfully.

A faithful Christian leader could also be compared with an athlete who competed in the Greek games. Twice in this verse Paul uses the term from which we get the word "athlete." A winning athlete trains in order not just to win but to play by the rules. Paul also expected Timothy not to be mentally and emotionally "soft," but disciplined enough to state the case for Christianity against those who would argue against it.

C. A successful farmer, 6

6 The husbandman that laboureth must be first partaker of the fruits.

The same hint of justification for taking a salary is made in the metaphor of a "husbandman," which means a gardener or farmer as well. The meaning is not that the minister must be the first in the church to dip into the contribution, as the KJV implies, but that it is right for him to share in the "firstfruits" or harvest.

II. General Charge—4:1-8

A. Preach the word!, 1-2

4:1 I charge thee therefore before God, and the Lord Jesus Christ, who shall judge the quick and the dead at his appearing and his kingdom;

2 Preach the word; be instant in season, out of season; reprove, rebuke, exhort with all longsuffering and doctrine.

Specfically, Paul expects Timothy (and presumably other ministers of the time as well) to focus especially on preaching. Proclaiming the way of salvation is primary because it is the Gospel that will make the difference between being saved or lost at the day of judgment.

This preaching is to be consistent, not convenient. It is to contain both the gentle, healing elements that encourage those who are faint in spirit, and the robust, challenging rebuke needed by those who think to "get by" in the faith by slacking instead of working—the kind of mentality rebuked by the German martyr Dietrich Bonhoeffer who preached so clearly against "cheap grace."

B. Approaching apostasy, 3-4

3 For the time will come when they will not endure sound doctrine; but after their own lusts shall they heap to themselves teachers, having itching ears;

4 And they shall turn away their ears from the truth, and shall be turned unto fables.

The phrase "sound doctrine" appears four times in the New Testament, and only in the pastoral epistles (1 and 2 Timothy and Titus). Positively, faithful preachers are to proclaim "healthy doctrine," referring to the basics of the Christian message. From the doctrinal emphasis in Paul's epistles, we can assume that "sound doctrine" includes preaching that Jesus is the Son of God, salvation by grace through faith, the role of the church as the gathering place of the saved, and the doctrine of judgment at the Last Day which Paul has just mentioned. Paul foresees the time when those with "itching ears" will not abide such basics. Negatively, "unsound doctrine" would neglect to emphasize these issues, resulting in the "sickness" or unsoundness of the soul.

C. Specific charge, 5

5 But watch thou in all things, endure afflictions, do the work of an evangelist, make full proof of thy ministry.

Paul is not seeking ministers who need to be served, but who want to serve others. The Church will not need weak-willed or spiritually sick preachers, but those who can stand up as leaders of people accustomed to the hardships of being a minority group, and who are roundly criticized from all sides. Not long before or after Paul wrote this letter, the Roman emperor Nero tried to place the blame for the great fire of Rome, which destroyed more than half the city, on Christians. They needed leaders who could defend the Church against such nonsense, but with the love and graciousness of the Good News. Pantywaists need not apply.

D. Paul's future, 6-8

6 For I am now ready to be offered, and the time of my departure is at hand.

7 I have fought a good fight, I have finished my course, I have kept the faith:

8 Henceforth there is laid up for me a crown of righteousness, which the Lord, the righteous judge, shall give me at that day: and not to me only, but unto all them also that love his appearing.

This passage closes with a kind of "epitaph in advance" that is one of the most beautiful in literature. It reveals a man who, while never boasting of his accomplishments, knows that he has given his best. He has been put to the test, and not found wanting. He is ready to go home to be with his Lord if that is God's will, and He is confident of the reward awaiting not just himself, but all the faithful. We are reminded of a similar statement, where the apostle says that if given the choice he could hardly choose between life or death. Either way "Christ shall be magnified in my body, whether it be by life, or by death" (Phil. 1:20).

ക്കോ

Evangelistic Emphasis

In another place the apostle quoted the Old Testament verse that promises, "Whosoever shall call upon the name of the Lord shall be saved." Then he asked rhetorically, "How then shall they call on him in whom they have not believed? and how shall they believe in him of whom they have not heard? and how shall they hear without a preacher?" (Rom. 10:13-14).

This still seems to be his concern when he instructs Timothy to teach the truths he has learned to good men who are qualified then to share them with yet another group of learners.

Like cells multiplying in a biologist's petri dish, this process set in motion by Paul through his younger helper should guarantee that the number of available gospel preachers would continue to expand with each passing generation.

In the fellowship he grew up in, my own father identified a serious shortage of trained leaders and preachers. Paul's concept of an unbroken chain of trained church workers in 2 Timothy 2:2 caught my father's fancy. It inspired him to spend over 50 years training ministers and other workers for the Kingdom.

Today the gospel is being preached literally all over the world by hundreds of people my father taught. We must give generous support to the training of tomorrow's preachers.

$$\mathcal{SO}\mathcal{CR}$$

Memory Selection

Be strong in the grace that is in Christ Jesus. And the things that thou hast heard of me among many witnesses, the same commit thou to faithful men, who shall be able to teach others also. Thou therefore endure hardness, as a good soldier of Jesus Christ.—*2 Timothy 2:1-3*

Between his first and second years in law school, my oldest son Jon decided to sign up for Officer Candidate School in the U. S. Marine Corps. He had taught high school and coached for a few years after college, so he was a bit older than most of the other officer candidates at Quantico that summer.

He soon found that those extra years made a difference as he and his comrades endured the grueling physical regimen Marines use to weed out the weak and strengthen the survivors. Under the searing sun in Virginia's sultry swamps they pushed Jon's squadron of wannabe officers to the very limits of their abilities. On the proud day when his mother and I came to Quantico to see him receive his lieutenant's bars, I marveled that any of those guys were able to complete the barrier courses they showed us.

By the end of that summer the band of young officers who made it through that rigorous training were hardened and tough both in body and spirit, ready to face almost any challenge.

You and I are supposed to be willing to go through equally demanding preparation for our service in the army of the Lord.

Weekday Problems

Second Timothy 4:2 admonishes us to "preach the word; be instant in season, out of season." The King James vocabulary baffled me when I first read that verse. I had no idea what it meant to "be instant." I began to catch on, though, when I compared the RSV, where Paul commands, "Be urgent."

Of all the words that I would use to describe my Christian friends today, "urgent" is not one of them. Most of them are loving. The majority are upright. I would describe them as faithful, or truthful, or merciful. But urgent? No. Most of us are not that.

We used to be. When I was a youngster, we often knocked on doors for Jesus. We passed out tracts, held revivals, and otherwise pestered our neighbors constantly to be sure they knew about Jesus. Today the evangelistic fervor in the churches I serve seems to burn at a much lower level. Current taboos on proselyting seem to have made most of us much quieter and more subdued in our attempts to share the gospel.

Perhaps we have learned better methods evangelism—ways more suited to these present times. Perhaps we have matured in Christ and repented of our past urgency to steal sheep. That sort of urgency we can do without.

What's so urgent about preaching Jesus? To begin with, Jesus might return tomorrow. Then there's my friend Ed. He found out yesterday that he has terminal liver cancer. In a few days he may be going to see Jesus. In either case, it's urgent that I be telling Ed that Jesus died for his sins.

On Preaching and Preachers

Though we live in a reading age and in a reading community, yet the preaching of the Gospel is the form in which human agency has been and still is most efficaciously employed for the spiritual improvement of men.—*Daniel Webster*

* * *

A pastor needs the tact of a diplomat, the strength of Samson, the patience of Job, the wisdom of Solomon—and a cast-iron stomach.—*James Street, in* The Gauntlet

* * *

No sermon is of any value, or likely to be useful, which has not the three R's in it; ruin by the fall, redemption by Christ and regeneration by the Holy Spirit. My aim in every sermon is loudly to call sinners, to quicken saints, and to be made a blessing to all.—*John C. Ryland*

This Lesson in Your Life

Yesterday's e-mail brought an urgent request for prayer from a missionary friend on the other side of the world.

Trouble has broken out in one of their key village churches, he told us. One of the native preachers in that church had also served in some capacity at the mission station, but the missionary had been forced to dismiss the man when he ignored repeated warnings about mishandling funds.

Now, the missionary told me, the man he fired has begun to preach openly against the missionary, slandering him and other mission workers as he tries to align the village church on "his side" by spreading ugly lies about mission policies.

As my missionary friend seeks prayer support and advice, he wrestles with the same sort of options most of us face when we are confronted by a fellow-believer's serious misbehavior.

Timing is always one of the hardest calls. Is it best to confront the wrongdoer immediately? Or will it be wiser to wait patiently for the Lord to work on the hearts of those involved? Sometimes it's mighty hard to know which option will yield the best results.

In 2 Timothy 4:2, when Paul tells Timothy to rebuke those who need it, he tells him to do so with "great patience" (NIV) and "doctrine" (KJV) or "teaching" (NKJV).

It is always gracious for us to assume that a person who is misbehaving simply doesn't know any better. Even Jesus on the cross prayed, "Forgive them, for they know not what they do." Sometimes all that is needed to correct a bad situation is some "careful instruction" (NIV).

Surely, patience is usually in order. All of us want others to be patient with our mistakes, so we owe at least as much to those we must correct. We do well to give the Spirit time to work in the hearts of those who desire to walk in His ways.

Still, the time comes when Christian leaders must have the courage to reprove and rebuke those who persist in doing evil. Failure to do so may allow the sin to spread inside the fellowship while it may also tarnish the reputation of the church in the eyes of outsiders.

When my missionary friend weighed all these possibilities, he felt led in his present situation to wait for the Lord instead of publicly and immediately confronting his antagonist.

This has not been an easy decision for him. Today he e-mailed his stateside counselors to tell us what he has decided to do, and he candidly admitted to us that only time will tell if he has chosen the right timing.

1. Where was Timothy supposed to find strength for his ministry?
In "the grace that is in Christ Jesus."

2. Where did Timothy first learn the gospel?
From the apostle Paul.

3. To whom did Paul want Timothy to pass it on? Why?
Paul told him to pass on the gospel message to faithful men, who would then be able to share it with others.

4. What example did Paul use to explain the kind of hardship Timothy should endure?
Timothy was to endure suffering as a good soldier would. In other verses, Paul used the metaphor of a soldier in basic training.

5. What reasons did Paul give for Timothy to consider his "charge" a serious one?
Paul's charge to Timothy was super-serious because it was given to him in the presence of God and of Christ.

6. What was the "charge" Paul gave him?
Paul charged Timothy to "preach the word."

7. How was Timothy supposed to "exhort" his listeners, according to Paul?
With patience, with meekness, and with doctrine.

8. Paul warned that a bad time was coming. How did he describe it?
Soon men and women would not be willing to receive "sound doctrine," Paul said, but they would want fancy fables from teachers who told them what they wanted to hear.

9. What kind of ears did Paul predict that Timothy's listeners would have? What did he mean by this description?
Paul referred to "itching ears," probably describing listeners who want to be entertained instead of taught solid truths.

10. How could Timothy obey Paul and "make full proof" of his ministry?
Paul wanted Timothy to keep proclaiming the pure gospel he had been taught, thereby producing converts who would be true to Christ, standing firm in the truth.

When we first read it, Paul's preface to his instructions to Timothy sounds intimidating to most of us modern Christians: "I charge you therefore before God and the Lord Jesus Christ, who will judge the living and the dead at His appearing and His kingdom . . . ." (2 Tim. 4:1, NKJV).

Sadly, many Christians in our age have been taught to cringe at the very thought of being judged by Jesus. We seem to be afflicted by a hangover of *The Late, Great Planet Earth* mentality.

Such a reaction would be on target if we were rebels against the Lord, bent on doing all manner of evil. Then we ought to cower at the prospect of being called to account by the Lord of the universe.

But Timothy is God's devoted servant. He is suffering for the Kingdom and working hard to spread the gospel to those who don't yet know Jesus. Timothy is one of the good guys. When Jesus comes to judge all humanity, Timothy won't have a thing to worry about. He's clothed in white, washed in the blood of Jesus.

So are we—if we are trusting in the Cross. So are we—if we are saved by grace through faith (Eph. 2:8).

Have we been washed in the blood of the Lamb? Then we don't need to fear His coming. Are we faithfully serving Him and growing each day more and more into His likeness? Then His judgment will mean His approval and reward for us. We will have nothing to fear and everything to anticipate with joy.

Then, instead of being like so many modern Christians who dread Jesus's return and desperately pray, "No, Lord, not yet," we will echo the first-century Christians who urgently prayed, "Even so, Lord Jesus, come quickly!" If we read Paul's words to Timothy in this light, then we can see that the apostle is not threatening him with divine disapproval. He is holding out to a faithful minister the prospect of heavenly reward.

Surely all of us who love Jesus should look forward along with Timothy to hearing our Lord say, "Well done, good and faithful servant."

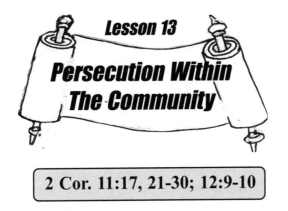

2 Cor. 11:17, 21-30; 12:9-10

That which I speak, I speak it not after the Lord, but as it were foolishly, in this confidence of boasting.

21 I speak as concerning reproach, as though we had been weak. Howbeit whereinsoever any is bold, (I speak foolishly,) I am bold also.

22 Are they Hebrews? so am I. Are they Israelites? so am I. Are they the seed of Abraham? so am I.

23 Are they ministers of Christ? (I speak as a fool) I am more; in labours more abundant, in stripes above measure, in prisons more frequent, in deaths oft.

24 Of the Jews five times received I forty stripes save one.

25 Thrice was I beaten with rods, once was I stoned, thrice I suffered shipwreck, a night and a day I have been in the deep;

26 In journeyings often, in perils of waters, in perils of robbers, in perils by mine own countrymen, in perils by the heathen, in perils in the city, in perils in the wilderness, in perils in the sea, in perils among false brethren;

27 In weariness and painfulness, in watchings often, in hunger and thirst, in fastings often, in cold and nakedness.

28 Beside those things that are without, that which cometh upon me daily, the care of all the churches.

29 Who is weak, and I am not weak? who is offended, and I burn not?

30 If I must needs glory, I will glory of the things which concern mine infirmities.

12:9 And he said unto me, My grace is sufficient for thee: for my strength is made perfect in weakness. Most gladly therefore will I rather glory in my infirmities, that the power of Christ may rest upon me.

10 Therefore I take pleasure in infirmities, in reproaches, in necessities, in persecutions, in distresses for Christ's sake: for when I am weak, then am I strong.

Memory Selection
2 Cor. 12:10

Background Scripture
2 Cor. 11:16–12:10

Devotional Reading
1 Cor. 1:18-25

Nov. 30

FOCUS

As he often does, the apostle Paul begins this section on one theme but soon shifts gears to another—yielding a twin focus. First he responds to criticism from "false apostles" who charge that Paul himself is a "wolf in sheep's clothing." Then he moves into one of the most powerful weapons in the Christian arsenal—the ability, through the power of Christ, to transform difficulty into victory.

Few people invite criticism, persecutions and other such difficulties. Paul's view, however, is that since every faithful Christian is likely to be criticized, and since Christ's grace and power flourish in such difficulties, "Bring it on!" In making his point, Paul also gives some interesting information about some of the suffering he has experienced as a Christian.

&)CR

For a Lively Start

Ask your group to share, from experience or reading, incidents when God was able to turn defeat into victory. For example, imagine how Paul must have felt, as a highly educated Jew, after his conversion experience "reduced" him to an oft-despised

Christian. Yet God used Paul's education to equip him for such challenges as to argue the case for Christianity before pagans on Mar's Hill (Acts 17:21ff).

Marriage is another life-arena in which victory has been wrested from the jaws of defeat, as when a divorce, or the death of a spouse results, long-range, in finding another life partner. The point is made by Paul: "My strength is made perfect in weakness" (2 Cor. 12:9).

Teaching Outline	Daily Bible Readings

I. Joking Boastfully—11:17, 21-30
  A. Permission to boast, 17, 21
  B. True identity, 22-23
    1. A true Jew, 22
    2. A Christian minister, 23
  C. Victories out of loss, 24-30
    1. Persecutions, 24-25a
    2. Natural disasters, 25b-27
    3. Care of the churches, 28-30
II. The Christian Paradox—12:9-10
	Mon. Persecution in the World
	     John 16:25-33
	Tue. Suffering in Similar Ways
	     1 Thess. 2:13-16
	Wed. Present Suffering, Future Glory
	     Rom. 8:18-25
	Thu. Through Many Persecutions
	     Acts 14:21-23
	Fri. Sharing Christ's Suffering
	     1 Pet. 4:12-19
	Sat. 'Come to Our Help!'
	     Ps. 44:17-26
	Sun. Perfect in Weakness
	     2 Cor. 11:16-18; 12:9-10

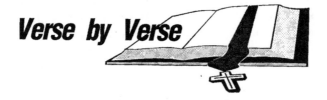

Verse by Verse

A. Permission to boast, 17, 21

17 That which I speak, I speak it not after the Lord, but as it were foolishly, in this confidence of boasting.

21 I speak as concerning reproach, as though we had been weak. Howbeit whereinsoever any is bold, (I speak foolishly,) I am bold also.

In chapters 9 and 10, God gives Paul permission to use the literary device of irony to deal with attacks from his enemies. Apparently these enemies consist of Jews who are either half-hearted Christians ("They lean that way"), or are spies working behind the lines and merely pretending to be Christians in order to undermine the Christian movement and/or expose its members.

One definition of irony is "the use of words to express something other than and especially the opposite of the literal meaning" (Webster). Paul uses irony to pretend to be boasting of his superior position as a Jewish Christian, when as anyone knows boasting is the opposite of a truly Christian attitude. This is why he mentions several times

that he is speaking "foolishly," and asks his audience to "bear with me a little in my folly" (11:1).

B. True identity, 22-23

1. A true Jew, 22

22 Are they Hebrews? so am I. Are they Israelites? so am I. Are they the seed of Abraham? so am I.

Why would anyone "boast" that he was a Hebrew? Because in the early days of the Church it was important to show that Christianity was the legitimate outgrowth of Judaism. It was not a "foreign growth" or weed growing out of the Mosaic system, but the true fulfillment of God's prophecy to Abraham, Isaac and Jacob. Jesus was the true Jewish Messiah, and the Church was the true people of God. Although Christ's death on the Cross had fulfilled the Law, Paul saw that Christ's followers were the "true Jews" or "the Israel of God" (Gal. 6:16). Paul himself was "circumcised the eighth day, of the stock of Israel, of the tribe of Benjamin, an Hebrew of the Hebrews; as touching the law, a Pharisee" (Philip. 3:5). No one had better Jewish credentials.

2. A Christian minister, 23

23 Are they ministers of Christ? (I speak as a fool) I am more; in labours more abundant, in stripes above measure, in prisons more frequent, in deaths oft.

On the other hand, in a day when Christianity was only emerging from its Jewish roots, some of Paul's enemies were bold enough to boast that they were "better" Christians than Paul. Some Judaizing teachers even went about baptizing people—but insisted that their converts follow Moses' Law.

Continuing to speak ironically, or "as a fool," Paul could also boast that he could prove by his suffering that he was a minister of Christ. He had the "work background," the stripes (or whip-marks), the nights in jail, and the death-threats—from both Jews and pagans, to prove his identity as a Christian minister.

C. Victories out of loss, 24-30

1. Persecutions, 24-25a

24 Of the Jews five times received I forty stripes save one.

25 Thrice was I beaten with rods,

The "five times" Paul was lashed by Jewish authorities are not further named or dated. Convicted prisoners were given only 39 lashes because of an interesting limitation in Deut. 25:2-3, where the text seems to go out of its way to say the convicted person may be given 40 stripes "and not exceed: lest . . . thy brother should seem vile unto thee"—which seems to be an attempt to allow the convict to retain some dignity. Paul distinguishes this from the three times he

was beaten with rods, which was a Roman way of beating.

2. Natural disasters, 25b-27

25b once was I stoned, thrice I suffered shipwreck, a night and a day I have been in the deep;

26 In journeyings often, in perils of waters, in perils of robbers, in perils by mine own countrymen, in perils by the heathen, in perils in the city, in perils in the wilderness, in perils in the sea, in perils among false brethren;

27 In weariness and painfulness, in watchings often, in hunger and thirst, in fastings often, in cold and nakedness.

Both "journeys" and "perils of waters" come to mind in connection with Paul's capture and "free ride to Rome" for trial, as recorded in Acts 27, when the story of his "journeyings" becomes a fascinating adventure story. Natural dangers are intermingled with attacks from Paul's enemies in a list designed to challenge all comers to see if any of the false apostles who are opposing Paul are willing to put their record of suffering for the cause up against his own. The proof of Paul's authentic apostleship was written on a scarred body and a severely tested but triumphant spirit.

3. The care of the churches, 28-30

28 Beside those things that are without, that which cometh upon me daily, the care of all the churches.

29 Who is weak, and I am not weak? who is offended, and I burn not?

30 If I must needs glory, I will glory of the things which concern mine infirmities.

Paul's suffering in behalf of the infant churches among whom he worked is less measurable but no less real. As "the apostle to the Gentiles," and driven by a desire to preach where no one else had gone before, he had voluntarily taken on the weaknesses and offenses borne by the new churches he established. Little wonder that he feels protective of them, longs to see them remain faithful, and to resist the impostors whose motives were sometimes material, being paid for their preaching while Paul was making tents.

II. The Christian Paradox—12:9-10

12:9 And he said unto me, My grace is sufficient for thee: for my strength is made perfect in weakness. Most gladly therefore will I rather glory in my infirmities, that the power of Christ may rest upon me.

10 Therefore I take pleasure in infirmities, in reproaches, in necessities, in persecutions, in distresses for Christ's sake: for when I am weak, then am I strong.

In addition to all these trials, God had visited His servant Paul with some bodily handicap or "thorn in the flesh" (vs. 7), apparently as yet another test. Paul had asked the Lord three times to remove it (vs. 8), but received the classic answer of "sufficient grace." Paul's response is heroic: he will gladly accept whatever life has for him if it means a greater measure of Christ's power in the Christian paradox: "for when I am weak, then am I strong."

సారు

Evangelistic Emphasis

What price will a person pay to take the gospel to the lost?

I know a Christian couple who repeatedly have spent thousands of dollars of their own money, spent weeks of their own precious time, and risked diseases and dangers of many kinds to visit distant lands in hopes of sharing Jesus with a handful of hungry souls who otherwise would never hear of Him.

I know a retired man who leaves his comfortable home, flies miles away from his doctor, and endures the aggravations of cantankerous local craftsmen to help mission stations build new facilities—without receiving one penny of pay.

Dozens of high school and college students I know give up their holidays to go sleep on dirt floors, to live without plumbing, to survive without computers or television in order to build modest houses for people who otherwise would live in flimsy, drafty huts. In the name of Jesus these kids brave insects, endure heat and cold, work from dawn to dark, and return home pumped by the whole experience.

Paul's example of facing dangers and difficulties to expand the Kingdom is being imitated today by thousands of dedicated people. In a generation addicted to luxury and comfort, these stalwart souls willingly renounce both in order to share Jesus' love.

ᔥᔦ

Memory Selection

He said unto me, My grace is sufficient for thee: for my strength is made perfect in weakness. Most gladly therefore will I rather glory in my infirmities, that the power of Christ may rest upon me. —*2 Corinthians 12:9*

My friend David was a strong, athletic fellow until he dived into the swimming hole, butted a rock, and broke his neck. He has not walked since. After years of intense therapy David remains quadriplegic, with barely enough arm and hand control to guide his motorized wheelchair.

How many times do you think David has pled with God to let him walk again?

I had another buddy named David, who was a highly trained medical doctor. He was about to complete his residency as an Air Force physician when a life-threatening drug reaction revealed that he suffered an acute form of lupus. Eventually this dreadful disease left my Christian friend blind and unable to practice medicine.

How often do you think my doctor friend begged God to remove his affliction or to slow its assault on his body?

No doubt you know several friends just like these two Davids—people who have prayed for God to heal them from some painful or disabling ailment. And so far, God has said No. That's exactly what God said to Paul, too. Could it be that His message to our suffering friends is also the same: "My grace is sufficient for you. Instead of healing, let me give you the power of Christ"?

Weekday Problems

An hour ago I stood in the room of an aging couple who now reside in the Alzheimer's unit of a local care facility. They are dear, sweet people who for years were active members—the kind of folks who are always there and can always be counted on.

He no longer knows where he is or who he is. It's sad. Her mind is much clearer, but she chooses to be in the locked-down unit with him. After 65-plus years of living side by side, she can't imagine being elsewhere.

In response to my questions about how she has been feeling lately, she replied, "I'm O.K., but it's frustrating to be 92 and not able to walk." I don't think she remembers her last small strokes, or the big one that took away her mobility. She just knows she's stuck all day long every day in her chair.

Instead of praying for this dear lady to walk again, I left their room asking in my heart that God would give her grace to make the most of what at best is a minimal situation. All of her days she has trusted in the Lord to get her through life's tough times. Now that trust is being challenged, perhaps as never before.

Even a great man like Paul must have wondered sometimes why he was going through some of his trials and whether he had what it took to get through those hard days. Hardest of all must have been the times when his own converts turned on him and trashed him. The Lord taught Paul to expect special grace when he was suffering the most. I hope my friend in the Alzheimer's unit can feel that grace.

Speaking of Sacrifice

I never made a sacrifice. We ought not to talk of "sacrifice" when we remember the great sacrifice which He made who left His Father's throne on high to give Himself for us.—David Livingstone

* * *

The altar of sacrifice is the touchstone of character.—O. P. Clifford

* * *

In this world it is . . . what we give up that makes us rich.—Henry Ward Beecher.

* * *

Self-preservation is the first law of nature; self-sacrifice the highest rule of grace.—Anonymous

* * *

Our virtues are dearer to us the more we have had to suffer for them. It is the same with our children. All profound affection admits a sacrifice.—Goethe

This Lesson in Your Life

My friend and his wife got home a couple of weeks ago from a self-financed mission trip to China. Proselyting is a serious violation of China's laws, so they knew they could not preach on street corners or assemble with underground churches. They would have to use great care in whom they talked to and how they went about it.

Along with a dozen other Christians, my friends signed on to teach English for one week each in two schools. Chinese students are required to study English from the third to the twelfth grades, but in these schools many miles from Beijing the students had never met a native English speaker. The Americans were welcomed warmly.

Their hope, of course, was to develop friendships that might eventually lead, perhaps in later visits, to conversations about Jesus. They knew, though, that anyone who dared to show even cursory interest in Jesus might pay an enormous price.

On a Sunday in Beijing my friend and his group attended worship in the registered (government permitted) Protestant church. He said about 2,500 worshipers showed up for that service, and four more services would be held that day. Any Chinese citizen attending worship there had to have the word "Christian" on their passport. Communist party officials were always there, checking to be sure nobody fudged on this.

Those who opt to be known as Christians in that officially atheist nation know they are opting for a life of hardship and poverty. They will be denied work. Cut off from good wages, they will be unable to afford decent housing or adequate food. Their kids will be ineligible for the best schools. Their neighbors will discount them as victims of some sort of weird insanity.

Still, knowing the price they will pay, between 10,000 and 12,000 people show up every Sunday at the registered Protestant church. As I heard my friend describing this, I found myself wondering how many of us would show up at church next Sunday if coming there would cost us our house, our food, our job, our wages, our children's future, and our neighbors' respect.

Besides the registered church—tightly controlled by Chinese authorities—underground Christian groups attract literally millions of believers. All of those disciples risk severe penalties if the party decides to make their group an example.

To run such risks and pay such a price, our Chinese brothers and sisters in Christ have to be really serious about their faith. Persecution and suffering like theirs and like Paul's will expose fake piety. As the apostle Peter says, it will refine our faith like gold in the fire. Only the genuine will last.

GETTING THE FACTS STRAIGHT

1. When Paul speaks of himself as a fool and says he is uttering foolish words, can we tell when he is serious and when he's speaking ironically?

Sometimes it's hard to know when the apostle shifts from irony and back again, but he does identify several sections in 2 Corinthians when he is using the exaggerations or sarcasm.

2. What were Paul's critics boasting about? Was he able to equal and surpass their claims?

Paul's detractors evidently were boasting of their ministries, but his list of dangers suffered and deeds done for Christ surely silenced their bragging.

3. How many times had Paul been flogged, shipwrecked, or imprisoned?

Paul tells us here that he has been flogged a total of eight times, shipwrecked three times, and put in jail multiple times.

4. What sort of dangers had he faced?

Note all the "perils" he lists in 11:26—everything from floods to false brethren.

5. Can we locate in the Book of Acts some of the times and places where Paul suffered the abuses he listed here?

Each of Paul's journeys, from the first one in Acts 13 to his shipwreck story in Acts 27, contain examples of what he lists here in his letter.

6. From what city did Paul escape in a basket let down through a window in the city wall?

Damascus. Right after his conversion to Christ.

7. Is the man who saw the vision Paul described actually Paul himself?

Probably.

8. What did he see in this vision?

Paul says he went to "the third heaven" and saw paradise—things no man can tell.

9. According to Paul, why did God give him the "thorn in the flesh"?

Whatever the physical ailment, Paul says the Lord sent it to keep him from getting too proud of his extraordinary visions.

10. When Paul prayed repeatedly for this "thorn" to be removed, what was God's answer?

God did not remove the physical problem. Instead He told Paul, "My grace is sufficient for thee."

Uplift

In these verses of 2 Corinthians and in the chapters before and after them, the irony in Paul's words cuts deep. Most of the time the apostle Paul writes in a loving, moderate, persuasive tone, so the uncharacteristic bitterness in this book lets us know how fiercely his enemies have assailed him. In his sarcasm we sense his disappointment and his pain.

Words that bite like these may distance us from a writer at first, but hearing how much Paul hurts prepares us to hear how much God's grace meant to him in this terribly difficult time in his ministry.

The famous devotional writer Henri Nouwen wrote a classic book that he called *The Wounded Healer*. In it he presents simply but eloquently the truth that we are truly able to help someone going through the fires of suffering only when we have been through the same fires ourselves.

I have seen this demonstrated many times. All of us in our congregation rush to encourage and pray for one of our group who faces heart surgery, but the best comfort and most meaningful advice come from one who has come through that same surgery himself.

When one of our people faces cataract surgery, I notice that they invariably seek the advice and reassurance of someone who has recently gone through it. By some sort of sixth sense we discern that a person who has suffered a wound like ours will be our best helper and healer.

Could this be why the Holy Spirit saw fit to preserve Paul's acid words about those who were trying to destroy him and discredit his ministry?

Perhaps the Spirit knew that we also would encounter stressful times of opposition in our service to the Lord.

Perhaps the Spirit knew that we would need the example of another faithful servant of Christ being harassed and hounded by wrong-spirited opponents.

Perhaps He knew that seeing Paul persevere—seeing him rely on God's grace when the going got so tough—would give us the encouragement we need to stand strong when it would be tempting just to give up and walk away.

Lesson 1

Mary's Commitment

Luke 1:26-33, 46-55

Unit I. Commitment to the Messiah

And in the sixth month the angel Gabriel was sent from God unto a city of Galilee, named Nazareth,

27 To a virgin espoused to a man whose name was Joseph, of the house of David; and the virgin's name was Mary.

28 And the angel came in unto her, and said, Hail, thou that art highly favoured, the Lord is with thee: blessed art thou among women.

29 And when she saw him, she was troubled at his saying, and cast in her mind what manner of salutation this should be.

30 And the angel said unto her, Fear not, Mary: for thou hast found favour with God.

31 And, behold, thou shalt conceive in thy womb, and bring forth a son, and shalt call his name JESUS.

32 He shall be great, and shall be called the Son of the Highest: and the Lord God shall give unto him the throne of his father David:

33 And he shall reign over the house of Jacob for ever; and of his kingdom there shall be no end.

46 And Mary said, My soul doth magnify the Lord,

47 And my spirit hath rejoiced in God my Saviour.

48 For he hath regarded the low estate of his handmaiden: for, behold, from henceforth all generations shall call me blessed.

49 For he that is mighty hath done to me great things; and holy is his name.

50 And his mercy is on them that fear him from generation to generation.

51 He hath shewed strength with his arm; he hath scattered the proud in the imagination of their hearts.

52 He hath put down the mighty from their seats, and exalted them of low degree.

53 He hath filled the hungry with good things; and the rich he hath sent empty away.

54 He hath holpen his servant Israel, in remembrance of his mercy;

55 As he spake to our fathers, to Abraham, and to his seed for ever.

Memory Selection
Luke 1:46-47

Background Scripture
Luke 1:26-38, 46-55

Devotional Reading
1 Sam. 2:1-1

FOCUS

As the church calendar moves once again toward the celebration of the birth of our Lord, this lesson prepares us by celebrating the commitment of Mary, the young woman in Israel whom God had selected to become the mother of the Christ-child, Jesus.

Think of how Mary, pregnant but unwed, could have given in to questions or to despair. What would Joseph, her betrothed, think of her? The classic question "What will the neighbors say?" becomes as intense as only a small village can make it. Instead of allowing herself to be overwhelmed by such questions, she sings "The Magnificat," the timeless words of which can help dispel any time of darkness by their example of praise to God, commitment to Him, and their spirit of submission to His will.

℘℘

For a Lively Start

If someone in your group is from a "high church" tradition, or can find a musical version of "The Magnificat," perhaps they could introduce this lesson by teaching the class to sing the passage, which consists of Luke 1:46-55. This text has been set to music more than any other piece of Scripture. It is said that nearly 1,000 different musical versions of Mary's song have been published by a single music publisher.

Alternately, the leader can lead the group in a responsive reading, consisting of alternating verses of Mary's song; or following the example of countless ancient churches, simply lead group members in reciting together the words of Luke 1:46-55.

Teaching Outline	Daily Bible Readings	
I. Visit from an Angel—1:26-33	Mon.	Prayer of Hannah *1 Sam. 2:1-10*
A. The Annunciation, 26-29	Tue.	Gabriel's Announcement *Luke 1:26-33*
B. 'Fear not . . . for favor,' 30-33	Wed.	Mary's 'Let It Be!' *Luke 1:34-38*
II. Mary's Song of Praise—46-55		
A. For remembering the humble, 46-48	Thu.	Simeon and Mary *Luke 2:25-35*
B. For being a mighty God, 49-53	Fri.	Do What He Tells You! *John 2:1-11*
C. For remembering the Covenant, 54-55	Sat.	Praying with the Disciples *Acts 1:6-14*
	Sun.	Praise for God's Mercy *Luke 1:46-55*

Verse by Verse

I. Visit from an Angel—1:26-28
A. The Annunciation, 26-29

26 And in the sixth month the angel Gabriel was sent from God unto a city of Galilee, named Nazareth,

27 To a virgin espoused to a man whose name was Joseph, of the house of David; and the virgin's name was Mary.

28 And the angel came in unto her, and said, Hail, thou that art highly favoured, the Lord is with thee: blessed art thou among women.

29 And when she saw him, she was troubled at his saying, and cast in her mind what manner of salutation this should be.

"In the sixth month" refers to the sixth month of the pregnancy of Elisabeth, Mary's older cousin, who has just had her own "annunciation" (Lesson 2). Two unexpected pregnancies in a Jewish culture where having babies—especially baby boys—it all makes quite a Christmas present!

The whole season of births is carefully timed. Social unrest in the ancient world at this time was causing many to look for the Messiah to bring relief. The "pax Romana," or Roman peace, is a phrase coined to describe the way Rome had pacified much of the known world, producing a degree of social and political peace beyond what had been the case.

Roman roads spanned much of the area, and Roman troops restrained robbers who had preyed on travelers. Greek had been established as a universal language, enabling travelers to spread the news of such events as the birth that was about to occur in a manger in the village of Bethlehem. It was, as the apostle Paul would call it, "the fullness of time" (Gal. 4:4)—just the right time for Gabriel to appear.

The angel's assertion that Mary would bear a child even though she is a virgin is sometimes dismissed as a myth. There are a few similar stories of miraculously-born gods, but none are located in history like this story of Jesus' birth. Further, they resort to gods having intercourse with humans—a story that Jews especially would never have allowed or adopted as the story of the beginnings of their new-found faith.

The fact is that the virgin birth fits precisely into the story to show both that God loves His creation enough to send Himself as the Son into the womb of a peasant girl, and that He identifies with humans enough to place His blessing on the human process of birth, both elements combining to show that Jesus qualifies to be our Savior because He is divine, and our "elder Brother" in order to empathize with our all-too-human struggles.

Mary is understandably troubled (vs. 29) because she is not married. She cannot fathom anything like a "virgin birth." It was customary for Jewish girls of the time to become engaged at about age 13. Bride- and groom-to-be were bound to be faithful during a long engagement or betrothal; and Mary has no idea how what the angel says might come about. She could only trust God—which will become the new way to God: salvation by faith.

B. 'Fear not . . . for favor,' 30-33

30 And the angel said unto her, Fear not, Mary: for thou hast found favour with God.

31 And, behold, thou shalt conceive in thy womb, and bring forth a son, and shalt call his name JESUS.

32 He shall be great, and shall be called the Son of the Highest: and the Lord God shall give unto him the throne of his father David:

33 And he shall reign over the house of Jacob for ever; and of his kingdom there shall be no end.

Amazingly, the reason Mary is found to be pregnant is because she has found favor (grace) with God, not because she took the usual way of human procreation. We can scarcely imagine her wonder as the angel says that the infant will be named "Jesus," which she knows means "Savior."

Equally wondrous is the connection with David (vss. 32-33), although this connection would at least begin to tie into the stories of King David that Mary had heard since birth. God had promised that there would always be a king on David's throne (2 Sam. 7:12-13). No doubt Mary would have been even more amazed if she had understood that this Davidic heir would reign over a worldwide spiritual Kingdom of which "the house of David" was only a symbolic name.

II. Mary's Song of Praise—46-55
A. For remembering the humble, 46-48

46 And Mary said, My soul doth magnify the Lord,

47 And my spirit hath rejoiced in God my Saviour.

48 For he hath regarded the low estate of his handmaiden: for, behold, from henceforth all generations shall call me blessed.

The Latin translation of verse 46 gives this immortal passage the title "The Magnificat." The full phrase is *Magnificat anima mea Dominum,* "My soul magnifies the Lord." This line, and several of the thoughts that follow, echo the song of Hannah as she also praised God for her own son Samuel (1 Sam. 1:1-10). As in the case of Jesus, who often quoted the Old Testament and applied it to crucial situations, Mary must have been thoroughly exposed to such texts through synagogue readings, even though opportunities for a girl to attend school were limited.

Mary's reference to her "low estate" shows that she shares Elisabeth's humility. Yet, by now, she has reflected on her lot enough to realize that future generations will remember that she was chosen for the awesome ministry of being the mother of Jesus, the Messiah.

B. For being a mighty God, 49-53

49 For he that is mighty hath done to me great things; and holy is his name.

50 And his mercy is on them that fear him from generation to generation.

51 He hath shewed strength with his arm; he hath scattered the proud in the imagination of their hearts.

52 He hath put down the mighty from their seats, and exalted them of low degree.

53 He hath filled the hungry with good things; and the rich he hath sent empty away.

Mary's song now contrasts her "low estate" with the magnificence of the mighty God who has done so great a thing as to enable a virgin, and a mere girl at that, to become pregnant by the Holy Spirit. (The word "mighty" is from a root that gives us the expression "mega"—Mary sings of a "mega-God"!)

In her outburst of pure praise, Mary sings in successive verses of God's holiness, mercy, and strength. Perhaps the reference to His holiness arises in defense of His choosing an unwed woman to bear a child. His mercy is seen in sending His Son into the world to bless all who will respond to Him in faith.

In verse 51, the strength or might of God's "arm" (a common way of refer-ring to God's doing great deeds) would have been high in Mary's consciousness because of the miracle of the virginal conception. This verse introduces a kind of "revolutionary" tone to Mary's song, praising God for opposing the world's power structures by choosing the humble to discount their arrogance. Certainly there is no better example of this than God's plan to allow the Son whom kings will ridicule to turn the tables on them by rising from the dead and being crowned king of kings, above them all.

C. For remembering the Covenant, 54-55

54 He hath holpen his servant Israel, in remembrance of his mercy;

55 As he spake to our fathers, to Abraham, and to his seed for ever.

In the final theme of Mary's magnificent hymn of praise, she emphasizes how God's promise that the Messiah will be born is in fulfillment of the Covenant with Abraham. For her to sing that God has "helped" (KJV "holpen") His servant Israel is to recall again the "servant" passages of Isaiah 40–55. Mary is awed to be the vessel for the fulfillment of God's promise to send His Servant to deliver His people.

Verse 55 again refers to Abraham as the original patriarch to receive the Covenant. This patriarch's "seed" or family will now not only consist of the children of Israel, but will include all those who will become a part of spiritual Israel and figurative children of Abraham by following His descendant Jesus, the Messiah (see Rom. 9:6; Gal. 6:16).

The chosen "seed" has taken root, and will now multiply!

Evangelistic Emphasis

I have watched with interest as a large old congregation with a proud history has tried to reinvent their identity and basic mission. For years they were an upper-middle class congregation, a comfortable place for doctors, lawyers, bankers, and yuppies. They were serious about spreading the gospel. Their members provided much-needed community leadership.

Then a generation with a new vision took the reins of this fine church. They were near the deteriorating center of the city. Many of their neighbors were destitute or homeless. So the church's new staff decided in to make social services for the poor their primary ministry.

It was a bold move that soon cost that church half its membership. Some of their people were excited about the new direction, but several hundred members decided one by one that they felt no calling to create a surrogate Salvation Army half a dozen blocks from the one that was already doing a fine job.

These have been hard years for this shrinking congregation, but the faithful remnant have been tenacious and courageous in their passion to reach the poor and downtrodden for Jesus.

As these good people re-tool and learn to preach the gospel to the neediest people in our community, they may want to emphasize the side of God that so impressed a peasant maid like Mary.

In her famous Magnificat (Luke 1:46-55), Mary praised God because He "scattered the proud" and "put down the mighty." She liked the fact that in her case God had "filled the hungry." A God like this has something to offer the poor.

Memory Selection

Mary said, My soul doth magnify the Lord, And my spirit hath rejoiced in God my Saviour.— *Luke 1:46-47*

During the Dark Ages, the Holy Scriptures were preserved for God's people primarily in the Latin translation known as the Vulgate. Taken from the same Latin root that gives us our English word *vulgar*, Vulgate means "of the people." It was a Bible for ordinary people.

Although the Church treasured rare copies of the Scriptures in Hebrew and Greek, the Latin Bible gave the holy text to common folks in a universal language. For many hundreds of years, it was the main Bible used by Christians worldwide.

Our English texts that tell us Mary "magnified" the Lord are not far removed from the Latin wording in the Vulgate. In the Latin text, Mary's outburst of praise to the Lord begins with the verb from which we draw her song's historic title, "The Magnificat." How do you and I respond when God comes up with a "common" or lowly assignment for us? Mary magnified the Lord. Some of us may be more likely to moan and postpone, hoping God will chose somebody else. Our response sometimes is more like Jonah's than like Mary's.

Weekday Problems

God's ancient rules against unmarried Israelite women hav-ing babies were shockingly harsh. The Torah mandates, "One of illegitimate birth shall not enter the assembly of the Lord; even to the tenth generation none of his descendants shall enter the assembly of the Lord" (Deut. 23:2, NKJV). Could it be that God made the penalty so severe because He knew how much havoc unwed parenting introduces to any culture?

Have you seen recent federal reports of the percentage of tax dollars required to house, doctor, and feed unmarried mothers and their progeny? The financial burden on our society is immense, and that is just dollars. The amount of human suffering involved is incalculable.

Even in an age when we try to be compassionate to the illegitimate, such people seem to live under what appears to be an inescapable curse of poverty and depri-vation. God loves His people too much to want more generations to live like that.

Almost all church people today do everything they can to make life better for unwed mothers and their offspring. All of us want to bless these sufferers instead of cursing or punishing them.

Our Lord Jesus, however, was born in a time when the stigma of illegitimacy was still quite cruel. When God decided to become one of us, He voluntarily suffered all the heartache and mistreatment life dishes out to babies born to single mothers.

Remember the Good Ol' Days . . .

1. When people were smarter than machines.

2. When you could buy steak for a dime a pound (but we forget we had to work an hour for the dime).

3. When a dish-washing machine had to be married, not bought.

4. When you put food in cans, instead of taking it out.

5. That when folks sat down for dinner they counted their blessings instead of their calories.

6. When a man's wife, not the government, was the one who withheld money from his paycheck.

7. When a bureau was a piece of furniture.

8. When rockets were just part of a fireworks celebration.

9. When there really were "bad" report cards.

10. When I could remember when . . . Oh, I forget.

This Lesson in Your Life

A buddy and I visited while we were sitting in a hospital waiting room during heart surgery for a mutual friend. I've known this guy since early high school days, but on this day he told me a personal story he had never shared with me before.

"We had just moved to town," he began. That would have been about 1955, right after his coach/teacher father died young. I knew they had lived at first with the family of his mother's twin sister—a family that included his cousin Jimmy. "Just before we moved to town," my friend continued, "Uncle Milton bought Jimmy a fancy bicycle—a Schwinn with white sidewall tires and all the bells and whistles. It was the first bike I'd seen that had its own built-in lock. Jimmy always locked it when he parked it, and he hid the key. I was strictly forbidden to touch that bike.

"But one day when Mom and Aunt Totsy and the whole family was gone somewhere," my buddy confessed, "I slipped that key out of the hiding place I had discovered, and I rode that swanky bicycle up the highway into downtown.

"I rolled past all the stores," he recalled, listing one by one the historic retail businesses that had once lined the main streets in our bustling center city. He stumbled on a few names, or due to lapsed memory transplanted one or two on the wrong block. We had fun recreating in our minds the familiar haunts of our youth, remembering banks and movie theaters and drugstores and five-and-dimes that long since have surrendered to the bulldozer.

"I was sailing down the middle of the sidewalk between Taylor and Polk Streets," my chum now got to the crux of his tale, "oblivious to anything but the thrill of coasting on that marvelous forbidden machine. I approached the alley that crossed the sidewalk in the middle of that block when, as if out of nowhere, the largest black man I ever saw stepped out and caught me. He just engulfed me in his arms, bicycle and body and all.

"Before I had time to wonder what was happening to me," my friend recounted with a resurrected look of relief on his face, "a huge delivery truck came roaring out of that alley, flying across the sidewalk where I would have been without the aid of my new friend."

My buddy sat there, quiet for a moment, before he reflected in a grateful voice, "That was my angel. At that hard time in my life, with Dad just dead and Mom and I living with kinfolks, I felt God's hand in my life. From that moment I told myself that God must have kept me around for a reason. He must have something for me to do."

Mary's angel was named Gabriel. I don't think my buddy ever knew the name of his. Have you met your angel?

1. Who brought God's message to Mary in Nazareth?
The angel Gabriel.

2. How does Luke describe Mary and her situation before she received that incredible message?
Mary lived in the town of Nazareth in Galilee. She was a virgin engaged to a man named Joseph, who belonged to the tribe of David, which was Judah.

3. If an angel had told you what this one told Mary, would you have interpreted it as an expression of God's favor?
It is hard to imagine an unmarried girl thinking that learning that she was pregnant was "good news."

4. What was Mary's first reaction to the news that she would have a baby?
She was troubled and she wondered what in the world the angel was trying to tell her.

5. How did the angel describe this baby and His future?
The baby would be great, the angel said. He would be called the Son of the Highest, and he would reign on David's throne forever.

6. Actually, the angel told of two miracles instead of one. What miracle was God working right then in the life of Mary's cousin, Elizabeth?
Elizabeth, a woman past menopause, was at that moment pregnant with John the Baptist.

7. In verse 37, how did the angel explain miracles such as a baby born to an old lady past menopause and another born to a virgin?
The angel told Mary, "With God nothing shall be impossible."

8. What was Mary's reply to the angel's instructions?
She said, "I belong to God. Let it happen to me as you have said."

9. When Mary "magnifies" the Lord, can we tell from her words if she belongs to a rich or powerful family?
Her family must have been poor and not influential.

10. Was Mary rejoicing that God had done embarrassing things to wealthy and influential people?
No. She was simply thanking God for choosing to send His Son through a lowly, poor person instead of a rich and noble one.

Uplift

Some of my dear Catholic friends address Mary with honor and reverence that seem to go beyond anything the New Testament commands or depicts in the practice of the first-century Christians.

On the other hand, some of my Protestant friends seem to go out of their way to ignore the Scriptures' clear picture of Mary's faith and courage. As the word *Protest*ant implies, they probably are extending the "protest" begun centuries ago by their anti-Catholic ancestors.

Actually, we likely do well to steer the middle course between excessive honor and no honor for the mother of our Lord.

Mary models for us the kind of faith it takes to be a follower of her son. She did not flinch or waver at Gabriel's promise that she, a maiden who had never had sex with any man, would bear a child. She knew this was biologically impossible, but she accepted Gabriel's assurance that "with God nothing shall be impossible" (Luke 1:37).

Years later, in Romans 4, Paul identifies this same kind of faith in Abraham. The aging patriarch believed God's promise that a promised child would come from his wife's dead womb. Paul tells us that God was so impressed with Abraham's faith that He counted it as righteousness.

Then, at the end of that great chapter in Romans, Paul makes his point that all of us who come to God through Christ are expected to have that kind of faith. God want us also to believe that He is a God who does impossible things. Abraham believed God could bring life out of a dead womb. We Christians are asked to believe that He brought life out of a tomb. Paul assures us that God will "credit righteousness" to us also if we "believe in him who raised Jesus our Lord from the dead" (Rom. 4:25, NIV).

The God we serve is not a hunk of stone or a fancy wood carving—a mindless, unconscious, powerless god.

Our God is not an absentee deity, lounging somewhere on a heavenly cloud, oblivious to the needs of His creatures.

The cherished Christmas story of our Savior's birth introduces God to us as a God who does the impossible.

What can He not do for you and me?

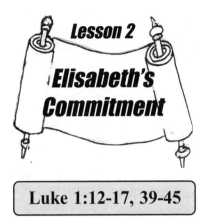

Lesson 2

Elisabeth's Commitment

Luke 1:12-17, 39-45

And when Zacharias saw him, he was troubled, and fear fell upon him.

13 But the angel said unto him, Fear not, Zacharias: for thy prayer is heard; and thy wife Elisabeth shall bear thee a son, and thou shalt call his name John.

14 And thou shalt have joy and gladness; and many shall rejoice at his birth.

15 For he shall be great in the sight of the Lord, and shall drink neither wine nor strong drink; and he shall be filled with the Holy Ghost, even from his mother's womb.

16 And many of the children of Israel shall he turn to the Lord their God.

17 And he shall go before him in the spirit and power of Elias, to turn the hearts of the fathers to the children, and the disobedient to the wisdom of the just; to make ready a people prepared for the Lord.

39 And Mary arose in those days, and went into the hill country with haste, into a city of Juda;

40 And entered into the house of Zacharias, and saluted Elisabeth.

41 And it came to pass, that, when Elisabeth heard the salutation of Mary, the babe leaped in her womb; and Elisabeth was filled with the Holy Ghost:

42 And she spake out with a loud voice, and said, Blessed art thou among women, and blessed is the fruit of thy womb.

43 And whence is this to me, that the mother of my Lord should come to me?

44 For, lo, as soon as the voice of thy salutation sounded in mine ears, the babe leaped in my womb for joy.

45 And blessed is she that believed: for there shall be a performance of those things which were told her from the Lord.

Memory Selection
Luke 1:41b-42

Background Scripture
Luke 1:5-24, 39-45

Devotional Reading
Isa. 7:10-14

There are so many similarities between the focus of this lesson and Lesson 1 that it would be a good idea to review last week's lesson to compare and contrast the spirit of commitment shared by the cousins Mary and Elisabeth. Elisabeth was much older, creating several similarities also with

the story of Hannah in 1 Samuel 1 and 2; so include that account in your preparation also.

All these lessons show the great contributions women of faith made to God's plan to bring the Messiah into the world and, in Elisabeth's case, to bring John the Baptist as well. They are testimony to God's power to overcome issues of gender, age, and other obstacles that may at first seem to tell us that we can't do what God calls us to do.

ॐ

For a Lively Start

You can introduce this lesson by leading a discussion on the kinds of difficulties and obstacles Satan sometimes places in our path in an attempt to foil our accomplishment of God's will.

What challenges have group members experienced in their own lives? Advanced age, as in the case of

Elisabeth? Or, as with Mary, the opposite issue of youth? Has anyone been called to overcome poor health or other physical handicaps in order to do God's will? Or can anyone report having overcome the kind of fear that affected old Zacharias in this story?

Alternately, tell the story of Helen Keller or some such inspiring historical figure who, with God's help, overcame unusual challenges to make their commitment to God firm, sure, and certain.

Teaching Outline	Daily Bible Readings

I. Zacharias' Fearful Encounter—1:12-17
 	
  A. Choosing Fear or Joy, 12-14
 	
  B. Prediction about John, 15-17
 	
II. Mary's Visit to Elisabeth—39-45
 	
  A. Spirit-filled response, 39-41
 	
  B. Elisabeth blesses Mary, 42-45
	Mon. Appearance to Abraham
	      Gen. 18:1-8
	Tue. Hope for the Barren
	      Gen. 18:9-14
	Wed. Righteous and Blameless
	      Luke 1:5-11
	Thu. Promise of a Son
	      Luke 1:12-20
	Fri. The Lord's Favor
	      Luke 1:21-25
	Sat. Faith in God's Promises
	      Luke 1:39-45
	Sun. 'Call Him John'
	      Luke 1:57-63

Verse by Verse

I. Zacharias' Fearful Encounter— 1:12-17

A. Choosing Fear or Joy, 12-14

12 And when Zacharias saw him, he was troubled, and fear fell upon him.

13 But the angel said unto him, Fear not, Zacharias: for thy prayer is heard; and thy wife Elisabeth shall bear thee a son, and thou shalt call his name John.

14 And thou shalt have joy and gladness; and many shall rejoice at his birth.

As mentioned earlier, the similarities between this account and other miraculous works of God are remarkable. In the story of the angel delivering the good news about Elisabeth and Zacharias having a child, the issue of age is parallel with the event, some 1,800 years earlier, when God promised a child also to Abraham and Sarah in their old age.

In that account, it is the woman, Sarah who finds it impossible to believe that she could have a child in her old age (90; Gen. 17:17; 18:12). In today's lesson, it is the man, Zacharias

the priest, who doubts (see Luke 1:18-22). The particulars of age and gender are not the main point, however. Each story is included to teach that "No!" is the correct answer to the question, "Is anything too hard for the Lord?" (Gen. 18:14; Luke 1:37).

As is often the case when God wants to bless us, we can choose joy by accepting God's promise, or self-pity and the spirit of failure by continuing to doubt. The angel encourages Zacharias not to accept the limitations of old age. Saying Yes instead of No to God will mean that the old priest will be able to be an instrument in blessing thousands through their son, who will become John the Baptist.

B. Prediction about John, 15-17

15 For he shall be great in the sight of the Lord, and shall drink neither wine nor strong drink; and he shall be filled with the Holy Ghost, even from his mother's womb.

16 And many of the children of Israel shall he turn to the Lord their God.

17 And he shall go before him in

the spirit and power of Elias, to turn the hearts of the fathers to the children, and the disobedient to the wisdom of the just; to make ready a people prepared for the Lord.

If the angel is able to predict that this older couple will have a child, we should not be surprised that he can also provide these details about his life and work. The fact that he will be great in God's sight is probably included to offset the tendency of some, after John takes up his ministry, to resent the fact that Jesus, in His Messiahship, can be considered greater than John. John himself showed no indication of jealousy (see Luke 3:16); but some of his followers appear to have become "John-ites" and to have formed a group following him even after his death.

The fact that John avoided strong drink may indicate that he took a Nazirite vow. Coming "in the spirit and power of Elias" is in direct fulfillment of the prophecy in Malachi 4:5. Jesus Himself endorsed the fact that John was symbolically "Elijah reincarnated" (Matt. 11:10-14). The angel's prediction that John would turn many in Israel to the Lord (vs. 16) is directly fulfilled in Luke 3:3—"repentance" literally means to turn, or to change one's mind.

All in all, the angel's testimony should have been enough to convince Zacharias that he is blessed beyond all other priests. His continued doubt, however, prompts the angel to pronounce a curse on him that strikes him dumb for a time (1:20), and when the time has come to name the infant, Zacharias has to write the child's name on a tablet (vs. 63-64).

II. Mary's Visit to Elisabeth—1:39-45

A. Spirit-filled response, 39-41

39 And Mary arose in those days, and went into the hill country with haste, into a city of Juda;

40 And entered into the house of Zacharias, and saluted Elisabeth.

41 And it came to pass, that, when Elisabeth heard the salutation of Mary, the babe leaped in her womb; and Elisabeth was filled with the HolyGhost:

Many women can testify to the pleasure of talking about their pregnancy with other women who are also "expecting." They enjoy sharing the excitement of bearing new life, the anticipation of adding a new member of the family, the reaction of husbands and siblings-to-be. It can even help to have someone with whom to compare notes on the discomforts of pregnancy.

Perhaps with all this and more in mind, Mary leaves Nazareth, to the north near the Sea of Galilee, and journeys south to her cousin Elizabeth's home in Judea. Since Elisabeth's husband Zechariah was a priest, they must have lived near Jerusalem, perhaps even in Bethlehem, where Jesus was born. The angel Gabriel had told Mary that Elisabeth was also with child (vs. 36). Although this was not a virginal conception, we know that it approached the status of a miracle becaue of Zacharias' advanced age and Gabriel's statement that nothing is impossible for God (vs. 37).

Elisabeth was six months pregnant when Gabriel made his stunning announcement to Mary; and since it is normal for a woman to feel the fetus move as early as four months, there was nothing unusual, on the surface, about

John "leaping" in his mother's womb. What is unusual is to attribute this activity to a "fetal emotion" such as joy (vs. 45), although many pregnant women have reported movement in the womb at a loud noise or even music. In this case, we are in no doubt that something supernatural is occurring, in light of the reference to the Holy Spirit's indwelling Elisabeth and prompting her to give voice to the blessing to follow.

B. Elisabeth blesses Mary, 42-45

42 And she spake out with a loud voice, and said, Blessed art thou among women, and blessed is the fruit of thy womb.

43 And whence is this to me, that the mother of my Lord should come to me?

44 For, lo, as soon as the voice of thy salutation sounded in mine ears, the babe leaped in my womb for joy.

45 And blessed is she that believed; for there shall be a performance of those things which were told her from the Lord.

Elisabeth's greeting acknowledges Mary's blessedness in being chosen as the mother of the Messiah. As early as the fifth century, her first words had been transformed into a part of the Catholic "Hail Mary" (*Ave Maria*) prayer. Its earliest form consisted of a chain of scriptures relating to Mary and the birth of Jesus.

ಬಐಛ

Evangelistic Emphasis

One of the most delightful fellows in my congregation recently turned 88. Fred spent his "prime" years raising a family and building a successful business. I'm sure he believed in the Lord, but Fred was so busy with his various responsibilities that he hardly found time for church. He was not anti-church. It just was not an important part of his day-to-day life.

In the last decades of his life, after I buried his first and second wives and married him to a delightful third lady, Fred discovered how much the church could add to his life and how much he could contribute to the ministries of God's people.

Like so many retirees, Fred had time and talent and funds to enhance our church's mission. People in our little church welcomed him with open arms because of his cheerful spirit and his sharp mind. And Fred, a gregarious guy by nature, found in our church new friends who added unexpected life and light to his later days.

With so many of us in America living longer and staying active in our advanced years, Fred's story may well be the story of people all over the land. The church's richest mission field may be the senior citizen centers and similar hangouts for the gray-haired folks in our communities.

These people need Jesus and His Church, and the Church needs the resources and manpower they can offer.

ℰℚℜ

Memory Selection

Thou shalt have joy and gladness; and many shall rejoice at his birth. For he shall be great in the sight of the Lord, and shall drink neither wine nor strong drink; and he shall be filled with the Holy Ghost, even from his mother's womb.—*Luke 1:14-15*

Our 13th grandchild was born three days ago. Weeks before his birth, we knew he would be a boy (the fifth male child among seven children in his family). "We had lots of girl names picked out," our youngest son e-mailed us, "but we're out of boy names. What do you suggest?" Like old Zecharias, I was speechless. They wound up calling him David Patrick to honor some of the child's illustrious ancestors. That suited me just fine.

Being a bit long in the tooth, I still haven't got used to this new world where we know so much about a baby before he's hatched. I kind of enjoyed the suspense of wondering whether we'd have a linebacker or a ballerina. Way back in New Testament times, however, it seems apparent from the story of John's birth that the Lord knew far more about that baby than even the most modern parents know today. Even before John was conceived, the Lord told Zecharias many exciting details about who the baby would grow up to be and what he would do for Israel.

If we knew that sort of thing about our babies-to-be, do you suppose today's horrendous abortion rates would go down?

Weekday Problems

How many times do you suppose Zecharias had gone through the motions of offering incense to God in the Holy Place? I suspect that he could do it in his sleep, just like we sometimes do while singing and praying. How surprised do you think Zecharias was when he was jolted from his reverie by that heavenly visitor? I don't doubt that this holy man believed in the reality of God, but did he really expect a response from heaven to his acts of worship that day?

Do we? When we gather to praise our Creator, how many of us expect a response from heaven? If God did talk back to us, would we believe it any more than Zecharias seemed to? Maybe the Lord would have to silence our tongues too, so we would believe that He was really speaking to us.

Staying alert in worship is a universal problem. Even the giants in the field of devotional practice confess that they struggle to stay focused in prayer, and not to daydream during ritual or sermons. Many of them feel guilty about this, just as we do.

Zecharias found out that his distraction that day in the Temple was actually God's priority for him at that moment. Could the same thing be true for you and me when our minds drift during worship?

Daffynitions of Marriage

Wedding ring—The smallest hand cuff in the world.

Wedding—1. A ceremony where the bridegroom starts kissing the bride and all the other guys stop. 2. A funeral where you smell your own flowers. 3. The point at which a man stops toasting a woman and begins roasting her. 4. A ritual in which rings are put on the finger of the lady and through the nose of the man.

Marriage license—A certificate that gives a woman the legal right to drive a man.

Marriage—1. A mutual partnership where the man is the mute. 2. A process of finding out what sort of guy your wife would have preferred. 3. The first union to defy management. 4. The only life sentence that can be suspended by bad behavior. 5. The process of a woman turning a rake into a lawn mower.

Marriage proposal—A speech often made on the purr of the moment.

This Lesson in Your Life

My mother was 42, my brother was two years into college studies, I was a senior in high school, and our sister was only three years behind me when my parents announced to us that Mom was going to have a baby.

We knew nothing about Planned Parenthood back then. Obviously. I can assure you that at first our sedate, middle-aged parents were nothing short of shell-shocked by this development.

But my mom and dad were young compared to Zecharias and Elisabeth. My parents proved that they were still of child-bearing age. No miracles were necessary for our family to grow. Not then. Not two years later when they purposely conceived another child so the first one—the accident—would not grow up as virtually an only child.

Can you think of better proof than the John the Baptist tale that God has a sense of humor? Can't you hear Him chuckling as He watched the reaction of Elisabeth when Zecharias came home that day and told her that accidents or miracles still happen?

Fifty years later it seems obvious to my family that God had a hand in giving us two younger—very much younger—brothers. He has used them mightily in the work of His Kingdom.

Are we ready for God to work His wonders through us? Being a key part of His plans to bless our world is not always convenient. Temple rules required Zecharias to retire soon. I wonder what he and Elisabeth would have done in their golden years if that unplanned baby had not livened up their world. Do you suppose they lived long enough to see their miracle baby become a Jerusalem headliner? Were they still around when he began to announce the Messiah's imminent arrival and the city crowds flocked to the Jordan to be baptized by him?

The only concern my godly parents shared with us—our first family—was their fear that they might not live long enough or they might not be healthy enough to raise their late babies to maturity. Surely this same anxiety must have troubled John's aged parents, but the Bible tells us John's birth was a source of delight for them.

Something inside me winces when I hear prospective parents describing a new pregnancy as a disaster in their lives. God have mercy on any child who finds out that his parents did not want him.

John's parents probably seemed ancient to his youthful eyes, but he did know from the moment of his first breath that they welcomed him as a genuine blessing from God. The angel was right when he called his prediction of Elisabeth's untimely pregnancy "glad tidings" (1:19, KJV) or "good news" (NIV). Do our children know that's how we feel about them?

STRAIGHT

1. What kind of people were Zacharias and Elisabeth?
They were righteous people, careful to do everything God asked them to. They were elderly and childless.

2. What was her greatest cause of disappointment and embarrassment?
The fact that she had no child. In her culture, barrenness was seen as a curse.

3. What was Zacharias doing when the angel appeared to him?
Offering incense during the daily rituals in the Jewish Temple.

4. What did the angel predict?
That Elisabeth would get pregnant and have a boy, who should be named John.

5. According to the angel, the child born to the old priest and his wife would do what?
This boy would be filled with the Holy Spirit from the time of his birth. He would be great in God's eyes. He would live a life of self-denial, drinking no wine or liquor, and his message would call many of God's people back to Him.

6. What Old Testament prophet would their son be like?
Elijah.

7. What sign did the angel give to Zacharias to prove that his prediction would come true, against Zacharias' doubt?
The angel made the old priest unable to speak until John was named.

8. How long did Elisabeth stay out of the public eye because of her pregnancy?
She "hid herself" for five months.

9. Who came to visit Elisabeth in Judea while she was pregnant?
Mary, Elisabeth's cousin, who would become the mother of Jesus.

10. How did Elisabeth know the identity of her cousin's baby?
The baby in her womb leaped and the Spirit filled her.

I am writing these words during a week when I am preaching a revival in a small-town church in West Texas. Like most rural congregations, this one has a preponderance of folks with gray hair (or no hair). So I have been absolutely delighted to see things livened up this week by an unexpected swarm of cute, sharp, rambunctious kids.

Three of the local pastor's grandkids are visiting Grandma and PawPaw this week. To their delight, a local man on furlough from a Ukrainian mission is home with his Ukrainian wife and their four boys.

All week long my heart has been made glad by the antics of these youngsters, who are so obviously totally enjoying one another.

During our preaching services, these kids—none of them older than 9—have been exemplary. Their godly parents obviously know which buttons to push to teach a kid how to behave. Even the preschoolers in the batch are quiet and orderly during worship. No need for children's church when you have parents like these.

Outdoors where it's proper, though, these delightful children romp and play with an energy level and with an abandon that telegraph how wholesome and happy they are. Watching these kids rollick and cavort together this week has warmed the heart of this old man.Sunday afternoon when my week of preaching here is finished, I will drive east about four hours where I will see seven more kids—my own grandkids—who are equally impressive. Line them up on a church pew and from the time they are toddlers they are attentive and quiet. Turn them loose on a playground or a ballfield and they have a blast.

You probably won't believe that I'm not telling you this just to brag about my grandchildren (although they are exceptional, now that you mention it).

Seeing so many extraordinary children being raised so well by godly parents with a strong commitment to the Lord's Church has reassured me this week that the future of the Kingdom indeed is in good hands. I hope you are seeing similar signs in your corner of the world.

Lesson 3

Shepherds Glorify God

Luke 2:8-20

A nd there were in the same country shepherds abiding in the field, keeping watch over their flock by night.

9 And, lo, the angel of the Lord came upon them, and the glory of the Lord shone round about them: and they were sore afraid.

10 And the angel said unto them, Fear not: for, behold, I bring you good tidings of great joy, which shall be to all people.

11 For unto you is born this day in the city of David a Saviour, which is Christ the Lord.

12 And this shall be a sign unto you; Ye shall find the babe wrapped in swaddling clothes, lying in a manger.

13 And suddenly there was with the angel a multitude of the heavenly host praising God, and saying,

14 Glory to God in the highest, and on earth peace, good will toward men.

15 And it came to pass, as the angels were gone away from them into heaven, the shepherds said one to another, Let us now go even unto Bethlehem, and see this thing which is come to pass, which the Lord hath made known unto us.

16 And they came with haste, and found Mary, and Joseph, and the babe lying in a manger.

17 And when they had seen it, they made known abroad the saying which was told them concerning this child.

18 And all they that heard it wondered at those things which were told them by the shepherds.

19 But Mary kept all these things, and pondered them in her heart.

20 And the shepherds returned, glorifying and praising God for all the things that they had heard and seen, as it was told unto them

Memory Selection
Luke 2:20

Background Scripture
Luke 2:1-20

Devotional Reading
Ps. 107:1-15

Luke's version of the Christmas story focuses on the way a band of shepherds on the hills near Bethlehem responded to the Good News of the birth of the Messiah, to his young mother, Mary, and to his earthly father, Joseph. It is significant that *Matthew's* version

of this timeless story focuses on the response of three kings—the wise men from afar—to the same news. Combined, the two stories show how the birth of Jesus has universal application—to the rich and the poor, to Jews and non-Jews.

The story also focuses on how God keeps His promises. The event in the stable of Bethlehem is the fulfillment of thousands of years of Bible prophecy, from Genesis 3:15 to Malachi 4:5-6. Our God keeps His Word!

ℰℭℛ

For a Lively Start

You can introduce this lesson with a discussion of the principle of *promises*—promises made, kept, and broken. Ask group members to share an experience, preferably from their childhood to avoid the problem of sharing unhappily broken marital promises, when their parents or other significant persons made a promise, then either

kept it or broke it. For example, was anyone promised a bike for Christmas? How did they feel when the promise was kept? Alternately, did they understand when circumstances required that the promise be broken?

Note that the world's greatest promise was that one day God would send "the seed of woman," the Messiah of the Jews, to right the wrongs caused by the serpent in the Garden of Eden. At Christmas we celebrate God's faithfulness in keeping this promise.

Teaching Outline	Daily Bible Readings
I. Announcement by Angels—2:8-14	Mon. God's Plan Fulfilled *Isa. 46:8-13*
A. Humble shepherds, 8-9	Tue. The King of Glory *Ps. 24*
B. Good News!, 10-12	Wed. Who Is Like the Lord? *Ps. 113*
C. Welcoming chorus, 13-14	Thu. Praise the Lord! *Ps. 148*
II. Redemptive Discovery—15-20	Fri. Glory Forever *Rom. 17:25-27*
A. Visit to Bethlehem, 15-16	Sat. Mary's First Baby *Luke 2:1-7*
B. The first evangelists, 17-20	Sun. Glory to God! *Luke 2:8-20*

Verse by Verse

I. Announcement by Angels—2:8-14
A. Humble shepherds, 8-9

8 And there were in the same country shepherds abiding in the field, keeping watch over their flock by night.

9 And, lo, the angel of the Lord came upon them, and the glory of the Lord shone round about them: and they were sore afraid.

What were Joseph and Mary doing in the area where shepherds were keeping watch over their flock by night? They had gone to Joseph's hometown, Bethlehem, to register for a tax roll (vss. 4-5). Although secular history does not confirm this particular taxation, it does confirm that the emperor Augustus was especially concerned to put the Roman Empire's finances in order, and that would have included the province of Judea. Joseph has accepted the angel's announcement that his bride-to-be, Mary, was with child "by the Holy Spirit," and the time for her delivery was too near to leave her at home in Nazareth.

Although the pastoral scene of shepherds caring for their flocks is thoroughly normal, there is nothing common about the angelic light that bursts over their heads. It was so brilliant, and its accompaniment by angels was such a unique event that it is little wonder that the shepherds are almost overcome by fear.

"Glory" is the standard Old Testament way of referring to the awesome presence of God (see Exod. 16:7; Ps. 63:3; Isa. 60:1). In Greek the term is *doxa,* which gives us "Doxology"— and there is no more fitting time than at Christmas to sing "Praise (or "Give glory to") God from whom all blessings flow!"

Some people in the society of the time looked down on sheepherders. The job required little skill, and—well, there's that *smell!* But Luke is intent throughout his book to show God's concern for the outcast, and the poor. It may also be that selecting shepherds to be among the first to hear of the

Messiah's birth would link Him with David, the shepherd-king from whom Messiah was descended.

B. Good News!, 10-12

10 And the angel said unto them, Fear not: for, behold, I bring you good tidings of great joy, which shall be to all people.

11 For unto you is born this day in the city of David a Saviour, which is Christ the Lord.

12 And this shall be a sign unto you; Ye shall find the babe wrapped in swaddling clothes, lying in a manger.

Fear is the nearly universal way people in Scripture respond to the appearance of an angel, and "Fear not!" are almost always the angel's first words. Although God is certainly capable of announcing gloom and doom through His angels, this announcement consists of "good tidings of great joy," designed to remove all dread at being in God's glorious presence.

Bethlehem was known as the "city of David," even though nearby Jerusalem was his royal city. "Bethlehem" means literally "house of bread," and the link with the eternal food of salvation is obvious.

The baby which the angel hints that the shepherds should search for is more than an infant; He is Christ the Lord—*christos* being the Greek for Messiah. Also, "Lord" was a frequent Old Testament word for God Himself; and connecting the two titles would have been more than enough to excite the shepherds, especially in light of what follows.

C. Welcoming chorus, 13-14

13 And suddenly there was with the angel a multitude of the heavenly host praising God, and saying,

14 Glory to God in the highest, and on earth peace, good will toward men.

No grand event has been more worthy of assembling a choir to celebrate it. "Host," which the NIV translates "great company," usually means "great company of soldiers," or army. These soldiers are divine warriors, not just choirboys. They fill the skies with more praise to the God of hosts, or of all armies, and we can only imagine the heavenly din, and the impact it would have had on these simple, rustic men. (It takes no imagination to contrast the "peace" that accompanies the birth of the Christ-child, with the fact that mankind has spent most of the time before and after His birth in war.)

II. Redemptive Discovery—15-20

A. Visit to Bethlehem, 15-16

15 And it came to pass, as the angels were gone away from them into heaven, the shepherds said one to another, Let us now go even unto Bethlehem, and see this thing which is come to pass, which the Lord hath made known unto us.

16 And they came with haste, and found Mary, and Joseph, and the babe lying in a manger.

Even had they not been simple men the shepherds would have wasted no time in theological debate about the meaning of skies filled with singing angels. They just leave their flocks immediately for the short journey to Bethlehem to see for themselves what the angels have announced.

By the time they arrive at the rude shelter which the innkeeper has arranged for the Holy Family, Jesus has been born. As promised, they find the infant already wrapped in "swaddling clothes," with the "royal bed" a mere manger from which cattle had no doubt recently eaten. Bethlehem was small enough and had few enough inns that the shepherds would have had little trouble locating the only one where a birth had occurred that night.

B. The first evangelists, 17-20

17 And when they had seen it, they made known abroad the saying which was told them concerning this child.

18 And all they that heard it wondered at those things which were told them by the shepherds.

19 But Mary kept all these things, and pondered them in her heart.

20 And the shepherds returned, glorifying and praising God for all the things that they had heard and seen, as it was told unto them.

The sight of Jesus, coupled with the angels' interpretation of His significance, was so wonderful that the shepherds could only tell everyone they met about it. The message was as yet so new and strange that it could only have prompted wonder in the hearts of those who heard it.

Luke, however, is careful to note that one member of this divine drama's cast has emotions deeper than excitement. Mary's response was more thoughtful. The word translated "pondered" meant literally to "throw back and forth" as in a ball game; and when applied to ideas it means to wonder first on this aspect of the notion and then another. Certainly what Mary has experienced would have prompted just such a "dialectic" or back-and-forth wonderment as she tried to fathom the meaning of, on the one hand, angels tossing grand titles for her baby back and forth, and, on the other hand, simply enjoying her first experience as a mother.

The shepherds return to their flocks, seemingly symbolizing the way believers today return to their daily tasks after the excitement of Christmas. Quiet now returns to the skies, to the Judean hillsides, and to the manger. Most of the world little realizes how both heaven and earth will be forever changed by what happened this night in Bethlehem.

Ꮧ᎐Ꮳ

155

Evangelistic Emphasis

How eager are we to do as the shepherds did? Luke tells us, "They made known abroad the saying which was told them concerning this child" (1:17).

Are we so full of excitement and enthusiasm about Jesus that we can't contain ourselves? Or, has the truth about God's Son become old hat to us—something so routine in our lives that it no longer causes our adrenaline to flow?

A childhood friend of mine—a fellow dearly loved by many and a "sweet singer of Israel"—lost his hearing totally. When the first news reports of the incredible cochlear implants was broadcast on TV, his telephone would not quit ringing. Friends literally from coast to coast could not wait to let him know about this fabulous invention. They had good news to share, and it could not wait. Today he sings again.

Luke tells us how the shepherds' message affected their friends. "All they that heard it wondered at those things which were told them by the shepherds" (1:18).

Friends who hear us telling about the Christ who has softened our prejudices, calmed our fears, tamed our tempers, or disciplined our desires, will wonder, too.

ဆာ⟩ဆ

Memory Selection

The angel said unto them, Fear not: for, behold, I bring you good tidings of great joy, which shall be to all people. For unto you is born this day in the city of David a Saviour, which is Christ the Lord.— *Luke 2:10-11*

One of the grandest Christmas sermons ever preached was Karl Barth's simple homily based on this glorious text.

"Unto you." This was Dr. Barth's first point. The Good News of a Savior comes to every person in every place in every age.

"Is born this day." Today is always the day of salvation for any person who hears about Jesus and accepts His salvation. Christ is born in our hearts and in our personal world that very day.

"A Savior." Jesus is not just a mythical character, an ancient hero, or a dead moralist. God sent Him to save us from the damage done by our sins. He saves us from sin's guilt and power.

"Who is Christ the Lord." Centuries of promises from God came true when Jesus was born in Bethlehem. Like the shepherds and the inhabitants of Bethlehem on that historic night, we are wonderfully blessed when we learn who that Baby really is.

"Who writes your sermons?" someone asked a pastor friend of mine. I don't think they meant to insult him. If anybody had asked Karl Barth who wrote this simple sermon, he could have truthfully replied, "An angel."

That heavenly messenger brought a message worth repeating, didn't he?

Weekday Problems

Not all of us have exciting jobs. Instead of being fighter pilots or NASCAR drivers, most of us have repetitive jobs that require us to faithfully perform routine functions over and over.

How many times a day does a secretary answer her business phone with the same greeting? How often in one day does a clerk at McDonald's ring up a Happy Meal? How many bed pans can a nurse empty, how many patients can she weigh, how many vitals can she measure before all the romance is gone from that part of her job? In such cases our performance will be judged not by how thrilled we are with our duties, but by how faithful we are in being sure they are done, and done right.

Watching over a flock all through the lonely Judean night sounds like a dreary job to me. How would a fellow keep from falling asleep and letting a wolf snatch a lamb? But bored minds and droopy eyes got cured instantly that night when the heavens erupted with angelic praise. In an instant every man in that field was alert and amazed.

Next time you go to work, listen closely for the voice of God. Be sensitive to the touch of His hand. Your job, like that of those shepherds, will come alive when heaven comes near.

Christmas Tide

Until one feels the spirit of Christmas—there is no Christmas. All else is outward display—so much tinsel and decorations. For it isn't the snow that is holy. It isn't the tree nor the firelight's glow. It's the warmth that comes to the hearts of men when the Christmas spirit returns again.—*Anonymous*

* * *

Probably the reason we all go so haywire at Christmas time with the endless unrestrained and often silly buying of gifts is that we don't quite know how to put our love into words.—*Harlan Miller*

* * *

There was a gift for each of us left under the tree of life 2,000 years ago by Him whose birthday we celebrate today. The gift was withheld from no man. Some have left the packages unclaimed. Some have accepted the gift and carry it around, but have failed to remove the wrappings and look inside to discover the hidden splendor. The packages are all alike: in each is a scroll in which is written, "All that the Father hath is thine. Take and live!"—*Anonymous*

This Lesson in Your Life

Although our Christmas traditions tend to merge them as part of a single event, the two "Christmas" episodes involving Luke's shepherds and Matthew's wise men evidently were separated by as much as two years.

The shepherds heard the angel's announcement of Jesus' birth and hurried to see Him in the manger on the night when he was born. The magi, however, clearly indicate to King Herod that the royal child they are seeking might be a two-year-old toddler.

In our community's spectacular Christmas pageant, for years now the shepherds have had to scramble off the civic center stage to keep from being stepped on by the magi, who come down the auditorium steps leading a llama, no less!

It's not a major biblical gaffe. In fact, the confusion may be bred by the King James Version's wording which tells us that the wise men came to Bethlehem "when Jesus was born" (Matt. 2:1). Newer versions clarify by translating it "*after* Jesus was born." This reading certainly fits better with the time references later in Matthew's account.

The same chronological confusion shows up in cartoons and on Christmas cards, which always include the star and the three dudes on camels as popular Christmas icons.

Churches that celebrate the Church calendar do tend to reflect the actual Scripture accounts more accurately. Epiphany, the Church's remembrance of that day when non-Jews came to worship the King, always comes in January, thus separating the magi from the shepherds just as the Scriptures do.

Does all of this matter? Not really. What does matter is that we feel drawn to bow down to Jesus—to pay homage to the King—as both the shepherds and the wise men did.

Can you imagine anything so important that you would walk away from your job and leave valuable possessions unsupervised to go check it out? The shepherds did.

Can you conceive of something so compelling that you would travel two years toward an indefinite destination to pay your respects? I hardly can, but Matthew tells us that's what the magi did.

Some people I know would give almost anything they have to *keep from* having to go to worship. The shepherds and the wise men made courageous, costly excursions to find the Christ child that they might bow down to Him and give Him praise.

Getting the shepherds and the wise men to Bethlehem at the right time and in the correct order is no big deal, but honoring Him enough to seek Him and praise Him truly is.

GETTING THE FACTS STRAIGHT

1. Who required Joseph and Mary go to Bethlehem?
The Roman Emperor Caesar Augustus required everybody in the empire to be registered for taxation.

2. Why Bethlehem and not some other place?
Each citizen had to registered in his family's hometown, and both Joseph and Mary traced their ancestry back to King David, who was born in Bethlehem.

3. How did Mary care for her newborn right after the birth?
Mary wrapped her baby in strips of cloth and put him to bed in the stable's feed trough.

4. Why were Joseph and Mary in lodging like that?
All the rooms in the inn were full.

5. What was the first reaction of the shepherds when the angel appeared to them?
The appearance of the angel frightened them.

6. What good news did the angel bring to the shepherds?
The angels announced that the Savior was being born that night right there in Bethlehem.

7. According to the angel, how would the shepherds know they had found the right baby.
He would be wrapped in cloths and his crib would be a manger. Not many babies in Bethlehem would be sleeping in a feed trough, would they?

8. Who praised God and His eternal plans for saving humanity right after the first angel finished his announcement?
A vast multitude of angels suddenly began to praise God for what was happening that night in Bethlehem.

9. What did the shepherds do immediately after that angelic praise team disappeared?
The shepherds hurried into town to find the baby the angels had described.

10. What was the reaction of people when the shepherds told them what they had seen and heard that night?
Everybody who heard their tale "wondered" at what the shepherds were telling.

159

Around Christmas time, most of us try to be a bit kinder and a bit less Scrooge-like, don't we? After all, this season is a time for goodwill, isn't it? The Bethlehem angels said so.

Or did they? Most of us who have grown up reading the Christmas story in the familiar King James have understood the text in this light. We have heard the angels calling men and women on earth to get along better—to show goodwill to one another.

Surely nobody would question that on this scrapping, fussing, violent globe we need all the peace and goodwill that can be mustered.

When the new Bible translation, the Revised Standard Version, was published, however, I was a young, novice pastor. My knowledge of Scripture was 10 miles wide and an inch deep.

The first time I read Luke 2:14 in the RSV, I caught my breath and wondered if I had got it right. For here the Christmas angels cry out to the shepherds:

"Glory to God in the highest, and on earth peace among men with whom he is pleased!"Instantly I heard the echo of God's words at Jesus' baptism, "This is my beloved Son, in whom I am well pleased" (Matt. 3:17). As you probably have guessed, I also recalled God saying the same thing about Jesus on the Mountain of Transfiguration (Matt. 17:5).

That God would say such words about His sinless Son seemed appropriate to me. I understood why God would affirm the ministry and faithfulness of Jesus. Hearing God speak those same words about all of humanity, however, boggled my mind. He was talking about a world full of evil men, like Judas Iscariot and Herod the Great and Pontius Pilate. How could He be "pleased" with wicked people like that?

God was talking about a world populated with people like you and me—weak, flawed, sin-prone people, who so often need to say, "I'm sorry," and too often forget to.

Here was the Almighty, announcing to the world through His messengers, that He is "pleased" with us. That was incredible to me.

When I finally absorbed the angels' grand message, then the implications of their words began to dawn on me.

If God sees something in His broken creatures that pleases Him, then it would be wrong for me to give up on them. If the Creator sees something about us humans that He values, something worth coming to Earth to save, then I need to try to see my neighbors through His eyes.

This is the glorious message of the angels at Christmas.

Lesson 4

John the Baptist Proclaims God's Message

Luke 3:7-18

7 Then said he to the multitude that came forth to be baptized of him, O generation of vipers, who hath warned you to flee from the wrath to come?

8 Bring forth therefore fruits worthy of repentance, and begin not to say within yourselves, We have Abraham to our father: for I say unto you, That God is able of these stones to raise up children unto Abraham.

9 And now also the axe is laid unto the root of the trees: every tree therefore which bringeth not forth good fruit is hewn down, and cast into the fire.

10 And the people asked him, saying, What shall we do then?

11 He answereth and saith unto them, He that hath two coats, let him impart to him that hath none; and he that hath meat, let him do likewise.

12 Then came also publicans to be baptized, and said unto him, Master, what shall we do?

13 And he said unto them, Exact no more than that which is appointed you.

14 And the soldiers likewise demanded of him, saying, And what shall we do? And he said unto them, Do violence to no man, neither accuse any falsely; and be content with your wages.

15 And as the people were in expectation, and all men mused in their hearts of John, whether he were the Christ, or not;

16 John answered, saying unto them all, I indeed baptize you with water; but one mightier than I cometh, the latchet of whose shoes I am not worthy to unloose: he shall baptize you with the Holy Ghost and with fire:

17 Whose fan is in his hand, and he will throughly purge his floor, and will gather the wheat into his garner; but the chaff he will burn with fire unquenchable.

18 And many other things in his exhortation preached he unto the people.

Memory Selection
Luke 3:8a

Background Scripture
Luke 3:1-20

Devotional Reading
Ps. 51:10–19

We have noticed how God chose John, son of Zacharias and Elisabeth, to be the forerunner of Jesus the Messiah. This lesson moves forward into John's adulthood and focuses on his work as "John the baptizer," giving us a glimpse of what it actually meant to be the Messiah's forerunner.

Perhaps the group will recall that John was to come "in the spirit" or after the style of the Old Testament prophet Elijah. Both chose the wilderness as the setting of much of their work. Both were rough-clothed and rough-spoken men, bluntly confronting evil in high places and caring little for what people thought of them. John the Baptist seemed totally committed to the task God gave him: preparing the way for the Lord.

☙◊❧

For a Lively Start

You can start this lesson by asking what it would mean for a modern church to have a man modeled after John the Baptist for their minister. Would it be a suitable arrangement to have a minister who spent most of his time up in the mountains or out in the desert, away from the crowds? What about a man who cared little about how he dressed, and wore the kind of rough clothing John did? What about a preacher who, like John, bluntly reproved people for their life-style?

Of course John had a unique ministry, and most such comparisons with modern times are unrealistic.

Aren't they . . . ?

Teaching Outline	Daily Bible Readings

I. Why Are We Here?—3:7-9
  A. The wrath to come, 7
  B. Worthy fruits, 8-9
II. What Shall We Do?—10-14
  A. The people, 10-11
  B. Publicans, 12-13
  C. Soldiers, 14
III. Could This be the Christ?—15-18
  A. 'I am not worthy,' 15-16a
  B. What Messiah will do, 16b-18
	Mon. More Than a Prophet
	     Luke 7:24-29
	Tue. Witness to the Light
	     John 1:6-9
	Wed. Voice in the Wilderness
	     John 1:19-27
	Thu. John's Testimony
	     John 1:29-34
	Fri. A Shining Lamp
	     John 5:30-35
	Sat. 'I Must Decrease'
	     John 3:22-30
	Sun. Call to Repentance
	     Luke 3:7-18

Verse by Verse

I. Why Are We Here?—3:7-9

A. The wrath to come, 7

7 Then said he to the multitude that came forth to be baptized of him, O generation of vipers, who hath warned you to flee from the wrath to come?

What an unusual evangelist! He is followed into the wilderness by throngs of people—any evangelist's dream—and then he speaks to them bluntly, as though he didn't care whether they were there or not.

Of course everything depends on the preacher's purpose. John the Baptist did not come to "get out the crowd," or even to baptize people, although he did both. He was the Lord's scouring pad, sent to scrub the people clean, and to prepare them for the coming of Jesus, the Messiah. So he greets the people almost rudely, asking facetiously who warned them to flee the wrath God has prepared for pretenders. People who came to hear him merely because it was the thing to do, or to impress John or the local priests—such folk had as well stay home.

The theme of moral reform before Messiah will come lasted well into the Christian era. Some conservative Jews to this day say that the Messiah will not come until His people show by their good works that they are ready for His righteous rule. It would seem that many of John's hearers had heard that he was preaching a message of reformed ethical living, and came to hear more to see if indeed the Messianic age was breaking in.

B. Worthy fruits, 8-9

8 Bring forth therefore fruits worthy of repentance, and begin not to say within yourselves, We have Abraham to our father: for I say unto you, That God is able of these stones to raise up children unto Abraham.

9 And now also the axe is laid unto the root of the trees: every tree therefore which bringeth not forth good fruit is hewn down, and cast into the fire.

John sees through the motives of some of his hearers. They want to be in on the first Messianic call, but they are not ready to reform. As for being "ready," are they not Abraham's de-

163

scendants, and therefore automatically part of the saved? John's response is to warn them that heart-felt reform, not their lineage, will prove whether they are Abraham's true descendants.

The reference to "stones" may be a sly hint of the coming days when God will invite Gentiles as well as Jews to be His children. Not only can God make children of whom He will; He will also "cut down" His own children (roots or trees) and cast them into the fire of punishment if they do not reform and come to God on His terms.

II. What Shall We Do?—10-14
A. The people, 10-11

10 And the people asked him, saying, What shall we do then?

11 He answereth and saith unto them, He that hath two coats, let him impart to him that hath none; and he that hath meat, let him do likewise.

It seems that John's stern message got through to some of the people. They want him to be more specific about what they should do to prepare for the Messianic Age. His answer, again, is in ethical terms. They are to share clothing and food with the have-nots among them. The answer implies that they have been focusing on going through the motions of ritual Judaism, offering the prescribed sacrifices and keeping the traditions taught by their leaders, while ignoring the needs of the needy.

B. Publicans, 12-13

12 Then came also publicans to be baptized, and said unto him, Master, what shall we do?

13 And he said unto them, Exact no more than that which is appointed you.

The "buzz" is spreading, and publicans (tax collectors) take up the question of what they should do. Matthew's account emphasizes that Pharisees and Sadducees are also among those who come to hear John, and they receive the same answer (Matt. 3:8).

The "fruits" of the publicans are to be honest in their work, which was to contract with the Romans. They collected enough taxes to allow for a certain percentage to be deducted as their pay, but they often went far beyond the contracted amount. Seeing that their hearts are hardly ready for a Messiah, John tells them straightforwardly that being honest is the place where they should begin, in order to prepare for His coming.

As Luke 3:3 has said, John's message connected the repentance or change of heart he preaches here with baptism, apparently to symbolize the cleansing of the heart to which John is calling them. Some four years later, a "baptism of John" was still being taught among some Jews, but it was replaced by baptism in the name of Christ because it took the death of Christ to actually wash away sins (see Acts 18:24-25).

C. Soldiers, 14

14 And the soldiers likewise demanded of him, saying, And what shall we do? And he said unto them, Do violence to no man, neither accuse any falsely; and be content with your wages.

Soldiers in the Roman army are another category who want to know more about John's message. Since it is unlikely that very many Roman soldiers, being Gentiles, would have been among the majority Jewish crowd, it is likely that these are Jews who have been conscripted into the army. Possibly they were back-up or enforcers for the taxpayers already mentioned. At any rate, they were very poorly paid, and were notorious for "doing violence" in order to fatten their thin purses. Once more, John perceives that the reform they need to demonstrate must begin in the heart; they are not simply to stop pressuring the people for money, they are to be content with their wages.

III. Could This be the Christ?—15-18

A. 'I am not worthy,' 15-16a

15 And as the people were in expectation, and all men mused in their hearts of John, whether he were the Christ, or not;

16 John answered, saying unto them all, I indeed baptize you with water; but one mightier than I cometh, the latchet of whose shoes I am not worthy to unloose:

John preaches with such authority, and has such ready answers to the people's question, "What shall we do?" that the talk inevitably turns to the possibility that he is the Messiah. As he does consistently, he quickly takes a humble position to relieve the people of any such misconceptions. He illustrates his position vividly by indicating that he is not worthy even to serve as the Messiah's valet, a task which would include latching and unlatching His sandals. In all ways, John is proving worthy of the task God has assigned him, instead of pressing for a higher position.

B. What Messiah will do, 16b-18

16b he shall baptize you with the Holy Ghost and with fire:

17 Whose fan is in his hand, and he will throughly purge his floor, and will gather the wheat into his garner; but the chaff he will burn with fire unquenchable.

18 And many other things in his exhortation preached he unto the people.

Finally, John says that Messiah's superiority will be shown by His greater baptism—one that probably implies a testing or judging (see also Mat. 20:22). Following Messiah will be more costly than following John because it will ask more of the follower. This makes a likely connection with the image of winnowing that follows, with the hulls from the grain being burned while the kernels are saved.

ഔങ

Evangelistic Emphasis

I first got to hear Billy Graham preach in person in Arizona. In the mid-1960's he came to Phoenix and held a crusade in the Arizona State University stadium.

Even before it was expanded to the Fiesta Bowl, the crowds who flocked to hear the famous preacher's message packed it night after night. I noticed that many in the bleachers were university students.

Do you remember that blatantly secular time? Hippies were damning the Establishment and their professors were proclaiming in the media that God is dead. So I suspected that the bulk of the students had come to scoff. Incredibly, many hundreds of them stayed to repent and bow down to the Savior. I was amazed at the power of the gospel the great evangelist preached.

What connected so clearly and gripped the hearts of the young people in that crowd? It seemed to me that the message moved them because the Spirit convicted them of their sins. Like the crowds who poured out of the cities to hear John the Baptist, those students in Arizona heard the preacher describing how they felt, who they were, what they wrestled with.

Like Jesus and John the Baptist before him, Billy Graham's main message in that crusade was, "Repent." Like the Baptizer, Graham called his hearers to Jesus as the solution to their sins.

ଇଠଔ

Memory Selection

All men mused in their hearts of John, whether he were the Christ, or not; John answered, saying unto them all, I indeed baptize you with water; but one mightier than I cometh, the latchet of whose shoes I am not worthy to unloose: he shall baptize you with the Holy Ghost and with fire.—*Luke 3:15-16*

Have you ever worn a shoe that had a "latchet"? Me neither. Of course, that was a perfect translation for folks in England in 1611. Lots of them wore shoes held on by latchets.Our newer Bible versions are probably on target when they have John the Baptist talking about sandals secured by leather thongs. That likely describes the footwear of Jesus' day. John's words would make more sense to us if our translators said something about shoe laces (at least they would have until the recent rage for flip-flops).

When my wife got her new knee last year, for a few weeks she needed me to tie her shoes, so most of the time she elected to wear slip-ons. Today, however, we live in a world without slaves or servants. So, even if we get John's words about sandals or latchets updated, his illustration still may go over our heads.

If John the Baptist were preaching today, can you think of some humiliating modern service John could refer to as something he would not be worthy to do for Jesus?

Weekday Problems

Have you ever known a pastor who did not celebrate when talented, committed people decide to join the pastor's church? Recently my congregation was blessed by the addition of a gifted couple who are widely known in our community as people who make good things happen. Do I need to tell you that I was elated?

Before these sweet people formally announced their decision, however, they sat down with the leaders of our church so their new shepherds would know what to expect from them.

"We're leaving a congregation where we have served for many years," they told us. We knew this. "Some time ago during a capital funds campaign at that church, we made a serious financial commitment which will last for several more months," they revealed. Then they explained, "Our tithes here will temporarily be short by that much, for we intend to fulfill that commitment."

Instead of being unhappy with this explanation, the leaders of my church were delighted to see that these were people who honor their commitments to the Lord and the Church. Is this what happens to the hearts of people whom Jesus baptizes with the Holy Spirit? The Spirit empowers us to carry through on serious commitments in our lives and in our discipleship.

What's in a Name?

A young girl, seeing names like "Surrender" and "My Sin" on the perfume counter, asked the clerk timidly, "Oh my goodness, don't you have any for a beginner?"

* * *

It happened on one of those lake cruises. Most of the women were on deck, while the men were down below. It grew cold, and a woman called out "Hey, isn't there a Macklnaw down there to keep a couple of ladies warm?"

"Nope," came a reply, "But there's a MacMillan that's willing to try."

* * *

"Why on earth," a man demanded of his friend Reggie, "did you name your boy Reginald Clarence?"

"Because, in our neighborhood, he's gotta be a good fighter, and I figure that any boy named Reginald Clarence will have to get to be a good fighter."

This Lesson in Your Life

Years ago a mature pastor told me about his experience at a dysfunctional church. After more than two years of struggling with that congregation's warped attitudes and dead-end philosophies, he decided it was time for him to confront the problems head-on. He was convinced that otherwise the church would never prosper.

"So," he told me, "after telling my wife what I intended to do, I packed my suitcase on Saturday night, and on Sunday morning I preached candidly about the foolish habits and the evil spirit that kept disrupting the governance of that congregation." That capable pastor knew full well what it would cost him to tell that congregation what they needed to hear.

Do you suppose John the Baptist realized the price he would pay for his forthright preaching? The tyrant king, Herod Antipas, had seduced Herodias, his brother's wife. Everybody in the country knew Antipas and his no-good sister-in-law were shamelessly living together. John the Baptist had the courage to preach publicly that this was wrong. Did he know what is would cost him to proclaim that truth?

Antipas was like his corrupt daddy, King Herod the Great, whose claim to fame was the slaughter of Bethlehem's babies. Herod Antipas played fast and loose with the Roman rules. He sold positions of power, shook down merchants, and indulged in just about every known form of immorality.

John the Baptist dared to expose the king's flagrant sins. Did John know his reproof to the wayward king would cost him his freedom at first, and finally his head? Luke and the other Gospel writers tell us what happened to the wilderness prophet, but they don't tell us if he saw it coming.

How do we know when to speak up and when to keep our peace? When we become aware of misdeeds in government, on the job, or in our families or our churches, how can we know when it will be wiser and—in the long run—more beneficial for us to look the other way or to blow the whistle on wrongdoers?

Wise parents know there are times when it's best not to see what their youngsters are up to. If we're going to win the war, one mother of teenagers told me recently, we've got to pick our battles carefully. That's true in every arena.

Did John the Baptist miscalculate the danger of trying to reform the profligate king? Did John think his bold preaching would really make any difference in the king's behavior?

"Be wise as serpents," Jesus warned His men about the time the preaching of John was cut short (Matt. 10:16). Those of us who really want to clean up our dirty world and set crooked things straight will do well to heed his warning.

1. How does Luke identify the precise historical date when John the Baptist began preaching in the wilderness of Judea?

He listed a group of government officials—the emperor, the governor, three tetrarchs, and two top priests—whose terms of office overlapped. Thus he pinpointed the exact time.

2. What message did John preach?

John preached "the baptism of repentance for the remission of sins" (3:3).

3. Who came to hear him preach?

John's crowds came from all the territories along the River Jordan.

4. Why did John call the religious leaders "vipers" or "snakes"?

He was comparing those evil men running from hellfire to the desert snakes who would escape wildfires by slithering to the nearest water hole or river.

5. What does it mean to bring forth "fruits worthy of repentance"?

He wanted them to behave in ways that would show that they really had turned from their sins.

6. What did John tell well-to-do people to do?

To share what they had with the poor.

7. What did John tell publicans (tax collectors) to do to reform their ways?

To stop overcharging people on their tax bills.

8. What kind of repentance did he require of soldiers (the law enforcement officers of that day)?

John told them not to abuse their authority by pushing people around, not to file false charges against anyone, and not to seek bribes.

9. Who did the people think John might be?

Some thought he might be the Christ (Messiah) predicted in the Scriptures.

10. What illustration did John use to describe the greatness of Jesus in comparison to himself?

John said Jesus was so much greater than he was that it would not be proper for John even to serve Jesus as a slave who might untie his shoes.

Do you understand what the prophet Isaiah was talking about in the quotation John the Baptist selected to describe his ministry?

All of us probably know that John's job was to get God's people ready for the coming Jesus. His was indeed, "The voice of one crying in the wilderness" (Luke 3:4). That description fit John perfectly.

What was that wilderness voice saying? According to Isaiah, John's message would be, "Prepare ye the way of the Lord, make his paths straight. Every valley shall be filled, and every mountain and hill shall be brought low; and the crooked shall be made straight, and the rough ways shall be made smooth" (Luke 3:4-5).

Isaiah was depicting John as a highway builder. When a mighty king moved in to assault an enemy city, he had to control the outlying territory and send road-building crews ahead of him. They had to "prepare his way." Only when hills were leveled and ravines filled in, only when winding local roads were replaced with straight, wide, flat super-highways could the royal armies haul in all their battle gear. They prepared the highway for the king.

God sent John the Baptist to prepare the way for the King. Isaiah's highway construction illustration fit him perfectly.

John's ministry was unique, of course. For centuries the Messiah had been promised, and now at last He was coming. John was privileged to wake up his people so they would be ready for Jesus.

In a very real way, however, all of who love Jesus get to mimic John. If God has given us sons or daughters, our task is to pave the way for Jesus to enter their hearts. If we have been blessed with honest mates who need salvation, God counts on us to remove any obstacles that might keep them from Jesus.

Some people must travel intimidating paths to reach the Lord. The hills they must climb are treacherously high, the valleys they must traverse are terrifyingly deep, the route for them is crooked and steep.

What can you and I do to ease their journey, to fill in the gullies, and to reduce the inclines they must cross to reach the Savior?

The King is coming. Let us do what we can to prepare His way.

Lesson 5

Midwives Serve God

Exodus 1:7-22

Jan. 4

And the children of Israel were fruitful, and increased abundantly, and multiplied, and waxed exceedingly mighty; and the land was filled with them.

8 Now there arose up a new king over Egypt, which knew not Joseph.

9 And he said unto his people, Behold, the people of the children of Israel are more and mightier than we:

10 Come on, let us deal wisely with them; lest they multiply, and it come to pass, that, when there falleth out any war, they join also unto our enemies, and fight against us, and so get them up out of the land.

11 Therefore they did set over them taskmasters to afflict them with their burdens. And they built for Pharaoh treasure cities, Pithom and Raamses.

12 But the more they afflicted them, the more they multiplied and grew. And they were grieved because of the children of Israel.

13 And the Egyptians made the children of Israel to serve with rigour:

14 And they made their lives bitter with hard bondage, in morter, and in brick, and in all manner of service in the field: all their service, wherein they made them serve, was with rigour.

15 And the king of Egypt spake to the Hebrew midwives, of which the name of the one was Shiphrah, and the name of the other Puah:

16 And he said, When ye do the office of a midwife to the Hebrew women, and see them upon the stools; if it be a son, then ye shall kill him: but if it be a daughter, then she shall live.

17 But the midwives feared God, and did not as the king of Egypt commanded them, but saved the men children alive.

18 And the king of Egypt called for the midwives, and said unto them, Why have ye done this thing, and have saved the men children alive?

19 And the midwives said unto Pharaoh, Because the Hebrew women are not as the Egyptian women; for they are lively, and are delivered ere the midwives come in unto them.

20 Therefore God dealt well with the midwives: and the people multiplied, and waxed very mighty.

21 And it came to pass, because the midwives feared God, that he made them houses.

22 And Pharaoh charged all his people, saying, Every son that is born ye shall cast into the river, and every daughter ye shall save alive.

Memory Selection
Exod. 1:17

Background Scripture
Exod. 1:7-22

Devotional Reading
Prov. 16:1-7

FOCUS

This is the first of several lessons that illustrate the principle of commitment to God from Old Testament incidents. The apostle Paul writes to New Testament Christians about why it is appropriate for us to draw lessons from the Old Testament: "For whatsoever things were written aforetime were written for our learning, that we through patience and comfort of the scriptures might have hope" (Rom. 15:4).

The first lesson in this series reminds us of the heroism of Hebrew midwives during their captivity in Egypt. At great personal risk, they defied Pharaoh's orders and saved the lives of newborn Hebrew boys. They knew well the ethical principle, "We ought to obey God rather than men" (Acts 5:29).

ഗ്രോ

For a Lively Start

You can introduce this lesson by drawing on the memory of group members to describe the setting of the lesson. Questions that will help do this include:

Why are the Hebrews in Egypt? (An Egyptian Pharaoh had invited their ancestors Jacob and his 12 sons to come to Egypt to flee a famine. Many scholars date this event about 1250 B.C.)

Why did the present Pharaoh order newborn boys to be killed? (He feared the Hebrews' population growth.)

What method of did Pharaoh try to use to control the growth of Hebrew boys? (He ordered the midwives to kill them.)

What slave labor did the Jews perform? (They built cities.)

Teaching Outline	Daily Bible Readings	
I. 'The Jewish Problem'—1:7-10	Mon.	Honor God-Fearers *Ps. 15*
A. Times change, 7-8	Tue.	Whom Shall I Fear? *Ps. 27:1-6*
B. Perceived threat, 9-10	Wed.	Fear No Evil *Ps. 23*
II. The Slave-Labor Option—11-14		
A. Building 'treasure cities,' 11-12	Thu.	Delivered from Fear *Ps. 34:4-14*
B. Bitter burden, 13-14	Fri.	Friendship of God *Ps. 25:12-21*
III. The 'Birth Control' Option—15-22		
A. Death upon birth, 15-19	Sat.	'Let All Fear the Lord' *Ps. 33:8-18*
B. Drowning, 20-22	Sun.	Courage Before Threat *Exod. 1:7-22*

Verse by Verse

I. 'The Jewish Problem'—1:7-10

A. Times change, 7-8

7 And the children of Israel were fruitful, and increased abundantly, and multiplied, and waxed exceedingly mighty; and the land was filled with them.

8 Now there arose up a new king over Egypt, which knew not Joseph.

Although the date for the events of this lesson is highly debated, probably a majority of scholars would place it in the 13th century, with the "new king over Egypt" Pharaoh Rameses II. He was known as an energetic builder, which fits the state of the Hebrews as providers of slave labor. Although the Hebrews have multiplied mightily, the days when Joseph was second in command are forgotten—reminding us of the fragility of people of faith relying on political means for their well-being.

B. Perceived threat, 9-10

9 And he said unto his people, Behold, the people of the children of Israel are more and mightier than we:

10 Come on, let us deal wisely with them; lest they multiply, and it come to pass, that, when there falleth out any war, they join also unto our enemies, and fight against us, and so get them up out of the land.

The remarkable growth of the Israelites must be dealt with. The NIV translates Pharaoh's state of mind better than the KJV. He calls for the Egyptians to deal "shrewdly," not just "wisely," with the population explosion among the Hebrews. The problem is not just that they might take the side of an enemy and fight against the Egyptians in case of war; the Egyptians need the forced labor provided by the Hebrews.

II. The Slave-Labor Option—11-14

A. Building 'treasure cities,' 11-12

11 Therefore they did set over them taskmasters to afflict them with their burdens. And they built for Pharaoh treasure cities, Pithom and Raamses.

12 But the more they afflicted them, the more they multiplied and grew. And they were grieved because of the children of Israel.

The "treasure" in the cities the Hebrews were forced to build consisted not of precious metals or crown jewels, but the "treasure" of grain and other goods that would be used in case of famine. Archeologists believe they have discovered the ruins of both these cities. Art work on their walls portrays apparently Semitic slaves at work on building projects. This was the very area of work that had been assigned to Joseph; but the change from his royal position to the state of slavery could not have been more sharply drawn.

The repetition of the assertion that the Hebrews were growing in numbers is probably a sign that the author (traditionally, Moses) believed that God was aiding and abetting their remarkable growth. This of course added an extra measure of "grief" to the Egyptians, beyond what natural reproduction would have brought upon them.

B. Bitter burden, 13-14

13 And the Egyptians made the children of Israel to serve with rigour:

14 And they made their lives bitter with hard bondage, in morter, and in brick, and in all manner of service in the field: all their service, wherein they made them serve, was with rigour.

Another repetition—the description of the Hebrews' work being "with rigour"—is designed to double the impact on the reader. The Egyptians are not merely bent on getting all the work they can from the Jews, but also on breaking their spirit and reducing them to a slave mentality as a defense against uprisings.

It is possible that the work with "brick" denotes "adobe"-like bricks made from the black mud of Goshen, the delta area that had originally been assigned to the Jews' as their homeland.

III. The 'Birth Control' Option— 15-22

A. Death upon birth, 15-19

15 And the king of Egypt spake to the Hebrew midwives, of which the name of the one was Shiphrah, and the name of the other Puah:

16 And he said, When ye do the office of a midwife to the Hebrew women, and see them upon the stools; if it be a son, then ye shall kill him: but if it be a daughter, then she shall live.

17 But the midwives feared God, and did not as the king of Egypt commanded them, but saved the men children alive.

18 And the king of Egypt called for the midwives, and said unto them, Why have ye done this thing, and have saved the men children alive?

19 And the midwives said unto Pharaoh, Because the Hebrew women are not as the Egyptian women; for they are lively, and are delivered ere the midwives come in unto them.

It seems unlikely that only two midwives could provide adequate services to a people said to be growing so rapidly. Possibly these two, whose names have remarkably been preserved, were in charge of a cadre of midwives. "The stools" were an ancient arrangement in which a woman giving birth would be positioned for efficient delivery. Although the directions to kill the male babies are clear enough, the mere edict of a king is not as powerful as the obedience of these believing servants.

B. Drowning, 20-22

20 Therefore God dealt well with the midwives: and the people multiplied, and waxed very mighty.

21 And it came to pass, because the midwives feared God, that he made them houses.

22 And Pharaoh charged all his people, saying, Every son that is born ye shall cast into the river, and every daughter ye shall save alive.

God honors the midwives' obedience by granting them "families" (NIV; not "houses," as in the KJV). Apparently their work ordinarily required them to be on call to the extent that it was impossible for them to have families of their own. Pharaoh, however, probably not believing the midwives' story about "lively" Hebrew women, now sets the entire Egyptian population against Hebrew male babies. As sad as this was, the author seems to be deliberately painting a grim picture in order to make God's approaching deliverance all the more joyful.

ഇന്ദ

Evangelistic Emphasis

In our recent literature and movies we have come through the era of the anti-hero. Gone are the simple days when Roy Rogers and Gene Autry wore white hats and vanquished cattle rustlers and train robbers wearing black ones.

"Crime does not pay," was the recurring theme of Dick Tracy comics when I was a boy. Now, "Crime pays handsomely and virtue may leave you poor," is the word on the street and in current Hollywood sleaze.

Even in our churches and our schools we are terribly short on heroes. When the President—regardless of his party—is vilified by the press, and top sport figures so often turn out to be dopers or thugs, who can we hold up to our young people as models to imitate?

In our hero-less age, our church people—young and old—need to know about heroines like Shiphrah and Puah. Those gutsy gals won't show up on anybody's Top Ten list of biblical greats, but we need to celebrate the kind of unflinching faith that allowed them to brave daunting risks to save the boy babies Pharoah wanted dead.

While giving thanks for all who authentically represent the cause of Christ, instead of the rich and famous, perhaps we should be putting forward our real heroes—those who, like the Hebrew midwives, dare to risk everything to stand up for what they know is right.

ఇం⊃Q⊰

Memory Selection

Now there arose up a new king over Egypt, which knew not Joseph. And he said unto his people, Behold, the people of the children of Israel are more and mightier than we: Come on, let us deal wisely with them; lest they multiply.—*Exodus 1:8-10*

Someone has said that racial prejudice is one part rational and nine parts fear. We might debate the percentages, but any of us who have felt the rising panic in a community experiencing a radical shift in ethnic mix will likely agree that when prejudice rears its ugly head, people get scared of one another.

When we lived on the gulf coast of Texas during World War II, my father was often invited to preach at a robust congregation in a small farming town. In that community the racial divide between Hispanics and Gringos was sharp. Twenty years later all the city officials were Hispanics and only two white kids attended the high school.

In his novel *Texas,* James Michener predicted that by 2020 the state's population might be 90 percent Hispanic. Does a demographic shift of this proportion in any locale set up a replay of the fear tactics in Goshen, Egypt? In places where the majority rapidly becomes the minority—areas like Los Angeles and Miami—does today's Church have enough influence to deter hate crimes and malicious political schemes? Can our love for Christ keep us from reenacting Egypt?

Weekday Problems

One of my sharpest high school Bible students, Rachel, went with a mission group to Nicaragua this summer. They slept on the ground, bathed in buckets of cold water, ate tasteless local mush, and worked at brutal, dirty construction jobs at least 12 hours a day.

Any contractor who had hired these students and subjected them to such abusive conditions would have been thrown in jail, or sued, or both. But Rachel came home telling us how grand it was.

In Egypt the brick-making and construction tasks were designed to repress the multiplying Hebrew population, and these jobs were perceived as bitter, hard bondage. About 3,500 years later in the southern reaches of the Nile rift, my brother helped establish a fruitful mission station. In the earliest days they hired local laborers who knew the age-old methods of molding and firing bricks made from straw mulched in Nile clay—just like the bricks of Moses' day. In one summer the workers produced tens of thousands of high quality bricks. Instead of feeling abused by their assignments, however, these brick-makers were delighted to be receiving higher than average wages, and they were proud when their bricks became the walls of a maternity clinic, a school, a village church, and a student dorm.

The next time you're tempted to complain about your job, let this story remind you that the real rub may not be the job itself, but the reasons behind it.

All in the Family

"How do you like your new baby sister, Tommy?"

"Oh, she's OK, I guess. But just like Pop says, there are lots of things we needed worse."

* * *

"John," said the wife, "I'm ashamed of the way we live. Mother pays the rent, Aunt Martha sends her hand-me-down clothes, and my sister sends us money for groceries. I don't like to complain, but I'm sorry we can't do better than that."

"Well, you should be," replied John indignantly. "You've got two uncles who don't send us a dime."

* * *

During a bad electrical storm, a mother thought her young son might be frightened, so she tiptoed into his room to comfort him.

Without opening his eyes, and before she could say anything, the wise little boy mumbled sleepily, "What's Daddy doing with the TV set now?"

This Lesson in Your Life

After my paternal grandfather buried his first wife, he lived alone for about a dozen years. Then, when he was almost 80, some of our friends in his small town tipped us off that Big George (as we all called him) was courting a local widow.

Every day, they told us, he would stop by the post office, pick up this lady's mail, and use the daily delivery as an excuse to share a cup of coffee in her big old house. That's how Mama Pearl came into our lives—and what a blessing she turned out to be. Mama Pearl was, among other things, an experienced midwife. Before she retired, well past 80, she had delivered more than 2,000 babies for families in the huts that encircled her back yard.

In the days before Medicaid and similar government programs dealing with indigent healthcare needs, Mama Pearl's nursing and midwifery provided the first line of medical service for hundreds of migrant farm families and bottom-line poor folks in the county. At all hours of the day or night pregnant women would show up on her doorstep already in labor. Almost always they brought with them their entire family. Mama Pearl would put the mother-to-be on a primitive birthing bed in one of her backyard shanties.

She charged $5 to deliver a baby. That fee covered meals for the entire family for however long the delivery might take. No organized church ministry or government medical program aided more people than Mama Pearl did all by herself with no outside funding.

This was my introduction to the work of a midwife. My wife and I stayed in the house with Big George and Mama Pearl for half a week in 1960. Late in the night while the rest of us were fast asleep, she delivered three babies there at her house that week.

Whenever I read the Exodus 1 account of those brave Hebrew midwives, I think immediately of my step-grandmother, Mama Pearl. She was cut from the same cloth they were. She shared their plucky spirit. She simply did whatever needed to be done for her poor clients whenever it was needed.

Mama Pearl also had a double dose of the hilarious effrontery of Shiphrah and Puah. Can you believe the explanation those cheeky Hebrew midwives gave Pharaoh when he complained that the Hebrews' boy babies were surviving? Mama Pearl knew the local doctors and county officials back then were not going to care for all those ailing migrant workers, so in a judicious way she basically told any nitpicking big-wig to take a hike.

How often are we tempted to defer to government programs as caretakers for the poor instead of taking personal initiative to be merciful and helpful whenever we can? Do we hide behind court rulings and bureaucratic regulations as reasons not to speak up against unjust or ungodly activities? Or, with these midwives and Peter do we say "We ought to obey God rather than man"?

1. At the beginning of this account, what was the Egyptian king concerned about?

The king was afraid the Hebrews were becoming so numerous that they might join with an attacking enemy against Egypt.

2. What did he propose to do about the problem?

His first plan was to force the Israelites to do oppressively hard labor.

3. When the Egyptians began making life hard for the Hebrews, what happened to the Hebrew birth rate?

They had more babies than ever. The harder they worked, the more kids they had.

4. What kind of labor were the Hebrew slaves forced to do?

They made bricks out of mud and straw, and they built royal cities.

5. Who were Shiphrah and Puah?

Hebrew midwives.

6. What did Pharaoh instruct them to do?

To kill the boy babies born to the Israelites.

7. Did these women obey the king?

No.

8. Why did they choose this option?

They feared God more than they feared the king.

9. What explanation did they give when the king questioned them?

They alibied to the king, telling him that the hardworking Hebrew mothers were so much stronger than the wimpy Egyptian maidens that they had their babies too rapidly for the midwives to get there in time to kill them.

10. Compare the reading of a new Bible version and tell how God rewarded the faithfulness of these women?

He gave these faithful ladies families. Children were born to them because they saved the Hebrew boys.

In the ancient Egypt of Exodus 1, it was deadly to be born a Hebrew boy. It's dangerous today to be born a female in China.

A recent news report told of a Chinese farmer who spotted a tiny hand sticking out of the soil on the edge of his field. He was shocked to see the hand move. Frantically he scooped away the loose dirt and unearthed a newborn girl. Thanks to his aid, the baby survived.

Why would anybody do such a heinous thing? Recent visitors to inland China cite two compelling reasons. First is the devastating economic consequences of raising a girl. When she gets married, her poor parents will likely be bankrupted and ruined just to pay her dowry, whereas a male child can grow up to earn wages and be paid dowry.

Still, baby girls might survive except for a second factor. The Chinese government penalizes any family that raises more than one child. So my friends who know China tell me over 80 percent of China's school children today are male.

Such lopsided male/female stats result both from gendercide and from widespread abandonment of female infants.

The latter cause does give rise to some heartwarming tales. Last week I ate breakfast with a former pastor who now works for our school district. He and his wife have a 2-year-old daughter they adopted in China, and he told me they hope soon to adopt another.

Several mornings a week I see a retired optometrist—a longtime church leader and friend—who often has with him his precious 3-year-old Chinese granddaughter, also adopted through an international Christian agency.

In Indianapolis a pastor friend and his wife whose marriage I performed a decade ago could hardly wait for me to see their new daughter—also an infant from China.

Although we live halfway around the world from China, these American Christians have rescued these little girls from a world where their families consider them an unbearable burden and their government basically sells them as a major export commodity.

"Blessed are the merciful," Jesus tells us, and He promises that those who do acts of mercy will receive the same. What kind of blessings do you suppose are in store for the hundreds of Christians who today are rescuing the endangered gender of China?

God saw what the midwives did to save the Hebrew boys in Egypt, so He rewarded them with children (KJV "houses") of their own. What reward does He have for those who save the girls of China?

Lesson 6

Rahab Helps Israel

Joshua 2:1-4, 12-14; 6:22-27

And Joshua the son of Nun sent out of Shittim two men to spy secretly, saying, Go view the land, even Jericho. And they went, and came into an harlot's house, named Rahab, and lodged there.

2 And it was told the king of Jericho, saying, Behold, there came men in hither to night of the children of Israel to search out the country.

3 And the king of Jericho sent unto Rahab, saying, Bring forth the men that are come to thee, which are entered into thine house: for they be come to search out all the country.

4 And the woman took the two men, and hid them, and said thus, There came men unto me, but I wist not whence they were:

12 Now, therefore, I pray you, swear unto me by the Lord, since I have shewed you kindness, that ye will also shew kindness unto my father's house, and give me a true token:

13 And that ye will save alive my father, and my mother, and my brethren, and my sisters, and all that they have, and deliver our lives from death.

14 And the men answered her, Our life for yours, if ye utter not this our business. And it shall be, when the LORD hath given us the land, that we will deal kindly and truly with thee.

6:22 But Joshua had said unto the two men that had spied out the country, Go into the harlot's house, and bring out thence the woman, and all that she hath, as ye sware unto her,

23 And the young men that were spies went in, and brought out Rahab, and her father, and her mother, and her brethren, and all that she had; and they brought out all her kindred, and left them without the camp of Israel.

24 And they burnt the city with fire, and all that was therein: only the silver, and the gold, and the vessels of brass and of iron, they put into the treasury of the house of the Lord.

25 And Joshua saved Rahab the harlot alive, and her father's household, and all that she had: and she dwelleth in Israel even unto this day; because she hid the messengers, which Joshua sent to spy out Jericho.

26 And Joshua adjured them at that time, saying, Cursed be the man before the Lord, that riseth up and buildeth this city Jericho: he shall lay the foundation thereof in his firstborn, and in his youngest son shall he set up the gates of it.

27 So the Lord was with Joshua; and his fame was noised throughout all the country.

Memory Selection
Josh. 2:11-12

Background Scripture
Josh. 2; 6:22-25

Devotional Reading
Heb. 11:23-31

FOCUS

Although it is hardly as colorful as several other possible reasons why the story of Rahab the harlot is so famous (see below), the historical significance of the account is probably the main reason it was included in Scripture.

Under the newly inaugurated leadership of Joshua, Israel has come up to the Jordan River, poised there to invade Canaan. Although many Bible maps do not show Shittim (or Abel-Shittim, see Num. 25:1; Josh. 2:1), it is located only about 10 miles from the northern tip of the Dead Sea. Moses was buried on nearby Mt. Nebo. So history has come full circle. After 40 years in the desert, the invasion of the Promised Land is imminent.

For a Lively Start

One way to start this lesson is to invite group members to try to use their imaginations to deduce why the story of Rahab the harlot has survived so famously down through the ages: (1) People instinctively like to see that a person of ill repute is also capable of good works, much like a pirate saving a person's life. (2) Remarkably, this person actually turns out to be included in the ancestry of the Messiah. (3) The story is quite simply a good adventure tale. (4) Rahab's assistance to the spies from Israel turns out to be a turning point in the history of God's people, since it facilitated their first entry into Canaan, (5) The story poses an ethical dilemma: Should Rahab lie to help God's people?

Be sure to emphasize the fact that Rahab is only one of several people in Scripture whom society rejects but God uses.

Teaching Outline	Daily Bible Readings	
I. Plot and Counter-Plot—2:1-4	Mon.	The Courage of Faith *Josh. 1:10-18*
A. Spies and counter-spies, 1-3	Tue.	Rahab: Example of Faith *Heb. 11:23-31*
B. Rahab's choice, 4		
II. Rahab's bargain, 12-14	Wed.	Rahab's Declaration *Josh. 2:8-11*
A. Plea for safe-keeping, 12-13	Thu.	Rahab's Agreement *Josh. 2:15-21*
B. Spies' agreement, 14		
III. Fulfilled promise,6:22-25	Fri.	Justified by Works *James 2:21-26*
IV. Curse on a city, 26-27	Sat.	Rahab's Legacy: A King *Matt. 1:1-6*
	Sun.	Rahab's Protection *Josh. 2:1-4; 12-14; 6:22-25*

Verse by Verse

I. Plot and Counter-Plot—2:1-4

A. Spies and counter-spies, 1-3

1 And Joshua the son of Nun sent out of Shittim two men to spy secretly, saying, Go view the land, even Jericho. And they went, and came into an harlot's house, named Rahab, and lodged there.

2 And it was told the king of Jericho, saying, Behold, there came men in hither to night of the children of Israel to search out the country.

3 And the king of Jericho sent unto Rahab, saying, Bring forth the men that are come to thee, which are entered into thine house: for they be come to search out all the country.

Forty years and many miles of wilderness wandering have marked Israel's history since our last lesson. Moses' career has risen and fallen, and since God is about to give Israel permission to invade the Promised Land, the reins of leadership have passed into the hands of a military man, Joshua (see Josh. 1:1-9). The people have camped at Abel-Shittim, just north of the Dead Sea and east of the Jordan River, a spot that will become a home camp from which the first attack on Canaan will be made.

The first target is the city-state of Jericho, just west of the Jordan. It was an important trading post, located on commercial crossroads. Some archeologists believe it is the oldest walled city in the world. In modern times it has become the focus of fierce arguments, with some archeologists believing they have discovered walls that have fallen outward, indicating God's miraculous help (see Josh. 6:20), and others stoutly disputing this claim.

Joshua may have been to Jericho 40 years earlier when he had been part of a team of spies who explored Canaan and assessed Israel's ability to conquer the land. He and Caleb were the only two out of 12 spies to urge that Israel could successfully invade the Promised Land then, but their counsel was overruled (see Num. 14:30), leading to 40 more years of wandering in the desert.

Why did the spies go to the house of a harlot as their first stop? Despite her

183

occupation, it is possible that Rahab is part Jewish—in Jesus' genealogy she is said to be the mother of Boaz (Matt. 1:5). She also may have been a Gentile who intermarried with a Jewish family. This possibility is strengthened by the fact that the king knows where to go for counter-intelligence about the Jewish spies (he may have known of some Jewish connection). Also, there would perhaps be no better place to go for information—especially about troop movement. The spies are on a fact-finding mission, not one on which they are interested in impressing local inhabitants about the company they keep, and they go to a place they know soldiers frequented.

B. Rahab's choice, 4

4 And the woman took the two men, and hid them, and said thus, There came men unto me, but I wist not whence they were:

Again we have no better answer to the question of why the harlot has cast her lot with the Jews, unless it be simply that she has heard how God seemed to have been winning victories for the Jews (2:9). At any rate, she faces a moral dilemma. In some way she has come to believe that the Hebrews serve the true God, and her dilemma is whether to lie to her own townsfolk about the spies' whereabouts, or to turn them in. For whatever reason, her choice to hide the spies will have far-reaching implications in helping God's people gain a foothold early in their campaign against the Canaanites. Apparently her choice has God's approval. She is commended twice in the New Testament—once for her faith (Heb. 11:31) and once for her works

(James 2:25).

II. Rahab's bargain, 12-14
A. Plea for safe-keeping, 12-13

12 Now, therefore, I pray you, swear unto me by the LORD, since I have shewed you kindness, that ye will also shew kindness unto my father's house, and give me a true token:

13 And that ye will save alive my father, and my mother, and my brethren, and my sisters, and all that they have, and deliver our lives from death.

Rahab is a shrewd woman. She has not hidden the Hebrew spies without thinking about the benefit she might gain from it. After all, she has been a factor in saving the lives both of the spies and of countless soldiers in the battle to come. It is not clear what "true token" she has in mind as a guarantee that her and her families' lives will be spared in return. Possibly it is only a promise or vow. If so, she is apparently satisfied with the spies' promise in verse 14, to follow.

B. Spies' agreement, 14

14 And the men answered her, Our life for yours, if ye utter not this our business. And it shall be, when the LORD hath given us the land, that we will deal kindly and truly with thee.

The formal nature of the language— "Our life for yours" may be a hint that this is the "token" or vow Rahab seeks from the spies. At any rate, both she and the spies seem satisfied with the bargain.

III. Fulfilled promise, 22-25

6:22 But Joshua had said unto the two men that had spied out the country, Go into the harlot's house, and

bring out thence the woman, and all that she hath, as ye sware unto her,

23 And the young men that were spies went in, and brought out Rahab, and her father, and her mother, and her brethren, and all that she had; and they brought out all her kindred, and left them without the camp of Israel.

24 And they burnt the city with fire, and all that was therein: only the silver, and the gold, and the vessels of brass and of iron, they put into the treasury of the house of the LORD.

25 And Joshua saved Rahab the harlot alive, and her father's household, and all that she had: and she dwelleth in Israel even unto this day; because she hid the messengers, which Joshua sent to spy out Jericho.

Now the story moves beyond the first encounter with Rahab and on past the colorful story of the Hebrews' crossing the Jordon, raising a memorial of stones and "flattening" of the walls of Jericho by the famous trumpet blast. Joshua orders the two spies whom Rahab had sheltered to seek her out, along with her family. Their sign is the red "string" or cord (2:18, NIV) by which Rahab had let them down through the window of her apartment on the wall. (A double wall, with spaces suitable for such dwellings, are a part of what archeologists have found.)

IV. Curse on a city, 26-27

26 And Joshua adjured them at that tie, saying, Cursed be the man before the LORD, that riseth up and buildeth this city Jericho: he shall lay the foundation thereof in his firstborn, and in his youngest son shall he set up the gates of it.

27 So the LORD was with Joshua; and his fame was noised throughout all the country.

Perhaps in tribute to this, his first conquest in Canaan, Joshua adds a curse to the burning of the city. If anyone tries to rebuild it, his firstborn son would die with the completion of the foundation, and his youngest with the hanging of the gates. Some 520 years later, either in ignorance of this curse, or blatant disbelief, Hiel the Bethelite defied it. He tried to rebuild the city, and sure enough, suffered the consequences (see 1 Kings 16:34).

෨෬

Evangelistic Emphasis

Yesterday I ate lunch in one of the poorest homes in the small community where I am preaching a revival. The leaders of the congregation asked, "Who will feed the preacher this week?" This good lady (let's call her Jane) could not wait to maneuver her power wheelchair to the table where she could sign up to provide a meal.

"It's been a marvelously cool morning with all the clouds and the showers," I observed as we sat down at the dinner table in Jane's un-air-conditioned home. Temps might normally have been near 100.

"Yes," she agreed, "but we're lucky it didn't rain hard. The roof leaks bad right over the spot where you're sitting."

At first Jane's kids and grandkids were ill at ease. I suspected they had not spent much time around a preacher. As lunch ended, Jane told me, "I told my boys they ought to come to church with me." Her sons offered no comment. "I told 'em this is the only church that ever treated me good. Most church people treat me shabby 'cause my clothes are shabby."

If they ever do come to the Church and to the Lord, likely it will be because they heard their mother's reports of its goodness, just as Rahab years ago heard the reports of Yahweh's greatness.

℘ℭ℞

Memory Selection

By faith the harlot Rahab perished not with them that believed not, when she had received the spies with peace.—*Hebrews 11:31*

Rahab was surrounded by people who disdained the God of Israel. Don't you wonder why she had faith when they didn't? Even in that pagan city the "good folks" in town probably would have singled out Rahab as a person of questionable morals, but the Bible singles her out as a person who had exemplary faith.

Isn't it refreshing to know that we are not doomed by our DNA? Doesn't it free our souls when we find out that we are not destined to repeat the mistakes of those before us and around us? Rahab rose above her reputation, above her neighborhood's destiny. The faith and valor in her own soul set her and her family free. Do you suppose anybody in that city suspected the goodness and the greatness that hid in that woman's heart? If they had been looking for an unforgettable hero in their town, would they have singled out Rahab? God did.

Could it be that you are the person in your family or your neighborhood whose faith will lift you up to new levels, just as Rahab's did? I have a friend who this fall will be the first in his family to go to college in four generations.

"My mother and my grandma got divorced several times. My marriage is lasting," one sweet lady told me.

It is possible to break loose from the limits of the past. Like these good people. Like Rahab.

Weekday Problems

In one of the largest businesses in the city where I live, an extremely sticky situation arose. During the first frantic investigations by the people in charge, a friend of mine—an employee in the affected department—was among those interviewed. "I always tell the truth, at least as I know it," my friend assured me, "but in that two-hour session, I don't think they believed much that I told them."

I trusted anything she told me, and I wondered why her superiors would react otherwise. "In my department," she lamented, "truth seems to be in short supply. We have far too many people who will simply tell you whatever they think you want to hear—whatever seems to make them look best at the moment. Since they lie all the time without a minute's hesitation, I guess they think everybody else does too."

Truth is a precious element of all our relationships. Without it marriages fail, friendships die, business deals go sour, and trust is betrayed.

Although Rahab lied to the soldiers to save her visitors' lives, she expected her newfound friends to tell her the truth. Do you agree that any agreement that works and lasts must be based on that expectation, and that any exception to the rule must be for the greater good, as in Rahab's case?

Driving Ourselves Crazy

The husband, hopelessly snarled in a traffic jam, was receiving from his wife multiple sets of instructions about what to do. When nothing worked, she demanded, "Well what are you going to do?"

"I have no idea," her husband replied, "but I'm sure if you climb into the back seat, you can figure it out."

* * *

Sign on the back of a truck: PLEASE DON'T HUG ME. I'M GOING STEADY.

* * *

The reason there were fewer accidents in ancient times when donkeys pulled carts is that the driver didn't depend entirely on his own intelligence.

* * *

Why are natives, who beat drums to beat off evil spirits, objects of scorn to civilized American motorists who lean on their horns to break up traffic jams?

* * *

Drinking before driving is putting the quart before the hearse.

187

This Lesson in Your Life

"The Scarlet Thread" was the clever title of a sermon I first heard preached years ago by a late preacher friend who let thd "scarlet" in this story represent the blood of Christ, and the "thread" stand for the ancestral line of our Lord Jesus. I suspect the sermon has been around in some form for centuries. At the time, I was hearing it for the first time and the insights it offered impressed me.

In a nutshell, this long-ago sermon noted that besides Mary, three other women are named in Jesus' family tree in Matthew 1, and all of those famous ladies are non-Jews. Evidently God is not a Nazi. It did not bother Him that His Son's bloodline was not "pure." Tamar is the first woman mentioned in Matthew's genealogy of Jesus (1:3). She was the daughter of a Canaanite neighbor to Jacob's family. Her story, told in Genesis 38, gave Shakespeare part of his plot for *The Merchant of Venice*.

Two verses later Matthew names two more foreign females as great-grandmothers of Jesus. You may recall the much-loved story of Ruth. When a drought drove Naomi's family to Moab, one of her sons married the local girl, Ruth. He died, and Ruth returned with Naomi to Bethlehem, where she then married an older farmer named Boaz.

Years earlier, Boaz had been the child of Rahab, Jericho's famous harlot and the second lady in that list in Matthew 1. I've often wondered if old Boaz found it easier to accept Ruth as a wife because of his own mother's non-Jewish roots. What do you think?

In his sermon my preacher friend traced the blood line of Jesus through these illustrious foreign ladies, down to Mary, and finally, to complete a grand gospel message, to the blood of Jesus running down the Cross. Of course, Rahab—our heroine in this week's lesson—was right there in the middle of that scarlet thread.

I heard that sermon before the names of people like Martin Luther King and Rosa Parks were known by all Americans. I heard it before riots shook Watts in Los Angeles and racial marches left permanent marks on Little Rock and Selma.

So, I must confess, as much as I enjoyed my friend's sermon, I missed part of the power of his message. It mattered far more than I realized at the time. Our nation's future depended then—and it still depends—on all of us learning that God does not draw racial lines. Instead, as Peter tells us, He accepts people from every race "who fear him and do what is right" (Acts 10:35).

1. Where did the Hebrew spies hide while they were checking out the city of Jericho?
They lodged in the house of a harlot named Rahab.

2. What did Rahab tell the soldiers who were sent by the king to arrest the spies?
She lied and told them the spies had left before the gates of the city had been closed that evening.

3. Where had Rahab hidden the spies?
They were concealed under stalks of flax that were drying atop Rahab's house.

4. Why did Rahab take such a huge chance to protect the spies?
Rahab told the spies that everybody in Jericho had heard how Israel's God had parted the Red Sea and how He had wiped out the armies east of the River Jordan. She knew who would win.

5. What deal did Rahab make with the spies?
She would save their lives if they would save hers.

6. How was Rahab supposed to mark her house so the army of Israel would know to spare her?
Rahab was given a scarlet cord and told to tie it in her window.

7. If Rahab or any of her family were not in the house marked with the red rope, what would happen to them?
The spies warned that they would not be responsible for the safety of anybody who was outside Rahab's house.

8. How did the spies elude the army that was searching for them?
They ran to a nearby mountain, as Rahab had instructed, and stayed hidden there for three days until Jericho's soldiers ended their search.

9. What report did the spies give to Joshua about Jericho?
They told him that God had given the city into Israel's hands, because all the people inside the city were scared and expected to be defeated by Israel.

10. What happened to Rahab and her family when the city of Jericho was destroyed by Israel?
Joshua had the spies escort Rahab and her family to safety.

When Moses sent spies into Canaan 40 years before the Jericho story, Israel turned away from the Promised Land and died in the desert because they were afraid of Canaan's armies.

Four decades later, however, when Joshua led his army to the assault on Jericho, it was the people of Canaan who were afraid. Rahab said their hearts melted with fear and all courage fled.

Guess who lost? In each case, fear was the main factor in determining who was victorious and who was defeated..

On every hand today, it seems, somebody wants to frighten us. I listen occasionally to tapes of sermons preached by a pastor friend of mine. I like the man. I like most of what he stands for. But I deplore his preaching style.

In almost every sermon this man tries to motivate his people by scaring them to death. His main product is fear. If he can frighten his people enough, then he can sell them on almost any solution.

My friend's pastoral approach seems to be the exact opposite of Christ's. Jesus often started off by telling people, "Fear not."

Fear is a favorite commodity of our media today. Turn on any channel any night and somebody will be issuing dire warnings about everything from calories to global warming. It's probably not nice to snicker at serious scientists who are trying to stave off man-made disasters for planet Earth, but I can't keep from it when I hear some of the best-educated people among us shifting into Chicken Little mode.

Not long ago I heard a wildlife biologist who was in a fret because his studies showed that polar bear genitals were shrinking. He attributed this earth-threatening disaster to global warming.

Scientist like that are almost as funny as clergymen when they start taking themselves too seriously, aren't they?

The planet you and I live on was made by an Almighty Creator whose grace and care are still sufficient to protect and sustain it. We who know this great God should know better than to let some secular alarmist replace our faith with fear.

In Christ we can relax and rejoice that "God has not given us a spirit of fear, but of power and of love and of a sound mind" (2 Tim.1:7, NKJV).

Lesson 7

Joshua Leads Israel

Joshua 3:1-13

And Joshua rose early in the morning; and they removed from Shittim, and came to Jordan, he and all the children of Israel, and lodged there before they passed over.

2 And it came to pass after three days, that the officers went through the host;

3 And they commanded the people, saying, When ye see the ark of the covenant of the LORD your God, and the priests the Levites bearing it, then ye shall remove from your place, and go after it.

4 Yet there shall be a space between you and it, about two thousand cubits by measure: come not near unto it, that ye may know the way by which ye must go: for ye have not passed this way heretofore.

5 And Joshua said unto the people, Sanctify yourselves: for to morrow the LORD will do wonders among you.

6 And Joshua spake unto the priests, saying, Take up the ark of the covenant, and pass over before the people. And they took up the ark of the covenant, and went before the people.

7 And the LORD said unto Joshua, This day will I begin to magnify thee in the sight of all Israel, that they may know that, as I was with Moses, so I will be with thee.

8 And thou shalt command the priests that bear the ark of the covenant, saying, When ye are come to the brink of the water of Jordan, ye shall stand still in Jordan.

9 And Joshua said unto the children of Israel, Come hither, and hear the words of the LORD your God.

10 And Joshua said, Hereby ye shall know that the living God is among you, and that he will without fail drive out from before you the Canaanites, and the Hittites, and the Hivites, and the Perizzites, and the Girgashites, and the Amorites, and the Jebusites.

11 Behold, the ark of the covenant of the Lord of all the earth passeth over before you into Jordan.

12 Now therefore take you twelve men out of the tribes of Israel, out of every tribe a man.

13 And it shall come to pass, as soon as the soles of the feet of the priests that bear the ark of the LORD, the Lord of all the earth, shall rest in the waters of Jordan, that the waters of Jordan shall be cut off from the waters that come down from above; and they shall stand upon an heap.

Memory Selection
Josh. 3:7

Background Scripture
Joshua 3

Devotional Reading
Ps. 142

The immediate focus of this lesson is on Israel's first military move in the conquest of Canaan. Much more is involved, however, than the crossing of the Jordan and the military maneuver that will lead to the Israelite victory over the city-state of Jericho. Behind those mo-

mentous steps is a morale issue.

For 40 years the Israelites have been led and guided by Moses. Just before his death, he turned the leadership over to the military leader, Joshua. With Moses having served so long, the question arises of how enthusiastic the people will be to follow Joshua. In this lesson, therefore, God takes definite steps to enlist their whole-hearted support of the new leader whom God has chosen for them.

ഇൻൽ

For a Lively Start

Lead your group in a brief discussion of specific character traits and other factors that would be involved if they were suddenly asked to follow a new leader in a specific new project with the church. Imagine a person, for example, with a building and loan company being asked to come in and inaugurate a building campaign or other

promotion that will require the full support of the people if it is successful.

What kind of personality will the new leader need—a dynamic and energetic spirit, or a steadier and more settled character? What might he or she do to win the trust of the people? What steps might be taken to involve "lieutenants" or other leaders at secondary levels? What pitfalls or mistakes could you name that would be important to avoid? What other factors that might affect whether a person such as Joshua succeeds?

Teaching Outline	Daily Bible Readings
I. Assembly at the Jordan—3:1-6	Mon. Military Leader *Exod. 17:8-16*
A. The ark goes first, 1-3	Tue. Optimistic Spy *Num. 14:6-10*
B. Sanctifying space, 4-6	Wed. Moses' Successor *Num. 27:12-23*
II. Magnifying Joshua—7-11	Thu. Charge to Joshua *Deut. 31:1-8*
A. 'As with Moses, so with thee,' 7-8	Fri. Spirit of Wisdom *Deut. 34:1-9*
B. Nations driven out, 9-11	Sat. 'The Lord Is With You' *Josh. 1:1-9*
III. Stopping the Jordan—12-13	Sun. Leadership Affirmed *Josh. 3:1-13*
IV. 'What Mean These Stones'?, 4:6-9	

Verse by Verse

I. Assembly at the Jordan—3:1-6

A. The ark goes first, 1-3

1 And Joshua rose early in the morning; and they removed from Shittim, and came to Jordan, he and all the children of Israel, and lodged there before they passed over.

2 And it came to pass after three days, that the officers went through the host;

3 And they commanded the people, saying, When ye see the ark of the covenant of the Lᴏʀᴅ your God, and the priests the Levites bearing it, then ye shall remove from your place, and go after it.

As mentioned earlier, Shittim (or Abel-Shittim) was about 10 miles to the northeast of the northern tip of the Dead Sea (or "Salt Sea"). Nearby was Mt. Nebo, where God led Moses for a glimpse into a Promised Land he would never see. The Bible says God Himself buried Moses atop Nebo, declining to let any of Moses' followers bury their leader lest they make a shrine of the place and elevate Moses in death

to the status of a god (see Deut. 34:1-6). The present scene, with the crossing of the Jordan once more at hand, is at the end of the 40-year wilderness sentence.

The presence of the ark and its attending priests at the head of the people signal a new attitude. With God and His supernatural forces leading them, perhaps they can "pass over" the Jordan instead of allowing their fears to cause them to turn back. The term "pass over" is used some 15 times in chapters 3–5. The repetition is a sign of demarcation. "This side" (the eastern side) of the Jordan now represents "the old Israel" that lacked the courage to invade Canaan 40 years earlier. "Passing over" represents the western side of the Jordan and "the new Israel," ready to follow Joshua and God's leadership, represented by the ark, in taking possession of the Promised Land that God had already given them.

B. Sanctifying space, 4-6

4 Yet there shall be a space between

you and it, about two thousand cubits by measure: come not near unto it, that ye may know the way by which ye must go: for ye have not passed this way heretofore.

5 And Joshua said unto the people, Sanctify yourselves: for to morrow the LORD will do wonders among you.

6 And Joshua spake unto the priests, saying, Take up the ark of the covenant, and pass over before the people. And they took up the ark of the covenant, and went before the people.

Although the ark is to have an important and visible part in the conquest of the land, Joshua's lieutenants go through Israel's army instructing them not to be on too familiar terms with what has come to be a holy—and hence untouchable—piece of ritual furniture. Ironically, the ark was made of shittim wood—the very name of Israel's final camp on the east side of the Jordan (see Exod. 25:10), overlaid within and without with pure gold. It contained a pot of manna, Aaron's rod that miraculously and continuously budded, and the two stone tablets containing the Ten Commandments.

Even more than its holy contents, the art was considered holy because it upheld "the mercy seat" and the cherubims of gold whose wings almost touched. Although it was forbidden to make a represention of God, it was considered that the invisible God dwelt upon the mercy seat—and thus atop the ark (Ps. 99:1). With all this symbolic holiness, it is not surprising that there were strict rules for carrying and even approaching the ark, witnessed by the well-meaning Uzzah who was stricken dead when he ventured to touch the ark (2 Sam. 6:6-7).

Here, on the verge of "crossing over" the Jordan, God seems to take up a special presence on the ark, since, not having traveled beyond the Jordan before, the people are instructed to follow it. Even so, they are to show their reverence for it by keeping three thousand feet away from it. They are also to "sanctify themselves," which probably consisted of washing their clothes (perhaps in the Jordan itself) and abstaining from sexual relationships (see Exod. 19:14-15). All this—the presence of the priests with the ark, the sanctifying of the people, and the promise that God is about to do amazing things for His people—lends a religious aura, not just that of a secular battle, to the preparations for "crossing over."

II. Magnifying Joshua—7-11
A. 'As with Moses, so with thee,' 7-8

7 And the LORD said unto Joshua, This day will I begin to magnify thee in the sight of all Israel, that they may know that, as I was with Moses, so I will be with thee.

8 And thou shalt command the priests that bear the ark of the covenant, saying, When ye are come to the brink of the water of Jordan, ye shall stand still in Jordan.

The presence of God, the ark, and the priests have already indicated that whatever victory Israel will win in the approaching battle against Jericho will be of the Lord's doing, not man's. Yet, as in most heavenly ventures, God needs earthly vessels through whom to work. In this case He has chosen the military leader Joshua as His strong right arm. As mentioned earlier, Moses has been that strength for more than 40 years, and the transition to a new leader will not be easy. God therefore chooses to perform one of his particularly "mighty works" in order to "magnify" (NIV "exalt") Joshua before all the people to convince them that Joshua is lacking in nothing when compared with Moses.

The miracle God chooses rivals the crossing of the Red Sea in dramatic effect. To prepare for it, the priests bearing the ark of the covenant are to hoist it on their shoulders, carrying it by the "staves" or poles made for this purpose, and march straight for the waters of the Jordan. When all the priests are standing in the near edge of the Jordan, they are to stop and await further orders.

B. Nations driven out, 9-11

9 And Joshua said unto the children of Israel, Come hither, and hear the words of the LORD your God.

10 And Joshua said, Hereby ye shall know that the living God is among you, and that he will without fail drive out from before you the Canaanites, and the Hittites, and the Hivites, and the Perizzites, and the Girgashites, and the Amorites, and the Jebusites.

11 Behold, the ark of the covenant of the Lord of all the earth passeth over before you into Jordan.

Now the commanding voice the people hear is that of Joshua himself. He reminds the people of God's enemies who now occupy the Promised Land. God is not arbitrarily taking the land from them merely out of favoritism for the Jews. The people there are guilty of some of history's most heinous crimes, including the violation of human rights by ruthless dictators, the worship of false gods, and even human sacrifice. Verse 10 names some of them, while other passages provide other names. "Canaanites" is something of a generic name, including smaller nations. "Jebusites" is the only group not attested in writings outside the Bible. With the naming of these nations, God is about to magnify Himself and His servant Joshua.

III. Stopping the Jordan—12-13

12 Now therefore take you twelve men out of the tribes of Israel, out of every tribe a man.

13 And it shall come to pass, as soon as the soles of the feet of the priests that bear the ark of the LORD, the Lord of all the earth, shall rest in the waters of Jordan, that the waters of Jordan shall be cut off from the waters that come down from above; and they shall stand upon an heap.

The role of the 12 men, one from each tribe, will be to carry one stone each for the building of a monument— a feat that will not be described until chapter 4. For now, the "wonder" God has chosen is to create a kind of "second exodus." The waters of the Jordan flowing from the north "stand upon an heap," or pile up as a wall, cut off from the waters that continue to flow south to the Dead Sea. The result is dry land, like that in the bed of the Red Sea, creating a path over which the armies of Israel, then finally the priests with the ark, march boldly into Canaan and on to Jericho.

Evangelistic Emphasis

From among my graduating class at a prominent Christian university, a mission team consisting of about a dozen couples formed and laid plans to take the gospel to a South American city.

During our last year in school, the committed members of the team spent many hours learning the language of their target area. They contacted dozens of churches and companies to raise support and to solicit equipment needed for their new work.

When this group of eager missionaries embarked, they were one of the best prepared, best equipped mission teams ever. Their awareness of their new culture and their technological tools for spreading the gospel were incredible.

By far the greatest response to their early efforts, however, came from the women in the villages. Before long these native ladies began to seek out the missionaries' wives. "Tell us what causes your husbands to be faithful to you," all of them wanted to know.

Evidently the men in that culture were just expected to have multiple lovers. The sexual faithfulness of the Christian husbands was a phenomenon there. "Hereby ye shall know that the living God is among you," Joshua said (3:10). What will people see in our churches that demonstrates God's presence?

৪০৩

Memory Selection

The LORD said unto Joshua, This day will I begin to magnify thee in the sight of all Israel, that they may know that, as I was with Moses, so I will be with thee.—*Joshua 3:7*

"Passing the torch" is always a delicate processes, especially if the outgoing leader has served a long time and is much loved. Dr. Winfred Moore pastored the largest church in our town for more than 20 years. He was a man about town, active in civic projects far beyond the scope of his congregation. Both inside and outside of his church people held him in high esteem, so all of us felt a deep sense of loss when he retired.

Wisely this good pastor discerned that it would be almost impossible for any successor to succeed if the former pastor stayed nearby. He accepted an invitation to go to Baylor University—far enough away to give the new man room to breathe. Still, I wonder how many times some thoughtless soul told him, "That's not how Winfred did it."

Winfred Moore is my dear friend and still a highly capable pastor. I rejoiced for his replacement, however, on the day when they stood side by side to preach the funeral of an influential member of their congregation. Both men did a good job, but, surprisingly, the new man out-preached the veteran. That day the torch passed. From that day on, Joshua could fill Moses' shoes and nobody in Israel would complain.

Weekday Problems

Some days require more faith than others, don't they?

How would you like to have been one of those priests who had to walk into the rampaging, flood-stage currents of the Jordan River? Water like that is treacherous. It can kill you. Stepping into torrents like that took a lot of faith.

If you can pilot an airplane, do you remember the first time you took off solo? Did you have butterflies in your belly?

If you can drive a car, do you remember the first time you got behind the wheel—even with a parent or a friend beside you?

If you are married, do you remember when you said "I do," and stepped into the vast unknown of marital responsibilities? Were you hit by a bad case of cold feet, wondering what in the world you were getting yourself into? If so, you were by no means the first bride or groom to feel that way.

I remember my first day on the job as a ground man in a utility substation construction crew. Working right under all that high voltage already had me a bit spooked. The first time I had to go looking for the restroom in the bowels of that huge power plant with the deafening roar of its steam-driven turbines overhead just about unnerved me.

Days like that—when we're daring visible dangers and stepping into the unknown—require extra faith. Without it, we will be crippled by our fears.

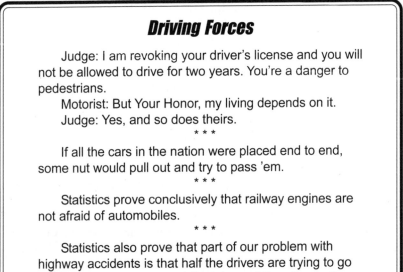

Driving Forces

Judge: I am revoking your driver's license and you will not be allowed to drive for two years. You're a danger to pedestrians.

Motorist: But Your Honor, my living depends on it.

Judge: Yes, and so does theirs.

* * *

If all the cars in the nation were placed end to end, some nut would pull out and try to pass 'em.

* * *

Statistics prove conclusively that railway engines are not afraid of automobiles.

* * *

Statistics also prove that part of our problem with highway accidents is that half the drivers are trying to go fast enough to thrill their girlfriends, and the other half are trying to go slow enough to please their wives.

This Lesson in Your Life

I have a standing annual gig at our community's finest retirement center. Several years ago the chaplain there invited me to speak at a special dinner for a unique group of their residents—people whose mates had died during the previous 12 months.

What could I say to a group like that? I had not walked in their shoes. Any comfort I tried to offer them surely would come off sounding hollow, at best. Finally I chose to base my brief remarks on the words in Joshua 1:4, "You have not passed this way before" (RSV). Joshua and his people were about to travel a new road into unfamiliar territory. That journey might stir in them a sense of dread or the thrill of adventure, for before them lay a land of giants, but also a land of milk and honey.

To that group of people on a new road, I pointed out that all of us eventually find ourselves on a road we have not traveled. Recently divorced, a friend of mine is single again for the first time in his adult life. Another friend is caring for a husband who has just been hit with Alzheimer's.

I shared those examples with my attentive hearers and affirmed to them that all of us at times feel like we're lost in the wilderness without a map— that we're groping in the darkness without a candle.

Then, out of Joshua 3, I offered these dear people some instructions for the new road. To begin with, Joshua told his people to *follow the Ark* (3:3). We are never on the road alone. If we stay close to Him, we have nothing to fear. He knows our needs, and He cares.

Then I pointed out that, like Joshua's people, we need to *obey the rules* (3:4) They had to keep a certain distance from the holy Ark. Joshua didn't explain why. It simply was God's way. Those who live by God's moral laws avoid many of the health problems and heartaches common to our time.

The third "instruction for the road" I shared that night was that we should *draw near to God.* Joshua told his people, "Consecrate yourselves, for tomorrow the LORD will do amazing things among you" (3:5, NIV).God's grace will be sufficient to see us through hard times.

A final rule for the unfamiliar road is that we should *remember God's past help.* Israel had crossed the Red Sea on dry ground. As children, many of them had seen God's victory there. Now it made sense to expect similar assistance from above.   40

Even so, I suggested to that group of new widows and widowers that they should expect the God who had seen them through past trials to aid them again. The same God still loves you, I assured them.

The Scriptures refer to Jesus as the Pioneer (RSV) or Trailblazer (Barclay) of our faith (Heb. 12:2). If we follow Him, I told my audience that night, we never have to be afraid to walk for the first time down any road.

1. How would the children of Israel know when to start packing up and preparing to cross the Jordan River?

Their cue would be when they saw the priests carrying the Ark of the Covenant toward the river.

2. How close were the people allowed to get to the Ark?

No closer than 2,000 cubits (1,000 yards—NIV).

3. How were the people supposed to prepare themselves for the great events of the coming day?

They people were to "sanctify" or "purify" (TEV) themselves. This entailed not eating any unclean food or touching anything that would defile them or make them unclean by the standards of Leviticus.

4. What did God tell Joshua He would do for him that day?

God promised that by the events of that day He would establish Joshua as Moses' rightful successor.

5. Where were the priests supposed to take the Ark of the Covenant?

To the river's edge.

6. When the priests got to the river, what were they supposed to do?

Joshua told them to stand in the water.

7. Whom did God promise to drive out of the land of Canaan so the Israelites could move in?

The seven nations who had lived there for centuries before this.

8. What does the Joshua account tell us about the level of the river on the day when Israel crossed it?

The river was at flood stage, so it should have been an impassable barrier keeping Israel on the eastern bank and out of Jericho's backyard.

9. What happened to the raging river when the priest's feet touched the water?

Immediately the water upstream began to pile up in a heap, so that the Israelites could pass through the riverbed downstream.

10. Where were the priests and what were they doing while the people crossed over the river?

The priests stood in the dry riverbed with the Ark on the shoulders until the last person in Israel's camp had safely crossed over to the bank near Jericho.

Uplift

Is there a more famous sport story that the one about Babe Ruth's legendary home run on October 1, 1932, at Wrigley Field in Chicago? In Game 3 of the 1932 World Series, when Babe Ruth came to the plate in the fifth inning, the Cubs players were riding him unmercifully. In the hubbub raised by the stadium full of Chicago fans, the famous Yankee slugger responded to the Cubs taunts with both gestures and shouts.

With the President of the nation, Franklin Delano Roosevelt, looking on from his box seat, Ruth took four pitches—a strike, two balls, and then another strike. At that point, according to Scripps-Howard sports editor Joe Williams, Babe Ruth pointed to center field. As Williams wrote in the next morning's newspaper, the slugger "called his shot," and on the next pitch he drove a screaming liner into the stands right where he said he would.

Although some later questioned some of the details in this sports story, without doubt Joe Williams' account of Babe Ruth's mighty blow made it the best-known homer in the history of major league baseball. This exploit became a core element of Ruth's larger-than-life image as the all-time hero of the game.

Joshua's chutzpah compares favorably with Babe Ruth's. How could he know that the flood-stage waters of the Jordan would be stanched when the priests stepped into the river? No doubt God had told him to expect it, but never before had Joshua done such an outlandish feat.

Wouldn't Joshua have looked silly to his people if he predicted a dry riverbed and the waters had continued to roll past unabated?

It takes special faith for us to believe that God really will do what He has promised. It takes even more faith for us to step out and act like we are sure His promises will come true.

Lesson 8

Samson's Mother Prepares for His Birth

Judges 13:1-13, 22-24

And the children of Israel did evil again in the sight of the LORD; and the LORD delivered them into the hand of the Philistines forty years.

2 And there was a certain man of Zorah, of the family of the Danites, whose name was Manoah; and his wife was barren, and bare not.

3 And the angel of the LORD appeared unto the woman, and said unto her, Behold now, thou art barren, and bearest not: but thou shalt conceive, and bear a son.

4 Now therefore beware, I pray thee, and drink not wine nor strong drink, and eat not any unclean thing:

5 For, lo, thou shalt conceive, and bear a son; and no razor shall come on his head: for the child shall be a Nazarite unto God from the womb: and he shall begin to deliver Israel out of the hand of the Philistines.

6 Then the woman came and told her husband, saying, A man of God came unto me, and his countenance was like the countenance of an angel of God, very terrible: but I asked him not whence he was, neither told he me his name:

7 But he said unto me, Behold, thou shalt conceive, and bear a son; and now drink no wine nor strong drink, neither eat any unclean thing: for the child shall be a Nazarite to God from the womb to the day of his death.

8 Then Manoah intreated the LORD, and said, O my Lord, let the man of God which thou didst send come again unto us, and teach us what we shall do unto the child that shall be born.

9 And God hearkened to the voice of Manoah; and the angel of God came again unto the woman as she sat in the field: but Manoah her husband was not with her.

10 And the woman made haste, and ran, and shewed her husband, and said unto him, Behold, the man hath appeared unto me, that came unto me the other day.

11 And Manoah arose, and went after his wife, and came to the man, and said unto him, Art thou the man that spakest unto the woman? And he said, I am.

12 And Manoah said, Now let thy words come to pass. How shall we order the child, and how shall we do unto him?

13 And the angel of the LORD said unto Manoah, Of all that I said unto the woman let her beware.

22 And Manoah said unto his wife, We shall surely die, because we have seen God.

23 But his wife said unto him, If the LORD were pleased to kill us, he would not have received a burnt offering and a meat offering at our hands, neither would he have shewed us all these things, nor would as at this time have told us such things as these.

24 And the woman bare a son, and called his name Samson: and the child grew, and the LORD blessed him.

Jan. 25

Memory Selection
Judges 13:5

Background Scripture
Judges 13

Devotional Reading
Ps. 91

Judges 13 provides encouragement to adults who are willing to make a commitment to raise, or help raise, children who have the opportunity to grow up to be faithful to the call of God on their lives. Samson's mother also shares the distinction of several other women in the Bible who, while barren at first, are granted children by a special act of God.

Of course not all adults become parents. Yet almost anyone can make himself available as official or unofficial "God-parent" for his friends' children. The church provides a special place for this kind of support, which the story of Samson illustrates and encourages.

ℛℭℛ

For a Lively Start

This lesson can be started with a light-hearted sharing of experiences which parents in the group have had with young children. Some women may, like Samson' mother, have had trouble conceiving at first, then, with or without special prayer, had far more children than they planned for.

Also include in your discussion whether any in the group have had God-parents or other special support from adult friends. How did this work? Did the God-parent provide any special support services, or was it mainly something like a best man at a wedding, where verbal or silent support was provided? In general, use this time to ask whether "It takes a church to raise a child."

Teaching Outline	Daily Bible Readings
I. Plans for Deliverance—13:1-5	Mon. Special Vows to God *Num. 6:1-8*
A. Philistine dominance, 1	Tue. Disobeying God *Judg. 2:1-5*
B. Angel's announcement, 2-5	Wed. A New Generation *Judg. 2:6-10*
II. Parents Conspire—6-13	
A. Woman's report, 6-7	Thu. Results of Unfaithfulness *Judg. 2:11-17*
B. Father's petition, 8-13	Fri. Judges Raised Up *Judg. 2:18-23*
III. Pleasing God—22-25	
A. Perception of Fear, 22-23	Sat. Offering to the Lord *Judg. 13:15-23*
B. Growing up blessed, 24	Sun. Promise of a Son *Judg. 13:1-13, 24*

Verse by Verse

I. Plans for Deliverance—13:1-5

A. Philistine dominance, 1

1 And the children of Israel did evil again in the sight of the LORD; and the LORD delivered them into the hand of the Philistines forty years.

The word "again" is, sadly, one of the most frequent words in the story of Israel during the period of the Conquest of Canaan. The people and their leaders can hold on to faithful living only sporadically, then they "*again* do evil in the sight of the Lord." The period of the Judges is so named because "the LORD raised up judges . . . and delivered [the people] out of the hand of their enemies" (Judg. 2:18). However, after the judge's death the pattern was for Israel to return to worshiping the gods of the pagans about them, to forget personal holiness and the sacrifices, and to neglect to do good to their neighbor. The Philistines, as here, were some of the most frequent tormentors of Israel during these times.

B. Angel's announcement, 2-5

2 And there was a certain man of Zorah, of the family of the Danites, whose name was Manoah; and his wife was barren, and bare not.

3 And the angel of the LORD appeared unto the woman, and said unto her, Behold now, thou art barren, and bearest not: but thou shalt conceive, and bear a son.

4 Now therefore beware, I pray thee, and drink not wine nor strong drink, and eat not any unclean thing:

5 For, lo, thou shalt conceive, and bear a son; and no razor shall come on his head: for the child shall be a Nazarite unto God from the womb: and he shall begin to deliver Israel out of the hand of the Philistines.

Through God's grace He plans to raise up another judge, this time out of the tribe of Dan, on the coast of the Mediterranean about even with the north shore of the Dead (or "Salt") Sea. We may well ask why God so often chooses a barren woman to be the mother of His special servants. Again, grace is the answer—first, because of the high value placed on having children, especially a son, the woman herself is graced; and second, for the same reason, she is graced in the eyes of her friends and neighbors, many of whom looked down on a woman who was without child.

The angel announced to the woman (she is nowhere named other than as "wife of Manoah") that when the child reaches maturity he will be identified as a special servant of God by reason of his uncut hair and abstinence from strong drink—two of the primary marks of "the Nazirite." (The third was not to touch or approach a dead body; see Num. 6:1ff.)

The KJV spelling is confusing because a "Nazirite" is not to be confused with a "Nazarite," which is simply a person from Nazareth. We are not given any reasons for taking the vow other than to "be separate," which the term "nazir" means. It could be taken for a limited period of time (as was possibly the case of the vow the apostle Paul took in Acts 18:18), or for a lifetime. In most cases the vow seems to have been voluntary, although, as indicated by the meaning "separate," it was taken as a sign of the level of spirituality among the people. The prophet Amos laments the fact that even when the vow was taken the people were careless about helping the committed person abstain from wine (Amos 2:11-12).

What is distinctive in the Nazirite vow in this case is that the rules apply to the Nazirite's mother as well to the chosen one. Although there were no prohibitions against a woman taking the vow, references to the vow in other accounts seem to apply only to the child, never to the mother.

II. Parents Conspire—6-13
A. Woman's report, 6-7

6 Then the woman came and told her husband, saying, A man of God came unto me, and his countenance was like the countenance of an angel of God, very terrible: but I asked him not whence he was, neither told he me his name:

7 But he said unto me, Behold, thou shalt conceive, and bear a son; and now drink no wine nor strong drink, neither eat any unclean thing: for the child shall be a Nazarite to God from the womb to the day of his death.

Again consistent with the patriarchal customs of the day, not only is Manoah's wife neither named nor called a Nazirite, she seems to have to have her encounter with the angel of the Lord confirmed by her husband. She identifies the angel as having a "terrible" countenance, which is interpreted by the NIV as "awesome."

B. Father's petition, 8-13

8 Then Manoah intreated the LORD, and said, O my Lord, let the man of God which thou didst send come again unto us, and teach us what we shall do unto the child that shall be born.

9 And God hearkened to the voice of Manoah; and the angel of God came again unto the woman as she sat in the field: but Manoah her husband was not with her.

10 And the woman made haste, and ran, and shewed her husband, and said unto him, Behold, the man hath appeared unto me, that came unto me the other day.

11 And Manoah arose, and went

after his wife, and came to the man, and said unto him, Art thou the man that spakest unto the woman? And he said, I am.

12 And Manoah said, Now let thy words come to pass. How shall we order the child, and how shall we do unto him?

13 And the angel of the LORD said unto Manoah, Of all that I said unto the woman let her beware.

Manoah, father-to-be of this special child, takes a special interest both in his wife's encounter with the angel and with how the child should be raised as well. However, the angel has no specific instructions for Manoah, but only enforces what he had told the woman about both her and the child's obedience to the rules of the Nazirite vow.

III. Pleasing God—22-25

A. Perception of Fear, 22-23

22 And Manoah said unto his wife, We shall surely die, because we have seen God.

23 But his wife said unto him, If the LORD were pleased to kill us, he would not have received a burnt offering and a meat offering at our hands, neither would he have shewed us all these things, nor would as at this time have told us such things as these.

In Exodus 33:20 and other places it seems to be against God's Law to look upon His face, although there are a few special exceptions. Manoah is not counting on an exception to the rule, however, and fears that merely looking on the face of the angel of God might mean death. His wife, more matter-of-fact, calmly observes that there would have been no benefit in appearing to them and making the announcement about their coming child-bearing, only to strike them dead. Also, it would be very inhospitable to enjoy a food offering and then say Thank-you by killing them.

B. Growing up blessed, 24

24 And the woman bare a son, and called his name Samson: and the child grew, and the LORD blessed him.

At the end of her pregnancy, Manoah's wife names the child Samson, which has the rather romantic meaning of "Serving like the sun." Unfortunately what most people recall are Samson's violations of the Nazirite vow (as when getting honey from the carcass of a lion), and allowing Delilah to cut his hair. He does, however, avenge Israel's servitude to the Philistines by killing many, then pulling down their temple and killing even more (16:25ff.).

ဆာ

Evangelistic Emphasis

I'm one of the luckiest guys on the planet. Every school day for the past 32 years I have been allowed to walk into a large public high school to teach a tough academic Bible course to eager students. I find out the paths my students are navigating, some of which have been steep and crooked.

I remember one student who was estranged from her parents. She lived in her own apartment with her boyfriend. She worked to pay her rent while struggling to graduate from school. I sensed a lot of hurt in her soul.

Right beside her sat two wholesome, happy, well-adjusted kids. They were so much fun—so alert and curious and excited to be alive. Both of them spoke often of their parents, always with warmth and respect. These were model kids. Peers and school staff alike esteemed them as straight, clean living, trustworthy young people.

In an age when many families turn out troubled children, homes that produce kids like the last two ought to be the envy of all their neighbors. Struggling parents who see other fathers and mothers doing it right must surely long to know the secret behind their success.

Manoah and his wife had something on the ball in the way they raised their son. This result of their faith must have impressed those who knew them. Does our parenting draw that kind of attention?

Memory Selection

ℰ)ℭℛ

Drink not wine nor strong drink, and eat not any unclean thing: For, lo, thou shalt conceive, and bear a son; and no razor shall come on his head: for the child shall be a Nazarite unto God from the womb: and he shall begin to deliver Israel out of the hand of the Philistines.—*Judges 13:4-5*

Recent studies reveal how much mental damage can be done to an infant if its mother drinks much alcohol during her pregnancy. Most women are aware of the horrid condition of crack babies born to addicted mothers. Until recently, however, a lot of people had no idea that a few innocent drinks during the early weeks of pregnancy can reduce a baby's I.Q. significantly. *Heavy* drinking by a pregnant woman can result in a baby with fetal alcohol distress syndrome. If such a baby survives, there is a high likelihood that such a child will have serious lifelong deficits.

Manoah and his wife didn't have access to all the modern medical studies about a mother's prenatal habits. What they did have was a plain instruction from heaven that implied that what she ate or drank during her pregnancy would affect her baby as much as his own diet would after he was born. All of this has interesting implications for the current legal and theological efforts to balance the rights of unborn children against those of mothers seeking abortions. Samson appears to have been Samson from the time of his conception. At least, his heaven-prescribed diet was in force even while he was in his mother's womb.

Weekday Problems

The word *Nazirite* is used in Judges 13:7 to describe the set of restrictions the angel specified for Samson's diet and lifestyle. The spelling of this term varies depending of the Bible version we consult, but in all of them it refers to a curious oath first described in detail in Numbers 6.

"Nazirite" sounds somewhat like "Nazareth," so some mistakenly conclude that it has some connection to the place of Jesus' birth. Moses described a Nazirite vow as "a vow of separation to the Lord" (Num. 6:2, NIV).

Moses indicates that either a male or a female might take such a vow, but later prohibitions about cutting hair or shaving during the time of the vow seems to imply predominantly male participation. All of the Bible accounts of someone taking such a vow involve men (Samson, Samuel, and Paul). In Samson and Samuel's cases, the vow lasted a lifetime. In Paul's case, the oath was only for a specific time.

The nearest equivalent in our culture would be a Lenten vow, where a believer agrees to give up some food item or pleasure for a certain number of days. (When we had three pre-schoolers at home, my wife often volunteered to give up her children for Lent—and we didn't even believe in Lent!)

The Nazirite vow was a voluntary form of selective fasting. It helped people deepen their spiritual discipline and draw near to the Lord. What spiritual exercises have you tried that help you do that?

Failures to Abstain

At the police station the indignant drunk demanded, "What I want to know is why I was brought in here."

"You were brought in for drinking too much," the sergeant said.

"Well, that's different," the pacified drunk replied. "When do we get started?"

* * *

A drunk was walking along the street, one foot on the curb and the other in the gutter. "Why are you walking that way?" a cop demanded. "You must be drunk."

"Oh thank heavens," said the drunk. "I thought I was lame."

* * *

A drunk in the Empire State Building pried open a closed elevator door, stepped into the shaft and fell 30 stories. Dazed, he got up, shook his fist angrily toward the 30th story, and exclaimed, "I said UP!"

This Lesson in Your Life

One of the ubiquitous e-mail forwards that gets recycled every few months is a series of letters purportedly written by children in a church school. You've probably seen them. Forgive me for doubting their source, but most of the letters sound to me like not-quite-clever-enough fabrications purposely worded to make them sound as if innocent kids had penned them.

Whether they are true or not, for our purposes on this page (which is being written by a white-haired old codger who is just rejoicing to be around to turn another calendar page), one of those too-cute letters strikes a note worth pondering.

"Dear God," this probably fictitious 8-year-old prayed, "I am doing the best I can. Really." Signed: "Frank."

Toward the end of the year just past, if we had been asked, "Are you doing your best?" I suspect many of us would have echoed Frank and said Yes. But are we really?

If our boss told us today that by doing a bit more each day at work we can earn a bonus of 10 percent of our wages at the end of this year, how many of us would reply, "Nah. Keep your money. I can't do one thing extra?"

If your coach told you that he would guarantee you a slot on the first string if you faithfully ran an extra lap after practice every day, would you turn him down? If an "extra lap" of attentiveness or consideration would transform your so-so marriage into one that is fun and warm again, could you do it?

Like long-distance runners, deep within us most of us have an unexpected reserve of energy—enough to provide that extra kick it often takes to win.

We think we're running full-out, but often it turns out we're not. All we need is the right motivation to reach deeper, push harder, climb higher.

Is that what the apostle Paul had in mind when he said, "I press on toward the goal of the prize of the high calling of God in Christ Jesus"? One Bible version says here, "I strain toward the finish line."

Right now would be a great time for each of us to take stock of who we are and to ask, "Am I really doing my best? Or have I been so tired, so bored, so discouraged that I have begun to coast without putting forth my best effort?"

When the Lord's angel outlined to Manoah and his wife what God wanted them to do, they could have told him, "No way. We're too old to take on a task like that. We never could get a kid to conform to those crazy rules." Content with life as they had come to know it, they could have turned their back on God's plans to bless them and to free their nation.

Of this much I am sure. You are the only person who can make you reach out for God's blessings by agreeing to do your best. That call is up to you.

1. Why had God allowed Israel to be oppressed by the Philistines for 40 years?
Because the nation had done evil.

2. How does the Bible describe Manoah and his wife?
They were a childless couple in the tribe of Dan.

3. What did the angel tell Manoah's wife?
He told her she would have a son who would be required to live as a Nazirite, drinking no wine, eating nothing unclean, never allowing a razor to touch his head.

4. According to the angel, what would this son of Manoah do for Israel?
The angel said God would use this lad to deliver the people of Israel from the oppression of the Philistines.

5. Was Manoah's wife sure that she had talked to an angel?
Evidently not entirely, but that was the best explanation she could give for the strange conversation she had.

6. What was Manoah reaction to his wife's tale about the angel?
He asked God to send the angel again so he would see him and make sure his wife had understood the instructions.

7. When the angel appeared a second time, did he come to Manoah or to Manoah's spouse?
The angel came again to the woman while she was alone in the field. She had to summon her husband.

8. How did Manoah respond to God's plans for him when the angel reaffirmed his earlier message to the woman?
Manoah agreed to be used by God. "Let thy words come to pass," he told the angel. Then he asked for fuller instructions.

9. What spectacular thing happened when the Manoah offered a sacrifice to God on a rock?
Jumping into the flames leaping up from the offering, the angel ascended to heaven and vanished from their sight.

10. What did Manoah and his wife name their baby boy, and what did God do for him?
They called their son Samson, and after he matured, God began to send His Spirit to motivate and empower the young man.

My legs ached at night so bad that I cried and could not sleep. At first my parents assumed I had played too hard the day before or perhaps had strained or bruised myself while rough-housing with my playmates or my siblings. But the pain persisted.

I was barely five years old when my mother got the crushing news that her middle child had rheumatic fever.

I was the sick one in the family. I was the one in pain. I was the one whose future health hung in the balance while doctors with their scant knowledge of this dread disease ran primitive tests to find out if it had damaged my heart valves or diluted my blood cell count.

The doctor's diagnosis, however, amounted to a year-long sentence for my mother. For most of the next year, my 30-year-old mom would be trapped in our small house nursing a bedfast child. Forget going to church, eating out in a restaurant, walking on the seashore, or just meandering around town. She was my full-time nurse.

Back then I was too young to worry about how my sickness was impacting my mother. All of my pity was reserved for me. During that endless year, I lay on a rented hospital bed. I can't begin to tell you how much I wanted out of that bed. Surely my mother wanted out of our house even more, but she never breathed a complaint to me.

When that hard year passed and I was healthy enough to go to first grade in September, both Mom and I felt liberated. I remember how careful she was for me, how concerned she was that I might over-exert myself and suffer a relapse.

Her concern backfired. All of her attempts to treat me like a hot-house pot plant made me that much more determined to prove I could do anything any kid could. Now that my mother is in heaven, I look back and realize how grateful I should be for all she gave up and all she did for me during those difficult years. Unintentionally, I cost her many a tear.

Years later when it was apparent that God would use my gifts and that my ministry would be fruitful, did my mother realize her earlier sacrifices had made this possible? I wonder.

Samson's Nazirite restrictions must have made life hard for his mother. As he matured, some of his decisions surely cost her some sleepless nights. He stretched her soul. I hope she lived long enough to see God using her son to set Israel free. Then she would know that her costly commitment had been worth it all.

Lesson 9

A Shunammite Woman Helps

2 Kings 4:8-17

And it fell on a day, that Elisha passed to Shunem, where was a great woman; and she constrained him to eat bread. And so it was, that as oft as he passed by, he turned in thither to eat bread.

9 And she said unto her husband, Behold now, I perceive that this is an holy man of God, which passeth by us continually.

10 Let us make a little chamber, I pray thee, on the wall; and let us set for him there a bed, and a table, and a stool, and a candlestick: and it shall be, when he cometh to us, that he shall turn in thither.

11 And it fell on a day, that he came thither, and he turned into the chamber, and lay there.

12 And he said to Gehazi his servant, Call this Shunammite. And when he had called her, she stood before him.

13 And he said unto him, Say now unto her, Behold, thou hast been careful for us with all this care; what is to be done for thee? wouldest thou be spoken for to the king, or to the captain of the host? And she answered, I dwell among mine own people.

14 And he said, What then is to be done for her? And Gehazi answered, Verily she hath no child, and her husband is old.

15 And he said, Call her. And when he had called her, she stood in the door.

16 And he said, About this season, according to the time of life, thou shalt embrace a son. And she said, Nay, my lord, thou man of God, do not lie unto thine handmaid.

17 And the woman conceived, and bare a son at that season that Elisha had said unto her, according to the time of life.

Feb. 1

Memory Selection
2 Kings 4:9-10

Background Scripture
2 Kings 4:8-17

Devotional Reading
Luke 6:32-36

For a Lively Start

In this series on Bible characters who exhibited outstanding commitment, we come now to one of the several stories in 2 Kings that highlight the work of the prophet Elisha. The focus, however, is not on Elisha but on the commitment of a woman who befriended the prophet. She lived in a place called Shunem, some 15 miles southwest of the Sea of Galilee. We do not know her name; she is called simply "the Shunammite."

We do know of the woman's care for the prophet. In appreciation, Elisha arranges for her to have the miraculous gift of a son. Suddenly he dies. How will a woman who received such a gift react?

This lesson follows several recent studies that emphasize the importance of women of Israel begging for, and eventually receiving as a gift from God, a son. Elisabeth and Sarah were both past the age of child-bearing, but through God's grace they bore sons anyway. In a similar way, Samson's mother had her prayer for a son answered.

To introduce this, yet another lesson involving a woman whom God miraculously graced with a child late in life, discuss this high value Israelite women of old placed on having children—especially a son. What do members of a modern Bible study group think of this value? What about women who wanted children but had no miracle worked to give them any? Evaluate this cultural fact both from our standpoint and that of ancient times.

Teaching Outline	Daily Bible Readings
	Mon. The Call of Elisha *1 Kings 19:15-21*
I. Hospitality for a Prophet—4:8-10	Tue. The Prophet's Mantle *2 Kings 2:9-15*
A. The prophet's path, 8	
B. Idea for comfort, 9-10	Wed. Prayer for a Child *2 Kings 4:27-37*
II. In Return for Hospitality—11-14	Thu. Death of Elisha *2 Kings 13:14-20*
A. No immediate needs, 11-13	
B. What about a son?, 14	Fri. Hurrying for Help *2 King 4:18-26*
III. A Son in Her Old Age, 15-17	Sat. Miracle of Life *2 Kings 4:27-36*
IV. Postscript (Summary: vss. 18-37)	Sun. Jesus on Elijah and Elisha *Luke 4:23-30*

Verse by Verse

I. Hospitality for a Prophet—4:8-10

A. The prophet's path, 8

8 And it fell on a day, that Elisha passed to Shunem, where was a great woman; and she constrained him to eat bread. And so it was, that as oft as he passed by, he turned in thither to eat bread.

Elisha was just as colorful a prophet as his predecessor Elijah, who had been taken into heaven in a whirlwind (2 Kings 2:1ff.), leaving Elisha as his successor. The careers of both prophets were filled with miracles, as though God was trying to convince Israel that He sent them, and that they and their unruly kings should listen to them.

One way God demonstrated His power in the life of these prophets was to whisk them away from one place to another. In the present scene, however, Elisha is afoot, and his work frequently takes him past a small village called Shunem (which is still identifiable, but is now called Solem). A well-to-do woman (the KJV "great woman" means great not in size but in material wealth!) simply called a woman of Shunem, or

"the Shunammite," notices this habitual pathway taken by Elisha and his servant Gehazi. Being given to hospitality, she begins to make a habit of providing the prophet with a snack as he passes by.

B. Idea for comfort, 9-10

9 And she said unto her husband, Behold now, I perceive that this is an holy man of God, which passeth by us continually.

10 Let us make a little chamber, I pray thee, on the wall; and let us set for him there a bed, and a table, and a stool, and a candlestick: and it shall be, when he cometh to us, that he shall turn in thither.

Providing a food break grows into the idea of providing the prophet with a small room in which to rest or even spend the night. Building the room "on the wall" probably means atop one of the walls, resulting in a small room on the roof, a common feature of houses in that day and time.

II. In Return for Hospitality—11-14

A. No immediate needs, 11-13

11 And it fell on a day, that he came thither, and he turned into the chamber, and lay there.

12 And he said to Gehazi his servant, Call this Shunammite. And when he had called her, she stood before him.

13 And he said unto him, Say now unto her, Behold, thou hast been careful for us with all this care; what is to be done for thee? wouldest thou be spoken for to the king, or to the captain of the host? And she answered, I dwell among mine own people.

Elisha is somewhat taken with the Shunammite woman's gracious efforts to make him comfortable as he makes his way to and fro in the area. He instructs his servant to ask the woman to speak to him about any needs which she might have, and which Elisha might meet. He even suggests that he might speak to the king if she has any needs which politics might meet. (Although both Elijah and Elisha are often at odds with the reigning kings of Israel, Elisha is on good terms with the present king, Jehoram.)

The Shunammite woman, however, can think of nothing Elisha can do for her. She has enough money to add a room to her house, and she says here that she lives close to her own family. Her needs seem to be met.

B. What about a son?, 14

14 And he said, What then is to be done for her? And Gehazi answered, Verily she hath no child, and her husband is old.

At a loss to know what to do for the woman, Elisha asks his servant for advice. We wonder why the prophet hasn't already noticed that the woman has no children, a fact which his servant Gehazi readily supplies when asked. We may also marvel that Gehazi thinks that Elisha might be able to do something about her family situation. Apparently he has seen the prophet work enough miracles that his confidence is unbounded.

III. A Son in Her Old Age, 15-17

15 And he said, Call her. And when he had called her, she stood in the door.

16 And he said, About this season, according to the time of life, thou shalt embrace a son. And she said, Nay, my lord, thou man of God, do not lie unto thine handmaid.

17 And the woman conceived, and bare a son at that season that Elisha had said unto her, according to the time of life.

The woman's response is somewhat surprising, but real. It would be a cruel joke to promise a child to a woman who is past the age of child-bearing, and the woman's response indicates that such a promise would be too good to be true. Sure enough, "about this season," about nine months or nearly a year later, she rejoices in bearing a son.

IV. Postscript (Summary: vss. 18-37)

Although space does not allow the rest of the story to be printed in the text, verses 18-37 are essential for giving further insight into the woman's commitment and trust.

While working with his father and the reapers, the son suffers what seems to be a sunstroke. Although a servant rushes the child to his mother, it is too late, and he dies. The woman takes the child into Elisha's new room and lays him on the bed. Then she has a servant drive her in a cart to Elisha, who is at Mt. Carmel. She is understandably upset, and her confrontation with the prophet has in it a touch of bitterness. She reminds him that she had not asked for a son, and in fact had begged the prophet not to deceive her. Now she feels betrayed.

Elisha instructs his servant Gehazi to go to the child and place the prophet's staff—which had belonged to Elijah—and to place it upon the child's face. Thinking to heal him by "long distance," he bids the woman to go home. However, she will not hear of it, and her response moves Elisha to go to her house himself. Sure enough, Gehazi has been unable to restore the lad to life.

Nonplussed, Elisha is not through. Strangely, he stretches himself out on top of the child, places his mouth on the child's mouth, and apparently breathes the breath of life back into the boy. Of course his mother is overjoyed, and bows herself before the prophet.

Thus does the story of the Shunammite woman end, except for a minor incident years later. In punishment for Israel's disobedience, God is about to send a seven-year famine on the land, through Elisha. The prophet does not fail to remember the woman of Shunem, and he is thoughtful enough to warn her to find refuge in Philistia until it is over (2 Kings 8:1ff.). She returns after the famine and raises a public cry against such evils as those that caused the famine. The king inquires of Gehazi about her history, and is so impressed that he restores to her the crops and fruit of the land destroyed by the famine.

Of course this story is not meant to teach that God will always reward such commitment materially. It does remind us that we serve a God whose power has been, can be, and in the end will be, exercised in behalf of the good of those who are committed to Him.

ഇൗ

Evangelistic Emphasis

If you wanted to encourage a pastor or a Christian leader who is busy spreading the gospel, what could you do for that person? The rich lady at Shunem added a room to her house for the prophet. It was his to use whenever he came through the area. Most of us are not rich, however. What could we do to assist a Kingdom worker?

My own minister father was invited every two or three years to a church in the Texas panhandle as a guest preacher. On almost every visit, one member there—not a wealthy fellow—took my dad to a local clothing store and bought him a new suit. My father never asked for such favors, but in those post-Depression days, it was a marvelous help to a poorly paid pastor who had a family to feed and clothe.

As I traveled to speak at churches all across America, hospitable people in literally dozens of towns opened their homes to me. Instead of staying in hotel rooms, I much preferred the company of such friends. In their homes I knew which bedroom was mine, and we often referred to it as my "Elisha's room."

These generous souls who temporarily turned their home into a pastor's bed and breakfast probably lacked my ability to write a sermon or to proclaim the word of God to large assemblies, but they made it possible for me to do so by doing what they could do well.

What could you and I do to assist those who preach the word?

෴

Memory Selection

Behold now, I perceive that this is an holy man of God, which passeth by us continually. Let us make a little chamber, I pray thee, on the wall; and let us set for him there a bed, and a table, and a stool, and a candlestick: and it shall be, when he cometh to us, that he shall turn in thither.—*2 Kings 4:9-10*

What picture comes to your mind when you try to envision "the little chamber" this well-to-do lady wanted to build for Elisha "on the wall"? From that description, it's hard for me to get a clear idea of where it was positioned and what it might have looked like. Some Bible versions tell us it was a small room on the roof of the rich woman's house. Others add that it was a room with walls on her roof, or "a small upper room on the wall."

Elisha's benefactor and her husband did furnish the room comfortably for the prophet. Instead of a "candlestick," all the newer versions probably are on target in telling us Elisha had a "lamp." Do these precise details matter? Not really. We can grasp the extent of the Shunammite's generosity even if we don't have the exact floor plan of Elisha's new diggings. But most of us do find that the Bible events tend to come alive for us more vividly if we can visualize their settings as the Bible depicts them.

Weekday Problems

My soul delights in one sterling couple in my church. In every way they are special people who make life better for all of us who know them. These are accomplished people, tops in their fields. Their home reflects their loving spirit. It is a warm, comfortable, welcoming place.

Whenever we see these delightful people they are smiling. Life has been good for them, and they radiate their gratefulness for this.

One dark cloud parked over their heads, however. Having grown up in happy, active homes, they longed for a family; but for years they had none. They traveled many miles and spent a fortune consulting with medical experts looking for help in getting pregnant, but, like that couple in Shunem, they had everything but a child.

Did you notice the Bible's rather strange description of the plight of the Shunammite couple? Unlike Bible stories where Scripture tells us the woman was barren, this story tells us in 8:14, "Her husband is old." It sounds almost like a Viagra commercial, doesn't it? In a world where so many pregnancies are aborted—where the prospect of the birth of a child is perceived as a disaster, this Bible story is refreshing. Elisha wanted to bless the lady who provided so kindly for him, and the best blessing he could think of was a baby.

After years of expensive, frustrating trying, the young couple I started telling you about were able to conceive a son. Today they have two. Like the Shunammite woman, they will tell you that these fine little boys are blessings sent to them by God.

More Daffynitons: A Diplomat Is . . .

- A person who prefers ironing out his differences to flattening his opponent.

- A person who thinks twice before she says nothing.

- A man who is able to convince his wife that she would only look stocky in a fur coat.

- A man who remembers a woman's birthday, but forgets her age.

- A person who can be disarming while his country is building up arms stockpiles.

- Someone who can juggle a hot potato long enough for it to become a cold issue.

- A person who can bring home the bacon without spilling the beans.

This Lesson in Your Life

In our cynical age it would be easy to conclude that every person we deal with has a selfish agenda, always asking "What can I get out of it?"

Not long ago I passed through the room where a swarm of my younger grandchildren were wrestling on the rug while a TV ballgame went largely ignored behind them. As I watched without comment, a commercial came on. As such advertising goes, it was a rather bland pitch—something about toothpaste or mouthwash, I think. It shocked me to hear a 3-year-old granddaughter look up briefly from her play to debunk the claims of the talking head in the commercial.

Whatever he was trying to sell, she wasn't buying. She doubted the veracity of his claims and the genuineness of his motives. And this child is just three!

At gut level, at bottom line, we expect the people we deal with in our world to be out to get something, don't we?

Do you remember the lady who tried to organize the Random Acts of Kindness efforts? I didn't follow it all that closely and I don't know many details of how all of it unfolded. I do know that after a surprising amount of fanfare in national media and magazines, the effort kind of fizzled.

Critics battered the RAOK founder. They took all the fun out of her dream project, mainly, it seems, because they simply could not believe she was not in it for fame and fortune.

In a greedy, grasping, ugly world it's hard to believe in generosity without strings attaching. Some folks like to doubt even Mother Teresa, simply because, like most of us, we occasionally have doubts.

Like Jesus, that awesome lady came not to be served, but to serve. She came, like our Lord, not to get but to give. Like Elisha's benefactor in Shunem, she offered a gift and was somewhat taken aback when anyone suggested that she should be rewarded in return.

How rare of those who do not expect at least a thank you, and often far more, in return for any good they have done.

In his autobiographical work, *The Seven-Storey Mountain*, Trappist monk Thomas Merton commented about how many religious people see their almsgiving as "an easy and simple way of wiping out sins." Even on this higher spiritual level of life, he says, too many of us give, expecting something in return. We go to church, put our dollars in the heavenly vending machine, and expect it to spit out blessings.

Seen in this light, that lady in Shunem must have been an extraordinary soul. God basically told her through His prophet, "Tell Me what you want." Incredibly, she asked for nothing.

GETTING THE FACTS STRAIGHT

1. Where was Shunem, the town Elisha visited?
Shunem was located just a few miles south of what we would later call the Sea of Galilee. It was in the tribal area of Issachar just east of the Jordan River and about 10 miles from Nazareth.

2. Who extended hospitality to Elisha in Shunem?
A "great" lady and her husband. Other versions describe her as wealthy or well-to-do.

3. What did they do for the prophet?
At first they provided him meals when he came to their area.

4. What did the lady suggest to her husband that they should provide for Elisha?
She proposed building and furnishing a small room where the prophet could lodge when he visited Shunem.

5. Why did the Shunnamite woman think they should do this for Elisha?
She told her husband that she could see that Elisha was really a great man of God.

6. Whom did Elisha send to visit with the hospitable lady?
He sent his servant Gehazi.

7. What did Elisha want to find out from the woman?
He asked Gehazi to find out what they could do for her to repay her kindness to them.

8. What did she ask for?
Nothing.

9. What idea did Gehazi come up with as he and Elisha pondered what they could do for their friend?
Gehazi pointed out to the prophet that this wealthy lady did not have a child.

10. What was the woman's reaction when Elisha told her she would have a baby in nine months?
She could not believe it. "Don't lie to me," she replied.

Uplift

In January, 1983, a portrait of the poet Robert Service appeared on the cover the Salvation Army's magazine *War Cry*. Among other things the Army was honoring him for writing some of his most unforgettable lines:

> I wanted the gold and I got it—
> Came out with a fortune last fall.
> Yet somehow life's not what I thought it,
> And somehow the gold isn't all.

Former chaplain of the U. S. Senate, Dr. Richard Halverson, told of riding from the airport in the luxury sedan of a rising young corporate executive.

They had not driven too far when this earnest fellow cut to the heart of who he was. "Dr. Halverson," he told the graying pastor, "I made more money last year than I ever hoped I could. My wife and I live in a mansion. We have six expensive cars parked in our garage. We can afford to travel anywhere any time. We are wealthy beyond our dreams. But something is missing. We're not happy."

What a wise man, and how fortunate he was, to discern the emptiness of his life before he used up his years. He had tumbled to the great truth spoken by Jesus centuries ago. Our lives really do not consist of our possessions.

In the *Caesar and Christ* volume of his 10-volume *History of Civilization*, Will Durant described the Roman culture about 150 years before Jesus was born. It was a prosperous, materialistic age. Durant said, "Everyone longed for money, everyone judged or was judged in terms of money."

"How are you doing?" I asked a good buddy rather flippantly one day. His reply was just as off-handed, "I'm fine." After a short pause, he added, "There's nothing wrong with me that a few more dollars wouldn't cure." He really was not as greedy or materialistic as that comment makes him sound. Little did he know how wrong he was. He had plenty of dollars in the bank when diabetes and cancer and kidney failure ended his life. "A few more dollars" didn't help.

Our heroine in Shunem understood the point I'm pressing here. She, too, had possessions to burn. She said herself that she didn't need anyone to lobby for her or to pull strings in high places. She had all the clout she needed to prosper. All of her wealth and power, however, could not make her happy. Not the way that baby did. Until the child came, she had everything—except happiness.

Lesson 10

Nathan Challenges David

2 Sam. 12:1-7a, 13-15, 19-23

And the LORD sent Nathan unto David. And he came unto him, and said unto him, There were two men in one city; the one rich, and the other poor.

2 The rich man had exceeding many flocks and herds:

3 But the poor man had nothing, save one little ewe lamb, which he had bought and nourished up: and it grew up together with him, and with his children; it did eat of his own meat, and drank of his own cup, and lay in his bosom, and was unto him as a daughter.

4 And there came a traveller unto the rich man, and he spared to take of his own flock and of his own herd, to dress for the wayfaring man that was come unto him; but took the poor man's lamb, and dressed it for the man that was come to him.

5 And David's anger was greatly kindled against the man; and he said to Nathan, As the LORD liveth, the man that hath done this thing shall surely die:

6 And he shall restore the lamb fourfold, because he did this thing, and because he had no pity.

7 And Nathan said to David, Thou art the man.

13 And David said unto Nathan, I have sinned against the LORD. And Nathan said unto David, The LORD also hath put away thy sin; thou shalt not die.

14 Howbeit, because by this deed thou hast given great occasion to the enemies of the LORD to blaspheme, the child also that is born unto thee shall surely die.

15 And Nathan departed unto his house. And the LORD struck the child that Uriah's wife bare unto David, and it was very sick.

19 But when David saw that his servants whispered, David perceived that the child was dead: therefore David said unto his servants, Is the child dead? And they said, He is dead.

20 Then David arose from the earth, and washed, and anointed himself, and changed his apparel, and came into the house of the LORD, and worshipped: then he came to his own house; and when he required, they set bread before him, and he did eat.

21 Then said his servants unto him, What thing is this that thou hast done? thou didst fast and weep for the child, while it was alive; but when the child was dead, thou didst rise and eat bread.

22 And he said, While the child was yet alive, I fasted and wept: for I said, Who can tell whether GOD will be gracious to me, that the child may live?

23 But now he is dead, wherefore should I fast? can I bring him back again? I shall go to him, but he shall not return to me.

Memory Selection
2 Sam. 11:27–12:1

Background Scripture
2 Sam. 12:1-23

Devotional Reading
Ps. 51:1-9

Feb. 8

In our survey of biblical figures who demonstrate outstanding commitment, we must not omit those whose commitment faces them with the unpleasant, the socially awkward, even the dangerous. This is the case with Nathan the prophet, whom God charged with the task of confronting King David with his sin with Bathsheba and the murder of her husband Uriah the Hittite.

Nathan approaches his task through the now-famous parable of the rich man who stole a poor man's only sheep, a pet lamb. To us the story is transparently about David; but Nathan has to point out the painfully clear point that the story describes the king himself. Nathan's life was on the line.

ℰℭℛ

For a Lively Start

Relate the following true story to the class, and discuss points from it that may be parallel to the point of this lesson, as described in the "Focus" section.

An Associate Minister was caught embezzling church funds. Knowing he was about to be exposed, the minister applied for, and won, an appointment at another church. The chair of the board at the first church learned about the new job before the minister moved. She wondered whether she should contact the church that was about to hire the minister and report his misdeed. Would that be unfairly letting his mistake follow him? Or would the new church possibly experience a similar problem if they weren't warned? What if anything should be done?

Teaching Outline	Daily Bible Readings

I. Confrontation with David—12:1-7a
  A. Rich man, poor man, 1-4
  B. The king's judgment, 5-6
  C. 'Thou art the man,' 7a
II. Confession and Punishment
  A. David's confession, 13
  B. Forgiveness and punishment, 14-15
III. Response to punishment, 19-23
  A. Death of the child, 19-20
  B. Realistic response, 21-23
	Mon. Lust and Adultery
	    2 Sam. 11:1-5
	Tue. Unsuccessful Cover-up
	    2 Sam. 11:6-13
	Wed. Contrived Murder
	    2 Sam. 11:14-21
	Thu. An Easy Conscience
	    2 Sam. 11:22-27
	Fri. Cry for Forgiveness
	    Ps. 51:1-9
	Sat. A Broken and
	    Contrite Heart
	    Ps. 51:10-19
	Sun. 'You Are the Man!'
	    2 Sam. 12:1-7, 13-15

Verse by Verse

I. Confrontation with David—12:1-7a

A. Rich man, poor man, 1-4

1 And the LORD sent Nathan unto David. And he came unto him, and said unto him, There were two men in one city; the one rich, and the other poor.

2 The rich man had exceeding many flocks and herds:

3 But the poor man had nothing, save one little ewe lamb, which he had bought and nourished up: and it grew up together with him, and with his children; it did eat of his own meat, and drank of his own cup, and lay in his bosom, and was unto him as a daughter.

4 And there came a traveller unto the rich man, and he spared to take of his own flock and of his own herd, to dress for the wayfaring man that was come unto him; but took the poor man's lamb, and dressed it for the man that was come to him.

This approach to justice was light-years ahead of any of the nations around Israel. In their systems, the king encompassed all three of the branches of our own government—legislative, executive and judicial. In Israel, however, the king had to write a copy of the Law of Moses by which he would make his judgments (Deut. 17:15-20). In the time of David, this written code was supplemented with the word of a prophet such as Nathan. Still, this system was often violated, and Nathan understandably could have trembled in fear, as had Samuel when he brought a word of rebuke from God to King Saul.

Nathan's parable—or God's through Nathan—realistically fixes the setting of the parable in the eternal conflict between the rich and the poor. Again, Israel's Law was supposed to provide for the poor (Exod. 23:11), and as "a man after God's own heart" David would have been sensitive to the blatant injustice of the rich man's theft of the poor man's ewe lamb. That the poor man fed his pet lamb at his own table heightens our sympathy for him.

The parable's reference points are

223

painfully clear to us, but David's infatuation with Bathsheba blinds him to the point of the story. Of course Uriah is the poor man, Bathsheba is his pet lamb, and the rich man and his flocks stand for David and his vast wealth.

B. The king's judgment, 5-6

5 And David's anger was greatly kindled against the man; and he said to Nathan, As the LORD liveth, the man that hath done this thing shall surely die:

6 And he shall restore the lamb fourfold, because he did this thing, and because he had no pity.

The Law of Moses had already written part of the judgment against such a case, requiring five oxen in repayment for the theft of one, and four sheep for one, as in Nathan's parable. David adds his own wrath at such a blatant miscarriage of justice, and supplements his ruling with the rich man's death, plus an oath: "As the Lord liveth." His own conscience has led him into Nathan's trap so neatly that we wonder if subconsciously David is ruling against himself and a huge case of unconfessed shame and guilt.

C. 'Thou art the man,' 7a

7 And Nathan said to David, Thou art the man.

We can almost see Nathan pointing a bony prophetic finger at the king as he brings the parable home in four memorable words: "Thou art the man." Psalm 51 shows how these words of judgment pierced David's heart: "I acknowledge my transgressions: and my sin is ever before me" (Ps. 51: 3).

II. Confession and Punishment
A. David's confession, 13

13 And David said unto Nathan, I have sinned against the LORD. And Nathan said unto David, The LORD also hath put away thy sin; thou shalt not die.

It is to the king's credit that he does not quibble or protest. He has obviously been struggling with his conscience, and his confession flows so quickly that it seems he was waiting for the prophetic word to bring to the surface the guilt that was eating away David's heart. Again from the Psalms, David's experience of sin and silence, followed by confession and forgiveness, seems to be expressed in Psalm 32:1-5. The fact that God has already "put away thy sin" or forgiven David shows the difference between David, or anyone ready to confess his sin, and Saul, who was too defensive for such an admission of guilt.

B. Forgiveness and punishment, 14-15

14 Howbeit, because by this deed thou hast given great occasion to the enemies of the LORD to blaspheme, the child also that is born unto thee shall surely die.

15 And Nathan departed unto his house. And the LORD struck the child that Uriah's wife bare unto David, and it was very sick.

Still, although God's grace has covered David's sin, there is the matter of consequences. David has not only done evil to Uriah and Bathsheba; his sin was so public that it gave Israel's enemies generous opportunity to blaspheme God. "He has preached righteousness and condemned our sin, but now he has shown himself to be a sinner. What sort of God would allow a murderer and adulterer to remain on the throne?" They do not understand grace, and they will not wait to see that David's child whom Bathsheba will bear will be the cost of forgiveness. The sickness that will claim the child's life seems to creep into the palace even before Nathan the prophet can be gone.

III. Response to punishment, 19-23
A. Death of the child, 19-20

19 But when David saw that his servants whispered, David perceived that the child was dead: therefore David said unto his servants, Is the child dead? And they said, He is dead.

20 Then David arose from the earth, and washed, and anointed himself, and changed his apparel, and came into the house of the LORD, and worshipped: then he came to his own house; and when he required, they set bread before him, and he did eat.

Verses 16-18 record David's battle with God in prayer, begging for the child's life to be spared. It is not God's will; and on the seventh day of the boy's illness, he dies. The king's servants, knowing of the depths of David's sorrow while the child struggled for his life, are afraid of what the king might do if he learns of his death. But David sees the servants whispering about it all, and asks if the child is dead. Learning that this was true, the king surprises his servants by washing his face, changing clothes, and eating.

B. Realistic response, 21-23

21 Then said his servants unto him, What thing is this that thou hast done? thou didst fast and weep for the child, while it was alive; but when the child was dead, thou didst rise and eat bread.

22 And he said, While the child was yet alive, I fasted and wept: for I said, Who can tell whether GOD will be gracious to me, that the child may live?

23 But now he is dead, wherefore should I fast? can I bring him back again? I shall go to him, but he shall not return to me.

David's explanation of his response to the child's death stands as an eternal guidepost for those who deal with the death of a loved one. The response does not encourage flippancy, but a measure of realistic resignation. It also reveals the depth of understanding in Israel at this time regarding the finality of death and the unbridgeable gap between this life and the other world.

As difficult as Nathan's task was, the value of his facing up to his duty as a prophet can now work itself out in the life of the king and the people. What David said about the child might also be said about Uriah, and about the moral scars left on David and Bathsheba. Although the account reveals the depth of grace in the heart of God, it also shows that the *consequences* of sin can often prove permanent.

ഇൗ

Evangelistic Emphasis

Storyteller Madeleine L'Engle is on to something important, I think. In her little book *Penguins and Golden Calves* she says, "God did not give answers; God gave himself, to save us, to free us from our sins."

So often in our efforts to win our neighbors to Jesus, we allow ourselves to get enmeshed with them in debates over religious minutiae. What our unchurched neighbors really need, of course, is not correct answers (often to the wrong questions). What they need is the assurance of grace to cover their mistakes and light for the path they must walk.

Fussing about doctrines often turns out to be an effective way to avoid dealing with the real issues that are keeping us from God.

Do you remember that Samaritan woman at the well in John 4? How much easier it was for her to banter with Jesus about "the correct place to worship" than to explore with Him the real causes of her serial marriages. She desperately needed God's grace. In her heart, surely she knew this. And so do our neighbors who have lost their spiritual way. If they once discover they can have the kind of forgiveness David found after his shameful fall, nothing will be able to keep them away from Jesus.

ℰℭ

Memory Selection

Have mercy upon me, O God, according to thy lovingkindness: according unto the multitude of thy tender mercies blot out my transgressions. Wash me throughly from mine iniquity, and cleanse me from my sin.—*Psalm 51:1-2*

In the 51st Psalm, penitent King David confessed his shame and poured out his heart to God because of the horrid sins he had fallen into. Until recently, David had been a good man, an upright man, a man after God's own heart (1 Sam. 13:14). Now he had done worse things than he ever believed he could. He had disgraced himself, shamed his family, and dishonored God, and all he could think about was the ugliness of his sins.

What lay ahead for David? Could he possibly be forgiven for sins so terrible? Could the sun ever shine again in world so darkened by his deeds? This is what David is asking the Lord in this famous psalm.

Richard Nixon must have felt like this after Watergate. So did Chuck Colson. So did nationally known pastor Gordon McDonald, when his affair made front-page nationwide headlines. My sins and yours may not be so widely known, but they still spell shame and ruin for us and for those we love.

David's prayer was answered. God told him He would forgive. And He tells us the same thing: "The blood of Jesus his Son cleanses us from all sin. . . . If we confess our sins, he is faithful and just, and will forgive our sins and cleanse us from all unrighteousness" (1 John 1:7-10, RSV).

Weekday Problems

A fine young school teacher I know was motoring down a new strip of highway concrete at what he thought was the usual speed limit, but he had failed to see the small construction-zone signs that reduced the allowable speed. He got a ticket for speeding. In Texas that means the offender pays double the usual fine.

According to the law of ancient Israel, a man who killed or sold a sheep he had stolen was required to repay the original owner fourfold—four sheep for the one that vanished. Being the king and therefore the chief magistrate of that era, David would have known this rule. Without having to consult his law library, in an outburst of outrage, David responded to Nathan's made-up tale by sentencing the dastardly sheep-stealer to restore the poor man's sheep four times over. It was the law.

In any state, any church, any union, any athletic league, we expect to conform to the rules, don't we? If doping tests show that a bicycle rider in the French Alps has been cheating, people in Wisconsin and Wyoming get livid. We demand punishment by the rules that govern such competition.

Isn't it strange, then, that investment advisers and corporate executives who get caught violating the clear rules against insider trading and mis-dated stock options cry foul and act abused when the courts assess the penalties provided by law? If we break the rules, we pay by the rules. Should any of us be exempt from that?

Investing in Sure Insurance (or Not . . .)

"So you don't believe Smith's widow is as sorry as she pretends?"

"Well, when I gave her the $50,000 insurance check, she stopped crying and said she'd cheerfully give $5,000 of it to have him back.

* * *

A farmer's barn burned down, and the insurance company said that instead of a cash payment they would build him another barn of similar size. The farmer was furious. "If that's the way your company does business," he said, "you can just cancel the policy on my wife."

* * *

The insurance salesman was having trouble finding out how much insurance the lady of the house had on her husband. "What I mean is, what would you get if he died?" he asked once more.

"Oh," said the woman brightly. "A parakeet."

This Lesson in Your Life

The late Dr. Francis Schaeffer, founder of the *L'Abri* renewal centers, challenged the Christians of his day with some of the deepest thinking and most turgid prose ever published. Most of his writing was hard for average folks to read, but it always yielded up a blessing to those who persevered.

Having struggled through several of his volumes, I was amazed and delighted when I discovered a book of his sermons, *No Little People*. Simply written in an easy-to-grasp, popular style, Schaeffer's sermons show how King David's indiscretions and cover-up crimes exacted a toll on the king's family for the rest of his days.

Nathan comforted the king by telling him, "The Lord has forgiven you" (2 Sam. 12:14, TEV). God's *forgiveness*, however, did not cancel the *consequences* of David's sins. In his series of *L'Abri* sermons Dr. Schaeffer traces one by one the upheavals that ripped David's family and broke his heart in the years that followed.

He shows in one sermon, for example, how the impetuous sexual sins of David's son, Crown Prince Amnon, were likely triggered by David's own sins. As Amnon began to realize that the crown he should have worn would belong instead to Bathsheba's son, Solomon, his future evaporated and his behavior showed it.

Dr. Schaeffer also suggests that David's sins may have cost him the right to discipline his children. Had the king reproved Amnon for having sex with a woman he was not married to, Amnon surely would have replied, "That's what you did, Daddy."

Later in Absalom's and Adonijah's stories we see again how David's own sins compromised his moral authority as a father and sowed discord among his sons. Look in 2 Samuel 3:2-5 at the list of princes who should have inherited David's throne. When his lover crashed the party, her son went to the head of the line.

Absalom explained his murder of Prince Amnon as the rightful punishment he deserved for raping Princess Tamar. In truth, however, Amnon's death removed the one man who legally stood between Absalom and the throne. In all of this, David watched in silence while one of his sons killed the other, for he knew Absalom could reply, "Daddy, how is that any different to what you did to Uriah?"

Dr. Schaeffer ties the threads together far better than I have here, but no story in Scripture more clearly reveals the inevitable price paid for their sins—even the ones the Lord forgives.

We hear people talking about "victimless crimes." Is there any such thing as a victimless sin?

STRAIGHT

1. In Nathan's parable, whom did (1) the rich man and (2) the poor man stand for?

The rich man stood for David and the poor man stood for Uriah.

2. Who did the one little lamb represent?

The lamb represented Bathsheba, Uriah's wife.

3. Why do you suppose the rich man took one of the poor man's sheep for his guest instead of a sheep from his own flock?

The rich man was so covetous that he didn't want to use a sheep from his own flock. Wealth often creates a lust for more wealth.

4. What impresses you most about Nathan in this story?

We may be impressed by his courage in confronting the king . . . or by his creativity in inventing the parable which fit so well . . . or by staying so close to God that he knew exactly how to apply the parable, as well as David's punishment.

5. Why did God tell Nathan so quickly that he had "put away" David's sin?

Because David immediately confessed and repented (vs. 13).

6. Although David was forgiven, what did he still have to face?

He had to work through the several *consequences* of his sin, such as the death of his and Bathsheba's son.

7. Wouldn't it have been more just for *David* to die for his sin, instead of his son?

No. David had to live with those consequences of his sin, whereas his son went immediately to "Abraham's bosom," or into God's presence.

8. Do you agree with David's actions before and after his son's death?

(Discuss. David seems to have thought it through.)

9. Who fulfilled the punishment that David's wives (or concubines) would be given to someone else in public (12:11-12; 16:22)?

Absalom, another of David's son, to deride his father.

10. What do you think is the most moving part of David's confession of sin in Psalm 51?

(Discuss the psalm,)

Uplift

One Sunday morning after worship time one of our sweet couples—an attorney and his wife—were halfway down the front sidewalk on the way to the car when he stopped and called back to me, "Hey, preacher!"

When I looked up and acknowledged him, he told me, "I really enjoy sermons like the one you preached today." Then he explained, "I like sermons that contain good stories."

My sermon that morning had ended with an extended, heart-touching story that drove home the point of my message. My attorney friend had turned and departed before I got a chance to confide in him that he is not the only person who likes sermons like that. I like to preach them.

When the Lord blesses me with the perfect narrative to convey some truth, in the pulpit I can feel it when the people and I connect. Stories are God's chosen vehicle for truth.

How else do you suppose Nathan could have penetrated David's misguided heart? Blinded by his own sins, the once-good king had been willing to connive and murder an innocent man to cover up his wickedness. What could he be expected to do to a preacher who threatened to expose his shamefulness?

Nathan's innocent story did the trick. It became the mirror in which David could see his own distorted soul. It broke open his heart and caused him to confess, "I have sinned."

Author Madeleine L'Engle recalls an insightful remark made to her. "Jesus was not a theologian," her friend said. "He was God who told stories." Disarmingly simple, those stories Jesus told are still touching hearts and changing lives. Unlike most of the sermons preached by pastors like me, our Lord's messages are unforgettable. Anyone who has read the Gospels remembers the Master's teaching—especially His stories.

Just as Nathan slipped up on David with his story about the stolen sheep, Jesus blindsided that questioning lawyer with His seemingly innocuous tale about the fellow who got mugged on the Jericho highway. In the ages since, none of us can dodge the example of that Good Samaritan. Jesus bids us, "Go, and do likewise."

Was there ever a story more convicting and illuminating that the one we call The Prodigal Son? Who can forget the truths Jesus hid in planted seeds, patched clothes, precious pearls, and empty lamps?

"He just told stories," the soldiers reported when they returned to their evil bosses empty-handed. Thank God He did.

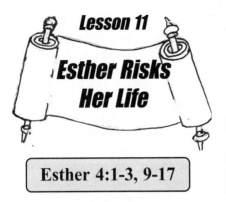

Lesson 11

Esther Risks Her Life

Esther 4:1-3, 9-17

When Mordecai perceived all that was done, Mordecai rent his clothes, and put on sackcloth with ashes, and went out into the midst of the city, and cried with a loud and a bitter cry;

2 And came even before the king's gate: for none might enter into the king's gate clothed with sackcloth.

3 And in every province, whithersoever the king's commandment and his decree came, there was great mourning among the Jews, and fasting, and weeping, and wailing; and many lay in sackcloth and ashes.

9 And Hatach came and told Esther the words of Mordecai.

10 Again Esther spake unto Hatach, and gave him commandment unto Mordecai;

11 All the king's servants, and the people of the king's provinces, do know, that whosoever, whether man or woman, shall come unto the king into the inner court, who is not called, there is one law of his to put him to death, except such to whom the king shall hold out the golden sceptre, that he may live: but I have not been called to come in unto the king these thirty days.

12 And they told to Mordecai Esther's words.

13 Then Mordecai commanded to answer Esther, Think not with thyself that thou shalt escape in the king's house, more than all the Jews.

14 For if thou altogether holdest thy peace at this time, then shall there enlargement and deliverance arise to the Jews from another place; but thou and thy father's house shall be destroyed: and who knoweth whether thou art come to the kingdom for such a time as this?

15 Then Esther bade them return Mordecai this answer,

16 Go, gather together all the Jews that are present in Shushan, and fast ye for me, and neither eat nor drink three days, night or day: I also and my maidens will fast likewise; and so will I go in unto the king, which is not according to the law: and if I perish, I perish.

17 So Mordecai went his way, and did according to all that Esther had commanded him.

Memory Selection
Esther 4:16

Background Scripture
Esther 4–5

Devotional Reading
Philip. 1:20-30

Feb. 15

No one demonstrates more vividly the principle of commitment than Esther, who, though Jewish, was also queen of Persia and wife of Ahasuerus (Xerxes). Reigning in the sixth century B.C., Xerxes had several wives in addition to Esther.

Esther is especially remembered by Jews who observe the Feast of Purim, which is the celebration of Esther's successful appeal that the planned "pogrom" or execution of the Jews be cancelled by the king. This lesson focuses on that notable event.

The story of Esther, whose name in Hebrew is Hadassah (Esther 2:7) also includes her uncle Mordecai. They were among Jews captured and taken in 586 B.C. to Babylonia, which in turn was occupied by Persia.

For a Lively Start

History records several people who seem, like Queen Esther, to have been raised up by God for special service at a crucial time. Of course it is easy for a particular nation to claim divine appointment for one of its favorite sons or daughters, so it is usually only after several years, decades, or even centuries that widespread agreement by believing historians is reached.

Who besides Esther would your group place in this class? What about George Washington, who won the title "Father of Our Country" even before his death? Some people who lived through "the Great Depression" would include FDR. In South America, Simon Bolivar is widely considered to be such a leader. Encourage as many contributions as your group can think of.

Teaching Outline	Daily Bible Readings	
	Mon.	Search for a Queen *Esther 2:1-11*
	Tue.	New Queen Selected *Esther 2:15-18*
I. Mordecai's Lament—4:1-3	Wed.	A Plot Is Thwarted *Esther 2:-19-23*
II. Esther's Concern—9-12	Thu.	An Evil Edict *Esther 3:7-13*
III. Mordecai's urging, 13-14	Fri.	Evil Intent Revealed *Esther 7:1-10*
V. Esther Agrees, 15-17	Sat.	The People Rescued *Esther 8:3-8*
	Sun.	'If I Perish, I Perish' *Esther 4:1-3, 9-17*

Verse by Verse

I. Mordecai's Lament—4:1-3

1 When Mordecai perceived all that was done, Mordecai rent his clothes, and put on sackcloth with ashes, and went out into the midst of the city, and cried with a loud and a bitter cry;

2 And came even before the king's gate: for none might enter into the king's gate clothed with sackcloth.

3 And in every province, whithersoever the king's commandment and his decree came, there was great mourning among the Jews, and fasting, and weeping, and wailing: and many lay in sackcloth and ashes.

"All that was done" refers to the events in chapter 3, leading up to a very real crisis for all Jews living in Persia. One Haman, a high Persian official, was able to persuade the king to issue an edict ordering people to bow before Haman whenever they approached each other. Whether this bowing had religious overtones, as though Haman were a kind of god, we are not told; but this would

explain why Mordecai the Jew refused to bow before him (3:2).

Haman, consumed with pride, was enraged, and went again to Ahasuerus the king. He had discovered that Mordecai was one of the Jews whom the Babylonians, the previous rulers of Persia, had captured in Judea. Mordecai was only one among thousands, but either his pride equaled Haman's, and he was willing to jeopardize the well-being of his people, or bowing down before a mere court official really was of some religious significance that would actually violate Mordecai's conscience. At any rate, Haman was able to paint a picture of Mordecai and all other Jews as a rebellious people whose refusal to obey the laws of Persia threatened the kingdom. Haman offered the king 10,000 talents of silver in return for a national sweep that would kill all Jews in the land.

The edict was posted throughout the land, prompting Mordecai to don

233

sackcloth and ashes and parade himself before the king's gate, which was against the law. Other Jews went into public mourning, realizing that their very existence as a nation was threatened not only in Persia, but that surrounding nations could follow suit.

II. Esther's Concern—9-12

As explained earlier in the book, Esther was Mordecai's niece. She had been named queen after a spat between the king and the previous queen, Vashti. Not knowing she was Jewish, the king had chosen Esther as his favorite wife. Mordecai had urged her to take advantage of her status and put a stop to the terrible plan to exterminate the Jews.

9 And Hatach came and told Esther the words of Mordecai.

Hatach was one of the eunuchs in charge of the king's harem. Queen Esther had charged him with personally going to her uncle Mordecai to get a clearer picture of the cause of the disturbance. Mordecai explains the entire plot, including the incentive of the large payment of silver. He sends Hatach back with a copy of the decree condemning Jews to death, which had been drafted at the palace in Shushan (a city which is among a host of historical details confirmed by secular writings from the same era).

Mordecai sees only one hope for the Jews. Esther the queen must approach the king personally and make supplication in behalf of her people.

III. Obstacle for Esther, 10-12

10 Again Esther spake unto Hatach, and gave him commandment unto Mordecai;

11 All the king's servants, and the people of the king's provinces, do know, that whosoever, whether man or woman, shall come unto the king into the inner court, who is not called, there is one law of his to put him to death, except such to whom the king shall hold out the golden sceptre, that he may live: but I have not been called to come in unto the king these thirty days.

12 And they told to Mordecai Esther's words.

Apparently Mordecai did not know that a strict protocol governed who could appear before the king, and when, as is usually the case in all nations. Not only did a personage as important as a king want control over his daily agenda and calendar; he needed protection from potential enemies. Furthermore, for some reason it had been a month since the king had summoned Esther. There might not be time to approach him through his deputies, and appearing unscheduled might be fatal even to the queen.

IV. Mordecai's Urging, 13-14

13 Then Mordecai commanded to answer Esther, Think not with thyself that thou shalt escape in the king's house, more than all the Jews.

14 For if thou altogether holdest thy peace at this time, then shall there enlargement and deliverance arise to the Jews from another place; but thou and thy father's house shall be destroyed: and who knoweth whether thou art come to the kingdom for such a time as this?

As badly as Mordecai wants his niece to try to intervene with the king, he makes a highly altruistic point. Even if Esther decides not to try to gain an

234

audience with the king, the Jews will be delivered in some other way. There is the hint that Esther would miss out on being the very means of saving her people. Such faith seems to indicate that her uncle has a higher motive than self-preservation.

Yet he is not finished trying to persuade Esther to try to obtain a personal audience before the king. He makes a logical point. Even if she does not make an appearance, it would no doubt come out that Esther herself was a Jew, and she would lose her own life in the general holocaust that would exterminate the Jews.

V. Esther Agrees, 15-17

15 Then Esther bade them return Mordecai this answer,

16 Go, gather together all the Jews that are present in Shushan, and fast ye for me, and neither eat nor drink three days, night or day: I also and my maidens will fast likewise; and so will I go in unto the king, which is not according to the law: and if I perish, I perish.

17 So Mordecai went his way, and did according to all that Esther had commanded him.

Finally, Queen Esther agrees to do as Mordecai urges. After throwing herself on the mercy of God in fasting (and presumably prayer, which usually accompanied fasting), she would make an unscheduled attempt to speak to the king. Her answer to her uncle has in it a mixture of great faith and resignation. If, when she suddenly appears before the king unannounced and he extends to her the golden scepter, she will confess her nationality and try to make her case for revoking the order to destroy them. However, it all depends on the king's mood. If he does not extend his scepter, both Esther and her people will be destroyed.

We cannot conclude this lesson without reminding ourselves of "the rest of the story." The king does extend the scepter that signals his willingness to grant Esther an audience. As it turns out, he is aghast that his own edict would destroy both Esther and her people. The king orders that Haman, who was behind the entire scheme, be hanged on the very scaffold he had built for Mordecai. Unfortunately the king reverses the edict so violently that the Jews are given permission to put to death those who would have destroyed them. At any rate, to this day observant Jews celebrate the "lot," or Pur, on the Feast of Purim, to celebrate at least one incident when their scheduled extermination failed.

ℰᎧℭᏒ

Evangelistic Emphasis

In his book *The Parables of Peanuts*, Robert L. Short reminds us that a pastor in the pulpit "stands between his congregation and the Bible not to dazzle his congregation with his oratory or his exceptional knowledge of biblical criticism, but simply to share the excitement that comes to him from the book."

Have we discovered the fun and excitement that charge the biblical story of Queen Esther?

As a young pastor I got to share this story with the neighborhood kids one summer in our Vacation Bible School. What an immense pleasure it gave me to see their eyes dance with delight as they grasped the intrigue and suspense and heroism pent up in Esther's grand tale.

An obvious part of our intent that summer was to teach those youngsters the details of the story of Esther. More important to me, however, was my aim to send these children away with the lasting impression that Bible reading can be great fun.

What ever happened to our conviction that the message we share about Jesus is *Good* News? Only when our own hearts are aflame with delight in God's word can we expect to strike the sparks of interest and faith in the souls of those we teach.

ಬಂಡ

Memory Selection

Go, gather together all the Jews that are present in Shushan, and fast ye for me, and neither eat nor drink three days, night or day: I also and my maidens will fast likewise; and so will I go in unto the king, which is not according to the law: and if I perish, I perish.—*Esther 4:16*

Smoke was rising in a plume of doom from the World Trade Center after the first jetliner crashed into one tower on that fateful morning in September, 2001.

Fire signals were blaring a warning. Elevators automatically refused to open, lest hapless riders get trapped somewhere between floors. So hundreds of people jammed the stairways, fleeing the deadly fires above.

As more and more panicked people crowded onto the stairs to make their way down to safety, they met policemen and firemen rushing up the same stairways carrying all sorts of rescue gear. These brave men and women were running toward the danger, not away from it.

In a shattered cocktail bar not far from Ground Zero, some firemen scrawled the name and number of his fire brigade on the broken mirror. Beside it he wrote, "Others run out; we run in!"

This rare kind of courage is the stuff of heroines and heroes. It causes people like Esther to dare to die if that's what it takes to save her people.

Weekday Problems

Pastor M. R. DeHaan, III, used to tell the delightful story about a band of post office customers who got fed up with the slow service. The lines "were moving slower than paint dries," one customer said later. Service must have been really bad that day. Another fellow told a newspaper reporter, "It was like watching grass grow."

The reporter's story the next morning documented that 26 postal patrons had been stuck there way too long, jammed into two lines that were not moving.

Finally a 73-year-old man in the lines got the inspiration to organize all of them into an impromptu cheering squad. "We want service!" all 26 customers began chanting together. This unprecedented show of unity turned out to be more effective than any of them dared to hope. Before long a clerk ambled up from the catacombs of the post office and, without cracking a smile, said, "Next?"

Now the 26 frustrated customers knew they were on to something, so they resumed their chant, "We want service!"

"You guessed it," Pastor DeHaan nodded. Soon a fourth clerk appeared and opened another service window.

The reporter quoted an amused customer who left smiling. "It was amazing," he said. "I got through that line in four minutes. I've never seen anything like it!"

Likewise, the unified efforts of God's people always get more done than the most zealous efforts of one of us alone. To survive and succeed, Esther knew she needed all of the Jews in the land backing her up with fasting and prayer.

Warning: False Advertising

The extermination of an estimated 6 million Jews by Nazi Germany in World War II is only the worst single slaughter of history's most persecuted people. Many other mass killings have their roots in the false document called "The Protocols of the Elders of Zion."

Originating in the Middle Ages, this pamphlet was apparently written by an unknown author in Paris who was working for the Russian secret police. A 20th century revision was issued in Russia in 1903, and the spurious document has been translated into all known languages. It describes an imaginary conference in which Jewish leaders plot to poison wells used by Christians, and to spread the plague among Christian communities. The "Protocols" was used to justify the holocaust launched by the Nazis. To this day this counterfeit material is required reading in schools in most Arab countries.

This Lesson in Your Life

The bride and groom in a recent wedding I performed were barely 20 years old. Some do get married even younger than that, I know, but these clean-cut kids appeared to be younger than they were. As I stood before them and heard them pledging "I do" to promises that are supposed to last a lifetime, I wondered, "Do these young people know what they're getting into?"

"For richer, for poorer" in my own case included some terribly lean years when my wife and I struggled to feed and clothe our kids on a small-church pastor's salary. Just how "poor" will these kids be able to tolerate?

"In sickness and in health" described some times for us that were distressing and confining. As that couple stood there before God and their families, promising to hang tough with each other through all sorts of medical woes, I suspected they thought they were signing on for a fairy-tale life in which they would always be robust, vigorous, and strong—with no bedpans or bandages or wheelchairs or walkers.

Marriage is not the only commitment we make that conceals later demands. A few days ago I talked to a soldier just home from Iraq. He told me that several of his battle-weary buddies had signed up for the military reserves primarily as an easy way to pay for college. They never really meant to leave their families stateside to go dodge IED's and jihadist snipers in the back alleys of Baghdad.

A talented fellow who grew up in my church changed jobs last week. After working out of his home for a couple of years, he chose the better salary and benefits of a new company, knowing from the start that it would cost him a 35-minute metro commute twice a day. But he was shocked when his new position soon took him several states east, away from his family for weeks at a time. He didn't know what he was getting into when he signed that lucrative contract.

When Esther decided to compete in the Queen-for-a-Day contest with the fairest ladies in the land, I wonder what she thought the permanent job of Queen would entail. Did her pre-queen dreams stop with endless banquets, full-time house help, a bottomless expense account, and closets full of costly gowns by the finest designers—all the luxuries reserved for the royal family of the most powerful nation on earth?

Like most of us, Esther probably failed to "read the fine print" in her new job description. I doubt we could find a doctor, a school principal, a pastor, or a social worker who, when they took their job, had any idea how much dirty work it would require of them.

Esther stepped up to the plate. Without flinching, she resolutely faced whatever dangers her role might throw at her. Few things will demonstrate our own faith and integrity more than when we stand strong and true to our promises in the face of unforeseen demands or perils.

GETTING THE FACTS STRAIGHT

1. Why were the Jews Mordecai and his niece Esther in Persia?

They were among the Jews who had been captured and taken there by the Babylonians, who were in turn conquered by the Persians.

2. How did Esther wind up as one of the wives of King Ahasuerus?

She was taken to the king's harem because of her beauty, then replaced the Persian queen Vashti.

3. Who hated Mordecai and the rest of the Jews so much that he persuaded the king to command that they be killed?

Haman, a chief prince in the king's court.

4. Why did the prince hate Mordecai?

Because Mordecai refused to bow down before the prince as though he were some sort of deity.

5. Why was Esther reluctant to go into the king and beg that the Jews be spared?

Because one could be killed by appearing before the king without an appointment. It had been a month since he had called for Esther, and she feared for her life if she went into the court uninvited.

6. How did Mordecai persuade Esther to risk her life and appeal to the king to spare the Jews?

By pointing out that she could lose her life anyway if the king's edict were not repealed.

7. What did Esther ask the Jews to do in support of her decision to enter the king's presence?

She asked that they gather together and fast, and probably pray, for her.

8. What happened to Prince Haman when the king learned he was behind the plot to kill all Jews in the land?

He was hanged on the very gallows he had prepared for Mordecai.

9. What were the Jews allowed to do after the king spared the Jews?

They were encouraged to kill all those who would have put them to death.

10. How do observant Jews celebrate Mordecai and Esther's victory?

With the Feast of Purim, which means "lots," referring to the lots cast by Haman to decide when he would try to have the Jews killed.

Uplift

In one of his most memorable lines, Shakespeare wrote in *Twelfth Night*, "Some are born great, some achieve greatness, and some have greatness thrust upon them."

I wonder if Esther knew what strength and courage lay within her until that day when it was so desperately needed.

Winston Churchill was that sort of hidden hero. Some of his early teachers thought he was a brat. School often bored him, it seems. At times he resisted their best efforts to educate him. Surely there must have been days when his parents wondered what kind of disgrace he might bring on their noble family.

Even the early political career of this legendary hero-to-be did not at times seem headed to the heights. By 1933, some historians note, his political future seemed dismal. No one would have predicted that less than a decade later that Sir Winston would successfully lead his own nation and much of the free world through their darkest days.

Looking back, one has to wonder if all three of Shakespeare's ways to become great mighty describe Churchill's ascent to fame. The most gripping biographies tend to be those of rise to greatness out of relative obscurity and appear to emerge on the public scene—like Esther did—for some special time and task.

In the Bible we recall the examples of people like Joseph and David and Daniel, whom God raised up at just the right time to bless their generation. Although we don't tend to think of the heroic leaders in the book of Judges as men and women of great stature, still each of their stories makes it clear that God put them in place to bless His people in a particular time and place.

Look around you at the kids on your street or the teens in your church. Which rowdy little ruffian might actually be a Samson or a Gideon in the making? Which demure lass might be Esther on the way to the throne—a potential first lady getting ready for a troubled moment in our nation's distant days?

God evidently didn't give Esther much advance notice. But when the fateful day did come, it was apparent to God's people that His hand been guiding, shaping, preparing her all the way.

Lesson 12

Isaiah Answers God's Call

Isaiah 6:1-13

1 In the year that king Uzziah died I saw also the Lord sitting upon a throne, high and lifted up, and his train filled the temple.

2 Above it stood the seraphims: each one had six wings; with twain he covered his face, and with twain he covered his feet, and with twain he did fly.

3 And one cried unto another, and said, Holy, holy, holy, is the LORD of hosts: the whole earth is full of his glory.

4 And the posts of the door moved at the voice of him that cried, and the house was filled with smoke.

5 Then said I, Woe is me! for I am undone; because I am a man of unclean lips, and I dwell in the midst of a people of unclean lips: for mine eyes have seen the King, the LORD of hosts.

6 Then flew one of the seraphims unto me, having a live coal in his hand, which he had taken with the tongs from off the altar:

7 And he laid it upon my mouth, and said, Lo, this hath touched thy lips; and thine iniquity is taken away, and thy sin purged.

8 Also I heard the voice of the Lord, saying, Whom shall I send, and who will go for us? Then said I, Here am I; send me.

9 And he said, Go, and tell this people, Hear ye indeed, but understand not; and see ye indeed, but perceive not.

10 Make the heart of this people fat, and make their ears heavy, and shut their eyes; lest they see with their eyes, and hear with their ears, and understand with their heart, and convert, and be healed.

11 Then said I, Lord, how long? And he answered, Until the cities be wasted without inhabitant, and the houses without man, and the land be utterly desolate,

12 And the LORD have removed men far away, and there be a great forsaking in the midst of the land.

13 But yet in it shall be a tenth, and it shall return, and shall be eaten: as a teil tree, and as an oak, whose substance is in them, when they cast their leaves: so the holy seed shall be the substance thereof.

Memory Selection
Isa. 6:8

Background Scripture
Isa. 6

Devotional Reading
Rev. 4

Feb. 22

241

FOCUS

Some people who enter fulltime Christian service do so after an experience that seems to say unmistakably, "Come do My will." Most, however, enter Christian ministry after more subtle "hints" from God. Perhaps they reach the conclusion that their personality is suitable for "church work," as is the case of those who easily "weep with those who weep" or otherwise identify with those who need what a minister has to offer.

This lesson on the call of Isaiah is of the first variety. Like the apostle Paul, who was struck down by a blinding light, Isaiah has a vision that leaves no doubt that God is calling him into His service. The vision is highly mystical, and we may have trouble identifying some of its figures. There is no mistaking the call, however: "Who will go for us," or Isaiah's answer: "Send me."

ℰↃ◯Ⴗ

For a Lively Start

One of the most frustrating experiences of ministers is to have them and their work stereotyped. Some feel that they are expected to speak in a "stained glass voice," to hold their hands just so when they pray, and otherwise act in ways that almost shout, *"I'm a minister, OK?"*

This lesson can be started with a free-style discussion of the traits the group expects a minister to have. Should a minister never say No? Should he or she seek to please as many types of people as possible? Should they all be evangelists? Should all be married and have 2.5 children? Should they dress the same way?

Ask these and other questions that encourage a broadening of expectations and a minimum of stereotyping.

Teaching Outline	**Daily Bible Readings**
I. Setting of Mysticism—6:1-4	Mon. An Emerald Rainbow Rev. 4:1-6a
A. Vision of God, 1	Tue. Thrice-holy God Rev. 4:6b-11
B. Seraphim and trembling, 2-4	Wed. Call to Leave Gen. 12:1-5
II. Sin and Salvation—5-7	Thu. Call to Stay Gen. 26:1-5
A. Sinful prophet, 5	Fri. Call to Deliver Judg. 6:11-23
B. Saving grace, 6-7	Sat. Answer for Uncertainty Judg. 6:36-40
C. Call and response, 8	Sun. 'Here Am I, Send Me' Isa. 6:1-8
III. Surprising message, 9-10	
IV. Seed and Remnant—11-13	

Verse by Verse

I. Setting of Mysticism—6:1-4
A. Vision of God, 1

1 In the year that king Uzziah died I saw also the Lord sitting upon a throne, high and lifted up, and his train filled the temple.

King Uzziah and Isaiah the prophet were on friendly terms. (Reading about Uzziah's 52-year reign can be confusing since Uzziah was his "throne name," and he is also called by his personal name, Azariah.) Although Uzziah was generally one of Judah's better kings, he was arrogant enough to encroach on the domain of the priests; and as a result he was stricken with leprosy and had to live in isolation for most of his reign.

Isaiah's vision might be called "surreal" or dream-like. By whatever name, it is overwhelming from the beginning. We are asked to imagine the huge Temple in Jerusalem filled with the flowing robes or train, perhaps symbolizing the fact that God is present everywhere. His presence fills His creation, although we recognize it all too little.

B. Seraphim and trembling, 2-4

2 Above it stood the seraphims: each one had six wings; with twain he covered his face, and with twain he covered his feet, and with twain he did fly.

3 And one cried unto another, and said, Holy, holy, holy, is the LORD of hosts: the whole earth is full of his glory.

4 And the posts of the door moved at the voice of him that cried, and the house was filled with smoke.

"Seraphim" literally means "burning ones." Since this is their only appearance in Scripture, we have little information about them. Like the cherubim, the winged creatures guarding Eden after the Fall, and sitting atop the Ark of the Covenant, they were apparently created for the explicit purpose of testifying to the glory of God.

Just as the seraphim had three sets of wings, so they acclaim God to be "three times holy," three being the number of perfection. Their exclamation triggers something of an earthquake,

243

for the doorposts of the Temple gates tremble and the place is filled with smoke. We can only imagine Isaiah's awe-struck heart at the sights and sounds before him.

II. Sin and Salvation—5-7
A. Sinful prophet, 5

5 Then said I, Woe is me! for I am undone; because I am a man of unclean lips, and I dwell in the midst of a people of unclean lips: for mine eyes have seen the King, the LORD of hosts.

The breathtaking scene of holiness appropriately causes Isaiah to feel his own unworthiness. He is not only personally guilty, if for nothing else for lacking perfection; he lives among people who have not been keeping God's law in general, and who have unclean speech in particular. Isaiah also feels guilty for having seen a representation of the holy God, which was forbidden in the Law. However, Scripture records several exceptions to this rule, with people allowed to see at least representations of God (such as "the angel of the Lord"; and cf. Exod. 24:9-1).

B. Saving grace, 6-7

6 Then flew one of the seraphims unto me, having a live coal in his hand, which he had taken with the tongs from off the altar:

7 And he laid it upon my mouth, and said, Lo, this hath touched thy lips; and thine iniquity is taken away, and thy sin purged.

If indeed one purpose of seraphim (the KJV "s" is not needed to make the plural) is to acclaim God's glory, they are at their best when they administer forgiveness to imperfect men like Isaiah. As a hot coal or ember cauter-izes and cleanses a wound, so the seraph's coal cleanses Isaiah's "wound" of sin. No part of this scene is more important. It is painted to draw us to worship the holy God. We move toward Him, but are hesitant to approach because of our sinfulness. Yet He who invites us to worship also "qualifies" us to do so by removing our sin. (The down side is we can no longer sleep in on Sunday morning with the excuse that we're not good enough to go to church!)

C. Call and response, 8

8 Also I heard the voice of the Lord, saying, Whom shall I send, and who will go for us? Then said I, Here am I; send me.

Here God emphasizes the evangelistic side of worship. Others need to be exposed to the beauty and fearfulness of the God whose train fills the Temple. It seems that the appeal for someone to "go for us" is hardly made before Isaiah answers in the famous phrase made so real by countless missionaries and other worshipers through the ages: "Here am I; send me."

III. Surprising Message—9-10

9 And he said, Go, and tell this people, Hear ye indeed, but understand not; and see ye indeed, but perceive not.

10 Make the heart of this people fat, and make their ears heavy, and shut their eyes; lest they see with their eyes, and hear with their ears, and understand with their heart, and convert, and be healed.

The message God wants Isaiah to take to the people surprises us. Instead of being filled with sweetness and light, it is a stern message of judgment. This is because the "missionary message" is set in a time when Israel is sinning with no twinge of conscience. In such cases, judgment precedes mercy. The "coal" of the cherubim cannot burn away the sin of those who refuse to admit they are sinning. The message is therefore filled with irony: actually, no one will be saved without seeing, hearing, and understanding the message of salvation.

IV. Seed and Remnant—11-13

11 Then said I, Lord, how long? And he answered, Until the cities be wasted without inhabitant, and the houses without man, and the land be utterly desolate,

12 And the LORD have removed men far away, and there be a great forsaking in the midst of the land.

13 But yet in it shall be a tenth, and it shall return, and shall be eaten: as a teil tree, and as an oak, whose substance is in them, when they cast their leaves: so the holy seed shall be the substance thereof.

Isaiah finds it unbearable to take such a stern message to the people, so he asks how long it is to be valid. The answer has two parts. The first part is no more comforting than the original message: the people are to live under God's rebuke until the land is desolate, and destruction is the rule, not the exception. This seems to refer Assyria's invasion of the northern kingdom of Israel in 721, which occurred during Isaiah's prophetic work during the 8th century B.C.

The second part of the message is more hopeful, and it appears throughout the times when God has to threaten His people with punishment. That message is that a *remnant*—here symbolized by a "tithe" or tenth—of the people will be preserved. Whether this refers to people who will never be deported by the Assyrians, or to others who are captured but later allowed to return, the Remnant is God's way of fulfilling His eternal promise of salvation. It is symbolized by the stump of a "terebinth" (also often simply called an oak, or KJV "teil") tree after the main trunk has been cut down. Something of the life of God will be left in His people despite the coming destruction.

245

Evangelistic Emphasis

"Go, and tell this people," the Lord commissioned Isaiah. Does He have a similar mission for us today?

In the spring of 1961, Dr. Elton Trueblood came to the town where I was completing my undergraduate schooling. To overflow crowds in the McMurray College chapel, this grand man of God delivered the lectures that eventually became his classic book, *The Company of the Committed.*

This diminuitive, white-haired theology professor was one of the true spiritual giants of the 20th century. He pulled no punches as he delivered a stinging indictment to those of us who were "at ease in Zion."

"Standard Protestantism is characteristically urbane and well-mannered," Trueblood said, "but it is sadly deficient in driving power and in the ability to imagine new and fresh ways of permeating the world."

I look back now and wonder if the candor of this exceptional fellow may have helped to jumpstart that generation of missionaries and pastors who reached millions for Christ. Perhaps the Lord sent Elton Trueblood to us and to our generation, just as He sent Isaiah to his people to touch the hearts of those who had stopped listening to God.

೮೧೦೩

Memory Selection

I heard the voice of the Lord, saying, Whom shall I send, and who will go for us? Then said I, Here am I; send me.—Isaiah 6:8

Shortly before the epochal year 2000 dawned, two young Christian men I know and admire made a personal "prayer trek" to the isolated nation of Nepal. Few places are more shut off from Christ and the gospel than this tiny land with some of Earth's most spectacular terrain. Evangelism is forbidden. Religious conversions are against the law. Distributing Bibles or Christian literature could land one in prison for a long time.

So my young friends did not go to Nepal to preach. They went to pray. At their own expense they spent ten days in that Far East country sitting in front of Buddhist shrines, government offices, and Nepalese universities wording silent prayers in their hearts, asking God to touch those institutions and save the men and women in them.

Just a few years later, two more Christian friends—a retired Texas couple—traveled to the isolated interior of China, again at their own expense. To a setting where all preaching is banned and conversion to Christianity is outlawed and heavily penalized, my friends went as volunteers to teach English as a second language. Their real purpose was to help somebody in that walled-off land to hear about Jesus. They knew the laws, however; so they taught English expertly and made friends wherever possible, praying all the while that one or two of those friends might ask for information about the Lord.

If not Nepal or China, where might the Lord send you?

Weekday Problems

Little did Isaiah know what he was getting into when he so readily volunteered, "Here am I. Send me!"

Send me where?

Send me to say what?

How could he have known that he would be the Billy Graham of his day—the personal confidant of kings for at least the next 60 years?

Nor did he know before he signed on as God's messenger that his message would be a grim one—a prediction of God's judgment on Israel for their corruption and immorality.

For several decades Isaiah preached in the palace and in the streets of Judah's cities. The longer and louder he preached, the worse things appeared to be. The kings were faithless and wicked men. The people seemed to hear little that God said through His spokesman.

Then, after Isaiah surely must have despaired at the futility of his task, along came King Hezekiah. Here was a king who responded to God's warnings with faith and penitence, and thereby saved his people.

You and I won't likely be sent to preach to kings, but the Lord may pick us out to carry His message to our neighbors or to our grandkids. Who knows? One of them just might wind up running a multi-national corporation that touches lives from China to the Czech Republic.

The God who called Isaiah—the God who calls us—sees a lot farther and thinks a lot bigger than we do.

Words on Worship

Worship is pictured at its best in Isaiah, when the young prophet became aware of the Father; aware of his own limitations; aware of the Fatheer's directives; and aware of the task at hand.—*David Julius*

* * *

The worship of God is not a rule of safety—it is an adventure of the spirit, a flight after the unattainable.—*Alfred North Whitehead*

* * *

The instinct to worship is hardly less strong than the instinct to eat.—*Dorothy Thompson*

* * *

Do not forget that even as "to work is to worship" so to be cheery is to worship also, and to be happy is the first step to being pious.—*Robert Louis Stevenson*

This Lesson in Your Life

Gene Perret says, "Probably the greatest opening line of all times was written for Johnny Carson by 'Tonight Show' writer Pat McCormick.

"It was penned on February 9, 1971. . . . That morning Los Angeles was rocked by a devastating earthquake that practically shut the city down, except for the 'Tonight Show.' After the trauma of that day, Carson opened his show with, 'The God Is Dead meeting that was scheduled for tonight is cancelled.'"

Perret says, "It was the perfect punchline for a straight line that registered 6.5 on the Richter scale."

What happens to a society that concludes that God is dead? Malcolm Muggeridge traded in his agnosticism for faith in Jesus in his last years. After spending years before British television cameras, Muggeridge commented in his book *Christ and the Media* on the decline of morality in our culture. "If it is the case, as I believe, that what we call Western civilisation is fast disintegrating," Muggeridge opined, "then the media are playing a major role in the process by carrying out, albeit for the most part unconsciously, a mighty brainwashing operation, whereby all traditional standards and values are being denigrated to the point of disappearing, leaving a moral vacuum in which the very concepts of Good and Evil have ceased to have any validity."

Had this wise old Brit dug a bit deeper, he probably could have told us that morals tend to vanish from any culture that begins to leave God out of the daily equations of life.

American professors and theologians began to announce in the early 1960s that God is dead—right before the decade of flower children and free love (sex anytime anywhere with anyone) and draft dodging and hippie communes.

When we come face to face with the Almighty, as Isaiah did, everything within us cries out with the angels that He is holy and we are not. "Woe is me!" the prophet-to-be began to wail. Beholding God's holiness made him desperately aware of his own sinfulness.

Do you recall the reaction of Peter when Jesus worked that first stunning fish-catching miracle that almost sank Peter's boat? Instantly, Peter felt the need to put distance between himself and Christ. "Depart from me!" Peter cried. Why? "Because," he said, "I am a sinful man."

Tom Williams asserts this truth when he says in his book *In Search of Certainty*, "Whether God exists is not merely a theoretical abstraction that has no practical bearing on our everyday lives. When belief in God wanes and dies, society loses its stable underpinnings and spins downward into a maelstrom of fragmented individualism with each person out for his or her own gain and each of us the potential victim of all the others."

Drawing near to God's Presence confronts us with a double truth. It makes us aware both of Who He is and of who we are.

GETTING THE FACTS STRAIGHT

1. Where was the Lord when Isaiah saw Him in his vision?
He was on the throne in the temple of Heaven.

2. Describe the seraphim (the angels) above the throne.
Each had six wings—two that covered their face, two that covered their feet, and two with which to fly.

3. What were the angels shouting in Isaiah's vision of Heaven?
They shouted, "Holy, holy, holy, is the Lord of hosts: the whole earth is full of his glory."

4. When the angel cried out, what happened to the temple?
The doorposts "moved" (KJV) or "trembled" (NASB), and it was filled with smoke.

5. What was Isaiah's reaction when he saw the vision of God on His throne?
Isaiah was frightened because he was aware of his own sinfulness in contrast to the holiness of the Lord.

6. What sin was Isaiah most aware of?
He mentioned the sins of his "unclean lips."

7. What did one of the angels do to take care of Isaiah's sinful lips?
With tongs he took a burning coal from the altar and laid it on Isaiah's mouth.

8. As the angel did this, what did he say to Isaiah?
"Lo, this hath touched thy lips; and thine iniquity is taken away, and thy sin purged."

9. What was Isaiah's answer when the Lord asked, "Whom shall I send, and who will go for us?"
Isaiah said, "Here am I; send me."

10. Was the message God told Isaiah to carry a message of hope or doom for His people?
God told Isaiah to predict that the people of Israel would become unable to hear God and that they would be exiled from their land.

Uplift

"High and lifted up" are the words Isaiah used to describe God in his famous vision. One familiar Old Testament name for God is the Most High.

No doubt, we're saying something like this when we pray the prayer Jesus gave His followers, "Our Father, who art in heaven . . . ."

Although some theologians in the 1960s decided they were too smart to use Earth's directions to locate God, both the wise and the simple through all generations have looked "up" to praise the Creator.

"Unto thee, O Lord, do I lift up my soul," the psalmist prayed (Ps. 25:1). Three psalms later we hear him saying, "I will lift up my hands toward your Most Holy Place" (Ps. 28:2, NIV).

Psalm 123:1 is even more specific: "Unto thee lift I up mine eyes, O thou that dwellest in the heavens."

Lamentations 3:41 bids God's people, "Let us lift up our hearts and our hands to God in heaven" (NIV). Do you suppose the apostle Paul had this in mind when he wrote, "I want men everywhere to lift up holy hands in prayer" (1 Tim 2:8, NIV)?

The Scriptures and the expressions men and women in all ages are consistent. We look *up* to God.

One good reason for this may well be that the most common response to any encounter with the Almighty is to prostrate ourselves before Him. When the apostle John saw the glorified Christ in Revelation 1, he fell on his face. This was precisely the response of Ezekiel when he saw the vision of God on His throne. He "fell facedown" (1:28, NIV).

Last Lord's day I sang with a joyous band of disciples the strains of the modern praise song, "We bow down, and we worship the King." Then we sang, "Come, let us worship and bow down. Let us kneel before the Lord, our God and Maker."

Nothing lifts up our souls more than bowing down before the God of Heaven and Earth.

Unit 3: The Promise of New Life

Lesson 1

A New Spirit

Ezekiel 11:14-25

Again the word of the LORD came unto me, saying,

15 Son of man, thy brethren, even thy brethren, the men of thy kindred, and all the house of Israel wholly, are they unto whom the inhabitants of Jerusalem have said, Get you far from the LORD: unto us is this land given in possession.

16 Therefore say, Thus saith the Lord GOD; Although I have cast them far off among the heathen, and although I have scattered them among the countries, yet will I be to them as a little sanctuary in the countries where they shall come.

17 Therefore say, Thus saith the Lord GOD; I will even gather you from the people, and assemble you out of the countries where ye have been scattered, and I will give you the land of Israel.

18 And they shall come thither, and they shall take away all the detestable things thereof and all the abominations thereof from thence.

19 And I will give them one heart, and I will put a new spirit within you; and I will take the stony heart out of their flesh, and will give them an heart of flesh:

20 That they may walk in my statutes, and keep mine ordinances, and do them: and they shall be my people, and I will be their God.

21 But as for them whose heart walketh after the heart of their detestable things and their abominations, I will recompense their way upon their own heads, saith the Lord GOD.

22 Then did the cherubims lift up their wings, and the wheels beside them; and the glory of the God of Israel was over them above.

23 And the glory of the LORD went up from the midst of the city, and stood upon the mountain which is on the east side of the city.

24 Afterwards the spirit took me up, and brought me in a vision by the Sirit of God into Chaldea, to them of the captivity. So the vision that I had seen went up from me.

25 Then I spake unto them of the captivity all the things that the LORD had shewed me.

Memory Selection
Ezek. 11:19

Background Scripture
Ezek. 11:14-21

Devotional Reading
2 Cor. 3:1-11

FOCUS

This quarter is based on the universal experience of feeling the need to "start over." Believers know of God's power to create life, and we instinctively turn to Him also when we need *new* life.

The first five lessons are based on the promise of new life that God gave

His people Israel during the captivity of the sixth-century B.C. Certainly in their idolatry and other forms of disobedience they had well earned the low ebb of life they felt as captives in strange lands. Yet, through God's promise to save a faithful Remnant and other acts of grace, God assures them that those who turn to Him will not be abandoned. They will yet experience new life, a new heart, and a new spirit from Him who first created life.

ഇ‍ാ

For a Lively Start

Think of illustrations of vigorous activity that, after showing great promise, then lapse into a downward spiral. For example, a distance runner may start off too fast, and be unable to maintain her original pace. A camper may put a match to kindling and watch the flames at first leap into a warming fire

. . . then sputter and die after coming upon some green twigs. A businessman invests too liberally in a start-up operation, then runs out of funds and is unable to make the first payment on a loan.

So it is in the moral and spiritual life. We may begin to follow Jesus with great enthusiasm, then allow a crisis to virtually squelch all hope. Is there a possibility of a new start, of new life? That question faces Israel in this lesson.

Teaching Outline	**Daily Bible Readings**
I. Rejection and Promise —14-16	Mon. Evil Hearts *Gen. 6:1-8*
A. Judah rejects Israel, 14-15	Tue. Willing Hearts *Exod. 25:1-9*
B. A 'little sanctuary,' 16	
II. Regathering of the People—17-18	Wed. Defiant Hearts *Deut. 2:26-30*
III. Recompense—19-21	Thu. Obedient Hearts *Deut. 5:28-33*
A. Real heart, renewed obedience, 19-20	Fri. Proud Hearts *Deut. 8:11-19*
B. Rebellious ways, 21	Sat. Loving Hearts *Deut. 10:12-21*
IV. Removal of the Spirit—22-25	Sun. One Heart, New Spirit *Ezek. 11:14-21*

Verse by Verse

I. Rejection and Promise —14-16
A. Judah rejects Israel, 14-15

14 Again the word of the LORD came unto me, saying,

15 Son of man, thy brethren, even thy brethren, the men of thy kindred, and all the house of Israel wholly, are they unto whom the inhabitants of Jerusalem have said, Get you far from the LORD: unto us is this land given in possession.

Ezekiel did his prophesying early in the period after Judah had been taken captivity into Babylon. There are some signs that he stayed in touch with the prophet Jeremiah, who remained longer in Jerusalem before going to Babylon. It is also possible that Ezekiel was allowed enough freedom to make some trips back to Judea. At any rate, we can see from these verses that some among his brethren in "the house of Israel," probably a remnant of the northern kingdom who had trickled down to Jerusalem, were taunting Ezekiel, as a Judean or "southerner," saying that the Promised Land, both northern and southern kingdoms, was theirs. Ezekiel, they say, should stay as far as he could away from home and accept captivity.

B. A 'little sanctuary,' 16

16 Therefore say, Thus saith the Lord GOD; Although I have cast them far off among the heathen, and although I have scattered them among the countries, yet will I be to them as a little sanctuary in the countries where they shall come.

God tells Ezekiel to reply to the taunting by quoting God as saying that although he and his companions have been taken into Babylon and other countries of the Diaspora (or "Scattering"), God will make of them a "little sanctuary" and keep them safe until it is time for them to return. This is the doctrine of the Remnant: no matter how unfaithful the main body of God's people become, because of His promise to Abraham He will preserve a part of the people through whom the Messiah will come. Those Jews in captivity who want to repent and return to

God may be included in this "little sanctuary" or Remnant if they wish.

II. Regathering of the People—17-18

17 Therefore say, Thus saith the Lord GOD I will even gather you from the people, and assemble you out of the countries where ye have been scattered, and I will give you the land of Israel.

18 And they shall come thither, and they shall take away all the detestable things thereof and all the abominations thereof from thence.

This promise to give the land of Israel to the Jews sounds almost identical to God's original promises to the patriarchs Abraham, Isaac, and Jacob. The difference is in the last phrase, where God says the Remnant who are given again the Promised Land will remove all the "detestable things" and "abominations." They had lost the land and been carried into captivity partly because they had failed to remove such idolatrous forms of worship; it is unthinkable that those who want to return would fail to rid themselves of such evils a second time. The tragic fact is that they actually did, on the whole, submit to foreign worship again after they returned, forfeiting the land except in the spiritual sense in which God gives the faithful His Kingdom.

III. Recompense—19-21

A. Real heart, renewed obedience, 19-20

19 And I will give them one heart, and I will put a new spirit within you; and I will take the stony heart out of their flesh, and will give them an heart of flesh:

20 That they may walk in my stat-utes, and keep mine ordinances, and do them: and they shall be my people, and I will be their God.

It is likely that God envisions now the very spiritual Kingdom mentioned above. Looking down through the future, He sees that Israel will largely abandon their renewed promise to be faithful, and God will find it necessary to spiritualize the Land Promise into His Kingdom promise. This realm will comprise those who have "one heart." They will have traded their hearts of stone for hearts of flesh. Because they have accepted the Messiah they will be the "true Jews" (see Gal. 4:6-9; 6:16).

B. Rebellious ways, 21

21 But as for them whose heart walketh after the heart of their detestable things and their abominations, I will recompense their way upon their own heads, saith the Lord GOD.

All of God's promises are like a two-sided coin, with blessings for obedience on one side and punishment for disobedience on the other. Moses had set before the people two ways, a way of blessing and a way of cursing (Deut. 11:26). Jesus spoke of two ways, one leading to eternal life and the other to eternal death. This future choice is what is being offered here to God's people in captivity.

This provision of choice does not mean that the people have to reform before God blesses them; in fact, as we saw in verses 19-20, God goes so far as to give the faithful a heart of flesh and take away their heart of stone. He who makes the demand supplies the means of obedience. The choice merely reveals the intent and motive; it is an example of God's *foreknowledge*, not

His *foreordination.*

IV. Removal of the Spirit—22-25

22 Then did the cherubims lift up their wings, and the wheels beside them; and the glory of the God of Israel was over them above.

23 And the glory of the Lord went up from the midst of the city, and stood upon the mountain which is on the east side of the city.

24 Afterwards the spirit took me up, and brought me in a vision by the Spirit of God into Chaldea, to them of the captivity. So the vision that I had seen went up from me.

25 Then I spake unto them of the captivity all the things that the Lord had shewed me.

The prophet Ezekiel had a unique means of transportation. When he was needed in Jerusalem, he was granted a set of "wheels" in a vision, which in turn would reverse themselves and return the prophet to Babylon when he was needed there. This latter trip is what is described here. God needs him to carry the message above to Chaldea (Babylonia).

In this "chariot-throne," as it has been called, the wheels are somehow coordinated with the *"cherubim,"* which were four-winged creatures whose flights seem to make the wheels turn. The whole visionary "vehicle" is also connected to the Holy Spirit, so where Ezekiel goes, the Spirit goes with him.

Chapter 10 has the most complete description of the whole complex vehicle—wheels, Spirit, cherubim, and all. There we learn, among other facts, that the cherubim each have four faces—the likeness of a lion, a man, an eagle, and a cherub itself (see 10:14). Note how different these awesome creatures are from the cute, plump, and cuddly cherubs of paintings from the Middle Ages.

&)Q

Evangelistic Emphasis

Sin is bad and brings consequences, but God is good and that makes all the difference. God is love, and He never stops loving us even when we sin. This is one of the messages we receive from Ezekiel's prophecy.

The Israelites had so grievously sinned against God that He allowed Nebuchadnezzar, ruler of Babylon, to conquer the city of Jerusalem and destroy the Temple. Leading inhabitants of the city were taken away to Babylon as captives.

They lived along a waterway connected to the Euphrates River, in the area that is now Iraq. It must have been a horrible existence for them, away from their homes, their city, and their sacred Temple. Their sins were costing them dearly.

God, though, never forgets His people. He is gracious and merciful. He is forgiving, and reaches out to His children even when they have sinned against Him. Second Peter 3:9 tells us that the Lord is not willing that any should perish, but wants everyone to come to repentance. This is good news for us all.

Memory Selection

And I will give them one heart, and I will put a new spirit within you; and I will take the stony heart out of their flesh, and will give them an heart of flesh—*Ezekiel 11:19*

Many years before our time of modern medical centers where heart transplants are performed, God promised to give new hearts to the Israelites who had sinned against Him.

He promised to replace their hardened hearts with tender ones. A stony heart would be hard and uncaring. It would be rebellious and obstinate. It would be easy to disobey God if one's heart were in this condition.

On the other hand, the replacement hearts God promised them would be of a different spirit. They would be cooperative and willing. These hearts would welcome God and want to do the right thing. They would believe. (Hebrews 3:12 warns about unbelieving hearts.) God promised them "one heart." It would be new, and focused on Him.

God is just as concerned about our hearts as He was for His children in Ezekiel's time. Hebrews 10:16-17 says, "…I will put my laws into their hearts, and in their minds will I write them; and their sins and iniquities will I remember no more."

Weekday Problems

Let's face it, and be honest with ourselves and God. It's not always easy to put Him first in our lives. Sometimes it's easier to do than others, but sooner or later we're likely to be tempted to set Him aside for the moment.

"No other gods" is the first Commandment (Exodus 20:3). No "graven images" is the second. The worship of other gods and idols can be a subtle sin. Covetousness (greed) falls into this category (Eph. 5:5; Col. 3:5). In a sense, any thing that stands between us and God is a form of idolatry.

Paul wrote about the "god of this world" (Satan), as distinct from Jesus Christ, who is the image of God (2 Cor. 4:4). We make decisions every day in which we choose to serve either "god" or God.

Jesus reminds us that we can't serve two masters (Matt. 6:24). Ezekiel 11:18 required that the Israelites get rid of detestable idols. Surely God expects no less of us.

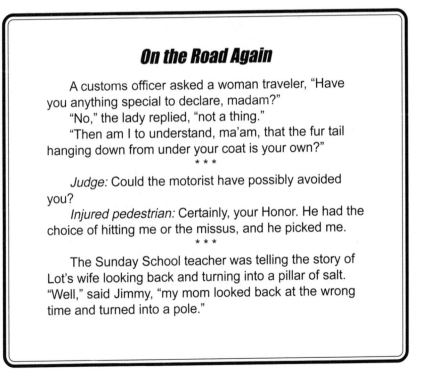

On the Road Again

A customs officer asked a woman traveler, "Have you anything special to declare, madam?"

"No," the lady replied, "not a thing."

"Then am I to understand, ma'am, that the fur tail hanging down from under your coat is your own?"

* * *

Judge: Could the motorist have possibly avoided you?

Injured pedestrian: Certainly, your Honor. He had the choice of hitting me or the missus, and he picked me.

* * *

The Sunday School teacher was telling the story of Lot's wife looking back and turning into a pillar of salt. "Well," said Jimmy, "my mom looked back at the wrong time and turned into a pole."

This Lesson in Your Life

As we first read the Ezekiel passage for this lesson, we might think that we don't have much in common with the people it describes. A closer look reveals that we do. There's a lesson here for our lives. What's described in Ezekiel speaks to the 21st century.

These people felt isolated from God. They were aliens in an unfriendly world. They felt abandoned. They were filled with anxiety. They were depressed. In such ways as these, they seem much like the people we know. Maybe they're just like you or me.

Our time has been called the age of anxiety, and we can't brush over the truth in that description. One British poet (admittedly a very pessimistic one) wrote, "I am a stranger and afraid, in a world I never made." It's a shame he felt that way. It wasn't really necessary.

We all have a bad day now and then, yet we realize there are more good days than bad ones. The mother of one of my childhood friends, as we were grumbling about something or another, reminded us that "If all the world were chocolate cake, there'd still be crumbs." Cheer up! There's more cake than crumbs.

Actually, surviving well in a troubled world calls for the deepest level of our Christian faith. "This is my Father's world," we sing in the hymn. We believe that God is sovereign in the universe He created.

The opening phrase in the Lord's Prayer is "Our Father which art in heaven." Believing this is not going to exempt us from troubles, but it gives us the key to handling them. We are children of the Father, not orphans. He loved us enough to send His Son to us. He gives us His Spirit. We have the comfort of Scripture. We are not abandoned. We are never alone. No one is friendless. Jesus loved us enough to die for us. There's no better friend than this.

Ezekiel's countrymen had lost their Jerusalem Temple. Even so, God said He would be their sanctuary. Neither does He leave us without assurance. Psalm 23 is an excellent place to begin finding it.

GETTING THE FACTS STRAIGHT

1. Our Devotional Reading states that the Corinthian Christians were a letter, written not in ink, but with what?

Written with the Spirit of the living God; not on stone, but in fleshly tables of the heart.

2. This same passage says that the letter kills. What does the Spirit do?

The Spirit gives life.

3. How did God describe to Ezekiel the location to which He had exiled the people?

He cast them far off among the heathen, and scattered them among the nations.

4. The Temple had been destroyed in Jerusalem. What (spiritually) would God be for them while in exile?

He would be for them "a little sanctuary."

5. What (geographically) did God promise to do for them?

He would gather and assemble them out of the countries where they were scattered, and give them the land of Israel.

6. When they returned to Israel, what were they to destroy?

They were to destroy all the detestable things and abominations ("vile images and detestable idols," NIV).

7. God would give them "one heart." What does this mean?

It was to be a new and undivided heart. They would serve God gladly and without reservation. He also gave them a new spirit.

8. How is their old heart described, and what will replace it?

Their old heart was a heart of stone. A heart of flesh will replace it.

9. What would be the difference between a heart of stone and of flesh?

A stone heart would be cold and uncaring. It would be stubborn and rebellious. A heart of flesh would be just the opposite of stone. It would be warm and caring, concerned about God's will.

10. In what way will their lives be different, with a new heart and spirit?

They will walk in God's statutes and keep His ordinances, rather than being rebellious and disobedient as they had been previously. They will be God's people, and He will be their God.

The Scripture passages in this lesson open up an exciting challenge for us. We've been reading about spirit and heart, newness and letter writing. Let's put them together and make something out of them.

Here's hoping that you know someone who exudes the joy of the Lord. Just being around this person makes you want to smile. When you see this individual, you see Christ in him or her. You're in the presence of a Christian optimist.

This wonderful friend is also a Christian realist, and knows that the world is not always a nice place, and may have even experienced the worst that a troubled world can throw at us.

This may have given depth to your friend, but hasn't diminished his or her spirit.

The challenge is, can each of us become this person?

The apostle Paul gives inspiration for this goal. His Philippian letter, written from prison and when a number of things had gone wrong, is filled with joy and rejoicing. He had the right kind of heart. We see Christ in him.

Lesson 1 is about receiving a new heart and a new spirit, one attuned to God. It's about having the Spirit (the one spelled with a capitol S). We can be living letters, written by the Spirit of the living God, known and read by all. Our friends will see Christ in us.

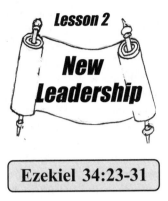

Lesson 2

New Leadership

Ezekiel 34:23-31

And I will set up one shepherd over them, and he shall feed them, even my servant David; he shall feed them, and he shall be their shepherd.

24 And I the LORD will be their God, and my servant David a prince among them; I the LORD have spoken it.

25 And I will make with them a covenant of peace, and will cause the evil beasts to cease out of the land: and they shall dwell safely in the wilderness, and sleep in the woods.

26 And I will make them and the places round about my hill a blessing; and I will cause the shower to come down in his season; there shall be showers of blessing.

27 And the tree of the field shall yield her fruit, and the earth shall yield her increase, and they shall be safe in their land, and shall know that I am the LORD, when I have broken the bands of their yoke, and delivered them out of the hand of those that served themselves of them.

28 And they shall no more be a prey to the heathen, neither shall the beast of the land devour them; but they shall dwell safely, and none shall make them afraid.

29 And I will raise up for them a plant of renown, and they shall be no more consumed with hunger in the land, neither bear the shame of the heathen any more.

30 Thus shall they know that I the LORD their God am with them, and that they, even the house of Israel, are my people, saith the Lord GOD.

31 And ye my flock, the flock of my pasture, are men, and I am your God, saith the Lord GOD.

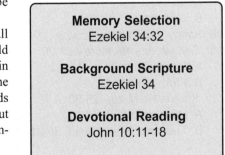

Memory Selection
Ezekiel 34:32

Background Scripture
Ezekiel 34

Devotional Reading
John 10:11-18

FOCUS

The various messages in the book of Ezekiel are addressed to various peoples—to the disobedient captives that have been taken to Babylon, to disobedient "shepherds" or leaders of the people, to the prophet himself, to the nations which, although used for a time by God to discipline His people, still are held accountable, and, as in today's lesson, to captives who have repented and indicated a willingness to return to the Lord.

Many of these captives are only victims of the treasonable leaders that have caused the disaster of the Diaspora (Scattering). The focus of this lesson is that God has not forgotten them. He will bring them together again under the leadership of the Messiah, as part of the Remnant preserved to testify to the faithfulness of God.

&)(&

For a Lively Start

This lesson, which predicts the return to the Holy Land of many who had been captured by their enemies, portrays the people as sheep. Ask your group what characteristics, good or bad, this characterization calls up.

For example, sheep tend to "follow the leader," whether the leader is a "bell-wether" or a trusted shepherd. Sheep are not "fighters" so they need to be protected, and contained in at least a temporary sheepfold at night. They are so timid that they often will drink only from a quiet pond, rather than rushing water. Because of the shape of their mouths and teeth, they tend to pull grass up by the roots, and thus must continually be shown new pasturage. Point out that the Messiah as the Good Shepherd offers just what we as sheep need.

Teaching Outline	Daily Bible Readings	
I. Safe Shepherds—34:23-24	Mon.	A Begotten Son *Ps. 2:4-11*
A. Messiah, 23	Tue.	The Good Shepherd *John 10:11-18*
B. God, 24	Wed.	Trusting in the Lord
II. Safety and Nurture—25-26		*Ps. 21:1-7*
III. Self-servers No More—27-28	Thu.	An Enduring Throne *Ps. 45:1-7*
A. From within, 27	Fri.	A Righteous King
B. From without, 28		*Ps. 72:1-7*
IV. Shame No More—29-30	Sat.	An Exalted King *Ps. 110*
A. Heathen banished, 29	Sun.	'You Are My Sheep'
B. The parable explained, 30-31		*Ezek. 34:23-31*

Verse by Verse

I. Safe Shepherds—34:23-24
A. Messiah, 23

23 And I will set up one shepherd over them, and he shall feed them, even my servant David; he shall feed them, and he shall be their shepherd.

Rather than kings or prophets, *chaos* has reigned supreme over Israel and Judah for generations. Unfaithful kings largely cancel out the work of faithful rulers. From the eighth century B.C. the threat—and often the reality—of foreign domination and even deportation and captivity has been very real.

Through it all, the word of faithful prophets and the lives of faithful Hebrews have been still, small voices—a committed minority largely overwhelmed by those who seem eager to follow foreign gods whom they can see instead of their own invisible God. Now, with most members of the northern kingdom of Israel in Assyrian captivity, and more recently the southern kingdom of Judah carried away into Babylonia, God decides it is time for a heartening word to the faithful, wherever they live.

It comes in the form of "Remnant theology," which we have noticed before. A small number of faithful Israelites will be allowed to return to the Promised Land and rebuild both the Holy City of Jerusalem and the Temple itself. This will require strong leadership, which is characterized here by "one shepherd," David. Only a few scholars think this is a prediction of a resurrected David, who has been dead for nearly 400 years. Rather, it is probably a veiled reference to the fact that God has promised that there will always be a member of the Davidic dynasty on the throne—the Messiah, who would one day be born of the *house* of David.

B. God, 24

24 And I the LORD will be their God, and my servant David a prince among them; I the LORD have spoken it.

Although there will be "one shepherd" (vs. 23), in the mystery of the godhead (or Trinity) He can be described either as the Father of the Son,

263

Messiah ("prince" of David) or the Lord. After generations of kings who over-tax the people and lead them to serve other gods, this must have been the most heartening word possible to those who are languishing captive in foreign lands. The final sentence, "I the Lord have spoken it," serves as a divine vow designed to make the promise too strong to be broken.

II. Safety and Nurture—25-26

25 And I will make with them a covenant of peace, and will cause the evil beasts to cease out of the land: and they shall dwell safely in the wilderness, and sleep in the woods.

26 And I will make them and the places round about my hill a blessing; and I will cause the shower to come down in his season; there shall be showers of blessing.

Now the oracle moves toward a parable of the faithful among Israel as sheep. In the first place, returning to Jerusalem will be as though a great sheep owner will make a covenant with the natural environment, assuring peace between the surroundings and the sheep. Usually sheep require a high degree of maintenance and an environment suitable for tame animals. Upon the people's return to Judea, however, it will be as though the land itself co-operates in meeting the needs of the sheep (people). They will not need to sleep in the safety of a sheepfold, but can sleep safely in the wilderness. Instead of needing the safety of a corral, they can stay in the woods.

In verse 26, "the hill" may be a figurative reference to the hill on which the Temple in Jerusalem will be rebuilt.

Instead of having to deal with storms out of season, the sheep and the land will cooperate by having gentle rains "in season." This will include what agriculture workers called "the early rains," in the Fall, and "the latter rains," in the Spring. Instead of "gully washers," the rains will be gentle—"There Shall Be Showers of Blessing" is a hymn appropriately drawn from this verse.

III. Self-servers No More—27-28
A. From within, 27

27 And the tree of the field shall yield her fruit, and the earth shall yield her increase, and they shall be safe in their land, and shall know that I am the LORD, when I have broken the bands of their yoke, and delivered them out of the hand of those that served themselves of them.

In 34:2ff., Ezekiel unleashed a harsh tirade against leaders in Israel whose first thought was of themselves: "Woe be to the shepherds of Israel that do feed themselves! Should not the shepherds feed the flocks? Ye eat the fat, and ye clothe you with the wool, ye kill them that are fed: but ye feed not the flock" (vss. 2-3). In other words, Israel had lapsed into its familiar cycle when judges and kings could be bribed, and priests and prophets were for sale to the highest bidder. It would do no good to be allowed to return to the Holy Land if its governance will be no better than it was when the people left it. That, the prophet now assures them, will not be the case. Apparently this will not be accomplished by a revolution of the people but by the Spirit of God working among the "shepherds."

B. From without, 28

28 And they shall no more be a prey to the heathen, neither shall the beast of the land devour them; but they shall dwell safely, and none shall make them afraid.

To balance his oracle, the prophet returns to the figure of the sheep, promising safety not only from within but from without. The "beasts" of the Philistines and other enemies will be tamed so that God's flock can live in safety.

IV. Shame No More—29-30

A. Heathen banished, 29

29 And I will raise up for them a plant of renown, and they shall be no more consumed with hunger in the land, neither bear the shame of the heathen any more.

Our understanding of this verse is enhanced by reading "planting" for "plant." The idea is that God, as the Great Gardener, will make a planting of His people in the land He gave them. Two main drawbacks in owning land include *hunger,* when the rains do not come on time, and *enemies* (here, "heathens") who come to steal, or "salt" the land. Neither of these elements will be present, God promises, when He restores the people to the land.

B. The parable explained, 30-31

30 Thus shall they know that I the LORD their God am with them, and that they, even the house of Israel, are my people, saith the Lord GOD.

31 And ye my flock, the flock of my pasture, are men, and I am your God, saith the Lord GOD.

Now God stops speaking in parables and explains His promises in literal terms. He, the Shepherd of the parable is their Lord and God. The house of Israel, His people, are the flock, and the pasture is the Land of Promise. It is unusual for parabolic language to receive such a plain explanation.

* * *

We can hardly avoid asking about the long-term meaning of these promises, when both biblical and secular history show that after only a few generations the people had returned to the ungodly lives for which God had punished them by allowing them to be carried into captivity. Once more they are defeated by their enemies. This problem is removed when, as the prophet no doubt intended, the "Land" and "Shepherd" promises are spiritualized. The Land can be read as the Kingdom of God, the Shepherd becomes Jesus the Messiah, and the flock becomes His followers.

Evangelistic Emphasis

What happens in Washington, D.C. will touch your life and mine. It's where our national leaders do their thing. If you've watched proceedings there on TV, have you wished we had more statesmen (and stateswomen) and fewer politicians on the job? Quality of leadership matters.

In recent years we've witnessed major corporations fail because of misdeeds of executive officers. Or perhaps you've had the good fortune of working for a company with excellent leadership.

Ezekiel describes a time when leadership of God's people was abysmal. His shepherds took care of themselves, but not the sheep.

Christians need to take note of leadership issues. We want to see the Good News about Jesus Christ spread around the globe, and for others to know about the grace of God. Christian leaders will help determine our success or failure. Let's accept the responsibility for producing godly leaders, and for encouraging and supporting them as they sacrificially shepherd us.

Memory Selection

And ye my flock, the flock of my pasture, are men, and I am your God, saith the Lord God.—*Ezekiel 34:31*

It's a reality that goes as far back as human memory reaches: Sheep need a shepherd. This is reinforced for us in Scripture and in art. We all have the mental image of the Good Shepherd enfolding the lost sheep in His arms.

The words in our Memory Selection were given to Ezekiel while the people were still scattered in the exile. It must have comforted them to hear God's assurance that even in a foreign land they were still His sheep and in His pasture.

God made the point clear that He is God, and people are people. We want to be careful about having such a fuzzy, feel-good feeling about the shepherd/sheep imagery that we forget this.

As we read Psalm 23 we affirm that the Lord is our shepherd. We feel assured as we read Jesus' words in John 10:11, "I am the good shepherd. The good shepherd lays down his life for the sheep." Such leadership is comfort food for our souls.

Weekday Problems

Do you suppose that sometimes sheep might get a little too frisky? Maybe it's night and they're all in the sheepfold, but one independent lamb jumps over the wall. Or maybe they're grazing on the hillside and one gets to wondering if the grass is greener on the other side. We remember Jesus' parable about the one sheep that got lost (Luke 15:3-7). How do you suppose that happened?

This might get a little embarrassing, so you can keep the answer between yourself and the Lord. But have you ever purposely wandered away from the Shepherd? Maybe a careless straying away is more likely. Either way, Jesus' parable lets us know that the Shepherd came searching. Even if He still has 99, He's concerned about the one that's missing.

At one time or another we've all been straying sheep. That's just a human-sheep problem. We don't always follow our Leader. The Lord helps solve the problem when He comes looking for us.

Down on the Farm

The book agent came to sell an Arkansas farmer a set of books on scientific approaches to agriculture. The leathery-skinned farmer thumbed through them, then said, "Nope, son, I ain't gonna buy these-here books."

"But sir," replied the salesman, "do you realize that if you had these books you could farm twice as good as you do now?"

"Well, see, that's the problem," said the farmer. "I ain't farmin' now half as good as I know how."

* * *

The farmer carried his milk pail up to the feisty cow with his teeth gritted. "Well, Bessie, what's it going to be? Am I going to have milk for supper tonight or hamburger?"

* * *

The woman went to the gardening store and asked the proprietor what to plant in a particular spot in her yard. "It gets very little rain, has too much late afternoon sun, the soil is clay, and it's on a rocky ledge. What should I plant there?"

"Well," said the gardener, "you might try a flagpole."

This Lesson in Your Life

It's fascinating to be reading in the Old Testament, as we are in this present lesson, and observe how God worked some of His long-term plans into the message He was giving to those long-ago children of His.

Through the message God gave Ezekiel, He dealt with the immediate problem facing the people then, and described for them how He would deal with their disobedience and remedy their lives. He also spoke words that must have left them wondering: words such as in 34:23, "And I will set up one shepherd over them, and he shall feed them, even my servant David; he shall feed them, and he shall be their shepherd." This must have been a puzzle for Ezekiel also. (Read 1 Peter 1:10-12.) We might assume that in the back of his mind, this prophet realized that part of his message was directed to the distant future, though he couldn't say exactly how or when.

With Christian hindsight we find a prophecy of the coming Good Shepherd, a descendant of David. The verse does not elaborate, but briefly makes its statement. The New Testament has numerous references to Jesus as the son of David. As a matter of fact, the first verse in the New Testament begins, "A record of the genealogy of Jesus Christ the son of David . . . ." Also, the angel Gabriel told Mary that God would give her child "the throne of his father David" (Luke 1:32).

As we read chapters such as Ezekiel 34, we are not just reading ancient history. We're reading background information about God's plans for our relationship with Jesus Christ.

Knowing how God dealt with those people in the distant past, gives light as to how He feels about us and our present situation. Sin brings consequences. God is gracious and loving. Sinners must repent. God makes us new, and gives us good hearts and a new spirit. God shepherds His flock, and in a time long after Ezekiel's, He sent David's son as the Good Shepherd. Acting on this information will help us get through life successfully.

GETTING THE FACTS STRAIGHT

1. In our Devotional Reading, Jesus identifies Himself as the good shepherd. What is the outstanding characteristic of such a shepherd?

The good shepherd lays down his life for the sheep.

2. We're studying about the importance of servant-leaders. How does Jesus describe the shepherd who cares nothing for the sheep?

If he sees the wolf coming, he will run away and abandon the sheep.

3. What kind of message was Ezekiel commanded to give to the shepherds of Israel?

He was to prophesy against them for failing to care for the people.

4. Instead of taking care of the sheep, what had the shepherds done?

They had taken care of themselves and neglected the sheep.

5. What kind of rule did the shepherds exercise over the sheep?

They ruled them "with force and with cruelty."

6. God took the flock away from the bad shepherds. After this, how were the sheep shepherded?

God would shepherd them and bring them back to the land of Israel.

7. After all the above had taken place, what did God say He would do about a shepherd?

"And I will set up one shepherd over them, and he shall feed them, even my servant David; he shall feed them, and he shall be their shepherd" (vs. 23).

8. What else is said about David?

God's servant David will be a prince among the people, and he shall be their shepherd.

9. In what way do we associate Jesus as being the David spoken of in these verses?

Such passages as Matthew 1:1, which speaks of Jesus Christ the son of David. Also Acts 2:25-36 and numerous other New Testament references.

10. What is the title of the Christian song that is a direct quotation from Ezekiel?

"There Shall be Showers of Blessing" (vs. 26).

Let's begin our Uplift Page with something of a put-down (with the promise of getting back up very quickly).

Some religious leaders can be a disaster. Ezekiel describes some really bad ones. Paul does also. While he was in prison some church leaders purposely preached Christ out of envy, strife, selfish and impure motives, hoping to cause Paul even more distress during his imprisonment (Phil. 1:12-18). That's about as low as anybody can get to be.

Now for the uplift: Paul rejoiced about it because Christ was preached.

Fortunately, church members normally have some input in selecting leaders. We can pray for and hope for Christ-honoring, Spirit-led, Scripture-loving servant leaders in our churches and other areas of Christian activity. We can work toward this goal, keeping our standards high, and as opportunities permit, be the best leader we can if leadership roles are opened for us.

When leadership is poor and there's nothing constructive we can do about it, we can try to have the same attitude Paul did, and rejoice for whatever successes there are in honoring Christ.

God's People Restored Again

Ezekiel 36:22-32

Therefore say unto the house of Israel, Thus saith the Lord GOD; I do not this for your sakes, O house of Israel, but for mine holy name's sake, which ye have profaned among the heathen, whither ye went.

23 And I will sanctify my great name, which was profaned among the heathen, which ye have profaned in the midst of them; and the heathen shall know that I am the LORD, saith the Lord GOD, when I shall be sanctified in you before their eyes.

24 For I will take you from among the heathen, and gather you out of all countries, and will bring you into your own land.

25 Then will I sprinkle clean water upon you, and ye shall be clean: from all your filthiness, and from all your idols, will I cleanse you.

26 A new heart also will I give you, and a new spirit will I put within you: and I will take away the stony heart out of your flesh, and I will give you an heart of flesh.

27 And I will put my spirit within you, and cause you to walk in my statutes, and ye shall keep my judgments, and do them.

28 And ye shall dwell in the land that I gave to your fathers; and ye shall be my people, and I will be your God.

29 I will also save you from all your uncleannesses: and I will call for the corn, and will increase it, and lay no famine upon you.

30 And I will multiply the fruit of the tree, and the increase of the field, that ye shall receive no more reproach of famine among the heathen.

31 Then shall ye remember your own evil ways, and your doings that were not good, and shall lothe yourselves in your own sight for your iniquities and for your abominations.

32 Not for your sakes do I this, saith the Lord GOD, be it known unto you: be ashamed and confounded for your own ways, O house of Israel.

Memory Selection
Ezekiel 36:23

Background Scripture
Ezek. 36

Devotional Reading
Ps. 25:11-22

271

FOCUS

On the surface, the focus of this lesson seems highly similar to earlier studies promising that God will restore His people in captivity to their former fortunes in Israel. Just beneath the surface, however, there is a drastic difference. Earlier promises emphasize how much better life will be for the people when they return from captivity. The motive for improving the Israelites' life in this lesson is far different. It is in order *to improve the way God is perceived among Israel's enemies* that He is granting His people a reprieve.

Still, even that is for the people's benefit. Think of how their lives would improve if their enemies were to begin to love God and glorify Him!

෨෨ශ

For a Lively Start

Tell this parable to your group:

Johnny stole a toy while playing next door with his friend Larry. He climbs up the fence and sees Larry's mom working in the garden. "Hi, Mrs. Brown," says Larry. "Can Larry stay for supper?"

Mrs. Brown thinks a minute. Johnny has been acting up all day, and certainly deserves no favors. Then she has an idea, and replies, "Sure," she says. "If it's OK with your mom, it is with me."

Her son Johnny swallows a lump in his throat. He knows he doesn't deserve this treat, and that Mrs. Brown would have been well within her rights to say No. Hmm, Johnny thinks. He's going to act better tomorrow.

How is this parable similar to the Focus, above? How is it different?

Teaching Outline	Daily Bible Readings

I. Blessing for God's Sake—22-24
  A. My name profaned, 22-23
  B. Yet you may return, 24
 	
II. Bringing You Home—25-28
  A. Sprinkling you clean, 25
  B. New heart, new spirit, 26-27
  C. New relationship, 28
 	
III. Blessing the Land—29-30
 	
IV. Blessing and Shame—31-32
	Mon. Restored with God's Help
	  Ps. 69:1-5, 11-12
	Tue. Restored to be Saved
	  Ps. 80:1-7
	Wed. Restored to Our Salvation
	  Ps. 85:1-9
	Thu. Restored to God
	  Lament. 5:15-21
	Fri. Restored through Repentance
	  Jer. 31:7-9, 16-20
	Sat. Restored to Service
	  Jer. 15:15-21
	Sun. For My Name's Sake
	  Ezek. 36:22-32

Verse by Verse

I. Blessing for God's Sake—22-24
A. My name profaned, 22-23

22 Therefore say unto the house of Israel, Thus saith the Lord GOD; I do not this for your sakes, O house of Israel, but for mine holy name's sake, which ye have profaned among the heathen, whither ye went.

23 And I will sanctify my great name, which was profaned among the heathen, which ye have profaned in the midst of them; and the heathen shall know that I am the LORD, saith the Lord GOD, when I shall be sanctified in you before their eyes.

The speaker here is God, and He is giving the prophet Ezekiel a surprising message. It is not surprising in content, but in motive. God has promised earlier that He would bring a remnant back from captivity among the Gentiles. Now, however, he reveals a surprising motive or reason for doing so. He is not doing it for the people's sake, but for His own sake!

This is in spite of the fact that the people have "profaned" God's name before the heathen among whom they have been living. Although we are not

given any specifics, we can imagine. The word "profane" means *outside* or *before* (pro-) *the temple* (from the Latin "fanum," temple). A profane person uses carelessly and shamefully language or names that are intended to exalt God in the Temple. Another way to say it is that such language *desecrates* that which is holy, or the name of God.

Some Jews taken into captivity were tempted to profane God's name beyond their capacity to resist. They may have simply used God's name "in vain" or sworn with it, in the hearing of the Babylonians. They may have participated in Babylonian worship, attributing holiness to pagan idols. Whatever the specific means of profanity, it degraded the true God before the Israelites' captors.

The surprising part of God's promise here is that He will allow some of the people to return to their homeland *for his own sake,* not to benefit the people. He knows that this will be viewed by the Jews' captors as an act of mercy. "Look at the Israelites' God," they may say. "He had every reason to

273

punish His people for profaning His name, and instead He blesses them!" This act of grace does the opposite of profaning God's name; it *sanctifies* it, meaning that His name is "set apart" and made distinct from ordinary gods.

In a way, this is an evangelistic act. Showing the Babylonians that He is a God of grace might win some from paganism out of admiration, and cause them to worship the true God. In a sense, then, allowing the people to return is in part for the pagans' sake as well for God's.

B. Yet you may return, 24

24 For I will take you from among the heathen, and gather you out of all countries, and will bring you into your own land.

Obviously, being allowed to return to their homeland actually does benefit the Israelites, not just God. One thing is certain: however God chooses to state the reason for the return it will not be for any selfish motive. As "God is light, and in him is no darkness at all" (1 John 1:5), so God is love and in Him is no selfishness at all.

"All countries" of course refers to all countries in the known world, or all countries where Jew have been relocated. In addition to Babylon, Jews had been resettled in lands as far as Egypt to the south, Spain to the west, India to the east, and countries around the Black Sea to the north.

II. Bringing You Home—25-28

A. Sprinkling you clean, 25

25 Then will I sprinkle clean water upon you, and ye shall be clean: from all your filthiness, and from all your idols, will I cleanse you.

Although some Jews could not see it, being spiritually cleansed was more important than being relocated in Jerusalem. To a large degree, their difficulties had much less to do with geography or where they lived than with the inner landscape of their hearts. Sprinkling with water had been a sign of asking God for spiritual cleansing from the beginning of Jewish worship. Sprinkling with blood and with anointing oil were also involved (see Exod. 29:21).

B. New heart, new spirit, 26-27

26 A new heart also will I give you, and a new spirit will I put within you: and I will take away the stony heart out of your flesh, and I will give you an heart of flesh.

27 And I will put my spirit within you, and cause you to walk in my statutes, and ye shall keep my judgments, and do them.

Closely akin to being sprinkled as a sign of being cleansed of sin is the concept of a new (or renewed) heart. Adding "a new spirit" is the same, not an additional element. Neither the Jews nor Christian worshipers today would have difficulty with false worship or other forms of sin if their hearts were "soft" or "fleshy" enough to be moved by God's Word and will. The combination of the spirit "within you" and keeping God's laws shows that the common Christian charge that the Law was *only* a matter of the letter, or outward observances, is not true. Keeping only the letter of the Law was an abuse of God's will, not in any way originally intended to be sufficient.

C. New relationship, 28

28 And ye shall dwell in the land that I gave to your fathers; and ye

shall be my people, and I will be your God.

As precious as any of the blessings in returning to Palestine was that it would be accompanied by a renewed intimacy with God, as described in this verse. Being God's people and having Yahweh as their God describes a spiritual family relationship with Him that was impossible as long as the people chose to live in disobedience to His will.

III. Blessing the Land—29-30

29 I will also save you from all your uncleannesses: and I will call for the corn, and will increase it, and lay no famine upon you.

30 And I will multiply the fruit of the tree, and the increase of the field, that ye shall receive no more reproach of famine among the heathen.

For all the importance of the Temple which was to be rebuilt in Jerusalem, the Israelites were at root an agricultural society. For God to promise that the weather would be favorable for growing corn, fruit, and other crops is one of the most valuable blessings He could give His people. The last phrase, "no more reproach of famine among the heathen," likely refers to the jeers and taunts of pagans who would point to famine as evidence that the Jews were not living in favor with their God.

IV. Blessing and Shame—31-32

31 Then shall ye remember your own evil ways, and your doings that were not good, and shall lothe yourselves in your own sight for your iniquities and for your abominations.

32 Not for your sakes do I this, saith the Lord GOD, be it known unto you: be ashamed and confounded for your own ways, O house of Israel.

The passage closes as it began, with the affirmation that God will arrange for the return of Jews from the Diaspora for His own sake, not theirs. Again, however, there is no hint of self-centeredness here. For a person living in sin to "lothe" (some KJV versions spell it "loathe") themselves or become ashamed of their sinfulness is the first step toward having God forgive them. If the return to the Holy Land accomplishes that, it will obviously benefit the people as well as God.

෨෮

Evangelistic Emphasis

The Israelites were God's chosen people, but they were giving Him a bad reputation. They had profaned His holy name among the Gentiles. It didn't speak well of God that His children were so unruly. God said He would cleanse them, bring them back to their own land, give them a new spirit, and cause them to keep His laws. This would be done not for their sake, but for the sake of His own holy name.

What we're seeing here is a far cry from Christian evangelism, but there are some similarities. God's power can change people; (He gave them a new heart.) He is a God of mercy; (He could have annihilated them). He is a forgiving Father; (they didn't respect him). He is a God of grace; (they weren't deserving.) He is love; (He loved them when they were otherwise unlovable).

There is a majestic splendor to God, whose great and holy name is part of our evangelistic message. (Suggested for further reading: 1 Tim. 6:15-16.)

Memory Selection

And I will sanctify my great name, which was profaned among the heathen, which ye have profaned in the midst of them; and the heathen shall know that I am the LORD, saith the Lord GOD when I shall be sanctified in you before their eyes.—*Ezekiel 36:23*

This is a powerful verse. It shows the power of a changed life. It shows the impact of holy living.

The Israelites had disgraced the name of God by their lives. They were not even worthy to retain the land He had given their ancestors. If these were chosen people, their lives didn't speak well of the God who had chosen them.

Consequently, God announced that He would turn these people around; He would renew their hearts and spirits and make different people of them. He would make them holy, and thus demonstrate His own holiness to the nations of the world.

That's just how influential a holy life can be. It can indicate to anyone who sees it the power that brought it about. It may well be that the only look some people get of God is what they see of Him in our lives. We'll certainly want to project the right image.

Does it seem that you've been given more than your share of difficult situations to handle?

Weekday Problems

Let's take a quick lesson from Ezekiel. We think of him as an important man. He might have evaluated his situation differently.

Chapter 2 describes the people to whom God sent him to minister. Using the NIV, they're said to be rebellious, obstinate, and stubborn. They're called thorns, briars, and scorpions. God didn't give this prophet an easy job. His work was cut out for him.

Some people seem to get more difficult assignments in life than others. Recently, someone who was helping a relative through some legal and financial difficulties asked me, "Why am I the one who has to do this?" My reply to him was, "Because you're the one who can and will."

If you've been given a life with heavy-duty obligations, it may be because you're the one who can handle them, and because the Lord knows you will.

ℰᗡᏃ

Bragging Rights?

Don't brag, puff, and blow. It isn't the whistle that pulls the train.

* * *

When a man gets "too big for his britches" his hat won't fit, either.

* * *

The man who falls in love with himself will have no competition.

* * *

An egotist is a self-made man who's in love with his creator.

* * *

He who claims to be a self-made man has relieved God of an embarrassing responsibility.

* * *

People who are carried away by their own importance seldom have far to walk back.

This Lesson in Your Life

Though the prophet Amos came many decades before Ezekiel, and preached to an entirely different group of Jewish people, there's a verse in his book (3:2 NIV) that perfectly fits the situation in Ezekiel's time. The verse is based on a principle that speaks to our lives today. "You only have I chosen of all the families of the earth; therefore I will punish you for all your sins." The Israelites were God's chosen people. They were His "treasured possession" (Ex. 19:5). Yet they did not live as if that were the case, and God punished them severely for their failure. They have been described as experiencing the peril of privilege. They were honored by being God's elect, but did not live up to the responsibilities that came with their privileged position.

There's a message in Ezekiel for Christians. Similar to the ancient Israelites, we Christians have received a new heart and a new spirit from God. Such a transformation is the essence of being Christian, and it enables us to live lives that honor God.

God does this for us, and it gives us the opportunity to show His holiness through our attitude and life. In this sense, we are Christians for His "holy name's sake" (36:22). He does us the honor of allowing us to be godly people who can show the world what He has done through us.

This is the key point that Ezekiel's fellow-Israelites neglected. Rather than honoring God they defamed His reputation by their ungodly lives. They sadly missed their high calling by rejecting God's expectations.

Jesus said, "From everyone who has been given much, much will be demanded; and from the one who has been entrusted with much, much more will be asked" (Luke 12:48 NIV0).

God has abundantly given us His grace, mercy, love, and His Son and Spirit. We have "been given much," and have been "entrusted with much." We are so blessed. With such privilege comes much responsibility.

GETTING THE FACTS STRAIGHT

1. In our Devotional Reading, for what reason does the psalmist ask God to forgive his sins?

He asks forgiveness for the sake of God's name.

2. In our Memory Selection, how would God sanctify (show the holiness of) His name before the heathen)?

By having His holiness shown through the reformed lives of the Israelites.

3. How had the Israelites dealt with the name of God in the presence of the heathen?

They had profaned His name by their sinful lives.

4. God said He would not bless the Israelites for their own sake, but for what reason would He do so?

He would bless them for His own holy name's sake.

5. What will the heathen know about God, once He has sanctified the Israelites?

They will know that He is the Lord.

6. For what purpose would God gather His people out of the heathen lands and all the countries?

He would take them to their own land from which they were exiled.

7. God says He will sprinkle clean water on the people. Why is this to be done?

So they will be clean from their filthiness and their idols.

8. In 36:26, a promise is repeated that had been made earlier. What is it?

God will give His people a new heart and new spirit. He will take away their heart of stone and give them one of flesh.

9. God will also give them a new spirit. When all this is done, what change will take place in the people?

They will walk in His statutes and keep His laws.

10. After all these beneficial changes take place with the Israelites, how will they feel about their former life?

They will feel ashamed and disgraced for their previous conduct.

Uplift

We occasionally see someone interviewed on the TV news who is on the waiting list to receive a vital organ transplant, perhaps a heart. We consider it a miracle of modern medicine that an otherwise terminally ill patient can receive a new heart.

God has performed so many heart transplants that their number must be astronomical. Much of our present study in Ezekiel is about this very thing.

God is still in the business of working on hearts, and there are some beautiful New Testament passages about it. Here are a few of them.

"And because ye are sons, God hath sent forth the Spirit of his Son into your hearts, crying, *Abba*, Father" (Gal. 4:6).

"[I pray] that Christ may dwell in your hearts by faith . . . " (Eph. 3:17).

"And he that searcheth the hearts knoweth what is the mind of the Spirit, because he maketh intercession for the saints according to the will of God" (Rom. 8:27).

"For with the heart man believeth unto righteousness; and with the mouth confession is made unto salvation" (Rom. 10:10).

"In your hearts set apart Christ as Lord" (1 Pet. 3:15, NIV).

Being a Christian is a *heart*felt experience.

Lesson 4

Prophesying New Life

Ezekiel 37:1-14

The hand of the LORD was upon me, and carried me out in the spirit of the LORD, and set me down in the midst of the valley which was full of bones,

2 And caused me to pass by them round about: and, behold, there were very many in the open valley; and, lo, they were very dry.

3 And he said unto me, Son of man, can these bones live? And I answered, O Lord GOD, thou knowest.

4 Again he said unto me, Prophesy upon these bones, and say unto them, O ye dry bones, hear the word of the LORD.

5 Thus saith the Lord GOD unto these bones; Behold, I will cause breath to enter into you, and ye shall live:

6 And I will lay sinews upon you, and will bring up flesh upon you, and cover you with skin, and put breath in you, and ye shall live; and ye shall know that I am the LORD.

7 So I prophesied as I was commanded: and as I prophesied, there was a noise, and behold a shaking, and the bones came together, bone to his bone.

8 And when I beheld, lo, the sinews and the flesh came up upon them, and the skin covered them above: but there was no breath in them.

9 Then said he unto me, Prophesy unto the wind, prophesy, son of man, and say to the wind, Thus saith the Lord GOD; Come from the four winds, O breath, and breathe upon these slain, that they may live.

10 So I prophesied as he commanded me, and the breath came into them, and they lived, and stood up upon their feet, an exceeding great army.

11 Then he said unto me, Son of man, these bones are the whole house of Israel: behold, they say, Our bones are dried, and our hope is lost: we are cut off for our parts.

12 Therefore prophesy and say unto them, Thus saith the Lord GOD; Behold, O my people, I will open your graves, and cause you to come up out of your graves, and bring you into the land of Israel.

13 And ye shall know that I am the LORD, when I have opened your graves, O my people, and brought you up out of your graves,

14 And shall put my spirit in you, and ye shall live, and I shall place you in your own land: then shall ye know that I the LORD have spoken it, and performed it, saith the LORD.

Memory Selection
Ezek. 37:6

Background Scripture
Ezek. 37

Devotional Reading
Rom. 6:1-14

The priest-prophet Ezekiel had the delicate task of warning the people (primarily of Judah) that doom awaited them if they did not reform, but that God would support any efforts they made if they did return to Him. Both of these emphases are seen in the famous vision of the "Valley of the Dry Bones," which is the topic of this lesson.

People who live in or near a desert know how disheartening it is to come upon the carcass of cattle or sheep that have died from thirst. Nothing signals the lack of life more graphically than such sun-bleached bones. Yet in this parable, the Spirit shows God's power in bringing life from death.

෴

For a Lively Start

Ask a singer to lead your group in the first verse of the old African-American spiritual, "Dry Bones," inspired by Ezekiel's vision in chapter 37:

Ezekiel connected dem dry bones! (Sing three times.)

De toe bone connected to de (pause) *foot bone.* (Repeat thrice, end with *"Now hear de word of de Lawd!"*

De foot bone connected to de (pause) *ankle bone* (Repeat as above.)

De ankle bone connected to de (pause) *leg bone.* (Repeat.)

De leg bone connected to de (pause) *thigh bone.* (Repeat.)

De thigh bone connected to de (pause) *hip bone.* (Repeat.)

De hip bone connected to de (pause) *back bone.* (Repeat.)

De back bone connected to de (pause) *shoulder bone.* (Repeat.)

De shoulder bone connected to de (pause) *neck bone.* (Repeat.)

De neck bone connected to de (pause) *head bone.* (Repeat; conclude with *Now hear de word of de Lawd!)*

Teaching Outline	Daily Bible Readings
I. Israel Dead and Scattered—37:1-2	Mon. God Will Do Something New Isa. 43:14-21
II. Incisive Issue—3-6	Tue. A New Strength Isa. 40:23-31
A. Piercing question, 3	
B. Life-giving power predicted, 4-6	Wed. A New Covenant Luke 22:14-23
III. Indwelling Spirit—7-10	Thu. A New Creation 2 Cor. 5:16-21
A. Stage I: external healing, 7-8	
B. Stage 2: internal life, 9-10	Fri. New Mercies Every Day Lament. 3:19-31
IV. Interpretation of the Vision, 11-14	Sat. A New Song Ps. 40:1-5
A. Sad state of affairs, 11	
B. Israel's 'resurrection,' 12-14	Sun. You Shall Live! Ezek. 37:1-14

Verse by Verse

I. Israel Dead and Scattered—37:1-2

1 The hand of the LORD was upon me, and carried me out in the spirit of the LORD, and set me down in the midst of the valley which was full of bones,

2 And caused me to pass by them round about: and, behold, there were very many in the open valley; and, lo, they were very dry.

We must skip down to verse 11 to have the bones of this famous vision definitely identified as the Jews who have been carried captive to Babylon. Although the name "Ezekiel" means "God will strengthen," this vision and other references we have seen in the book show that God will first punish disobedient Israel before strengthening a remnant to return to the Holy Land. Ezekiel was among the Jews deported from Jerusalem to Babylon, when it invaded Judah (2 Kings 25). He may have witnessed a battle that left a valley filled with literal bones, as the Babylonians overran the Holy City.

The location is unimportant, and the vision obviously symbolic. Israel has been disassembled as a skeleton whose flesh and sinews have rotted away, leaving the bones to be picked over and scattered by beasts and birds of prey. Although Ezekiel has previously prophesied both destruction and restoration of God's people, this vision is unsurpassed in its graphic imagery.

II. Incisive Issue—3-6

A. Piercing Question, 3

3 And he said unto me, Son of man, can these bones live? And I answered O Lord GOD, thou knowest.

Many Bible prophecies ask this rhetorical question (see Rev. 7:13-14). Usually the prophet answers that only God can give its meaning. In the context of the Old Testament, which says very little about a resurrection to life after death, Ezekiel might have been expected to answer "No!" Even speaking symbolically, as though the question means "Can Israel be *restored*?" an optimistic reply would be difficult, given the continual rebellion of God's people. Yet it is not Ezekiel's burden to pronounce judgment, but only to be a vehicle for the vision.

B. Life-giving power predicted, 4-6

4 Again he said unto me, Prophesy upon these bones, and say unto them, O ye dry bones, hear the word of the LORD.

5 Thus saith the Lord GOD unto these bones; Behold, I will cause breath to enter into you, and ye shall live:

6 And I will lay sinews upon you, and will bring up flesh upon you, and cover you with skin, and put breath in you, and ye shall live; and ye shall know that I am the LORD.

As dismal as are Israel's prospects to "come to life," the God of second chances charges the prophet to address the lifeless bones with a word of hope. "Ye shall live"—not because of any inherent vitality in Israel itself, but because the God who is able to create life is also able to *re*-recreate it. As He breathed breath into Adam, he will breathe the breath of life into the scattered bones, and the flesh and sinews will reappear and reconnect the bones.

The Hebrew word *ruach,* translated "breath" in verse 5, is translated "wind" in verse 9, and "spirit" in verse 14. It literally means "air-in-motion," and the context determines how it is translated.

A. Stage 1: external healing, 7-8

7 So I prophesied as I was commanded: and as I prophesied, there was a noise, and behold a shaking, and the bones came together, bone to his bone.

8 And when I beheld, lo, the sinews and the flesh came up upon them, and the skin covered them above: but there was no breath in them.

Ezekiel is faithful to the charge to prophesy to the apparently dead bones

as though they can hear. The noise and shaking are from the "wind" or breath of God sweeping through the valley. Instead of scattering the bones more, it pulls them together and supplies the soft tissue necessary for bones to become a body.

Yet something is seriously missing. God's breath has reassembled what appears to be the bodies of the disobedient Israelites destroyed by the Babylonians, but they have no life within them. "Stage 1" of Ezekiel's vision has resulted only in a group of assembled corpses like cadavers in a morgue. At this stage of the drama there are plenty of bodies, but God obviously wants us to ask, "Of what use are mere corpses?"

B. Stage 2: internal life, 9-10

9 Then said he unto me, Prophesy unto the wind, prophesy, son of man, and say to the wind, Thus saith the Lord GOD; Come from the four winds, O breath, and breathe upon these slain, that they may live.

10 So I prophesied as he commanded me, and the breath came into them, and they lived, and stood up upon their feet, an exceeding great army.

Now the rest of the vision supplies what is so seriously lacking: the enlivening spirit that is the difference between a corpse and a person. The wind of God is summoned from the four corners of the earth, which is both an ancient and a modern way of saying "from all directions." It is a reversal of the Diaspora or Dispersion which scattered the Jews in the first place.

Even more important is the fact that the bodies that are reunited by God's breath or Spirit are also reanimated with a spirit of their own. We are probably to understand this to mean that the Jews whom God reassembles for the return to Judah will have the "new heart" predicted by Jeremiah (31:33; see also Ezek. 11:19.)

IV. Interpreting the Vision, 11-14

A. Sad state of affairs, 11

11 Then he said unto me, Son of man, these bones are the whole house of Israel: behold, they say, Our bones are dried, and our hope is lost: we are cut off for our parts.

Now Ezekiel is given the benefit of a clear explanation of what he has witnessed in the Valley of the Dry Bones. The defeat and deportation suffered by Israel have made a deep impression on them, as God intended. They finally realize that the idolatry and injustice to which they had descended was "the death of them," and had cut them off from a relationship with God.

B. Israel's 'resurrection,' 12-14

12 Therefore prophesy and say unto them, Thus saith the Lord God; Behold, O my people, I will open your graves, and cause you to come up out of your graves, and bring you into the land of Israel.

13 And ye shall know that I am the Lord, when I have opened your graves, O my people, and brought you up out of your graves,

14 And shall put my spirit in you, and ye shall live, and I shall place you in your own land: then shall ye know that I the Lord have spoken it, and performed it, saith the Lord.

Ezekiel is now instructed to reassure God's people that their "graves"—that is, the nations to which they were taken captive or "buried"—are now to be opened, and that they are to be restored to their homeland. The most notable example of the fulfillment of this prophecy is recorded in the books of Ezra and Nehemiah, who led a return from exile that included the rebuilding of the Temple in Jerusalem.

Some authorities believe the vision recorded here also applies to the restoration of all Israel at the Second Coming of Christ. Others see the fulfillment of the vision in the gathering of Jews "from every nation under heaven" in Acts 2:5, and the resulting formation of the Church, the spiritual Israel.

಄಄

Evangelistic Emphasis

Ezekiel's vision of the valley filled with dry bones reminds us that even if our evangelistic efforts appear unlikely to be successful, God can turn things around.

In all the history of the universe, prospects for reaching an audience with a meaningful message couldn't have been deader than what Ezekiel faced. Do you suppose this prophet felt a little uncertain as he delivered his sermon to bleached bones? Perhaps his past experience had prepared him for the likelihood that God would do something unexpected.

One thing we learn from Ezekiel's bone-sermon experience is never to give up too easily. We also learn to depend on God. He is the one who touches hearts and opens them to receive his grace.

Paul told the evangelist Timothy to be prepared in season and out of season (2 Tim. 4:2). The dry bones sermon appeared to be out of season, but when God is involved, maybe we should expect unexpected results.

Memory Selection

And I will lay sinews upon you, and will bring up flesh upon you, and cover you with skin, and put breath in you, and ye shall live; and ye shall know that I am the LORD.—*Ezekiel 37:6*

God works in an orderly fashion. He puts first things first, and builds from there. He finishes the jobs He begins. The results are good. This almost sounds like a description of Creation, doesn't it? In a sense it is a new creation, as we see Him give new life to bleached bones.

After He formed the bodies, He put breath into them, "And they lived, and stood up upon their feet, an exceeding great army" (vs. 10). This is a graphic word-picture of the restoration of Israel. Through this great rescue mission, He tells Israel that "ye shall know that I am the LORD."

We should be impressed, and appreciative. We take special note of Ezekiel's prophecies, because above and beyond the immediate message for Israel, there is a Christian connection. We, along with Israel, are assured that God is "the LORD."

Weekday Problems

Christian living is not a do-it-yourself project. I suspect that even though we know this, we may tend to depend largely on ourselves and not very much on God. (This is not to say that we don't have personal responsibilities, and are accountable for them.)

When God showed Ezekiel what covered the valley floor, He asked the prophet if those bones could be made to live. Do you suppose Ezekiel's first thought was, "Oh, no! Surely He doesn't expect me to do that!" He never did really answer the question. He just told God that He was the one who knew about such things.

God was much more qualified to re-work old bones than Ezekiel was. Ezekiel knew this and didn't volunteer for the job. There may be a lesson here for us. We need to know our limitations as well as our strengths. We might avoid some problems if we learn to say, "Please, God. I need help with this."

ഇരു

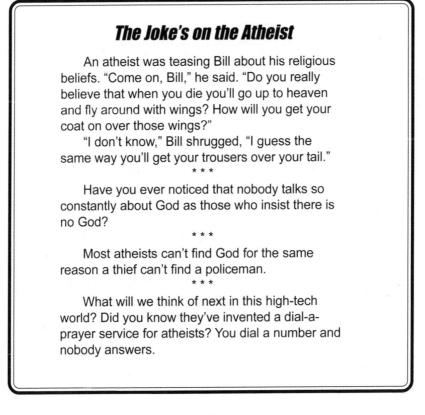

The Joke's on the Atheist

An atheist was teasing Bill about his religious beliefs. "Come on, Bill," he said. "Do you really believe that when you die you'll go up to heaven and fly around with wings? How will you get your coat on over those wings?"

"I don't know," Bill shrugged, "I guess the same way you'll get your trousers over your tail."

* * *

Have you ever noticed that nobody talks so constantly about God as those who insist there is no God?

* * *

Most atheists can't find God for the same reason a thief can't find a policeman.

* * *

What will we think of next in this high-tech world? Did you know they've invented a dial-a-prayer service for atheists? You dial a number and nobody answers.

This Lesson in Your Life

Ezekiel went through some very strange experiences during his prophetic ministry. Bluntly put, we'd say some weird ones. Considering the exciting and unusual visions he had, we're made to wonder if his dreams while sleeping didn't seem pretty dull.

Ezekiel's writing doesn't make easy reading. His message, though, fits us well. Actually, we Christians are on the receiving end of much of it.

For example, he preached about being dead and finding new life. As a Christian each of us has experienced this. Paul wrote about being dead in transgressions and sins, but being made alive with Christ (Eph. 2:1, 5). He says this is "by grace." (It was also by the free gift of God that Ezekiel's countrymen were restored.)

In our Devotional Reading (Romans 6:1-14) Paul paints a word-picture for us about being dead to sin and alive in Christ. He says that "all of us who were baptized into Jesus Christ were baptized into his death." He calls it being "buried with him by baptism into death," and says "we shall be also in the likeness of his resurrection" (vss. 4-5).

If we have shared Christ's resurrection, sin no longer has mastery of our lives. In this sense, we have died to sin and are alive to God in Christ Jesus.

There's no reason to think that Ezekiel comprehended the full implications of his messages as they applied to us. (Besides, he had his hands full just keeping herd on his cantankerous Israelite sheep.)

We, though, as unexpected as it might be as we first look into Ezekiel's activities, discover that he said much that is basic to our Christian faith. Every day of our lives we are enjoying some of the blessings he foretold. (Also, in addition to what he wrote about new life, we pick up on his references to David and the shepherd, both pointing to Jesus.)

1. Romans 6:11 says that we are "dead indeed unto sin, but alive unto God through Jesus Christ our Lord." What do the following two verses say should result from that?

We should not let sin reign in our bodies, and neither should we yield our members as instruments of unrighteousness.

2. As Ezekiel is about to be taken to the bone-filled valley, how does he describe getting there?

He says "The hand of the LORD was upon me, and he brought me out . . . ."

3. After Ezekiel was shown the bones, what question was he asked, and how did he answer?

He was asked, "Son of man, can these bones live?" His reply was, "O Lord GOD, thou knowest."

4. What kind of preaching was he instructed to do that seems quite strange?

He was to prophesy to the bones, and tell them to hear the word of the LORD.

5. What was the message he gave them?

They would be made alive. They would receive sinews, flesh, skin, breath, and would live.

6. As he prophesied to the bones, what happened?

He heard a noise, there was a shaking, and the bones came together, bone to its bone.

7. At this point there was no breath in the bodies. How was the next prophecy to be directed?

It was directed to the wind. Breath was to come from the four winds and breathe on the bodies so they could live.

8. After the breath came, what happened?

"They lived, and stood up upon their feet, an exceeding great army."

9. How did God identify "these bones"?

He said they were "the whole house of Israel."

10. As this episode closed, what did God say He would do for His people and that they will know about Him?

He said He would put His spirit in them so they shall live, He will place them in their own land, and they will know that He is the LORD.

Uplift

Here is some wonderful news that will certainly make you feel better: God is in charge of the world. He has not placed the burden of that responsibility on any of us.

It's not framed in these exact words, but through the book of Ezekiel God keeps telling the Israelites, "You people don't seem to realize that I'm God."

Let's not make that mistake. We'll want to honor Him in every way possible, including keeping our moral and spiritual lives in the condition that our Father expects and deserves from His children. (The Israelites, we remember, had dishonored His name by sinful living, including idolatry.) Keeping the name of God "hallowed" (as in the Lord's Prayer), is not just a feeling we have, but includes our lifestyle as well. (We might think in terms of our own families. We don't want our kinfolks besmirching the family name.)

You or I would be very inefficient in keeping the universe moving along. That's another reason we're glad God is running things, even though He sometimes behaves in unexpected ways. For instance, He gave His sinful, exiled Israelites a new heart, a new spirit, and new lives back in their own homeland. They had no right to expect that. He treated them nicer than they deserved. That's how He does things.

That's why we're glad He's God and is in charge. He treats us nicer than we deserve. We call it grace. We call it love.

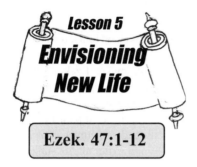

Lesson 5
Envisioning New Life

Ezek. 47:1-12

Afterward he brought me again unto the door of the house; and, behold, waters issued out from under the threshold of the house eastward: for the forefront of the house stood toward the east, and the waters came down from under from the right side of the house, at the south side of the altar.

2 Then brought he me out of the way of the gate northward, and led me about the way without unto the utter gate by the way that looketh eastward; and, behold, there ran out waters on the right side.

3 And when the man that had the line in his hand went forth eastward, he measured a thousand cubits, and he brought me through the waters; the waters were to the ankles.

4 Again he measured a thousand, and brought me through the waters; the waters were to the knees. Again he measured a thousand, and brought me through; the waters were to the loins.

5 Afterward he measured a thousand; and it was a river that I could not pass over: for the waters were risen, waters to swim in, a river that could not be passed over.

6 And he said unto me, Son of man, hast thou seen this? Then he brought me, and caused me to return to the brink of the river.

7 Now when I had returned, behold, at the bank of the river were very many trees on the one side and on the other.

8 Then said he unto me, These waters issue out toward the east country, and go down into the desert, and go into the sea: which being brought forth into the sea, the waters shall be healed.

9 And it shall come to pass, that every thing that liveth, which moveth, whithersoever the rivers shall come, shall live: and there shall be a very great multitude of fish, because these waters shall come thither: for they shall be healed; and every thing shall live whither the river cometh.

10 And it shall come to pass, that the fishers shall stand upon it from En-gedi even unto En-eglaim; they shall be a place to spread forth nets; their fish shall be according to their kinds, as the fish of the great sea, exceeding many.

11 But the miry places thereof and the marishes thereof shall not be healed; they shall be given to salt.

12 And by the river upon the bank thereof, on this side and on that side, shall grow all trees for meat, whose leaf shall not fade, neither shall the fruit thereof be consumed: it shall bring forth new fruit according to his months, because their waters they issued out of the sanctuary: and the fruit thereof shall be for meat, and the leaf thereof for medicine.

Memory Selection
Ezek. 47:9

Background Scripture
Ezek. 47:1-12

Devotional Reading
John 4:7-15

FOCUS

The message of Ezekiel takes a great leap forward in chapter 40, becoming, like the last two chapters of the book of Revelation, a pictorial vision of the peaceful and blessed nature of the fulfillment of the Kingdom of God. It does so in part by picturing a new Jerusalem with a new Temple, so "the tabernacle of God is with men, and he will dwell with them, and they shall be his people, and God himself shall be with them, and be their God" (Rev. 21:3).

All this makes Ezekiel, like most other end-time prophecies, highly symbolic and non-literal. We can therefore expect the scenes it paints to be often difficult and sometimes controversial to interpret. After all, its subject matter is "a new heaven and a new earth"; it is not surprising that the language is "new" as well.

&⊃CZ

For a Lively Start

This lesson from Ezekiel describes the Holy Land as believers might see the Kingdom in God's future—with abundant streams of life-giving water, fertile hillsides with flourishing crops, lakes teeming with fish, and forests replete with wildlife.

Invite members of your group to tell of places like that which they have visited. Think of Yellowstone National Park, the Shenandoah Valley, Yosemite National Forest, or the white sands along the Gulf of Mexico. Such places are attractive spots to visit partly because they are so different from the dry and barren areas where many of us live. Note that this lesson from Ezekiel presents a picture-post-card view of the Kingdom of God after all of God's children are settled and safe (and maybe even catching a trout or hiking down a mountain trail!).

Teaching Outline	Daily Bible Readings	
I. River of Life—47:1-5	Mon.	Wash Yourselves *Isa. 1:12-17*
A. Stream to the east, 1-2	Tue.	Water of Rebirth *Titus. 3:1-7*
B. Deepening waters, 3-5	Wed.	Like Showers and Rains *Hosea 6:1-6*
II. Healing of the Sea—6-10	Thu.	Planted by the Water *Ps. 1*
A. Trees at the bank, 6-7	Fri.	Give Me Living Water *John 4:7-15*
B. Dead Sea Enlivened, 8-10	Sat.	The Water of Life *Rev. 22:12-17*
III. Briny Bog—11	Sun.	Water from the Sanctuary *Ezek. 47:1-12*
IV. Tree of Healing—12		

Verse by Verse

I. River of Life—47:1-5
A. Stream to the east, 1-2

1 Afterward he brought me again unto the door of the house; and, behold, waters issued out from under the threshold of the house eastward: for the forefront of the house stood toward the east, and the waters came down from under from the right side of the house, at the south side of the altar.

2 Then brought he me out of the way of the gate northward, and led me about the way without unto the utter gate by the way that looketh eastward; and, behold, there ran out waters on the right side.

Ezekiel is being given a tour that seems to be of Jerusalem and the Temple in "the time after time"—after time has come to an end, and the struggles in the Kingdom have resulted in victory for the Lord and His people. One of the primary features in this fulfilled Kingdom is a new Temple—at least its dimensions and accommodations are far different from Solomon's Temple and the one that was rebuilt after the Jews returned from Babylonian captivity.

The word translated "house" in the KJV is simply that—a house. Yet the NIV is probably correct in translating it "temple," since it seems to be a new house of God. One of the several differences between this temple and Solomon's, in Jerusalem, is the stream or brook that flows from under the building, first to the south of the altar and then eastward. The meager flow will grow steadily stronger, perhaps symbolizing the small Remnant that returned from Babylon, which would be transformed in the Messianic Age to a mighty river of salvation. (The "utter" gate means "outer.")

B. Deepening waters, 3-5

3 And when the man that had the line in his hand went forth eastward, he measured a thousand cubits, and he brought me through the waters; the waters were to the ankles.

4 Again he measured a thousand, and brought me through the waters; the waters were to the knees. Again

he measured a thousand, and brought me through; the waters were to the loins.

5 Afterward he measured a thousand; and it was a river that I could not pass over: for the waters were risen, waters to swim in, a river that could not be passed over.

A man with a measuring line has been accompanying Ezekiel now and then since 40:3. He measures the brook that was at first a mere trickle, and finds that it has grown in both length and depth—evidently symbolizing the steadily growing Kingdom of God that began its greatest period of growth in Acts 2 at the first Pentecost after Christ's resurrection. The river begins only ankle-deep, but as Ezekiel follows it south, toward the brook Kidron, it burgeons up the knees, then to the loins, then becomes so deep a man must swim to traverse it.

Ezekiel is seeing that the small number of the faithful allowed to return are being rewarded by seeing their number grow. The prophet is preaching an "object sermon" showing the rewards of remaining faithful even against opposition. That this is the meaning is supported by the similar language in the victory chapter of Revelation 22:1—"And he shewed me a pure river of water of life, clear as crystal, proceeding out of the throne of God and of the Lamb."

II. Healing of the Sea—6-10
A. Trees at the bank, 6-7

6 And he said unto me, Son of man, hast thou seen this? Then he brought me, and caused me to return to the brink of the river.

7 Now when I had returned, behold, at the bank of the river were very many trees on the one side and on the other.

Another sign of new and vigorous life is that the formerly barren land near the southeast corner of Jerusalem has suddenly blossomed into a veritable orchard, on both sides of the river. In countryside like Palestine, trees were a welcome sign of relief from the unrelenting sun. They were also a sign of water, an oasis providing both relief from the heat and fruits such as dates and olives. What is happening here? A few Israelites with the grit and stamina to remain faithful are being given a glimpse into how their labor will be rewarded in the future.

B. Dead Sea Enlivened, 8-10

8 Then said he unto me, These waters issue out toward the east country, and go down into the desert, and go into the sea: which being brought forth into the sea, the waters shall be healed.

9 And it shall come to pass, that every thing that liveth, which moveth, whithersoever the rivers shall come, shall live: and there shall be a very great multitude of fish, because these waters shall come thither: for they shall be healed; and every thing shall live whither the river cometh.

10 And it shall come to pass, that the fishers shall stand upon it from En-gedi even unto En-eglaim; they shall be a place to spread forth nets; their fish shall be according to their kinds, as the fish of the great sea, exceeding many.

The Kidron is part of a long gash in the earth, a "rift valley" that begins far to the north of the Sea of Galilee and continues south through the Gulf of Akaba, the upper reaches of the Red Sea, then the Nile River in Africa. The Dead Sea is a part of this geographical feature, but since it has no outlet it is widely known as the Salt Sea as well. Its waters are too briny to support sea-life—unless it is time for God's Spirit to show us a symbolic future in which the Sea teems with fish and fishermen with nets make their living from it. The removal of the brine is described as a "healing," just as the hearts of people under Messiah's rule are healed.

III. Briny Bog—11

11 But the miry places thereof and the marishes thereof shall not be healed; they shall be given to salt.

The bright future is not 100 percent lovely. Until the Kingdom is firmly transformed into heaven there will al-ways be some who prefer the unhealed waters of brine, "given to salt." ("Marish" is of course a KJV spelling for "marsh.")

IV. Tree of Healing—12

12 And by the river upon the bank thereof, on this side and on that side, shall grow all trees for meat, whose leaf shall not fade, neither shall the fruit thereof be consumed: it shall bring forth new fruit according to his months, because their waters they issued out of the sanctuary: and the fruit thereof shall be for meat, and the leaf thereof for medicine.

Again the vision merges with Revelation's description of "the tree of life" (Rev. 22:2). "Meat" in the KJV often, as here, means "food," not necessarily flesh. The fruit and leaves that heal our spiritual wounds are in both Ezekiel's and Revelation's lovely landscape.

கை

Evangelistic Emphasis

It's a study in contrasts, a visual image of opposites! We see pure water, clear and cool, a life-giving stream flowing down into the hot, desolate, dead desert. The water flows from the Temple.

Ezekiel uses this imagery to illustrate what a marked change there will be when the exiled Israelites return home. It's also a metaphor we Christians can use.

Without an authentic spiritual base, life is something like a barren desert. The emptiness invades every area of a person's being. Such a life is an unhealthy one, with the possibility of mental, emotional, as well as physical consequences.

Jesus' words to the woman at the well bring Ezekiel's metaphor full circle. He said: "But whosoever drinketh of the water that I shall give him shall never thirst; but the water that I shall give him shall be in him a well of water springing up into everlasting life" (John 4:14). Christians have a refreshing message to share. Thirsty, barren hearts need it badly.

❧

Memory Selection

And it shall come to pass, that every thing that liveth, which moveth, whithersoever the rivers shall come, shall live: and there shall be a very great multitude of fish, because these waters shall come thither; for they shall be healed; and every thing shall live whither the river cometh—*Ezekiel 47:9*

We are presented with an impressive river scene. The water that flows from God's Temple grows deeper as it goes down into the valley and reaches the Dead Sea. The sea's brackish water, previously good for nothing except producing salt, is "healed" and becomes fresh. Now, where the river flows, everything will live, and the sea is filled with a wide variety of fish. We even see the fishermen's nets drying along the shore.

God uses this imagery to show Ezekiel how wonderful things will be when Israel is restored. This is the language of visions and we learn to love it. It tells us about the healing power of the Lord. With expansive words and vivid scenes we are impressed by what God can do.

What God did with the unproductive Dead Sea He can do with spiritually dead people. There's no reason for anyone to endure an empty, dead life. "Where the river flows everything will live" (NIV).

Weekday Problems

Change can be frightening. Though we may not like the way things are in our lives now, at least we are familiar with them. We dealt with our problems yesterday. We can do it again today and tomorrow. If we tried to make a change for the better, who knows?

Old habits are hard to break, especially addictive ones. The life-path we have followed may have created deep ruts. If you've ever driven a car on a muddy, boggy road, you know that if you leave the ruts you might slip into the ditch.

How do you suppose the woman at the well (in our Devotional Reading) managed to change her lifestyle? She must have been addicted to husbands. She'd had five, and now had a live-in.

Jesus knew that she, as well as we, could climb out of ruts, and that our lives can be radically changed. We need to remember that.

*What changes did Jesus bring to the life of the woman at the well?

*What changes happened in the lives of the townspeople because of Jesus' encounter with her?

Heaven's Healing

Taking the first footstep with a good thought, the second with a good word, and the third with a good deed, I entered Paradise.—*Zoroaster*

* * *

As much of heaven is visible as we have eyes to see.—*William Winter*

* * *

To get to heaven, turn right and keep straight.—*Wesleyan Methodist*

* * *

Heaven's the perfection of all that can be said or thought—riches, delight, harmony, health, beauty; and all these not subject to the waste of time, but in their height eternal.—*James Shirley*

* * *

A man may go to Heaven with half the pains it cost him to purchase Hell.—*Henry Fielding, in* Jonathan Wild, IV

This Lesson in Your Life

Ezekiel wrote about the healing water that flowed from God's presence in the Temple, and Jesus spoke to the woman at the well about life-giving water. There's another passage (please read John 7:37-39) where Jesus speaks in similar terms. In doing so, He touches our lives in a very intimate way.

It was during the Jewish Feast of Tabernacles that He spoke the words we'll be examining, and just a bit of background information will be helpful.

As the Feast was observed during Jesus' time, on each of its seven days a priest went to the Pool of Siloam and filled a golden pitcher. Then he led a procession to the Temple, where he poured the water out as part of the "drink offering."

One of the names given to this celebration is the Festival of Drawing Water. In his commentary on John, Leon Morris quotes the Talmud as saying, "Why is the name of it called The drawing out of water? Because of the pouring out of the Holy Spirit, according to what is said: 'With joy shall ye draw water out of the wells of salvation'" (Isa. 12:3).

So now, back to John 7:37 (NIV). After six days of drawing and pouring water as part of the Feast of Tabernacles, "On the last and greatest day of the Feast, Jesus stood and said in a loud voice, 'If anyone is thirsty, let him come to me and drink. Whoever believes in me, as the Scripture has said, streams of living water will flow from within him. By this he meant the Spirit ...."

In our minds we see and hear what's taking place there. As is described in Edersheim's *Life and Times of Jesus,* there have been trumpet blasts and the chanting of Psalms. Two priests have climbed steps toward the altar, one with water from Siloam, the other with wine. Simultaneously they pour out their offering.

The Jewish festival itself recognized the poured water as representing God pouring out His Holy Spirit. With this as background, we hear the words of Jesus as He applies the entire process as pointing to what He will do for those who believe in Him. He gives us streams of living water. He gives the Holy Spirit.

In our studies in Ezekiel we have read quite a bit about life-giving water and receiving a new spirit. Jesus' experience with the woman at the well expands and enriches Ezekiel's imagery. And this episode with Jesus at the Feast of Tabernacles helps bring it all home to each of us in a way we can personally experience.

1. From what source did the river in Ezekiel's vision originate?

The river flowed from the Temple.

2. As the river flowed, what happened to its depth?

It continued to get deeper, going from ankle deep to deep enough to swim in—"a river that no one could cross."

3. When the river emptied into the Dead Sea, what happened to the water in the sea?

The KJV uses the expression, "the waters shall be healed." The NIV says it "becomes fresh."

4. After the water had been healed and became fresh, what occurred with the sea?

The sea became productive and was filled with fish of all kinds, like the fish of the Great Sea (the Mediterranean).

5. What happened along the banks of the river?

Along what previously had been barren desert, thriving trees produced never-failing fruit and leaves that did not wither, but furnished food and healing.

6. What beautiful expression can be quoted describing what happened with the changed landscape?

"Every thing shall live whither the river cometh" (vs. 9). Or, "So where the river flows everything shall live" (NIV).

7. Ezekiel's descriptions were telling about the restoration of the exiled Israelites. In what way does it apply to us today?

We can use it as a metaphor describing the new life and radical changes that Jesus Christ brings into the world.

8. What description did Jesus give of the water he could give to the woman at the well?

It would be living water, a well of water springing up to everlasting life.

9. What was there about this woman's history that suggested she needed a new start in life?

She was now living with a man to whom she was not married, and she had five husbands in the past.

10. At the Feast of Tabernacles when Jesus spoke of rivers of living water, to what was he referring? (See John 7:37-39.)

He was speaking of the Holy Spirit.

In John 4, Jesus told the woman at the well that if she drank the water He supplied, she would never thirst again. In John 7, He told the crowds at the Feast of Tabernacles that if anyone thirsts, "Let him come to me and drink." Both these offers are attractive and promising.

However, in John 7 he adds an extra dimension to His promise. He said that not only can a person drink and satisfy his own spiritual needs, but "streams of living water will flow from within him." What's taking place here? We expect the streams of living water to come from Christ, but how can they flow from those of us who believe in Him?

He is speaking about the Spirit, whom believers are to receive. When we believe and receive this gift, we are able to bless others. The imagery is expressed in terms of streams of living water flowing out from the believer. We are well aware that the ultimate source of blessings is the Lord, but He also uses us to provide blessings for others.

It's uplifting to know that we can be the stream that brings encouragement and new hope to others. It gives us our own personal involvement and participation in Ezekiel's river metaphors, and reminds us of John Bunyan's words: "There was a man, the world did think him mad, the more he gave away, the more he had." We want to drink so deeply into the Holy Spirit, that He flows out from our lives and touches the people around us.

Lesson 6

Suffering Unto Death

Luke 23:32-46

And there were also two other, malefactors, led with him to be put to death.

33 And when they were come to the place, which is called Calvary, there they crucified him, and the malefactors, one on the right hand, and the other on the left.

34 Then said Jesus, Father, forgive them; for they know not what they do. And they parted his raiment, and cast lots.

35 And the people stood beholding. And the rulers also with them derided him, saying, He saved others; let him save himself, if he be Christ, the chosen of God.

36 And the soldiers also mocked him, coming to him, and offering him vinegar,

37 And saying, If thou be the king of the Jews, save thyself.

38 And a superscription also was written over him in letters of Greek, and Latin, and Hebrew, THIS IS THE KING OF THE JEWS.

39 And one of the malefactors which were hanged railed on him, saying, If thou be Christ, save thyself and us.

40 But the other answering rebuked him, saying, Dost not thou fear God, seeing thou art in the same condemnation?

41 And we indeed justly; for we receive the due reward of our deeds: but this man hath done nothing amiss.

42 And he said unto Jesus, Lord, remember me when thou comest into thy kingdom.

43 And Jesus said unto him, Verily I say unto thee, To day shalt thou be with me in paradise.

44 And it was about the sixth hour, and there was a darkness over all the earth until the ninth hour.

45 And the sun was darkened, and the veil of the temple was rent in the midst.

46 And when Jesus had cried with a loud voice, he said, Father, into thy hands I commend my spirit: and having said thus, he gave up the ghost.

Apr. 5

Memory Selection
Luke 23:46

Background Scripture
Luke 23:32-46

Devotional Reading
1 Cor. 15:1-11

As we approach Easter, it is important to do so with an appreciation of Jesus' approach to that last Passover—His arrest and crucifixion, His suffering and death. Also, since our lesson is drawn from Luke's Gospel, we can give special attention to his unique contribution to the classic Good Friday story.

Only Luke records Jesus' intercessory prayer from the cross, "Father, forgive them, for they know not what they do"; and only Luke tells of the thief on the cross who was penitent, and to whom Jesus offered hope in the face of death.

Be especially aware of anyone in your group who has recently lost a loved one. If someone is still mourning, the teacher can keep the focus on Jesus' death instead of making the lesson too intensely personal.

§)(§

For a Lively Start

Remind your group of some of the possible reasons there are four Gospels. (1) The story can be told to different kinds of audiences [Matthew is thought to have written especially to Jews, Mark to Romans, Luke to Greeks;] and (2) it offers each Gospel writer the opportunity to give his own special emphasis. (John wrote a "spiri-tual gospel"; Luke emphasized prayer, women, the poor, and the Holy Spirit.)

Note also that today's lesson, being from Luke, describes two prayers not recorded in the other Gospels. One is Jesus' prayer that God would forgive His murderers; and the other is the prayer of one of the thieves, who repented and asked Jesus to remember him when He comes again. The world would be poorer in spirit if we did not have this diversity of accounts of Jesus' death.

Teaching Outline	Daily Bible Readings	
I. Jesus Is Crucified—23:32-38	Mon.	The Message of the Cross *1 Cor. 1:18-25*
A. Three crosses, 32-34	Tue.	The Suffering Servant *Isa. 53:1-9*
B. Taunts and derisions, 35-39	Wed.	A Ransom for Many *Mark 10:32-44*
1. People and rulers, 35		
2. Soldiers, 36-38	Thu.	Sacrifice of Atonement *Rom. 3:21-26*
II. Different Attitudes—39-43		
A. Mocking, 39	Fri.	Single Sacrifice for Sin *Heb. 10:10-18*
B. Penitence, 40-42	Sat.	Bought with a Price *1 Cor. 6:12-20*
C. Paradise, 43		
III. Final Events—44-46	Sun.	The Death of Jesus *Luke 23:32-46*

Verse by Verse

I. Jesus Is Crucified—23:32-38
A. Three crosses, 32-34

32 And there were also two other, malefactors, led with him to be put to death.

33 And when they were come to the place, which is called Calvary, there they crucified him, and the malefactors, one on the right hand, and the other on the left.

34 Then said Jesus, Father, forgive them; for they know not what they do. And they parted his raiment, and cast lots.

From a purely human standpoint, this lesson lies at the lowest point of the Gospel story; for what could be "Good News" about the Messiah being crucified? The story is also at the heart of the mystery of the faith; a tragic crime for which the perpetrators will be held accountable, becomes a part of the scheme of redemption planned from the "foundation of the world" (Rev. 13:8). Jesus' intercessory prayer for those putting Him to death fits with this eternal plan. It is also a guide for Jesus' followers; we should

have a forgiving spirit for both Jews and Romans, for we ourselves are sinners, too.

The place of crucifixion was called "Calvary" in Latin, which in turn was derived from the Greek *kranion,* from which we get our word for "skull." Early tradition says the name came from an odd formation on a hillside with features that resembled a skull. Nailing a live human being to a cross involved a good deal of work, so it was not uncommon to include more than one person, so two "malefactors" (lit. "evil-doers") join Jesus here. A variety of crosses were used, some shaped like the traditional cross, or like a T, an X, A, Y, or even just a single upright stake. Both hands and feet were usually nailed, partly to help support the body's weight and keep it from tearing loose. Luke's description is mercifully brief.

John's Gospel adds the note that Jesus' garment was "seamless," indicating unusual quality; hence the competition among the soldiers about who would get it. Yet John also says that the garment was divided by four and distributed among four soldiers, hinting that they may have guessed that Jesus was a personage whose garment might come to be valuable, even in pieces.

B. Taunts and derisions, 35-39

1. People and rulers, 35

35 And the people stood beholding. And the rulers also with them derided him, saying, He saved others; let him save himself, if he be Christ, the chosen of God.

From Luke 4:23 we can see that the biting taunt about a savior being unable to save himself was a common proverb of the day. Of course in Jesus' case it is both true and false. Had He wanted to, He could have called down legions of angels to save Him; yet, had He taken this way out, the world could not have been saved. "The rulers" are probably rulers of the synagogue, since Roman rulers would not have enough at stake to bother to hurl the taunt. For them it was just another crucifixion.

2. Soldiers, 36-38

36 And the soldiers also mocked him, coming to him, and offering him vinegar,

37 And saying, If thou be the king of the Jews, save thyself.

38 And a superscription also was written over him in letters of Greek, and Latin, and Hebrew, THIS IS THE KING OF THE JEWS.

Among the remarkable prophecies fulfilled at the crucifixion is the note that "They gave me also gall for my meat; and in my thirst they gave me vinegar to drink" (Ps. 69:21). The taunt that began in verse 35 grows into a louder and more challenging chant, punctuated by the sign "labeling" Jesus

as the Jews' king in the three main languages in Jerusalem at that time. Pilate probably allowed this sign gladly, since it implied that the Jewish king was now dead, leaving Pilate alone to be their ruler.

II. Different Attitudes—39-43

A. Mocking, 39

39 And one of the malefactors which were hanged railed on him, saying, If thou be Christ, save thyself and us.

One of the two thieves joins heartily with those who mock Jesus' lack of power. Perhaps this thief's challenge is triggered by the erection of the sign labeling Christ as a King. If a king, then He must be the long-awaited Christ, or Messiah; and if so, why not save me? is this thief's reaction.

B. Penitence, 40-42

40 But the other answering rebuked him, saying, Dost not thou fear God, seeing thou art in the same condemnation?

41 And we indeed justly; for we receive the due reward of our deeds: but this man hath done nothing amiss.

42 And he said unto Jesus, Lord, remember me when thou comest into thy kingdom.

Luke is the only Gospel writer who records this second thief's rebuke of his fellow criminal, his defense of Jesus, and his more humble plea for salvation. Note also that since he is guilty he does not even plead to be released from the charge, but for Jesus, as "Lord," to do so at the fulfillment of the Kingdom. This thief must have heard Jesus preach, or otherwise know a good deal of His teachings, since he knows Jesus has "done nothing amiss," that He has claimed to be "Lord," that He thus has authority to admit the thief into His Kingdom, and that He is in fact coming into an after-life in which the man's sins might be forgiven.

C. Paradise, 43

43 And Jesus said unto him, Verily I say unto thee, To day shalt thou be with me in paradise.

Although this verse raises questions for us, the thief was no doubt too happy to have Jesus approve of his request to bother with raising questions about the details. In the pictures of Judgment Day in passages such as Revelation 20, the evil, at least, are consigned to a place of waiting and suffering until the end of time. Here Jesus seems to be promising the penitent thief immediate blessedness in "paradise" *today*. Possibly the two different pictures can be reconciled by using the picture of the rich man and Lazarus, where the good and the evil are consigned to one place or the other immediately, but with actual entrance postponed.

III. Final Events—44-46

44 And it was about the sixth hour, and there was a darkness over all the earth until the ninth hour.

45 And the sun was darkened, and the veil of the temple was rent in the midst.

46 And when Jesus had cried with a loud voice, he said, Father, into thy hands I commend my spirit: and having said thus, he gave up the ghost.

Since the Jewish day began at 6 a.m., the "sixth hour" of darkness would have begun at noon. It is remarkable that the death of the Messiah seems to make more impact on the onlookers than this three-hour period of darkness.

Equally sparse is Luke's account of the tearing of the Temple veil, the curtain that separated the Holy of Holies from the rest of the Temple. Although the meaning of this remarkable event is not explained, it is generally considered to stand for the removal of the barrier between God and man under the Old Covenant system of worship. With the destruction of the separating veil, "the tabernacle of God is with men, and he will dwell with them, and they shall be his people" (Rev. 21:3).

The final event in our passage is the death of Jesus, which, like the crucifixion, Luke understates. There is only a simple but moving statement of ultimate trust that Jesus' spirit would be adequately welcomed by His Father. The word translated "ghost" is *pneuma,* and signifies the giving up of the life force—but, by faith, with the full assurance of its acceptance and care by the Father.

ଓ୨ଓଃ

Evangelistic Emphasis

The word "gospel" as used by Christians refers to the good news about Jesus Christ. We actually use the word with different shades of meaning. For instance, we refer to the "four Gospels," which are books about Jesus. Mark's Gospel, the first one written, begins with "The beginning of the gospel of Jesus Christ, the Son of God . . . ." He uses the word here as a broad term that includes all Christian teaching.

In 1 Corinthians 15, Paul reduces the term to absolute basics about Jesus, and says this is the gospel that saves us. Here's what he taught. (1) Christ died for our sins; (2) He was buried; and (3) He rose again the third day.

This is getting the gospel down to its bare essentials. There are many things about Jesus that are true and important, and we want to know about them. However, the Cross and the empty tomb are central. Without them all else is meaningless. Any evangelistic effort we make must stay focused on these points.

Memory Selection

And when Jesus had cried with a loud voice, he said, Father, into thy hands I commend my spirit: and having said thus, he gave up the ghost.—*Luke 23:46*

When I was a child growing up in a small southern village, one of the elderly men who often led prayer in our church always included "Give us a peaceful hour in which to depart this life." This is something for which we all wish, but we're realists enough to know that our death might come unpleasantly.

Jesus' death did not come in a "peaceful hour." It was a cruel affair. However, the manner in which He handled it says much. He had full assurance that His Father's hands would be there to receive His spirit. His intimate relationship with the Father made all the difference. His "into thy hands" anticipates a reunion.

We can find an object lesson here in how Jesus faced death. Our own deaths will be much easier if we have full confidence in the Father. Even in death (and regardless of the circumstances in which we experience it) we can look forward to life with God.

Weekday Problems

Quite a number of years ago I knew a man who insisted that he was not good enough to become a Christian. He had the wrong perspective. Christ didn't die for us because we're good. He died for us because we're sinners. (Romans 5:8 says that God demonstrated his love for us in that Christ died for us while we were still sinners.)

If we had to qualify through our own virtue before we came to Christ, we'd never come. We probably all know this, but even so there's something of a do-it-yourself impulse that tends to pull us in the wrong direction.

The concept of being saved by grace through faith, not works (Eph. 2:8-9) takes away our feeling of independence and our capacity to be "good enough" to be saved. That's good. We need to depend on God, not ourselves. "But God forbid that I should glory, save in the cross of our Lord Jesus Christ, by whom the world is crucified unto me, and I unto the world" (Gal. 6:14).

The Death of Dying

When Henry David Thoreau, the naturalist, was close to death, he was visited by a very pious aunt who asked, Henry, have you made your peace with God?"

Replied Thoreau, "I didn't know that we ever quarreled."

* * *

A good man, being asked during his last illness, whether he thought he was dying, replied, "Really, friend, I care not whether I am or not; for if I die I shall be with God; if I live, He will be with me."

* * *

Alexander the Great, seeing the philosopher Diogenes examining carefully a parcel of bones, asked him what he was looking for. "That which I cannot find," was the reply—"the difference between your father's bones and those of his slaves."

This Lesson in Your Life

Something horrible happened on the day we call Good Friday. Christ died. Obviously, there must be some substantial reason why we use the word "good" to describe such a day as this. There is.

Good Friday was the day Christ showed us how much He loves us. As a matter of fact, what happened on that day is what gives meaning to the word love. "Hereby perceive we the love of God, because he laid down his life for us: and we ought to lay down our lives for the brethren" (1 Jn. 3:16).

In the very next chapter (4:10), John writes "Herein is love, not that we loved God, but that he loved us, and sent his Son to be the propitiation for our sins." Good Friday lets us know how much God loves us.

Your life has value. You are important to God. Jesus regards you as significant, and died to prove it. You are loved by both the Father and the Son. These things being true, there are certain personal responsibilities that follow.

After telling us how much God loves us, John adds (4:11), "Beloved, if God so loved us, we ought also to love one another." John had already told us (3:16) that because Jesus has demonstrated to us what love is, we should be willing to lay down our lives for our brothers (and sisters).

It becomes quite clear just how the death of Christ impacts our lives. Among other things, we become loving, sacrificial people. We sometimes hear the expression, "I can love because I am loved," and this is true. Because the love of the Lord is in us, we can be gracious and loving to others.

First Corinthians 6:19-20 tells us that we are not our own; we were bought at a price. We should therefore honor God with our bodies. Good Friday was the day Jesus lovingly paid the cost. It's with our own lives that we respond to his love.

GETTING THE FACTS
STRAIGHT

1. Read 1 Corinthians 15:1-2 very carefully, and list four things Paul said about the gospel.

(1) He had preached the gospel to them. (2) They had received it. (3) They took their stand on it. (4) By this gospel they would be saved.

2. What "if" did Paul attached to the above verses?

The gospel would save them *if* they kept it in memory, or "unless ye have believed in vain."

3. What three specific points defined the gospel, for Paul? (vss. 3-4)?

Christ died, was buried, and rose again. (Additional reading: Rom. 4:25; 6:1-14; 8:11, 32; Eph. 2:1-10.)

4. What request did Jesus make to God concerning those who had crucified him?

"Father, forgive them; for they know not what they do."

5. What happened to the clothing Jesus had been wearing?

The soldiers cast lots for it and divided it among themselves. (Additional details in Matt. 27:35; Mark 15:24; John 19:24.)

6. What Psalm makes reference to the above?

Psalm 22:18, "They parted my garments among them, and cast lots upon my vesture." (In addition, see Ps. 22:1 Matt. 27:46.)

7. One of the criminals crucified beside Jesus cast insults at Him. The other one made what request of Him?

He asked the Lord to remember him when He came into His Kingdom.

8. What response did Jesus give to this request?

Jesus told the crimnal that he would be with Him that day in paradise.

9. What exceptional events does Luke mention that occurred at the crucifixion (one in nature, the other in the Temple)?

There was darkness from the sixth to the ninth hour, and the curtain of the Temple was torn in two.

10. What did Jesus say just before death that indicated His assurance about the Father, and that can comfort us in our own dying?

"Father, into thy hands I commend my spirit."

God does indeed work in mysterious ways. At first glance it seems a puzzle that good news can result from the Crucifixion. In fact, though, Calvary is the most uplifting event we can imagine. As an example, let's look at just one thing that occurred there.

The very heart of Temple worship was disrupted and a symbolic truth about Christ was revealed as the veil of the Temple was torn down the middle (Luke 23:45).

Inside the Jerusalem Temple there was an enormous, elaborately decorated curtain (veil). Behind it was the holy of holies, which represented the presence of God. The high priest, and no one else, could enter there once each year. The curtain represented the remoteness, the separateness, of God. When the curtain was torn in two, symbolically the way to God was opened, a new and living way was revealed (Heb. 10:19-20).

These verses tell us that we can boldly "enter into the holiest by the blood of Jesus." We are no longer separated from God. Because of Jesus' blood shed on the cross, we have access to the presence of God.

Hebrews 4:14-16 tells us that Jesus, our great high priest, has passed into the heavens (remember the symbolism of the torn curtain), and that we can boldly come to the throne of grace, where we can "obtain mercy, and find grace to help in time of need." The blood of Jesus opened the way to heaven for us. This is the best of good news and the greatest of uplifts.

Lesson 7

Resurrected Unto New Life

Luke 23:50–24:12

And, behold, there was a man named Joseph, a counsellor; and he was a good man, and a just:

51 (The same had not consented to the counsel and deed of them;) he was of Arimathaea, a city of the Jews: who also himself waited for the kingdom of God.

52 This man went unto Pilate, and begged the body of Jesus.

53 And he took it down, and wrapped it in linen, and laid it in a sepulchre that was hewn in stone, wherein never man before was laid.

54 And that day was the preparation, and the sabbath drew on.

55 And the women also, which came with him from Galilee, followed after, and beheld the sepulchre, and how his body was laid.

56 And they returned, and prepared spices and ointments; and rested the sabbath day according to the commandment.

24:1 Now upon the first day of the week, very early in the morning, they came unto the sepulchre, bringing the spices which they had prepared, and certain others with them.

2 And they found the stone rolled away from the sepulchre.

3 And they entered in, and found not the body of the Lord Jesus.

4 And it came to pass, as they were much perplexed thereabout, behold, two men stood by them in shining garments:

5 And as they were afraid, and bowed down their faces to the earth, they said unto them, Why seek ye the living among the dead?

6 He is not here, but is risen: remember how he spake unto you when he was yet in Galilee,

7 Saying, The Son of man must be delivered into the hands of sinful men, and be crucified, and the third day rise again.

8 And they remembered his words,

9 And returned from the sepulchre, and told all these things unto the eleven, and to all the rest.

10 It was Mary Magdalene, and Joanna, and Mary the mother of James, and other women that were with them, which told these things unto the apostles.

11 And their words seemed to them as idle tales, and they believed them not.

12 Then arose Peter, and ran unto the sepulchre; and stooping down, he beheld the linen clothes laid by themselves, and departed, wondering in himself at that which was come to pass.

Memory Selection
Luke 24:5

Background Scripture
Luke 23:50–24:12

Devotional Reading
1 Cor. 15:12-26

They tried—for both good and bad reasons, they tried to keep Jesus' body in the tomb. His enemies who crucified Him asked for an extra guard. Good and honest people like Joseph of Arimathea tried. He found that rocky cavity and tenderly placed the body there to protect it from grave robbers. Everyone went to unprecedented lengths to keep His body in the tomb.

But earth could not, would not, contain it, you see. There were promises to fulfill, and a Kingdom to run. There was a Covenant to keep, one that required the body and soul of Jesus to be reunited in a spiritual state that defied all "natural law." There was an empty throne to occupy there by the Father's right hand.

Stand back! The earth will shake the folds of its heavy skirts and the body will come forth. No matter how hard they try.

ഇൗൠ

For a Lively Start

A lively introduction can be initiated by getting members of your group to open up and really discuss how they feel about the empty tomb. Predictably, if you ask, most will say they believe in a literal resurrection, But why? Is it because most other Christians do? Or perhaps some will be bold and honest enough to admit that they have some doubts. After all, they haven't *seen* a resurrection themselves. Imagine how many natural laws were broken if the story is really true. Taking a doubter's side for a moment, why do some *not* believe? Are they bad people?

Urge your class to have open minds. Then present the lesson in a way that builds faith.

Teaching Outline	Daily Bible Readings	
I. Friends Ask for the Body—23:50-56	Mon.	God Raised Him from the Dead! *Acts 13:26-33*
A. Joseph and the tomb, 50-53	Tue.	God's Power for Us *Eph. 1:15-23*
B. Women prepare spices, 54-56	Wed.	First-fruits from the Dead *1 Cor. 15:12-26*
II. The Tomb Is Empty!, 1-12	Thu.	Buried and Raised with Him *Col. 2:6-15*
A. Sunday morning surprise, 1-3	Fri.	Walk in Newness of Life *Rom. 6:3-11*
B. 'He is not here, but is risen!' 4-7	Sat.	Seek the Things Above *Col. 3:1-11*
C. Telling the news, 8-11	Sun.	Christ Has Risen! *Luke 24:1-12*
D. Running to see, 12		

Verse by Verse

I. Friends Ask for the Body—23:50-56
A. Joseph and the new tomb, 50-53

50 And, behold, there was a man named Joseph, a counsellor; and he was a good man, and a just:

51(The same had not consented to the counsel and deed of them;) he was of Arimathaea, a city of the Jews: who also himself waited for the kingdom of God.

52 This man went unto Pilate, and begged the body of Jesus.

53 And he took it down, and wrapped it in linen, and laid it in a sepulchre that was hewn in stone, wherein never man before was laid.

The location of Joseph's home, Arimathea, is unknown. He may have moved to Jerusalem to make tending to his duties on the Sanhedrin more convenient, and bought a tomb since he spent so much time there. To be called a "counselor" (or councilor) was equivalent to saying that he was a member of the "council," the Sanhedrin, the ruling council of the Jews. To Luke's compliment that Joseph was a good man and just, Mark adds that he was

"respected," and Matthew says plainly that he was "a disciple of Jesus." Since the vote condemning Jesus was apparently unanimous, Joseph must have been absent from that meeting.

Burial customs usually required that spices be tucked into the linen cloth as the body was wrapped; that they are not mentioned until later is an indication that Joseph had to hurry to get some covering on it because of the oncoming Sabbath.

B. Women prepare spices, 54-56

54 And that day was the preparation, and the sabbath drew on.

55 And the women also, which came with him from Galilee, followed after, and beheld the sepulchre, and how his body was laid.

56 And they returned, and prepared spices and ointments; and rested the sabbath day according to the commandment.

The women cooperate with Joseph in preparing the spices for use after the Sabbath, but refraining from breaking the Law by working on the Sabbath.

Exactly what kind and how much work was allowed depended on tradition as rabbis on the council changed through the years and the issue was debated.

Leaving "the women" unnamed leaves room for the various women whom some Gospels include or omit.

II.The Tomb Is Empty!—23:1-12

A. Sunday morning surprise, 1-3

24:1 Now upon the first day of the week, very early in the morning, they came unto the sepulchre, bringing the spices which they had prepared, and certain others with them.

2 And they found the stone rolled away from the sepulchre.

3 And they entered in, and found not the body of the Lord Jesus.

After resting on the Sabbath as the Law required, the women who had helped Joseph plus certain others arise early Sunday morning to finish the embalming process, the Sabbath having ended Saturday evening. Matthew and Mark say that Joseph had rolled a great stone against the tomb's opening, so those who come to tend to Jesus' body will need plenty of help to roll it away. However, they find that the stone has already been removed, and are further shocked when they enter the tomb and find it empty.

B. 'He is not here, but is risen!' 4-7

4 And it came to pass, as they were much perplexed thereabout, behold, two men stood by them in shining garments:

5 And as they were afraid, and bowed down their faces to the earth, they said unto them, Why seek ye the living among the dead?

6 He is not here, but is risen: remember how he spake unto you when he was yet in Galilee,

7 Saying, The Son of man must be delivered into the hands of sinful men, and be crucified, and the third day rise again.

The more details we begin to be given, the more variety there is in the way the various Gospels report them. Here Luke says the women are greeted by "two men," but they are in "dazzling apparel," which fits the term "angel" in Matthew. Mark says "young man." There would seem to be little to be gained from lengthy discussions trying to discern why such small details differ. Apparently they have simply come down through differing oral, then written, traditions. This can be said to show that they are unvarnished and genuine, instead of having been "fixed up" to agree in ever minor detail.

The angel or young man seems a little impatient in the question he asks, "Why seek ye the living among the dead?" His main purpose of course is to help them recall that Jesus had in effect predicted this moment earlier while they were still in Galilee. It is not surprising that they have forgotten; each time Jesus spoke of his coming death they tended not to listen or, not understanding, promptly to forget.

C. Telling the news, 8-11

8 And they remembered his words,

9 And returned from the sepulchre, and told all these things unto the eleven, and to all the rest.

10 It was Mary Magdalene, and Joanna, and Mary the mother of James, and other women that were with them, which told these things unto the apostles.

11 And their words seemed to

them as idle tales, and they believed them not.

Knowing that, as verse 11 says, they are likely to be disbelieved by the apostles, the women hurry from the gravesite since it may take a while to convince the men to listen to them. They too have been slow to listen and to understand not only the women but even their Lord when He had tried to tell them of His coming death and resurrection. It was simply an account that did not fit their preconceived version of the Messianic story.

D. Running to see, 12

12 Then arose Peter, and ran unto the sepulchre; and stooping down, he beheld the linen clothes laid by themselves, and departed, wondering in himself at that which was come to pass.

Finally Peter goes to check on what the women are saying, perhaps to si-lence them as much as anything else. The linen clothes he finds are those used by Joseph or his helpers when he did the hasty and only partial task of embalming the body. Later, on the road to Emmaus (vs. 24), Peter will speak of "those who were with us," while he seems to be alone according to verse 12, here. It may be for this reason that the RSV and other translations omit the verse. The fact that Peter goes away wondering to himself indicates that while he may be slow to come to a firm belief in the resurrection, he knows that something mysterious and not immediately explicable has happened.

The fact that both the women and the men among Jesus' followers do not know what to make of what they see is an indication that a resurrection was the last thing they were expecting, and adds a note of authenticity to the Gospel records.

ଽୄୠ

Evangelistic Emphasis

Good Friday is past and Easter has come. The tomb is empty. He is not there! He is risen, and on Resurrection morning the world is a different place.

The Crucifixion was not in vain. Jesus did not sacrifice His life and shed His blood to no purpose. He was "declared to be the Son of God with power, according to the spirit of holiness, by the resurrection from the dead" (Rom. 1:4).

Someone has pointed out that every book in the New Testament either directly affirms or assumes the Resurrection.

The first two gospel sermons recorded in Acts were preached by Peter. In both of them he emphasized the Resurrection (Acts 2:14-36; 3:12-26). We would have no authentic Christian message without a living Lord. The Crucifixion does not stand alone. It requires the Resurrection, and these two together furnish us the emphasis we need for evangelizing.

Memory Selection

And as they [the women] were afraid, and bowed down their faces to the earth, they [the men in shining garments] said unto them, Why seek ye the living among the dead?—*Luke 24:5*

It was early morning, the first day of the week. Jesus had been in the tomb since Friday. Now that Sabbath was past, the women came to the tomb, spices in hand, expecting to anoint the corpse.

They were in for a series of surprises. First, they found the stone rolled away from the sepulcher. Then they entered the tomb and found it empty. So far things had been confusing, but now fright sets in. Two men in shining clothing were standing beside them, and what they said was the most surprising of all. "Why seek ye the living among the dead?" they asked, "He is not here, but is risen."

Suddenly, these women discover that their mission has changed. There is no corpse. Jesus is alive. They rush back to tell the 11 and others in the group the good news. Nobody believes them. Later on, the apostles will face the challenge of proclaiming the message they first heard from the women: He is risen.

Weekday Problems

Probably most of us know that Scripture instructs us to live worthy of our Christian calling (See Eph. 4:1; Col. 1:10; 1 Thess. 2:12.) That's not always easy to do. It's a large order to fill, and we're likely to need all the help we can get.

There are several passages that tie the solution to this very problem to the Resurrection. Paul told the Ephesians he was praying that God would enlighten them about the incomparably great power He supplies to believers. It's power like that which God exerted in Christ when He raised Him from the dead (Eph. 1:19-20). This is an astounding piece of information. God, whose great power raised Jesus from the dead, will work in us with this same "mighty power."

Living right takes a lot of effort. It's a real problem. God has the strength to help. (See also Col. 2:9-15; 3:1-4.)

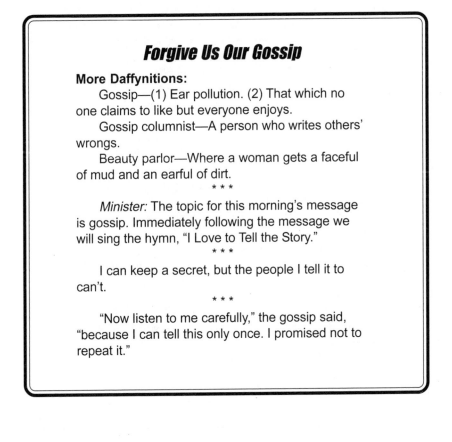

Forgive Us Our Gossip

More Daffynitions:

Gossip—(1) Ear pollution. (2) That which no one claims to like but everyone enjoys.

Gossip columnist—A person who writes others' wrongs.

Beauty parlor—Where a woman gets a faceful of mud and an earful of dirt.

* * *

Minister: The topic for this morning's message is gossip. Immediately following the message we will sing the hymn, "I Love to Tell the Story."

* * *

I can keep a secret, but the people I tell it to can't.

* * *

"Now listen to me carefully," the gossip said, "because I can tell this only once. I promised not to repeat it."

This Lesson in Your Life

I almost never read the obituaries in the newspaper. Today was an exception, and here's some of what I found.

> Mary, age 99, who in life was forthright and witty.
> Dave, age 20, who was gifted and had a great heart.
> Latinka, age 83, was active in the Serbian Orthodox Church.
> Patti, age 34, had worked in a health clinic.

There were others, but these are enough to make a point. At some time we're all going to need to find a remedy for death.

"Remedy for death" is not a bad description for the Resurrection, for we all benefit from what happened to Christ on the third day. First Corinthians 15:22 says that "in Christ shall all be made alive." Basically, the things we do at a funeral will be reversed. When the Lord returns, He will undo what we've done. The body that we lovingly placed in the grave will "come forth" (John 5:28-29).

First Corinthians 15:42-44 describes it this way: The body is sown in corruption, and raised in incorruption. It is sown in dishonor, but raised in glory. What is sown in weakness is raised in power, and the natural body we bury is raised a spiritual body.

We'll come up from the grave. We'll be changed, but we will still be "us." "As we have borne the image of the earthly [Adam], we shall also bear the image of the heavenly [Christ]" (1 Cor. 15:49). We look for the Savior, the Lord Jesus Christ, to come from heaven and "change our vile body, that it may be fashioned like unto his glorious body . . ." (Phil. 3:20-21).

The apostle John has this to say: Even now we are children of God, but we don't know what we will be in the hereafter, "but we know that, when he shall appear, we shall be like him; for we shall see him as he is" (1 Jn. 3:2).

John places a moral imperative on this. In verse 3 he says that people who have this hope in Christ should purify themselves, even as Christ is pure.

He is risen indeed! Have a blessed Easter.

GETTING THE FACTS STRAIGHT

1. Apparently some Corinthians were holding that there was no such thing as a resurrection. What contradiction did Paul see in this concerning the gospel? (15:12)

Paul had taught the Resurrection. If they accepted his teaching,, how could they deny the reality of their resurrection?

2. If there is no resurrection, and Christ has not risen, what does this mean about Paul's preaching and their faith?

It is vain, they are still in their sins, and Paul is a false witness. Also, those who had died were lost.

3. If in this life only we have hope in Christ, what does Paul say about us?

He says we are of all men most miserable.

4. How long must Christ reign?

Until He has put all enemies under his feet.

5. What is the "last enemy" to be destroyed?

Death.

6. When did the women come to the tomb to anoint the body of Christ with spices?

They came very early in the morning on the first day of the week.

7. What were the first two things they discovered when they arrived at the tomb?

The stone was rolled back and the tomb was empty.

8. What did the two men in shining clothing say to them?

Why do you seek the living among the dead? He is not here, but is risen.

9. What gentle reprimand did the men give them?

They asked if the women didn't remember that Jesus had told them he would be crucified and rise again the third day.

10. What kind of reception did the women get when they reported this to the apostles and others who were gathered?

They were not believed. Their news sounded like idle tales.

Christ's resurrection was a many-faceted event, something like a diamond cut so that we see light shining through from many angles. Every sparkle is uplifting and exciting.

In Romans 4, Paul takes notice of one of these aspects. He reminds us that Abraham had faith, and God gave him credit for righteousness because of it. He writes that God will do this "for us also," "if we believe on him that raised up Jesus our Lord from the dead" (vs. 24).

In the next verse Paul continues, "[Jesus] was delivered for our offences, and raised again for our justification." It's easy to understand that it was our offences (sins) that delivered Jesus to the cross. The part about His being raised for our justification may not be so easily understood. The TEV might help. It says "he was raised to life in order to put us right with God."

We know we are sinners, and are responsible for the Crucifixion. We know also that God counts us as blameless (justified, put right with Himself) because of the Resurrection.

In Romans 8:34 (NIV) Paul writes, "Christ Jesus, who died—more than that, who was raised to life—is at the right hand of God and is also interceding for us." We are more than conquerors. Our Lord won the victory over death, and we share the victory.

Lesson 8

Witnesses To New Life

Luke 24:36-53

And as they thus spake, Jesus himself stood in the midst of them, and saith unto them, Peace be unto you.

37 But they were terrified and affrighted, and supposed that they had seen a spirit.

38 And he said unto them, Why are ye troubled? and why do thoughts arise in your hearts?

39 Behold my hands and my feet, that it is I myself: handle me, and see; for a spirit hath not flesh and bones, as ye see me have.

40 And when he had thus spoken, he shewed them his hands and his feet.

41 And while they yet believed not for joy, and wondered, he said unto them, Have ye here any meat?

42 And they gave him a piece of a broiled fish, and of an honeycomb.

43 And he took it, and did eat before them.

44 And he said unto them, These are the words which I spake unto you, while I was yet with you, that all things must be fulfilled, which were written in the law of Moses, and in the prophets, and in the psalms, concerning me.

45 Then opened he their understanding, that they might understand the scriptures,

46 And said unto them, Thus it is written, and thus it behoved Christ to suffer, and to rise from the dead the third day:

47 And that repentance and remission of sins should be preached in his name among all nations, beginning at Jerusalem.

48 And ye are witnesses of these things.

49 And, behold, I send the promise of my Father upon you: but tarry ye in the city of Jerusalem, until ye be endued with power from on high.

50 And he led them out as far as to Bethany, and he lifted up his hands, and blessed them.

51 And it came to pass, while he blessed them, he was parted from them, and carried up into heaven.

52 And they worshipped him, and returned to Jerusalem with great joy:

53 And were continually in the temple, praising and blessing God. Amen.

Apr. 19

Memory Selection
Luke 24:48-49

Background Scripture
Luke 24:36-53

Devotional Reading
Acts 2:22-32

FOCUS

"Famous Last Words" has become a category of speech all its own because of the emotional weight they bear. Sometimes they also carry sensory significance, if loved ones are present when they are uttered. This lesson focuses on the last words of Jesus, and the importance they had in helping the

disciples overcome doubt after His crucifixion.

In Luke's Gospel, Jesus' last words follow his appearance to two disciples on the road to Emmaus. Despite this appearance, He vanished again. If we had been the disciples, would we have wondered if what we saw and heard was real? Jesus graciously appears once more to all the disciples, removing all doubt with both physical and spiritual confirmation. Only then does He ascend into heaven leaving them to tell the world of their experience.

ഇറ

For a Lively Start

Tell your group that although this lesson includes Jesus' last words to His disciples, *their* last words to *Him* would also have been important. Challenge them to creatively put themselves in the disciples' shoes for this, the last

scene in the drama of their Lord's life.

What would be on your heart? Keeping in mind His expectations of you after He leaves, do you feel adequately equipped? Has your understanding of who He really is deepened after a time of doubting? Do you feel that He has left you with some unanswered questions? The lesson is on our Lord's last words to us, His disciples. What would be *your* last words to Him?

Teaching Outline	Daily Bible Readings

I. The Reality of Being—36-43
  A. More than a spirit, 36-39
  B. Evidence of flesh, 40-43
II. Opening the Understanding—44-48
  A. Moses fulfilled, 44-45
  B. Message to preach, 46-48
III. Waiting and Worshipping—49-53
  A. Wait in Jerusalem, 49
  B. Blessing and ascension, 50-53
	Mon. Women at the Tomb
	        Matt. 28:6-10
	Tue. Mary Magdalene
	        John 20:11-18
	Wed. On the Road to Emmaus
	        Luke 24:13-23,28-31
	Thu. Thomas
	        John 20:24-29
	Fri. Seven Disciples
	        John 21:1-14
	Sat. Witnesses of Resurrection
	        1 Cor. 15:1-8
	Sun. You Are Witnesses
	        Luke 24:44-53

Verse by Verse

I. The Reality of Being—36-43

A. More than a spirit, 36-39

36 And as they thus spake, Jesus himself stood in the midst of them, and saith unto them, Peace be unto you.

37 But they were terrified and affrighted, and supposed that they had seen a spirit.

38 And he said unto them, Why are ye troubled? and why do thoughts arise in your hearts?

39 Behold my hands and my feet, that it is I myself: handle me, and see; for a spirit hath not flesh and bones, as ye see me have.

Our lesson begins with the disciples gathered in Jerusalem discussing the moving event when Jesus revealed Himself to two of the disciples on their walk to nearby Emmaus. We can imagine their confusion. The Christ they thought would usher in the last phase of the Kingdom in the flesh had been crucified and buried. Then there was a report from some women that he was alive. Now the two disciples from the short walk to

Emmaus say that they also saw Him alive. What are they to think?

Suddenly Jesus appears before all of them! Their concept of life after death was much like ours: the body decays and the spirit dwells somewhere invisibly, except in certain ghostly appearances accepted by some, who are usually "terrified and affrighted," and rejected by others.

Jesus questions them as though they should have overcome this conventional view. Their fear is a sign that after all this time they do not accept their Master's power over both life and death. When Jesus asks why *"thoughts"* arise in their hearts, He uses a word that implies not just an idea but *conflicted thoughts,* as when we weigh a difficult thought back and forth. In verse 39 Jesus urges them to "handle" or touch him, and not to think of him as a ghost "for a spirit hath not flesh and bones."

B. Evidence of flesh, 40-43

40 And when he had thus spoken, he shewed them his hands and

his feet.

41 And while they yet believed not for joy, and wondered, he said unto them, Have ye here any meat?

42 And they gave him a piece of a broiled fish, and of an honeycomb.

43 And he took it, and did eat before them.

The fact that Jesus has a real body is so important that Jesus presses the issue. Looking into the future, He knows that people called "Gnostics" will teach that if He were really God's Son He could not have flesh and bones, because all matter is evil. Even after handling Him, His disciples are waffling on the subject. We know the feeling described in verse 41, where the disciples "believed not for joy." We express this feeling when we say that something is "too good to be true."

So Jesus decides to give His disciples an illustration of his "fleshliness," one for which he will need meat. He asks if they have any leftovers. They supply the ingredients—a piece of fish and a honeycomb—for a demonstration that should prove His point: *a spirit lacks the physical apparatus to eat.*

Even after this demonstration, all our questions aren't answered. We have also read that Jesus somehow passed through a closed door—a feat which we can perhaps imagine a spirit performing, but not one that is clothed with a body. Apparently Jesus has the kind of "spiritual body" of which the apostle Paul speaks when he tries to explain the resurrected body. When we die, our body "is sown a natural body; it is raised a spiritual body. There is a natural body, and there is a spiritual body" (1 Cor. 15:44). That which is an oxymoron to us was very real to Paul, and to Jesus. After taking the food and eating it, perhaps Jesus convinced His disciples as well.

II. Opening the Understanding—44-48
A. Moses fulfilled, 44-45

44 And he said unto them, These are the words which I spake unto you, while I was yet with you, that all things must be fulfilled, which were written in the law of Moses, and in the prophets, and in the psalms, concerning me.

45 Then opened he their understanding, that they might understand the scriptures,

For these disciples, steeped as they are in the Old Covenant Scriptures, seeing is not enough. They need to have what they seem to be seeing confirmed by God's Word. After all, Satan has the power to work "signs and lying wonders" too (2 Thess. 2:9). Jesus has already had a brief Bible study with the two disciples on the road to Emmaus (Luke 24:27), and he takes it up again here.

The "law, the prophets, and the psalms" were a common way of dividing up the Old Testament in Jesus' day. It was important that He show that all three sections point to the dying and rising Messiah, and the works that He has fulfilled among them. Now they have had two important avenues toward faith presented to them: *experience,* having seen Jesus in the flesh after seeing Him put to death; and *the Scriptures,* which point to the Coming One and the works He would perform, and which Jesus has fulfilled.

There is one more avenue to faith down which Jesus leads His disciples, one that is explained in verse 45: *He opened their understanding.* Many people no doubt saw the resurrected Jesus. Countless more have read about Him in the Old and New Covenant Scriptures. Yet many of these do not believe—some no doubt because God has not "opened their understanding." This does not mean that God plays favorites, but that faith depends on a person's *willingness* to understand and believe, and that this willingness comes from God.

B. Message to preach, 46-48

46 And said unto them, Thus it is written, and thus it behoved Christ to suffer, and to rise from the dead the third day:

47 And that repentance and remission of sins should be preached in his name among all nations, beginning at Jerusalem.

48 And ye are witnesses of these things.

The same Scriptures that speak of the coming Messiah, and of the works that He would do, tell us also that He will suffer and die, then rise on the third day, and that this message will be preached throughout the world, beginning at Jerusalem. It is in this way that Israel, God's "Suffering Servant" will be a "light to the nations" (Isa. 49:6).

We can imagine that silence may have fallen upon the little group when Jesus drops the final words of this passage, verse 48, on them: *We are witnesses of these things.* The unspoken message is that since the disciples are the only ones in the room, this word is

especially for them. It is to be 12 men sent to the world! (And then whatever numbers, like this group, who are gathered and hear of this message, as well as its tremendous responsibility.)

III. Waiting and Worshipping—49-53

A. Wait in Jerusalem, 49-52

49 And, behold, I send the promise of my Father upon you: but tarry ye in the city of Jerusalem, until ye be endued with power from on high.

50 And he led them out as far as to Bethany, and he lifted up his hands, and blessed them.

51 And it came to pass, while he blessed them, he was parted from them, and carried up into heaven.

52 And they worshipped him, and returned to Jerusalem with great joy:

Apparently the disciples stay in Jerusalem some 40 days (see Acts 1:3) before going to the Mount of Olives, where Bethany was located. There, while Jesus is in the act of blessing them, He ascends into heaven. We may rightly exclaim, "What a way to go!" With all doubts removed, His disciples worship Him, then return again to Jersalem.

B. Blessing and ascension, 53

53 And were continually in the temple, praising and blessing God. Amen.

With Christianity not yet divorced from Judaism, it was natural for Jesus' followers to assemble in the Temple. There is much to discuss, more still to wonder about, and they wait for the Holy Spirit to supply the power they will need to "go unto all the world" (Acts 1:8).

Evangelistic Emphasis

In his commentary on the book of Luke, Charles R. Erdman refers to the man Luke as "the careful historian, the intelligent physician." We see the accuracy of this description in our Scripture reading for this lesson, as Luke assures his contemporaries (and future generations) of the actuality of the Resurrection.

As Luke was to record later in the Book of Acts, when the apostles preached they did not declare that "The tomb was empty." They said "We have seen the Lord." A tomb might be empty for any of several reasons. The actual appearance of the resurrected Lord was positive, not negative, evidence.

Christ's appearance (24:36-53) to the 11 in the upper room was carefully calculated to remove doubt. Jesus invited them to look and to touch Him. His crucifixion scars were evident. He ate food in their presence. He explained that what had happened to Him fulfilled the prophecies.

As Luke records this, he is authenticating gospel teaching. He assures us that we can confidently declare that Jesus lives.

Memory Selection

And ye are witnesses of these things. And, behold, I send the promise of my Father upon you: but tarry ye in the city of Jerusalem, until ye be endued with power from on high.—*Luke 24:48-49*

Luke omits the Galilee appearance of the risen Christ, as recorded by Matthew and Mark. He places his emphasis on Jerusalem, where the apostles were to wait until they receive empowerment from the Holy Spirit. This will happen at Pentecost (Acts 2), which comes 50 days following Passover (when the Crucifixion occurred).

They have just been told that repentance and remission of sins should be preached to all nations, beginning at Jerusalem. Bit by bit, the Lord is preparing them to do this. They were with him for three years during his earthly ministry. They witnessed the Crucifixion. Nobody witnessed the actual Resurrection, but they had unquestionably seen the risen Lord.

Things are in place, and they now await the promised Holy Spirit. He will enable them to evangelize the world.

Weekday Problems

When Jesus appeared to the eleven in the upper room, they weren't ready to accept the evidence before their eyes. They were terrified and thought they were seeing a ghost. They were so filled with joy and amazement, that even after examining his hands and feet they still couldn't believe.

How do you fare in this department? My assumption is that Christians believe intellectually. We accept the fact, otherwise we wouldn't be Christians. It may be, though, that many of us don't utilize the power of the Resurrection in our day by day experience. It should motivate us for Christian living, and form the core of who we really are. Together we can all sing:

> He lives! He lives! Christ Jesus lives today!
> He walks with me, and talks with me
> Along the narrow way. He lives! He lives!
> Salvation to impart: You ask me how I know he lives?
> He lives—within my heart.

He Is Risen!

Little Billy was puzzled after the Sunday School lesson on Easter Sunday. "But how did Jesus get to heaven?" he asked.

Sister Sue, a knowing veteran of countless such lessons, illustrated by paper puppets, supplied the answer. "Well, silly, it was easy. Somebody up there has Scotch tape and string, and they just *pulled* him up."

* * *

The drunk took a short-cut home through the cemetery and fell into a freshly dug, empty grave. He tried several times to climb out but finally decided to wait until someone came along who might help. As luck would have it, another drunk came along and also fell into the grave. He too tried unsuccessfully to climb out.

Not wanting to scare him, the first drunk finally said softly, "Friend, don't you know you can't get out of here that way?"

But he did.

This Lesson in Your Life

My friends and I were with an American Christian missionary nurse in a large city in India. She was an American, but had been born in India to missionary parents. Actually, she was the third generation of her family ministering in that country. She spoke the Indian dialects used in the area. She knew the customs, and how the people lived. She had a Christian work-ethic, and did not live a pampered life. She lived plainly, dressed simply, and worked among the poor. She would never be mistaken for a rich American.

An influential Muslim gentleman had asked her to come to his home. He had something to discuss with her. Most of her work was done out in the villages, so she was accustomed to walking. We walked over a mile with her to his home. (My friends and I would have been content, being spoiled Americans, riding in a cab. It was a hot day.)

The man we went to see was wealthy, and had been in the foreign service of India, serving in several countries. He was a published author, and looked the part of an aristocrat. He received us graciously, concerned because we had walked so far, and had a servant bring us tea.

He wanted to hire our friend to operate a Muslim charitable organization with which he was associated. He said he knew she wasn't afraid to get her hands dirty, would see that the job got done, and would be honest. He wanted to hire a Christian. No Muslim. No Hindu. No one but a Christian, and he knew the reputation of this lady.

What is so special about our friend that he should seek her out? She believes that Jesus Christ is the Son of God. She believes that He sacrificially and voluntarily went to the Cross because He loved us. She believes that He rose the third day from the grave, ascended to the Father, and sent the Holy Spirit to be our helper.

She believes these things strongly enough that they motivate her life, and have led her into sacrificial, loving service to others.

The Muslim gentleman may or may not know it, but these are the reasons he wanted to hire this Christian missionary. He saw the end result of her faith. We know the details of what was dear to her heart, and made her a living representative of Jesus Christ.

There's a lesson here for all our lives.

Post Script: She did not accept his job offer. The kind Muslim man had his driver return us to the hotel in his car, and she returned to the villages where she continued to portray Jesus by her life.

GETTING THE FACTS STRAIGHT

1. When Jesus appeared to the 11 in the upper room, He said "Peace be unto you." Did they receive His presence as a peaceful gesture?

No. They were terrified and afraid, and thought they saw a ghost.

2. Jesus could see that they didn't believe, so what did He tell them to do?

He told them to look at His hands and feet, to touch Him, because a spirit does not have flesh and bones.

3. They still did not believe. What did He do to convince them?

He asked for something to eat, and ate a piece of fish and honeycomb in their presence.

4. He reminded them of some previous teaching. What was it?

He told them that the things written about Him in the Law of Moses, the prophets, and the psalms must be fulfilled.

5. How did he sum up this Resurrection teaching for them?

It was written that Christ must suffer and rise from the dead on the third day.

6. After the above took place, what message would be preached?

Repentance and remission of sins should be preached to all nations, beginning at Jerusalem.

7. What part did the apostles have in validating this message?

They were to be witnesses of these things.

8. What would be sent upon them from the Father?

They would be sent the Father's promise (the Holy Spirit).

9. In the meantime, what were they to do?

They were to wait in Jerusalem until they were "endued with power from on high."

10. What was Jesus' last act before the apostles?

He blessed them and then was carried up into heaven.

Has any one event definitely changed your life for the better? Perhaps it led you out of despondency and into peace? Maybe it gave you a perspective by which to evaluate life, and determine what was really significant.

These are not intended as trick questions, and maybe you saw from the start where they were headed. The fact is, the Resurrection has the potential to make such positive changes.

There was probably never so desperate a group of people anywhere as Christ's disciples, following the Crucifixion.

After the Resurrection, though, and their having received the Holy Spirit, they joyfully faced persecution and martyrdom as they traveled the world declaring that Jesus rose from the grave. Without the Resurrection there would be no Church. There would be no New Testament, and the Holy Spirit would not have been given. You would not be involved in this study, for Christianity could not exist without its core doctrine.

This one event, the Resurrection, has changed the life of every believer for the better. Those who do not yet believe in Him, but come to faith, have the blessing waiting.

Lesson 9

Bringing New Life To Those in Need

Acts 9:32-43

And it came to pass, as Peter passed throughout all quarters, he came down also to the saints which dwelt at Lydda.

33 And there he found a certain man named Aeneas, which had kept his bed eight years, and was sick of the palsy.

34 And Peter said unto him, Aeneas, Jesus Christ maketh thee whole: arise, and make thy bed. And he arose immediately.

35 And all that dwelt at Lydda and Saron saw him, and turned to the Lord.

36 Now there was at Joppa a certain disciple named Tabitha, which by interpretation is called Dorcas: this woman was full of good works and almsdeeds which she did.

37 And it came to pass in those days, that she was sick, and died: whom when they had washed, they laid her in an upper chamber.

38 And forasmuch as Lydda was nigh to Joppa, and the disciples had heard that Peter was there, they sent unto him two men, desiring him that he would not delay to come to them.

39 Then Peter arose and went with them. When he was come, they brought him into the upper chamber: and all the widows stood by him weeping, and shewing the coats and garments which Dorcas made, while she was with them.

40 But Peter put them all forth, and kneeled down, and prayed; and turning him to the body said, Tabitha, arise. And she opened her eyes: and when she saw Peter, she sat up.

41 And he gave her his hand, and lifted her up, and when he had called the saints and widows, presented her alive.

42 And it was known throughout all Joppa; and many believed in the Lord.

43 And it came to pass, that he tarried many days in Joppa with one Simon a tanner.

Apr. 26

Memory Selection
Acts 9:38

Background Scripture
Acts 9:32-43

Devotional Reading
John 14:8-14

FOCUS

Jesus' last words to His disciples before ascending back to the Father were a rough outline of the missionary work they were expected to do: "Ye shall be witnesses unto me both in Jerusalem, and in all Judea, and in Samaria, and unto the uttermost parts of the earth" (Acts 1:8). Today's lesson finds the apostle Paul working in Judea and the first phase of this agenda. In that area he found opportunity to heal a man who had been bedfast for eight years, and to raise to life a godly woman who had died.

Here is the beginning of proof that Jesus' followers, not just their Master Teacher, have been blessed with the ability to transmit the New Life He had brought to them. They hold nothing back, but cast their net of salvation and healing as broadly as they can.

ഇരു

For a Lively Start

Most churches have a formal or informal ministry to the sick. If they had existed in the time Peter was doing his work of healing in this lesson, chances are that Aeneas and Tabitha would have already been tended to by a visitation committee or committee member.

If your church does not have such an organized ministry, discuss ways it could be formed; or if it has one, mention its name, the ministries it does, and the chair person who presides. Some churches appoint people to visit the sick. Others extend this work to include carrying in food as necessary. Some take a flower to everyone admitted to the hospital, regardless of church affiliation. Are there other works you can suggest in this area?

Teaching Outline	Daily Bible Readings	
I. Making the Sick Whole—9:32-35	Mon.	God Is Glorified *John 14:8-14*
A. Sick six years, 32-33	Tue.	The Promise of Healing *Isa. 57:14-21*
B. An immediate healing, 34-35	Wed.	'O Lord, Heal Me!' *Ps. 6*
II. Bringing the Dead to Life—36-41	Thu.	'Heal My Sin!' *Ps. 41*
A. A woman of good works, 36-37	Fri.	Return and Be Healed *Jer. 3:19-23*
B. Sending for Peter, 38-39	Sat.	Joy Comes with the Morning *Ps. 30:1-5*
C. Bringing Dorcas to life, 40-41	Sun.	God Heals Through Peter *Acts 9:32-43*
III. Spreading the Word—42-43		

Verse by Verse

I. Making the Sick Whole—9:32-35

A. Sick six years, 32-33

32 And it came to pass, as Peter passed throughout all quarters, he came down also to the saints which dwelt at Lydda.

33 And there he found a certain man named Aeneas, which had kept his bed eight years, and was sick of the palsy.

Although Saul of Tarsus, who will become known as the apostle Paul, has been converted, Peter is still in the forefront of the early Christian movement at this point. He seems to be roving in the province of Judea as the Spirit moves him, or as he hears of opportunities that present themselves.

Lydda was probably a village toward the Mediterranean Sea from Jerusalem. Since Peter finds there a man who has been bedfast for eight years, we can assume that he and most of the other converts were Jews, since the early Christian communities have not yet had time either to become separate from the synagogues, or to organize ministries to the sick.

The word for "palsy" gives us our word "paralysis," but was a general term for muscular ailments; so we do not know whether this man had been hurt in an accident or had polio or any number of other diseases that immobilize the muscles. We do know that the man was in distress from the simple fact he had been bedridden for so long.

B. An immediate healing, 34-35

34 And Peter said unto him, Aeneas, Jesus Christ maketh thee whole: arise, and make thy bed. And he arose immediately.

35 And all that dwelt at Lydda and Saron saw him, and turned to the Lord.

Peter wastes no time in conversation with the sick man but simply announces that "Jesus Christ maketh thee whole." Perhaps this immediacy was partly because Peter had seen Jesus heal a man of the palsy (Matt. 8:6). It is also a sign that Peter is not interested in making a name for himself as a healer, but wants the man and all who are present to know the true source of the healing.

This directness has the desired effect of causing all those in the area who learned of the healing incident to turn to the Lord (not to Peter). Luke (the assumed author of Acts) wants to be sure that we realize that Jesus is fulfilling His promise to send His disciples out to preach and to heal with the assurance of success. As pagan and Jews turn against them, they will need to recall times such as these where success was not blocked by opposition.

II. Bringing the Dead to Life—36-41

A. A woman of good works, 36-37

36 Now there was at Joppa a certain disciple named Tabitha, which by interpretation is called Dorcas: this woman was full of good works and almsdeeds which she did.

37 And it came to pass in those days, that she was sick, and died: whom when they had washed, they laid her in an upper chamber.

Continuing west, Peter comes to the larger town of Joppa, on the coast. This city, modern Jaffa or Yafo, has been an archeologist's dream, with seven different layers of long-term living having been discovered. It wasn't a large city, but its location made it a good seaport, and it was here that King Hiram of Tyre floated timber to, for some of Solomon's many building projects (see 2 Chron. 2:16; Ezra 3:7).

At Joppa Peter met Dorcas, or Tabitha, the kind of woman who is the backbone of many a church. She was especially known for her nimble fingers in needle work, keeping her busy making garments for the poor. Unfortunately she became ill and died.

B. Sending for Peter, 38-39

38 And forasmuch as Lydda was nigh to Joppa, and the disciples had heard that Peter was there, they sent unto him two men, desiring him that he would not delay to come to them.

39 Then Peter arose and went with them. When he was come, they brought him into the upper chamber: and all the widows stood by him weeping, and shewing the coats and garments which Dorcas made, while she was with them.

The kind of off-hand remark in verse 38, just mentioning that some disciples had heard that Peter was at Lydda, provides helpful glimpses of some of the life and times in Peter's day. It is remarkable that the disciples had such an efficient communications network with only word-of-mouth.

Peter has no reason to delay. He goes to Joppa promptly, soon enough that the mourners are still at their mourning, and were still displaying some of the garments she had made.

C. Bringing Dorcas to life, 40-41

40 But Peter put them all forth, and kneeled down, and prayed; and turning him to the body said, Tabitha, arise. And she opened her eyes: and when she saw Peter, she sat up.

41 And he gave her his hand, and lifted her up, and when he had called the saints and widows, presented her alive.

We are not told why Peter puts the mourners and guests out of the room. Perhaps he is only following Jesus' example (Mk. 5:40). Peter's body-language is of note. He prays to God, but turns to Tabitha as though expecting her to hear him, in answer to his prayer. In a gentle scene, Peter gives Tabitha his hand as though having no doubt but that she would arise at his command. One of the remarkable omissions from these stories is the lack of self-consciousness by Christ's miracle-working disciples, so confident are they in the power of their Lord.

III. Spreading the Word—42-43

42 And it was known throughout all Joppa; and many believed in the Lord.

43 And it came to pass, that he tarried many days in Joppa with one Simon a tanner.

Just as was the case with the healing of Aeneas at Lydda, the news of the healing spread with the result of many converts. Although it is not mentioned, we can assume that these healings are being accompanied by words of forgiveness, and the gospel message of sin and salvation. Indeed, one of the words for "healing" (*therapeuo*) can refer to making both body and soul "well," and its connection with our word "therapy" is obvious.

80C8

Evangelistic Emphasis

Jesus told Philip that those who believe in Him would do even greater works than He had done. He would go to the Father, He explained, but the Holy Spirit would come to be with them. (John 14:12, 16, 17, 26).

The apostles were instructed by Jesus (shortly before the Ascension (Luke. 24:49), to wait in Jerusalem until they were clothed with power from on high. At Pentecost (Acts 2) the promised Holy Spirit came. Peter stood up with the eleven to preach (v.14), and this marks the beginning of their empowered apostolic ministry.

How does this fit in with the disciples doing greater work than Christ did? Jesus traveled in a very limited area, and His earthly ministry lasted for only three years. There was only one of Him. Acts 1:15 mentions that He had about 120 followers.

On Pentecost alone about 3,000 were added to their number. With daily converts (v. 47), there were soon 5,000 men (4:4). In the past 2,000 years, countless millions have come to Christ.

Memory Selection

And forasmuch as Lydda was nigh to Joppa, and the disciples had heard that Peter was there, they sent unto him two men, desiring him that he would not delay to come to them.—*Acts 9:38*

Peter came to Lydda, where he healed a man who had been paralyzed for eight years. In the meantime, in nearby Joppa, Tabitha had died. The disciples in Joppa sent for Peter to come quickly. (Perhaps they had heard about the recent healing.)

Peter was ushered into the room where Tabitha lay dead. He kneeled down and prayed, then said "Tabitha, arise." As word spread about this miracle, many believed in the Lord. (The healing in Lydda had also resulted in new converts.)

In the account of Tabitha, on every level we notice how much the believers cared for each other. Every person mentioned cared for the others, consequently they knew they could depend on each other. We also see in Peter not only a preaching ministry, but one of healing and restoring.

We also see how the Lord confirmed the apostle's preaching by the signs (accompanying miracles) that followed (See Mk. 16:20).

Weekday Problems

Prayer is a significant part of Christian life. Making requests of God is an important (but by no means the only) part of our prayer life (Phil. 4:6; 1 Tim. 2:1).

Have you ever felt your prayers were not answered in the way you wanted? Paul had "a thorn in the flesh." He asked God three times to remove it, but it did not happen (2 Cor. 12:7-10). God told him that His grace was sufficient. Paul did not let this deter him. He preached the gospel "through infirmity of the flesh" (Gal. 4:13).

Do you suppose that either you or I might have responded differently than Paul did? He accepted God's answer humbly and graciously. His ailment continued to be a problem, but he had no problem with God's decision not to remove it. Could we, even if God gives what seems a negative answer, continue to cast our care upon Him, still believing He cares for us (1 Pet. 5:7)?

*How do you suppose the disciples at Joppa would have reacted if Peter had not restored life to Tabitha?

Church Chuckles

"Well," said the tavern keeper, teasing an old customer, "I see you've been over to the revival meeting. Guess you gave your last dollar, and now you'll have to walk home."

"Guess so," said his customer, rather pleased with himself, "And many's the time I've given you my last dollar and *couldn't* walk home."

* * *

A minister met the town scoundrel on the street and struck up a conversation. "Bill, just what do you have against coming to church?"

"Plenty!" Bill snarled. "First time I went they threw water on my head, the second time they tied me to a woman I've had to support ever since."

"I see," said the minister, "and the next time they'll throw dirt on you."

* * *

Message on the church bulletin board: WANTED: MEN, WOMEN, AND CHILDREN TO SIT IN SLIGHTLY USED PEWS SUNDAY MORNINGS, 11 TO 12 O'CLOCK.

This Lesson in Your Life

In Jesus' conversation with Philip, as well as Peter's experience in Lydda and Joppa, we can see Christianity in its embryonic stage. The principles and basic truths and practices we view there have expanded around the globe, and now find expression in all our Christian lives.

Jesus gave Philip the astounding news that His disciples would do even greater works than He had done. He laid out a plan, indicating how this would begin. First, the disciples would witness in Jerusalem. After this, in Judea (the surrounding area), and from there to Samaria (just to the north), and then "to the uttermost part of the earth" (Acts 1:8). From this systematic beginning, and with the help of the Holy Spirit, Christian history has progressed to this present moment. You are a part of it.

Peter's healing the paralyzed man and raising Tabitha, both resulting in the addition of new believers, are examples of what Jesus described to Philip. (And we assume that while Peter was doing this, other apostles were busy elsewhere.) As you have the opportunity to show a kindness or help the helpless, you are carrying on this tradition.

The apostles and other believers would have learned compassion from Jesus (See Mtt. 9:35-36; 14:14; 20:34). It must have been a tender moment for Peter as he performed these two miracles. We cannot imagine Christianity without compassion and a sense of caring.

In our churches and Christian organizations, we carry on the Lord's loving concern for one another. Many of our hospitals have a Christian connection. (A quick look in my city's Yellow Pages shows at least four with Christian-associated names: Good Samaritan, for example.) Health care and education frequently go hand in hand with preaching in missions to undeveloped countries.

Christians are "People of the Book." This may have something to do with the fact that many educational institutions have Christian origins. The compassion of Jesus is reflected in elder-care facilities, homes for battered women and children, orphan-care, hospices, and other areas where Christians can fill a need.

As individuals we are concerned. We pray, we show kindness and do good deeds. We help the helpless. We teach. When we do this, we help fulfill what Jesus told Philip, as well as carry on the tradition of Peter and his associates.

1. What two things did Jesus say about the relationship between Himself and the Father?

He said that he who had seen the Father had seen Him (Jesus). Also, He was in the Father, and the Father in Him.

2. If anyone did not believe what Jesus said, what other reason would there be for believing?

They should believe for His works' sake.

3. What was the contrast between the works Jesus did, and those that would be done by His disciples?

Those who believe in Him shall do greater works.

4. To what place was Jesus going?

He was going to the Father.

5. Jesus told Philip that whatever they asked in His name, He would do for them. What would be the result of this?

The Father would be glorified in the Son.

6. When Peter went to Lydda to visit the saints, whom did he find that had a serious health problem?

He found Aeneas.

7. What was Aeneas' problem, and how long had he been in bed with it?

He had had the palsy (was a paralytic) for eight years.

8. When Aeneas was healed, to whom did Peter give the credit?

Peter said, "Jesus Christ maketh thee whole."

9. Tabitha is an Aramaic word meaning gazelle. What is the other name by which this lady was called?

Her other name was Dorcas, which is Greek for gazelle.

10. When Aeneas was healed and Tabitha was raised from the dead, what effect did this have on people in the surrounding area?

A large number of people became believers.

Uplift

The lady whom Peter raised from the dead was an uplifting person. We feel good just reading about her. Her name was Gazelle. We know her better as Tabitha or Dorcas, which were Aramaic and Greek for gazelle. In any language a gazelle is a delicate and graceful creature, and this is the name she bore.

She had a caring heart and a soft spot for those in need. She didn't just feel sorry for them and wish them well. She did something about it. When good works and helping the poor are associated with her name, the Bible says "which she did."

The apostles preached, performed miracles, and some of them traveled the world. Dorcas stayed home and sewed. The apostles had their gift. She had hers, and that suited her fine. She wasn't trying to be great. She just wanted to be useful.

1 Corinthians 12:28 says that God has made various appointments in the Church: apostles, prophets, and others. This verse also says some are to be "helps." That describes Dorcas. The NIV words this as "those able to help others."

Dorcas took her needle and served God with it. She served Him by helping needy ladies who were glad to have the quality clothing she produced.

Now! Doesn't Dorcas cheer you up a bit? We'll feel even better knowing we have our own equivalent of her needle and thread, serving God by serving others.

Lesson 10

New Family In Christ

Eph. 1:3-14

Blessed be the God and Father of our Lord Jesus Christ, who hath blessed us with all spiritual blessings in heavenly places in Christ:

4 According as he hath chosen us in him before the foundation of the world, that we should be holy and without blame before him in love:

5 Having predestinated us unto the adoption of children by Jesus Christ to himself, according to the good pleasure of his will,

6 To the praise of the glory of his grace, wherein he hath made us accepted in the beloved.

7 In whom we have redemption through his blood, the forgiveness of sins, according to the riches of his grace;

8 Wherein he hath abounded toward us in all wisdom and prudence;

9 Having made known unto us the mystery of his will, according to his good pleasure which he hath purposed in himself:

10 That in the dispensation of the fulness of times he might gather to- gether in one all things in Christ, both which are in heaven, and which are on earth; even in him:

11 In whom also we have obtained an inheritance, being predestinated according to the purpose of him who worketh all things after the counsel of his own will:

12 That we should be to the praise of his glory, who first trusted in Christ.

13 In whom ye also trusted, after that ye heard the word of truth, the gospel of your salvation: in whom also after that ye believed, ye were sealed with that holy Spirit of promise,

14 Which is the earnest of our inheritance until the redemption of the purchased possession, unto the praise of his glory.

May 3

Memory Selection
Eph. 1:5
Background Scripture
Eph. 1:3-14
Devotional Reading
Exod. 19:1-8

In the previous unit we considered the *path* to new life in Christ made possible by His gift of salvation. That is the start of new life. What then? This unit is about the *dailiness* of new life. What difference does being "born again" make on the job, around the house, in our families (even if it's a family of one!) Five lessons from Paul's letter to the Ephesians provide the study material for this topic.

The first principle to understand is that this "new life way" is more *gift* than *demand*. As Ephesians 1 emphasizes, believers are *blessed, chosen, predestined, adopted,* and *called* to live the born-again life, *but . . . .* It's like being adopted into a loving family. We're welcome to the family; but we're expected to live a cut above the way we lived on the street.

ജ്ഞ

For a Lively Start

How is church like a family? In this lesson and in other places in Ephesians, Paul speaks of salvation in terms of being adopted into His family. He specifically uses the term "family" in 3:15. You can introduce this lesson by asking your group how being saved is like being in a family. Ask if anyone in the group was adopted, or have adopted children of their own, and whether they have any experiences that compare with being brought into God's family. What role does *God* play in the Church, our spiritual family? What *responsibilities* do members of a particular family have which those outside the family don't have? What *blessings*? What happens. or should happen, when a member of a family flagrantly disobeys the father?

Teaching Outline	**Daily Bible Readings**
I. What's Expected of the Children? 1:3-4	Mon. A Priestly Kingdom *Exod. 19:1-8*
II. What Has God Done for Them?—5-10	Tue. An Inheritance Promised *Gal. 3:15-18*
A. Predestination, 5a	Wed. God's Children by Faith *Gal. 3:23-29*
B. Adoption, 5b-6	Thu. Adoption as God's Children *Gal. 4:1-7*
C. Redemption, 7	
D. Revealed the Mystery, 8-10	Fri. Inheriting Eternal Life *Matt. 19:23-30*
III. Who Gets the Praise?—11-14	Sat. Guided by the Spirit *Gal. 5:16-25*
A. Predestined for *His* glory, 11-12	Sun. God's Own People *Eph. 1:3-14*
B. Sealed by the Spirit, 13-14	

Verse by Verse

I. What's Expected of the Children? 1:3-4

3 Blessed be the God and Father of our Lord Jesus Christ, who hath blessed us with all spiritual blessings in heavenly places in Christ:

4 According as he hath chosen us in him before the foundation of the world, that we should be holy and without blame before him in love:

The letter to the Ephesians is famous for the "showers of blessings" that it promises those who are "in Christ." In fact that two-word phrase is used *27 times* in the book. It describes those who have responded to God's call through His Son, and who have therefore been plucked out of the world and put in God's sheepfold, the Church, "Which is his body."

Today many Christians carelessly speak of "Going to church" as though it were the place they meet. For the author to the Ephesians (probably Paul) the Church is Christ's Body. It consists of *people,* not bricks and mortar; and

getting to be "in" that Body is the safest, most wonderful place in the world (or "out of the world"!) one can be.

Before getting into those blessings for those "in Christ," and skipping down to the latter part of verse 4, we discover that being in Christ brings with it some expectations, too. In fact, we are expected to *"be holy and without blame before him in love."* Not to worry, though—if we but try to be holy, we have the incredible blessing of being accredited with the holiness of Christ. God doesn't expect us to be holy on our own; as the saying goes, "Where God guides, God provides." Paul just mentions holiness early on to show that being in Christ has some responsibilities.

Yet, partaking of *Christ's* holiness is one of the most amazing blessings those who are "in Christ" receive. It's a blessing that was credited to us "before the foundation of the world." Long before we chose to be holy, God chose to set aside, or "elect" a group of people who *could* be holy because of what Christ would accomplish on the Cross as a part of His pre-ordained plan.

II. What Has God Done for Them?—5-10

A. Predestination, 5a

5a Having predestinated us ...

After holiness, the next blessing those "in Christ" have is being *predestined to be adopted.* We won't be able to answer all the questions about predestination in this short lesson. It's been a battleground among Protestants since it was emphasized by Martin Luther, then John Calvin. For many, predestination takes away free will. One way to think about it that avoids this problem is to think of predestination as God's pre-selecting *a body*—the Body, the Body of Christ—but allowing individuals the free will to decide whether they want to be *in* that predestined body or not.

B. Adoption, 5b-6

5b unto the adoption of children by Jesus Christ to himself, according to the good pleasure of his will,

6 To the praise of the glory of his grace, wherein he hath made us accepted in the beloved.

Paul compares being saved to being adopted. The prospective family comes to the orphans' home. They *can't* adopt all the children, and the fact that they adopt any is a matter of "the good pleasure of [their] will." They look around at the runny noses and uncombed hair and untied shoes, and it's a wonder that they adopt any of us. When they do, it's not because we look like good prospects for good kids; it's *"to the praise of the glory of his grace, wherein he*

hath made us accepted in the beloved"—that is, in that beloved family of God, or again, "in Christ." Yet the visiting prospective parents respect the free will of the kids in the orphanage. They won't adopt any who don't want to be, or who they can tell will be too rebellious to follow the rules in their new home. That wouldn't bring any praise for their grace at all.

C. Redemption, 7

7 In whom we have redemption through his blood, the forgiveness of sins, according to the riches of his grace;

Another evidence of the grace of adoption is that God has already ordained that whoever accepts His offer to be a part of His family has had the price of adoption already paid. This way of speaking of salvation grew out of the Old Covenant system of animal sacrifices. Man's sin constitutes slavery to Satan, the father of sin. In His love, God graciously paid the price in blood sacrifices to "buy" or redeem us from that bondage. The animals sacrificed under the Law of Moses were only a token of the ultimate sacrifice of God Himself, in the form of His Son (Heb. 9:12). Paul emphasizes the important point that this grand plan was not concocted by man, but is solely out of the riches of God's grace.

D. Revealed the Mystery, 8-10

8 Wherein he hath abounded toward us in all wisdom and prudence;

9 Having made known unto us the mystery of his will, according to his good pleasure which he hath purposed in himself:

10 That in the dispensation of the

fulness of times he might gather to- gether in one all things in Christ, both which are in heaven, and which are on earth; even in him:

Most world religions have devised ways to reconnect sinful man with a holy God or gods. Just how to do this was often called a "mystery," and wise sages have tried, through human wisdom, to developed the wisest system. Paul insists that this cannot be done: "the world by wisdom knew not God" (1 Cor. 1:21).

Fortunately, as verse 9 says, *God's* wisdom penetrates this mystery. He did not leave it to human wisdom. Some pagan religions in Paul's world were actually called "the mysteries." New converts were shown sacred objects and given secret phrases to chant as signs that they had penetrated the mystery of the way of salvation. Paul, however, insists that the true mystery is not a secret at all. It is the simple story of Jesus, which was not to be kept secret but broadcast to "all the world."

A part of this mystery, according to verse 10, is that at a time decided on by God, not man ("the fullness of time"), those who choose to join this elect Body can all be one people. Instead of the constant warfare between nations and races, the elect can be one—again, *in Christ.* This great body unites with "things in heaven," too, not with so-called "mysteries" on earth.

III. Who Gets the Praise?—11-14
A. Predestined for *His* glory, 11-12

11 In whom also we have obtained an inheritance, being predestinated according to the purpose of him who worketh all things after the counsel of his own will:

12 That we should be to the praise of his glory, who first trusted in Christ.

Ever since the doctrine of predestination began to be emphasized, some have treated it as a badge of their favored position in Christ. Paul says that the purpose of the inheritance promised to the elect is to be to the praise of *His* glory, not to the glory of the elect. In fact, we can easily relieve ourselves of all pride in being among the elect by remembering that the earliest Christians often had to die for the privilege! They sometimes felt like Tevya in "Fiddler on the Roof," whose life as part of the "chosen race" was so hard that he prayed for God to choose someone else for awhile!

B. Sealed by the Spirit, 13-14

13 In whom ye also trusted, after that ye heard the word of truth, the gospel of your salvation: in whom also after that ye believed, ye were sealed with that holy Spirit of promise,

14 Which is the earnest of our inheritance until the redemption of the purchased possession, unto the praise of his glory.

Perhaps anticipating the discouragement that some "chosen" believers would suffer when they realize that being part of the elect sometimes feels like they're going over a cliff, Paul gives them some "limbs" to hang on to: *the word of truth, the gospel,* and *the seal of the Holy Spirit*—all of which constitutes the earnest or promise of our inheritance, and all of which is ours if we "choose to be chosen to the praise of His glory."

Evangelistic Emphasis

The Israelites had been slaves in Egypt for about four centuries. By its very nature, slavery robs its victims of personal identity and a feeling of self-worth. For generations, the lives of these people had been dominated by the whims of their masters. As we find them in Exodus 20 they have been free for exactly three months, and God sends Moses to them with wonderful news.

If they keep the covenant that God will make with them, they will be His "peculiar treasure," "a kingdom of priests, and an holy nation" (vss. 5-6). Not only will they be free, but they are promised a special relationship with God. This is a far cry from slavery.

Romans 6:16-18 tells us that we are slaves of whomsoever we obey. We can be servants to sin, and that brings death. Or we can be God's servants, which brings righteousness (a right relationship with God). Those who obey God's teaching are free from being sin's slave, and free to become servants of God. We have a choice. It's an easy one to make. Everyone should be told about it.

Memory Selection

Having predestinated us unto the adoption of children by Jesus Christ to himself, according to the good pleasure of his will.—*Ephesians 1:5*

Arriving at an understanding of predestination is not the easiest of tasks. Good and honest Christians have worked on this for centuries without coming to one clear-cut conclusion.

There are, however, some valuable truths that are obvious for us all. To begin with, what the Bible says about predestination lets us know that God is God. Even before time existed He was making decisions about us. Before He laid the foundations of the world He was making choices, and one of them was that we should be adopted as His children (vss. 4-5).

In Ephesians predestination is rooted in the grace of God (2:4-10). It glorifies His grace (1:6). We are His workmanship, created in Christ for good works, "which God hath before ordained" (2:10).

You may enjoy working your way through the intricacies of this fascinating subject. Or, you might prefer to relax and be content that God is in control of His universe. Predestination adds to the awe, the majesty, the mystery of God. It's for our benefit.

Weekday Problems

Do you remember a few years ago when the world got its first view into some Romanian orphanages? Some children had received no love, no attention, and a minimum of adult contact. They couldn't relate to people or to life situations about them.

I have recently become aware of a child in the States who has Attachment Reactive Disorder, the name given to this condition. This child was born to a drug addicted, alcoholic, frequently absentee parent, and otherwise all-around dysfunctional situation. Those who know his case say that the outlook is not favorable.

God doesn't treat His children like that. Quite to the contrary, he planned far in advance (before the foundation of the world) to adopt us. It was a decision on His part. Something He wanted to do. He did it through love and grace.

Being unattached to our Father is a problem we'll never have, unless, of course, we should become rebellious children and run away from home. Even then, He'd come looking for us.

ASSIGNMENT FOR NEXT WEEK

On May 10 our lesson will include the threat of "passions of the flesh" in our society. Bring to class a pasted up poster-montage of newspaper or magazine head-lines, photos, and stories illustrating this danger (omitting pornography, of course). Although lust and sexual sins such as rape usually come to mind first, remember that Scripture also includes such sins as **gossip, warring, pride, and hatred** as "sins of the flesh."

These montages can be displayed as an introduction to next week's lesson.

347

This Lesson in Your Life

As my sister and I were growing up, we had two cousins who had been adopted. It would be an exaggeration to say that this made my sister and me feel like second-class citizens, but there were times when we wondered. Little children can be brutally honest and maybe a little cruel. Our cousins reminded my sister and me that they had been selected, picked out on purpose. We, on the other hand, had been born into our family, and the implication may have been that our parents were stuck with us whether they wanted to be or not. Our parents didn't get to select us. They had to take the luck of the draw. (These childhood goings-on are written light-heartedly and were never really an issue.) The fact truly is, though, that adoption is something quite special.

God made a choice. He chose us. Paul points out in Ephesians 1:5 that before time existed, God predestined us for adoption "by Jesus Christ to himself." We're an important part of His long-term plan. In 2:8-10 we learn that our salvation is by grace, and that He had "before ordained" that we should do good works. Christ came so "that we might receive the adoption of sons" (Gal. 4:4-5). Because of this we can say "Abba, Father."

Paul is the only New Testament writer who uses the term "adoption." There are other doctrines that bear a similarity to it, or at least have points in common. Regeneration (the new birth) is one of them. Someone has made the observation that adoption places emphasis on an act of God. Regeneration (the new birth) places emphasis on renewal of the believer (new spirit, new heart, being born again).

Ephesians says that our adoption is "by Jesus Christ." Galatians 4 says that "when the fullness of time was come, God sent forth his Son," "that we might receive the adoption of sons." We want to remember that there is no adoption apart from Christ. God used Christ's coming in the flesh, His teaching, the Crucifixion, Resurrection, and Ascension, to secure our adoption. It's all by grace. Abba, Father, thank You.

1. In the third month to the very day since the Israelites left Egypt, where did they encamp?

They came to the desert of Sinai and encamped "before the mount."

2. In what picturesque language did God describe His bringing the Israelites out of Egypt?

"I bare you on eagles' wings, and brought you unto myself."

3. If the Israelites would keep God's covenant, what kind of nation would He make of them?

He would make them a kingdom of priests, and a holy nation.

4. Did the people agree to keep the covenant?

Yes. (See also Exod. 24:3, 7.)

5. Through what kind of pre-planning did God determine to adopt children?

Through predestination.

6. God predestined the adoption of children to Himself. Through whom would this be accomplished?

"By Jesus Christ."

7. Through what motivation or intention did God do this?

"According to the good pleasure of his will."

8. What kind of credit or praise would be given for this action?

"To the praise of the glory of his grace."

9. What kind of mystery did God make known to us?

He has "made known unto us the mystery of his will, according to his good pleasure which he hath purposed in himself."

10. We are accepted in "the beloved" [Christ], in whom we have what?

"We have redemption through his blood, the forgiveness of sins, according to the riches of his grace."

349

Relationships are fragile. They're precious. Family and friends are a blessing from God and we want to preserve them. God Himself gives us a great object lesson on their importance.

It's impossible for us accurately to conceive of God before He created the world. Possibly we can think of Him as the Spirit, the Loving Force, the Eternal I AM, out in the Great Beyond (except there was nothing created yet for Him to be "beyond.") But supposing we can somehow bring Him into focus. What would He have on His mind? That part's easy. He was thinking about you, me, and all his future children.

He chose us in Christ before the foundation of the world. He predestined us by Jesus Christ to be adopted for Himself. Even before His Spirit moved across the face of the waters and the heavens and earth were formed, God was planning His family.

This whole thing about predestination and adoption is something that he "purposed in himself." It's bigger than any of us. It's part of the "counsel of his own will." We can't fathom the depth of His thinking. It's "to the praise of the glory of his grace."

Maybe when we get to heaven we'll understand more about this. Until then it calls us to worship and adoration "to the praise of the glory of his grace." (Quotations from Ephesians 1.)

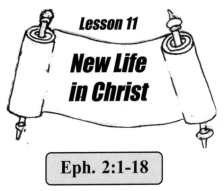

Lesson 11

New Life in Christ

Eph. 2:1-18

And you hath he quickened, who were dead in trespasses and sins;

2 Wherein in time past ye walked according to the course of this world, according to the prince of the power of the air, the spirit that now worketh in the children of disobedience:

3 Among whom also we all had our conversation in times past in the lusts of our flesh, fulfilling the desires of the flesh and of the mind; and were by nature the children of wrath, even as others.

4 But God, who is rich in mercy, for his great love wherewith he loved us,

5 Even when we were dead in sins, hath quickened us together with Christ, (by grace ye are saved;)

6 And hath raised us up together, and made us sit together in heavenly places in Christ Jesus:

7 That in the ages to come he might shew the exceeding riches of his grace in his kindness toward us through Christ Jesus.

8 For by grace are ye saved through faith; and that not of yourselves: it is the gift of God:

9 Not of works, lest any man should boast.

10 For we are his workmanship, created in Christ Jesus unto good works,

which God hath before ordained that we should walk in them.

Wherefore remember, that ye being in time past Gentiles in the flesh, who are called Uncircumcision by that which is called the Circumcision in the flesh made by hands;

12 That at that time ye were without Christ, being aliens from the commonwealth of Israel, and strangers from the covenants of promise, having no hope, and without God in the world:

13 But now in Christ Jesus ye who sometimes were far off are made nigh by the blood of Christ.

14 For he is our peace, who hath made both one, and hath broken down the middle wall of partition between us;

15 Having abolished in his flesh the enmity, even the law of commandments contained in ordinances; for to make in himself of twain one new man, so making peace;

16 And that he might reconcile both unto God in one body by the cross, having slain the enmity thereby:

17 And came and preached peace to you which were afar off, and to them that were nigh.

18 For through him we both have access by one Spirit unto the Father.

May 10

Memory Verse
Eph. 2:8

Background Scripture
Eph. 3:1-10

Devotional Reading
Ps.86:1-13

FOCUS

This lesson comes close to lending itself to the kind of sermon which, when asked what the topic was, the answer was "sin"; and when asked "What did the preacher have to say about it?" the answer was "He was agin' it." The author (perhaps Paul) was not only "agin" sin; he knew both Jew and Gentile were guilty.

He also raises the way self-righteous Jews habitually criticized Gentiles as being sinners, when in fact Jews needed the cleansing blood of Christ as much as Gentiles. He appeals to the fact that new life in Christ both appealed for righteous living and provided the grace to live righteously. The theme is *good works made possible not by human righteousness but by grace,* and *good works as the evidence of a grace-filled life.*

୧୨୯୨

For a Lively Start

At the end of our last lesson, an Assignment (p. 347) suggested that group members bring poster-sized montages of newspaper and magazine clippings that illustrate our society's immersion in "passions of the flesh." You won't have to look far to find headlines such as "47 killed in Iraq," "28 arrested in prostitution ring," "Meth labs said to be doing big business," "3 indicted for murder." The Bible also labels as "fleshly" less lurid "crimes" such as gossip and character assasination. With or without the paste-ups, discuss various ways such activities threaten law and order in society as well as violate God's Word and will.

Teaching Outline	Daily Bible Readings
I. Former Sinfulness—2:1-3	Mon. Full of Grace and Truth *John 1:14-18*
A. Gentiles dead in sin, 1-2	Tue. Wait for the Gracious Lord *Isa. 30:15-21*
B. Jews dead also, 3	Wed. No Good Withheld *Ps. 84:9-12*
II. Future Glory—4-10	
A. Saved and raised, 4-6	Thu. The Throne of Grace *Heb. 4:14–5:10*
B. Through grace, not works, 7-10	Fri. Set Your Hope on Grace *1 Pet. 1:10-16*
III. Fleshly Difference—11-12	
IV. Forever One—13-18	Sat. The Blessing of Grace *Num. 6:22-27*
A. Divisive Law Abolished, 13-15	Sun. Saved by Grace / Faith *Eph. 2:1-10*
B. Uniting Cross and Spirit, 16-18	

Verse by Verse

I. Former Sinfulness—2:1-3
A. Gentiles dead in sin, 1-2

1 And you hath he quickened who were dead in trespasses and sins;

2 Wherein in time past we walked according to the course of this world according to the prince of the power of the air, the spirit that now worketh in the children of disobedience:

Certain catch-phrases such as "the prince of the power of the air" would tentatively identify Satan as in control of the former lives of Gentile members of the church at Ephesus. Indeed, Paul makes this explicit in 3:1 when he refers to the special calling God had given him "for you Gentiles." Yet we know from Paul's first visit to Ephesus that there was also a Jewish synagogue there (Acts 19:1-8). We can only conclude therefore that the Ephesian church was a typical "Diaspora" ("scattered") church, composed both of Jews brought there when various campaigns against their homeland resulted in many being carried away to foreign countries but allowed to practice their religion; and of Gentiles, some of whom had become Jewish "proselytes" and others who had been converted by Paul and other early Christian missionaries. They had been "quickened" or made alive—saved—from their former pagan manner of living.

B. Jews dead also, 3

Among whom also we all had our conversation in times past in the lusts of our flesh, fulfilling the desires of the flesh and of the mind; and were by nature the children of wrath, even as others.

Both Jew and Gentile are in the same boat. A Jew who boasted of keeping the Law of Moses perfectly was as "fleshly" as a Gentile whose past life was characterized by sexual immorality. All are "test cases," proving our natural inclination to be sinners and the universal need for the gospel. ("Conversation" is the KJV for "manner of living.")

II. Future Glory—4-10
A. Saved and raised, 4-6

4 But God, who is rich in mercy, for his great love wherewith he loved us,

5 Even when we were dead in sins, hath quickened us together with Christ (by grace ye are saved;)

7 And hath raised us up together, and made us sit together in heavenly places in Christ Jesus:

Just as both Jew and Gentile were equally lost, now, by the grace of God, they are equally saved. Here Paul moves toward the over-arching theme of his letter to the Ephesians: *unity in Christ*. Modern Christians and Jews who have little to do with each other can hardly realize the radical nature of Paul's affirmation that this racial division is erased in Christ; that in Him we are raised *together* to jointly occupy the position of brothers and sisters—*priests*—in one Body, the Church. Indeed it is so revolutionary that Jews and Christians have never succeeded for long in actually *practicing* the theological fact of unity in Christ.

It is important to note the past tense of the verbs Paul uses. Jew and Gentile are not *awaiting* equality, or being raised to be given roles in the Kingdom of God. We are *already*, in this life, made spiritually alive. The afterlife will only confirm for eternity the eternal life that is already ours, so firm is the promise! Using the Greek word for "last things," theologian C. H. Dodd called this truth "realized eschatology"—God is so dependable that the victory and the unity that has been promised is already the spiritual possession of Jews and Gentiles who come together in Christ. Does it not behoove us to *practice* the unity that is already ours?

B. Through grace, not works, 7-10

7 That in the ages to come he might shew the exceeding riches of his grace in his kindness toward us through Christ Jesus.

8 For by grace are ye saved through faith; and that not of yourselves: it is the gift of God:

9 Not of works, lest any man should boast.

10 For we are his workmanship, created in Christ Jesus unto good works, which God hath before ordained that we should walk in them.

For the unity Paul preaches to be something other than an empty cheer; for it to be a fact that can be lived out in practical ways; and for the death of Christ to retain its meaning—something must be said about the Jew/Gentile views of salvation. Verses 8-9 show that we cannot compromise by saying that we are saved by a little work and a little grace. Although Moses had not intended for his Law to become a works-system, it was inevitable that it become one. Any system of law was partly a humanistic, pull-yourself-up-by-the-bootstraps attempt to be saved. Despit good intentions, such systems were based on "the desires of the flesh," providing us something to boast about; and boasting is of the devil (vss. 1-3). It also lent itself to division instead of unity. Since our achievements of goodness vary, we are tempted to boast one against another. Unity is possible only if we all confess our unworthiness. Then we can all "be raised together" as the workmanship not of our own devising but of Christ's, in a plan pre-ordained for us.

III. Fleshly Difference—11-12

11 Wherefore remember, that ye being in time past Gentiles in the flesh, who are called Uncircumcision by that which is called the Circumcision in the flesh made by hands;

12 That at that time ye were without Christ, being aliens from the commonwealth of Israel, and strangers from the covenants of promise, having no hope, and without God in the world:

"At that time" and "in time past" refer of course to the era when Jew and Gentile were estranged. Most of Paul's audience were Gentiles "in the flesh" (3:1)—that is, their difference from Jews was not merely racial but bore with it the fleshly mark of Jewish circumcision. Paul, however, had been shown how superficial this mark is. What was needed was a circumcision of the heart, an operation on the will. *Anyone,* Jew and Gentile alike, can submit to this kind of circumcision, not "made by hands."

The list of labels that could be applied to Gentiles before this spiritual circumcision is formidable. Verse 12 finds five terms that apply to their unjustified state before coming to Christ. However, "the bigger they come, the harder they fall"; only those who admit their desperate condition outside of Christ could fully enjoy their new equality as spiritual Jews sitting *in* the covenant and the commonwealth of the true Israel.

IV. Forever One—13-18
A. Divisive Law Abolished, 13-15

13 But now in Christ Jesus ye who someimes were far off are made both one, and hath broken down the middle wall of partition between us;

14 For he is our peace, who hath made both one, and hath broken down the middle wall of partition between us;

15 Having abolished in his flesh the enmity, even the law of commandments contained in ordinances; for to make in himself of twain one new man, so making peace;

For generations it had been necessary to allow the law to keep a pure line of Jewish descent through which the Messian could come. Now we can say, "That was then; this is now." Now, *anyone* who accesses the blood of Christ by faith can enjoy peace with God, with Christ, and with their former enemies, the Jews.

B. Uniting Cross and Spirit, 16-18

16 And that he might reconcile both unto God in one body by the cross, having slain the enmity thereby:

17 And came and preached peace to you which were afar off, and to them that were nigh.

18 For through him we both have access by one Spirit unto the Father.

Whereas there were two "bodies," Jew vs. Gentile, now there are one. With the former enmity between them slain on the Cross, both now have equal access to the Father through one Spirit.

Evangelistic Emphasis

In his commentary on Ephesians, R. Kent Hughes remarks that the first three verses in chapter 2 take us into the Death Valley of the soul, and the next four verses take us to "heavenly places in Christ Jesus." It is only in Christ that we make this journey.

John R. W. Stott's *God's New Society* notes that "you," "we," and "others" in the first three verses, describes people who are in the clutches of moral and spiritual death. Without Christ, that's everybody. Without Him there is no spiritual life for anybody.

This realization should trigger some significant reactions in all Christians. Sincere gratitude and praise easily come to mind. Ephesians 1:3 points us in that direction: "Blessed be the God and Father of our Lord Jesus Christ, who hath blessed us with all spiritual blessing in heavenly places in Christ."

We also realize that this news is too good not to be shared. Let's not forget the "others," who may not have heard about it.

Memory Selection

For by grace are ye saved through faith; and that not of yourselves: it is the gift of God.—*Ephesians 2:8*

"This is one of the great evangelical summaries of the New Testament," says F. F. Bruce in his Ephesians commentary. He goes on to point out that our salvation springs only from God's grace, and is appropriated by us through faith alone.

Other passages reinforce this truth. Romans 11:6, for instance, says "And if by grace, then it is no more of works: otherwise grace is no more grace. But if it be of works, then it is no more grace: otherwise work is no more work."

This is an either/or situation. Grace is a free gift. When we work we earn. Romans 4:4 emphasizes this: "Now to him that worketh is the reward not reckoned of grace, but of debt." We can't present God with a "Due and Payable" statement. He can (and does) present us with a free gift.

Weekday Problems

A number of years ago I was visiting a church on the East Coast, and as the morning's worship service was closing, the final remark before the benediction was this: "We have done our duty for the week."

That jarring mis-statement is still tucked away in the part of my brain where I remember upsetting things. It's true that we had gathered to share in praise to God, and that was good. But supposing that we had "done our duty for the week" mean that we could check God off our "to-do" list until the next Sunday?

Ephesians 2:10 says that we are "created in Christ Jesus unto good works, which God hath before ordained that we should walk in them." When we think we've "Done our good deed for the day," maybe we should look around for another one to do.

Racial Warfare

A German was the guest of a Frenchman who asked him how they distinguish between an optimist and a pessimist in Germany. "It is very simple," replied the German. "The optimists are learning English and the pessimsts are learning Russian."

* * *

"Who are those people cheering?" asked the recruit as the soldiers marched toward the train.

A wise veteran standing by said solemnly, "They're the people who aren't going."

* * *

"This slaughter is shocking," said the wife, commentng on the war. "Can nothing be done to stop it?"

"I'm afraid not," her husband answered.

"Why don't both sides get together and arbitrate?" she asked.

"They did," said her husband. "That's how this whole thing got started."

This Lesson in Your Life

Ephesians chapter 2 is filled with contrasts. Within the first three verses we read about death, sin, and wrath. In the next verse we find the words mercy and love. The difference couldn't be greater. To one extent or another, we all either have been, now are, or may be in the future, involved in everything suggested by these words. It's describing lives that either have been, or have not been, made alive by Christ.

This makes getting to verse 5 very important. It says, "Even when we were dead in sins, he hath quickened us [made us alive] together with Christ (by grace ye are saved)."

However, there's a human element that can complicate our response to God's grace. It can pull us downward toward death and sin, or upward toward God and glory. A few lines from a Studdard Kennedy poem express how our human nature feels both the upward and downward tug:

> I'm a man and a man's a mixture
> Right down from his very birth;
> For part of him comes from heaven
> And part of him comes from earth.

Assuming grace has touched our humanity and changed it, we all "sit together in heavenly places in Christ Jesus" (v. 9). This is just a way of saying that we receive a little bit of heaven here on earth. Not all of it by any means, but just a touch; enough to make us want the fullness of it.

Verse 10 says that we are God's workmanship. We are His new creation in Christ Jesus, a masterpiece that only He could make. He has created us "unto good works."

God, the creator of the universe, is the master workman. There's a trickle-down effect as we become more godly and good works result.

We realize that we are not saved *by* works. We are, however, saved *for* good works. Good works will be the fruit of salvation, and are a characteristic of the Christian lifestyle.

Take a moment and see the progression that takes place between verses 1 and 10. We began with death, sin, and wrath. By God's grace we have advanced to life, mercy and love. We're His children, doing the works he ordained for us.

STRAIGHT

1. In Psalm 86:5, how does God respond to those who call on Him?
He is good, ready to forgive, and plenteous in mercy.

2. How does Paul describe the evil influences in which the Ephesians previously walked (Eph. 2:1f.)?
He describes them as being directed by the course (or way) of this world, the prince of the power of the air, and the spirit that works in the children of disobedience.

3. By nature, what kind of children are we?
The children of wrath.

4. Christ has raised us up together, and we now sit together. Where does He have us sit?
We sit together in the heavenly places.

5. Why did God raise us up to sit in heavenly places?
To show the exceeding riches of His grace and His kindness toward us.

6. Our salvation is the gift of God. How does He give it to us?
He gives it by grace through faith.

7. Why does this passage say our salvation is not by works?
If it were by works, we could boast about it.

8. By whose workmanship have we been created in Christ Jesus?
We have been created by His (God's) workmanship.

9. For what purpose has He created us in Christ?
We are created for good works.

10. How does God fit in with the good works we are to do?
He has ordained them. He enables us to do them.

Paul was not stingy with words. Neither was he afraid to express his fervor. This being so, he does a marvelous job in using adjectives, or otherwise selecting his words, to pour out the fullness of his heart.

He doesn't deal in half measures. In Ephesians 2:4, for instance, he doesn't just refer to God's love and mercy. Rather, he tells of God's *great* love for us, and His *rich* mercy. In verse seven we read about the *exceeding riches* of His grace.

In 1:3 God does not bless us modestly, but with *all* spiritual blessings, and in verse eight, He *abounds* toward us in *all* wisdom and understanding.

In 3:10 Paul uses what F. F. Bruce describes as a rare poetical adjective: "manifold." It comes across as a very ordinary word in English, in the reference to the manifold wisdom of God. What he's actually describing, Bruce says, is the masterpiece of God's wisdom, His diversified, "many colored" wisdom.

In 3:16 and 19, Paul writes of the *riches* of God's glory and our being strengthened with *might* by His Spirit. He wants us to know about Christ's love that *passes understanding*, and for us to be filled with *all the fullness* of God.

Paul (being led by the Holy Spirit) blesses us by emphasizing the full import of the topics he's discussing. It's as though he goes the extra mile to encourage and uplift us by expanding on his basic thoughts. He wants to give us nothing less than all the fullness of God.

Lesson 12

New Revelation In Christ

Eph. 3:1-13

For this cause I Paul, the prisoner of Jesus Christ for you Gentiles,

2 If ye have heard of the dispensation of the grace of God which is given me to youward:

3 How that by revelation he made known unto me the mystery; (as I wrote afore in few words,

4 Whereby, when ye read, ye may understand my knowledge in the mystery of Christ)

5 Which in other ages was not made known unto the sons of men, as it is now revealed unto his holy apostles and prophets by the Spirit;

6 That the Gentiles should be fellowheirs, and of the same body, and partakers of his promise in Christ by the gospel:

7 Whereof I was made a minister, according to the gift of the grace of God given unto me by the effectual working of his power.

8 Unto me, who am less than the least of all saints, is this grace given, that I should preach among the Gentiles the unsearchable riches of Christ;

9 And to make all men see what is the fellowship of the mystery, which from the beginning of the world hath been hid in God, who created all things by Jesus Christ:

10 To the intent that now unto the principalities and powers in heavenly places might be known by the church the manifold wisdom of God,

11 According to the eternal purpose which he purposed in Christ Jesus our Lord:

12 In whom we have boldness and access with confidence by the faith of him.

13 Wherefore I desire that ye faint not at my tribulations for you, which is your glory.

Memory Selection
Eph. 3:8-9

Background Scripture
Eph. 3:1-13

Devotional Reading
Isa. 40:1-11

May 17

361

God called the apostle Paul to be His special messenger to the Gentiles, proclaiming to them the good news that they had been included in "the chosen race." Previously this status had been preserved for the Jews; but with the coming of Jesus, the Messiah, all people were eligible to become believers, and heirs to the promises of salvation in the Kingdom.

Who, though, was this man named Paul? And how could he prove to his opponents that God had called him to this task? For one thing, he had been given the ability to work miracles like the other apostles. For the rest, it remained for the hardships and sacrifices Paul made to convince people his call was genuine. All this was to back up his message not as self-invented, but as a revelation direct from God through His Spirit.

℘

For a Lively Start

Ask members of your group to put themselves in the place of a Jewish member of the synagogue at Ephesus, or a "hanger on" or proselyte—someone interested but not an official member. One day a messenger comes to the city with a document claiming to be from one "Paul the apostle." The chief of the synagogue and several leaders have heard of him; but what are they to make of his message that the Gentiles are now to be included among God's people? What questions would you ask to confirm the genuineness of the message? What might convince you that Jew and Gentile may now intermingle freely? What is this "church" the message speaks of? What clues in this lesson that might convince you of the truth of Paul's communiqué?

Teaching Outline	Daily Bible Studies

I. Mystery Made Known—1-4
  A. Prisoner of Christ, 1
  B. Dispensation of grace, 2-4
II. Gentiles Are Fellow-heirs—5-6
III. Paul's Commission—7-9
  A. Made a minister, 7
  B. Fellowship of Gentiles, 8-9
IV. God's Manifold Wisdom—10-13
  A. To the 'heavenlies,' 10-12
  B. That you faint not, 13
	Mon. God's Dominion Over All
	     Job 12:13-25
	Tue. Secrets of the Kingdom
	     Matt. 13:10-17
	Wed. God Reveals Mysteries
	     Dan. 2:25-30
	Thu. God's Secret Revealed
	     Amos 3:1-8
	Fri. The Son Reveals the Father
	     Matt. 11:25-30
	Sat. Stewards of God's Mysteries
	     1 Cor.4:1-5
	Sun. Sharing the Promise in Christ
	     Eph. 3:1-13

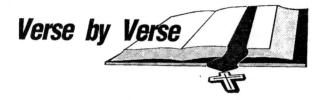

Verse by Verse

I. Mystery Made Known—1-4
A. Prisoner of Christ, 1

1 For this cause I Paul, the prisoner of Jesus Christ for you Gentiles,

The "cause" Paul speaks of here is the over-riding purpose of the entire book of Ephesians—the union of Jew and Gentile in one Body, the Church. (The total content of chapter 2.) By the time he wrote this, probably in prison in Rome, he had truly become a "prisoner" not only of Jesus Christ but of the specific purpose of being the apostle to the Gentiles. Yet there is no hint of unhappiness or surliness at being jailed; he had far rather be given this commission than to wander free, but aimless.

B. Dispensation of grace, 2-4

2 If ye have heard of the dispensation of the grace of God which is given me to youward:

3 How that by revelation he made known unto me the mystery; (as I wrote afore in few words,

4 Whereby, when ye read, ye may understand my knowledge in the mystery of Christ)

We are not to confuse the term "dispensation" here with what many call "dispensation theology," with one stage of world events after another. The original term gives us our word "economy," and simply means "system"—here, the system of grace that God has installed for all, but especially, again, for the Gentiles, who are never far from Paul's mind in this letter. Verse 1 had sounded like Paul was about to give thanks for his role in this dispensation in a prayer; but if so, as he so often did, he became enthralled in another topic. He doesn't get back to the prayer until verse 14, after our lesson text.

What captures his attention now is making sure his readers realize that they had heard of his having received this stunning message of Jew-Gentile unity by *revelation*. He had not convened a meeting of the apostles and worked it out with them. Who could have thought of such a sweeping plan? Rather, God gave it to Paul just as He gave him instructions on the Damascus Road; so those who read it can be confident of its truth. He "wrote afore" about it, meaning he had touched on it earlier in the book, and now wanted to get back to it.

Paul often uses the word "mystery" in a way we should be careful of. As mentioned earlier, the secret religions of some gnostics were also sometimes called "mysteries," but that was because they were *secret*. Paul, however, was caught up in the joy of being allowed to write of a mystery that had been *revealed*—the unity of all races and peoples in Christ.

II. Gentiles Are Fellow-heirs—5-6

5 Which in other ages was not made known unto the sons of men, as it is now revealed unto his holy apostles and prophets by the Spirit;

6 That the Gentiles should be fellowheirs, and of the same body, and partakers of his promise in Christ by the gospel:

The exciting thing, for Paul, is that this mystery is just now being revealed through him and the other apostles and New Covenant prophets. Earlier, God's plan of salvation had the exclusive element of God's Covenant with the patriarchs and their descendants, the Jews. Only now has it been revealed that it also included Gentiles, as fellowheirs right along in the same Body with Abraham, Isaac, and Jacob. This was made possible by Christ, as Paul affirmed in the gospel

III. Paul's Commission—7-9
A. Made a minister, 7

7 Whereof I was made a minister, according to the gift of the grace of God given unto me by the effectual working of his power.

Again Paul exults in his own role in disseminating the news of this grand union. The word for "minister" is *diakonos,* which may also be translated

"deacon," but because of Paul's office as an apostle it is better to use "minister" here. Notice again, that whether Paul is speaking of being a servant, a slave, or a prisoner of Christ, he does so in joyful terms, with no hint of resentment or surliness at what he had to go through.

B. Fellowship of Gentiles, 8-9

8 Unto me, who am less than the least of all saints, is this grace given, that I should preach among the Gentiles the unsearchable riches of Christ;

9 And to make all men see what is the fellowship of the mystery, which from the beginning of the world hath been hid in God, who created all things by Jesus Christ:

In verse 5, Paul had mentioned that God had revealed the Good News to "his holy apostles." Lest readers think he has a high opinion of himself for being in that group, he explains clearly here that arrogance is simply not part of his make-up. He thinks of himself as less than the least of all saints, possibly because he had "persecuted the church of God" (Gal. 1:13) before his conversion. Yet the same grace that has brought Jew and Gentile together was extended to him, and in fact is no doubt part of the reason Paul could continue to preach that message against all opposition. He had experienced personally what he was urging others to accept.

Verse 9 now shows why the miracle of grace was called a "mystery." It had been concealed from the beginning of the world, having been in the mind of God even before creation. Also, the Christ who died on the Cross to accomplish the union among all peoples was the Christ through whom God made the world. What more mysterious and ultimately unfathomable fact could we conceive of? No wonder Paul is so often overwhelmed that his planned sentences are interrupted by an outburst of prayer or praise.

IV. God's Manifold Wisdom—10-13
A. To the 'heavenlies,' 10-12

10 To the intent that now unto the principalities and powers in heavenly places might be known by the church the manifold wisdom of God,

11 According to the eternal purpose which he purposed in Christ Jesus our Lord:

12 In whom we have boldness and access with confidence by the faith of him.

Picking up the sentiment in verse 9, Paul's mission to "make all men see" in verse 9, is to the intent that others see it, too—and this presents us with another mystery. "Principalities and powers in (lit.) the heavenlies" are looking on as well. That was a phrase that the Gnostic religions forming even as Paul wrote used to describe the whole "economy" of creation. To them, there were layers upon layers of such powers. Whether they were real or not, to Paul they were mere onlookers at

the greater scheme that was being unfolded before men and angels and powers alike: God was in Christ, reconciling the world to Himself. Some of those principalities and powers seem to be named in 1:21; but neither principalities, or powers, or might, or dominion are as great, Paul says as the unfolding "manifold wisdom of God" which had united in Christ people who had for so long been enemies.

No wonder Paul could have "boldness and confidence" in his message and ministry. God and Christ were the authors of his message and behind the purpose of it all. Paul could therefore be bold in his preaching; and little wonder: he had access not just to the limited amounts of faith he might have, but Christ's faith, too!

B. That you faint not, 13

13 Wherefore I desire that ye faint not at my tribulations for you, which is your glory.

With so much going for him, Paul does not want anyone to pity him or "faint" at the tribulations he underwent, such as the imprisonment he was experiencing even as he wrote. He would not want to be released if it meant "robbing" them of the glory they were experiencing not only in Christ but in their union with other believers.

෨෦෫

Evangelistic Emphasis

Paul had an impeccable Jewish background. He went so far as to describe himself as a "Hebrew of the Hebrews" (Phil. 3:5). Though born in Tarsus, he grew up in Jerusalem surrounded by orthodox Jewish influences, and attended the prestigious school of Gamaliel (Acts 22:3).

Paul tells us that at the time of his conversion he was advancing in Judaism beyond his contemporaries. He was so zealous for Judaism that he persecuted the Church and tried to destroy it (Gal. 1:13-14).

Then Paul, the epitome of Judaism, unexpectedly finds himself selected by God to be the apostle to the Gentiles (Acts 9:15; 22:21; 26:17-18; 2 Tim. 4:17). As he tells us in Ephesians 3, he marvels that God has given him the grace to perform His Gentile ministry. It was only by the working of God's power that such a turn-about could have come into Paul's life.

Have you ever felt that you don't have what it takes to witness for Christ? Perhaps God knows differently.

ഇൻ

Memory Selection

Unto me, who am less than the least of all saints, is this grace given, that I should preach among the Gentiles the unsearchable riches of Christ. And to make all men see what is the fellowship of the mystery, which from the beginning of the world hath been hid in God, who created all things by Jesus Christ.—*Ephesians 3:8-9*

You and I think of Paul as a hero of the faith, a man who took up his cross, followed the Lord, and suffered gladly. We rank him as the greatest of missionaries. He is the predominate apostle in the book of Acts, and wrote much of the New Testament. How could any Christian worker outrank him?

Yet he considered himself as less than the least among all saints. (In the New Testament, all Christians are called saints.) He could never forget that he had persecuted the church of God, and in 1 Corinthians 15:9 stated that he was the least of the apostles, and not fit to be called an apostle.

This great man teaches us all a lesson in humility. He took to heart the first of Jesus' Beatitudes, "Blessed are the poor in spirit" (those who know they are spiritually impoverished): "for theirs is the kingdom of heaven" (Matt. 5:3). "Just as I am! without one plea, / But that Thy blood was shed for me" is an awareness that we should hold in common with all God's saints, Paul included.

366

Weekday Problems

There are different kinds of energy. An apple contains stored energy. It will stay inside the apple until we eat it. On the other hand, there is kinetic, moving energy, such as a snowball has rolling down a steep hill, getting larger and gaining speed.

The apple won't jump out of the bowl and hit us. If we're smart, though, we'll get out of the way of the snowball. It doesn't want its forward motion disturbed.

There's a life-metaphor here. We all have potential energy stored within us, just waiting to be used; something like the apple. We also have an active life, busy as a run-away down-hill snowball. We might not like it if someone got in our way and interfered with our lifestyle.

Paul was operating at full speed defending Judaism. God stopped him in his tracks and changed the direction of his life. Paul accepted this as being done by God's power and grace.

*This raises a question. Would you or I graciously accept any major changes in our lives to help us conform to God's will?

Higher Education ... or Not

The young man had just received his college degree. He rushed out of the auditorium and cried out, "Here I am, world! I have an A.B.!"

And the world replied, "Sit down, son, and I'll teach you the rest of the alphabet."

* * *

Sophomore: "Hey Dad! Do you know what a lucky man you are?"

Dad: "How's that?"

Sophomore: "You won't have to buy new books for me this year. I'm taking last year's work over again!"

* * *

The father, passing through his son's college town late one night, thought he would pay his son a surprise visit. He knocked on the door of the fraternity house but could rouse no one. Finally from a second-floor window came a sleepy voice. "Whaddya want?"

"Does Steve Jones live here?" asked the father.

"Yeah," the voice replied. "Bring him on in."

This Lesson in Your Life

In the New Testament there is often a distinction made between Jews and Gentiles. In the original language of the New Testament, the word Gentile basically just means nation, or people,,and is the same word (*ethne*) from which we get the term "ethnic." To the Jews, non-Jews were simply all the other people in the world. God made His covenant with Jews, and that's what counted.

Jesus was a Jew, as were the apostles and earliest Christians. It required a special vision given to Peter (Acts 10) to establish that God would accept Gentiles into the Church. Even after that, acceptance did not always come easily.

Paul was about the last person in the world who might have had kind feelings about the Church, or want any association with Gentile people. This all changed with his conversion. (See Acts 9:1-22. Especially notice verse 15.)

Actually, God had intended all along to include Gentiles as His people. This was prophesied in the Old Testament, but not made clear to the people at that long-ago time. God knew it, but it was a mystery to the people. Thus, Paul writes in Ephesians 3:5-6 that by revelation he learned the mystery which in past generations was not known, but is now revealed by the Spirit. He learned that the Gentiles would be heirs together with Israel, of the same body, and partakers of the promise God gave through Christ.

On a very personal level this is highly important to all of us who are not ethnic Jews. Without what Paul has been explaining, Christianity would not be open for us. We would still be separate from Christ, non-citizens, spiritual foreigners, and without God and Christ (Eph. 2:12). Ephesians teaches oneness in Christ. It is our privilege to participate. Thanks be to God for the adoption.

Red and yellow, black and white, all are precious in His sight. We're one in Him.

STRAIGHT

1. **Isaiah 40:8 says that the grass withers and the flower fades. What does the word of the Lord do?**
The word of our God shall stand forever.

2. **In Ephesians 3, what did Paul say about his imprisonment?**
He was the prisoner of Jesus Christ for the Gentiles.

3. **How do we know that Paul believed in revelation?**
He said that it was by revelation that he knew about the mystery concerning the Gentiles.

4. **The mystery was not known in previous generations. By what source was it revealed to Paul and others?**
It was revealed by the Spirit.

5. **What was the mystery?**
The mystery was that the Gentiles should be fellow-heirs, of the same body, and partakers of the promise in Christ through the gospel.

6. **How did Paul become a minister to the Gentiles?**
It was by God's grace and through the working of His power.

7. **In what words did Paul express his position relative to other Christians?**
He said he was less than the least among all the saints.

8. **What did Paul preach among the Gentiles?**
He preached the unsearchable riches of Christ.

9. **Paul wanted everyone to know about the fellowship of the mystery. For how long had God known about it?**
Since before the foundation of the world.

10. **What is it that the Church has the responsibility of making known to all principalities and powers?**
The Church is to make known the manifold wisdom of God.

In Ephesians Paul ecstatically describes what God has done for the Gentiles, and says that it was by a gift of God's grace that he "should preach among the Gentiles the unsearchable riches of Christ" (3:8). This should be exciting to us, also. It's not just every day that unlimited riches are shared. This is an exceptional uplift.

It's interesting to see how various Bible expositors search for ways to describe these unsearchable riches. Here are some examples.

John R. W. Stott explains that His riches are available because of the Cross. They include:

- resurrection from the death of sin,
- victorious enthronement with Christ in the heavenlies,
- reconciliation with God,
- incorporation with Jewish believers in His new society,
- the end of hostility and the beginning of peace,
- access to the Father through Christ and by the Spirit,
- membership in the kingdom and household of God.

R. Kent Hughes lists the riches by categories: sanctifying, relational, practical, and eternal.

Here's a verse with an interesting take on Christ's riches.

> Thou art coming to a King;
> Large petitions with thee bring;
> For His grace and power are such,
> None can ever ask too much.

370

Lesson 13

New Life in The Home

Eph. 5:21–6:4

Submitting yourselves one to another in the fear of God.

22 Wives, submit yourselves unto your own husbands, as unto the Lord.

23 For the husband is the head of the wife, even as Christ is the head of the church: and he is the saviour of the body.

24 Therefore as the church is subject unto Christ, so let the wives be to their own husbands in every thing.

25 Husbands, love your wives, even as Christ also loved the church, and gave himself for it;

26 That he might sanctify and cleanse it with the washing of water by the word,

27 That he might present it to himself a glorious church, not having spot, or wrinkle, or any such thing; but that it should be holy and without blemish.

28 So ought men to love their wives as their own bodies. He that loveth his wife loveth himself.

29 For no man ever yet hated his own flesh; but nourisheth and cherisheth it, even as the Lord the church:

30 For we are members of his body, of his flesh, and of his bones.

31 For this cause shall a man leave his father and mother, and shall be joined unto his wife, and they two shall be one flesh.

32 This is a great mystery: but I speak concerning Christ and the church.

33 Nevertheless let every one of you in particular so love his wife even as himself; and the wife see that she reverence her husband.

6:1 Children, obey your parents in the Lord: for this is right.

2 Honour thy father and mother; (which is the first commandment with promise;)

3 That it may be well with thee, and thou mayest live long on the earth.

4 And, ye fathers, provoke not your children to wrath: but bring them up in the nurture and admonition of the Lord.

Memory Selection
Eph. 5:21

Background Scripture
Eph. 5:1–6:4

Devotional Reading
1 Cor. 1:4-17

May 24

As he usually does, Paul lays down theological principles in the first part of his letters, then in the latter part deals with practical ways those principles should be lived out. A major part of the last part of Ephesians is devoted to how the ordinary family can reflect the love and unity Paul has said should now be true of Jews and Gentiles.

Don't assume that the structure of each family represented in your class consists of father, mother, and 2.5 children! Remember that one person can make a family, and that, more and more, *life together* defines "family" as much as *biological relationships*. Also, since the Bible was not intended to be a textbook on the family, allow room for more than one answer to many questions.

&)(&

For a Lively Start

You may want to start this lesson by leading a brief discussion on the question, *"What is a family?"* Webster defines a family as "A group of individuals living under one roof and usually under one head." In the Old Testament many families included more than wife, and Paul probably had to address some leftover examples of that sort of family. Some families include grandparents, while others don't. Can one person comprise a family?

Alternately, you may want to discuss the question, *"What are the benefits of living in a family?"* Unfortunately, the level of strife and discord in many families can make older teens want to move out—and parents to encourage it!

Teaching Outline	**Daily Bible Readings**
I. The Principle of Submission—5:21-24 A. Mutual submission, 21 B. Wives and husbands, 22-24 II. The Principle of Love—25-30 A. Husband and wives, 25-27 B. The Golden Rule in the Home, 28-30 III. Leaving and Cleaving—31-33 IV. Parents and Children—6:1-4	Mon. Trained by God's Grace *Tit. 2:1-13* Tue. Partnership in Marriage *Gen. 2:18-25* Wed. Interpreting Traditions *Exod. 12:21-28* Thu. Parental Advice *Prov. 4:1-9* Fri. Spirituality and Family *Col. 3:12-24* Sat. Providing for the Family *1 Tim. 5:1-8* Sun. Family Relationships *Eph. 5:21–6:4*

Verse by Verse

I. The Principle of Submission—5:21-24

A. Mutual submission, 21

21 Submitting yourselves one to another in the fear of God.

Paul seems to be starting his teaching on family relationships in the middle of a paragraph. This is because he has been working through a variety of behavioral principles that begin with participles like "speaking," "singing," "making melody," and "giving thanks" (vss. 19-20). Turning to family relationships, the structure of his writing makes it natural to start with another participle, even though he will write far more on the subject of family relationships, roles, and behavior than he did on the previous topics.

Few Bible principles have been discussed more—and more loudly!—than the teaching that wives should submit to their husbands. We discuss with fervor whether this was meant to apply for all time. Less often do we notice that this teaching in verse 22 is preceded by a "mutual submission" verse which, if followed, would turn down

the heat of our other concerns. In fact most of the rest of this lesson would be unnecessary if each family member would make an effort to submit to the other.

B. Wives and husbands, 22-24

22 Wives, submit yourselves unto your own husbands, as unto the Lord.

23 For the husband is the head of the wife, even as Christ is the head of the church: and he is the saviour of the body.

24 Therefore as the church is subject unto Christ, so let the wives be to their own husbands in every thing.

Some interpreters say that Paul did not mean for the submission of wives to be an eternal principle any more than he meant for the behavior of slaves or servants to be forever (6:5). The difficulty with that argument is that Paul ties the submission of wives to the submission of Christians to their "head," Christ, which is certainly an eternal principle. The analogy between Christ and the husband can go only so far, however, since husbands are hardly the "savior" of their wives as Christ is of the Church. What is certain is that if a husband would never ask of his wife anything that is not for her good, the passage would rarely come up for argument.

II. The Principle of Love—25-30
A. Husbands and wives, 25-27

25 Husbands, love your wives, even as Christ also loved the church, and gave himself for it;

26 That he might sanctify and cleanse it with the washing of water by the word,

27 That he might present it to himself a glorious church, not having spot, or wrinkle, or any such thing; but that it should be holy and without blemish.

Verse 25 contains another principle which, if followed, would make for far fewer arguments about submission. Husbands are to love their wives "*as Christ also loved the church.*" He never loved the Church imperiously or demandingly. He loves the Church in ways that "*sanctify*" it. The term can mean to "make holy," but its more basic meaning is to "set apart." Husbands, then, are to "set apart" their wives as someone to love as no other, in ways that make her feel that she, like the Church with Christ, is in a relationship that is for her good.

Since, as verses 32-33 will say, most of this material begins first with the relationship between Christ and the Church, and only secondarily with human relationships, Paul pauses in verses 26-27 to say more about that. The Church is formed by the Word, and people enter it by the figurative "washing" of baptism (see also 1 Pet. 3:21). All this is because Christ is preparing us to live in heaven, where there is nothing unclean. The application here is on a "clean church" more than a "clean wife." The husband who sets out to mandate how his wife can live a sanctified life risks making an object of her. He would serve her better by seeing that she has the freedom to develop her own relationship with Christ and the family.

B. The Golden Rule in the Home, 28-30

28 So ought men to love their wives as their own bodies. He that loveth his wife loveth himself.

29 For no man ever yet hated his own flesh; but nourisheth and cherisheth it, even as the Lord the church:

30 For we are members of his body, of his flesh, and of his bones.

In verse 25, Paul had noted that Christ had given Himself for the Church, a reference of course to the crucifixion. Continuing his analogy between Christ and the Church on one hand, and husbands and wives on the other, he can exhort husbands to live a sacrificial life for their wives. This of course removes any possibility of a husband demanding submission of a wife in the sense of forcing his will against hers. Ideally, spouses will be strong enough to allow each other to have his or her way unless it is to the detriment of the family.

Paul seems to be taking special measures to prevent husbands from lording it over their wives. The principle in verses 29 and 30 should apply to both husband and wife. They cherish each other as themselves, and Paul rightly assumes that since right-thinking spouses will not abuse themselves, they will not abuse each other. "Doing unto others as we would do to ourselves" is especially important in a marriage.

III. Leaving and Cleaving—31-33

31 For this cause shall a man leave his father and mother, and shall be joined unto his wife, and they two shall be one flesh.

32 This is a great mystery: but I speak concerning Christ and the church.

33 Nevertheless let every one of you in particular so love his wife even as himself; and the wife see that she reverence her husband.

In verse 31 Paul quotes most of Genesis 2:24, reinforcing what he has just said about loving one's spouse as we love ourselves. Paul cannot exchange his role as an apostle and theologian for that of a marriage counselor, so he returns to the Christ-Church theme. He has used the word "mystery" several times in referring to God's eternal plan to unite Jew and Gentile in one Body through the sacrifice of Christ. Now he calls the husband-wife and Christ-Church analogy a "mystery," again not because it is a secret but because it is profound. He is asserting that the real basis for all this analogical material is Christ's relationship with the Church,

not the husband-wife relationship. "Nevertheless," he says, the practical application between husband and wife must never be ignored.

IV. Parents and Children—6:1-4

6:1 Children, obey your parents in the Lord: for this is right.

2 Honour thy father and mother; (which is the first commandment with promise;)

3 That it may be well with thee, and thou mayest live long on the earth.

4 And, ye fathers, provoke not your children to wrath: but bring them up in the nurture and admonition of the Lord.

Finally, Paul turns to the parent-child relationship. Speaking directly to children implies a setting in which children are present as this letter is read. He bases his command for children to obey their parents on the Fifth Commandment. Since it is not the first to be followed by a promise, that phrase probably means that it is of "first importance to children." Also, there is no literal promise here that an obedient child will live longer than other children. The promise is more general: obedient children contribute to the happiness and harmony of the family, which in fact might lead to longer lives because the "nurture and admonition of the Lord" is simply the best way to live.

ℰᗞᏟᏜ

Evangelistic Emphasis

It has been said that good doctrine produces good morals. Both Scripture and life confirm this. In Ephesians Paul leads us into some significant doctrinal areas as we study such topics as predestination, adoption, redemption, and the mystery that had been hidden but has now been revealed.

As we move toward the end of this book, Paul shifts gears. Building on the sound doctrine he has taught us, he gives some specific instruction about Christian living. He encourages us to preserve unity, and to be gentle, loving, and patient toward those with whom we share our Christian faith. He stresses sexuality and other areas of purity and right living. He discusses mutual submission, and lays out the foundation for Christian homes. He gives instructions to each member of the family.

The good behavior that comes from good doctrine will be obvious even to unbelievers. There will be a correlation between Scripture, Church, and Christian life. This will validate the gospel message and make it more attractive to everyone.

Memory Selection

Submitting yourselves one to another in the fear of the Lord.—*Ephesians 5:21*

The topic of submission is going to be an interesting one. Let's approach our Memory Verse by defining just what each part means. What do we mean by submitting ourselves to one another? What about doing it "in the fear of the Lord"?

We're not talking about one person dominating another individual. Nobody holds anybody captive. This verse describes a reciprocal action where each person respects and honors the other. Each person will subject himself for the benefit of the other.

We do this out of fear (respect) for Christ. The Cross calls us to such action. If God so loved us, we should love one another (1 Jn. 4:11).

There's a sense in which submitting to each other has a liberating effect. It frees us from egotism. We are no longer bound by selfishness. We have the freedom to do what Jesus would have done.

Weekday Problems

Rex, his wife and two teenagers, were members of a church where the teens were active in the youth groups. A new Youth Minister replaced one who had been there for some time.

When Rex and his wife met him for the first time, Rex was not impressed, though his wife thought he was quite nice. When the new man replaced the study materials the teens were using, Rex felt strongly that the previous curriculum was much better. When schedules were changed and recreational activities were adjusted, he became even more disgruntled. He was an unhappy man.

Rex began to complain to the parents of other teens. He felt that the Youth Minister had ruined the youth department, and should be replaced. He finally convinced one other family to agree with him. Word reached the Youth Minister that "There are people who think you are not doing a good job, and should be replaced."

*Evaluate Rex's behavior in the light of 1 Corinthians 1:10-12 and Ephesians 5:21.

All in the Family

Child psychologists say the modern child treats his parents with awe. This confirms the common observation: it's always "Aw, why can't I have the car?" or "Aw, why can't I have a bigger allowance?"

* * *

A father was scolding his son for telling an extra-big fib. "I never told lies when I was your age," he said.

The lad looked down at his shoes for a second, then looked up and asked, "Well, how old were you when you started?"

* * *

Dad was tired and irritable when he got home from work and when his son kept asking what he did he barked, "Nothing!"

Thinking a minute, his son asked, "Well how did you know when you got through?"

This Lesson in Your Life

Paul gives us quite an impressive "submissive list." We all submit to each other. Wives submit to their husbands. The Church submits to Christ. Husbands love their wives to the point of dying for them if necessary (the ultimate submission). Children obey parents. Slaves obey their masters.

This is all quite interesting in view of the fact that we're living in an age of liberation. How can we make this work when everybody wants to "do his own thing?"

Paul's background for submission reaches back as far as 5:2, where he says Christ loved us and gave Himself up for us. Another essential for a submissive attitude is in 5:18, which tells us to "be filled with the Spirit." Philippians 2:1-8 is a companion section to this.

It's important that we realize what these passages do *not* teach.

There's nothing here about tyranny. Nobody is being brow-beaten. We're not talking exploitation. Quite to the contrary, love, respect, gentleness, meekness, honor for all, and genuine concern for others, make Christian submission a viable, wholesome accomplishment. Think in terms of Jesus, wash basin and towel in hand, on His knees washing the disciple's dirty feet.

Before Paul lists categories (wives, children, etc.) he tells us that we all should be submissive to each other. That's just the Christian way. Under this overall heading, he gets specific.

The idea that a wife should be submissive to her husband will draw a lot of flack these days. Those who try to shoot it down may not realize what Paul is saying. It's simply that there has to be structure and order, and God has assigned responsibilities. It has nothing to do with inferiority.

If both the husband and wife are aware that verse 21 says we all should submit to one another out of reverence for Christ, and they both realize that the husband will do for the wife what Christ did for the Church, this will remove the fear of any authoritarian or overbearing behavior. It places responsibility on the husband and gives assurance to the wife.

It's a blessing when children are brought up in a well-regulated home. They have a head-start in life when they learn respect and responsibility.

Paul sets a lofty goal for the Christian family when he entwines its relationship with Christ and the Church. It's a touch of heaven on earth when it happens.

STRAIGHT

1. Our Devotional Reading indicates that there were contentions in the Corinthian church. What three things did Paul ask of them?
He asked that they all speak the same thing, that there be no divisions among them, and that they be perfectly joined together in the same mind and judgment.

2. Why was Paul glad that he had personally baptized no more of them than he had?
He did not want them saying they had been baptized in his name (and saying "I am of Paul").

3. Paul encouraged the Ephesians to be imitators of God. If we do this, what kind of life will we live?
We will live lives of love, just as Christ loved us and gave Himself up for us.

4. Paul gave instructions for Christians not to get drunk with wine (that leads to excess), but instead to be filled with what?
They should be filled with the Spirit.

5. What two things does he immediately say will result from being filled with the Spirit?
They will be singing and giving thanks.

6. It seems as if Paul is continuing a list of things that result from being filled with the Spirit. What does he say about Christian relationships?
He says we should submit ourselves one to another in the fear of God.

7. Why does Paul say wives should submit to their husbands?
Because the husband is the head of the wife, as Christ is head of the Church, and is the savior of the body.

8. In what way does the husband's love for his wife add tremendous responsibility for him?
He is to love his wife as Christ loved the Church and sacrificed Himself for it.

9. A husband should love his wife as much as he loves what other person?
He should love her as much as he loves himself.

10. What is the first commandment with promise?
To honor father and mother is the first commandment with promise (Exod. 20:12).

Stable homes are a scarce commodity in today's world. Unfortunately, "dysfunctional" is a word that gets used too often in describing families. It doesn't have to be that way.

A home will not rise above the people who comprise it. People make up a family, so it is what they are. And Paul tells us what they should be. It's interesting that the Spirit could use a bachelor such as Paul to teach so much about families. Ephesians is a virtual outline for successful living and great families.

In this letter Paul gives us a solid doctrinal footing. He teaches us about God's Church, and about Christ, its savior. He instructs us about sexual morality and other appropriate conduct. The parenting he describes will pass these values on to the children, as they are brought up in the training and instruction of the Lord.

All Christians, including married couples, will have a Christ-like servant spirit, and will be subject one to the other. The husband will love his wife so dearly that he will sacrifice anything for her benefit, even his life. The wife will have no qualms about the husband being the head. They will, in words that go back to the beginning, be joined to each other and be one flesh. Paul says this is a great mystery, and he speaks concerning Christ and the Church.

Paul gives us a look into the organization and functioning of a stable Christian family. How many families are you aware of that fit this description?

Equipped for New Life

Eph. 6:10-20

Finally, my brethren, be strong in the Lord, and in the power of his might.

11 Put on the whole armour of God, that ye may be able to stand against the wiles of the devil.

12 For we wrestle not against flesh and blood, but against principalities, against powers, against the rulers of the darkness of this world, against spiritual wickedness in high places.

13 Wherefore take unto you the whole armour of God, that ye may be able to withstand in the evil day, and having done all, to stand.

14 Stand therefore, having your loins girt about with truth, and having on the breastplate of righteousness;

15 And your feet shod with the preparation of the gospel of peace;

16 Above all, taking the shield of faith, wherewith ye shall be able to quench all the fiery darts of the wicked.

17 And take the helmet of salvation, and the sword of the Spirit, which is the word of God:

18 Praying always with all prayer and supplication in the Spirit, and watching thereunto with all perseverance and supplication for all saints;

19 And for me, that utterance may be given unto me, that I may open my mouth boldly, to make known the mystery of the gospel,

20 For which I am an ambassador in bonds: that therein I may speak boldly, as I ought to speak.

Memory Selection
Eph. 6:13

Background Scripture
Eph. 6:10-20

Devotional Reading
Luke 11:14-23

In this lesson, Paul nears the end of his letter to the Ephesians with a virtual sermon encouraging his readers/hearers to be faithful. Even today it is not uncommon for sermons to be built around analogies or metaphors such as those selected by Paul. He envisions the Christian walk as a battle, and the

equipment we need as figurative pieces of armor.

The battle, of course, is spiritual. We do not fight "against flesh and blood, but against principalities, against powers, against the rulers of the darkness of this world, against spiritual wickedness in high places." Paul himself, probably writing from a Roman prison, is facing some of these powers as he writes. We could not be urged to faithfulness by a more genuine and authentic warrior.

ଞୀଔ

For a Lively Start

You can introduce this lesson with a "pre-test," explaining that Paul will list several pieces of ancient *armor* and asking how many pieces group members can name. Make this a light exercise, being sure not to be critical of fading memories! Most of your group will be somewhat acquainted with

those Paul names.

Predictably, the *helmet* will be mentioned, since that is still a part of a suit of armor in modern warfare. The *sword* will likely rank high, too. The other pieces Paul uses in his "sermonette" are the *girdle* or *belt*, the *breastplate*, *footwear* (sandals) and the *shield*.

Some may mention *prayer* also, which certainly should be accepted although Paul may discuss it apart from his own list.

Teaching Outline	Daily Bible Readings

I. The Battle Before Us—6:10-13
  A. Stand strong!, 10-11
  B. A spiritual war, 12
II. The Armor We Possess—13-17
  A. Stand girdled, 13-14
  B. Footwear, 15
  C. Shield of faith, 16
  D. Helmet and sword, 17
III. Persevering Prayer—18-20
  A. In general, 18
  B. For Paul's boldness, 19-20
	Mon. Truth
	      Ps. 25:1-5
	Tue. Righteousness
	      Prov. 11:1-10
	Wed. Good News of Peace
	      Isa. 52:7-12
	Thu. Faith
	      Heb. 10:35–11:3
	Fri. Salvation
	      Isa. 12:1-6
	Sat. The Word of God
	      Ps. 119:105-112
	Sun. The Whole Armor of God
	      Eph. 6:10-18

Verse by Verse

I. The Battle Before Us—6:10-13
A. Stand strong!, 10-11

10 Finally, my brethren, be strong in the Lord, and in the power of his might.

11 Put on the whole armour of God, that ye may be able to stand against the wiles of the devil.

This entire section of metaphors for spiritual armor reflects Paul's training as a rabbi and a wordsmith. He calls the entire set of equipment we need "the whole armor of God," twice (here and in vs. 13). The original word gives us our term "panoply," meaning a full set of armor, or a sturdy tent used for a war room on an ancient battlefield. It appears in the old hymn, "Soldiers of Christ Arise":

But take to arm you for the fight,
The panoply of God.

This introduction to what might be called a "sermonette" is pure poetry, especially in the KJV, both in its rhythm and word choice. For example, Paul chooses three words meaning power,

packing the sentence with dynamite (the root of which appears in the phrase "be strong"), and making the whole sentence a stirring call to arms.

B. A spiritual war, 12

12 For we wrestle not against flesh and blood, but against principalities, against powers, against the rulers of the darkness of this world, against spiritual wickedness in high places.

Unfortunately, the forces of Christ have too often taken Paul literally and armed themselves not for spiritual warfare but for bloody battle. Paul, however, could not make it clearer that he is not calling us to a *jihad—a* "flesh and blood" war. Instead, he names our enemies with four terms. *Principalities,* is from a word that describes high-placed officials. In the spirit world these include Satan and his angels. Second, we fight against *powers,* from a word often translated "authorities," as in our only half-joking line "You can't fight City Hall."

Third, we fight *the rulers of the darkness of this world,* obviously referring again to Satan and his lieutenants, which can take many forms. And fourth, we fight *spiritual wickedness in high places.* Satan's home is referred to here as "beyond the heavens," although it can also be described as below the earth. Either place is meant to infer a spirit-place beyond—above or below—all goodness.

II. The Armor We Possess—13-17
A. Stand girdled, 13-14

13 Wherefore take unto you the whole armour of God, that ye may be able to withstand in the evil day, and having done all, to stand.

14 Stand therefore, having your loins girt about with truth, and having on the breastplate of righteousness;

What defense do Christians have against such spiritual evils? We have, again, the "panoply" or whole armor of God, some of which Paul draws from Isaiah 59:17. He urges us not to put it aside but to wear it constantly because "the evil day" that calls us to battle may occur at any time.

The first piece of the armor Paul mentions is the broad leather girdle or belt that pulled the rest of a suit of armor together and gave strength to the mid-section. It was fitted with loops or hooks for hanging clubs or swords, and was therefore a very basic piece of equipment. It is the "girdle of truth," signaling that we will not stoop to the lying strategies of the enemy.

Next there is the *breastplate of righteousness.* The word for righteousness often refers to the right-ness that is imputed to us as we are justified by the grace of God, not our own right-ness. Here, however, used so close to the "girdle of truth," it probably refers to the righteous *character* which God seeks in all His soldiers, so we can never rightly be charged with any of the subterfuges of the enemies of righteousness. The word for "breastplate," which fit on the chest of the soldier, gives us our word "thorax."

B. Footwear, 15

15 And your feet shod with the preparation of the gospel of peace;

Third, Paul recalls the physical demands placed on a soldier—the need to be prepared to move quickly, sometimes while carrying a heavy pack. Being prepared to make such moves will enable us to "fight" with *peace,* one of the ironies of spiritual warfare. Perhaps Paul, writing from prison, is reminded of the hobnail sandals of the Roman soldiers guarding him.

C. Shield of faith, 16

16 Above all, taking the shield of faith, wherewith ye shall be able to quench all the fiery darts of the wicked.

Most of the elements of spiritual armor are defensive, and no defensive piece of armor was more important than the *shield.* How often have we experienced the need for the *shield of faith,* when the enemy is using psychological warfare to frighten or depress us? As the well-known list of battleworn heroes in Hebrews 11 reminds us, no piece of armor is more important than faith. Roman shields were often made of wood covered with leather, which could extinguish literal "fiery darts" or arrows. Some shields were notched to fit into a recess carved in the shield of the soldier next to it. This made the two fit each other, posing an almost impenetrable "phalanx" or wall of soldiers outfitted with a wall of shields.

D. Helmet and sword, 17

17 And take the helmet of salvation, and the sword of the Spirit, which is the word of God:

Mentioning the sword, an offensive weapon, in the same breath as the defensive helmet, shows that our warfare must sometimes be taken to the enemy. Paul himself was doing that in prison, sharing the word of God with his captors, fellow-prisoners, judges, and anyone else who would listen. The regular soldier's helmet was usually made of thick, heavy leather, while officers would more commonly wear helmets of metal. Spiritually, our hope of salvation provides the morale needed for battle (1 Thess. 5:8).

III. Persevering Prayer—18-20
A. In General, 18

18 Praying always with all prayer and supplication in the Spirit, and watching thereunto with all perseverance and supplication for all saints;

Although prayer is rightfully a part of the Christian's armor, it seems to be separated here from Paul's more militant pieces of figurative armor. Yet what spiritual soldier can do without both the offensive and defensive power of prayer? The fact that it is "supplication in the Spirit" reminds us that we are in a spiritual battle, not what many of our Christian forebears called "carnal warfare." The prayer Paul urges us to make here is general in nature, praying for "all saints" or all Christians. Unless the angels in heaven tell us, we will never know the power prayer has in spiritual warfare.

Encouraging examples of the effectiveness of prayer have emerged in recent years in the arena of praying for the sick. A century ago, "faith healing" was looked down on and generally left to extremists and raucus and rowdy services with the atmosphere of a traveling circus. Now, with scientific studies providing proof of the effectiveness of some kinds of prayer, it is often a part of more mainstream church services.

B. For Paul's boldness, 19-20

19 And for me, that utterance may be given unto me, that I may open my mouth boldly, to make known the mystery of the gospel,

20 For which I am an ambassador in bonds: that therein I may speak boldly, as I ought to speak.

Paul is in a precarious position, at the mercy of his guards. Yet he is bold enough to ask the Ephesians to pray for *more* boldness, that he may be an "ambassador" for Christ, speaking as he "ought to speak" despite the risk of reprisal. This is no arm-chair general urging the troops far to the front lines to pray, but an officer boldly serving and praying himself at his post, despite his bonds.

Evangelistic Emphasis

You will notice an abrupt change between our previous lesson and this one. Paul now emphasizes the necessity for battle preparation.

In our earlier studies he told us about the wonderful and sometimes mysterious working of God, and we have just finished studying his description of the ideal Christian family. Suddenly, though, he now says it's time for "On-ward Christian soldiers."

Though Christ brought us peace through the Cross, to enjoy it we must fight constantly with His (and our) adversary, the devil. Satan is a dirty fighter. He does not recognize any civilized rules of warfare. We'd hardly expect him to be anything less than scheming and treacherous.

Paul prepares us for both defensive and offensive battle. If there's any truth to the saying that the best defense is a good offense, this is the time for it. The word of God is the Spirit's sword (6:17). Let's polish up our swords and go to war!

Memory Selection

Wherefore take unto you the whole armour of God, that ye may be able to withstand in the evil day, and having done all, to stand.—*Ephesians 6:13*

Paul is preparing us for Christian warfare so we can stand our ground in the evil day. The evil day is now. It's here. In 5:16 Paul has already admonished us to take advantage of every opportunity because the days are evil. It doesn't require a close observer to be aware of the evil that surrounds us constantly.

There's truth in the expression that to be forewarned is to be forearmed. Paul is warning us, and instructing us to get armed for battle.

We're in a fight to the finish. There can be no backing down. Notice that four times (including verses 11 and 14) Paul mentions *standing*. He says we "stand against the wiles of the devil," we "withstand in the evil day," and having done all, "to stand." He says "stand therefore" with our armor in place.

At the risk of redundancy, let's summarize. Get prepared. Take a stand. There's an evil world out there.

Weekday Problems

Earlier this week a young man showed me a medallion he kept on his keychain. It had been given to him by his drug addiction support group. He's had 18 months of sobriety. Without the encouragement and support of this group it's not likely he could have done so well.

The devil will be persistent in his efforts to defeat us. We're going to need all the help we can find to make sure he's not successful. We're told to submit ourselves to God, to resist the devil and he will flee from us (James 4:7). We pray for the Lord's help in resisting temptations. We want to be alert and receptive to whatever methods He uses as He responds to our request.

It may be that God has blessed you with a Christian family to help strengthen your resolve. We find encouragement through church participation. In extreme situations such as addictions we may need support groups or professional help. Paul reminds us to "be strong in the Lord, and in the power of his might" (6:10).

Soldiering On

A letter sent home by a private at the front lines read, "I sure like this army life. It's nice to lie in bed every morning until 5:30."

Of course he was a milkman when he was a civilian.

* * *

Said the speaker at a marriage conference: "Marry an army man, girls. He can cook, make beds, sew, is in perfect health, and is already used to taking orders."

* * *

An icy voice cut into the sergeant's telephone conversation that was getting out of hand at an army post. "Do you know whom you are addressing?" a stern voice broke in.

"No," said the sergeant."

"Well, this is Col. Humdinger."

"Colonel," said the sergeant. "Do you know whom *you* are addressing?"

"*No!*" thundered the colonel.

"Thank God!" said the sergeant, and quickly hung up.

This Lesson In Your Life

There's one point about which we need to be perfectly clear. We're all sinners (1 Jn. 1:8). The devil is too often successful at his evil work. On the battlefield of life he wins some skirmishes. We don't want him to win the war.

Paul wants to make sure that the victory will be ours. He uses the imagery of a Roman soldier's equipment, and with this metaphor he outfits us for battle. We're actually more interested in what the armor represents than in the armor itself. Let's take a look.

We'll go on the battlefield with truth, righteousness, the gospel of peace, faith, salvation, and the word of God (the sword of the Spirit) in our arsenal. In another passage Paul adds love to the armament (1 Thess. 5:8).

As we consider what kind of battle we'll be fighting, we'll see that Paul has outfitted us correctly. He tells us (vs. 12) that it's not flesh and blood we're struggling with, but we'll be going "against principalities, against powers, against the rulers of the darkness of the world, against spiritual wickedness in high places."

We're fighting against a spiritual enemy. That's why we need spiritual resources. The real battle is not against the physical manifestations of evil (bad people, bad things), but against the powers that cause evil. Whatever the spiritual forces are that exist, whatever outreach Satan has, whatever his control over the dark world that carries out his bidding, this is our enemy.

The horrible events of 9/11 were evil. At the memorial service conducted in Washington's National Cathedral following that sad day, Billy Graham said that evil had always been a mystery to him. We can see the results of evil, but how are we to comprehend the dark power that fuels it? We don't have to understand all there is to know about "spiritual wickedness in high places." Paul has, however, told us how to deal with it.

In addition to wearing the armor, Paul says we should keep praying and keep watching (v.18). The need for prayer and alertness, and the value of using the equipment God has given us, is a lesson Paul wants us to remember.

1. Luke 11 records a time when Jesus cast out a devil from someone. Through what power was he accused of doing this?

They said he did it through Beelzebub, the chief of the devils.

2. If the chief of devils cast out a devil, that means his house is divided. What did Jesus say about this?

He said a divided kingdom is brought to desolation, and a divided house falls.

3. Jesus said that if He cast out devils by the finger of God, what did that indicate for the people who accused him?

It meant that the Kingdom of God had come upon them.

4. In Ephesians, what would allow believers to stand against the wiles of the devil?

Putting on the full armor of God.

5. In our struggle against evil, what does Paul tell us we're not wrestling against?

We do not wrestle against flesh and blood.

6. What are the four influences Paul says we do oppose?

We fight against principalities, powers, the rulers of the darkness of this world, and against spiritual wickedness in high places.

7. If we have the whole armor of God we will be able to stand in the evil day. When is the evil day? (See 5:16)

In that verse he says "the days *are* evil." That means they are *now.*

8. Name the qualities that Christians need as represented by the Roman soldier's armor.

The Christian will need the weapons of truth, righteousness, the gospel of peace, faith, salvation, and the sword of the Spirit (the Word of God).

9. Paul adds two things that should be done along with wearing the armor. What are they?

We should continue praying and being watchful.

10. These are unusual preparations for a battle. Why does Paul list these spiritual qualities?

Because it is a spiritual battle.

One of the first rules of warfare is that you don't go into battle unless you're prepared to win. Jesus told a short parable about a king who figured the odds of winning with 10,000 troops before he went out to battle against 20,000 men (Luke. 14:31-32).

We Christians are in a winnable war against the devil. The Cross and the Resurrection assure us of ultimate victory. We're assured that those who believe that Jesus Christ is the Son of God will overcome the world (1 Jn. 5:4-5). Paul said "I can do all things through Christ which strengtheneth me" (Phil. 4:13).

True, it's a disturbing thing to read about the spiritual power of the devil. Romans 8:37-39, though, gives assurance that this will never separate us from the love of God. Against all obstacles we are more than conquerors.

Words from Martin Luther's great hymn, "A Mighty Fortres," echo our confidence:

> Did we in our own strength confide
> Our striving would be losing;
> Were not the right One on our side
> The Man of God's own choosing.
> Dost ask who that may be?
> Christ Jesus, it is He;
> Lord Sabaoth is His name,
> From age to age the same,
> And He must win the battle.

Unit I: Called Out of Egypt

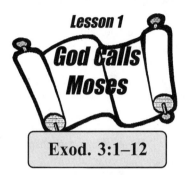

Lesson 1

God Calls Moses

Exod. 3:1–12

Now Moses kept the flock of Jethro his father in law, the priest of Midian: and he led the flock to the backside of the desert, and came to the mountain of God, even to Horeb.

2 And the angel of the LORD appeared unto him in a flame of fire out of the midst of a bush: and he looked, and, behold, the bush burned with fire, and the bush was not consumed.

3 And Moses said, I will now turn aside, and see this great sight, why the bush is not burnt.

4 And when the LORD saw that he turned aside to see, God called unto him out of the midst of the bush, and said, Moses, Moses. And he said, Here am I.

5 And he said, Draw not nigh hither: put off thy shoes from off thy feet, for the place whereon thou standest is holy ground.

6 Moreover he said, I am the God of thy father, the God of Abraham, the God of Isaac, and the God of Jacob. And Moses hid his face; for he was afraid to look upon God.

7 And the LORD said, I have surely seen the affliction of my people which are in Egypt, and have heard their cry by reason of their taskmasters; for I know their sorrows;

8 And I am come down to deliver them out of the hand of the Egyptians, and to bring them up out of that land unto a good land and a large, unto a land flowing with milk and honey; unto the place of the Canaanites, and the Hittites, and the Amorites, and the Perizzites, and the Hivites, and the Jebusites.

9 Now therefore, behold, the cry of the children of Israel is come unto me: and I have also seen the oppression wherewith the Egyptians oppress them.

10 Come now therefore, and I will send thee unto Pharaoh, that thou mayest bring forth my people the children of Israel out of Egypt.

11 And Moses said unto God, Who am I, that I should go unto Pharaoh, and that I should bring forth the children of Israel out of Egypt?

12 And he said, Certainly I will be with thee; and this shall be a token unto thee, that I have sent thee: When thou hast brought forth the people out of Egypt, ye shall serve God upon this mountain.

Memory Selection
Exod. 3:10

Background Scripture
Exod. 2:23–3:12

Devotional Reading
Heb. 3:1-13

Much of the Bible was produced under the pressure of *enslavement*—of the Egyptians over the Hebrews, of pagans of every stripe, of false religions, and ultimately of *sin*. The Scriptures are therefore a *liberation manual*.

Previous quarters have shown how God formed a *"Community of Free-*

dom," the Church; then how *"Human Commitment"* is the necessary response to God's grace; and the *"New Creation in Christ."* This last quarter comes full circle with *"Call Sealed with a Promise,"* the story of Moses and the Jews' call to freedom.

So the Bible is about *liberty,* about singing "Let My People Go," about God's grace in defeating the slave-master called sin. This first lesson of the last quarter is about an important chapter in this crucial and colorful story.

ℬↄⵙↄ

For a Lively Start

Ask group members to recall some of their most vivid memories about Moses. Of course the earliest memory will have to do with his having been hidden in the rushes on the banks of the Nile River and found by Pharaoh's daughter. They may also remember

how he killed an Egyptian who had killed a fellow-Hebrew, how he fled to the desert for 40 years, then returned (with a good deal of persuasion) to lead his people through the Red (or "Reed" Sea), and to freedom.

Note that this is the first of four lessons on the adventure of Moses and the Jewish people. They discover both the exhilaration of freedom and the consequences of not paying the price.

Teaching Outline	Daily Bible Readings	
I. Moses in Midian—3:1	Mon.	Moses' Birth *Exod. 2:1-10*
II. God in a Bush—2-6	Tue.	Moses Flees *Exod. 2:11-22*
A. Moses' call, 2-4	Wed.	Purpose Misunderstood *Acts 7:23-29*
B. The Awesome God, 5-6	Thu.	Moses' Call *Acts 7:30-34*
III. Rescue in Mind—7-12	Fri.	Moses' Death Foretold *Deut. 32:48-52*
A. Response to a problem, 7		
B. Plan for a land, 8-10	Sat.	Moses' Uniqueness *Deut. 34*
C. Promise over protest, 11-12	Sun.	'Come, I Will Send You' *Exod. 3:1-12*

Verse by Verse

I. Moses in Midian—3:1

1 Now Moses kept the flock of Jethro his father in law, the priest of Midian: and he led the flock to the backside of the desert, and came to the mountain of God, even to Horeb.

The Israelites had been led into Egypt by Joseph, one of the partriarch Jacob's sons, who enjoyed Pharaoh's favor. However, "there arose up a new king over Egypt who knew not Joseph" (Exod. 1:8), and as our story opens here the descendants of Jacob have been held in cruel Egyptian captivity for more than 400 years (Exod. 12:40). Now God begins to enact a plan to deliver them through His chosen leader, Moses. After being born a Hebrew but raised in Pharaoh's court, Moses struck a cruel Egyptian taskmaster and had to flee for his life (Exod. 2:11-15).

The land of Midian, where Moses found refuge, was probably in the arid region across the Red Sea and toward the southern tip of the Sinai peninsula (see a Bible map). If the land was named for Midian, fourth son of Abraham (Gen. 25:1-2), Moses was seeking asylum among distant relatives. Yet, when Israel became a threat to their territory, the Midianites became entrenched enemies (see Num. 31).

In Midian Moses married the daughter of a priest who is at first called Reuel (Exod. 2:18-21), and becomes a shepherd. Here Moses' father-in-law is called Jethro, which was possibly Reuel's second name. Although not an Israelite in the sense of a descendant of Jacob, it is possible that Jethro was a priest of the true God, like Melchizedek, who, long ago, had blessed Father Abraham (Gen. 14:18-24), showing that the true God had not left Himself without witness even in pagan lands before the Hebrews were welded into a nation.

Horeb is called "the mountain of God" because it becaue identified with Mt. Sinai, where Moses would later receive the Law after leading Israel out of Egypt (Deut. 4:15). It is possible that Sinai was the name of a mountain range, while Horeb was a specific peak in the area.

II. God in a Bush—2-6
A. Moses' call, 2-4

2 And the angel of the LORD appeared unto him in a flame of fire out of the midst of a bush: and he looked, and, behold, the bush burned with fire, and the bush was not consumed.

3 And Moses said, I will now turn aside, and see this great sight, why the bush is not burnt.

4 And when the LORD saw that he turned aside to see, God called unto him out of the midst of the bush, and said, Moses, Moses. And he said, Here am I.

Some scholars suggest that Moses saw a brightly-colored thornbush or some other strikingly-hued plant, rather than a bush that was actually afire. Verse 2, however, says clearly that "the bush burned with fire." The main point is that it was necessary for God to use a sensational sign to arrest Moses' attention. Moses was still in a "flight mode," had no plans to return to Egypt, and was not in a frame of mind to hear what any bush had to "say." Furthermore, he was heir to the patriarchs' belief that God was invisible. God chose to speak to Moses from a material bush to convince him that he was not just listening to his own inner voice.

Moses' response, "Here am I," will be echoed by the young Samuel (1 Sam. 3:4), and the prophet Isaiah (Isa. 6:8), when God calls them. Yet, while the answer indicates a willingness to listen, Moses will soon raise some defenses against the call.

B. The awesome God, 5-6

5 And he said, Draw not nigh hither: put off thy shoes from off thy feet, for the place whereon thou standest is holy ground.

6 Moreover he said, I am the God of thy father, the God of Abraham, the God of Isaac, and the God of Jacob. And Moses hid his face; for he was afraid to look upon God.

The place becomes sacred not because of some mysteriously holy chemical make-up in the soil or shrubbery, but because God chose to make Himself known to Moses there. Taking off one's footwear to show reverence is still practiced in some religions. Since slaves went without shoes in many cultures (Luke 15:22), the gesture implied the recognition of the unworthy status of a mere human before God, and the willingness to serve him.

This attitude of humility is also seen in Moses' unwillingness to show his face after God identifies Himself as the God of Moses' forebears, the patriarchs. "Thy father" probably refers to Father Abraham, father of Isaac and grandfather of Jacob. Moses was a descendant of Jacob's son Levi.

III. Rescue in Mind—7-12
A. Response to a problem, 7

7 And the LORD said, I have surely seen the affliction of my people which are in Egypt, and have heard their cry by reason of their taskmasters; for I know their sorrows;

For God to say that He has heard the cry of His enslaved people at the time of Moses does not imply that He could not hear it all along, but that delivering them now fits His timetable. The Jews have grown numerous to form their own nation, and their taskmasters have grown too harsh (vs. 9). It is time to begin the next chapter in the unfolding story of the history of salvation.

B. Plan for a land, 8-10

8 And I am come down to deliver them out of the hand of the Egyptians, and to bring them up out of that land unto a good land and a large, unto a land flowing with milk and honey; unto the place of the Canaanites, and the Hittites, and the Amorites, and the Perizzites, and the Hivites, and the Jebusites.

9 Now therefore, behold, the cry of the children of Israel is come unto me: and I have also seen the oppression wherewith the Egyptians oppress them.

10 Come now therefore, and I will send thee unto Pharaoh, that thou mayest bring forth my people the children of Israel out of Egypt.

A part of God's ancient covenant with Abraham, Moses' ancestor, was that his descendants would receive the very land described here (Gen. 13:14-15). Modern travelers to Israel and its surrounding territory know that much of it is desert land, and might not describe it is being filled with milk and honey. Yet the Jordan Valley was a paradise compared to the barren reaches of Midian. At any rate, the land's primary richness was the spiritual fertility with which God invested it as he enabled the chosen race to carve out a place for themselves.

Some of the tribes mentioned here cannot now be identified. The term "Perrizite" may have meant "villager," indicating that the list does not describe distinct racial groups but social differences such as nomads and city-dwellers.

Some have questioned the justice of God's allowing the Hebrews to wrest the land from its previous inhabitants. It can be noted that (1) these tribes forcibly took the land from previous inhabitants; (2) their own level of internal justice and morality was depraved, earning their expulsion; and (3) God's plan included the higher justice of separating a people for His own possession, through whom the Messiah, who would bring justice to all the earth, would one day come.

Verse 10 lays the groundwork for one of the major "hinges of history." God's plan to send Moses to demand that the Egyptian pharaoh release the Hebrews marks a watershed change in history more dramatic than the fall of the Berlin Wall and the collapse of Soviet communism in our own day.

C. Promise over protest, 11-12

11 And Moses said unto God, Who am I, that I should go unto Pharaoh, and that I should bring forth the children of Israel out of Egypt?

12 And he said, Certainly I will be with thee; and this shall be a token unto thee, that I have sent thee: When thou hast brought forth the people out of Egypt, ye shall serve God upon this mountain.

Like several of God's chosen servants, Moses at first cannot even envision himself as a leader (see Isa. 6:5; Judg 6:13-15). The primary evidence of his ability will be the privilege of service, which even today is often the most compelling sense that one of God's leaders is where he needs to be.

Evangelistic Emphasis

Moses fled Egypt after killing that Egyptian who was beating a Hebrew slave. He wanted to live as a stranger in the wilderness of Midian. But he did not remain a stranger for long. Through his kindness to the daughters of Jethro, he was welcomed into the family. He married, fathered a son, and settled down to life as a shepherd. No doubt Moses was thankful that he could now live in comfort and in peace. Isn't that what we all desire? All seemed to be quiet until God showed up in that bush, and laid a burden on his heart.

Few of us have stories as dramatic Moses', but all of us can tell of the highs and lows in our lives. We can all relate to the longing for a life that is comfortable and peaceful. The problem is that we serve a God who has things to do. While He is loving and gracious to help us in our struggles, He is also known to find us in our comfort and lay a burden on our hearts. Chances are we will never see a bush that is burning but not consumed by the fire. We might never have a lengthy a conversation with the Angel of the Lord. But we can be certain that God will take the initiative and lay a burden before us. We will come to know a person who does not know God. We will find a co-worker who is being treated unjustly. We will be asked to teach a children's class or help with an after-school outreach. And we will have the opportunity to seek our own comfort rather than respond to the call of God. Even after knowing the story of Moses, we may choose to turn aside from the call of God, but we will never be able to claim that we did not hear His voice.

ଈଠ

Memory Selection

Come now therefore, and I will send thee unto Pharaoh, that thou mayest bring forth my people the children of Israel out of Egypt.—*Exodus 3:10*

Some of our favorite scriptures contain God's invitation for us, "Come." What a joy it is to know that God does not hide Himself from us or keep us at a distance. He bids us to "Come." In our memory passage, God invites Moses to come to Him. He also says, "I will send you." This is the natural rhythm of God. He calls us to Himself to bless us and strengthen us, and then He sends us out to take His blessings to others.

As a child who has scraped a knee runs to the arms of the parent to be comforted, we—when thirsty or weary—respond to the call of our Father to come to Him. But the child does not remain in the parent's arms. The child is enabled to rejoin life with renewed confidence and purpose.

May we always have our ears tuned to hear God calling to us, "Come." May we respond to this call with relief and joy. But we must keep listening—for He will soon say, "And now I send you."

Weekday Prob ems

I knew Jim's story and had always considered him a great example of what hard work and the opportunities offered in America could produce. Jim had been born into inner-city poverty—one of six children reared by a single mother. Though his brothers and sisters had succumbed to the pressures and temptations of early retirement, Jim was different. After graduation from university, he was hired by a large company, and, through his work ethic and his God-given abilities, he rose to the position of vice-president. Financially successful beyond any of his dreams, Jim himself attained the ultimate American dream of early retirement.

At his retirement celebration I asked him what his plans were. He smiled and said, "I think my wife and I will be moving on." He went on to tell me that some of the people in the church back in his old neighborhood had contacted him and asked if he might move back to help them. "You know," he said, "there's a lot of kids just like me down there." I knew the neighborhood and tried to imagine Jim living there again. "So," I said hesitantly, "you want to take God back to your old home." Jim sighed, "No, God is already there. He's the one who's calling me to come."

*What would be your dream retirement?

*Do you think there could be any connection between the blessings Jim had received and his willingness to be used by God to serve others?

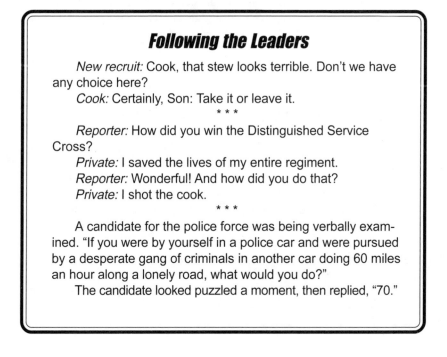

Following the Leaders

New recruit: Cook, that stew looks terrible. Don't we have any choice here?
Cook: Certainly, Son: Take it or leave it.

* * *

Reporter: How did you win the Distinguished Service Cross?
Private: I saved the lives of my entire regiment.
Reporter: Wonderful! And how did you do that?
Private: I shot the cook.

* * *

A candidate for the police force was being verbally examined. "If you were by yourself in a police car and were pursued by a desperate gang of criminals in another car doing 60 miles an hour along a lonely road, what would you do?"
The candidate looked puzzled a moment, then replied, "70."

This Lesson in Your Life

Few, if any of us, have pastured a flock of sheep in the wilderness. None of us has ever encountered God in a burning bush and been told to go to Egypt to lead his people out of captivity and into the Promised Land. Yet many of us can identify with receiving a call from God, as Moses did. His voice might not have been audible, but we heard the call in our heart. The call may have come embodied in a struggling friend or neighbor. We may have heard it in the grief of a co-worker. God can speak to us through an evening news program showing a tragic need in our city or on the other side of our world. It is at that point—when we realize that God is calling us—that we share the same feeling all of God's servants have experienced when God spoke: *inadequacy*. The questions immediately come to our minds. "What can I possibly do?" "Who am I to address this need?"

Do these questions sound familiar? They are the same questions Moses asked as he stood before God. "Who am I, that I should go unto Pharaoh?" (Exodus 3:11). Gideon asked the same question when the angel of the Lord called him: "How can I deliver Israel?" (Judges 6:15). Isaiah shared the same thought when he saw a vision of God in the temple: "Woe is me! I am lost, for I am a man of unclean lips . . ." (Isaiah 6:5). And we remember Jeremiah's objection to God's call: "I am only a boy" (Jeremiah 1:6). In fact, most stories we read in Scripture about people receiving a call from God express doubt they are capable of doing the task God has assigned. Could the message be that a sense of unworthiness and inadequacy is pre-requisite to being called by God?

Perhaps God only calls those who realize their own weaknesses. Paul realized this when he struggled with his own inadequacies. He prayed to be made strong, but God's reply was "My grace is sufficient for thee: for my strength is made perfect in weakness." (2 Cor. 12:9). Realizing that God would work through him, he wrote, "whenever I am weak, then I am strong." (vs. 10). An awareness of our own weakness is akin to our awareness of sin in our lives. To own our sin opens our hearts to the grace and mercy of God. To be aware of our inadequacies and weaknesses opens our hearts to His strength and power of God. As the old hymn says, "I am weak but Thou art strong."

In the story of Moses—as well as the stories of Gideon, Isaiah, Jeremiah, and Paul—we learn that doubting our own abilities is no reason to ignore the call of God in our lives. Those doubts are actually our qualifications for the job. The next time God calls, let your doubts arise in your heart and consider them confirmation of your calling. The next time God calls, keep listening. You will soon hear the words that Moses heard as well: "Certainly I will be with you" (Exod. 3:12).

1. What was Moses' occupation after he fled from Egypt to Midian?

Moses kept the flock of his father in law Jethro who was the priest of Midian (Exod 3:1).

2. What other name is given to Mount Horeb?

Horeb is described as the mountain of God (3:1). This mountain is also known as Mount Sinai.

3. What attracted Moses' attention to Mount Horeb?

He saw a bush on the mountain that was burning but was not being consumed by the fire (3:2).

4. Who spoke to Moses from the midst of the bush?

Scripture describes the one speaking as "the angel of the LORD" in Verse 2 and as "the LORD" and "God" in verse 4.

5. What was Moses told to do to show reverence in the presence of God?

Moses was told not to come near the bush and to take off his shoes because he was standing on holy ground (3:5).

6. How did God identify himself to Moses?

God said that he is the God of Moses' father, the God of Abraham, the God of Isaac, and the God of Jacob (3:6).

7. What task did God call Moses to perform?

God called Moses to deliver His people from the hand of the Egyptians and to bring them to the land He had promised them (3:7,8).

8. What had moved God to deliver His people?

God had seen the affliction of the people and had heard their cries to Him. He knew their sorrow (3:7).

9. What was Moses' first objection to the call of God?

Moses questioned his ability and qualifications for the task. He asked, "Who am I that I should go unto Pharaoh?" (3:11).

10. What was God's reassurance to Moses when he doubted he could do the task?

God promised to be with Moses and to bring him and the people to this very mountain (Horeb) to worship God (3:12).

Moses experienced what many of us long for—a face to face meeting with God. If we were so favored, we would discover what Moses—as well as other servants such as Elijah and Isaiah—found. The majesty and glory of God is too much for us as humans to bear. Moses hid his face from God. A mere mortal cannot look at God and live.

It is interesting how—in the glory of this moment—that God chose to introduce himself to Moses. God began by saying, "I am the God of your father." We do not have a lot of information about Moses' father. We know he was a descendent of Levi named Amram, son of Kohath, husband of Jocabed, father of Aaron, Moses, and Miriam, and that he participated in the exodus from Egypt. We also know, by this word from God, that he was a Godly man. What a blessing to have God identify Himself as the "God of your father."

Many of us first came to know God as the God of our parents. If we were reared in a home that honored God, the first face of God we knew was that of a Godly mother or Godly father. This is how God intended us to meet Him. Psalm 78 encourages us, "We will not hide them from their children, showing to the generation to come the praises of the LORD, and his wonderful works that he has done." Perhaps this is why God chose to describe his relationship with us as the relationship of a father and child. He has called parents to live in such a way as to introduce him to the next generation. If you first met God through a godly parent, include in your prayers your gratitude for such a gracious gift—something you did nothing to deserve—yet a gift that has opened to you eternal life with the Heavenly Father.

However, the sad truth is that not all children meet God through their parents. Some parents are abusive. Others are loving and nurturing parents but they do not know God in a way they can introduce Him to their children. If this is your experience, this verse still calls you. You can be the blessing. What greater joy would there be to think that one day in the heavenly kingdom God would meet your children and say, "I am the God of your mother," or "I am the God of your father." The circle can be even wider. Can God approach your friends and identify himself as "the God of your friend"?

Moses met God on Mount Horeb, but he already knew his voice and his face. He had seen and heard God in the face and voice of his father. May we so live that those who have encountered us will recognize God when they come face to face with him.

Lesson 2
Moses and Aaron Respond

Exod. 4:10-16, 27-31

And Moses said unto the LORD, O my Lord, I am not eloquent, neither heretofore, nor since thou hast spoken unto thy servant: but I am slow of speech, and of a slow tongue.

11 And the LORD said unto him, Who hath made man's mouth? or who maketh the dumb, or deaf, or the seeing, or the blind? have not I the LORD?

12 Now therefore go, and I will be with thy mouth, and teach thee what thou shalt say.

13 And he said, O my Lord, send, I pray thee, by the hand of him whom thou wilt send.

14 And the anger of the LORD was kindled against Moses, and he said, Is not Aaron the Levite thy brother? I know that he can speak well. And also, behold, he cometh forth to meet thee: and when he seeth thee, he will be glad in his heart.

15 And thou shalt speak unto him, and put words in his mouth: and I will be with thy mouth, and with his mouth, and will teach you what ye shall do.

16 And he shall be thy spokesman unto the people: and he shall be, even he shall be to thee instead of a mouth, and thou shalt be to him instead of God.

27 And the LORD said to Aaron, Go into the wilderness to meet Moses. And he went, and met him in the mount of God, and kissed him.

28 And Moses told Aaron all the words of the LORD who had sent him, and all the signs which he had commanded him.

29 And Moses and Aaron went and gathered together all the elders of the children of Israel:

30 And Aaron spake all the words which the LORD had spoken unto Moses, and did the signs in the sight of the people.

31 And the people believed: and when they heard that the LORD had visited the children of Israel, and that he had looked upon their affliction, then they bowed their heads and worshipped.

Memory Selection
Exod. 4:30

Background Scripture
Exod. 4:10-31

Devotional Reading
Prov. 1:20-33

FOCUS

In this lesson, God is speaking to Moses from the burning bush in the wilderness, trying to persuade him to return to Egypt and convince Pharaoh to release Israel from captivity.

Moses presents the last of four excuses for not doing as God requests; but who is more fit for the task? Although an Israelite, Moses was raised as a son of Pharaoh: he knows both sides. Yet perhaps because of the murder charge against him, or because he is "meek" in character (Num. 12:3), Moses is reluctant.

Finally God convinces Moses to take his brother Aaron with him as an aide; and wheels are set in motion that will result in the famous mass "exodus" of the Israelites out of Egyptian captivity. There are ample opportunities in the lesson to apply it to how we respond when God asks of us more than we believe we can do.

&CR

For a Lively Start

Before time for the meeting to begin, recruit four group members to participate in a brief "readers theater" that covers this lesson. You will need someone to read *Moses'* part (4:10, 13, 28); *God's* (4:11-16); *Aaron's* (recounting what the Lord said in 4:16); and a *narrator's* (4:29-31).

You may want to provide four copies of a modern-speech translation such as the Revised Standard Version or the New Living Translation for the role-players to use. Reading from such versions as these will not only introduce some variety into the readings, but in some places, such as 4:13, they will clarify some language that is difficult in the KJV.

Teaching Outline	**Daily Bible Readings**
I. 'I Am Not Eloquent'—4:10	Mon. The God Who Calls *Exod. 3:13-18a*
II. 'Who Made the Mouth?'—11-12	Tue. The God Who Equips *Exod. 4:1-9*
III. 'Take Aaron If You Must!'—13-16	Wed. The God Who Sends Back *Exod. 4:18-23*
A. 'Anyone but Me!,' 13	Thu. 'Do Not Be Afraid' *Zech. 8:11-17*
B. Aaron's potential, 14-16	Fri. 'God Will Help You' *Isa. 41:8-13*
IV. Moses Reports to Aaron—27-28	Sat. Refusing God's Call *Prov. 1:20-33*
V. The Report to the People—29-31	Sun. A Team of Two Exod. 4:10-16, 27-31

Verse by Verse

I. 'I Am Not Eloquent'—4:10

10 And Moses said unto the LORD, O my Lord, I am not eloquent, neither heretofore, nor since thou hast spoken unto thy servant: but I am slow of speech, and of a slow tongue.

Moses had begun to protest God's assignment to go back to Egypt back in 3:11, where he had seemed to lack the self-confidence to do so ("Who am I that I should go unto Pharaoh, and that I should bring forth the children of Israel out of Egypt?"). Note that God does not try to overrule Moses' objection here by saying that he is perfectly eloquent enough for the task. His fault is in not trusting God to loosen the creator of tongues, if indeed it was "slow," as the following verses will show. There is also a hint of actually rebuking God as Moses seems to say, "I wasn't eloquent before we began this conversation, and I am no better even now."

II. 'Who Made the Mouth?'—11-12

11 And the LORD said unto him, Who hath made man's mouth? or who maketh the dumb, or deaf, or the seeing, or the blind? have not I the LORD?

12 Now therefore go, and I will be with thy mouth, and teach thee what thou shalt say.

God's retort to Moses' excuse is brilliantly obvious: if Moses is being asked to use an organ (the tongue) which in fact was "invented" by Yahweh, He can surely enable Moses to use it effectively—as He could if they were discussing any other of the senses. This is the fourth and final excuse Moses has made, and God seems to be running out of patience. Although He will provide Aaron as a mouthpiece for Moses, even Aaron's speech will be what God says ("I will be thy mouth").

III. 'Take Aaron If You Must!'—13-16
A. 'Anyone but Me!,' 13

13 And he said, O my Lord, send, I pray thee, by the hand of him whom thou wilt send.

This verse is difficult in the KJV, but

exceedingly plain in other versions. The NIV says, "O Lord, please send someone else to do it," with the implication that God is perfectly capable of accomplishing His will with Pharaoh through anyone He chooses. He doesn't actually have to use Moses.

B. Aaron's potential, 14-16

14 And the anger of the LORD was kindled against Moses, and he said, Is not Aaron the Levite thy brother? I know that he can speak well. And also, behold, he cometh forth to meet thee: and when he seeth thee, he will be glad in his heart.

15 And thou shalt speak unto him, and put words in his mouth: and I will be with thy mouth, and with his mouth, and will teach you what ye shall do.

16 And he shall be thy spokesman unto the people: and he shall be, even he shall be to thee instead of a mouth, and thou shalt be to him instead of God.

Although God is angry and exasperated with Moses, He will not allow the "meekness" or hesitance of Moses to thwart His plans; so he arranges to have Moses' brother Aaron to be his spokesman as suggested earlier. To say that Aaron is coming to meet Moses implies that he is making a journey into Midian from Egypt, perhaps with the news that those who sought to punish Moses for killing the Egyptian were dead—especially the Pharaoh (see 4:19).

It seems strange, since Aaron and Moses are brothers, both sons of Levi, to call him "Aaron the Levite." Perhaps this is a title given to Aaron in Egypt,

and the author of the material picks it up. Recalling that the Levites would be the priestly tribe, it is possible that Aaron was already functioning in this arena in some way, and came by his ability to speak well because of his work.

At any rate, the scene speaks of a God of grace who is willing to compromise with Moses and allow his brother to "be to thee instead of a mouth." As it turns out, Aaron proves to be a faithful servant-brother, except for the terrible incident when he allowed the people to make the golden calf when they grew impatient while waiting for Moses (Exod. 32:19ff.).

IV. Moses Reports to Aaron—27-28

27 And the LORD said to Aaron, Go into the wilderness to meet Moses. And he went, and met him in the mount of God, and kissed him.

28 And Moses told Aaron all the words of the LORD who had sent him, and all the signs which he had commanded him.

Sure enough, just as God predicted, Aaron meets Moses at the "mount of God," or Horeb. We can well imagine how eager Moses is to tell his brother all that has happened, from the bush that burned to the rod that turned to a snake, and back to a rod again. He would especially have been glad to tell Aaron how God has appointed him to be Moses' mouthpiece. It seems that Moses is not reluctant to accept the assignment, but only the speaking role. Sure enough, in most of the appearances of the two brothers before Pharaoh in the days to come, the language indicates that Moses and Aaron work in tandem. When they confront Pharaoh, the text says "they said," or "Moses and Aaron said."

V. The Report to the People—29-31

29 And Moses and Aaron went and gathered together all the elders of the children of Israel:

30 And Aaron spake all the words which the Lord had spoken unto Moses, and did the signs in the sight of the people.

31 And the people believed: and when they heard that the Lord had visited the children of Israel, and that he had looked upon their affliction, then they bowed their heads and worshipped.

After the encounter with God in the bush, Moses wastes no time returning to Egypt and beginning the process of winning the release of the people, just as God had commanded. The brothers gather "the elders" of the people together and recount their experience with God in the wilderness. Note that although by now many other non-Egyptians have been pressed into service along with the Israelites, some form of organization headed by elders has developed, and the non-Israelites will be allowed to accompany the Israelites as they make their escape. This acceptance includes all "strangers" and "sojourners," with the exception that if they want to participate in the religion of the Israelites they must be circumcised (see 12:45-49).

Verse 30 indicates that Moses and Aaron did again "the signs" before the Israelites, apparently speaking of such incidents as the rod-snake incident, perceiving the need for some miraculous evidence that God actually spoke to Moses. By now, Moses had no doubt developed a reputation as "that man who murdered the Egyptian," and we can understand a certain reluctance on the part of the people to accept his leadership on pure hearsay. No doubt Aaron's skill at speaking contributed to their being able to convince the elders and people of the authenticity of their "call."

Despite their steadily deteriorating status in Egypt, and after giving up hope, the people can now take heart. God has not forsaken them, but has remembered their plight. The response to this grace is, appropriately, worship. Unfortunately, the worshipful attitude will become short-lived when they reach the wilderness and grow tired of quail, manna, and a shortage of water (see 16:2-3).

ဆာ၇ဢ

Evangelistic Emphasis

If there is one thing very clear in this passage, it is that Moses is unsure of his ability to perform the task to which God has called him. First he asked the question, "Who am I to do this?" Then he pleaded that he did not even know God's name. He claimed that the people of Israel would not believe him. He points out his speech impediment. Finally, he just says, "Why don't you send someone else?" Through all these objections, God continued to call Moses—patiently at first—then even in anger at his reluctance. Try as he might, Moses could not silence God.

We know that Moses eventually did answer the call of God and go to Egypt with his brother Aaron. That is when something remarkable happened. In Exodus 4:31 we read that the people did believe the words God had given Moses, and they bowed their heads and worshipped because God had looked upon their affliction. Notice that they had not yet been delivered from Israel. Their comfort came simply in Moses coming to them and speaking the word of God. Through this act, they knew that God still cared for them.

As God's servants, we must not be so focused on results that we fail to respond to His call. Maybe we will not be able to do amazing things in His name. Maybe we will appear clumsy and inept. But we can bring the presence of God in a time of need. Someone will know that God still cares. That is reason enough to put aside all our excuses.

෨ල

Memory Selection

And Aaron spoke all the words which the LORD had spoken unto Moses, and did the signs in the sight of the people.—*Exodus 4:30*

This is one of Aaron's finest moments. Here we find him speaking the words that God had given Moses and doing the signs God had promised Moses—humbly willing to be used by God in less than a starring role. Sadly, Aaron was not to remain content to be in the background. In a few short months, he would step forward into the spotlight and lead the people into sin. But for now he was a servant of God, Moses, and his people.

Most of us do not always need to be the center of attention, but our humility is often tested when others overlook our contributions—especially if they credit our success to someone else. The way of God has always been the way of the humble servant. From the Suffering Servant of Isaiah 53 to the Suffering Servant Jesus on his way to the cross, God has taught us to lay aside our pride and seek to serve Him and others. Even Jesus' own apostles struggled with this. We remember that they were caught by Jesus arguing about who was the greatest (Mark 9:33-34). Jesus responded by saying, "Whoever wants to be first must be last of all and servant of all" (Mark 9:35 NRSV).

Weekday Problems

Michael shifted uneasily in the pew as his friend James made his appeal from the pulpit once again. "We still need volunteers to go with us on our mission to Mexico this summer." Michael felt embarrassed and guilty for not signing up to help with the mission. James had listened patiently to Michael's explanations. He had lots of reasons not to go, but they were not the whole truth. The truth was that Michael was afraid to go—afraid he would not know what to say to others about God and the church—afraid of the weakness of his own faith.

That evening the Mission Team was gathering at James' house for dinner and a planning session. James had asked Michael to help him grill the hamburgers. Although Michael dreaded having to explain again to the others why he was not going, he was relieved to find some way to contribute to the effort. If there was one thing he could do, it was cook burgers. As expected, many on the team encouraged Michael to join them. "Why don't you come along with us?" "You would really be encouraged by the spirit of the Christians in Mexico." "Hey, these burgers are great. You ought to come with us and be our cook." At each invitation, Michael would smile and repeat one of his reasons for not going. By the end of the evening, he was tired—tired and angry—angry with the team for their continual asking—angry with himself for the fear in his heart.

*Have you ever passed up an opportunity for ministry because you felt inadequate?
*What would you tell Michael in this situation?

Moses in a Muddle

"Moses," God said, "maybe you could memorize a message for that man Pharaoh for me. I'm miffed that he makes my men make so many massive mortarless materials for his mansions."

"Maybe you could make someone else take this mission," Moses mumbled. "My mind doesn't mind such matters, but my mouth makes a mess of things, and in my case I know you don't want the medium to be the message."

"Most men I mention missions like this to muse that it's a monumental miracle for a message to come from a bush," God mention," mentiioned. "I have a monopoly on it, remember. And maybe it might mean a promotion for you.

"Let me meditate on it a minute," Moses said. "Man!" he finally said, mysteriously motivated. "Might Aaron help me?"

—Anonymous

This Lesson in Your Life

When God wills to do something, it will be done. This is a basic precept of our faith. Through the prophet Isaiah, God said: "So shall my word be that goeth forth out of my mouth: it shall not return unto me void, but it shall accomplish that which I please, and it shall prosper in the thing whereto I sent it (Isa. 55:11).

In these opening chapters of Exodus, we learn that God wills to deliver his people from the hand of the Egyptians. He calls Moses to be his servant in this task and patiently answers each of Moses' objections—growing angry with Moses only when he says, "You need to send someone else" (Exod. 4:13). Eventually, Moses did make the faithful decision to be God's instrument in the deliverance of His people.

Our usefulness to God depends in part on our character. Paul encouraged his young friend Timothy to turn away from wickedness so that he would be available to God. "If a man therefore purge himself from these, he shall be a vessel unto honor, sanctified, and meet for the master's use, and prepared unto every good work" (2 Tim. 2:21).

Being available to God is also a matter of humility. We can easily recognize pride when it causes us to think we are too good to perform a lowly task of ministry. But we must also realize that pride can tell us we are not good enough to do the bidding of God. Pride can be a focus on ourselves—whether we think too highly or too lowly of ourselves. Humility is focused on God and others. Humility is a matter of faith—believing that God will keep His promise to strengthen us.

How will we hear the call of God? Moses heard the voice of God from a burning bush on a wilderness mountainside. We can very well experience a burning in our heart through which God calls us to serve. Have you ever heard yourself say, "Someone needs to do something about . . . ." The one who sees the need can very well be the one whom God has prepared to meet that need.

When God's call comes in our lives, the story of Moses becomes meaningful to us. As we shake our heads over his reluctance to answer the call, we make it difficult to believe our own excuses for refusing God's bidding. As we see Moses embrace his calling, we are encouraged to step out in faith ourselves. After all, few will ever be asked to do something as frightening as challenging face to face the richest and most powerful man on earth as did Moses. Most importantly, through the story of Moses, we hear the voice of God as he speaks through His written Word the promise to all His servants: "Certainly I will be with you" (Exod. 3:12).

1. How did God answer Moses' concern about his speaking ability?

God promised, as the God who created mouths and all human senses, to be with Moses' mouth and teach him what to say (4:11-12).

2. How did God react to Moses' plea to send someone in his place?

God's anger was kindled against Moses (4:14).

3. Whom did God send to help Moses?

God sent Moses' brother Aaron (4:14).

4. How would God speak through Aaron?

God would teach Moses what to say, and Moses would tell Aaron (4:15).

5. In contrast to Moses' reaction to God's call, how did God say Aaron would respond?

God said Aaron would come to meet him and be glad in his heart (4:14).

6. Where did Aaron meet Moses and what did Aaron do when he saw his brother?

Aaron met Moses at the mount of God (Horeb) and kissed him (4:27).

7. What did Moses do when Aaron came to him?

Moses told Aaron all the Lord had said and showed Aaron the signs God had given him (4:28).

8. With whom did Moses and Aaron first meet when they went to Egypt?

They gathered the elders of Israel together, told them what the Lord had said, and performed the signs God had given them.

9. How did Israel respond to the message from Aaron and Moses?

They believed them (4:31).

10. What moved the people to bow their heads and worship?

They heard that the Lord had visited the children of Israel and looked on their affliction (4:31).

I first met Robert when I was a young ministry student. It was difficult not to notice him as his caregiver wheeled him into the church. Robert suffers with cerebral palsy. His drawn limbs and his constant movement attract your attention to him even in a crowded church. Following worship, I made an effort to meet Robert. I supposed it was the compassionate thing to do—although the thought did cross my mind that he had rather not draw a crowd of well-wishers every where he went. Robert was gracious when we met. I tried to visit with him, but his speech was difficult to understand—especially amidst the noise of the crowded room. As I left, I remembered being grateful for my health and mobility.

Several years later, I heard Robert's name again. Someone mentioned that it might be good to invite him to preach at our church. Could this be the same wheelchair-bound young man I had met before? I was assured it was. How could he possibly address a large congregation? I was assured he would be more than up to the task. Despite my skepticism, the invitation was issued and accepted.

That Sunday morning, Robert was rolled down the aisle and parked beside the front pew. Throughout the worship I noticed the congregants looking at him—most with sincere expressions of compassion and pity. I wondered if they had any idea he was to preach that morning. When it came time for the sermon, several men lifted Robert and his chair onto the dais. It struck me that even in our age of open access, we had never considered the need to provide a way for a person with a disability to ascend to the teaching platform of the church. At first, a questioning murmur ran through the crowd, but all grew quiet as Robert began to speak. Just as I remembered, his speech was difficult to understand. But I also noticed that the congregation visibly moved to the edge of their pews and leaned forward—making every effort to hear what this remarkable man was saying.

Robert preached on the joy of the Lord that morning—an interesting topic for someone with so many physical limitations. Due to the slowness of his delivery, he was able to say only a fraction of what an able-bodied preacher might have said during the same time. But his message moved through the church as a cool summer breeze—refreshing the weary and calling them to the comfort of the Lord. A dark, cynical voice whispered within me that people were listening so intently only because of Robert's disability. But I knew that was not true. They were hearing his message because of the authenticity of his heart and the obvious presence of the Lord in his life.

I had heard it said before, but now I knew it was true: God does not call perfect people to ministry. He calls us to witness to His perfect love and grace. As I greeted Robert later, I was no longer moved by pity but by awe. I had experienced what Paul wrote long ago: God chooses what is weak in the world to shame the strong (1 Cor. 1:26-29).

Lesson 3

Pharaoh Ignores God's Call

Exod. 5:1-9, 22-6:5

And afterward Moses and Aaron went in, and told Pharaoh, Thus saith the LORD God of Israel, Let my people go, that they may hold a feast unto me in the wilderness.

2 And Pharaoh said, Who is the LORD, that I should obey his voice to let Israel go? I know not the LORD, neither will I let Israel go.

3 And they said, The God of the Hebrews hath met with us: let us go, we pray thee, three days' journey into the desert, and sacrifice unto the LORD our God; lest he fall upon us with pestilence, or with the sword.

4 And the king of Egypt said unto them, Wherefore do ye, Moses and Aaron, let the people from their works? get you unto your burdens.

5 And Pharaoh said, Behold, the people of the land now are many, and ye make them rest from their burdens.

6 And Pharaoh commanded the same day the taskmasters of the people, and their officers, saying,

7 Ye shall no more give the people straw to make brick, as heretofore: let them go and gather straw for themselves.

8 And the tale of the bricks, which they did make heretofore, ye shall lay upon them; ye shall not diminish ought thereof: for they be idle; therefore they cry, saying, Let us go and sacrifice to our God.

9 Let there more work be laid upon the men, that they may labour therein; and let them not regard vain words.

22 And Moses returned unto the LORD, and said, Lord, wherefore hast thou so evil entreated this people? why is it that thou hast sent me?

23 For since I came to Pharaoh to speak in thy name, he hath done evil to this people; neither hast thou delivered thy people at all.

6:1 Then the LORD said unto Moses, Now shalt thou see what I will do to Pharaoh: for with a strong hand shall he let them go, and with a strong hand shall he drive them out of his land.

2 And God spake unto Moses, and said unto him, I am the LORD:

3 And I appeared unto Abraham, unto Isaac, and unto Jacob, by the name of God Almighty, but by my name JEHOVAH was I not known to them.

4 And I have also established my covenant with them, to give them the land of Canaan, the land of their pilgrimage, wherein they were strangers.

5 And I have also heard the groaning of the children of Israel, whom the Egyptians keep in bondage; and I have remembered my covenant.

Memory Selection
Exod. 5:1

Background Scripture
Exod. 5:1—6:5

Devotional Reading
Ps. 10:1-14

God has convinced Moses to return to Egypt and, with Aaron's help, to try to persuade Pharaoh to set the Israelites free. Although they surely must have known that the king of Egypt would have a negative response, and consider their request frivolous, they make a request that gives him complete opportunity to release them without bloodshed. Too much is at stake, however—not only Pharaoh's reputation, but his work force as well.

Instead of even considering emancipating the Hebrews, Pharaoh increases their work load. Surprisingly, Moses at first blames God for this. Equally surprisingly, God is amazingly patient, and instead of punishing Moses for unbelief only says, "Wait and see!"

ಬಿಂಡ

For a Lively Start

Moses and Aaron are faced with a difficult assignment. How can they persuade Pharaoh to release thousands of Hebrew workmen? They decide on an approach that could be called "situation ethics." Discussing this could make an interesting introduction to the lesson.

Instead of presenting God in truth as the Holy God whom they and their forefathers have served for generations, they pretend that they have only just met with Him in the wilderness. Instead of being straightforward about their plans to leave Egypt permanently, they pretend that it is only for a few feast days.

Is their liberty worth this misrepresentation, or should they have been more honest with Pharaoh about their plans?

Teaching Outline	Daily Bible Readings

I. Request to Leave—5:1-3
  A. Attempted ruse, 1
  B. 'Who is the Lord?, 2-3
	Mon. Bricks Without Straw
	  Exod. 5:10-21
	Tue. The Voice of the Lord
	  Ps. 29

II. Response of Harshness—4-9
  A. 'Gather your own straw,' 4-7
  B. The same with less, 8-9
	Wed. Return to God
	  Deut. 4:25-31
	Thu. God's Good Plan
	  Zech. 10:6-12

III. Report to God—5:22—6:1
  A. 'Why have you sent me?'
  5:22-23
  B. 'Wait and see!' 6:1-5
	Fri. God's Deliverance
	  Ps. 18:13-19
	Sat. All Shall Worship God
	  Zech. 14:12-19
	Sun. Moses' Complaint
	  Exod. 5:1-9, 22—6:1

Verse by Verse

I. Request to Leave—5:1-3

A. Attempted ruse, 1

1 And afterward Moses and Aaron went in, and told Pharaoh, Thus saith the Lord God of Israel, Let my people go, that they may hold a feast unto me in the wilderness.

Moses had accepted the fact that those who had sought his life had died. After all, it had been 40 years since the incident that resulted in the death of the Egyptian who was abusing the Israelite (2:12). Also, with God's reassurance that Aaron would help with the task of confronting Pharaoh, Moses accompanies Aaron back to Egypt. They call a meeting of the leaders of Israel, and prove, probably with the rod that became a serpent, how God's power rested now on Moses. The leaders therefore agree to follow Moses and Aaron's plan. The importance of this step is often overlooked; but it would be ludicrous for the two leaders to strike out toward the wilderness only to look back and discover that the people are not following. In fact, the authority of Moses and his leadership will often be questioned even after the miraculous escape from Egypt.

Another scene sometimes neglected is the appearance of Moses and Aaron before Pharaoh with the message from God to "Let my people go." As we shall see, this simple command is taking a great deal for granted.

B. 'Who is the Lord?, 2-3

2 And Pharaoh said, Who is the Lord, that I should obey his voice to let Israel go? I know not the Lord, neither will I let Israel go.

3 And they said, The God of the Hebrews hath met with us: let us go, we pray thee, three days' journey into the desert, and sacrifice unto the Lord our God; lest he fall upon us with pestilence, or with the sword.

Pharaoh knows of many gods in Egypt, but his pantheon does not include a god named Yahweh (note the capitals and small caps, "Lord," indicating that Moses frequently uses God's proper [and holy] name in speaking of Him to Pharaoh. From Pharaoh's perspective, it would be foolish to let the people go on the authority of a god he did not know. It would seem that this natural reluctance prompts the two Israelite leaders to concoct the story of the three-day sacrifice on the spot, as a note to add a concrete command that might lend credibility to the story. Otherwise, they say, their God might punish them with disease or the sword. The ruse does not work.

II. Response of Harshness—4-9
A. 'Gather your own straw,' 4-7

4 And the king of Egypt said unto them, Wherefore do ye, Moses and Aaron, let the people from their works? get you unto your burdens.

5 And Pharaoh said, Behold, the people of the land now are many, and ye make them rest from their burdens.

6 And Pharaoh commanded the same day the taskmasters of the people, and their officers, saying,

7 Ye shall no more give the people straw to make brick, as heretofore: let them go and gather straw for themselves.

Pharaoh now accuses Moses and Aaron of "letting" (KJV for "preventing" or "hindering"; see Rom. 1:13) the people from their work of brick-making. He not only intends to prevent them from attending the purported three-day feast in the wilderness; he will add to their burden as punishment for even asking.

Mixing straw with clay was one way bricks were made in Egypt, the straw acting as a bonding agent. Formerly, the Hebrews had been allowed to use hay or the stubble of grain crops for this purpose, and there is a hint that Egyptian workers would gather the material for the Israelite worker-slaves. Now Pharaoh expects them to range far and wide in the Nile Valley in search of their own bonding material, using straw if necessary instead of the more suitable stubble. Pharaoh is willing to build with inferior materials in order to punish the Hebrews.

B. The same with less, 8-9

8 And the tale of the bricks, which they did make heretofore, ye shall lay upon them; ye shall not diminish ought thereof: for they be idle; therefore they cry, saying, Let us go and sacrifice to our God.

9 Let there more work be laid upon the men, that they may labour therein; and let them not regard vain words.

Despite having to search for their own straw, the Israelite laborers are expected to make as many bricks as before. "Tale" is pronounced "tally" here, and means "number," rather than "story.") Pharaoh charges that the Hebrews had asked for time off to worship in the wilderness because they haven't had enough to do; so "more work" was assigned to them in order to teach them not to use "vain words."

III. Report to God—5:22—6:1
A. 'Why have you sent me?' 5:22-23

22 And Moses returned unto the LORD, and said, Lord, wherefore hast thou so evil entreated this people? why is it that thou hast sent me?

23 For since I came to Pharaoh to speak in thy name, he hath done evil to this people; neither hast thou de-

livered thy people at all.

We can discern here that Moses' faith in God and the assignment he has given him was weak. He resents Pharaoh's reaction to the request to go to the wilderness, and virtually blames God for the "evil" Pharaoh has done to the Israelites. We can see here not only a tendency to blame, but some defensiveness on Moses' part. He is trying to win the loyalty of the Hebrews so they will trust his leadership, and to him it does not seem that God is co-operating. From his perspective, he should have stayed with the sheep in the wilderness, for he can see no evidence that God is fulfilling His promise.

B. 'Wait and see!' 6:1

6:1 Then the LORD said unto Moses, Now shalt thou see what I will do to Pharaoh: for with a strong hand shall he let them go, and with a strong hand shall he drive them out of his land.

God is being exceedingly patient with Moses and his weak faith. As is so often the case, the servant chosen to do God's work—being unable to see His entire plan—is impatient and lacking in faith. Moses cannot see the plagues that are facing Pharaoh, nor the agony that will finally prompt him not merely to "let my people go," but actually to *drive* them from Egypt "with

a strong hand," indicating the extent of his wrath at their presence. Not only Moses but the people need a strong reminder of just who God is.

2 And God spake unto Moses, and said unto him, I am the LORD:

3 And I appeared unto Abraham, unto Isaac, and unto Jacob, by the name of God Almighty, but by my name JEHOVAH was I not known to them.

4 And I have also established my covenant with them, to give them the land of Canaan, the land of their pilgrimage, wherein they were strangers.

5 And I have also heard the groaning of the children of Israel, whom the Egyptians keep in bondage; and I have remembered my covenant.

The Hebrews have been living among pagans so long that they have forgotten the vast difference between their false gods and the one true God, Yahweh—the holy Name by whom they had not known Him. They needed to be reminded of the covenant He made with their forefathers, the patriarchs, and the covenant-keeping power and love He has for His people. The coming liberation will be a powerful lesson not only for Pharaoh and the Egyptians, but for God's people as well.

Evangelistic Emphasis

Although Moses was sent to announce God's deliverance of Israel, Pharaoh saw it as the threat to his power that it was. His reaction was to exert his power to hold the people in captivity—which made the lives of the Israelite people even more difficult. This was not what Moses had expected. He had resisted the call of God, and it had taken all his strength and faith to be responsive to God. Now, the leaders of the people blamed him for making things worse, and Moses blamed God for not doing what He said He would do. Maybe it would have been better to have stayed in Midian and never tried. But—if this was what Moses was thinking—he was underestimating God's power to deliver, and he was underestimating the power of evil to resist the will of God.

We, too, may find it difficult to take the good news of deliverance to others. When we do find the strength to share the Gospel, we wish we could see immediate results. We especially hate to see evil fight back with all its fury. Remember that when Jesus himself embraced God's mission in his baptism, Satan scheduled a face-to-face meeting with him. Let us not underestimate the determination of evil to oppress—nor let us ever doubt that God's will to deliver is stronger than all the objections evil can bring.

Memory Selection

And afterward Moses and Aaron went in, and told Pharaoh, Thus saith the LORD God of Israel, Let my people go, that they may hold a feast unto me in the wilderness.—*Exodus 5:1*

At first glance, it appears Moses and Aaron are not being totally honest with Pharaoh. Their demand that the people of Israel be allowed to go into the wilderness to have a worship service sounds as if they are asking only that the people be given a brief time away from their work. Of course, their intent was for the people to leave the slavery of Egypt permanently and enter the freedom of the Promised Land. All this sounds a little like the employee who says he is running an errand when he is really headed for the golf course.

But Moses and Aaron were not misleading Pharaoh—and we know from his reaction that Pharaoh understood the meaning of the request. Maybe we do not fully understand the liberation that is involved in the worship of the Lord. In the United States, we often express gratitude for the freedom of worship. By this, we mean that we are free to worship God according to our beliefs without fear of government interference. While this is a great blessing, it is not the greatest blessing. The blessing of worship is in the freedom experienced in worship itself. In worship we are free to be who God created us to be. We find in worship the fullest expression of God's intent for us.

416

Weekday Problems

Jim couldn't believe the situation in his family had grown to the point that he feared losing his marriage and his child. It had all started with a disagreement between his wife and him over how to discipline their son. Tempers had flared. Accusations had been made. Now his wife and son were staying with a friend, and Jim was enlisting my help in deciding what he should do next. I knew we were in trouble when the first words from Jim's mouth were, "It's all my wife's fault." I asked him to explain, and he went into a detailed account of how his wife was too tolerant of his son's disobedience. In the course of telling his story, Jim emphasized how often his son had caused problems in the family.

"So, you're really saying that it's your son's fault?" I asked. This took Jim by surprise. He thought about it for a moment and said,

"No, I think the real problem is that we didn't have more children. I think it would be better if we didn't have just one child. We tend to spoil him."

"Why didn't you have more children?" I asked.

"We wanted to. It just didn't happen. Maybe God didn't think we needed them," Jim replied.

Our conversation had served the purpose of playing the "blame game" to its ultimate conclusion. Like the Israelites who blamed Moses for their problems and Moses who blamed God. Or Adam, faced with his sin, blamed his wife— pointing out that it was God who had given her to him. I asked Jim if he was ready to start working on the problems rather than assigning the blame.

*Why do we want to focus on assigning blame rather than addressing problems?

Covenants and Conquests

The Smiths were on the balcony and could hear the young couple talking on the balcony below them. Mrs. Smith nudged her husband and whispered, "I think he wants to propose. We ought not to listen. Whistle at him."

"Why should I?" her husband asked. "Nobody whistled at me."

* * *

A sultan kept his harem three miles from where he lived. His marriage covenant called for him to send a servant every day to bring a wife to the palace. The sultan lived to be 83, but the servant died when he was only 30.

The moral of this story is: It's not the women that will kill you, it's running after them.

This Lesson in Your Life

Moses and Aaron met with Pharaoh and demanded that he free the Israelite slaves. Can we appreciate the full impact of that scene? One man, a slave and a fugitive from the legal system is addressing the most powerful man in the most powerful nation on the earth—telling him to give away one of his most financially lucrative resources. The events that follow are in no way surprising. Pharaoh acts to assert his authority and dispel any hope of liberation. He increases the workload of the people, and the people turn against Moses and Aaron. They accuse Moses and Aaron of making their situation worse with their dreams of freedom.

Pharaoh's system is typical of any oppressive system where the few benefit from the work and deprivation of many. When an oppressive system is challenged by the workers, the system will act to deplete the energy of the oppressed. The goal is that the harsh reality of physical exhaustion will remove any inclination to organize or work toward any change. The system will seek to convince the oppressed that their very existence depends on the strength of the system itself—that it offers their only hope of living. And the system will blame any problems the oppressed are suffering on the lack of character of the workers themselves (cf. "You are lazy," 5:8, 17).

We can see all these forces and strategies at work in Pharaoh's government, and we can recognize them in other oppressive systems throughout history. Whether it be the system of slavery in the young United States, the system of communism in 20th century Europe and Asia, or the system of oppression that ruled for so long in South Africa, the forces follow much the same game plan; and they have yet to die out in our world today.

The one thing that Pharaoh and other historical oppressors failed to reckon with is that God is a God of liberation. As He announced through his prophet Isaiah and as He brought into reality through His Son Jesus, He is the one who proclaims release for the captives and lets the oppressed go free (Luke 4:18-19). Freedom and dignity for all individuals is a cornerstone of the Kingdom of Heaven that is now breaking into the world. Liberation of the oppressed is within the very fabric of the Good News that we preach.

What is a disciple of the Great Liberator to do with such a text as Exodus 5? The text is to serve as warning that freedom from oppression does not come easily and without a price. The chapter maps out the expected response to be endured when oppression is challenged. But the text also presents the hope that God's heart is with the captive, and He will stand with those who rise to fight such forces in His name. This text urges us today to continue seeking out oppressive systems and, through faith in God, having the strength and courage to challenge them.

1. What reason did Moses and Aaron give Pharaoh when they demanded that he let the Israelites go out of Egypt?

They said God told them, "Let my people go, that they may hold a feast unto me in the wilderness" (Exod. 5:1).

2. What reason did Pharaoh give for refusing to let Israel go?

Pharaoh said that he did not know the Lord that he should obey him (5:2).

3. What did Pharaoh accuse Moses and Aaron of doing?

Pharaoh accused Moses and Aaron of interfering with the people's work—of making them rest from their burdens (5:4, 5).

4. What did Pharaoh tell his taskmasters to do in order to increase the burden of the people's work?

Pharaoh commanded that the people would have to gather their own straw to make their bricks (5:7).

5. Why did Pharaoh think the people wanted to go sacrifice to their God?

He said that the people were idle—or lazy (5:8).

6. Who were punished when the people could not produce as many bricks as before?

Pharaoh's taskmasters beat the officers of the children of Israel for not making enough bricks (5:14).

7. To whom did the officers of the children of Israel first complain about their punishment?

They cried out to Pharaoh, but he repeated his claim that the people were idle (5:15-17).

8. To whom did the officers next complain?

They met with Moses and Aaron and accused them of putting a sword in the hands of the Egyptians to slay them (5:20-21).

9. To whom did Moses complain?

Moses complained to God that He had brought evil on Israel by sending him to them (5:22).

10. How did God respond to Moses' complaint?

God said that Moses would see what He would do to Pharaoh—that with a strong hand he would let the people go (6:1).

Uplift

In Annie Dillard's book *Teaching a Stone to Talk,* she bemoans the way most Christians treat their religion as a powerless diversion. "On the whole, I do not find Christians, outside of the catacombs, sufficiently sensible of conditions. Does anyone have the foggiest idea what sort of power we so blithely evoke? Or, as I suspect, does no one believe a word of it? The churches are children playing on the floor with their chemistry sets, mixing up a batch of TNT to kill a Sunday morning. It is madness to wear ladies' straw hats and velvet hats to church; we should all be wearing crash helmets. Ushers should issue life preservers and signal flares; they should lash us to our pews. For the sleeping god may wake someday and take offense . . . ."

Do we truly believe in a God who changes things? Do we believe that He can and will address long standing systems of oppression and injustice? Would He dare call us to be instruments in His hands to address the evils of this world? His call to action has rung out to individuals over the centuries:

"Go at once to Nineveh, that great city, and cry out against it!"

"Go in this might of yours and deliver Israel from the hand of Midian!"

"Go, sell what you have and distribute the money to the poor!"

Has God changed His agenda, or have we?

Each year, as Christmas draws near, many of us gather in our churches to watch our children present the Nativity Story. We wrap the account of God's entrance into our world as a human in cuteness and warmth. Our hearts are thrilled to hear the angelic voices of children recite in unison: "Glory to God in the highest, and on earth peace, good will toward men." But rarely do we allow the words of Mary to disturb our peaceful reflection.

He has shown strength with his arm;
he has scattered the proud in the thoughts of their hearts.
He has brought down the powerful from their thrones,
and lifted up the lowly;
he has filled the hungry with good things,
and sent the rich away empty.
    Luke 1:51-53 (NRSV)

Maybe it is time for us to invest in a crash helmet—maybe a pair of work boots and gloves.

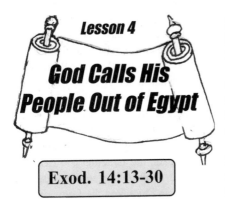

Lesson 4

God Calls His People Out of Egypt

Exod. 14:13-30

And Moses said unto the people, Fear ye not, stand still, and see the salvation of the LORD, which he will shew to you to day: for the Egyptians whom ye have seen to day, ye shall see them again no more for ever.

14 The LORD shall fight for you, and ye shall hold your peace.

15 And the LORD said unto Moses, Wherefore criest thou unto me? speak unto the children of Israel, that they go forward:

16 But lift thou up thy rod, and stretch out thine hand over the sea, and divide it: and the children of Israel shall go on dry ground through the midst of the sea.

17 And I, behold, I will harden the hearts of the Egyptians, and they shall follow them: and I will get me honour upon Pharaoh, and upon all his host, upon his chariots, and upon his horsemen.

18 And the Egyptians shall know that I am the LORD, when I have gotten me honour upon Pharaoh, upon his chariots, and upon his horsemen.

19 And the angel of God, which went before the camp of Israel, removed and went behind them; and the pillar of the cloud went from before their face, and stood behind them:

20 And it came between the camp of the Egyptians and the camp of Israel; and

it was a cloud and darkness to them, but it gave light by night to these: so that the one came not near the other all the night.

21 And Moses stretched out his hand over the sea; and the LORD caused the sea to go back by a strong east wind all that night, and made the sea dry land, and the waters were divided.

22 And the children of Israel went into the midst of the sea upon the dry ground: and the waters were a wall unto them on their right hand, and on their left.

23 And the Egyptians pursued, and went in after them to the midst of the sea, even all Pharaoh's horses, his chariots, and his horsemen.

24 And it came to pass, that in the morning watch the LORD looked unto the host of the Egyptians through the pillar of fire and of the cloud, and troubled the host of the Egyptians,

25 And took off their chariot wheels, that they drave them heavily: so that the Egyptians said, Let us flee from the face of Israel; for the LORD fighteth for them against the Egyptians.

26 And the LORD said unto Moses, Stretch out thine hand over the sea, that the waters may come again upon the Egyptians, upon their chariots, and upon their horsemen.

27 And Moses stretched forth his hand over the sea, and the sea returned to his strength when the morning appeared;

(Χοντινυεδ βοττομ οφ π. 425)

June 28

Memory Selection
Exod. 14:30

Background Scripture
Exod. 13:17—14:30

Devotional Reading
Exod. 15:1-13

FOCUS

Just as God had predicted, Pharaoh's refusal to let the Israelites leave Egypt leaves God no choice but to use force. One after the other, God sends 10 plagues on the Egyptians, the last one being the most terrible—the death of the firstborn in each Egyptian family. Pharaoh seems to be defeated, and tells the Hebrews to leave. Then he changes his mind and pursues the fleeing Hebrews across the Reed (or Red) Sea.

In what is surely history's greatest trap, God causes the waters of the sea to part so the Hebrews can cross on dry land; then the walls of water crash together, killing the Egyptians. After 400 years, the Israelites are free. For awhile, at least, "the people feared the LORD, and believed the LORD, and his servant Moses" (Exod. 14:31).

ഇൻൟ

For a Lively Start

The "exodus" or flight from Egypt is one of the most famous miracles in all of Scripture. You can introduce this lesson by leading a brief discussion on just why this is so. What is there about this incident that makes it so unforgettable? Here are some possibilities in a list you can use for points of discussion.

• The parting, then, the crashing together, of the waters.

• The terror of the 10 plagues, or the special horror of the death of the firstborn.

• The amazing stubbornness of Pharaoh that caused him to pursue Israel even after witnessing the power of their God.

• The overall display of God's power, even to the extent of using evil to convince Pharaoh to release the Hebrews.

Teaching Outline	**Daily Bible Readings**
I. 'The Lord Shall Fight for You'—13-18	Mon. Led to Freedom *Exod. 13:17-22*
A. 'Fear not, stand still,' 13-14	Tue. Pursued by the Enemy *Exod. 14:1-9*
B. Hardened hearts, 15-18	Wed. Overtaken by Fear *Exod. 14:10-14*
II. Division of the Waters—19-22	Thu. 'God Is Our Refuge' *Ps. 46*
A. Darkness and light, 19-20	Fri. Trust in the Lord *Prov. 3:3-10*
B. Night-long wind, 21-22	Sat. Celebrating Deliverance *Exod. 15:1-13*
III. Egyptians Are Overthrown–23-30	Sun. Saved from the Enemy *Exod. 14:15-25, 30*
A. Wheel-less chariots, 23-25	
B. Crashing seas, 26-28	
C. Hebrews live, Egyptians die, 29-30	

Verse by Verse

I. 'The Lord Shall Fight for You'— 13-18

A. 'Fear not, stand still,' 13-14

13 And Moses said unto the people, Fear ye not, stand still, and see the salvation of the LORD, which he will shew to you to day: for the Egyptians whom ye have seen to day, ye shall see them again no more for ever.

14 The LORD shall fight for you, and ye shall hold your peace.

If ever a people needed the Lord to fight for them, the Hebrews did. They were a minority, poor, and virtually without weapons. They had not distinguished themselves by their faith; but if they could just hold on for this battle, God would prove Himself faithful and they would never see these Egyptians again. To urge them to "hold your peace" is another way to plead for them to believe that the Lord will fight their battle for them. One reason this is important is that during hard times through years to come they will be able to tell each other how God fought for them, and thus renew their failing faith.

B. Hardened hearts, 15-18

15 And the LORD said unto Moses, Wherefore criest thou unto me? speak unto the children of Israel, that they go forward:

16 But lift thou up thy rod, and stretch out thine hand over the sea, and divide it: and the children of Israel shall go on dry ground through the midst of the sea.

17 And I, behold, I will harden the hearts of the Egyptians, and they shall follow them: and I will get me honour upon Pharaoh, and upon all his host, upon his chariots, and upon his horsemen.

18 And the Egyptians shall know that I am the LORD, when I have gotten me honour upon Pharaoh, upon his chariots, and upon his horsemen.

Exactly what Moses said when he cried to the Lord (vs. 15) is not recorded. Perhaps he had complained to God when the people complained to him (vs. 12). It is not a time to cry to God, however, but a time to "go forward."

Moses is rarely without his miracle-working rod (see 4:2-5). Now God will call on him to use it for the greatest miracle of all. Although Pharaoh has only recently given the Hebrews permission to leave the land, God knew from from the beginning that the king would harden his heart and change his mind (3:19). Now, while that mental process is going on, Moses is using his rod to divide the water in a shallow lake into two opposing walls.

Although most scholars now believe that the waters where Israel cross the Nile delta area were the *"Reed"* Sea, the older term "Red" Sea is more time-honored and persists. In Hebrew the name is *Yom (Sea) Suph (of Reeds)*. Even if the sea were shallow enough for reeds to appear, this does nothing to take away from the miraculous element. However, as verse 21 will explain, the event occurred with both natural and supernatural aid—the rod of Moses and a strong wind.

Since Pharaoh and the Egyptians have hardened their hearts, God responds in kind. He encourages them to pursue the Israelites between the walls of water, saying that what will happen to them there will "get me honor," or show the greatness of good over evil.

II. Division of the Waters—19-22
A. Darkness and light, 19-20

19 And the angel of God, which went before the camp of Israel, removed and went behind them; and the pillar of the cloud went from before their face, and stood behind them:

20 And it came between the camp of the Egyptians and the camp of Israel; and it was a cloud and darkness to them, but it gave light by night to these: so that the one came not near the other all the night.

The pillar of a cloud, here, and a pillar of fire later, are other miraculous elements God used in this unforgettable event. Here the cloud stands in the middle of the sea because the two armies will pass each other during the night, and God does not want a battle to break out and spoil His plan. The cloud clothes the Egyptians in darkness, but is bright enough to glow on the side of the Hebrews.

B. Night-long wind, 21-22

21 And Moses stretched out his hand over the sea; and the LORD caused the sea to go back by a strong east wind all that night, and made the sea dry land, and the waters were divided.

22 And the children of Israel went into the midst of the sea upon the dry ground: and the waters were a wall unto them on their right hand, and on their left.

Some would lower the element of the miraculous in this entire event by noting that the waters were said to be divided here by the wind, not Moses' uplifted rod. Actually, both are involved; and at any rate, it is as miraculous to be able call upon the east wind to blow upon demand as it would be to divide waters by Moses' rod.

III. Egyptians Are Overthrown–23-30
A. Wheel-less chariots, 23-25

23 And the Egyptians pursued, and went in after them to the midst of the sea, even all Pharaoh's horses, his chariots, and his horsemen.

24 And it came to pass, that in the morning watch the LORD looked unto the host of the Egyptians through the pillar of fire and of the cloud, and troubled the host of the Egyptians,

25 And took off their chariot wheels, that they drave them

heavily: so that the Egyptians said, Let us flee from the face of Israel; for the LORD fighteth for them against the Egyptians.

Now the Egyptians are able to see through the cloud to some extent, and to see some of the Israelites. Conditions are far from clear, however, and the Egyptian chariots seem to have trouble from at least two sides. The drivers are having difficulty seeing clearly, and their chariot wheels are having difficulty in the mud. Some translations indicate that the Lord took the wheels off, while others seem to say that the charioteers removed the wheels, thinking that they were a handicap in the sea-bed, which was not quite dry. Either way, things are going so badly that the Egyptians conclude (correctly) that God is fighting for the Hebrews, and the charioteers attempt to wheel about and make it to the near bank.

B. Crashing seas, 26-28

26 And the LORD said unto Moses, Stretch out thine hand over the sea, that the waters may come again upon the Egyptians, upon their chariots, and upon their horsemen.

27 And Moses stretched forth his hand over the sea, and the sea re- turned to his strength when the morning appeared; and the Egyptians fled against it; and the LORD overthrew the Egyptians in the midst of the sea.

28 And the waters returned, and covered the chariots, and the horsemen, and all the host of Pharaoh that came into the sea after them; there remained not so much as one of them.

It is interesting that Moses *divides* the waters with his rod (14:16), but *brings them together* with his hand. The Egyptians are trapped, while the Israelites have made it safely to the far bank.

C. Hebrews live, Egyptians die, 29-30

29 But the children of Israel walked upon dry land in the midst of the sea; and the waters were a wall unto them on their right hand, and on their left.

30 Thus the LORD saved Israel that day out of the hand of the Egyptians; and Israel saw the Egyptians dead upon the sea shore.

A sobering scene greeted the Israelites when dawn broke. God has protected them and, as promised, fought their battle for them, while a gruesome collection of Egyptian bodies litter the sea shore.

ಐೞ

Evangelistic Emphasis

As we read the story of the Israelites crossing the Red Sea, we picture it mainly as an account of God's great deliverance of His chosen people at the terrible expense of the Egyptians. In fact, we might assume that *God's* attention is focused solely on the deliverance of Israel as well—that He, along with us, sees the Egyptians only as a problem with which to deal. A careful reading of the text reveals something else.

In Exodus the liberation of Israel is actually in the background of the story. God's stated purpose for taking them across the sea is found in Exodus 14:18—which is an echo of 14:4. God said he was doing this so that "the *Egyptians* [author emphasis] shall know that I am the LORD." While he is watching over the Israelites walking through the dry lake bed and while he is eliminating the threat of Pharaoh's army, His eye is also on the people of Egypt. His heart is for them as well. Here is an opportunity for them to realize that He truly is the LORD—the one true God.

Centuries later, Paul repeated this same theme when he said that God had chosen to save him—the worst of sinners—so that all of us could believe God is able to save us as well (1 Tim. 1:15-17). Any time God rescues one of us, His eye is on those around us who see our deliverance and come to know God as LORD as well. This is why we continue to tell the story of the Red Sea. This is why we continue to tell the story of Jesus on the Cross.

℘℺

Memory Selection

Thus the LORD saved Israel that day from the Egyptians.—*Exodus 14:30*

"The Lord saves!" This statement is basic to our faith—so basic it occurs numerous times in various contexts throughout Scripture. And from what does He save us? Perhaps the first answer that comes to our minds is, "He saves us from our sins," or, "He saves us from eternal damnation." But in our verse for today, God is very specific: He saved His people from the Egyptians.

Can we look back in our lives and name some specifics from which God has saved us? Perhaps our testimony includes deliverance from an addiction that was destroying our lives. We have heard testimonies of deliverance from gang involvement and lives of crime. Maybe you can tell of a time of crisis where you faced immediate danger—and the Lord delivered you. Or maybe you have to stop to think—what would I be and where would I be if the Lord had not saved me?

It is wonderful to be able to say, "The Lord saved me." But it is even better to be able to say, "The Lord saved me from *this*!" Such testimony invites us to live in specific gratitude before God. Such testimony brings hope to those who struggle with what once enslaved them. From what has the Lord saved you this day?

Weekday Problems

Justine kicked off her shoes, collapsed into the chair, and sighed. The end of another day. She slowly rubbed her sore foot— 10 hours of retail was tough on feet—10 hours at minimum wage was tough on living expenses—and her mind went to the place it usually did in the evenings. How did she end up like this? Forty years old and starting over again. She thought of her carefree childhood and promising high school days. All that was before Jim. Her mother had begged her not to give up her future for Jim. Her mother had warned her that Jim had problems and would always be trouble. But Justine was sure she could change him. She had tried for 20 years, and then, one day, Jim was gone. If only she could go back and make different decisions. If only she had gone to college and to nursing school as she had planned. How different her life would be now.

As the children of Israel camped beside the Red Sea, their thoughts were much like Justine's. Following Moses had seemed to set a course toward destruction. They wished they could go back and do it all over. At least in Egypt they had life's basic necessities. With the sea before them and the Egyptian army behind them, they could see no future. This was when God spoke to Moses and said, "Tell the Israelites to go forward." Could they find the strength to keep from looking back? Could they find the faith to dare to look ahead?

*Do you think this story has anything to say to Justine?

*What would you tell Justine at this time in her life?

Time for Church

After everyone was seated, a bus driver sauntered into the sanctuary and took a seat up front, where the only open pews were available.

"'Scuse me, sir," he said to the minister. "I'm a bus driver, and I just dropped in to see how you get everybody to sit at the rear."

* * *

The minister's new secretary formerly worked at the Pentagon. Walking into her office, the minister found her busily reorganizing the filing system. She labeled one drawer, "Sacred," and the next "Top Sacred."

The man still had his hat on when an usher went up to him in the sanctuary and asked him to remove it. "I thought that would do it!" exclaimed the man. "I've been attending here five months and you're the first person who's spoken to me."

This Lesson in Your Life

Even those who know few stories from the Bible know the story of the children of Israel crossing the Red Sea. Whether they have read it, heard it in Sunday School, or seen it in a movie, they can tell the basic events of this amazing miracle. But in order for this story to become a force in our own lives, we must spend some time camped with the children of Israel beside the sea, and relive with them the recent events of their lives.

They had been in captivity—forced to work long hours with little reward—treated as second class citizens—the threat of disaster constantly hanging over their heads. Most of us can find something in our own lives that enables us to identify with such a situation. And now their whole world had been turned upside down. In a whirl of events, they had left their familiar surroundings to go into the wilderness. Filled with both hope and fear, they realized that nothing would ever be the same again for them. There was no going back. Again, if we spend some time with the Israelites, we can find these same emotions within us. We can travel with them until they come to the sea—and we can be ready to hear the story of their deliverance. Then we will be able to find within the story of their deliverance hope for our own.

Just when there seemed to be no hope for a future, Moses—under the direction of God—stretched out his hand toward the sea. The wind of God began to blow and the waters parted. Once again, as in that second day of Creation, God had brought forth dry ground from the sea. Now it was up to the Israelites. Could they trust this new act of creation? Would the dry land support their weight? Would the walls of the sea canyon hold while they passed through? It was in faith they stepped into the sea bed—trusting that the God who had created the past would be the creator of the future as well.

It is at that first step of faith that the story of Israel can become our story as well. As we come to a time in our lives when there seems to be no possibility for a future, can we trust God to be Creator? Even though we cannot see what can be done to give us hope, do we trust the one who can make something out of nothing to act once again? Too often we cry out to God to revive the past—just as the children of Israel cried out to go back to Egypt. We think the only answer to our problems is for God to put things back the way they were. But we are called to believe in a God who creates light out of darkness and hope out of hopelessness. Our calling is to have the faith to step onto the freshly created dry ground before us and, as God told the Israelites, "go forward" (Exod. 14:15).

GETTING THE FACTS STRAIGHT

1. What action was Moses to perform as God opened the Red Sea for the Israelites to cross?
He was to lift up his rod and stretch out his hand over the sea (Exod. 14:15).

2. What did God say would be the result of the destruction of the Egyptian army in the sea?
God would be honored and the Egyptians would know that He is the LORD (14:17,18).

3. What did God do to separate the Egyptian army from the children of Israel during that night at the sea?
The pillar of the cloud that had gone before the Israelites moved behind them to separate them from the Egyptians (14:19).

4. What force did God use to divide the water of the sea?
God caused a strong east wind to blow all that night to divide the waters and dry the land (14:21).

5. What did the Egyptian army do when they saw the Israelites walking through the sea?
The Egyptians pursued the Israelites into the sea (14:24).

6. What did the Lord do to the Egyptian chariots in the sea?
God caused the chariot wheels to bog down in the sea bed and to come off the chariots (14:25).

7. What did the Egyptian army realize when they began having trouble crossing through the sea?
They said they should flee from the face of Israel because the Lord was fighting for them against the Egyptians (14:15).

8. What happened when Moses once again stretched out his hand over the sea?
The waters of the sea returned to the sea bed and the Egyptian army was destroyed (14:27,28).

9. What time of day did these events occur?
The sea returned to its original place at dawn (14:27).

10. How did Israel react to this deliverance?
They feared the Lord, and they believed the Him and His servant Moses (14:31).

She thought her life was over when her husband told her he had found someone else. We grieved with her through the months of the divorce and its aftermath. We were relieved to see her begin to smile again, and we listened as she talked about going to various meetings for Christian Singles. She confided to us that she felt God had a special man out there for her and she would find him soon. But as time passed, God's chosen man did not appear. We worried that she would sink into despair once again. But now, years removed from her crisis, she is vibrant—alive with purpose and meaning. A volunteer position at a local shelter for abused women has evolved into a new career. She is the chairperson for the church's fellowship committee. Her smile, her gentle words, and her kind acts are a constant source of encouragement to all who are in crisis.

A few days ago we sat and talked about her journey. She confessed that she had gone through a time of bitterness—not just because of the divorce but because God was not rebuilding her life in the way she wanted Him to. It was during a late night prayer time that she strongly felt God's presence and His word to her heart. "I felt God was telling me to let Him do something new for me," she said. "I realized I was trying to direct God in what He should do when He knew of far more possibilities than I had ever dreamed."

The apostle Paul once wrote, "Now to him who by the power at work within us is able to accomplish abundantly far more than all we can ask or imagine, to him be glory. . ." (Eph. 3:20 NRSV). And to the Roman church, Paul said, "We know that all things work together for good for those who love God. . ." (Rom. 8:28 NRSV). These two passages encourage us to depend on God in our times of need, but to depend on Him as a God who can see more possibilities for us than we can see for ourselves.

The next time you are overwhelmed by life, lift your concerns to God. But be careful not to decide what God should do and how he should do it. Pray for patience to be still and wait. Pray for wisdom to see the path he will surely open before you.

Unit II: Called to Be God's People

Lesson 5
God Calls People To Covenant

Deut. 5:1-9a, 11-13, 16-21

And Moses called all Israel, and said unto them, Hear, O Israel, the statutes and judgments which I speak in your ears this day, that ye may learn them, and keep, and do them.

2 The LORD our God made a covenant with us in Horeb.

3 The LORD made not this covenant with our fathers, but with us, even us, who are all of us here alive this day.

4 The LORD talked with you face to face in the mount out of the midst of the fire,

5(I stood between the LORD and you at that time, to shew you the work of the LORD: for ye were afraid by reason of the fire, and went not up into the mount;) saying,

6 I am the LORD thy God, which brought thee out of the land of Egypt, from the house of bondage.

7 Thou shalt have none other gods before me.

8 Thou shalt not make thee any graven image, or any likeness of any thing that is in heaven above, or that is in the earth beneath, or that is in the waters beneath the earth:

9 Thou shalt not bow down thyself unto them, nor serve them:

11 Thou shalt not take the name of the LORD thy God in vain: for the LORD will not hold him guiltless that taketh his name in vain.

12 Keep the sabbath day to sanctify it, as the LORD thy God hath commanded thee.

13 Six days thou shalt labour, and do all thy work:

16 Honour thy father and thy mother, as the LORD thy God hath commanded thee; that thy days may be prolonged, and that it may go well with thee, in the land which the LORD thy God giveth thee.

17 Thou shalt not kill.

18 Neither shalt thou commit adultery.

19 Neither shalt thou steal.

20 Neither shalt thou bear false witness against thy neighbour.

21 Neither shalt thou desire thy neighbour's wife, neither shalt thou covet thy neighbour's house, his field, or his manservant, or his maidservant, his ox, or his ass, or any thing that is thy neighbour's.

Memory Selection
Deut. 5:1

Background Scripture
Deut. 5:1-27

Devotional Reading
Matt. 22:34-40

431

FOCUS

One of the most distinctive identifying traits of the ancient Hebrews was the idea of *the covenant*. One popular way of defining that term is "promise-law." God promised to care for humankind in return for keeping God's laws. The earliest relationship to be called a "covenant" was God's promise to save Noah, his family, and the animals if Noah would build the ark and care for those who rode out the storm in it.

The most famous covenant is the one between God and the patriarchs Abraham, Isaac, and Jacob. This lesson focuses on the core of that covenant, the Ten Commandments. These commandments are still the basis for law, order, and justice in many nations, including our own.

For a Lively Start

This lesson can be effectively introduced by a brief discussion of the value of *traffic laws*. Despite how much many people complain about them, imagine the chaos trying to get to work every morning if we had no laws! Ask what traffic rules are most irritating. More than likely it will be *traffic lights*. Now ask what laws are the most useful. *Right! Traffic lights again!* What other traffic laws are most helpful? (Look in the rear-view mirror before changing lanes? Observe stop signs? Observe speed limits?)

Point out that life in general goes more smoothly when we keep the rules. Although we sometimes complain about them, they are for our safety. Much the same can be said of the Ten Commandments. God gave them not to aggravate us, but "that it may go well with thee" (Deut. 5:16).

Teaching Outline	Daily Bible Readings
I. Remembering the Law—5:1-5 II. Foundation: One God—6-9a III. Two More Laws About God—11-13 IV. People-related Laws—16-21 　A. Honor parents, 16 　B. No murder, 17 　C. No adultery, 18 　D. No stealing, 19 　E. No false witness, 20 　F. No covetousness, 21	Mon.　Covenant by Sacrifice 　　　*Ps. 50:1-6* Tue.　Listening to the Prophet 　　　*Acts 3:17-25* Wed.　Covenant of Obedience 　　　*Ps. 132:11-18* Thu.　A Better Covenant 　　　*Heb. 8:6-12* Fri.　Covenant of Mercy 　　　*Rom. 11:25-32* Sat.　Greatest Commandment 　　　*Matt. 22:34-40* Sun.　God Makes a Covenant 　　　*Deut. 5:1-9, 11-13, 16-21*

Verse by Verse

I. Remembering the Law—5:1-5

1 And Moses called all Israel, and said unto them, Hear, O Israel, the statutes and judgments which I speak in your ears this day, that ye may learn them, and keep, and do them.

2 The LORD our God made a covenant with us in Horeb.

3 The LORD made not this covenant with our fathers, but with us, even us, who are all of us here alive this day.

4 The LORD talked with you face to face in the mount out of the midst of the fire,

5 (I stood between the LORD and you at that time, to shew you the work of the LORD: for ye were afraid by reason of the fire, and went not up into the mount;) saying,

This is the second time that the Ten Commandments, the heart of the "covenant" or Law of Moses, has been listed. This is why the book is called "Deuteronomy," which means "second [stating of the] law." The first

stating, with only slightly different wording, is in Exodus 20. It was given before the 40 years' wandering in the wilderness, and this one afterward, just before Israel enters the Promised Land. This is why Moses emphasizes that *this* stating of the Law is with *us,* not with "our fathers."

There could not be a more appropriate time to restate God's expectations and the people's obligations. Three verbs capture what is expected of Israel regarding these laws: they are to *learn, keep,* and *do* them. In one sense, Western culture has done just that, since the basic moral and legal codes of almost every nation in the West has been founded on what the Hebrews called "the Ten Words."

As Exodus 19 recorded, the first giving of this code was accompanied by impressive fireworks and awe-inspiring dramatics—so much that the people trembled and Moses had to stand between them and God to keep

433

them from fleeing in fear.

The code is divided into roughly two parts, with the first four dealing mainly with laws pertaining to people's relationship to God and the second six with people's relationship with each other.

II. Foundation: One God—6-9a

6 I am the Lord thy God, which brought thee out of the land of Egypt, from the house of bondage.

7 Thou shalt have none other gods before me.

8 Thou shalt not make thee any graven image, or any likeness of any thing that is in heaven above, or that is in the earth beneath, or that is in the waters beneath the earth:

9 Thou shalt not bow down thyself unto them, nor serve them:

First God identifies Himself as the only true God, establishing His authority to give such a code in the first place. The fact of monotheism is the basic law on which all others rest. Unfortuately, it will be the one violated the most, as the Israelites allow polytheistic nations about them to influence them; and with the violation of this law, the moral, person-to-person laws collapsed also. Verse 7 is therefore usually considered the first law.

One reason this law was violated so often is the nature of an invisible God. If the Philistines, for example, could see their God, and even carry him along to bless them in battle, why couldn't the Hebrews? Thus verse 8, the second law, follows quickly. The forbidding of "graven images" does not reflect an anti-art bias, but the fact that creating a likeness of a god inevitably lends credibility to it; and the next step

is polytheism. It may seem unlikely that making a likeness would lead so quickly to worshiping such a god; but for a primitive people in a time when artistic creations were so often endowed with life it was a very real danger.

III. Two More Laws About God—11-13

11 Thou shalt not take the name of the Lord thy God in vain: for the Lord will not hold him guiltless that taketh his name in vain.

12 Keep the sabbath day to sanctify it, as the Lord thy God hath commanded thee.

13 Six days thou shalt labour, and do all thy work:

Both God's name and the seventh day of the week are to be "kept holy" or sanctified. Regarding the name of God, this law is violated both when the name is used frivolously and in a context that actually has nothing to do with His name. In later years this was taken so seriously that God's proper name, Yahweh, would not even be pronounced; the word "Lord" would be used instead.

Regarding the seventh day, honoring God by not advancing one's own material wealth was a way to recall His magisterial power at creation, when he "rested" or finished His work (Gen. 2:1-3). This is the only one of the Ten Commandments that is not repeated, at least in principle, in the New Covenant. This of course is because the first day of the week, not the seventh, would become honored as the day of Jesus' resurrection (Acts 20:7). Because of the New Covenant's emphasis on honoring God in the inner life, the prohibitions against work were not carried over, although it was the early 20th century before the grip of custom and the unbiblical idea of a "Christian Sabbath" could be relaxed.

IV. People-related Laws—16-21

A. Honor parents, 16

16 Honour thy father and thy mother, as the LORD thy God hath commanded thee; that thy days may be prolonged, and that it may go well with thee, in the land which the LORD thy God giveth thee.

The force of this commandment has been remarkably powerful, as even "secular" Jews are often more respectful of parents than Gentiles are. The prolonging of days may be related to the need to keep large families thriving until the Promised Land could be conquered.

B. No murder, 17

17 Thou shalt not kill.

Some pacifists in later times used this commandment as a prohibition against all killing, a practice obviously at odds with the Old Testament itself, where killing was prescribed as punishment and where God was planning war even as He was giving the commandment. Surely, however, this is no excuse for the excess of instances when everyone who goes to war is happy to claim that God authorized it.

C. No adultery, 18

8 Neither shalt thou commit adultery.

Even many pagan moral codes forbade adultery, at least for women. We may wonder why there is no word against pologamy, since "from the beginning" God's ideal was monogamy (Matt. 19:8). Perhaps it was allowed because of the more difficult economic situation single women found themselves in the ancient world.

D. No stealing, 19

9 Neither shalt thou steal.

Stealing could be especially serious in a desert economy, as when the loss of a donkey or camel could cost a person his life.

E. No false witness, 20

20 Neither shalt thou bear false witness against thy neighbour.

This was often expanded to include lying of all kinds, since it is in fact lying against one's neighbor. Perhaps as a measure to discourage false witness, the first person to witness a capital offense was required to "cast the first stone."

F. No covetousness, 21

21 Neither shalt thou desire thy neighbour's wife, neither shalt thou covet thy neighbour's house, his field, or his manservant, or his maidservant, his ox, or his ass, or any thing that is thy neighbour's.

The word for "desire" can also be translated "covet," which the KJV does in Exod. 20:17. It is actually a morally neutral word unless directed, as here, toward something that belongs to someone else—thus "or any thing."

ຂດ

Evangelistic Emphasis

"Covenant" is a rich and an important word. Our God is a covenant-making God. When He called Abraham, God made a covenant with him. When God called the people of Israel from Egypt, He made a covenant with them. And when God called us through His Son Jesus, He made a covenant with us.

In its strictest sense, a covenant is a legal or binding agreement between two parties; but in the hands of God, a covenant is much more about two beings entering into an intimate relationship. This aspect of covenant is preserved in our primary use of the term in our society—the marriage covenant.

At Sinai, God entered into a covenant relationship with Israel. When Moses reminded the people of the covenant, he told them that the covenant was not with their ancestors but with those who were alive that day (Deut. 5:3). This statement is true for all generations. God's covenant is a living, breathing relationship—not a historical document.

The message of the New Testament (or New Covenant) is that we too have been called into a covenant relationship with God. Though this covenant was given almost 2,000 years ago through Jesus (a covenant in His blood), it is far from being only a historical or doctrinal document. The covenant is alive. We go out as witnesses to a God who has come to live in peace with others. When our lives show this kind of intimacy with God, evangelism is simply a way of life.

෨෮ඔ

Memory Selection

Hear, O Israel, the statutes and judgments which I speak in your ears this day, that ye may learn them, and keep, and do them.—*Deuteronomy 5:1*

Here is a memory verse that promotes memory verses. As God was about to give Israel what we refer to as the Ten Commandments, he first encouraged Israel to listen to them and to learn them. Have you learned the Ten Commandments? Can you list them? While that is important, it is even more important that they be written in the hearts of God's people.

When we have taken time to impress His words deep inside us, these words can minister to us in any situation of life we may face. Immediately following Jesus' baptism, the Spirit led Him into the wilderness where he fasted and prayed for 40 days and nights. Tempted by Satan, Jesus responded with the Word of God written in His heart. He found within it the power to overcome the efforts of Satan. The same is true for us today. Without a portion of the Word in our hearts, we are more prone to yield to temptations—in fact, we are more prone not to recognize a temptation for what it is.

One of the best places to begin in memorizing the Word of God is to know the basic commandments. So, we ask again. Can you list them?

436

Weekday Problems

Sunday morning Devon was challenged to learn the Ten Commandments. He had heard them all his life, but he was embarrassed that he could not repeat them—even out of proper sequence! That evening, he had opened his Bible and committed them to memory. He went to bed with a good feeling of accomplishment. But by Monday afternoon, he was wondering if he had done a dangerous thing.

By 5 p.m. on Monday, Devon realized that he had witnessed the breaking of at least eight of the Ten Commandments in his office building. He had never noticed before how much some of his co-workers loved money more than God. He heard God's name used in vain. He heard two co-workers discussing how hung over they were from a party on Sunday. A friend complained to him about how selfish and bothersome her elderly mother was. Then there was the current office romance that was violating two marriages. He noticed someone taking home a box of paper for personal use. And there were the lies and the comments about the boss's new "trophy wife."

Devon was not naive, and he knew that some of these people considered themselves "church folks." But until he had God's word fresh on his heart, he had not been aware of how widespread the abuse of God's basic commandments is. What was he to do with this new-found awareness? He thought about getting a plaque of the Ten Commandments for his desk, or pointing it out each time he saw one violated. Somehow, these did not seem like very workable solutions.

*What would you advise Devon to do as a witness to God's commandments in this environment?

*Have you ever learned a Bible verse and immediately seen its relevance?

Right 'n' Wrong

A department store decided to honor its two millionth customer. She was welcomed by the store president, interviewed on the radio, and loaded down with gifts.

Then she went on to her original destination: the complaint desk.

* * *

Wife (reading her husband's fortune cookie): "You are dynamic, a leader of men, and admired by women for your good looks and strength of character. It's got your weight wrong, too."

This Lesson in Your Life

I saw an old rerun of "The Andy Griffith Show" the other day. Gomer was convinced that Andy had saved his life. In gratitude, Gomer spent every waking moment trying to please Andy—with the predictable result that Andy couldn't get anything done with Gomer always there. The point of the show was to laugh at Andy's predicament, but the sincere attempts of Gomer to express his gratitude to Andy rang very true.

When we hear the story of God's giving the Law on Mount Sinai, we usually think first of the Ten Commandments and the other regulations God gave to Moses to tell the people. But that is not how the story actually begins. The story begins with God's saving the lives of the Israelites. The first statement He makes is, "I am the Lord thy God which brought thee out of the land of Egypt, from the house of bondage" (Deuteronomy 5:6).

God's Word to His people always begins with a word of grace. Without God's grace and mercy, we cannot hear Him. If we begin our reading of His commandments with Deut. 5:7—"You shall have no other gods before me"—we can get the idea that God is telling us the things that we must do in order for Him to love us. But the love is already there. The freedom from bondage is already there. What we learn in the Ten Commandments (and all God's commandments) is how to live gratefully before Him. Because He has rescued us, this is how we live.

In fact, the Commandments themselves are words of grace. In them, God does not reveal arbitrary rules of life He has set. Rather, He reveals to us the destructiveness of sin. Each thing he tells us to avoid is for our own spiritual—and sometimes physical—health. These things are sinful because they are not in the nature of God Himself, and anything not in the nature of God is hurtful to our lives and the lives of those around us as well. So we receive these commandments with grateful hearts.

What does the realization of God's grace in our lives change? Everything. It changes us from living under the burden of duty to living in the freedom of gratitude. The apostle Paul was well aware of this. "And be thankful," he said. "Let the word of Christ dwell in you richly; teach and admonish one another in all wisdom; and with gratitude in your hearts sing psalms, hymns, and spiritual songs to God. And whatever you do, in word or deed, do everything in the name of the Lord Jesus, giving thanks to God the Father through him" (Col. 3:15c-17).

Let us remove from our hearts any feelings of duty or drudgery in keeping the gracious commandments of our Lord. Let us rejoice in gratitude that He has saved us and has given us His wisdom in how we can live productive and effective lives.

1. When Moses called to Israel to tell them the statutes and judgments from God, what did he encourage them to do with these commandments?

He said they must hear them, learn them, keep them, and do them (Deut. 5:1).

2. Where did God make His covenant with Israel?

At Mount Horeb—also known as Mount Sinai (5:2).

3. How did the Lord first address Israel?

He spoke to them face to face out of the midst of the fire (5:4).

4. Why did Israel ask Moses to listen to the Lord and to speak His words to them?

They were afraid of the fire and would not go up on the mountain (5:5).

5. How did God identify Himself to Israel?

He said He was the LORD their God who brought them out of the land of Egypt and the house of bondage (5:6).

6. What is the first—and primary—commandment of God?

You shall have no other gods before me (5:7).

7. What reason did God give for not having graven images?

He said He is a jealous God, punishing those who reject Him but showing steadfast love to those who love Him (5:9).

8. What promise was given to the Israelites if they honored their parents?

God promised that they would live long, and that it would go well for them in the land He was giving them (5:16).

9. In what form were the commandments given to Moses to give to the people?

God wrote them on two stone tablets (5:22).

10. What promise did Israel make to Moses if he would listen to God and bring them God's commandments?

They promised they would listen to and keep the commandments (5:27).

When we think of the Ten Commandments, the first words that likely come to our minds are "Thou shalt not." It is true that eight of the ten are stated in this way. However, the Ten Commandments are far from being negative statements meant to limit our lives. They are positive guides that point us in the direction of living in a way that benefits us as well as those around us.

One way we can uncover the positive nature of the Ten Commandments is to restate them as questions. Use the following questions based on the commandments in examining your own life or in discussing the godly life with others.

1. How can I recognize God as God more fully in my life? In what areas of my life do I conduct myself with little or no thought about God?

2. Is there something in my life more important to me than God? Do I place my concern for my job or any possession above my love for God?

3. Do I use my speech to praise and exalt God other than when I am worshipping at church?

4. What time do I set aside as holy in my life?

5. How can I bring honor to my parents (or other family members)? Can I do better in demonstrating a more loving attitude, listening more, communicating, or showing respect?

6. How can I promote life? Can I be involved in protecting the lives of the unborn or of the abused? Can I find ways to ease the burden of the elderly or sick?

7. What can I do to promote marriage? Can I be involved in preserving the biblical intention of marriage? Can I be a better model of what God intended when He described marriage as two becoming one? How can I honor and bless the marriages of my friends?

8. What more can I give? When was the last time I gave when it was not expected or required? (See Eph. 4:28.)

9. How can I bless others with what I say? How can my speech be a vessel of grace in their lives? (See Eph. 4:29.)

10. How can I help others succeed rather than trying to hold them back? How can I celebrate the blessings of my family and friends?

By simply observing the positive direction the Commandments give us, we can utilize them to fill our days with Godly activity and thoughts.

Lesson 6
God Calls People To Remember

Deut. 16:1-13

Observe the month of Abib, and keep the passover unto the LORD thy God: for in the month of Abib the LORD thy God brought thee forth out of Egypt by night.

2 Thou shalt therefore sacrifice the passover unto the LORD thy God, of the flock and the herd, in the place which the LORD shall choose to place his name there.

3 Thou shalt eat no leavened bread with it; seven days shalt thou eat unleavened bread therewith, even the bread of affliction; for thou camest forth out of the land of Egypt in haste: that thou mayest remember the day when thou camest forth out of the land of Egypt all the days of thy life.

4 And there shall be no leavened bread seen with thee in all thy coast seven days; neither shall there anything of the flesh, which thou sacrificedst the first day at even, remain all night until the morning.

5 Thou mayest not sacrifice the passover within any of thy gates, which the LORD thy God giveth thee:

6 But at the place which the LORD thy God shall choose to place his name in, there thou shalt sacrifice the passover at even, at the going down of the sun, at the season that thou camest forth out of Egypt.

7 And thou shalt roast and eat it in the place which the LORD thy God shall choose: and thou shalt turn in the morning, and go unto thy tents.

8 Six days thou shalt eat unleavened bread: and on the seventh day shall be a solemn assembly to the LORD thy God: thou shalt do no work therein.

9 Seven weeks shalt thou number unto thee: begin to number the seven weeks from such time as thou beginnest to put the sickle to the corn.

10 And thou shalt keep the feast of weeks unto the LORD thy God with a tribute of a freewill offering of thine hand, which thou shalt give unto the LORD thy God, according as the LORD thy God hath blessed thee:

11 And thou shalt rejoice before the LORD thy God, thou, and thy son, and thy daughter, and thy manservant, and thy maidservant, and the Levite that is within thy gates, and the stranger, and the fatherless, and the widow, that are among you, in the place which the LORD thy God hath chosen to place his name there.

12 And thou shalt remember that thou wast a bondman in Egypt: and thou shalt observe and do these statutes.

13 Thou shalt observe the feast of tabernacles seven days, after that thou hast gathered in thy corn and thy wine:

Memory Selection
Deut. 16:1

Background Scripture
Deut. 16:1-16

Devotional Reading
1 Cor. 5:1-8

Today's text reflects the establishment of three major feasts celebrated by the Hebrews as remembrances of the great acts of God that helped form them as a people: the feast of *Passover*, of *Weeks*, and of *Tabernacles*.

Passover, the best known of these feasts, observed the terrible night when God killed the firstborn of humans and beasts among the Egyptians for not having released the Jews, but "passed over" the Jews' houses marked with the blood of a lamb. "Weeks" observed harvest-time, and "Tabernacles" celebrated the giving of the Law. Other feasts were observed with less regularity, but these three were of special importance as times of thanksgiving for God's deliverance of the Jews and the giving of the Law.

ഇരു

For a Lively Start

You can begin this lesson on Jewish feast days "close to home" by sharing ways you and your family celebrate family reunions or other events such as birthdays, anniversaries, Thanksgiving, Christmas, and other times together.

How do you decide where to have the special events? How do you keep them alive and interesting instead of "same ol' same ol'"? Do you play any particular games such as Dominoes, or Chess? Do some among you always manage to go fishing and/or have a fish fry? Do you try to have a religious element to them, or are your groups too diverse for that? Perhaps you can help others in your group give their celebrations new life by sharing openly some of your own traditions.

Teaching Outline	Daily Bible Readings	
	Mon.	Remember and Rejoice *Eccles. 11:7–12:1*
I. Passover—16:1-8	Tue.	Remember God's Deeds *Ps. 77:3-15*
A. Unleavened bread, 1-4		
B. Roast at evening, 5-8	Wed.	Remember and Give Thanks *Ps. 105:1-11*
II. Weeks—9-12	Thu.	Keeping the Covenant *2 Kings 23:1-3, 21-23*
A. The harvest feast, 9-10		
B. A feast of joy, 11-12	Fri.	Preparing for Passover *Luke 22:7-13*
III. Tabernacles—13-17	Sat.	Christ, Our Paschal Lamb *1 Cor. 5:1-8*
	Sun.	The Passover Observance *Deut. 16:1-8*

Verse by Verse

I. Passover—16:1-8

A. Unleavened bread, 1-4

1 Observe the month of Abib, and keep the passover unto the Lord thy God: for in the month of Abib the Lord thy God brought thee forth out of Egypt by night.

2 Thou shalt therefore sacrifice the passover unto the Lord thy God, of the flock and the herd, in the place which the Lord shall choose to place his name there.

3 Thou shalt eat no leavened bread with it; seven days shalt thou eat unleavened bread therewith, even the bread of affliction; for thou camest forth out of the land of Egypt in haste: that thou mayest remember the day when thou camest forth out of the land of Egypt all the days of thy life.

4 And there shall be no leavened bread seen with thee in all thy coast seven days; neither shall there anything of the flesh, which thou sacrificedst the first day at even, remain all night until the morning.

"Abib" was the name of a Canaanite month; Israel apparently adopted it as the "beginning of months," or of its calendar year, in commemoration of the exodus from Egypt. (After the Captivity the name of the month was changed to Nisan.) It corresponded to our months of March–April. Certainly it was appropriate to name the beginning of the calendar after the beginning of the nation; for the flight from Egypt was the formative event that melded several different ethnic groups with the Abrahamic tribes as one nation.

It was equally appropriate to begin the year with a feast commemorating the night God "passed over" the homes of the Hebrews and claimed the lives of the firstborn among man and beast, punishing the Egyptians for enslaving the Hebrew for more than 400 years. For generations the feast was a "pil-

443

grimage" event, held at a central spot such as Shechem, and later Jerusalem. Then it was changed to an event celebrated by clans and families, or groups of friends (as Jesus and the apostles, 22:1ff.).

Recall that on the night they fled from Egypt the Hebrews had no time for yeast-bread to rise; hence the tradition of eating unleavened bread at Passover.

B. Roast at evening, 5-8

5 Thou mayest not sacrifice the passover within any of thy gates, which the LORD thy God giveth thee:

6 But at the place which the LORD thy God shall choose to place his name in, there thou shalt sacrifice the passover at even, at the going down of the sun, at the season that thou camest forth out of Egypt.

7 And thou shalt roast and eat it in the place which the LORD thy God shall choose: and thou shalt turn in the morning, and go unto thy tents.

8 Six days thou shalt eat unleavened bread: and on the seventh day shall be a solemn assembly to the LORD thy God: thou shalt do no work therein.

The KJV wording of verse 5 may be confusing. It means "thou mayest not sacrifice the Passover at *just any* place, but only where God designates—which varied from year to year. The roast was lamb, symbolizing the slaughtered lamb from which came the blood that was put on the doorposts of the Hebrews' houses. Note that the Sabbath regulations such as not working took on double meaning during Passover.

II. Weeks—9-12

A. The harvest feast, 9-10

9 Seven weeks shalt thou number unto thee: begin to number the seven weeks from such time as thou beginnest to put the sickle to the corn.

10 And thou shalt keep the feast of weeks unto the LORD thy God with a tribute of a freewill offering of thine hand, which thou shalt give unto the LORD thy God, according as the LORD thy God hath blessed thee:

The second great pilgrim-feast was the Feast of Weeks, which came to be called Pentecost ("fiftieth") because it was observed on the fiftieth Sabbath from the beginning of Passover. Along with both the other primary feasts, Weeks also came to be a harvest festival—hence the regulation of a "freewill offering . . . according as the Lord thy God hath blessed thee" in the harvest.

Obviously this feast took on more importance after Israel had conquered a large part of Canaan, since it was more appropriate for the life of settled farmers than for nomadic tribes. This change in living conditions also occurred as harvest times varied from north to south. The period of 50 days was long enough to allow for variation in harvest times, with barley ripening in April and wheat somewhat later. In the hill country reaping may not start until the end of May or early June. This feast obviously lasted longer into the Christian era because of the coming of the Holy Spirit on the day of Pentecost (Acts 2).

B. A feast of joy, 11-12

11 And thou shalt rejoice before the LORD thy God, thou, and thy son, and thy daughter, and thy manservant, and thy maidservant, and the Levite that is within thy gates, and the stranger, and the fatherless, and the widow, that are among you, in the place which the LORD thy God hath chosen to place his name there.

12 And thou shalt remember that thou wast a bondman in Egypt: and thou shalt observe and do these statutes.

Although joy was a special feature at all these feasts, it was emphasized more than ever at the Feast of Weeks. There was also supposed to be a special effort made to include strangers and foreigners who were helping with the harvests or otherwise working in the area. Recalling their forefathers' years of slavery in Egypt was supposed to be a strong motive for looking out for the stranger at this and other feasts.

III. Tabernacles—13

13 Thou shalt observe the feast of tabernacles seven days, after that thou hast gathered in thy corn and thy wine:

As mentioned above, harvest was a prominent theme in all these feasts, but no more so than in the Feast of Tabernacles (or "booths"). City-folk would take branches and limbs like modern campers leave town for a camp-out weekend, commemorating the wandering in the wilderness and the transient labor during corn and wine harvest. Booths such as these were what Peter had in mind when he suggested that the disciples build memorial "tabernacles" for Moses, Elijah, and Jesus (Matt. 17:4).

As the following verses emphasize, these three feasts (plus other minor celebrations), were marked by a mixture of solemnity and joy. This allowed for a much wider range of emotions than became typical in early Christian worship gatherings, which very soon became dominated by the sacrifice of Christ on the Cross. In the Jewish background, the sadness of Egyptian slavery was balanced by the glad celebration of the memories of the exodus, and thanksgiving for abundant crops.

Although these three feasts were ideally attended by all males three times a year, especially after the Diaspora, when the Jews were scattered throughout the known world, being able to attend once a year, or even once a lifetime, was something to be joyful about.

෨ාශ

445

Evangelistic Emphasis

When Christians think of the Passover, we recognize it as the commemoration of a great event of deliverance in the history of God's people. We know that the exodus of Israel from Egypt played a significant role in our own salvation that has come to us through the Son of Israel—Jesus Christ our Lord. When we think of Jesus and the Passover together, we recall the last night before His death when He took bread and wine from the Passover meal and instituted our own commemoration—the Lord's Supper. In 2 Corinthians 11:23-26, the apostle Paul recounts that final Passover meal Jesus shared with His disciples. He took the bread and the wine and invited His disciples to share them "in *remembrance* of me."

The apostle Paul added additional significance to the eating of the Lord's Supper. Besides the Supper serving as a remembrance of Jesus, it also becomes *proclamation* of the deliverance He has brought. Paul wrote, "For as often as you eat this bread and drink the cup, you proclaim the Lord's death until he comes" (2 Cor. 11:26 NRSV). Each time we place the bread in our mouths and sip the wine, we proclaim our faith—what we believe and who we are.

Memory Selection

Observe the month of Abib, and keep the Passover unto the LORD thy God: for in the month of Abib the LORD thy God brought thee forth out of Egypt by night.—*Deuteronomy 16:1*

This verse fixes the time for the observation of the Passover Feast in the month of Abib (later known as the month of Nisan). At least once a year, every Israelite was reminded of the grace and mercy, the power, and the steadfast love of God, in delivering them from Egypt.

Do we have such dates marked on our calendars? Certainly we can point to our Sunday morning assemblies where we hear once again of the death, burial, and resurrection of Jesus. We can think of our yearly observances of Christmas and Easter. These events we celebrate as the people of God. But do we also have times to remember those moments of personal deliverance—when God has interacted with us as individuals? These are important times in our lives, too.

All of us have experienced specific moments of salvation. There was that moment in time when we gave ourselves in faith fully to our Lord and received the blessing of His forgiveness and His Spirit. Do we have that date marked on our calendar so we can once again lift up our hearts in gratitude and praise? We can think of times of crisis when God mercifully delivered us. Consider making a calendar recalling these moments of deliverance They are too precious to lose in the multitude of events that crowd our lives.

Weekday Problems

Shirley dug her cell phone from her purse and glanced at the caller ID. She wasn't surprised to find Miranda's name there. She was expecting the call. Shirley took a deep breath. These conversations with Miranda were always difficult. Shirley loved her friend, but she had a way of letting problems send her into a panic. This time it was Miranda's supervisor who—as Miranda saw it—was making unreasonable demands on her. Finally Miranda grew frustrated and asked, "Aren't you going to say anything?"

Shirley replied, "Let me just ask a question. When is the last time God helped you with a problem?"

"What?" Miranda asked, "You know God has helped me lots of times."

"Yes," Shirley continued, "But tell me the last time. Be specific. Maybe the best thing you can do tonight is to sit quietly and list as many times as you can remember when God has helped you through a crisis. Pray over that list, and then give Him your current problem. Go to bed, get some sleep, and face tomorrow with the confidence He will help you again."

*Do you think Shirley's advice was good? If so, why?

*Have you ever practiced this kind of confidence in God's continuing care?

Fast Feasting

Little Johnny had returned from a birthday party. His mother, apprehensive lest his appetite might have overcome his manners, asked, "Are you sure you didn't ask Mrs. Eldridge for a second piece of cake?"

"Oh I'm sure," said Johnny. "I only asked her for the recipe so you could make a cake just like it, and she insisted on giving me two more pieces!"

* * *

Billy wouldn't eat, and the psychologist was so desperate he said, "I'll eat half a plate of worms if you will." And he did.

Billy, however, burst into tears, saying, "But you ate my half!"

* * *

"Oh what lovely pearls," the rather arrogant woman said at the dinner party. "I suppose they're genuine. Let me bite one, and see."

"Sorry, dear," said her dinner partner. "That method requires genuine teeth."

447

This Lesson in Your Life

This scripture details God's command that the children of Israel remember the exodus by observing the Passover each year. In the passage, God is specific about the time of year for the feast, the offering of the sacrifice, and the eating of unleavened bread. But the detail most emphasized is the place for the observance. It was to be in a place "that the LORD God would choose" (16:6,7). Israel was not at liberty to select a place of their choice to worship God in the Passover. It was to be ordained by God Himself.

In John 4 we read of a discussion between Jesus and a Samaritan woman about the proper place of worship. The Samaritans maintained that God's chosen place of worship was the Mount Gerizim—the mountain near Jacob's well where Jesus and the woman were talking. The Jews, on the other hand, said the chosen place of worship was the city of Jerusalem. The woman wanted to know which was correct. In Jesus' reply, He indicated that the proper place was Jerusalem, but He added that even that was changing. The "place" that God was now calling people to worship Him was "in Spirit and truth."

The phrase "in Spirit and truth" has been much discussed. We are tempted to interpret this phrase as meaning that we should worship God sincerely. But it is a deeper and richer phrase than that. Throughout John's Gospel, Spirit and truth are identified with Jesus himself. And in the opening of the Gospel, John announced that in Jesus the Word had become flesh and "tabernacled" (or "lived") among us. With the coming of Jesus, the site of true worship to God changed from a place to a person. The only way we can offer acceptable worship to God is through His Son Jesus.

When we read God's careful instructions to Israel about worship, we realize how important worship is in the lives of God's people. Though we no longer are called to go to a specific geographical place to worship, we are, nonetheless, called to take the command to worship very seriously in our lives. Consistent worship is the lifeblood of God's people. Without it, we are in danger of forgetting His gracious gift of salvation. Without it, we are in danger of losing the needed fellowship and encouragement of fellow believers. This is why the writer of Hebrews admonished his readers not to neglect meeting together but to encourage each other as they saw the Day approaching (Heb. 10:25). We can be grateful that we no longer are asked by God to make long pilgrimages to worship Him. Our access to worshiping Him in the name of His Son Jesus is as near to us as gathering with other Christians. Let us not interpret this gracious provision of God as a softening of His call to us to worship. Let us seek every opportunity to gather in "solemn assembly" to lift up our hearts in gratitude to Him—knowing full well that in doing so we are being empowered to live our lives to His glory.

1. In what month were the Israelites commanded to observe the Passover and the Feast of Unleavened Bread?

They were to observe these feasts in the month of Abib—which corresponds to our late March and early April (Deut.16:1).

2. Why did God choose the month of Abib for the Passover?

It was the month in which God brought them out of Egypt (16:1).

3. Where were the Israelites to celebrate the Passover?

They were to celebrate the Passover in the place that God would choose to place His name (16:2).

4. What were the Israelites to eat for seven days during the celebration of the feast?

They were to eat unleavened bread for seven days (16:3).

5. Why was this kind of bread chosen for them to eat?

Unleavened bread (called the "bread of affliction") reminded them that they left Egypt in haste. They had not had time to let their bread rise (16:3).

6. Where were the Israelites not allowed to offer the sacrifice of the Passover?

They were not allowed to sacrifice the Passover within any of their gates (16:5).

7. How much of the Passover sacrifice were the people told to eat?

They were told to eat the entire sacrifice. None of it could remain until the morning (16:4).

8. What were the Israelites to do following the feast of the Passover?

They were to remain at the Passover all night and return to their tents in the morning (16:7).

9. What was to happen on the seventh day of the Feast of Unleavened Bread?

They were to gather in a solemn assembly (16:8).

10. What is another way they were to make the seventh day of the feast holy?

They were to do no work on the seventh day of the feast (16:8).

In Rob's Sunday School Class, they had been discussing the Passover and how holy that day had been for the children of Israel. It occurred to Rob that he could never remember having set aside an entire day as holy in his life. He had been faithful in attending church and special religious events, but he could not recall laying aside all duties of his life and giving the day to God. He decided to change that.

Rob called a friend who owned a small cabin about an hour from Rob's house and asked if he could use the cabin for a day. Then he took a vacation day from work, gathered his needed supplies, and drove to the cabin. His intent was that an entire 24-hour period—from 6 p.m. that evening until 6 p.m. the following day—would be holy time.

He arrived at the cabin excited about the evening that lay before him. Grabbing a sandwich and a soda, he settled into a chair to read through the Gospel of John—his favorite New Testament book. He followed his reading time with prayer—spending more time talking to God than he had in the past month. Finishing his prayer time, he glanced at his watch. It was 8:30. Now what? For the first time, it occurred to him that he did not know how to spend so much time with God. He realized that even while he was reading and praying, he was constantly finding his mind wandering back to work and to projects he needed to do around the house. How does a person learn to be still in the presence of God?

As he picked up his Bible to once again read, a small booklet fell from it to the floor. It was a copy of Brother Lawrence's *Practicing the Presence of God* that a friend of his had given to him. He had never taken the time to read it, but now time was something he had. He settled back into his chair and let the gentle writer instruct him on enjoying the presence of God in the simplest of tasks and being aware of sharing all moments of his life with God's holy presence. As he read, he began to realize that while he was dedicating this day to God, he was still in control of the agenda. He had prayed for almost an hour, but he had done all the talking. How could God speak if he was not willing to listen? For perhaps the first time in his life, Rob listened. As he grew quiet, he became deeply aware that he was not alone in the isolated cabin. He heard no voice, but he learned much about the love that God had for him.

Following a restful night of sleep, Rob spent the next morning and afternoon with God. He walked with Him through the woods. He enjoyed lunch with Him on the porch. He read His word again in the Gospel of John and discovered a message of peace and comfort he had never found before. His day ended much too quickly, but he packed the car to leave with the conviction that holy time would become a regular part of his life. He was only beginning to learn what God had told his people long ago—"Be still and know that I am God."

God Calls People to Special Service

Lev. 8:1-13

And the LORD spake unto Moses, saying,

2 Take Aaron and his sons with him, and the garments, and the anointing oil, and a bullock for the sin offering, and two rams, and a basket of unleavened bread;

3 And gather thou all the congregation together unto the door of the tabernacle of the congregation.

4 And Moses did as the LORD commanded him; and the assembly was gathered together unto the door of the tabernacle of the congregation.

5 And Moses said unto the congregation, This is the thing which the LORD commanded to be done.

6 And Moses brought Aaron and his sons, and washed them with water.

7 And he put upon him the coat, and girded him with the girdle, and clothed him with the robe, and put the ephod upon him, and he girded him with the curious girdle of the ephod, and bound it unto him therewith.

8 And he put the breastplate upon him: also he put in the breastplate the Urim and the Thummim.

9 And he put the mitre upon his head; also upon the mitre, even upon his forefront, did he put the golden plate, the holy crown; as the LORD commanded Moses.

10 And Moses took the anointing oil, and anointed the tabernacle and all that was therein, and sanctified them.

11 And he sprinkled thereof upon the altar seven times, and anointed the altar and all his vessels, both the laver and his foot, to sanctify them.

12 And he poured of the anointing oil upon Aaron's head, and anointed him, to sanctify him.

13 And Moses brought Aaron's sons, and put coats upon them, and girded them with girdles, and put bonnets upon them; as the LORD commanded Moses.

July 19

Memory Selection
Lev. 8:12

Background Scripture
Lev. 8:1-13

Devotional Reading
Rom. 11:33–12:2

Most religions have a priesthood—a system that functions both to provide access to the deity who is worshiped, and to see that this worship is done in the way the deity wishes. Today's focus is on the early Israelite priesthood under Aaron, its first "director of priests."

This lesson may seem somewhat foreign to Christians with a strong Protestant background, whose training includes an emphasis on "the priesthood of all believers." The teacher will need to recall the *setting*, which is the very beginning of worship under the Law of Moses. The rich finery of the priests' garments described here was needed to distinguish Moses' way from life in Egypt. The priesthood of all believers will come some 500 years later.

ഇരു

For a Lively Start

You can introduce this lesson by describing the sharp difference in religion as described by C. S. Lewis: (1) Some religion is *"clear."* It seeks to explain all mysteries, and give straightforward answers to all questions. Above all, it must *make sense.* (2) Other approaches to religion are *"thick."* For these worshipers, God Himself is an unfathomable mystery. He is best approached not by seeking answers but by encouraging awe.

The book of Leviticus is more *thick* than *clear.* Elaborate priestly garments encourage awe more than providing answers. *Which kind of religion appeals to you most?* By the way—Lewis himself thought both approaches are essential. It shouldn't be "either/or," but "both/and." He finished his comments on this topic by saying, "Let us pray for each other."

Teaching Outline	Daily Bible Readings
I. Gathering for Ordination—1-5	Mon. We Are God's *Ps. 100*
A. Candidates for priests, 1-2	Tue. Sanctify the Congregation *Joel 2:12-16*
B. Assembly's ordination, 3-5	
II. Garments of Ordination—6-9	Wed. The Ministry of Generosity *2 Cor. 9:6-12*
A. Binding, 6-7	Thu. Doing the Father's Will *Matt. 21:28-32*
B. Adorning, 8-9	
III. Anointing, Sanctifying—10-13	Fri. Present Your Bodies *Rom. 11:33–12:2*
A. Of altar and vessels, 10-11	Sat. The Example of Christ *Rom. 15:1-6*
B. Of Aaron and clothing, 12-13	Sun. Consecrated for Service *Lev. 8:1-13*

Verse by Verse

I. Gathering for Ordination—1-5
A. Candidates for priests, 1-2

1 And the LORD spake unto Moses, saying,

2 Take Aaron and his sons with him, and the garments, and the anointing oil, and a bullock for the sin offering, and two rams, and a basket of unleavened bread;

Previous references have gone into great detail describing the garments of the high priests and of lesser priests (see Exod. 28–29). The present passage therefore does not repeat the description of the garments in as much detail, but describes the *ordination* or appointment to official capacity of the priests who wore them.

In Old Covenant Scriptures such as these, Christians instinctively look for New Covenant parallels. In this case, however, the New Testament references in general show more *differences* than *similiarities* between these priestly adornments and any New Testament parallels. Their general effect,

for example, is to show the *distance* between the priests and the ordinary Hebrew worshiper, while the New Testament is concerned to elevate all worshipers to the priesthood (Rev. 1:6). This emphasis was of course needful for worshipers just coming out of more than 400 years' captivity among pagan worshipers. It was necessary to show the holiness of the one true God and His mediators, or priests (see 2 Sam. 2:6-7). In contrast, the followers of Christ were urged to consider themselves Christ's brothers and sisters (Mark 3:35).

Still, the value of this kind of study is obvious. God is still as worshipful as ever. Especially in a day when many Christians not only "dress down" on Friday at the office but on Sunday at church, and in general seem to consider Jesus as a "cool dude" instead of Alpha and Omega, King of kings and Lord of Lords, and our high priest, a lesson reminding us of how primitive

Hebrews honored Him in the way they dressed their priests is certainly appropriate.

Verse 2 describes the primary elements needed for ordaining Aaron as high priest and his sons as lesser priests—the anointing oil ("anointing" being from the same word as "Messiah," reminding us that as Messiah, Jesus is "the anointed One"); a bull and two rams for the live offerings, and a basket of unleavened bread.

B. Assembly's ordination, 3-5

3 And gather thou all the congregation together unto the door of the tabernacle of the congregation.

4 And Moses did as the LORD commanded him; and the assembly was gathered together unto the door of the tabernacle of the congregation.

5 And Moses said unto the congregation, This is the thing which the LORD commanded to be done.

Although God had from the beginning chosen Aaron as second in command, it was necessary for the people to ordain him as high priest before the regular worship could begin, establishing a "democratic" note even while describing a hierarchy in worship. Note that they gather at the door of the "tabernacle," indicating that they are now worshiping in the holy "tent of meeting," the "portable temple" which those Hebrews consigned to wandering in the wilderness for 40 years used for worship.

Verse 5 becomes a refrain repeated continually throughout the passage. It emphasizes the fact that the ordination of the priests itself is *not* a democratic idea thought up and voted on by the people. It is commanded by the Lord to be done; so they did it.

II. Garments of Ordination—6-9
A. Binding, 6-7

6 And Moses brought Aaron and his sons, and washed them with water.

7 And he put upon him the coat, and girded him with the girdle, and clothed him with the robe, and put the ephod upon him, and he girded him with the curious girdle of the ephod, and bound it unto him therewith.

Some scholars think that washing the priestly candidates with water is a forecast of Christian immersion for baptism. While possible, this seems unlikely in a desert environment far different from the settings of most New Testament baptisms, where rivers and water holes were much more prevalent.

The items in verse 7 were bestowed upon the high priest alone. Some of the terms come from various Canaanite languages; and which ones would be kept in Hebrew worship is problematic. The "coat" is translated "tunic" in the NIV, and the difference between this and the "robe" is debated. This difficulty of translation is present in almost every one of these elements, although the girdle (NIV "waistband") seems clear enough.

The "ephod" is one of the more striking elements of dress. It was apparently an ornamental piece or sleeveless garment onto which 12 precious stones were woven. The stones were woven into fine linen of gold, blue, purple and scarlet, and set in four rows of three stones each, representing the 12 tribes of Israel (see Exod. 28:17-21). The ephod, or something like it, was not only a part of the high priest's ceremonial wear; it could also be used as an oracle which sometimes divined God's will (1 Sam. 30:7-10); or even, when true spirituality was at a low ebb, an almost magical accompaniment for idols (Judg. 18:14ff.). It was sewn into what the KJV calls a "curious" girdle, meaning "well- "or "cunningly" woven.

B. Adorning, 8-9

8 And he put the breastplate upon him: also he put in the breastplate the Urim and the Thummim.

9 And he put the mitre upon his head; also upon the mitre, even upon his forefront, did he put the golden plate, the holy crown; as the LORD commanded Moses.

The breastplate was apparently considered a part of "the Lord's armor" since it was also a part of the armor or dress of many ancient soldiers (see Eph. 6:14). In the case of the priest's garments, it probably was worn as a covering of the precious stones in the ephod.

No one knows for sure what the Urim and Thummin were. Some believe the words themselves mean "oracle and truth." They may have been wood or stone objects carried in a pocket that was sewn into the breastplate. They apparently were connected with perceiving God's will, for with them the breastplate was called "the breastplate of judgment," and worn over the high priest's heart. Since the words begin and end with the first and last letters of the Hebrew alphabet, some have speculated that they represent the entire word and will of God, and when used to cast lots could be counted on to reveal His will.

The "mitre" was an ornamental headpiece, set off royally by a golden plate on which was engraved with the words "HOLINESS TO THE LORD" (Exod. 28:36).

III. Anointing, Sanctifying—10-13

10 And Moses took the anointing oil, and anointed the tabernacle and all that was therein, and sanctified them.

11 And he sprinkled thereof upon the altar seven times, and anointed the altar and all his vessels, both the laver and his foot, to sanctify them.

12 And he poured of the anointing oil upon Aaron's head, and anointed him, to sanctify him.

13 And Moses brought Aaron's sons, and put coats upon them, and girded them with girdles, and put bonnets upon them; as the LORD commanded Moses.

With the complex garments fitted on Aaron and the other priests, Moses finally anoints them, as well as the tabernacle, its furnishings, and Aaron's foot, with oil made of various precious ground spices (see Exod. 30:23-25). The anointing oil represented "sanctification," or being set apart for God's special use. This is a good definition of the priests and their duties, so verses 12-13 also describe the anointing and sanctification of the priests.

Evangelistic Emphasis

Our text for today describes the ordination of Aaron and his sons as priests before God for the benefit of the people of Israel. To serve as a priest is to be a bridge between God and people. In fact, the word "pontiff"—another word for priest—has the same root as our word "pontoon."

Under the Old Covenant, Aaron and his descendents served as priests for the people of God with one priest being designated "high priest." Under the New Covenant, we have been given a perfect high priest—Jesus Christ (Heb. 5:8-10). And now every believer is called to fulfill the role of priest (1 Pet. 2:9). How do we function as priests un-der our covenant with God? One way is to see ourselves as bridge builders.

We do this through living holy lives that display the blessings of being who God intended us to be. We serve as priests when we find opportunity to speak His word of love and forgiveness. We build bridges between God and people when we minister to those who are hurting and bring His comfort and peace. And, just as importantly, we fulfill our calling as priests when we hold our fellow human beings up before our heavenly Father.

Most of us are faithful in praying for family and friends. Can we expand our priesthood to pray for those for whom few—if any—ever pray? As faithful priests, let us bring before God the names and the struggles of some who might never be mentioned in the throne room of our Father unless we think to lift them up.

೫ೲ

Memory Selection

(Moses) poured of the anointing oil upon Aaron's head, and anointed him, to sanctify him.— *Leviticus 8:12.*

The anointing of Aaron sanctified him. To be sanctified means to be set apart from what is common to serve God in a special way. Under the New Covenant we read of the early Church setting aside people for special purposes (cf. Acts 13:1-3; 1 Timothy 4:14). Most churches continue the practice of ordaining special servants to minister among the people of God; and in one sense, all believers have received the anointing of the Holy One (1 Jn. 2:20) and should have an awareness of being in God's service.

Items that Aaron would use in his ministry were sanctified as well. The altar, the basin, and all the utensils he would need as a priest were sprinkled with the anointing oil. Certainly Christians respect our copy of the Bible and would never use it in an unholy way. I know some Christians who have set aside a place in their home where they go to pray and to meditate on God's word. Others sanctify a portion of their income (in addition to their tithe) that will be used only in service to God. Such practices may seem strange to outsiders, but they are reminders to us that we have a calling from God to be useful for His purposes.

Weekday Problems

The annual office fishing trip was a week away, and Zach was in a dilemma. For the most part, he had always enjoyed having a few days away with some of his co-workers, but as a committed Christian Zach had always been uncomfortable with some of the activities the fishing trip included. Most of the men drank far too much. The language was beyond just being coarse or vulgar. Some of his co-workers took advantage of the nightlife in a nearby town.

The reason Zach was having second thoughts about this year was that he had recently been ordained a deacon in his church. Zach took this responsibility very seriously, and he was concerned that his going on the trip was a tacit approval of the men's behavior. Thinking back over the past trips, he could not see that his example had been effective. Maybe he should be more vocal about his disapproval—but he felt sure that would just alienate him from his co-workers. Perhaps the best thing was to find some reason to stay home this year.

*What advice would you give Zach?

*Do you think his assessment of the impact of his example was fair?

*How have you handled similar situations?

Points to Ponder... or Not

- I planted some birdseed. A bird came up. Now I don't know what to feed it.
- I had amnesia once . . . or was it twice?
- What is a "free gift"? Aren't all gifts free?
- They told me I was gullible, and I believed them.
- Teach a child to be polite and courteous, and when he grows up he'll never be able to merge onto the freeway.
- One nice thing about egotists: they never talk about other people.
- My weight is perfect for my height . . . which varies.
- The cost of living hasn't affected its popularity.
- How can there be self-help *groups*?
- If swimming is so good for your figure, how do you explain whales?
- Is it I, or do buffalo wings taste like chicken?

This Lesson in Your Life

Perhaps the best way to enter this lesson is to place ourselves in the congregation gathered at the entrance of the tabernacle. As we watch, Moses brings Aaron and his two older sons before the congregation. Moses gestures for our attention and says, "This is what the Lord has commanded to be done." We wait in silence as Moses ceremonially washes Aaron and his sons. He dresses Aaron in beautiful clothing—a tunic, a robe, an ephod, and a breastplate. Within the breastplate are the Urim and Thummin—those mysterious objects that God uses to reveal His will to the people. On top of Aaron's head, Moses places a mitre adorned with a golden crown. Then, with great reverence, Moses takes the anointing oil and anoints the tabernacle to sanctify it. He anoints the altar seven times along with all the utensils used at the altar. He anoints the basin and its base to dedicate them to the Lord. Then he pours the anointing oil on Aaron's head. We watch as the precious oil washes over his hair and down onto his beard. Aaron is consecrated to do the work of the Lord.

How would we respond to such a solemn ceremony? Surely we would realize that a momentous event has occurred in our presence.

In our informal society, only a few such rites remain. We baptize to consecrate another of God's children. We ordain a minister to sanctify a servant for work in the Kingdom. We witness wedding vows to make holy the coming together of two as one. We pray that those who have been so sanctified will take the significance of their calling to heart—that the beautiful ceremony that marks the beginning is lived out in the reality of their lives.

As we reflect on the anointing of Aaron as priest, we are struck not only by the unusual aspects of the ceremony but also by the similarity of our own experience of consecration. While we will never wear the title of "High Priest"—as that is reserved for our Lord Jesus—we are sanctified as priests before God (1 Pet. 2:9). Like Aaron and his sons, we are washed by water—the water of baptism. And we are anointed—by the Holy Spirit (1 Jn. 2:20). Some Christian traditions continue to use the symbol of oil in visualizing this anointing. We are dressed for our work, having clothed ourselves in Christ (Gal. 3:27). In Ephesians 6:11ff, Paul tells us about the armor of God that enables us to fulfill our calling.

But do we have any parallel with the Urim and Thummin, those mysterious objects that revealed the will of God to the priest? Paul certainly believed we have. He wrote to the Colossian Christians, ". . .we have not ceased praying for you and asking that you may be filled with the knowledge of God's will in all spiritual wisdom and understanding" (Col. 1:9). How blessed to be priests of God!

1. Whom did the Lord command Moses to bring before the congregation at the door of the tabernacle?

God commanded Moses to bring Aaron and his sons before the people at the tabernacle (Leviticus 8:2).

2. What items was Moses to take with him as he brought Aaron and his sons before the people?

The priestly garments, the anointing oil, a young bull and two rams, and a basket of unleavened bread (8:2).

3. What justification did Moses give to the people for assembling them at the tabernacle?

Moses said, "This is the thing which the LORD commanded to be done" (8:5).

4. What was the first thing Moses did in consecrating Aaron and his sons?

He washed them with water (8:6).

5. What garments did Moses place on Aaron?

He put a coat (tunic) on him and bound it with a girdle (sash). He then covered him with a robe and tied the ephod around him. He placed a breastplate on him containing the Urim and Thummin (8:7-8).

6. What did Moses place on Aaron's head?

He put a mitre (or turban) on his head, and on the front of the mitre he placed a golden plate as a crown (8:9).

7. What did Moses first anoint with oil?

He anointed the tabernacle and all that was in it to sanctify them (8:10).

8. How many times did Moses anoint the altar?

He anointed the altar seven times—along with its vessels, the basin, and the base of the basin (8:11).

9. How did Moses anoint Aaron?

He poured the anointing oil on his head to sanctify him (8:12).

10. What actions did Moses do to consecrate Aaron's sons?

He put coats (tunics) on them, tied girdles (sashes) around them, and placed headdresses on their heads (8:13).

We love David. We love him because of his heart for God and the courage of his faith. But we also love him because we know of his struggles, his failures, and his repentance. We can relate to David, and we find encouragement in his story.

We love Peter. Peter was bold in his faith. He was willing to step out of the boat and walk on the sea. He boldly declared that Jesus was the Christ, the Son of God. But he was also the one who denied his Lord and wept bitterly in his contrition. We can relate to Peter.

What about Aaron? In some ways, Aaron is a secondary character in the Bible. His significance is tied to his relationship to Moses. But if we stop to think about Aaron's life, we can find in him yet another reason to be encouraged that God can use us—just as he used David and Peter for his purposes.

We don't meet Aaron until he is eighty-three years old—when he is called to assist Moses by being his spokesman. Obviously Aaron was gifted in speech, and he was faithful in responding to God. We must also acknowledge his courage as he and Moses went to Pharaoh to demand the release of the Israelites. He carried the staff of God's authority—the staff that became a snake—the staff that Aaron stretched out to initiate the plagues on Egypt—the staff that budded and produced almonds. And, as we have seen in our text for this lesson, God chose Aaron as His priest before the people. There is much to admire about this man.

But there is another side of Aaron. While Moses was on Mount Sinai speaking with God, it was Aaron who yielded to the people's panic and crafted for them a golden calf to worship. Even when confronted with his sin, Aaron denied responsibility—blaming the idolatry on the people and saying that the golden calf just appeared from the fire. At this time, God was so angry with Aaron that He would have destroyed him had not Moses interceded for his brother (Deut. 9:20). And then there was the time that Aaron and Miriam were jealous of the people's devotion to Moses. "Has not the LORD spoken through us, too?" they asked (Num. 12). At least in this instance Aaron did repent and pleaded for God to remove the leprosy that had been placed on Miriam as punishment.

So, in Aaron, we have another example of a devoted yet flawed servant of God. We are thankful that God in His wisdom included in scripture accounts of Aaron's sin along with his faithfulness. In Aaron's story we can find ourselves—loving God one moment and stumbling in our weakness the next. And we find great encouragement and consolation that God could still use Aaron for His purposes. That, also, is true for us.

Lesson 8

God Calls People To Jubilee

Lev. 25:8-24

And thou shalt number seven sabbaths of years unto thee, seven times seven years; and the space of the seven sabbaths of years shall be unto thee forty and nine years.

9 Then shalt thou cause the trumpet of the jubile to sound on the tenth day of the seventh month, in the day of atonement shall ye make the trumpet sound throughout all your land.

10 And ye shall hallow the fiftieth year, and proclaim liberty throughout all the land unto all the inhabitants thereof: it shall be a jubile unto you; and ye shall return every man unto his possession, and ye shall return every man unto his family.

11 A jubile shall that fiftieth year be unto you: ye shall not sow, neither reap that which groweth of itself in it, nor gather the grapes in it of thy vine undressed.

12 For it is the jubile; it shall be holy unto you: ye shall eat the increase thereof out of the field.

13 In the year of this jubile ye shall return every man unto his possession.

14 And if thou sell ought unto thy neighbour, or buyest ought of thy neighbour's hand, ye shall not oppress one another:

15 According to the number of years

after the jubile thou shalt buy of thy neighbour, and according unto the number of years of the fruits he shall sell unto thee:

16 According to the multitude of years thou shalt increase the price thereof, and according to the fewness of years thou shalt diminish the price of it: for according to the number of the years of the fruits doth he sell unto thee.

17 Ye shall not therefore oppress one another; but thou shalt fear thy God: for I am the LORD your God.

18 Wherefore ye shall do my statutes, and keep my judgments, and do them; and ye shall dwell in the land in safety.

19 And the land shall yield her fruit, and ye shall eat your fill, and dwell therein in safety.

20 And if ye shall say, What shall we eat the seventh year? behold, we shall not sow, nor gather in our increase:

21 Then I will command my blessing upon you in the sixth year, and it shall bring forth fruit for three years.

22 And ye shall sow the eighth year, and eat yet of old fruit until the ninth year; until her fruits come in ye shall eat of the old store.

23 The land shall not be sold for ever: for the land is mine; for ye are strangers and sojourners with me.

24 And in all the land of your possession ye shall grant a redemption for the land.

July 26

Memory Selection
Lev. 25:10

Background Scripture
Lev. 25:8-24

Devotional Reading
Matt. 18:21-35

This lesson outlines a radical plan for taking care of the poor in Israel—a plan in fact so radical that there is no evidence that it was ever practiced.

The plan was called "Jubilee," which means "the year of the ram's horn." At the end of a cycle of seven "Sabbaths" of years (seven-times-seven or 49 years), a ram's horn was blown signaling the beginning of Jubilee. At that point, land that had been bought or leased was to revert to the original owner. Also, men who had "indentured" themselves, or made a contract to work for so many years to avoid poverty, were to be set free.

The lesson should emphasize the *principle* of Jubilee, and the fact that it may have been practiced in small local areas, since it was apparently never practiced widely or as a hard and fast law.

80⊗

For a Lively Start

Explain that compassion for the poor prompted God to enact the laws of Jubilees and Sabbath Years, which included several principles about which you can lead a discussion to begin this lesson. (Even though Christians are released from Moses' Law, Jesus had a heart for the poor of the land.)

1. "The land shall not be sold forever: for the land is mine;" (Lev. 25:23). Do you agree with this principle?

2. Read *Lev. 25:20-21.* If you were an ancient Israelite farmer, do you think you could trust the Lord to provide all you need during a year when you did not sow or reap?

3. Read *Lev. 25:29-42.* What is the difference between being an Israelite *bondservant* and a *slave?*

Teaching Outline	Daily Bible Readings

I. Jubilee and the Land—Lev. 25:8-13
  A. The trumpet sound, 8-9
  B. Restoration of the land, 10-13
 	
II. Jubilee and the Man—14-17
  A. Restoration of labor, 14-16
  B. The principle at work, 17
 	
III. Jubilee and the Promise—18-24
  A. What would it take?, 18-21
  B. Who owns the land?, 22-24
	Mon. Jesus' Vision of Ministry
	    Luke 4:14-19
	Tue. Forgiveness and Mercy
	    Matt. 18:21-35
	Wed. Compassion and Mercy
	    Luke 10:25-37
	Thu. Compassion for the Helpless
	    Matt. 9:35-38
	Fri. Compassion for the Bereaved
	    Luke 7:11-17
	Sat. Ministry to the Needy
	    Matt. 25:31-40
	Sun. The Year of Jubilee
	    Lev. 25:8-23,24

Verse by Verse

I. Jubilee and the Land—Lev. 25:8-13
A. The trumpet sound, 8-9

8 And thou shalt number seven sabbaths of years unto thee, seven times seven years; and the space of the seven sabbaths of years shall be unto thee forty and nine years.

9 Then shalt thou cause the trumpet of the jubile to sound on the tenth day of the seventh month, in the day of atonement shall ye make the trumpet sound throughout all your land.

Although the Law of Jubilee as it has come down to us leaves some unanswered questions, the principles behind it are both clear and unique in the history of national law. The plainest principle is to attack the problem of poverty. Although, as Jesus said, "Ye have the poor always with you" (Matt. 26:11), it is rare to have a nationwide law to minimize the number in the first place, and to give a second chance to those whose poor choices made them economically poor.

A second principle, and one that raises several unanswered questions, is in Leviticus 25:23: "The land shall not be sold for ever: for the land is mine; for ye are strangers and sojourners with me." Unfortunately the fact that this leaves some questions had prompted even biblically-minded people simply to drop the custom, instead of trying to work out the questions. As mentioned in the "Focus" section, there is no record of the Jews ever having actually put the Law of Jubilee into practice; and many Christians have never even heard about it.

On the surface, the law is simple: After every "Sabbath" (seven times) of Sabbaths, that is, after every 49th year, land is to revert to its original owner. If practiced, this would prevent the common problem of the poor working harder to have less; or, as the folksong "Sixteen Tons" has it:

463

Y'load 16 tons
And whattya get?
Another day older
And deeper in debt.

As verse 9 says, the law is also connected to the Day of Atonement, showing concern even for those among the poor who are blamed for being carelessly or even sinfully poor.

B. Restoration of the land, 10-13

10 And ye shall hallow the fiftieth year, and proclaim liberty throughout all the land unto all the inhabitants thereof: it shall be a jubile unto you; and ye shall return every man unto his possession, and ye shall return every man unto his family.

11 A jubile shall that fiftieth year be unto you: ye shall not sow, neither reap that which groweth of itself in it, nor gather the grapes in it of thy vine undressed.

12 For it is the jubile; it shall be holy unto you: ye shall eat the increase thereof out of the field.

13 In the year of this jubile ye shall return every man unto his possession.

These verses explain that the 49th year of Jubilee is to be treated as the Jews were commanded to treat the seventh day of the week, the Sabbath: no sowing or reaping or other kinds of work was to be done. Also, as verse 13 re-emphasizes, those who sold or leased land 49 years ago are to be allowed to reclaim the land. Some scholars believe, on the principle stated in verse 23 that the land belongs to God, that in practice this refers only to land that had been *leased;* it could not be sold because God owned it, not man. However, the fact is the land *was*

bought and sold, and one of the unanswered questions is how, given that situation, adequate records leading back to the *first* sale could be kept.

II. Jubilee and the Man—14-17
A. Restoration of labor, 14-16

14 And if thou sell ought unto thy neighbour, or buyest ought of thy neighbour's hand, ye shall not oppress one another:

15 According to the number of years after the jubile thou shalt buy of thy neighbour, and according unto the number of years of the fruits he shall sell unto thee:

16 According to the multitude of years thou shalt increase the price thereof, and according to the fewness of years thou shalt diminish the price of it: for according to the number of the years of the fruits doth he sell unto thee.

"Ye shall not oppress one another" is, again, the primary principle of the Law of Jubilee. However, another principle arises when we ask how we are to figure *services*, not just *goods, merchandise,* or farm produce, are to be handled, in light of changing prices from year to year and, again, how sufficient records of such transactions could be kept in a primitive society. The NIV tries admirably to offer some clarification, but at the cost of a good deal of liberty with the original text:

When the years are many, you are to increase the price, and when the years are few, you are to decrease the price, because what he is really selling you is the number of crops.

Jubilee was also to be a time of releasing *themselves himself"* as a product, as a bond-servant or slave. Actually, Jews were forbidden to enslave fellow-Jews (Lev. 25:39-42, but that code was sometimes broken (Neh. 5:1-5).

B. The principle at work, 17

17 Ye shall not therefore oppress one another; but thou shalt fear thy God: for I am the Lord your God.

Again we can see that the primary principle underlying the otherwise idealistic and confusing laws of forbidding oppression is the fact that not only the land but *people,* both the poor and the rich, are not ours to buy, sell, or oppress in any other way. The serious degree to which we are to take these laws is seen in the phrase that also starts the Ten Commandments: "I am the Lord your God."

III. Jubilee and the Promise—18-24

A. What would it take?, 18-21

18 Wherefore ye shall do my statutes, and keep my judgments, and do them; and ye shall dwell in the land in safety.

19 And the land shall yield her fruit, and ye shall eat your fill, and dwell therein in safety.

20 And if ye shall say, What shall we eat the seventh year? behold, we shall not sow, nor gather in our increase:

21 Then I will command my blessing upon you in the sixth year, and it shall bring forth fruit for three years.

It should not be too much for Jews who were delivered from Pharaoh's hand to believe that if they treat God's world right, the world will respond in kind. If they observe His judgments they shall dwell in safety (v. 18), and if they wonder what they shall eat during the seventh year, when, as in the Jubilee year, they were not to sow or reap, they were to trust that God will give us double harvest during the sixth year.

B. Who owns the land?, 22-24

22 And ye shall sow the eighth year, and eat yet of old fruit until the ninth year; until her fruits come in ye shall eat of the old store.

23 The land shall not be sold for ever: for the land is mine; for ye are strangers and sojourners with me.

24 And in all the land of your possession ye shall grant a redemption for the land.

The promise that God will provide is repeated in verse 22, and the affirmation that the land is God's in the first place is restated in verse 23.

Finally, yet another question arises as we look back over the rules and promises of this code of Sabbath years and Jubilee, and realize that it seems to apply entirely to agricultural land and its yield. It does not answer the question of whether it applies to city property—whether blocks or lots of land on which there is only a dwelling, and no crops. Still, its basic concern for the poor is a principle we can emulate in any time or place.

༄ এ৩

Evangelistic Emphasis

The Year of Jubilee, as described in Leviticus 25:8-24, is about social justice. It presents God's plan for preventing the amassing of wealth in a way that is abusive to the poor and disadvantaged. Because the Year of Jubilee was to be celebrated every 50 years, each generation lived in hope of liberation—knowing that mistakes and weaknesses of the past had not destroyed their own future.

We have no biblical record that the Jubilee year was ever literally observed, but there were at least two symbolical "Jubilees." The prophet Isaiah used Jubilee language when he described God's liberation of Israel from Babylonian captivity. "The Spirit of the Lord God is upon me," Isaiah said, "because the LORD has anointed me; he has sent me to bring good news to the oppressed, to bind up the broken hearted, to proclaim liberty to the captives, and release to the prisoners; to proclaim the year of the LORD's favor" (Isa. 61:1-2). In their return to their homeland, the Jewish people were given back their future —a symbolic Jubilee.

A few hundred years later, a young rabbi sat in a synagogue in Nazareth. He was handed the scroll of Isaiah, and he stood and read, "The Spirit of the Lord is upon me . . . ." At the completion of the reading he sat down and announced, "Today this scripture has been fulfilled in your hearing" (Luke 4:16-21). Finally, the Year of Jubilee had arrived in its fullness. Through the ministry of Jesus the poor were hearing good news, the captives were released, the blind received their sight, and the oppressed were set free.

Memory Selection

ಸಿ)ಲ.

And ye shall hallow the fiftieth year, and proclaim liberty throughout all the land unto all the inhabitants thereof: it shall be a jubilee unto you; and ye shall return every man unto his possession, and ye shall return every man unto his family.—*Leviticus 25:10*

The very thought of a Year of Jubilee—literally "the year of the trumpet," which announced the beginning of jubilee—speaks hope to the heart. No generation would be bound to suffer for the mistakes of the past generation. Any abusive power structure would be dismantled, and the oppressed would be given hope once again.

Have you ever considered how much faith would be involved in celebrating a true Year of Jubilee? Though we do not celebrate Jubilee today, we are called to be generous givers. A real concern for those who have little might require us to move beyond giving only what we do not need for ourselves. We might find ourselves needing to give that which we feel we need to provide for ourselves. To give in this way requires both faith and love on our part. God, give us a heart for Jubilee!

Weekday Problems

Jim shuffled into my office and slowly sat down in the chair. It pained me to see how weak and feeble he was. Though well into his eighties, as recently as a few months ago he had been such a vibrant man. But a series of serious health problems had taken their toll on Jim, and he was struggling with his limitations. Having started with very little, Jim had worked hard and become a very wealthy man with most of his fortune in rental properties. He had called to ask if he could come by and talk about a problem.

"I can't keep up with all the houses I have," he began, "so I've decided to sell some of them." This was good news to me because we had worried about Jim's attempts to maintain his old work schedule. "There's this one house that's a problem, though," he continued. "Good family there. They've rented from me for 20 years. I went by and visited with the man and offered to sell him the house, but he says he can't afford it. I've got another buyer for it, but the buyer wants to move his daughter into it. So, this family needs a place to live. Do you think the church can help them out? They're really good people—they just don't have much money."

I took a deep breath. Did I dare say what I was thinking? "Let me ask you a question, Jim. Over those 20 years has the family paid you more rent than the house is worth?"

"Oh, sure," Jim replied. "At least twice as much."

"Why don't you just give them the house?"

*What is it about our economic system that makes this proposal difficult for Jim to comprehend?

*Do you think it would be a just thing to do? Would you be able to do it?

Proverbs on Poverty

Poverty of possessions may easily be cured, but poverty of soul never.—*Michel E. de Montiagne*

* * *

O God! That bread should be so dear,
And flesh and blood so cheap!
　　　　　　　　—Thomas Hood

* * *

The greatest man in history was the poorest.
　　　　　　　　—*Ralph Waldo Emerson*

* * *

Poverty is the wicked man's tempter, the good man's perdition, the proud man's curse, the melancholy man's halter.
　　　　　　　　—*Edward G. Bulwer-Lytton*

This Lesson in Your Life

Through His prophets, God continually called His people to live in such a way that all people in the land were treated equitably and fairly. Through Micah he said, "What does the LORD require of you but to do justice, and to love kindness, and to walk humbly with your God?" (Micah 6:8 NRSV). And in the Year of Jubilee, God gave His people a definite way to insure that every generation had fair opportunity to prosper and provide.

When God gave Israel the land of Canaan, each family was assigned a portion of the land so that no person would be in need. Actually, as our text points out in Leviticus 25:23, the people did not become landowners but tenants. The land belonged to God. But God is well aware of the nature of our hearts. He knows that some of us will be lazy or make poor decisions with our wealth while others of us will be greedy for more than we have. Knowing that land would change hands and a poorer class would develop, God instituted Jubilee. Every 50th year the land was to be returned to the families to whom it had been assigned. In fact, any contract that transferred land from one family to another was to be drawn up with the date of the next Jubilee in mind.

While we can recognize the fairness of such a system, we are probably not surprised to learn that there is no definite record in Scripture that Jubilee was ever observed. We are people prone to acquisition, and those who have prospered from the amassing of wealth are reluctant to release it. The result is described in the old saying—"the rich become richer and the poor poorer." But before we are too critical of the people of Israel for letting their greed keep them from following the call of God, we need to examine our own lives. Are we willing to work within our system to provide opportunity for the poor and the oppressed?

On a worldwide scale, many third-world nations owe huge debts to prosperous western countries. These debts require that funds needed for infrastructure, health care, food, and schools be paid instead toward the interest on the loans. Many of these loans were given to dictators who used the funds for their own interests rather than those of the people. Even though many of the loans have been paid several times over, the interest keeps compiling—keeping the nations in poverty.

What can we as individuals do to find the spirit of Jubilee? We can make our voices heard in the political process—insisting that injustices be addressed. We can volunteer in local efforts that seek to give the disadvantaged an opportunity to share in the wealth of this nation. Most directly, we can give of our own goods—being willing to sacrifice out of our plenty to help those who are in need.

GETTING THE FACTS STRAIGHT

1. **Why was the Jubilee set to occur every 50 years?**
Seven years comprised a "Sabbath" of years. The Jubilee was to follow a cycle of seven Sabbath years (49 years; see Lev. 25:8).

2. **On what day was the Jubilee to begin?**
Jubilee began on the day of atonement—the tenth day of the seventh month (25:9).

3. **How was the beginning of Jubilee supposed to be announced to the people?**
By the blowing of a trumpet (a ram's horn; 25:9).

4. **What was returned to people in Jubilee year?**
All family land was to be returned to its original family, and any indentured servants returned to their families (25:10).

5. **What was not to be done during Jubilee year?**
They were not to plant or harvest their fields or vineyards (25:11).

6. **When land was bought, what was the limit on the time the contract would be effective?**
Land could be bought only for the amount of time remaining until the next Jubilee. The price of the land depended on the number of years it would be owned (25:15,16).

7. **What was God's promise if Israel would faithfully observe Jubilee?**
God promised they would dwell in the land in safety (25:18).

8. **What promise for provision of food did God make concerning Jubilee.**
God promised that the sixth year of the Sabbath year preceding Jubilee would provide enough food for three years (25:19).

9. **Why could land not be sold forever?**
The land could not be sold forever because it belonged to the Lord.

10. **What did God encourage the people to think about themselves as they lived in the land.**
God reminded the people that they were strangers and sojourners with God (25:23).

I remember hearing a story of a group of migrant workers who would celebrate the end of harvest with a festive party. Days of planning went into the event. With decorations fashioned out of simple materials, they were able to create an atmosphere that revived memories of their homeland. Each family brought heaping dishes of their favorite foods. Dancing and laughter filled the room as they savored the few weeks of rest that lay before them. The highlight of the evening was the drawing for a treasured prize—a round trip airline ticket home. Every worker who contributed $50, a sacrificial sum, could write his or her name on a slip of paper for the drawing. This was their one chance to visit family and friends.

One particular year they invited a local foreman to attend their celebration. The foreman had befriended many of the workers and had even helped one man receive proper medical treatment following an injury. The foreman, accustomed to seeing the workers toil and sweat under an unrelenting sun, enjoyed seeing them having such a good time together. When the time for the drawing arrived, the workers asked the foreman to do the honors. He was flattered—knowing how important this moment was for each of them. As he stepped up on a chair and held the bowl containing the names of the workers, his eyes came to rest on Oscar. Oscar was older than most of the laborers and was no longer as productive in the fields as his younger friends. But Oscar was loved by all for his kindness and compassion. Oscar was faithful in sending most of his salary to his family—keeping for himself only enough to survive. The foreman knew that it had been many years since Oscar had been home, but he wondered if Oscar had enough money even to buy a chance at the trip.

The foreman dipped his hand into the bowl and rifled through the paper slips—realizing that each one represented so much hope. He selected one, removed it from the bowl, and unfolded it. He couldn't believe his eyes. There, printed in bold letters was the name "Oscar." With tears forming in his eyes, he found enough voice to say, "The winner is . . . *Oscar!*" The room erupted into cheers. The workers and their families rushed to Oscar and hugged him. Oscar collapsed into their arms in disbelief—his own tears streaking his smiling face.

As the party began to wind down, the foreman was helping to clean up. He took the bowl with the remaining names to empty it into the trash. But something led him to select another slip and read it. "Oscar," it said. He began going through the bowl reading all the slips. Each one read, "Oscar." Now his tears flowed freely—tears celebrating such sacrificial love that would give up something so dear to bless the life of one humble man.

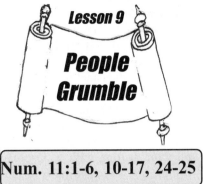

Lesson 9

People Grumble

Num. 11:1-6, 10-17, 24-25

And when the people complained, it displeased the LORD: and the LORD heard it; and his anger was kindled; and the fire of the LORD burnt among them, and consumed them that were in the uttermost parts of the camp.

2 And the people cried unto Moses; and when Moses prayed unto the LORD, the fire was quenched.

3 And he called the name of the place Taberah: because the fire of the LORD burnt among them.

4 And the mixt multitude that was among them fell a lusting: and the children of Israel also wept again, and said, Who shall give us flesh to eat?

5 We remember the fish, which we did eat in Egypt freely; the cucumbers, and the melons, and the leeks, and the onions, and the garlick:

6 But our soul is dried away: there is nothing at all, beside this manna, before our eyes.

10 Then Moses heard the people weep throughout their families, every man in the door of his tent: and the anger of the LORD was kindled greatly; Moses also was displeased.

11 And Moses said unto the LORD, Wherefore hast thou afflicted thy servant? and wherefore have I not found favour in thy sight, that thou layest the burden of all this people upon me?

12 Have I conceived all this people? have I begotten them, that thou shouldest say unto me, Carry them in thy bosom, as a nursing father beareth the sucking child, unto the land which thou swarest unto their fathers?

13 Whence should I have flesh to give unto all this people? for they weep unto me, saying, Give us flesh, that we may eat.

14 I am not able to bear all this people alone, because it is too heavy for me.

15 And if thou deal thus with me, kill me, I pray thee, out of hand, if I have found favour in thy sight; and let me not see my wretchedness.

16 And the LORD said unto Moses, Gather unto me seventy men of the elders of Israel, whom thou knowest to be the elders of the people, and officers over them; and bring them unto the tabernacle of the congregation, that they may stand there with thee.

17 And I will come down and talk with thee there: and I will take of the spirit which is upon thee, and will put it upon them; and they shall bear the burden of the people with thee, that thou bear it not thyself alone.

24 And Moses went out, and told the people the words of the LORD, and gathered the seventy men of the elders of the people, and set them round about the tabernacle.

25 And the LORD came down in a cloud, and spake unto him, and took of the spirit that was upon him, and gave it unto the seventy elders: and it came to pass, that, when the spirit rested upon them, they prophesied, and did not cease.

Aug. 2

Memory Selection
Num. 11:4-6

Background Scripture
Num. 11

Devotional Reading
Ps. 142

FOCUS

The immediate focus of this lesson is the folly of complaining about our lot simply because others have more than we do, or because we have not gained as much in this world's goods as we had expected. The example in the text is the complaint raised by he Israelites for having only manna to eat in the wilderness after they fled from Egypt.

A secondary focus is what we can do to prevent or cure this "attitude of ingratitude" when it breaks out in a community of believers as it did in the camp of the Israelites in the wilderness. In this case, Moses raised an *intercessory prayer* in behalf of the people, and *asked God for spiritual assistance*. Without a positive plan for dealing with widespread complaints, we can be guilty of simply complaining ourselves.

ಣೞ

For a Lively Start

You may want to try a change-of-pace activity to introduce this lesson: *having a time of prayer in behalf of your congregation, and for specific congregational needs.*

Regardless of a congregation's needs, every church would do well to pray to be more faithful in dealing with our opportunities. Regardless of how well we are doing with our opportunities, we would do well to pray for the ability to do better, or to perceive new works and new needs for which to pray.

Prayer sessions such as this are more fruitful when group members are given time to think about needs and opportunities facing your church. Suggest a time of silence, then select a person to open and someone else to close this time of asking "what to do about the manna."

Teaching Outline	Daily Bible Readings
I. Complaint in the Camp—11:1-6 　A. Fire from the Lord, 1-3 　B. 'Nothing but manna,' 4-6 II. Complaint from Moses, 10-25 　A. 'All is upon me,' 10-12 　B. 'It is too heavy,' 13-15 　C. Burden-bearers appointed, 　　16-17, 24-25	Mon. 'Give Heed to My Cry,' Ps. 142 　　*Ps. 142* Tue. A Test of Obedience 　　*Exod. 16:1-12* Wed. Living Bread 　　*John 6:41-51* Thu. Complaining, Turning Back 　　*John 6:60-68* Fri. Example to Instruct Us 　　*1 Cor. 10:1-11* Sat. Faith, Love, and Mercy 　　*Jude 1:14-23* Sun. Complaining About Hardships 　　*Num. 11:1-6, 10-15*

Verse by Verse

I. Complaint in the Camp—11:1-6
A. Fire from the Lord, 1-3

1 And when the people complained, it displeased the Lord: and the Lord heard it; and his anger was kindled; and the fire of the Lord burnt among them, and consumed them that were in the uttermost parts of the camp.

2 And the people cried unto Moses; and when Moses prayed unto the Lord, the fire was quenched.

3 And he called the name of the place Taberah: because the fire of the Lord burnt among them.

Since the specific complaint of the people is not recorded here, the reference is probably to the whole series of complaints that had begun even before the Israelites were well out of Egypt. It had begun when Pharaoh changed his mind about letting them go, and had pursued them while they were camped by the Reed (or Red) Sea (Exod. 14:9-

10). Despite God's dividing the water and bringing them safely through, the people complained shortly afterward when they could not immediately find suitable drinking water (15:24). Shortly afterward they complained about not have bread and meat, and the Lord provided manna and quail (Exod. 16). In each case, the Lord's case against His people was not that they were actually facing difficulty, but that there was a gradual build-up of complaints that indicated that they had not built up trust that God would provide for them, despite His consistent rescue operation. It was this pattern that eventually led God to refuse passage into the Promised Land for everyone except Joshua and Caleb—beginning a pattern of saving a "remnant" of the people.

At this point in the people's history of complaints, God seems about ready to abandon the entire nation and to destroy them with the very pillar of fire

473

that had been their guide in the wilderness. Yet, when they complain to Moses, He in turn prays to God in their behalf and the fire is quenched. This too is developing into a pattern—the "intercessory prayer" of Moses seems to be the only thing standing between the people and destruction. Although God hears Moses' prayer, he marks the place where the fire was His response to the people's complaining, calling it simply "The Burning."

B. 'Nothing but manna,' 4-6

4 And the mixt multitude that was among them fell a lusting: and the children of Israel also wept again, and said, Who shall give us flesh to eat?

5 We remember the fish, which we did eat in Egypt freely; the cucumbers, and the melons, and the leeks, and the onions, and the garlick:

6 But our soul is dried away: there is nothing at all, beside this manna, before our eyes.

This time the complainers are identified as the "mixed multitude"—probably the non-Hebrew ex-slaves that had found themselves sharing both the captivity and the release of the Hebrews, who outnumbered them. Nowhere does Scripture further identify these peoples. Secular sources mention a "Hyksos" or "shepherd" peoples whom some scholars identify as the Hebrews themselves, while others speculate that the "mixed multitude" are the Hyksos. At times their fortune rose and they found themselves, as Joseph, in leadership roles in Egypt. Whether former leaders or "rabble," they "lust" now, probably not in a sexual sense but, as the NIV says, they "crave other food"—which set the Israelites

themselves to complaining again.

This is the complaint to which God will respond by sending huge flocks of quail on a wind from off the sea, but paying for it with a plague for the attitude that brought the birds to them (11:31-33). For now, the people complain that the manna God previously sent was all they had to eat. Their displeasure takes the form of a "menu" of surprising variety which they say they enjoyed in Egypt—everything from fish to garlic (11:5). The NIV says they got all this "free"; and if this is the correct translation it indicates a very short memory, for the Hebrews paid for whatever food they received with cruel treatment and hard labor at the hands of the Egyptians.

We recall that the manna (which means "What is it?") was a flaky, white substance. Verses 7-8 seem designed to show the variety of ways it could be prepared, although to have it as the only staple in the people's diet makes complaints unsurprising.

II. Complaint from Moses, 10-17, 24-25

A. 'All is upon me,' 10-12

10 Then Moses heard the people weep throughout their families, every man in the door of his tent: and the anger of the LORD was kindled greatly; Moses also was displeased.

11 And Moses said unto the LORD, Wherefore hast thou afflicted thy servant? and wherefore have I not found favour in thy sight, that thou layest the burden of all this people upon me?

12 Have I conceived all this people? have I begotten them, that

thou shouldest say unto me, Carry them in thy bosom, as a nursing father beareth the sucking child, unto the land which thou swarest unto their fathers?

Up to now, Moses has taken the Lord's part when the people complain; but now he bursts forth with his own charges, feeling that God has left him to nursemaid a nation when he had not asked for the task.

B. 'It is too heavy,' 13-15

13 Whence should I have flesh to give unto all this people? for they weep unto me, saying, Give us flesh, that we may eat.

14 I am not able to bear all this people alone, because it is too heavy for me.

15 And if thou deal thus with me, kill me, I pray thee, out of hand, if I have found favour in thy sight; and let me not see my wretchedness.

The task of providing meat for the thousands of Israelites (some have estimated as many as 3 million) is overwhelming, and Moses finally gives vent to his feelings. He had rather die than to be try to deal with the psychological burden not only of providing for the people but of feeling that God has abandoned him. Like Job, He asks God to take his life.

C. Burden-bearers appointed, 16-17, 24-25

16 And the LORD said unto Moses, Gather unto me seventy men of the elders of Israel, whom thou knowest to be the elders of the people, and officers over them; and bring them unto the tabernacle of the congregation, that they may stand there with thee.

17 And I will come down and talk with thee there: and I will take of the spirit which is upon thee, and will put it upon them; and they shall bear the burden of the people with thee, that thou bear it not thyself alone.

God seems immediately sympathetic with Moses. He needs the assistance for which he asks. So God authorizes him to organize 70 elders and officers from among the people, wise leaders who can at least stand at the entrance of the tabernacle and listen to the list of complaints that Moses felt he was having to bear alone.

24 And Moses went out, and told the people the words of the LORD, and gathered the seventy men of the elders of the people, and set them round about the tabernacle.

25 And the LORD came down in a cloud, and spake unto him, and took of the spirit that was upon him, and gave it unto the seventy elders: and it came to pass, that, when the spirit rested upon them, they prophesied, and did not cease.

Moses does not need to be told twice that he can fulfill his request. The most telling response God could have given His servant at this time was not more food for the people but a more robust spirit. Taking a part of the Spirit of Moses and distributing it to the elders was equivalent to giving Moses a greater share, too. Remarkably, giving the elders this greater share also gives them the power to prophecy, which probably in this case includes speaking in tongues, as in the case of Saul, much later (1 Sam. 10:11).

Evangelistic Emphasis

Let's be honest. There are times that the call to spread the Good News of Jesus weighs as a burden on our hearts. We are grateful for those moments when we are carried along by the Spirit to speak freely the word of God to others. But often, we are frightened to speak or frustrated with the lack of response. We can echo the words of Moses as he dealt with the complaints of the children of Israel, "It is too heavy for me" (Num.11:14). We wish we could be released from our responsibility.

God responded to Moses' complaint by appointing 70 elders of Israel to share the Spirit who had been given to Moses. This is the second time that God had provided help for Moses in his leadership role. The appointing of the seventy also reminds us of Jesus' appointment of 70 to go and preach where He had intended to go. There was just too much to be done for any one person to bear. As Jesus sent out these men, he encouraged them by saying, "The harvest is plentiful, but the laborers are few; therefore ask the Lord of the harvest to send out laborers into his harvest" (Matt. 10:1, 2 NRSV). Isn't it interesting that even as Jesus was sending out helpers, he was telling them that they should be asking for even more laborers?

ಬಿಂಬ

Memory Selection

And the mixed multitude that was among them fell a lusting: and the children of Israel also wept again, and said, Who shall give us flesh to eat? We remember the fish, which we did eat in Egypt freely; the cucumbers, and the melons, and the leeks, and the onions, and the garlic: but now our soul is dried away: there is nothing at all, beside this manna, before our eyes. —*Numbers 11:4-6*

For some reason the voice of nostalgia always seems to be able to attract a following. It is all too easy to transform our past into something that is better than our present. When facing challenges, it is tempting to look back and wish things could be the way they once were.

This was true for the Israelites in the wilderness. Even though God had brought them miraculously through the sea, had spoken to them on Mount Sinai, and provided for their needs—now faced with difficulties—they were able to look back on their days in slavery with fondness. We too, at some point in our lives, have uttered the phrase, "If only things could be the way they were."

To fall into this attitude is to forget the struggles and problems that were in the past. But even more dangerous, it overlooks the grace of God in our lives today. As God was providing daily manna for the Israelites, they complained that they did not have an adequate diet. As God continues to bless us with his presence and grace, let us not allow the problems before us to cause us to miss His blessing.

Weekday Problems

Celina went to bed, but she couldn't sleep. The announcement by the church board at evening services still rang in her ears. The board had announced that they had voted to use the budget surplus for new carpet in the sanctuary. Celina had always been supportive of the church leaders. This time, however, she had to admit she was extremely disappointed in their decision.

Celina believed God had put on her heart the need to help with a new shelter for battered women. She had volunteered many hours at the shelter and was aware of the desperate need of the women and children who sought refuge there. The shelter needed many repairs. The plumbing was a disaster waiting to happen. Often the heater would not work. There was a troublesome leak in the roof.

Celina prayed her frustration to God. Still unable to find peace, she turned on the bedside lamp and opened her Bible. She happened to come across the story of Moses' frustration with the Israelites in Numbers 11. In the reading, God pours his Spirit on 70 elders to share in the leadership with Moses. Joshua was offended that others among the people would prophesy, but Moses replied that he wished all God's people were prophets. Was this a word to Celina? Could she dare petition to board to reconsider? Would God speak through her?

*Do you think institutional leadership sometimes forgets that God has often spoken to his people from the fringes?

*Would you advise Celina to approach the board again?

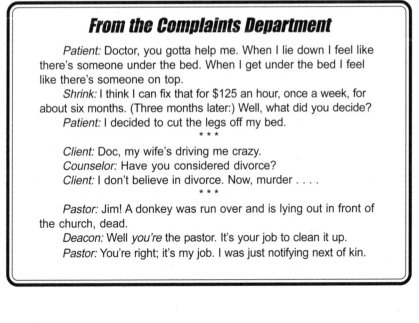

From the Complaints Department

Patient: Doctor, you gotta help me. When I lie down I feel like there's someone under the bed. When I get under the bed I feel like there's someone on top.

Shrink: I think I can fix that for $125 an hour, once a week, for about six months. (Three months later:) Well, what did you decide?

Patient: I decided to cut the legs off my bed.

* * *

Client: Doc, my wife's driving me crazy.

Counselor: Have you considered divorce?

Client: I don't believe in divorce. Now, murder . . . .

* * *

Pastor: Jim! A donkey was run over and is lying out in front of the church, dead.

Deacon: Well *you're* the pastor. It's your job to clean it up.

Pastor: You're right; it's my job. I was just notifying next of kin.

This Lesson in Your Life

Israel was complaining again. This was nothing new. Immediately after the miraculous crossing of the Red Sea, they complained that the water they had to drink was bitter (Exod.15:22). Shortly after that, they complained that they did not have enough to eat (16:2). In fact, their words echoed the words they speak in Numbers 11: "If only we had died by the hand of the LORD in the land of Egypt, when we sat by the fleshpots and ate our fill of bread" (16:3, NRSV). It seemed that every time a problem or challenge arose, Israel's first response was to complain to Moses and to God.

What is different about the story of Israel's complaining in Numbers 11 is the response of God. Previously, when the people complained, God seemed patient with them. Each time He addressed their need with a gracious act. But this time God responds differently. His anger burns against them, and He sends a fire that consumes the outer parts of the camp. And when He does send quail to satisfy the people's hunger for meat, He sends so much that it becomes a problem itself—and along with the quail He sends a plague. The people have not changed. They are still the same complainers. Why is God reacting differently than before?

Perhaps the answer lies in the timing of their complaints. When they first cried out to God for water and bread and meat, they had recently been delivered from slavery. They were still in the process of becoming God's covenant people. But the story in Numbers 11 occurs well after the people had heard the voice of God on Mount Sinai and had received the blessing of His covenant. Now they were expected to know God and to trust in His provision. In short, they were expected to know better.

It is no accident that God describes Himself to His people as Father. While He will fulfill His role as parent, the children are expected to fulfill their role as maturing children. What could be tolerated in their infancy could not be tolerated in their adolescence—and certainly not in adulthood.

We would be wise to recognize this dynamic in our churches. We must learn to be patient and nurturing with the young among us—both those who are young in years and those who are young in Christ. But those who have walked with God long enough to have experienced His mercy and His provision bear greater responsibility. When faced with difficulties, have we walked with God long enough that we can trust Him to provide? Do we have the faith and strength to speak encouragement to others rather than criticism? As David wrote, "As a father has compassion for his children, so the LORD has compassion for those who fear him. For he knows how we were made; he remembers that we are dust" (Psalm 103:13, 14 NRSV). God is a compassionate father, but He is a father that expects His children to grow up.

478

GETTING THE FACTS STRAIGHT

1. When the people complained, what was God's response?

His anger was kindled, and His fire burned the outer portions of the camp (Num. 11:1).

2. What did the people do in response to the fire?

They cried out to Moses, and Moses interceded for them. The fire was quenched (11:2).

3. Who incited the complaining of the people of Israel?

The mixed multitude that had come out of Egypt with them (cf. Exod. 12:38; 11:4).

4. What were the people complaining about?

They were remembering the variety of foods they had in Egypt and were complaining that they had no meat to eat (11:4,5).

5. What was the only food the Israelites had to eat?

All they had to eat was the manna which God provided (11:6).

6. What did the people do with the manna to prepare it for eating?

They ground it and baked it into cakes (11:8).

7. How was the manna given to the people?

It came with the dew each evening (11:9).

8. What did Moses tell God that the people had become to him?

Moses said that the people were a burden God had laid on him (11:11).

9. To what did Moses compare the people?

Moses said the people were like nursing children having to be carried to the land God had promised them (11:12).

10. What did Moses ask God to do to him?

Moses asked God to take his life so that he would not have to see his wretchedness (11:15).

Jay slipped into the back booth of the coffee shop and stared across the table at his pastor. The pastor didn't have to say anything. Jay immediately launched into a list of all the things that were bothering him. Things were not going well at work. Things were not going well at home. He was into the third day of a terrible headache. The pastor nodded sympathetically and listened until Jay finally paused to take a breath.

"Why don't we pray about all this, Jay?"

"Here?" Jay asked, looking around the coffee shop.

"I don't think anyone is near enough to hear us. Let's pray together—and why don't you pray first."

"I'd rather you prayed for me."

"I'll pray after you."

Jay knew the pastor well enough to know he wasn't going to win that argument. He bowed his head and thought for a moment—uncomfortable with his public display of piety. "Dear God," he began, "thank you for your blessings this day . . . ."

"Wait a minute, Jay," the pastor interrupted. "Is that how you really feel? Are you thankful right now?"

"Well . . . no. But I probably should be."

"True," the pastor said. "We should be thankful in all circumstances. But if you're not, you're not. Don't you think God knows how you're feeling right now? Why lie to Him?"

"I didn't think about it as lying to God. I was just trying to be nice."

"God appreciates your being nice. But He appreciates honesty more. Do you think you would be the first person ever to complain to God?"

"I don't know."

"Actually, Jay, you would be in good company. David did it. Elijah did it. Moses did it. And things worked out pretty good for them."

"But I thought people got into trouble for complaining about God."

"Maybe that's the difference. They were complaining about God rather than to God. They were complaining to everyone around them rather than expressing their frustration to the one being who could most help them through it."

"So God won't be disappointed in me?"

"I didn't say He wouldn't be disappointed in you. I just mean that if you put it out there for Him, He can work with you on it. Even if He chooses to deal with your anger in ways you wish He wouldn't, He'll bring you to a better place."

Jay shifted uneasily in the booth. "So, I'm just supposed to tell God what's really going on, huh?"

"Yes," the pastor said, "and He will be as real with you as you have been with Him."

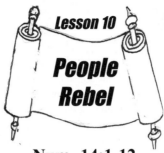

Lesson 10

People Rebel

Num. 14:1-12

And all the congregation lifted up their voice, and cried; and the people wept that night.

2 And all the children of Israel murmured against Moses and against Aaron: and the whole congregation said unto them, Would God that we had died in the land of Egypt! or would God we had died in this wilderness!

3 And wherefore hath the LORD brought us unto this land, to fall by the sword, that our wives and our children should be a prey? were it not better for us to return into Egypt?

4 And they said one to another, Let us make a captain, and let us return into Egypt.

5 Then Moses and Aaron fell on their faces before all the assembly of the congregation of the children of Israel.

6 And Joshua the son of Nun, and Caleb the son of Jephunneh, which were of them that searched the land, rent their clothes:

7 And they spake unto all the company of the children of Israel, saying, The land, which we passed through to search it, is an exceeding good land.

8 If the LORD delight in us, then he will bring us into this land, and give it us; a land which floweth with milk and honey.

9 Only rebel not ye against the LORD, neither fear ye the people of the land; for they are bread for us: their defence is departed from them, and the LORD is with us: fear them not.

10 But all the congregation bade stone them with stones. And the glory of the LORD appeared in the tabernacle of the congregation before all the children of Israel.

11 And the LORD said unto Moses, How long will this people provoke me? and how long will it be ere they believe me, for all the signs which I have shewed among them?

12 I will smite them with the pestilence, and disinherit them, and will make of thee a greater nation and mightier than they.

Aug. 9

Memory Selection
Num. 14:3

Background Scripture
Num. 14:1-25

Devotional Reading
Ps. 78:5-17

FOCUS

God has taken the Hebrews from slavery in Egypt, and destroyed the Egyptian armies that would detain them further. When they complained in the wilderness about a lack of food and good water, He led them to sweet water and fed them with the miraculous manna and quail. All His works have led them up to the moment in Number 13, when 12 spies return and give a report.

Just as God had promised, they found Canaan to be a good land. All they had to do was to depend on His leadership and the land was theirs. However, all the spies except Joshua and Caleb, quake in fear at the size of the opposition; and the people choose fear over faith. They vote to return to Egypt. This lesson shows the fruit of such fear and disobedience.

ഇറ൦

For a Lively Start

What more could we ask for than to have God on our side? You can introduce this lesson by leading a discussion that imagines the thinking of the doubters and the fearful people who say No to entering Canaan even though God promises to be on their side.

Invite the group to scan chapter 13 to pick up the thinking of these Hebrews who "vote down" Joshua and Caleb. What factors influenced their decision? What justification did they have for wanting to go back to Egypt? Can you think of similar times when we have allowed our own fear to overcome faith? How do you think Moses, Joshua, and Caleb would have felt?

Teaching Outline	Daily Bible Readings

I. Anguish and Woe—14:1-5
  A. The people, 1-4
  B. Moses and Aaron, 5
II. Appeal and Response—6-10
  A. Two spies' demand, 6-9
  B. People's rebellion, 10
III. Anger of the Lord—11-12
	Mon. Rebelling Against God
	  Ps. 78:5-17
	Tue. Reaping the Whirlwind
	  Hosea 8:1-10
	Wed. Offering for Sin?
	  Micah 6:1-8
	Thu. Mourning for Rebellion
	  Lam. 1:16-21
	Fri. Return to the Lord
	  Lam. 3:39-50
	Sat. A Compassionate God
	  Micah 7:14-20
	Sun. Return to Egypt?
	  Num. 14:1-12

Verse by Verse

I. Anguish and Woe—14:1-5

A. The people, 1-4

1 And all the congregation lifted up their voice, and cried; and the people wept that night.

2 And all the children of Israel murmured against Moses and against Aaron: and the whole congregation said unto them, Would God that we had died in the land of Egypt! or would God we had died in this wilderness!

3 And wherefore hath the LORD brought us unto this land, to fall by the sword, that our wives and our children should be a prey? were it not better for us to return into Egypt?

4 And they said one to another, Let us make a captain, and let us return into Egypt.

Except perhaps for its intensity, this exclamation of woe is almost identical to previous times when the Hebrews complained of inconveniences along the way. The level of grievance is higher here because they anticipated that they had finally reached the end of their long and arduous journey.

Chapter 13 tells in more detail what happened when the Hebrews came up to the Jordan River from the east side and sent the 12 men to spy out the land. There the focus is on the heroic role of Rahab the harlot. Here the theme is how carefully the whole nation is represented on the reconnaissance trip. The spies consist of one prominent man (KJV "ruler," 13:2) for each tribe. They spend 40 days surveying the fruitfulness of the land, returning to say "Surely it floweth with milk and honey," and displaying a huge cluster of grapes along with other fruit (13:23, 27).

What they fail to bring back from their appraisal is a positive spirit—one that shows that they trust the Lord to help them conquer the land. Only Joshua and Caleb have that spirit: "We are well able to overcome it [the land]," they say. The other 10 return telling of how much stronger the Canaanites look: "We saw in it . . . men of a great stature . . . and we were in our own sight as grasshoppers" (13:32-33).

It is this majority report that the mass of the people accept. They spend all night wailing, and the next day turn their wrath against Moses and Aaron. They say it would have been better to have died either in Egypt or the wilderness, and clamor for new leadership to lead them back into Egyptian slavery or death.

B. Moses and Aaron, 5

5 Then Moses and Aaron fell on their faces before all the assembly of the congregation of the children of Israel.

The reaction of Moses and Aaron, falling on their faces, is the recognized sign of mourning and grief, not of fear. At least if they are fearful it is of God, not the people. They know how often God has come close to destroying His own people because of their lack of faith and their fearfulness. Since the people have failed this last and greatest test, God may consider it the last straw.

II. Appeal and Response—6-10
A. Two spies' demand, 6-9

6 And Joshua the son of Nun, and Caleb the son of Jephunneh, which were of them that searched the land, rent their clothes:

7 And they spake unto all the company of the children of Israel, say-ing, The land, which we passed through to search it, is an exceeding good land.

8 If the LORD delight in us, then he will bring us into this land, and give it us; a land which floweth with milk and honey.

9 Only rebel not ye against the LORD, neither fear ye the people of the land; for they are bread for us: their defence is departed from them, and the LORD is with us: fear them not.

Caleb and Joshua, the two faithful spies, join Moses and Aaron, tearing their clothes in their grief and anguish. They reaffirm what the entire team of spies found: a land flowing with milk and honey. All that remains is for the Lord to find within the hearts of his people the heart and courage to follow Him as their leader. Unfortunately, He finds fear and rebellion instead. The size of the "giants" in the land looms larger to them than the parting of the Red Sea, the manna, the sweet water, the quail. The two stout-hearted spies beg them to remember how much greater the power of God is than the power of the Canaanites, which would be "bread" for God's people, in comparison. Whatever stories they have heard about the strength of the pagan armies across the river, that meager power has left them before the power of the God who creates nations and divides the land among whom He will. They finish their stirring speech with a battle cry: "The Lord is with us: fear them not."

B. People's rebellion, 10

10 But all the congregation bade

stone them with stones. And the glory of the LORD appeared in the tabernacle of the congregation before all the children of Israel.

Caleb and Joshua's call to arms had no effect, and the people call for them to be stoned. Little did they know what awesome defense the two loyal spies had at their command: the *"glory"* of the Lord. This is the mysterious brilliance that signifies the presence of God, before which no mere mortal could stand.

III. Anger of the Lord—11-12

11 And the LORD said unto Moses, How long will this people provoke me? and how long will it be ere they believe me, for all the signs which I have shewed among them?

12 I will smite them with the pestilence, and disinherit them, and will make of thee a greater nation and mightier than they.

Verse 11 is a rhetorical question, of course, but it signals God's impatience in trying to deal with a people who are more impressed with large soldiers (in Canaan) than they are with God's miracles such as the parting of the waters for them. God would be within His

rights to do all that he mentions in verse 12 and more. Because Moses is faithful, God is of a mind to make of him the great nation He had planned to make of Israel.

As it works out, however, Moses plays his usual role of mediator. In verses 13ff. he suggests that if God were to destroy His own people it would embarrass Him before the Egyptians. Also, the nations that heard of the event will say:

Because the LORD was not able to bring this people into the land which he sware unto them, therefore he hath slain them in the wilderness (14:16).

True to form, Moses proceeds to plead the case for his people—an especially gracious gesture in light of God's previous statement that He is willing to make of Moses a greater nation than the Israelites.

Yet, as the next lesson will show, even Moses has his errors to pay for, and of all those who left Egypt only Caleb and Joshua will be allowed to enter the prized and promised land, because of their faithfulness in believing that God could enable His people to conquer the land.

ഇരു

Evangelistic Emphasis

Following their harrowing escape from Egypt and their long journey through the wilderness, the people of Israel were finally near their goal. Before them was the Promised Land that flowed with milk and honey. Unfortunately their smoldering fears, fanned into flames by the discouragement of the 10 faithless spies, stopped them in their tracks. Moses, who had led them to the edge of promises fulfilled, fell on his face in frustration and despair. But God was faithful. Though these would not enter, He told Moses, their "little ones" would (Num.14:31).

Perhaps Jesus had this story in mind when He told the parable of the Great Banquet recorded in Luke 14:15-24. In that story, several guests were invited to a great feast. But, as the people of Israel hesitated before the feast of the Promised Land, the guests began to make excuses about why they could not attend. The host of the feast had a solution. Those invited would never eat the feast, but the "little ones"—the poor, the crippled, the blind, and the lame—would enter his house and enjoy the feast.

Not all whom we invite to attend the feast prepared by our God and Savior will respond. But we must never give in to despair to the point of abandoning our mission of inviting. God's feast *will* be enjoyed. He will not forget his promise to bring His people into the Promised Land and to welcome guests to his glorious banquet. His eye will turn to the "little ones." Let us be faithful in turning our eyes to them as well.

ෙ◌ඏ

Memory Selection

And wherefore hath the LORD brought us unto this land, to fall by the sword, that our wives and our children should be a prey? Were it not better for us to return into Egypt?—*Numbers 14:3*

Previously, God had worked with His impatient and rebellious people to move them toward Canaan. This time, however, they had pushed God's patience too far. Those responsible for this decision—those old enough to be responsible—the very ones who had seen God's power in delivering them from Egypt and preserving their lives in the wilderness—that generation would not see the Promised Land. They were violating the very first commandment of God—thou shalt have no other gods before me.

In his *Small Catechism*, Martin Luther wrote that this commandment means, "You shall fear, love and trust God above anything else." The people, however, feared the inhabitants of Canaan more than God. They loved themselves and trusted their own appraisal of the situation more than they loved God and trusted His promise. May we be among the faithful generation of hope that confidently marches forward into the land where God is leading.

486

Weekday Problems

The rapid growth and revitalization of the church had caught many of the long time members by surprise. They had grown content to be a small church occupying a stately old building near downtown. Evidently God had other plans for the church. With the arrival of a new pastor and with several Christian  families relocating to downtown to join the church, it had suddenly sprung to life. They had added more services on Sunday. Their ministry to the inner city youth kept the church open almost 24 hours a day, seven days a week. Something had to be done about the facilities. Repairs were needed, and more flexible multi-use space must be built.

The church met to discuss the possibilities. Some were excited and spoke about what God was doing and would do if they launched out in faith. Then others began expressing their doubts. They pointed out that most of the new members had little money. The church offerings had not grown nearly as rapidly as the attendance and participation. This was just not the time to consider a building project. The initial excitement of the evening began to wane.

The pastor had listened to the discussion quietly, but he had come prepared. He stood and asked if anyone knew when this old grand and glorious building had been constructed. Someone called out from the back of the room, "1932." The pastor smiled and asked, "Anyone want to talk about those times?"

*Do we ever exaggerate our fears about moving forward with God's work?

*How would you vote in this meeting?

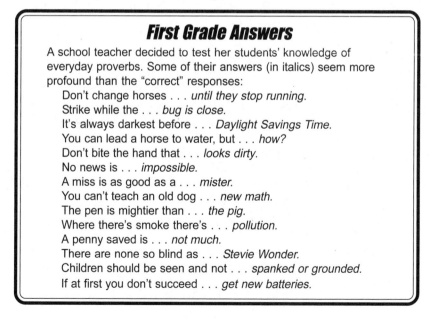

First Grade Answers

A school teacher decided to test her students' knowledge of everyday proverbs. Some of their answers (in italics) seem more profound than the "correct" responses:

Don't change horses . . . *until they stop running.*
Strike while the . . . *bug is close.*
It's always darkest before . . . *Daylight Savings Time.*
You can lead a horse to water, but . . . *how?*
Don't bite the hand that . . . *looks dirty.*
No news is . . . *impossible.*
A miss is as good as a . . . *mister.*
You can't teach an old dog . . . *new math.*
The pen is mightier than . . . *the pig.*
Where there's smoke there's . . . *pollution.*
A penny saved is . . . *not much.*
There are none so blind as . . . *Stevie Wonder.*
Children should be seen and not . . . *spanked or grounded.*
If at first you don't succeed . . . *get new batteries.*

487

This Lesson in Your Life

The people's rejection of God's Promised Land foreshadows the world's later rejection of God's Messiah, Jesus. We can always compare their lack of faith and their fear to our own. On the other hand, the example of the faithfulness of Joshua and Caleb calls us to imitate their courage and faith. Central to this story is Moses' intercession for the people.

When God announced that He intended to destroy the people of Israel and start over with Moses himself, Moses immediately opened his heart to God and pleaded for the people. This is an amazing act of humility on the part of Moses. In interceding for the rebellious nation, Moses was passing up possible glory for himself. Remember that the people were not only rejecting God, they were rejecting Moses' leadership as well. Can we find it within ourselves to pray for the benefit of those who have attacked us personally? Need we be reminded of Jesus' command to "pray for our enemies, and pray for those who persecute you" (Matt. 5:44)? Before Jesus uttered these words, Moses put them into practice with his beautiful prayer pleading for the life of Israel.

The fact that Moses would pray for these who had become his enemies stands as an example for us. Notice that Moses does not defend the worthiness of the people to be forgiven. Indeed, we cannot claim such worthiness for others or for ourselves. Moses begins by expressing concern for how others will see God himself. God had chosen the descendants of Abraham to be a blessing for all the nations, and Moses recognized that any act of mercy by God toward them would be of even greater benefit to those who saw it.

Moses also reminded God of the promises He had made to Israel and expressed faith that God was faithful in keeping His promises. He trusted in God's power to keep His word even in the face of the weakness of the people. And, finally, he called on God's steadfast love. This certainly is the only appeal we as sinners have before a righteous God. When David was overwhelmed by the evil of his sin with Bathsheba, he knew that he had nothing to offer God for forgiveness. All he could appeal to was God's love and mercy, as in Psalm 51:1 (NRSV):

Have mercy on me, O God,
according to your steadfast love;
according to your abundant mercy
blot out my transgressions.

Since we are in no position to make any claims or demands, all we can do is remind God—no, we actually remind ourselves—of who God is and why He bears with us.

GETTING THE FACTS STRAIGHT

1. When the people murmured against Moses and Aaron, what did they wish had happened?
They wished they had died in Egypt or in the wilderness (Num. 14:2).

2. What were they afraid of this time?
They feared the inhabitants of Canaan would kill them and take their wives and children as prey (14:3).

3. What plan of action did the people devise?
They wanted to elect a new leader who would take them back to Egypt (14:4).

4. How did Moses and Aaron react to this rebellion?
Moses and Aaron fell on their faces before the children of Israel (14:5).

5. What did the faithful spies Joshua and Caleb do when they heard the people's plan?
Joshua and Caleb tore their clothes and spoke to the people (14:6).

6. What did Joshua and Caleb tell the people?
They said the land was good and that the Lord would bring them into the land. They begged the people not to rebel, nor to fear the inhabitants of Canaan (14:7-9).

7. How did the congregation of Israel react to Joshua and Caleb's plea?
The people gathered stones to stone Joshua and Caleb (14:10).

8. Where did the Lord appear to the people of Israel?
The glory of the Lord appeared in the tabernacle of the congregation before all the children of Israel (11:10).

9. Why was the Lord so angry with the people for their lack of faith?
The Lord was angry because the people had ignored the many signs He had shown them (14:11).

10. What plan did God reveal to Moses in the tabernacle?
God said He would destroy the people with pestilence and make from Moses a mightier nation than they (14:12).

Three brothers received small fortunes as inheritances from their father's estate. One brother was a bold investor. He researched the stock market diligently and invested his money wisely. Soon his small fortune grew five-fold, and he was able to live comfortably and do much good for others. The second brother was more cautious. He invested in more secure bonds and high yield money market accounts. But he was able to double his funds, and he, too, was able to live comfortably and do much good. The third brother trusted no investments. He kept his money in a box in his house—carefully watching over it. Over the years, as expenses mounted, his inheritance was slowly spent until he had nothing at all.

Of course, you recognize this story as a retelling of the story Jesus told about the master and his three servants recorded in Matthew 25:14-30. We know the lesson well—that our Master expects us to use what He has given us so that it grows and becomes even more effective. It is interesting that in Jesus' story, the servant who was too fearful to invest his money was fearful because he mistrusted his master (Matt. 25:24, 25). Any reluctance on our part to use boldly what our Master has given us reflects on our faith in the Master.

God had delivered the children of Israel from the mightiest army in the world, and He had nurtured and cared for them through one of the most desolate wildernesses in the world. But as they stood on the brink of entering the Promised Land, they did not trust their Master enough to put themselves on the line. From our perspective, it is difficult to understand why they did not think that the God who had given them life and freedom would continue to bless them in their next challenge.

Or is it that difficult to understand? Certainly our master has given us much in our lives. In fact, He has given us life itself. When He calls upon us to use our gifts in His service, do we ever hold back out of fear? And isn't that fear usually fear—not of death—but of some type of ridicule or rejection that really is of small consequence? Jesus once told His disciples, "For those who want to save their life will lose it, and those who lose their life for my sake, and for the sake of the gospel, will save it" (Mark 8:35). The children of Israel turned away from the calling of God in order to save their lives—which they lost in the wilderness. Do we have enough faith to believe real life is to be found in faithfully following the Master wherever He might lead?

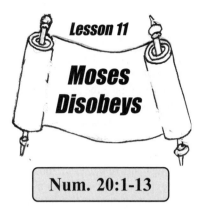

Lesson 11

Moses Disobeys

Num. 20:1-13

Then came the children of Israel, even the whole congregation, into the desert of Zin in the first month: and the people abode in Kadesh; and Miriam died there, and was buried there.

2 And there was no water for the congregation: and they gathered themselves together against Moses and against Aaron.

3 And the people chode with Moses, and spake, saying, Would God that we had died when our brethren died before the LORD!

4 And why have ye brought up the congregation of the LORD into this wilderness, that we and our cattle should die there?

5 And wherefore have ye made us to come up out of Egypt, to bring us in unto this evil place? it is no place of seed, or of figs, or of vines, or of pomegranates; neither is there any water to drink.

6 And Moses and Aaron went from the presence of the assembly unto the door of the tabernacle of the congregation, and they fell upon their faces: and the glory of the LORD appeared unto them.

7 And the LORD spake unto Moses, saying,

8 Take the rod, and gather thou the assembly together, thou, and Aaron thy brother, and speak ye unto the rock before their eyes; and it shall give forth his water, and thou shalt bring forth to them water out of the rock: so thou shalt give the congregation and their beasts drink.

9 And Moses took the rod from before the LORD, as he commanded him.

10 And Moses and Aaron gathered the congregation together before the rock, and he said unto them, Hear now, ye rebels; must we fetch you water out of this rock?

11 And Moses lifted up his hand, and with his rod he smote the rock twice: and the water came out abundantly, and the congregation drank, and their beasts also.

12 And the LORD spake unto Moses and Aaron, Because ye believed me not, to sanctify me in the eyes of the children of Israel, therefore ye shall not bring this congregation into the land which I have given them.

13 This is the water of Meribah; because the children of Israel strove with the LORD, and he was sanctified in them.

Memory Selection
Num. 20:12

Background Scripture
Num. 20:1-13

Devotional Reading
Ps. 95

Aug. 16

In one sense, the focus of this lesson is the same as in the preceding lesson, with a surprising twist as a difference. In Lesson 10 the Israelites come up to the border of the Promised Land, then because of their complaints are refused entrance. In this lesson, we are surprised by the disobedience of Moses

and Aaron, who are denied entrance into the land of Canaan.

This means that of all those who left Egypt, only Caleb and Joshua, the two faithful spies, enter the Promised Land. Aaron was buried atop Mt. Hor, south of the Dead Sea. Moses was buried tantalizingly close to Canaan, on Mt. Nebo, on the northeast tip of the Dead Sea. The bones of the rest of those who left Egypt were left strewn in the wilderness where they had wandered for 40 years.

ഇരു

was allowed into the Promised Land.

It has been widely assumed that surely they committed some other infraction for such a serious punishment to be assigned. You can introduce this lesson by leading a brief discussion in which your group speculates on whether some other infraction might have been involved. Since Scripture is silent, you can accept virtually any answer, but encourage the answers to be as reasonable as possible.

For a Lively Start

God told Moses to "take (his) rod" and "*speak* ye unto the rock" apparently to reveal a hidden spring for life-saving water for the Israelites. Instead, he *struck* the rock with his rod—not once, but twice, and apparently with Aaron's help. For this, neither leader

Teaching Outline	Daily Bible Readings
I. Miriam's Death—1:1	Mon. Small Rebellion *Num. 20:22-29*
II. More Complaints, 2-5	Tue. Tested at Meribah *Ps. 81:1-10*
A. 'Would we had died!' 2-3	Wed. 'Do not Harden Your Hearts *Ps. 95*
B. No fruit, no water , 4-5	Thu. 'Trust in the Lord' *Jer. 17:5-10*
III. Moses' Response, 6-11	Fri. Foundation of Faith *Matt. 16:13-18*
A. Prayer, 6	Sat. Water for the Thirsty *Rev. 21:1-7*
B. Instructions for water, 6-8	Sun. Result of Doubting *Num. 20:1-13*
C. Actual reaction, 9-11	
IV. Meribah's Tragedy, 12-13	

Verse by Verse

I. Miriam's Death—1:1

1 Then came the children of Israel, even the whole congregation, into the desert of Zin in the first month: and the people abode in Kadesh; and Miriam died there, and was buried there.

The Israelites were nearing the end of their 40-year sentence of wandering in the desert country north of Mt. Sinai. God therefore now leads them northeastward, retracing the route they took before they sent the 12 spies into Canaan, and rejected the favorable report of Caleb and Joshua in favor of the less courageous recommendation of the 10, which had resulted in the punishment of the Wilderness Wandering. They are in the Rift Valley that includes Kadesh and the Desert of Zin, south of the Dead Sea, when Miriam, Moses' sister dies.

The sister of both Moses and Aaron, Miriam has had a colorful and fruitful life. It was Miriam who had tended to the infant Moses in the pitch-sealed basket among the rushes of the Nile, and who saved his life by telling Pharaoh's daughter about him (Exod. 2:5-10). A prophetess, it was Miriam who had led Israelite maidens in singing the song that celebrated the escape from Egypt through the dry ground of the Red Sea (Exod. 15:20-21). Her life had not been without its down side as well, as when she was smitten with leprosy for criticizing Moses after he had married an Ethiopian woman (Num. 12:1ff.). Unfortunately, none among this remarkable family will enter the Promised Land that had been their zealous dream for so many years.

II. More Complaints, 2-5
A. 'Would we had died!' 2-3

2 And there was no water for the congregation: and they gathered themselves together against Moses and against Aaron.

3 And the people chode with Moses, and spake, saying, Would God that we had died when our brethren died before the LORD!

Once more the people complain to Moses and Aaron about the lack of water. They chided (KJV "chode") Moses as though he is the one who makes deserts short on water. Also once more, they forget the hardships of life as slaves in Egypt, when so many of their brethren died, foolishly adding that they would choose that over their present situation. Apparently both God and Moses are reaching the breaking point over this pattern. The people's complaint, ". . . when our brethren died before the LORD," seems to overstate the piety that characterized their life in Egypt, when most of them had hardly, if at all, known the Lord.

B. No fruit, no water , 4-5

4 And why have ye brought up the congregation of the LORD into this wilderness, that we and our cattle should die there?

5 And wherefore have ye made us to come up out of Egypt, to bring us in unto this evil place? it is no place of seed, or of figs, or of vines, or of pomegranates; neither is there any water to drink.

The people's over-stated piety continues as they describe themselves as "the congregation of the LORD," when in fact Moses and Aaron have had their hands full even to coax them to live differently from the pagans about them, and to be grateful to the Lord, and to Moses and Aaron, for leading them out of Egypt. All Moses had to do was leave them momentarily to go up on the mountain to receive the Law for them to have an orgy in honor of a golden calf. Although there had been some dissenters who voiced objections to following Moses in the first place, most of the people had given their approval for this opportunity to escape their captors. Now they want pomegranates!

III. Moses' Response, 6-11

A. Prayer, 6

6 And Moses and Aaron went from the presence of the assembly unto the door of the tabernacle of the congregation, and they fell upon their faces: and the glory of the LORD appeared unto them.

Instead of rebuking the people for their complaint, Moses' and Aaron's first response is to throw themselves before the Lord in prayer. As a result, the mysterious "glory of the Lord" makes itself visible to them, as though to reassure them of God's support. This "glory" (Heb. *kabod*) was originally a weight, then a way to describe the "weightiness" of God's power and glory. It is a sign that something powerful is about to break loose before the complaining and rebellious people claiming to be "the congregation of the Lord."

B. Instructions for water, 7-8

7 And the LORD spake unto Moses, saying,

8 Take the rod, and gather thou the assembly together, thou, and Aaron thy brother, and speak ye unto the rock before their eyes; and it shall give forth his water, and thou shalt bring forth to them water out of the rock: so thou shalt give the congregation and their beasts drink.

Once more the miraculous rod of Moses is about to be put to use, although it is important to note that God only tells Moses and Aaron to pick it up and speak with it in their hands, not to hit anything with it. Whatever they are to do with it, God promises that it will provide enough water for both man and beast. Perhaps there is a spring just under or within the rock, or perhaps it is a miracle, pure and simple.

C. Actual reaction, 9-11

9 And Moses took the rod from before the LORD, as he commanded him.

10 And Moses and Aaron gathered the congregation together before the rock, and he said unto them, Hear now, ye rebels; must we fetch you water out of this rock?

11 And Moses lifted up his hand, and with his rod he smote the rock twice: and the water came out abundantly, and the congregation drank, and their beasts also.

In view of the millions that some scholars envision the Israelites numbering, the rock they stand before must be huge. Not mincing words, Moses calls them "rebels," using a word that refers to people who habitually provoke others—a fitting description when one adds up the times they have raised complaints to their leaders. Apparently they have provoked Moses to his limit. Having been told only to "speak" to the rock, he strikes it—not once, but twice. This has the desired immediate consequences, providing water for both man and beast; but the unauthorized longterm effect of the method Moses uses is tragic.

IV. Meribah's Tragedy, 12-13

12 And the LORD spake unto Moses and Aaron, Because ye believed me not, to sanctify me in the eyes of the children of Israel, therefore ye shall not bring this congregation into the land which I have given them.

13 This is the water of Meribah; because the children of Israel strove with the LORD, and he was sanctified in them.

Surely there is more at stake here than God's ego in wanting His methods followed precisely. The most obvious possibility is that the people need a cure for their continual lack of respect for God, and for His word and will. Perhaps only *speak*ing to the rock will have this "sanctifying" effect. Another unanswered question is Aaron's role in what seems to us to be a minor infraction but what apparently has more to do in the way of trust and obedience than meets the eye.

Whatever is at work, it represents *striving* with or disobedience to God, and it is serious enough to name it. "Meribah" whih means a provocation or deliberate strife. Of course the real seriousness of the infraction is that it costs Moses and Aaron the privilege of entering the Promised Land, after all their efforts. Moses is buried atop Mt. Nebo, to the northeast of the Dead Sea—and, more importantly, outside the borders of Canaan. Aaron, after having his priestly garments given to his son Eleazar, is buried with honors on Mt. Hor, far to the south of the Dead Sea (Num. 20:25-29).

Evangelistic Emphasis

Many people, when they hear someone described as an "evangelist," visualize a man or woman dressed in expensive clothes, sporting a stylish hairdo, preaching in a large auditorium filled with thousands of people. Sometimes it seems that such evangelists enjoy their powerful position and thrive on the attention of the crowd. Certainly anyone who has been put into the position of bringing the Word of God to large crowds could attest to the temptation of pride—the tendency to focus on self rather than on the message of God.

Jesus encouraged His disciples not to hide their light but to let it be seen (Matt. 5:16). However, the purpose of the light was to bring glory to God, not to the light bearer. As good lighting is essential in an art gallery, it becomes a distraction if patrons notice the light rather than the beauty of the art.

As this story in the life of Moses demonstrates, even the best of God's servants can take their eyes off God and look to their own glory. As we bear God's word, we must realize the danger of self-focus. If our attention is on ourselves and our message is received in faith, we are in danger of being filled with pride. Then, if our message is rejected, we are in danger of being filled with despair and discouragement. Our commission is to carry the Word of God and trust that the power is in God and His word—as is the glory.

ഈോരു

Memory Selection

And the LORD **spake unto Moses and Aaron, "Because ye believed me not, to sanctify me in the eyes of the children of Israel, therefore ye shall not bring this congregation into the land which I have given them."**—*Numbers 20:12*

We find it difficult to accept that Moses would be punished after faithfully leading the children of Israel out of Egypt and through the wilderness. We must trust that God could see Moses' heart and the punishment was just. This story serves to remind us of an important truth we may have forgotten as we have studied the remarkable career of Moses as leader of the people. The truth is that Moses was a human being—a flawed, sometimes weak, struggling human being. The mighty works performed through him were not of his own doing. They were the work of a God who can use flawed, sometimes weak, struggling human beings to accomplish His will.

This event in the life of Moses reminds us always to give God the glory in any great work that is done. However, maybe even more important for most of us, the story reminds us that God can use flawed individuals to do mighty things. Even though Moses made his mistakes, the people were given water by God. It's usually not that God finds us too weak to be useful to Him—rather, he finds us too proud.

Weekday Problems

Allen and Ray met for dinner before the committee meeting at church. For the most part, the conversation was positive. This was a relief to Ray because he sometimes grew weary of Allen's tendency to be negative. But in the car, Allen brought up one his favorite subjects to complain about—the pastor. He felt the pastor was a control freak and that his ego was too big. Ray listened patiently. He knew it was useless to argue with Allen about this.

After the meeting, however, on the way home, Allen was on the topic again. He accused the comittee chairman of not listening to the other members. "He just wants to do things his way all the time," Allen said.

"You know, Allen," Ray responded. "I once read something by C. S. Lewis that really helped me in situations like this. Lewis said that the only thing that is offended by the pride of another is our own pride."

"What do you mean by that?" Allen asked.

"What it meant to me is that when I'm bothered by something someone is doing, I need to stop and ask if it's because that same fault is in me."

"So, you think I want to be in control of everything? Is that what you're saying?" Allen snapped.

"Just sharing something I learned about myself," Ray responded.

*Do you think that Allen might have a control problem himself?

*Have you ever thought about what bothers you most in other people and had the courage to look for those things in yourself?

Overdue Statements

- The dead batteries were given out free of charge.
- If you take a laptop for a run you could jog your memory.
- A dentist and a manicurist fought tooth and nail.
- A bicycle can't stand alone because it's two tired.
- A will is a dead giveawayl
- A backward poet writes inverse.
- A chicken crossing the road is poultry in motion.
- If you don't pay your exorcist you can get repossessed.
- With her marriage she got a new name and a dress.
- A guy fell into an upholstery machine but completely recovered.
- He had a photographic memory but it was never developed.
- A lot of money is tainted. 'Tain't yours, and 'tain't mine.

This Lesson In Your Life

This is a story full of surprises. It begins with the Israelites back in the same area where they had received the report of the twelve spies and had rebelled against God. Sadly, it is noted that Miriam—the sister of Moses and Aaron who had served as a leader of the people herself—died there and was buried. Then there is the problem of the lack of water, and the people of Israel respond in their usual way. They turn against Moses and Aaron and accuse them of bringing them into the wilderness to die. They feel it would have been better for them to have stayed in Egypt. Moses and Aaron once again fall on their faces and the glory of God appears to them.

It is at this point in the story that the surprises begin. When God speaks to Moses, He is not angry with the people for their complaints. It seems that this time the complaint is legitimate. He does not accuse the people of being faithless, but acts to provide the needed water. God simply instructs Moses to take the staff, to assemble the people before a rock, and to command the rock to bring forth water. Then we are surprised to hear Moses address the people in anger and to strike the rock rather than speaking to it. Though God does provide the water through Moses' faithless act, we next read the greatest surprise of all—because of their disobedience Moses and Aaron will not enter the Promised Land.

Does the punishment given Moses and Aaron seem too harsh for their sin? In fairness, we do need to realize that within this brief account lie several major problems for Moses. First of all, he misrepresented God when he spoke angrily to the people and called them rebels. God had not expressed either anger nor frustration with the people when He gave Moses his instructions. Secondly, Moses draws attention to himself when he says that "we must fetch water out of the rock." There is no mention of God at all—leaving the impression that Moses was the one with the power. And, lastly, Moses struck the rock rather than speaking to it as God had commanded. In fact, he struck it twice, in direct disobedience to God's instructions.

Perhaps the most valuable lesson for our lives in this story is that we not confuse our own feelings for the feelings of God. There can be times when we attribute wrath to God when it is really we ourselves who are angry. The same Lord who condemned adultery spoke words of kindness and mercy to a woman caught committing adultery (John 8). As we read of Moses angrily striking the rock in the wilderness, let us examine our own lives to see if there are times when we react angrily to those on whom God is seeking to bestow mercy and love. There are certainly times for us to express righteous indignation—but perhaps there are many more times for us to express His patience and gentle kindness.

1. Where did Miriam die?
Miriam died at Kadesh in the desert of Zin (Numbers 20:1).

2. What problem at Kadesh caused the people to rise up against Moses and Aaron?
There was no water in that place (20:2).

3. What did the people once again wish had happened?
They wished they had died with the others who had died in the wilderness (20:3, 4).

4. What complaints did the people add to their complaint about the lack of water?
They complained there were no seed, figs, vines or pomegranates (20:5).

5. What did Moses and Aaron do when the people complained to them?
They fell on the faces at the door of the tabernacle (20:6).

6. What three things did God tell Moses to do to provide water for the people?
God told Moses to take the staff, gather the people, and command the rock to bring forth water (20:8).

7. What did Moses call the congregation after he gathered them?
Moses called them rebels (20:10).

8. What did Moses do rather than commanding the rock to bring forth water?
Moses struck the rock twice with the staff (20:11).

9. What reasons did God give for punishing Moses and Aaron?
God said they had not believed Him or sanctified Him in the eyes of the children of Israel (20:12).

10. What punishment was given to Moses and Aaron?
They would not bring the congregation into the land which God had given them (20:12).

Have you ever tried to go to sleep with a water faucet dripping? The sound of water dripping is not extremely loud, nor do the first few drips disturb us much. But it's the constant dripping that finally wears us down and causes us to get up and address the problem. When we think of Moses leading the people of Israel through the wilderness, the analogy of dripping water might be very appropriate. The people had complained numerous times to Moses, and Moses had always been able to meet the challenge in a faithful way. But finally in Kadesh, the constant complaining—the constant dripping—had worn him down. In anger he lashed out at the people and—in the process—disobeyed God.

We can wear our leaders down through constant complaining and dissension. This is not only a problem for them, but it becomes a problem for us as well. In the book of Hebrews, the writer encouraged his listeners: "Obey your leaders and submit to them, for they are keeping watch over your souls, and will give an account. Let them do this with joy and not with sighing—for that would be harmful to you" (Heb. 13:17, NRSV). This writer knew that good leaders are made by good followers. Though we may always reserve the right to challenge poor leadership, we must first of all be concerned with helping leaders do their job well. A constant onslaught of criticism and complaining can break the best of leaders.

There has never been a time when the Church was in greater need of faithful leadership than now. Let us all commit to doing our part in encouraging the best in our leadership. We can do this by being faithful to remember our leaders in our personal prayers. We can give words of encouragement written and verbal. We can protect their reputation by refusing to criticize them to others. We can befriend them—for the place of leadership can often be a lonely place.

Lesson 12

God Calls For Obedience

Deut. 6:1-9, 20-24

1 Now these are the commandments, the statutes, and the judgments, which the LORD your God commanded to teach you, that ye might do them in the land whither ye go to possess it:

2 That thou mightest fear the LORD thy God, to keep all his statutes and his commandments, which I command thee, thou, and thy son, and thy son's son, all the days of thy life; and that thy days may be prolonged.

3 Hear therefore, O Israel, and observe to do it; that it may be well with thee, and that ye may increase mightily, as the LORD God of thy fathers hath promised thee, in the land that floweth with milk and honey.

4 Hear, O Israel: The LORD our God is one LORD:

5 And thou shalt love the LORD thy God with all thine heart, and with all thy soul, and with all thy might.

6 And these words, which I command thee this day, shall be in thine heart:

7 And thou shalt teach them diligently unto thy children, and shalt talk of them when thou sittest in thine house, and when thou walkest by the way, and when thou liest down, and when thou risest up.

8 And thou shalt bind them for a sign upon thine hand, and they shall be as frontlets between thine eyes.

9 And thou shalt write them upon the posts of thy house, and on thy gates.

20 And when thy son asketh thee in time to come, saying, What mean the testimonies, and the statutes, and the judgments, which the LORD our God hath commanded you?

21 Then thou shalt say unto thy son, We were Pharaoh's bondmen in Egypt; and the LORD brought us out of Egypt with a mighty hand:

22 And the LORD shewed signs and wonders, great and sore, upon Egypt, upon Pharaoh, and upon all his household, before our eyes:

23 And he brought us out from thence, that he might bring us in, to give us the land which he sware unto our fathers.

24 And the LORD commanded us to do all these statutes, to fear the LORD our God, for our good always, that he might preserve us alive, as it is at this day.

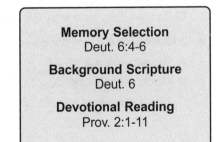

Memory Selection
Deut. 6:4-6

Background Scripture
Deut. 6

Devotional Reading
Prov. 2:1-11

Aug. 23

Deuteronomy 6:4, which is included in this lesson's opening verses, begins with the word "Shemah," which means "Hear." It came to be the name of a confession of faith for the Jews. If, as we have noted earlier, the word "Deuteronomy" means "the second [stating of] the Law," then the Shemah

For a Lively Start

As this lesson will show, many ancient Jews (and some Orthodox today) took literally the commands to bind the Scriptures over the heart or around an arm, and to fasten them to the doorposts of their house. One purpose of such practices was to keep the thought

can be considered a summary-introduction to that "second statement."

The material begins to take on the tone of a valedictory address, for it contains the last words of Moses. In a few weeks he will go to the top of Mt. Nebo, from where he can see the Promised Land, then die and be buried there. This lesson is therefore a pep talk exhorting the people to listen to all the words of the Law and to take seriously the exhortation, *"Hear, O Israel!"*

ഇൻരു

of God and their need to obey Him before them at all time.

Do we as Christians need something like that today? Or would it merely draw attention to the person wearing them? If so, what else could be done to keep our minds centered on God throughout the day? What about carrying a card with a verse of Scripture in our shirt pocket or purse? Any other ideas?

Teaching Outline	Daily Bible Readings	
I. To Keep All His Statutes—6:1-9	Mon.	Rewards of Obedience *Lev. 27:3-13*
A. To fear the Lord, 1-2	Tue.	Penalties of Disobedience *Lev. 26:14-26*
B. To hear the Lord, 3-5	Wed.	Consequences of Disobedience *1 Sam. 15:17-26*
C. To bind them for a sign, 6-9	Thu.	Disobeying the Son John 3:31-36
II. To Remember the Testimonies—20	Fri.	Listening and Obeying *Ps. 81:11-16*
A. We were slaves, 20-21	Sat.	Treasure God's Commands *Prov. 2:1-11*
B. God's mighty signs, 22-23	Sun.	Observe God's Law Deut. 6:1-9, 20-24
C. Man's humble obedience, 24		

Verse by Verse

I. To Keep All His Statutes—6:1-9
A. To fear the Lord, 1-2

1 Now these are the statutes, and the judgments, which the Lord your God commanded to teach you, that ye might do them in the land whither ye go to possess it:

2 That thou mightest fear the Lord thy God, to keep all his statutes and his commandments, which I command thee, thou, and thy son, and thy son's son, all the days of thy life; and that thy days may be prolonged.

Although Israel has again approached the Jordan River and the Promised Land, Moses has been told that he will not be allowed to enter for his presumptuousness in striking the rock (Num. 20:11). Thus he finds it necessary to restate the Law (Deuteronomy = "Second Law")—if the people will not be occupying the land under his guidance, at least they will go in with the Law freshly imprinted on their mind. He has restated

the Ten Commandments (Deut. 5; first stated in Exod. 20); now he gives some more general principles, stating the reasons for some of the laws and affirming that keeping them is for the good of the people, not just to satisfy the whims of a tyrannical God.

Moses uses three powerful words for what the people are to "keep" in the land of Promise: *statutes, judgments,* and *commandments.* While all three can be used as synonyms, there are shades of difference. The word for *statute* means a "decree" or "ordinance"; a *judgment* means a "commandment," and the term for *commandment* implies "justice." We can see that Hebrew is not lacking in legal terms. The point here is that whatever the fine points, the Israelites are to *do* them as they pass over into the Promised Land, that their days may be prolongedand and their children are to do them also.

503

B. To hear the Lord, 3-5

3 Hear therefore, O Israel, and observe to do it; that it may be well with thee, and that ye may increase mightily, as the LORD God of thy fathers hath promised thee, in the land that floweth with milk and honey.

4 Hear, O Israel: The LORD our God is one LORD:

5 And thou shalt love the LORD thy God with all thine heart, and with all thy soul, and with all thy might.

From just studying the legal terms of the Law of Moses we might think his religion is a Pharisaical collection of externals. Although that is certainly an emphasis that stands out when we compare it with the New Covenant, verse 3 here shows that the Law has heart and soul and inner force also. Doing the Law is not in order to have God check off commandments kept; it is in order that "it may be well with thee." Stated in this way the Law is similar to the modern "Promise Keepers" movement. The promises are kept so the participants can experience the joy of the Lord in their home. Here the commands are kept so the experience of occupying the Promised Land results in milk and honey "flowing in heart."

Verse 4-5 are the beginning of "the Shemah," which as the "Focus" section explains means is the first word, "Hear." When verse 6 is included, it forms an adage or maxim that the faithful Jew repeats several times a day.

It is important to note that the saying is not just a commandment, but has the important doctrinal basis for keeping them: "the Yahweh our God is one Yahweh." The faithful Jew will not be faced suddenly with another set of Laws from another god; there is one God, and one Law.

Again, the first commandment is not a Pharisaical command to boast about keeping; it is a law of love. We recognize verse 5 as part of the "Great Commandment" which Jesus uses to sum up the Law in Matthew 22:37.

C. To bind them for a sign, 6-9

6 And these words, which I command thee this day, shall be in thine heart:

7 And thou shalt teach them diligently unto thy children, and shalt talk of them when thou sittest in thine house, and when thou walkest by the way, and when thou liest down, and when thou risest up.

8 And thou shalt bind them for a sign upon thine hand, and they shall be as frontlets between thine eyes.

9 And thou shalt write them upon the posts of thy house, and on thy gates.

The words in verse 6 are to be "in thine heart" and talked about diligently as we walk about doing our daily tasks at work and home. They are words so important to remember that they are to be bound for a sign on our hand, as a frontlet between our eyes and on the door posts and gates of our homes. Many Jews took this literally, copying one or more especially meaningful verses on vellum or parchment, tying them up in a roll called a *tephillin* (or, in the New Testament, a *phylactery*), and wearing them on the hand or over the heart and posting them in a conspicuous place at the entrance of their home.

Not all Jews took these outward signs literally, but they neglected them at their peril. They are a classic illustration of Jewish psychology, which is correctly reluctant to separate body from mind. The verses from 4-6 that are written on papyrus and actually rolled up and bound around the forehead as a headband are thought of as virtually seeping through the skull to the heart to become a way of life. Obviously this fusion did not always "work"; but it tends to establish a singleness of heart and act that results in a *person* instead of a thought plus a body. It is a psychology that is at the heart of the Protestant principle of a "sacrament" as "an outward sign of an inward grace"—a unitary principle that is far too often neglected in favor of subconsciously defining our religion either as an inner mentalism or an outer deed. Not only is "the Lord our God one Lord," but the *person* is a unitary whole as well.

II. To Remember the testimonies?—20

A. We were slaves, 20-21

20 And when thy son asketh thee in time to come, saying, What mean the testimonies, and the statutes, and the judgments, which the Lord our God hath commanded you?

21 Then thou shalt say unto thy son, We were Pharaoh's bondmen in Egypt; and the Lord brought us out of Egypt with a mighty hand:

Wearing little scrolls of Bible verses is much more likely to elicit a question from children in the home about their meaning, than never having a visible reminder of the faith. The answer is a recital first of the mighty acts of God.

B. God's mighty signs, 22-24

22 And the Lord shewed signs and wonders, great and sore, upon Egypt, upon Pharaoh, and upon all his household, before our eyes:

23 And he brought us out from thence, that he might bring us in, to give us the land which he sware unto our fathers.

This is "theology from memory." Eventually of course it was written down (hence we have something to study!); but for generations Hebrew doctrine was a matter of *recital* and *memory*. Amazing heights of memory skills resulted. (The present author knew a Jew who could recite the entire "Torah," or first five books of the Old Testament.)

C. Man's humbe obedience.

24 And the Lord commanded us to do all these statutes, to fear the Lord our God, for our good always, that he might preserve us alive, as it is at this day.

In response to the mighty acts of God, His followers are to keep the statutes, commandments, and judgments (6:1). Although these laws grew into books, then sets of books, they are all based on the doctrine of one God (cf. "the Shemah,") and the Ten Commandments.

Evangelistic Emphasis

The impression of many people is that the Christian faith is a list of rules and regulations. When asked what information the Bible contains, the first thing that might come to their minds is the phrase, "Thou shalt not." Though God has given us commands to keep, this picture of our relationship with Him is far from accurate.

In the sixth chapter of Deuteronomy, the people of Israel are encouraged to pass on to their children the commands of God. But notice, too, that they are told to explain why these commands were given. The reason the statutes and ordinances made sense was because the people had a story to tell. "We were Pharaoh's slaves in Egypt," they were to say, "but the LORD brought us out of Egypt with a mighty hand. The LORD displayed before our eyes great and awesome signs and wonders" (Deut. 6:21-22). To know the commands of God is important, but primary to His commands is the story of our experience with Him.

Sharing our faith can be a daunting task if we think of it in terms of teaching all that God has revealed to us. But if we begin with the *story*—with what we have seen and heard, both in Scripture and the times God has embraced us and lifted us out of despair, sharing our faith is like telling a story with a joyful ending.

୭୬ଔ

Memory Selection

Hear, O Israel: The LORD our God is one LORD: and thou shalt love the LORD thy God with all thine heart, and with all thy soul, and with all thy might. And these words, which I command thee this day, shall be in thine heart.—*Deuteronomy 6:4-6*

This is one of the most familiar passages in all Scripture. As Christians, we recognize it as the passage Jesus quoted when a scribe asked Him, "What is the greatest commandment?" Jesus combined this passage with the command, "Love your neighbor as yourself," and stated that this was a summary of all the law and the prophets (Mark 12:28-31). Of course, this scripture was already familiar to the scribe and to all Israel. Known as the "Shema"—the Hebrew word for "hear"—this passage was recited by Israel at least twice a day every day.

Why is this passage so foundational to all that Israel and the church believe? Because it demands that we constantly make the decision that we will honor God as God. There is so much in our world that bids for our attention and our worship. The list of what we can place before our devotion to God is long. First on this list is often ourselves—to live to do what pleases us. But our jobs, our families, our possessions, and more can compete with our affection for God. As our minds and our hearts are so easily distracted, it is good for us to begin and end our days with the reminder that it is the Lord who is God, and none other.

Weekday Problems

Cassandra sat in the darkness of the family room wiping the tears from her eyes. As one who loved God deeply, she had always been committed to having a Godly home. A part of that commitment was having evening devotionals with her children. When they were younger, they seemed to enjoy the quietness and holiness of the moment. But as they had grown older, they began to resent having to interrupt their activities for these few minutes of worship with their mother. Tonight her daughter had gone to bed early and her teenage son had stayed out late with his friends, and came in sayng he was too tired for devotional time. Cassandra felt like a failure.

The next morning Cassandra shared her frustration with a friend from church. The wise friend encouraged Cassandra from Deuteronomy 6. "It says we should talk about God's Word when we're home and when we're away; when we lie down and when we rise. In other words, our whole lives should be filled with the word of God—not just at "devotional time." Your children may not conform to your scheduled teaching times, but they are definitely watching to see who we are. And seeing that, they will know who God is, too."

*Do you agree with the advice of Cassandra's friend?

*What do you think Cassandra should do about her devotional time? Should she continue insisting her children join her?

Leaning on the Law

Laws can discover sin, but not remove it.—*John Milton*

* * *

The laws of nature are but the ways in which the great Almighty Lawgiver operates; they have no efficiency except as channels of His will; rightly understood they cannot but be seen to agree with His written word.—*Tryon Edwards*

* * *

Every instance of a man's suffering the penalty of the law is an instance of the failure of that penalty in effecting its purpose, which is to deter from transgression.—*Whately*

* * *

Where law ends, tyranny begins.—*William Pitt*

* * *

Multitude of laws are signs, either of much tyranny in the prince, or much rebellious disobedience in the subject.—*John Marston*

This Lesson in Your Life

"Hear, O Israel: The LORD our God is one LORD." So begins the scripture cited by Jesus as the greatest commandment of all. This one brief sentence says much. Through it we affirm our belief that there is only one true God. When we repeat these words we commit to placing nothing else before Him as our god. But we also make a statement about God Himself—that God is not divided—He is one. He is not divided in His heart or His soul or His might. As His name reveals, "I AM WHO I AM." He will always be who He was and who He is. Because of His oneness, we can trust Him completely. He is faithful and consistent. His steadfast love is forever.

The oneness of God is a call to oneness within us. God's desire for us is that we, too, can have this consistency within us. When we pledge our love to him, we love him with heart, soul and mind. In other words we give him our complete loyalty (heart), the willingness even to die for our belief (soul), and pledge all our substance, wealth and possessions to His purposes (might). God is consistent in who He is, and He loves consistency in our lives, too. Note that this consistency continues in His command for teaching the word of God to our children. We are not to separate when we speak of God—such as in church on Sunday morning—but we are to be consistent in our witness to Him in all times of our lives. God knew well that children learn from the example of their parents more than from the words spoken occasionally—no matter how sincerely we might speak those words. And this theme continues at the end of the chapter as God through Moses encourages us not just to share the commandments of God but to share our own experiences with God as well (6:20-25). All children will someday ask the question, "Why?" They will ask their parents verbally or nonverbally, "Why should we believe what you tell us about God?" The answer to that question lies in our journey with God. As the first generation of Israelites in the Promised Land could recount how God had delivered them out of captivity and cared for them in the wilderness, we must share our own story of how God has delivered and nurtured us. It is our story that gives credibility to our devotion to the commandments.

There is also a warning in this passage. Between the two exhortations to teach our children to obey the commands of God (6:4-9 and 6:20-25), God warns against becoming so complacent in His blessings that we forget their source. For some reason, it is more our nature to cry out to God in our distress than it is to lift up His praise in our comfort. When was the last time our children—or anyone else in our lives—heard us express appreciation to God for what He has given? Would they be surprised to hear such language from us at home? Or would they simply smile and say, "We know. We've heard you say it so many times before."

1. What were the Israelites to observe in the land that were about to possess?

They were to keep the commandments, the statutes, and the judgments which the Lord commanded they be taught (Deut. 6:1).

2. If the people kept the commandments of God, what promises did He make to them?

God promised their days would be prolonged, it would go well with them, and they would increase mightily (6:2-3).

3. In the *Shema* ("Hear, O Israel"), what were they to know about the Lord?

They were to know that the Lord their God is one Lord (6:4).

4. To what extent was Israel called to love God?

They were to love the LORD their God with all their heart, and with all their soul, and with all their might (6:5).

5. To whom were the people to teach the commands of God?

They were to teach them diligently to their children (6:7).

6. How were the people to teach their children the commandments of God?

They were to talk about the commandments when they sat in their houses, when the walked in the way, when they lay down, and when they rose up (6:7).

7. Where were the commandments of God to be displayed?

The commandments were to be bound on their hands, fixed as frontlets on their foreheads, and written on the posts of their houses and gates (6:8-9).

8. What were the people to tell their children when the children asked about the meaning of the commandments?

The people were to tell their children the story of the Exodus, the great signs and wonders they had seen, and how God had brought them into the land He had promised (6:20-23).

9. What blessings were the people to tell their children God would give them?

They were to tell them keeping the commandments was for their good and so that God would preserve their lives (6:24).

10. What would be the righteousness of Israel?

If they observed all the commandments God had given, it would be their righteousness (6:25).

Uplift

We fear for the faith of the next generation. With the attacks of secularism in our own society and the rising storm of extremists in the world, we wonder if our children and our children's children will have faith. This is a concern of our age, but we are not the first age to have this concern. The generation of Israel that entered the Promised Land had grown up in the wilderness and had developed a deep faith in God. They had seen God's care for them through the forty years of wandering, and they witnessed the power of God as He led them to conquer the inhabitants of Canaan. But would their children share this same faith? Along with the bounty of the land, there would be many temptations. How could they pass their faith to the next generation?

God gives explicit instructions in how to pass faith to our children. First of all, we are to make sure that they know what the commandments of God are. We are to talk about the commandments—not just in church—but in all activities of our lives. And we are to share our own stories with our children. While they need to know what God has done long ago, they also need to hear and see what God has done in the lives of their parents and grandparents. The commandments of God will make sense to them only if the lives of their parents align with the commandments.

In his book *Illustrations Unlimited* (Tyndale, 1972, p. 381), James S. Hewett tells the story of two college students who went to hear a lecture by the notorious skeptic Robert Ingersoll. As they walked down the street after the lecture, one student said to the other, "Well, I guess he knocked the props out from under Christianity, didn't he?"

"No, I don't think he did," said the other. "Ingersoll did not explain one thing—he did not explain my mother's life. Until he can explain my mother's life, I will stand by my mother's God."

We do not need to underestimate the power of the world in attacking the faith of our children, but neither let us underestimate the power of the Godly lives of parents and family. If what we say and what we do are the same—and our walk of faith displays abundant hope and joy—the next generation will be eager to follow the same God who has produced such lives.

Lesson 13

God Calls For Decision

Deut. 30:1-14

1 And it shall come to pass, when all these things are come upon thee, the blessing and the curse, which I have set before thee, and thou shalt call them to mind among all the nations, whither the LORD thy God hath driven thee,

2 And shalt return unto the LORD thy God, and shalt obey his voice according to all that I command thee this day, thou and thy children, with all thine heart, and with all thy soul;

3 That then the LORD thy God will turn thy captivity, and have compassion upon thee, and will return and gather thee from all the nations, whither the LORD thy God hath scattered thee.

4 If any of thine be driven out unto the outmost parts of heaven, from thence will the LORD thy God gather thee, and from thence will he fetch thee:

5 And the LORD thy God will bring thee into the land which thy fathers possessed, and thou shalt possess it; and he will do thee good, and multiply thee above thy fathers.

6 And the LORD thy God will circumcise thine heart, and the heart of thy seed, to love the LORD thy God with all thine heart, and with all thy soul, that thou mayest live.

7 And the LORD thy God will put all these curses upon thine enemies, and on them that hate thee, which persecuted thee.

8 And thou shalt return and obey the voice of the LORD, and do all his commandments which I command thee this day.

9 And the LORD thy God will make thee plenteous in every work of thine hand, in the fruit of thy body, and in the fruit of thy cattle, and in the fruit of thy land, for good: for the LORD will again rejoice over thee for good, as he rejoiced over thy fathers:

10 If thou shalt hearken unto the voice of the LORD thy God, to keep his commandments and his statutes which are written in this book of the law, and if thou turn unto the LORD thy God with all thine heart, and with all thy soul.

11 For this commandment which I command thee this day, it is not hidden from thee, neither is it far off.

12 It is not in heaven, that thou shouldest say, Who shall go up for us to heaven, and bring it unto us, that we may hear it, and do it?

13 Neither is it beyond the sea, that thou shouldest say, Who shall go over the sea for us, and bring it unto us, that we may hear it, and do it?

14 But the word is very nigh unto thee, in thy mouth, and in thy heart, that thou mayest do it.

Memory Selection
Deut. 30:6

Background Scripture
Deut. 30

Devotional Reading
Josh. 24:14-24

Aug. 30

It has been a long journey—40 years and more for those who refused to accept God's first challenge to enter the Promised Land. Now history has repeated itself. The people find themselves drawn up before the Jordan and addressed again by Moses. He has de-livered to them God's blessings for obedience (Deut. 28:1-14), and His cursing for disobedience (28:15-68).

Sometimes in our own lives it is *decision time*. We serve a God of grace, who does not expect perfection. Yet he does expect general obedience. He expects a decision. He sets before us life and death, then steps back, respecting our right of choice, but urges, as he does here through Moes, *"Choose life!"* (30:19).

ॐ

For a Lively Start

You can introduce this lesson by leading a brief discussion that helps your group focus on the grounds the Israelites have for making the decision Moses calls for in this lesson. What events during the last 40 years have occurred that might help them say Yes to God, assuring Him that they will keep His covenant? On the other hand, if you had stood before Moses reflecting on the previous 40 years, what negative events have occurred that might tempt you to say No, and decline to enter the Promised Land? (God's frequent miraculous care in the desert might lead them to say Yes. Yet, to be honest, they have faced enemies, starvation, and thirst. Is there more weight for saying Yes or No?

Teaching Outline	Daily Bible Readings

I. Foreseeing Fateful Days—30:1-5
  A. Scattered and gathered, 1-3
  B. Pursued by the Lord, 4-5
II. Fruitful Days Are Possible—6-10
  A. Circumcised hearts, 6
  B. Curses on your enemies, 7
  C. Plenteous days of obedience, 8-10
III. A Doable Challenge, 11-14
  A. Not too high, 11-12
  B. Not beyond the sea, 13
  C. A charge in the heart, 14
	Mon. Observe God's Laws
	    Ps. 105:37-45
	Tue. Obey Christ's Commmands
	    Matt. 28:16-20
	Wed. A Gracious God
	    Neh. 9:16-20
	Thu. A Pledge of Obedience
	    Josh. 24:14-24
	Fri. To Love God Is to Obey
	    1 John 5:1-5
	Sat. I Love You, O Lord
	    Ps. 18:1-6
	Sun. Return to the Lord
	    Deut. 30:1-10

Verse by Verse

I. Foreseeing Fateful Days—30:1-5

A. Scattered and gathered, 1-3

1 And it shall come to pass, when all these things are come upon thee, the blessing and the curse, which I have set before thee, and thou shalt call them to mind among all the nations, whither the LORD thy God hath driven thee,

2 And shalt return unto the LORD thy God, and shalt obey his voice according to all that I command thee this day, thou and thy children, with all thine heart, and with all thy soul;

3 That then the LORD thy God will turn thy captivity, and have compassion upon thee, and will return and gather thee from all the nations, whither the LORD thy God hath scattered thee.

These poignant last words of Moses to Israel are set in a section of blessings and curses that portray Moses' powers as a prophet at their best. At times it seems that they are presented as a *choice*—the people may obey and

be blessed or disobey and be cursed. At other times they seem to reflect Moses' long years of experience with a people who can be fickle and erratic in their convictions and commitments, and Moses seems to be saying that he knows the people will be *both* faithful and unfaithful. For example, in verse 1 Moses says that he knows that "all these things are come upon thee, the blessings and the curse."

They will remember what he said when they find themselves "among all the nations, whither the LORD thy God hath driven thee." This seems to show Moses' certain conviction that something like the Captivity will descend on the Israelites in punishment for their disobedience; yet that they will afterward return to God—a precise picture of what happens when the Dispersion is followed by the Return.

Both the beauty of the blessings and the tragedy of the curses are laid out in 28:1-14 and 15-68, respectively, in one of the Pentateuch's more powerful sections from a literary standpoint.

B. Pursued by the Lord, 4-5

4 If any of thine be driven out unto the outmost parts of heaven, from thence will the Lord thy God gather thee, and from thence will he fetch thee:

5 And the Lord thy God will bring thee into the land which thy fathers possessed, and thou shalt possess it; and he will do thee good, and multiply thee above thy fathers.

This almost sounds as though God's people can do no wrong that would keep them from inheriting the Promised Land; wherever they are driven "from thence will he fetch thee." Yet in light of all the "if . . . then" pledges made in this entire section it seems unlikely that God will now announce that His people have a free ticket to act as they please and still inherit the land. It is much more likely that God is speaking of the Remnant that always returns to Him to inherit the blessing, rather than all the people in general. In that way His election and grace are always fulfilled.

II. Fruitful Days Are Possible—6-10
A. Circumcised hearts, 6

6 And the Lord thy God will circumcise thine heart, and the heart of thy seed, to love the Lord thy God with all thine heart, and with all thy soul, that thou mayest live.

Israel, as so many of God's people, has such a difficult time remaining steadfast and faithful over a long period of time, and in such a variety of temptations that this promise must surely have been heartening. They have

not been very successful at "circumcising" their own hearts—that is, of "wanting to want" to serve God consistently in all circumstances. It would therefore be "gospel" or good news to learn that *God* will do the operation on their hearts Himself. No doubt this will not release them from making personal moral effort; but it is a reassuring promise of God's grace, and of the fact that He will not allow them or their "seed" (children) to "be tempted above that ye are able; but will with the temptation also make a way to escape, that ye may be able to bear it" (1 Cor. 10:13).

B. Curses on your enemies, 7

7 And the Lord thy God will put all these curses upon thine enemies, and on them that hate thee, which persecuted thee.

This promise that the curses God threatens to be bring on disobedient Israel will fall on their enemies if they will but obey God shows the universal nature of the one God of the Hebrews. It is easy for those of us brought up from childhood to think in terms of monotheism. Moses' people, however, would have had more difficulty grasping the idea of a God whose power extends beyond the people who can carry him into battle or set him up in a temple of stone. This threat is also a promise that they serve just such a universal God.

C. Plenteous days of obedience, 8-10

8 And thou shalt return and obey the voice of the Lord, and do all his commandments which I command thee this day.

9 And the Lord thy God will make

thee plenteous in every work of thine hand, in the fruit of thy body, and in the fruit of thy cattle, and in the fruit of thy land, for good: for the LORD will again rejoice over thee for good, as he rejoiced over thy fathers:

10 If thou shalt hearken unto the voice of the LORD thy God, to keep his commandments and his statutes which are written in this book of the law, and if thou turn unto the LORD thy God with all thine heart, and with all thy soul.

Here is one of the more forthright promises of holistic well-being for obedience that God gives His people. Although the phrase "book of the law" usually refers to the Torah, or the first five books of the Bible, in the context of the promises made for obedience it probably refers to this book that is being written as Moses speaks. Even with such a positive promise, it would not have meant that a farmer would not have had to deal with a stillborn calf or child, or a hailed-out crop occasionally. It is more of a general promise like God's people depend on today. Every promise requires faith; none is automatic.

III. A Doable Challenge, 11-15
A. Not too high, 11-12

11 For this commandment which I command thee this day, it is not hidden from thee, neither is it far off.

12 It is not in heaven, that thou shouldest say, Who shall go up for us to heaven, and bring it unto us, that we may hear it, and do it?

God's commandments are not too difficult to obey. He does not expect the impossible of us. He does not play a game of hide and seek, or tuck His will away in a heavenly chest to which we do not have access. This is an encouraging statement designed to enable God's people to live a joyful and happy life instead of one of fearfulness that we have "failed to tag the base as we rounded second."

B. Not beyond the sea, 13

13 Neither is it beyond the sea, that thou shouldest say, Who shall go over the sea for us, and bring it unto us, that we may hear it, and do it?

Neither are God's commandments beyond the reach of land-bound people who are not skilled in sea-faring ways, or have to hire experienced sailors to retrieve it. It is made to be accessible to all who *want* to find it.

C. A charge in the heart, 14

14 But the word is very nigh unto thee, in thy mouth, and in thy heart, that thou mayest do it.

Instead of hiding it beyond the heavens or the seas, God has placed His charge to do His will well within our reach, in our mouth and heart. Only those who care nothing about it need fear that it will be difficult to understand and obey.

೫೦೧೩

Evangelistic Emphasis

Not all evangelism is calling someone to faith for the first time. Evangelism also includes taking the grace of the gospel to Christian brothers and sisters living in exile. The text in Deuteronomy 30 assumes that exile is in the future for the nation of Israel, and the promise it gives is that if the people will return to the Lord that He will restore their fortunes and have compassion on them (Deut. 30:3). The New Testament also recognizes that people of the New Covenant will find themselves in exile because of disobe-dience (Jas. 5:19-20; Gal. 6:1). It offers helpful advice in taking the gospel to such believers.

Perhaps transparency is the most needed attribute of one who would bring the mercy of God to a wandering fellow believer. We are one sinner encouraging another. If we have practiced the disciplines of repentance and confession, we will be well aware of both the difficulty of what we are calling another to do and the blessing of experiencing the forgiveness of God in our lives anew. Only such honesty with our own struggles gives us insight on how to approach another. To "speak the truth in love" includes speaking the truth about ourselves. It is our own stories of God's restoration that will bring hope to the exiles.

ഉറ

Memory Selection

And the LORD thy God will circumcise thine heart, and the heart of thy seed, to love the LORD thy God with all thine heart, and with all thy soul, that thou mayest live.—*Deuteronomy 30:6*

Circumcision was a sign of God's covenant with His people. It was a physical reminder that God had entered into a lasting relationship with them. One truth that God repeatedly stressed to His people was that He is a God of steadfast love. He will hold onto His people through all circumstances.In the New Covenant with God, we have received the sign of a spiritual circumcision—the circumcision of Christ when we were "buried with him in baptism" (Col. 2:11-12). That sign is a reminder of God's steadfast love for us. Jesus said that He would hold onto His sheep, and that "no one can snatch them out of my hand" (Jn. 10:28).

The circumcision mentioned in this passage from Deuteronomy is a circumcision of the heart that produces within the people a desire to do the will of God. In it God "cuts away" evil desire, and enables us "both to will and to work for his good pleasure" (Philip. 2:13, NRSV). God's desire for His people has always been that we keep His commandments—not out of duty or drudgery, but out of a sincere desire to do His will and to please Him. Let us receive with gratitude His pledge of steadfast love toward us, and allow that love to transform us into willing servants who love the Master.

Weekday Problems

Out of desperation and despair, Robert called his friend Kevin. "I've messed up my life, Kevin," Robert began, choking back the tears. "I know," Kevin acknowledged. Robert's life had appeared to be almost perfect—a wonderful wife, two children, and a good job. But Robert, to the surprise of those who knew him, had walked away from that life to begin an affair with a woman from his office. The weeks that followed had been predictable. Robert's wife had begun divorce proceedings. His children, once model teenagers, were struggling with school and with behavior problems. And Robert had lost his job for violating company policy on office relationships.

"I don't think I can put my life back together," Robert continued.

"No, you can't, Robert. That's beyond your power," Kevin replied.

"So what do I do then?" Robert asked. Kevin paused. He and Robert had taught together in the church's Bible study program.

"You know what God wants you to do, Robert. You need to repent," he said.

Robert sighed, "And what good would that do? This is too big for repentance to fix."

Kevin continued, "Robert, do you remember that last lesson we taught in class? It was on Deuteronomy 30—about how when Israel found itself in exile because of sin, the nation was to repent? Do you remember the point we made? We told the class that no matter how big of a mess we're in, our repentance will give God the opportunity to rebuild us."

Robert was quiet for a moment, then said, "You're saying if I repent, I'll get my family back?"

"No, Robert," Kevin replied, "I'm not saying that. You might; but God might do something else. We don't know. All we can do is return to Him, and trust that He will restore us in His way."

*What form do you think Robert's repentance should take, and what do you think God's response to such repentance might be?

Just Justice

"Judge, I don't know what to do."

"Why? How's that?

"Well, I swore to tell the truth, but every time I try, some lawyer objects."

* * *

Judge: My good man, under the American system of law, you are presumed to be innocent.

Defendant: Then why all this effort to prove me guilty?

This Lesson in Your Life

The context of Deuteronomy 30 is found in the blessings and curses detailed in Deuteronomy 28. The beginning of the text assumes that the nation of Israel will find itself in exile experiencing the curses of God, because they will choose the path of disobedience (30:1). Moses is encouraging the people to remember the blessings and to trust that God's compassion will bring about restoration if the people will repent and become obedient again. The text that says, "with God all things are possible" (Matt. 19:26), is best remembered when we are in the pits of despair and failure.

Paul used portions of this chapter in his letter to the church in Rome. In Romans 10:5ff, he quotes from this passage to encourage the Roman church to realize that God has given us all we need to respond to Him in faithful obedience. In Deuteronomy, Moses reminds the people that God has made His word accessible to them. He did not put it out of their reach by placing it up in heaven or across the sea. He had brought it very near—to their very mouths and hearts. According to Paul, God's act of grace toward us is even greater because God has made Himself available through Christ. What we could not do for ourselves—go into heaven to bring God down—God did for us. Now He Himself is near to us—the word of confession is on our lips and in our hearts. Because of God's grace, restoration of our relationship with Him is always within our grasp—no matter what situation we have created to destroy it.

Moses concluded his sermon to Israel by saying, "I have set before you life and death, blessing and cursing: therefore choose life, that both you and your children may live" (Deut. 30:19). The charge to "choose life" is realistic for any of us given God's mercy. Since He has done for us what we cannot do for ourselves, the opportunity to choose to live is viable.

This is the message we live by each day. This is the message we carry to a world lost in despair and hopelessness. There is always hope, for we serve a God who has created hope. If we truly believe that God has made Himself available and remains available through His steadfast love, we can join with Paul in joyously proclaiming, "For one believes with the heart and so is justified, and one confesses with the mouth and so is saved" (Rom. 10:10 NRSV). And the merciful truth of the statement, "No one who believes in him will be put to shame" (Romans 10:11) washes over us like cool water.

The God who restored the fortune of a people who abandoned Him to serve other gods can restore the fortune of any of us who have abandoned Him. The God who rebuilt the city of Jerusalem from its ashes can rebuild our lives from the ashes of our sins. If we will trust God with our hearts, He can change those hearts to be willing to serve and love Him. The rebuilding begins with our willingness to return.